CHRONOLOGICAL ENCYCLOPAEDIA OF WORLD HISTORY

other recent reference works from cosmo publications . . .

THE BUDDHISTS.
Encyclopaedia of Buddhism
in 5 Volumes
Edited by Subodh Kapoor

THE HINDUS.   *Bestseller*
Encyclopaedia of Hinduism
in 5 Volumes
Edited by Subodh Kapoor

THE MUSLIMS.   *Bestseller*
Encyclopaedia of Islam
in 11 Volumes
Edited by Subodh Kapoor

ENCYCLOPAEDIA OF INDIAN HERITAGE.
A Descriptive Work of Indological Research in Philosophy, Religion,
Sacred Literature, Society, Thought, Traditions, and Ancient Sciences.
in 90 Volumes
Edited by Subodh Kapoor

Also Available . . .

INDIAN HISTORICAL RESEARCHES
By Several Indologists of International Repute
in 78 Volumes

THE INDIAN ENCYCLOPAEDIA   *Bestseller*
Biographical, Historical, Religious, Administrative,
Ethnological, Commercial, and Scientific
Edited by Subodh Kapoor
in 25 Volumes

SIR AUREL STEIN'S CENTRAL ASIA   *Bestseller*
Aurel Stein
in 12 Volumes

ENCYCLOPAEDIA OF INDIAN RULERS   *Bestseller*
Ed. W. W. Hunter
in 24 Volumes

ENCYCLOPAEDIA OF ANCIENT INDIAN GEOGRAPHY
Ed. S. Kapoor
new edition
in 2 Volumes

CHRONOLOGICAL
ENCYCLOPAEDIA
OF
WORLD HISTORY

ANCIENT, MEDIEVAL AND MODERN

A REVISED AND MODERNIZED
VERSION OF PLOETZ'S "EPITOME"

COMPILED AND EDITED
BY
WILLIAM L. LANGER
COOLIDGE PROFESSOR OF HISTORY, HARWARD UNIVERSITY

SET IN THREE VOLUMES

VOLUME I

COSMO PUBLICATIONS
2006   New Delhi

**CHRONOLOGICAL ENCYCLOPAEDIA
OF WORLD HISTORY**
set in three volumes

First published in 2006 by
Cosmo Publications

First Published in India by
COSMO PUBLICATIONS

ISBN 81-307-0287-8 (set)
81-307-0288-6 (volume 1)

Published by
COSMO PUBLICATIONS
Div. of
GENESIS PUBLISHING PVT. LTD.
24-B, Ansari Road,
Darya Ganj, New Delhi-110 002,
INDIA

Printed at
Mehra Offset Press

COLLABORATORS

JAMES B. HEDGES
Professor of History, Brown University

WILLIAM THOMSON
Associate Professor of Arabic, Harvard University

CRANE BRINTON
Associate Professor of History, Harvard University

PENFIELD ROBERTS
Associate Professor of History, Massachusetts Institute of Technology

MICHAEL KARPOVICH
Associate Professor of History, Harvard University

ROBERT H. PFEIFFER
*Lecturer in Semitic Languages and Curator of the Semitic Museum
Harvard University*

MASON HAMMOND
Assistant Professor of History, and of Greek and Latin, Harvard University

CHARLES S. GARDNER
Assistant Professor of Chinese, Harvard University

DONALD C. McKAY
Assistant Professor of History, Harvard University

LAURISTON WARD
*Lecturer on Anthropology and Curator of Asiatic Archaeology in the Peabody
Museum, Harvard University*

JOHN K. FAIRBANK
Instructor in History, Harvard University

PAUL P. CRAM
Instructor in History, Harvard University

ROBERT O. SCHLAIFER
Teaching Fellow in History, Harvard University

EDWIN O. REISCHAUER
Teaching Fellow in Chinese, Harvard University

ROBERT S. CHAMBERLAIN
Formerly Assistant in History, Harvard University

Preface

THIS *Epitome of History* itself has a long and interesting history. More than seventy years ago Dr. Karl Ploetz, in his time a well-known German teacher, published an *Auszug aus der alten, mittleren und neueren Geschichte,* intended as a factual handbook for the use of students and for the convenience of the general reader. That his compilation filled a real need is attested by the fact that within a few years it went through seven editions, and by the further fact that to date more than twenty editions have appeared in Germany, revised and edited by noted scholars. The book has easily held its own despite competition of numerous similar works.

Ploetz' *Epitome* was translated into English by William H. Tillinghast and published by Houghton Mifflin Company in this country in 1883. The translator, recognizing that the original was designed particularly to meet the needs of the German student and that therefore the history of central Europe was weighted as against the history of France, England, and America, took the opportunity to enlarge a number of sections and to add others. No less a scholar than Edward Channing contributed the new sections on modern England and the United States. Furthermore, Tillinghast first added brief sections on the Middle and Far Eastern countries, which had been completely omitted from the German version. The book appeared under the title *An Epitome of Ancient, Mediaeval and Modern History,* and proved so popular that no less than twenty-four printings were necessary before 1905. Occasional revisions were made and in 1915 the title was changed to *A Handbook of Universal History.*

Since historical knowledge and historical conceptions are notoriously fluid, it is not to be wondered at that even so sound and reliable a book as the old Ploetz-Tillinghast *Epitome* should ultimately have fallen behind the times. After the World War the publishers therefore commissioned Dr. Harry Elmer Barnes to overhaul the book and bring it up to date. The new editor, with a number of collaborators, left the kernel of the old work (the Greek and Roman history, the mediaeval sections, and the early modern parts) as it was, judging quite rightly that in the large it was not so badly out of line as to justify rewriting and resetting. But the sections dealing with the early Near East, of which little was known in Ploetz' day, were completely redone, and a great deal of material on the period from 1883 to 1923 was added. The *Epitome,* thus revised, was published in 1925 as *A Manual of Universal History.* Like the preceding versions it has been widely used by students and laymen alike.

But despite revisions of one kind or another, it became increasingly clear that sooner or later the original book would require drastic changes if it were to keep abreast of modern knowledge and meet contemporary requirements. It stands to reason that in seventy years our command of the facts and our views of even those subjects best treated by Ploetz and Tillinghast have changed substantially. Above all, the past fifty years have witnessed the expansion of western influence over the entire globe and, as a result, there is now a much greater need to know something of the past of non-European countries and cultures, and a much livelier interest in formerly neglected fields. To fill the new requirements no amount of revision of the old book would do, for the original author wrote as a German and treated European history primarily as it touched his own country's development. Tillinghast attempted to give the English translation a somewhat more Anglo-American slant, and Dr. Barnes did what was humanly possible to adapt the old text to a more world-wide approach. But the point had been definitely reached where adaptations and adjustments would no longer suffice. The publishers therefore invited me to undertake a complete rewriting of the entire book, securing the aid of collaborators qualified to treat of special fields where it seemed desirable. It was my great good fortune to be able to interest fifteen of my colleagues to take over particular sections and to secure from them the most whole-hearted co-operation in what, after all, was an enterprise of some magnitude. Their names, with the sections for which they made themselves responsible, are listed at the end of the preface.

When embarking upon this project I still had hope that considerable parts of the old book might yet be salvaged and that a thoroughgoing revision would prove adequate for the ancient, mediaeval, and early modern sections. But it soon became apparent to all of us engaged in the work that the whole plan and approach required rethinking and that, consequently, there was but little use in trying to adhere to the old text. Here and there a few pages (thoroughly emended) have been retained, but they are relatively so few in number as to be hardly worth mentioning. Almost nothing of the substance of the old book remains; every single section has been gone over in thorough fashion, reduced or expanded and, above all, brought into line with present-day knowledge. Many other sections, naturally, have been newly written, so that I think we can honestly say that the book is no longer a manual of European history with some perfunctory reference to other countries, but genuine world history, in which the geographical divisions are dealt with on their merits.

In the course of rewriting we have, however, stuck by Ploetz' original conception. That is, we have tried to compile a handbook of historical facts, so arranged that the dates stand out while the material itself flows in a reasonably smooth narrative. Individual judgments have been kept in the background and divergent interpretations have been adduced only where they seemed to be indispensable. The great diversity of type which had crept into the old book has been done away with and we have broken the uniformity of the print only by the use of small and capital boldface and very occasional employment of italics. The number of genealogical charts has been much increased: new tables have been added for some of the non-European dynasties and all charts have been brought up to date. Furthermore, a considerable number of maps have been included, not with the idea of supplying a complete historical atlas, but simply for the convenience of the user who, when he is checking one event or another, cannot be expected to have always at hand the necessary map material.

In the preface to the 1925 edition Dr. Barnes referred to the growing interest in non-political aspects of history and to his attempt to expand sections dealing with economic and cultural developments. Though deeply interested in these phases of history, Dr. Barnes felt obliged to recognize that the majority of those who would use the book would come seeking information on political, military, and diplomatic history and that therefore those angles would have to be primarily considered. I subscribe entirely to this view, but I take this opportunity to point out further that cultural history does not lend itself readily to the method of treatment upon which this particular work is based. The backbone of this book is chronology which, in the case of general economic trends, religious and artistic movements and intellectual currents, is both hard to define and of relatively less significance. For methodological reasons, if for no other, we could therefore give but slight emphasis to these aspects of history. In addition we had to consider the further difficulties presented by space limitation: obviously anything like adequate treatment of literature, art, science, and economics would have taken us so far afield that the results could not possibly have been enclosed within two covers. In some sections the reader will find brief summaries of cultural activities, in others not; but in any case we offer them only for what they may be worth, as a matter of convenience, without any thought of sufficiency, much less exhaustiveness. And these remarks apply equally to the special sections at the beginning of the nineteenth century, entitled *Social Thought and Social Movements*, *Scientific Thought and Progress*, and *Mechanical Inventions and Technical Achievements*. The material we adduce in these sections appeared to us indispensable for an understanding of nineteenth-century development. It cannot be suitably included under any one country, for its application is general. We could not aim or hope for completeness; hence our only objective in these sections has been to bring together an irreducible minimum of pertinent information.

Each successive editor of this *Handbook* has come away from his task impressed with the difficulties of attaining accuracy in dealing with so vast a number of dates covering so wide a range of time and territory. I am no exception to the rule and am far from being arrogant enough to suppose that this new book is even more free from error than the old. There is some consolation, however, in the thought that we collaborators have all done what we reasonably could to guard against blunders and that, as a matter of fact, many dates are so uncertain or disputed that they will probably never be satisfactorily fixed.

The success of the *Epitome of History* over a period of more than two generations is ample proof of the need for a manual of this type. In the revised and extended form here presented, it ought to be more valuable than ever. Its use for students of history is obvious enough, but it ought to prove as helpful to many others. Students of the history of literature and of art should find a concise guide to political history a great boon and all readers of historical novels or biographies should welcome a book of reference to events of the past, to genealogical relationships, and so on. My own experience with the old book was that I used it more as I became better acquainted with it. Nothing would please me more than to have the new edition find a secure place on the shelves of all book-lovers.

In presenting the new *Epitome* I cannot refrain from expressing my profound gratitude to all the contributors and also to Professors Walter Clark and Vincent Scramuzza, to Dr. Sterling Dow, Mr. Eugene Boardman, and to Miss Katharine Irwin for the ready help they gave in reading proof. My secretaries, Mrs. Elizabeth Fox and Mrs. Rosamund Chapman, took care of countless loose ends and deserve more than a little credit for whatever merit the book may have.

CONTRIBUTORS

Dr. Lauriston Ward: The Prehistoric Period (Section I).

Professor Robert Pfeiffer: Early Empires of Africa and Asia (exclusive of India and China; Section II, A, 1–9 inc.).

Mr. Robert O. Schlaifer: Ancient Greece (Section II, B; D).

Professor Mason Hammond: Roman History (Section II, C; E; F).

Professor Charles Gardner: India and China through the 18th century (Sections II, A, 10–11; G, 2–3; III, E, 2–3; IV, F, 3–4).

Mr. Edwin O. Reischauer: Japan and Korea throughout (Sections II, G, 4–5; III, E, 4–5; IV, F, 5–6; V, J, 6–7; VI, F, 11).

Mr. Paul Cram: Western Europe in the Middle Ages (Section III, A, 1; B, 1, 3c; C, 1).

Professor William Thomson: The Moslem World in the Middle Ages (Sections II, G, 1; III, A, 3; B, 3, b, e, f, g).

Professor Michael Karpovich: Russia and Poland throughout and Scandinavia since c. 1500 (Sections III, B, 2, a, c, d; C, 2, a, b, c; IV, A, 7–9; B, 8–10; V, D; VI, B, 12–15).

Professor Crane Brinton: Western and Central Europe c. 1500–1815 (Section IV, A, 1–6; B, 1–7; V, B).

Mr. Robert S. Chamberlain: Latin America throughout (Sections III, F; IV, C; V, H; VI, D).

Professor James B. Hedges: North America, exclusive of Mexico, throughout (Sections IV, D; V, G; VI, C).

Professor Donald C. McKay: Western and Central Europe, 1815–1914 (Sections V, A, 1, 2, 3; C).

Dr. John Fairbank: India and China since c. 1800 (Sections V, J, 3, 4, 5; VI, F, 8, 9, 10).

Professor Penfield Roberts: Western and Central Europe since 1918 (Section VI, B, 1–9).

For all other sections the editor is alone responsible.

In the absence of Mr. Schlaifer, Professor Hammond and Professor Gardner, proofs of their sections were read as follows:

Greek History by Dr. Sterling Dow (Harvard).

Roman History by Professor Vincent Scramuzza (Smith College).

Indian History by Professor Walter C. Clark (Harvard) and Miss Katharine Irwin.

Chinese History by Dr. John Fairbank and Miss Irwin.

Far Eastern History since 1918 by Mr. Eugene P. Boardman.

NOTE

All the dates in this volume are uniformly in the New (Gregorian) Style.

Contents

CHRONOLOGICAL LIST OF IMPORTANT DATES, September 3, 1939–October 18, 1940 xxix

I. THE PREHISTORIC PERIOD

A. INTRODUCTION 1
   1. Definition, Data, and Methods 1
   2. The Origin of Man 1
   3. Cultures and Their Dating 2
      a. Cultures and Periods 2
      b. Relative Dating 2
      c. Absolute Dating 3

B. THE PALAEOLITHIC PERIOD 4
   1. Culture and Industries 4
   2. Europe 4
   3. Africa 5
   4. Asia and Oceania 6
   5. America 7
   6. Interrelationship of Palaeolithic Cultures 7
   7. The Dates of Palaeolithic Cultures 8
   8. Physical Types of Palaeolithic Man 8

C. THE POST–PALAEOLITHIC PERIOD 10
   1. Nature and Sequence of Post-Palaeolithic Cultures . . . 10
      a. Mesolithic Period 10
      b. Neolithic Period 10
      c. Chalcolithic Period 11
      d. Bronze Age 11
      e. Iron Age 11
   2. Modern Races of Man 12
   3. Regional Distribution of Post-Palaeolithic Cultures . . . 13
      a. Asia 13
      b. Europe 14
         (1) Climatic Changes and Time-Scale 14
         (2) Cultural Changes and Periods 15
         (3) Movements of Peoples 15
         (4) Regional Distribution of Cultures 16
      c. Africa 18
      d. Oceania 18
      e. America 19

II. ANCIENT HISTORY

A. EARLY EMPIRES OF AFRICA AND ASIA 21
   1. Egypt 21
   2. Mesopotamia 24
      a. Sumer and Akkad 25
      b. Babylonia 26
      c. Assyria 26
   3. Upper Mesopotamia (Mitanni) 28
   4. Palestine 29
      a. Israel and Judah 29
      b. The Jews 31

5. Phoenicia 32
    a. Carthage 33
6. Syria 34
    a. Damascus 35
7. Asia Minor 35
    a. Hittites 36
    b. Phrygians 36
    c. Lydians 37
    d. Hellenistic Monarchies 37
8. Armenia 38
    a. The Kingdom of Van (Urartu) 38
    b. Armenia 38
9. Iran 39
    a. Elamites 39
    b. Medes 40
    c. Persians 40
10. India 40
11. China 44

B. GREECE 46

1. The Early Period, to C. 500 B.C. 46
    a. Geographical Factors 46
    b. The Aegean Civilization 46
    c. The Invasions 47
    d. Aristocracy and Tyranny; Colonization and Trade . . . 47
    e. Formation of the Greek States 48
        (1) Asia Minor 48
        (2) The Peloponnese 50
        (3) Athens 50
        (4) Central and Northern Greece 52
        (5) Sicily and Magna Graecia 53
2. The Persian Wars 53
3. The Fifth Century 54
    a. The Peloponnese, 479–461 54
    b. Athens and the Delian League, 479–461 55
    c. The First Peloponnesian War 55
    d. Athens, 460–431 56
    e. Sicily, 499–409 57
    f. The Great Peloponnesian War 58
    g. Economic and Social Conditions 61
4. The Rise of Macedon 62
    a. Spartan Hegemony 62
    b. Theban Hegemony 63
    c. Macedon under Philip and Alexander the Great . . . 64
    d. The West during the Fourth Century 66
    e. Greek Culture in the Fourth Century 67

C. ROME, TO 287 B.C. 68

1. The Early Period 68
    a. Geographical Factors 68
    b. Early Populations of Italy 68
    c. The Roman Monarchy 69
2. The Early Republic 70

D. THE HELLENISTIC WORLD 75

1. Cultural Development 75
2. The Wars of the Diadochi 77

3. Sicily to the Roman Conquest 78
4. Macedon and Greece to the Roman Conquest 78
5. The Seleucid Empire and Pergamum 80
6. Parthia 82
7. Bactria 83
8. Ptolemaic Egypt, to the Roman Conquest 83

E. ROME, THE MIDDLE AND LATER REPUBLIC 85
  1. The Punic and Macedonian Wars 85
  2. Domestic Strife and Eastern Conquest 91

F. THE ROMAN EMPIRE 101
  1. The Early Empire (31 B.C.-192 A.D.) 101
  2. The Third Century (192-284) 113
  3. The Later Empire (284-527) 117

G. THE EMPIRES OF ASIA 124
  1. The Neo-Persian Empire of the Sassanians (226-651 A.D.) . 124
  2. India, to 500 A.D. 128
    a. Northern India 128
    b. Southern India 132
    c. Ceylon 132
  3. China, to 618 A.D. 132
  4. Korea, to 562 A.D. 137
  5. Japan, to 645 A.D. 138

III. THE MIDDLE AGES

A. THE EARLY MIDDLE AGES 141
  1. Western Europe 141
    a. The Early Papacy 141
    b. Invaders of the West 142
      (1) The Huns 143
      (2) The Visigoths 143
      (3) The Vandals 144
      (4) The Burgundians 145
    c. The Ostrogoths in Italy, 489–554 145
    d. The Frankish Kingdom, 481–752 147
    The Carolingians 149
    e. The Lombards and the Popes, 568–774 150
    The Papacy in the Carolingian Period 152
    f. The Empire of Charlemagne and Its Disintegration . . 153
    g. The West Franks under the Carolingian Kings, 843–987 . 158
    h. Germany under the Carolingian and Saxon Emperors, 843–1024 159
    i. Spain 163
      (1) The Visigothic Kingdom, 466–711 163
      (2) Moslem Spain, 711–1031 163
      (3) Christian Spain 164
    j. The British Isles 164
      (1) England to 1066 164
      (2) Scotland to 1034 168
      (3) Ireland to 1171 168
    k. Scandinavia 170

  2. Eastern Europe 170
    a. The Eastern Empire to 1025 170
    b. The First Bulgarian Empire to 1018 181
  3. The Moslem World 184
    a. Mohammed and Islam 184
    b. The Omayyad Caliphate, 661–750 186
    c. The Abbasid Caliphate, 750–c. 1100 188

B. THE AGE OF THE CRUSADES 191
  1. Western Europe 191
    a. The British Isles 191
      (1) England, 1066–1307 191
      (2) Scotland, 1034–1304 201
      (3) Ireland, 1171–1307 201
    b. Scandinavia 203
      (1) Denmark, 950–1320 203
      (2) Sweden, 993–1319 203
      (3) Norway, 872–1319 204
    c. Germany under the Salian and Hohenstaufen Emperors, 1024–
      1268 205
      (1) The Teutonic Knights 215
    d. Italy and the Papacy, 888–1314 216
      (1) The Norman Kingdom in South Italy and Sicily, 1105–1194 . 224
      (2) The Development of Italian Towns 224
      (3) The Rise of Venice to 1310 225
    e. France, 987–1314 226
    f. The Iberian Peninsula, 1037–1284 234
      (1) Moslem Spain 234
      (2) Castile 234
      (3) Barcelona and Catalonia 237
      (4) Navarre 239
      (5) Aragon 239
      (6) Portugal to 1279 240
  2. Eastern Europe 241
    a. The Slavs 241
    b. Bohemia and Moravia, to 1306 241
    c. Poland, to 1305 243
    d. Russia, to 1263 244
    e. Hungary, to 1301 247
    f. Serbia, to 1276 249
    g. The Second Bulgarian Empire 250
  3. The Near East 251
    a. The Eastern Empire, 1025–1204 251
    b. The Seljuk Turks 257
    c. The Crusades 258
    d. Latin and Greek States in the Near East, 1204–1261 . . 262
    e. The Mongols 264
    f. Moslem Egypt 266
    g. Moslem Dynasties of North Africa 266

C. THE LATER MIDDLE AGES 268
  1. Western Europe 268
    a. The British Isles 268
      (1) England, 1307–1485 268
      (2) Scotland, 1305–1488 276
      (3) Ireland, 1315–1485 276

b. France, 1314–1483 277
c. The Iberian Peninsula 284
   (1) Castile, 1312–1492 284
   (2) Aragon, 1276–1479 286
   (3) Portugal, 1279–1495 288
d. Italy and the Papacy 290
   (1) The Papacy, 1305–1492 290
   (2) Sicily and Naples, 1268–1494 294
   (3) Florence, to 1492 297
   (4) Milan, to 1500 300
   (5) Venice, 1310–1489 302
e. The Holy Roman Empire 303
   (1) Bohemia, 1306–1471 308
   (2) The Swiss Confederation, to 1499 309
   (3) The Hanseatic League 312
   (4) The Teutonic Knights 315
f. Scandinavia 315
   (1) Denmark, 1320–1387 315
   (2) Sweden, 1319–1387 316
   (3) Norway, 1320–1387 316
   (4) The Union of Kalmar, to 1483 316
2. Eastern Europe 318
a. Poland, 1305–1492 318
b. Lithuania 320
c. Russia, 1263–1505 321
d. Hungary, 1301–1490 322
e. The Serbian States, 1276–1499 323
f. The Eastern Empire, 1261–1453 325
g. The Ottoman Empire, 1300–1481 328

D. AFRICA DURING THE MIDDLE AGES 333

E. ASIA DURING THE MIDDLE AGES 335
1. Persia 335
2. India 335
a. Northern India 335
b. Western India 337
c. Southern India 341
d. Ceylon 345
3. China, 618–1471 345
a. Burma 353
b. Siam 353
c. Malaysia 353
4. Korea 354
5. Japan, 645–1543 355

F. PRE-COLUMBIAN AMERICA 366

G. THE GREAT DISCOVERIES 368
1. Asia 368
2. Africa 369
3. America 371
a. Pre-Columbian Discoveries 371
b. The Voyages of Columbus 372
c. Post-Columbian Discoveries 373

IV. THE EARLY MODERN PERIOD

A. EUROPE AND THE NEAR EAST, 1500–1648 375

   1. England, Scotland, and Ireland, 1485–1649 375
   2. The Netherlands to 1648 385
   3. France, 1483–1641 387
   4. The Iberian Peninsula 393
     a. Spain, 1479–1659 393
     b. Portugal, 1495–1640 396
   5. Italy 398
     a. The Italian Wars, 1494–1559 398
     b. The Papacy 401
     c. Venice 403
     d. Other Italian States 403
   6. Germany 404
     a. Germany, 1493–1618 404
     b. The Thirty Years' War 409
       (1) The Bohemian Period, 1618–1625 . . . 409
       (2) The Danish Period, 1625–1629 . . . 410
       (3) The Swedish Period, 1630–1635 . . . 411
       (4) The French-Swedish Period, 1635–1648 . . 412
     c. The Swiss Confederation 414
   7. Scandinavia 416
     a. Denmark and Norway, 1513–1645 416
     b. Sweden, 1523–1654 416
   8. Poland-Lithuania, 1492–1648 419
   9. Russia, 1505–1645 421
  10. Bohemia, 1471–1627 424
  11. Hungary, 1490–1648 425
  12. The Ottoman Empire, 1481–1656 426

B. EUROPE AND THE NEAR EAST, 1648–1789 431

   1. England, Scotland, and Ireland 431
   2. The Dutch Republic 443
   3. France 446
   4. The Iberian Peninsula 454
     a. Spain 454
     b. Portugal 458
   5. Italy and the Papacy 460
     a. Italy (general) 460
     b. The Papacy 460
     c. Savoy (Sardinia) 463
     d. Naples 463
     e. Other States 464
   6. The Swiss Confederation 465
   7. Germany 466
   8. Scandinavia 475
     a. Sweden 475
     b. Denmark and Norway 480
   9. Poland 480
  10. Russia 483
  11. The Ottoman Empire 487

C. LATIN AMERICA 491

   1. Nature of the Conquest 491
   2. The West Indies and the Isthmus 491

3. Venezuela and New Granada 493
4. Peru and the West Coast 494
5. The Rio de la Plata 495
6. New Spain 495
   a. The Conquest of Mexico 495
   b. Expansion to the South 496
   c. Expansion to the North 497
   d. The Gulf Coast, Florida, and the Carolinas 498
7. Foreign Encroachments and Territorial Changes 498
8. The Spanish Colonial System 500
   a. Population 500
   b. Administration 501
   c. The Church and the Missions 503
   d. Economic Conditions and Policies 504
   e. Education, Learning, and Fine Arts 505
9. Portuguese America 505
10. The Portuguese Colonial System 507

D. NORTH AMERICA 509

1. Exploration and Settlement 509
   a. The French in North America 509
   b. The English in North America 510
      (1) Exploration 510
      (2) Virginia 512
      (3) New England 512
         (a) Massachusetts 512
         (b) Connecticut and Rhode Island 513
      (4) Maryland 514
      (5) Island Settlements 514
   c. Dutch and Swedish Settlements 514
2. Colonial History 515
   a. New England 515
   b. New York, New Jersey, Pennsylvania 516
   c. Virginia, Delaware, and Maryland 517
   d. The Southern Colonies 517
3. Wars of England with France and Spain 518
4. The American Revolution 521

E. AFRICA, 1517–1800 528

F. ASIA 531

1. Persia, 1500–1794 531
2. Afghanistan, to 1793 535
3. India 535
4. China 541
   a. Burma 547
   b. Siam 547
   c. Malaysia 547
5. Korea 548
6. Japan, 1542–1793 548

V. THE NINETEENTH CENTURY

A. SCIENCE AND SOCIETY 557

1. Social Thought and Social Movements 557
2. Scientific Thought and Progress 559
3. Mechanical Inventions and Technical Achievements . . . 560

4. Arctic Exploration 566
   a. Earliest Explorations 566
   b. The Sixteenth Century 566
   c. The Seventeenth and Eighteenth Centuries 568
   d. The Nineteenth Century 569
   e. The Twentieth Century 573
      (1) Conquest of the Pole 573
      (2) The Canadian Arctic 574
      (3) Greenland 575
      (4) The Spitsbergen Area 576
      (5) The Russian Arctic 577
5. Antarctic Exploration 578

B. THE REVOLUTIONARY AND NAPOLEONIC PERIOD . . . 585

  1. Background of the Revolution 585
  2. The National Assembly 586
  3. The Legislative Assembly 587
  4. The National Convention 588
  5. The Directory 591
  6. War of the Second Coalition 593
  7. The Consulate 594
  8. The First Empire 597
  9. The War of the Third Coalition 598
 10. The Peninsular War 600
 11. The War Against Austria 601
 12. Europe, 1810–1812 602
 13. The French Invasion of Russia 604
 14. The Wars of Liberation 605
 15. The Peace Settlements 608
 16. The Hundred Days 609

C. WESTERN AND CENTRAL EUROPE 611

  1. The Congress System, 1815–1822 611
  2. The British Isles 611
   a. The End of the Tory Régime, 1815–1830 611
   b. An Era of Reform, 1830–1846 614
   c. Palmerston and Russell, 1846–1868 619
   d. Disraeli and Gladstone, 1868–1894 621
   e. A Decade of Unionism, 1895–1905 625
   f. The Liberal Régime, 1905–1914 626
  3. The Low Countries 628
   a. The Kingdom of the Netherlands, 1815–1830 (1839) . 628
   b. The Kingdom of Belgium, 1831–1914 630
   c. The Kingdom of the Netherlands, 1830–1914 . . . 632
  4. France 633
   a. The Restoration Monarchy, 1814–1830 633
   b. The July Monarchy, 1830–1848 635
   c. The Second Republic, 1848–1852 637
   d. The Second Empire: the Authoritarian Period, 1852–1860 . 639
   e. The Liberal Empire, 1860–1870 640
   f. The Third Republic, 1870–1914 643
  5. The Iberian Peninsula 650
   a. Spain 650
   b. Portugal 655
  6. Italy 657
   a. The Italian States, 1815–1848 657

b. The Italian War of Independence, 1848–1849 661
c. The Unification of Italy, 1849–1870 662
d. The Kingdom of Italy, 1870–1914 666
7. The Papacy, 1815–1914 670
8. Switzerland 672
9. Central Europe 674
a. Germany,1815–1848 674
b. The Hapsburg Monarchy, 1815–1848 677
(1) Austria 677
(2) Hungary 678
c. The Revolution of 1848–1849 in the Hapsburg Dominions . 680
d. The Revolution of 1848–1849 in Germany 681
e. The Austrian Empire, 1849–1867 685
f. The Unification of Germany 685
g. The German Empire, 1871–1914 695
h. Austria-Hungary, 1867–1914 700
(1) Austria, 1867–1914 700
(2) Hungary, 1867–1914 702

D. NORTHERN AND EASTERN EUROPE 704

1. Scandinavia 704
a. Denmark 704
b. Sweden and Norway 706
2. Russia 708

E. THE BALKANS AND THE NEAR EAST 717

1. The Balkan States 717
a. Greece 717
b. Serbia 719
c. Montenegro 722
d. Bulgaria 722
e. Rumania 726
2. The Ottoman Empire 728

F. INTERNATIONAL RELATIONS, 1870–1914 740

G. NORTH AMERICA 772

1. The United States 772
a. The United States, 1789–1861 772
b. The Civil War, 1861–1865 784
c. The United States, 1865–1921 788
2. British North America, 1783–1914 800
a. The Dominion of Canada 800
b. Newfoundland 806
3. Alaska 807

H. LATIN AMERICA 808

1. The Wars of Independence 808
a. Causes 808
b. Earlier Insurrections, 1721–1806 808
c. The Río de la Plata 809
d. Paraguay 810
e. The Banda Oriental (Uruguay) 810
f. Chile 810
g. Peru and Bolivia 810
h. Venezuela 811

   i. Great Colombia (New Granada, Venezuela and Quito) . . . 811
   j. New Spain (Mexico) 812
   k. Guatemala and Central America 813
   l. Brazil 814
  2. Latin America, 1825–1914 815
   a. Argentina 815
   b. Chile 817
   c. Paraguay 819
   d. Uruguay 819
   e. Bolivia 820
   f. Peru 821
   g. Ecuador 822
   h. Colombia (New Granada) 823
   i. Venezuela 825
   j. Brazil 826
   k. Panama and the Panama Canal Zone 827
   l. Central America 828
    (1) General 828
    (2) Territorial Adjustments 829
    (3) Nicaragua 829
    (4) Honduras 830
   m. Mexico 830
   n. The West Indies 832
    (1) Cuba 832
    (2) Puerto Rico 833
    (3) The Dominican Republic 833
    (4) Haiti 834

I. AFRICA 835
  1. General: Exploration 835
  2. Egypt and the Sudan 837
  3. Ethiopia and the Red Sea Area 843
  4. Northern Africa (Morocco, Algeria, Tunisia, Libya) . . . 846
  5. West Africa and the Sudan (French West Africa, Gambia, Sierra Leone, Gold Coast, Togoland, Nigeria, Cameroons, Rio de Oro, Portuguese Guinea) 848
  6. The Congo Region (French Equatorial Africa, Spanish Guinea, Belgian Congo, Angola) 852
  7. East Africa (British East Africa, Uganda, German East Africa, Nyasaland, Mozambique) 855
  8. South Africa (Cape of Good Hope, Orange Free State, Natal, South African Republic, Rhodesia, German Southwest Africa) . . . 859
  9. Madagascar 869

J. ASIA 872
  1. Persia 872
  2. Afghanistan 876
  3. India 878
  4. Indo-China 881
   a. Burma 881
   b. Siam 882
   c. French Indo-China 883
   d. British Malaya 885
   e. The Malayan Archipelago 886
  5. China 888
  6. Korea 896
  7. Japan 898

K. THE PACIFIC AREA 905
    1. General: Exploration and Annexation 905
    2. Australia 907
    3. New Zealand 915
    4. The Philippines 919
    5. Hawaii 921
    6. Samoa 921

VI. THE WAR AND POST–WAR PERIOD

A. THE WORLD WAR 923
    1. The Western Front, 1914 923
    2. The Eastern Front, 1914 925
    3. The War at Sea, 1914 928
    4. The War in the Colonies, 1914–1918 929
    5. The Ottoman Front, 1914–1915 930
    6. The Western Front, 1915 932
    7. The Eastern Front, 1915 932
    8. Naval Operations — Submarine Warfare 933
    9. The Intervention of Italy 934
    10. The Balkan Situation, 1914–1915 936
    11. The Mesopotamian Campaign, 1914–1916 938
    12. Political Changes, 1915–1916 939
        a. England 939
        b. France 939
        c. Italy 940
        d. Russia 940
        e. Austria-Hungary 940
        f. Germany 940
    13. Verdun and the Somme, 1916 940
    14. The War at Sea. Battle of Jutland 941
    15. The Italian Front, 1916 942
    16. The Eastern Front, 1916 942
    17. The Balkan Front, 1916 942
    18. The Intervention of Rumania 944
    19. Peace Negotiations, 1916–1917, and the Intervention of the United
        States 944
    20. Campaigns in Asiatic Turkey, 1916–1917 946
        a. Arabia 946
        b. Nejd 947
        c. Arab Revolt 947
        d. Mesopotamia 947
    21. The Western Front, 1917 948
    22. The Submarine War, 1917 948
    23. The British Offensives, 1917 949
    24. The Russian Front, 1917 949
    25. The Balkan Situation, 1917 950
    26. The Collapse of Italy, 1917 950
    27. Political Developments, 1917–1918 951
        a. France 951
        b. Austria-Hungary 951
        c. Germany 951
        d. Italy 951
    28. The Settlements in the East, 1917–1918 952
    29. Operations in the West, 1918 953

30. The Action at Zeebrugge and Ostend 955
31. The War in the Air, 1914-1918 955
32. The Russian Situation, 1918 956
33. The Collapse of Turkey 957
34. The Collapse of Bulgaria 957
35. The End of the Hapsburg Monarchy 958
36. The Allied Victory in the West 959
37. The Peace Settlements 961
     a. The Treaty of Versailles 961
     b. The Treaty of St. Germain 962
     c. The Treaty of Neuilly 963
     d. The Treaty of Trianon 963
     e. The Treaty of Sèvres 963

B. EUROPE 964

1. International Affairs 964
     a. The Period of Settlement 964
     b. The Period of Fulfillment 968
     c. The Period of Repudiation and Revision 970
2. The British Isles 976
     a. Great Britain 976
     b. Ireland 980
3. The Low Countries 984
     a. Belgium 984
     b. The Kingdom of the Netherlands 985
4. France 986
5. The Iberian Peninsula 991
     a. Spain 991
     b. Portugal 995
6. Italy and the Papacy 996
     a. Italy 996
     b. The Papacy 1003
7. Switzerland 1004
8. Greater Germany 1006
     a. The German Reich 1006
     b. The Republic of Austria 1015
9. Czechoslovakia 1019
10. Hungary 1024
11. The Balkan States 1027
     a. Yugoslavia 1027
     b. Albania 1029
     c. Greece 1031
     d. Bulgaria 1033
     e. Rumania 1035
12. Russia (Union of Socialist Soviet Republics) 1038
13. Poland 1047
14. The Baltic States 1051
     a. General 1051
     b. Lithuania 1052
     c. Latvia 1053
     d. Estonia 1054
15. The Scandinavian States 1055
     a. General 1055
     b. Denmark 1056
     c. Norway 1056
     d. Sweden 1057
     e. Finland 1057

C. NORTH AMERICA 1059

  1. The United States 1059
  2. The Dominion of Canada 1067
  3. Newfoundland 1070

D. LATIN AMERICA 1072

  1. General 1072
  2. Argentina 1074
  3. Chile 1074
  4. Paraguay 1075
  5. Uruguay 1076
  6. Bolivia 1077
  7. Peru 1078
  8. Ecuador 1078
  9. Colombia 1079
 10. Venezuela 1080
 11. Brazil 1080
 12. Central America 1081
    a. General 1081
    b. Panama 1082
    c. Costa Rica 1082
    d. Nicaragua 1083
    e. Honduras 1083
    f. Salvador 1084
    g. Guatemala 1084
 13. Mexico 1084
 14. The West Indies 1087
    a. Cuba 1087
    b. Haiti 1088
    c. The Dominican Republic 1088
    d. Puerto Rico 1089
    e. Virgin Islands 1089

E. AFRICA 1091

  1. General 1091
  2. Egypt and the Sudan 1091
  3. Ethiopia 1095
  4. North Africa: Morocco, Algeria, Tunisia, Libya 1096
  5. West Africa and the Sudan 1098
  6. The Congo Region: French Equatorial Africa, Spanish Guinea, Belgian Congo, Angola 1099
  7. East Africa: Kenya, Uganda, Tanganyika, Nyasaland, Mozambique 1100
  8. South Africa and Southwest Africa 1101
  9. Madagascar 1102

F. ASIA 1103

  1. Turkey 1103
  2. Syria 1107
  3. Palestine and Transjordania 1109
  4. Saudi Arabia and Yemen 1112
  5. Iraq 1114
  6. Iran 1116
  7. Afghanistan 1118
  8. India 1120

9. Indo-China 1124
   a. Siam 1124
   b. Other States 1124
10. China 1126
11. Japan 1132

G. THE PACIFIC AREA 1137
  1. General 1137
  2. Australia 1137
  3. New Zealand 1140
  4. The Philippines 1141
  5. Hawaii 1143

APPENDICES

   I. Roman Emperors 1145
  II. Byzantine Emperors 1146
 III. The Caliphs, to 1256 1147
 IV. Roman Popes 1148
  V. Holy Roman Emperors 1150
 VI. British Ministries since Walpole 1151
VII. French Ministries, 1815-1870 1152
VIII. Presidents and Prime Ministers of the Third French Republic . 1152
 IX. Italian Ministries since 1860 1154

INDEX i

Genealogical Tables

The Julian-Claudian House 104
The Merovingian Kings 148
The House of Pepin 149
The Carolingian Dynasty 156
The Saxon Emperors 161
The Macedonian Emperors 178
The Norman and Plantagenet Kings 195
The Scottish Succession 202
The Salian Emperors 205
The Welf and Hohenstaufen Families 210
The Capetian Kings 227
Rulers of Leon and Castile 236
The Houses of Navarre, Aragon, and Barcelona 238
Kings of Portugal, Burgundian House 240
The Comneni and Angeli 254
Lancaster and York 273
The French Succession, 1328 278
The Valois House 279
The House of Castile 285
The House of Aragon 287
Kings of Portugal 289
The House of Anjou 295
The Neapolitan Anjous 296
The Medici Family 299
Rulers of Milan 301
The House of Hapsburg 304
The House of Luxemburg 305
The House of Wittelsbach 307
Rulers of Denmark, Norway, and Sweden, 1263-1533 . . . 317
The Palaeologi 326
Succession to the English Crown, 1553-1603 377
The House of Burgundy 386
The French Succession, 1498 388
House of Lorraine and Guise 389
The House of Bourbon, to 1610 391
The Portuguese Succession, 1580 397
The Hapsburg House in the Sixteenth Century 405
Cleve-Jülich Succession, 1609 409
Kings of Denmark, 1448-1670 417
The House of Vasa in Sweden, 1523-1660 418
Kings of Poland, 1445-1668 420
Russian Rulers, 1462-1676 423
Ottoman Sultans, 1451-1649 427
The House of Stuart 439
The Houses of Orange and Nassau, 1559-1843 444
The French Bourbons, 1589-1803 447
The Spanish Succession, 1700 450
The Spanish Bourbons, 1700-1868 455
The House of Braganza, 1640-1826 459
The House of Savoy, 1553-1878 462
The German Hapsburgs, 1556-1835 468
The Hohenzollern House, 1415-1840 470
The House of Vasa, 1523-1818 476
The Danish House of Oldenburg, 1588-1906 479

The House of Romanov, 1613-1801 484
Ottoman Sultans, 1649-1839 488
The Safavid Dynasty 532
The Mogul Emperors 537
The Manchu (Ta Ch'ing) Dynasty, 1644-1795 544
The Tokugawa Shogun, 1603-1867 552
The House of Bonaparte 596
The British Royal House (Hanover, Saxe-Coburg, Windsor) 617
The House of Coburg, 1800-1939 631
The Dutch Royal House, 1815-1939 632
The French Bourbons, 1715-1883 634
The House of Bourbon-Orléans 636
The Spanish Bourbons, 1814-1931 651
The House of Coburg-Braganza 656
The Neapolitan Bourbons 658
The House of Savoy 659
The House of Savoy-Carignan 659
The House of Hapsburg-Lorraine 679
The House of Hohenzollern 686
The Kings of Hanover 689
The Kings of Saxony 690
The Kings of Württemberg 691
The Kings of Bavaria 692
Kings of Denmark since 1746 705
Kings of Sweden since 1751 707
Russian Tsars, 1796-1917 710
Kings of Greece (Danish House) 719
Rulers of Serbia (Yugoslavia) 720
Rulers of Montenegro 723
Rulers of Bulgaria 724
Kings of Rumania 728
Ottoman Sultans, 1703-1922 737
Khedives and Kings of Egypt since 1811 838
The Kajar Dynasty 873
The Barakzai Dynasty 877
The Manchu (Ta Ch'ing) Dynasty, 1795-1912 889
The (Wahabi) Dynasty of Ibn Saud 1113
The Hashimite Dynasty of Iraq 1115
The Pahlavi Dynasty of Iran 1117
Rulers of Afghanistan since 1929 1119
Japanese Emperors since the Restoration 1133

List of Maps

Ancient Empires (Egyptian, Assyrian, Babylonian, Persian) 22
Greek City-States 49
The Kingdoms of Alexander's Successors 76
The Roman Empire Before the Barbarian Invasions 100–101
The Frankish Empire 154
England in Alfred's Day 165
The Byzantine Empire Under Justinian 171
The Mohammedan World About 732 185
Dominions of Henry II 192
Holy Roman Empire and Southern Italy About the Year 1000 . . 206
Christian Expansion in Spain 235
Russian Principalities of the Middle Ages 245
The Eastern Mediterranean During the Crusades 259
The Mongol Empire and Routes to the Far East 265
Italy in the Fifteenth Century 291
The Swiss Confederation, 1291-1453 310
The Hanseatic League and the Teutonic Knights 313
Poland, Lithuania, and Russia in the Fifteenth Century 319
Conquests of the Ottoman Turks 329
Asia about 627 A.D. 336
China in the Last Half of the Twelfth Century 344
India to the Mohammedan Conquest 344
Europe at the Opening of the Sixteenth Century 374–375
Growth of Russia in Europe to 1725 422
Europe After the Treaty of Westphalia (1648) 430–431
The Partitions of Poland 481
Colonial Latin America 492
Early Settlements on the Continent of North America 511
The United States During the Revolution 522
Africa in the Early Sixteenth Century 529
Growth of British Power in India 536
The Manchu Empire 542
Sixteenth-Century Japan 549
The Arctic Regions 567
Antarctic Claims in 1939 579
The Napoleonic Empire at its Height 603
Europe in 1815 610–611
Unification of Italy 663
Europe in 1900 674–675
Central Europe, 1815-1866 675
The Balkan Nations in 1914 718
The Expansion of the United States 773
The United States During the Confederation Period 775
The Civil War, 1860-1865 785
Canada Before Confederation 801
The Growth of Canada 803
Latin-American States After the Revolutions 816
The Partition of Africa 836
The Development of South Africa 860
Asia in 1914 879
The East Indies 887
Australia and New Zealand 908
The Western Front 924

The Eastern Front 926
The Italian Front 935
The Near Eastern Theater of War 938
The Balkan Front 943
Europe After the World War 965
Modern Ireland 981
South America in 1930 1073
Africa in 1939 1092
Western Asia 1108
Eastern Asia in 1937 1125

Chronological List of Important Dates

SEPTEMBER 3, 1939, TO OCTOBER 18, 1940

1939, Sept. 3. **Great Britain and France declared war** on the German Reich in reply to the German invasion of Poland.

Sept. 4. Sinking of the British ship *Athenia* with considerable loss of life. The origin of the attack was never determined.

Sept. 5. The German forces swept on victoriously in Poland, cutting off the Polish Corridor and overrunning Upper Silesia. In South Africa, **Gen. Smuts** succeeded Gen. Hertzog as premier, after the legislature had rejected the Hertzog proposal to maintain neutrality.

Sept. 6. Anglo-French forces began an **advance into the Saar** region, but were forced to withdraw again after some six weeks.

Sept. 8. The Germans appeared before **Warsaw,** which offered valiant resistance, despite heavy bombardment from the air. The city finally surrendered on Sept. 27.

Sept. 10. **Canada declared war** on Germany.

Sept. 14. The Polish resistance, except at Warsaw, suddenly crumbled.

Sept. 16. Soviet Russian forces began to invade Poland from the east. The Polish government fled to Rumania.

Sept. 18. The German and Russian forces met in the vicinity of Brest-Litovsk. On Sept. 22 a provisional agreement was made for the partition of Poland.

Sept. 21. Premier **Calinescu** of Rumania was assassinated by members of the Iron Guard. Gen. George Argeseanu succeeded him, only to be himself replaced by Constantine Argetoianu on Sept. 28. Drastic repression of the Iron Guard by the government.

Sept. 29. Germany and Soviet Russia reached a definitive **agreement on Poland.** At the same time Russia concluded a mutual assistance **pact with Estonia** (also with Latvia, Oct. 5), by which Russia was given naval and air bases in the Baltic countries, as well as the right to garrison certain points.

Oct. 6. Hitler proposed a conference to discuss terms of peace. The suggestion was rejected by England and France (Oct. 10, 12).

Oct. 8. Russia and Germany concluded a trade agreement by which Germany arranged for supplies of vital war materials.

Oct. 10. Conclusion of an **agreement between Russia and Lithuania,** by which the latter was given the disputed town of **Vilna** in return for extensive military rights.

Oct. 18. **Conference at Stockholm** of the three Scandinavian rulers and the president of Finland, apropos of Russian demands presented to Finland on Oct. 9.

Oct. 19. Conclusion of a **pact between England, France, and Turkey,** the three powers promising each other mutual assistance in the event of aggression in the Balkans or eastern Mediterranean.

Nov. 3. The United States Congress voted a **neutrality bill** (cash and carry) as proposed by the administration.

Nov. 7. Queen Wilhelmina of the Netherlands and King Leopold of Belgium, after a conference, offered mediation in the war. England and France declined (Nov. 12).

Nov. 21. Britain declared a **blockade against German exports** and maintained this position despite protests from many neutral powers.

Nov. 24. **George Tatarescu** became prime minister in Rumania.

Nov. 26. Acute tension between Russia and Finland, Russia demanding the withdrawal of troops from the frontier.

Nov. 28. Russia denounced her non-aggression treaty with Finland.

Nov. 30. Beginning of the **RUSSIAN-FINNISH WAR.** The Russian government at once recognized a Bolshevik People's government set up in a frontier town by Risto Ryti. The war was fought on three fronts, from the Arctic (Petsamo) through the center (waist of Finland) to the Karelian Isthmus (Mannerheim Line), the Finns at first scoring a number of successes.

Dec. 13. The German battleship *Graf Spee* was attacked and badly damaged by British cruisers off the Uruguayan coast. It took refuge at Montevideo and, when obliged to leave, was blown up at sea by the commander (Dec. 17).

Dec. 14. Russia was expelled from the League of Nations after refusing the League's demand that negotiations with Finland be reopened.

Dec. 19. The British and French decided to grant the Finns material aid.

Dec. 31. Russia and Japan reached an agreement regarding the disputed fisheries and the Manchukuan debt.

1940, Jan. 13-15. Acute danger of German invasion of the Low Countries.

Jan. 14. A new Japanese cabinet was formed by Admiral Mitsumasa Yonai.

Jan. 15. A permanent Pan-American neutrality committee was set up at Rio de Janeiro.

Jan. 26. Expiration of the trade treaty of 1911 between the United States and Japan.

Feb. 2-4. Conference of the Balkan Entente at Belgrade.

Feb. 14. The Russians began a concerted assault upon the Mannerheim Line.

Feb. 15. A new Bulgarian cabinet was set up by Bogdan Philov.

Feb. 16. A British destroyer rescued British prisoners from the German ship *Altmark*, thereby violating Norwegian territorial waters.

Feb. 26-Mar. 19. Mission of the American diplomat, **Sumner Welles**, to Italy, Germany, France, and England.

Mar. 6. Peace terms submitted by Russia to Finland through the good offices of Sweden.

Mar. 8. England and France offered Finland aid if she would formally ask for it.

Mar. 13. **Russia and Finland concluded peace,** Finland ceding the Karelian Isthmus, with Viborg, the western and northern shores of Lake Ladoga, and various islands in the Gulf of Finland. Russia received a 30-year lease of the Hankö Peninsula and the right to build a railroad across the waist of Finland to the Bothnian Gulf.

Mar. 18. Meeting of Hitler and Mussolini at Brennero.

Mar. 26. Victory of the Liberal Party in the Canadian elections.

Mar. 30. A Chinese government under Japanese auspices was set up at Nanking under the leadership of **Wang Ching-wei.**

Apr. 8. England and France announced the mining of Norwegian territorial waters in order to prevent transit of German ships and supplies.

Apr. 9. **THE GERMANS OCCUPIED DENMARK AND BEGAN THE INVASION OF NORWAY,** seizing most of the seaports by ruse.

Apr. 13. British naval forces attacked the Germans at Narvik in the effort to block the rail connection with the Swedish iron fields.

Apr. 20. England and France landed an expeditionary force in Norway and began an advance inland.

May 2-3. The Anglo-French forces were obliged to withdraw again from southern Norway under acute pressure from superior German forces.

May 10. **GERMAN ARMIES ATTACKED AND INVADED THE NETHERLANDS AND BELGIUM.** The Netherlands were overrun in a short time, the queen and government fleeing to England (May 13).

May 10. **Resignation of the Chamberlain government** in England. **Winston Churchill** formed a coalition government in which the Labour Party was represented.

May 19. **Gen. Maxime Weygand** replaced Gen. Gamelin as commander of the Allied forces in France and Belgium. The Germans advanced rapidly through the frontier defenses, took Sedan and forced a wedge across northern France to Abbéville on the Channel coast (May 21).

May 26. Boulogne fell to the Germans, who thereupon began a movement to encircle the Allied forces in Belgium.

May 28. **King Leopold and the Belgian army surrendered to the Germans,** leaving the British forces and some of the French in an extremely precarious position.

May 29-June 4. Spectacular **evacuation of the British forces from Dunkirk.** The major part of the army was saved, though all equipment was lost.

June 5. Beginning of the **BATTLE OF FRANCE,** the Germans advancing along the whole front of the Somme and Aisne Rivers.

June 9. End of the Norwegian campaign — evacuation of Narvik by the British.

June 9. Russia and Japan came to an agreement regarding the long-disputed Manchukuan frontier.

June 10. **ITALY DECLARED WAR** on England and France and began an advance into southern France.

June 14. The **Germans occupied Paris,** which had been proclaimed an open city. At the same time they began to take the Maginot Line from both front and rear.

June 15. **Russian forces began the occupation of Lithuania, Latvia, and Estonia.**

June 16. Marshal Pétain replaced Reynaud as head of the French government, which had fled first to Tours and then to Bordeaux.

June 17. **The French government sued for peace.**

June 18. **Meeting of Hitler and Mussolini** at Munich to discuss terms of the armistice.

June 18. The **United States Congress reaffirmed the Monroe Doctrine** and devoted itself to an unprecedented program of defense.

June 19. The United States government issued a warning against transfer of territory in the Western Hemisphere from one non-American power to another.

June 21. Rumania became transformed into a totalitarian state.

June 22. Conclusion of an **armistice between Germany and France** at Compiègne. The French were obliged to disarm and to permit the occupation of three-fifths of the country by German troops.

June 23. **Gen. Charles de Gaulle** set up a French National Committee at London to continue the struggle against Germany. This committee was recognized by the British government, which severed relations with the government of Marshal Pétain, ultimately established at Vichy.

June 24. Conclusion of the **armistice between France and Italy.**

June 25. Arrival of Japanese warships at Indo-Chinese ports. Acute uncertainty about the future of **French Indo-China,** through which Japan demanded the right to send armies against China.

June 27. **Rumania ceded Bessarabia** and northern Bukovina to Soviet Russia, under pressure.

June 28. The Republican Convention at Philadelphia nominated **Wendell L.** Willkie and Charles L. McNary as candidates for the presidency and vice-presidency.

July 1. Rumania renounced the Anglo-French guaranty of territorial integrity and turned to Nazi Germany for support.

July 3. **Battle of Oran.** The British called upon the French naval forces to surrender and, on their refusal, opened fire, sinking or capturing an important part of the French fleet in order to keep it from German control.

July 3. **Ion Gigurtu** formed a new cabinet in Rumania.

July 7. Elections for the presidency in Mexico, followed by warm dispute as to the results.

July 10. The French parliament voted to introduce a totalitarian form of government, making Marshal Pétain dictator.

July 16. **Prince Fumumaro Konoye** became premier of Japan, with a program of national reorganization along totalitarian lines.

July 18. The Democratic Convention at Chicago nominated **President Roosevelt** to run for a third term, with Henry A. Wallace as vice-presidential candidate.

July 18. The British government yielded to the Japanese demand that the **Burma Road** to China be closed. In return Japan promised to try to make peace with Nationalist China.

July 20. President Roosevelt signed a bill providing for the construction of a **"two-ocean" navy,** as part of a tremendous defense plan.

July 21-30. **Meeting of American foreign ministers at Havana.** Agreement for action against "fifth-column" activities and provision for the joint administration in trust of derelict European colonies in the Western Hemisphere.

July 21. **Lithuania, Latvia, and Estonia,** under governments controlled by Russia, **asked incorporation in the Soviet Union,** which was graciously granted.

Aug. 4-19. The Italian **campaign against British Somaliland.** The British, with but few forces available, were obliged to fall back on Berbera and finally evacuate the whole colony.

Aug. 9. The British withdrew their garrisons from Shanghai and northern China.

Aug. 11. Acute tension in **Italian-Greek relations.** Mysterious attacks on Greek warships.

Aug. 11. Beginning of the **BATTLE OF BRITAIN,** in the form of large-scale air attacks on many parts of the country, including London (Aug. 15). The British air forces retaliated by widespread raids on German bases in France and the Low Countries, as well as upon the German and Italian industrial centers.

Aug. 17. President Roosevelt and Premier Mackenzie King of Canada set up an **American-Canadian Joint Defense Board.**

Aug. 30. Rumania, threatened by attack from Hungary and subjected to great pressure from Germany and Italy (Vienna Conference), was obliged to agree to the **cession of the northern half of Transylvania** to Hungary.

Sept. 3. The United States and Great Britain concluded an important agreement by which the United States turned over fifty World War destroyers in exchange for two naval and air bases and the 99-year lease of six others, extending all the way from Newfoundland to the South American coast.

Sept. 6. Gen. Antonescu became dictator in Rumania and opened negotiations with the Iron Guard. In the midst of grave disorders, King Carol was obliged to flee. He was succeeded by his son as **Michael V.**

Sept. 7. Beginning of the great **German air offensive against London.**

Sept. 7. Rumania signed an agreement with Bulgaria providing for the **retrocession of the Southern Dobrudja.**

Sept. 15. Beginning of the **Italian invasion of Egypt** from Libya.

Sept. 16. Passage of the **Selective Training and Service Act,** in the United States. This provided for the registration of all men between 21 and 36 years of age and for the training, for one year, of 1,200,000 troops and 800,000 reserves.

Sept. 21. The Bulgarians occupied the Southern Dobrudja, in accordance with the agreement with Rumania.

Sept. 22. The Japanese began to occupy parts of French Indo-China after the French government had agreed to the use of the three airfields and other concessions.

Sept. 23-25. Gen. de Gaulle and a force of "free Frenchmen," supported by the British navy, attempted to take over **Dakar** in French West Africa. Resistance of French warships in the harbor and of shore batteries led to severe fighting and finally to abandonment of the attempt.

Sept. 27. **CONCLUSION OF THE GERMAN-ITALIAN-JAPANESE PACT,** a ten-year military and economic alliance by which the contracting powers promised each other mutual assistance in the event of any one of them becoming involved in war with any power not yet a belligerent.

Oct. 4. Second **meeting of Hitler and Mussolini** on the Brenner Pass, evidently with the purpose of discussing new moves in the Balkans and Near East.

Oct. 11. German forces began to **arrive in Rumania** in considerable numbers, officially in order to train the Rumanian forces and to protect the oil wells against British designs. Rumania passed under German control.

Oct. 18. The British government reopened the **Burma Road,** in order to facilitate the shipment of supplies to China.

I. The Prehistoric Period

A. INTRODUCTION

1. DEFINITION, DATA, AND METHODS

HISTORY in its broadest sense should be a record of Man and his accomplishments from the time when he ceased being merely an animal and became a human being. The efforts to reconstruct this record may be classed under two heads: (1) **History** (in the stricter sense), which is based on written documents and covers part of the last five thousand years of Man's activities, and (2) **Prehistory**, which is based largely on archaeological evidence and covers all the long preceding period, which probably amounts to more than one million years.

The prehistoric period is important, not only by reason of its vast length, but also because during this time Man made almost all his major discoveries and adaptations to environment and group-life (except those connected with the recent machine age) and evolved physically into the modern racial types. Hence at least a brief summary of the prehistoric period is a necessary introduction to any account of the recorded history of Man.

The main body of material upon which the work of prehistoric reconstruction is based comprises: first, remains left by early peoples, largely in the form of tools and other artifacts, found by excavation in old habitation sites or burials; secondly, other traces of their activities, such as buildings and rock-carvings or rock-paintings; and lastly, the bones of the people themselves. This material gives good evidence of the physical type of prehistoric peoples and their material culture, very slight evidence of their social, intellectual, and religious life and no evidence of their language. It can be supplemented to some extent — and with great caution — by a comparative study of the physical types, languages, and material culture of modern peoples.

The time when prehistory ends and true history begins varies greatly in different parts of the world. Traditional history often covers the borderline between the two and can sometimes be successfully correlated with the archaeological evidence.

In prehistory, dates are entirely a matter of estimate and cannot be used as fundamental landmarks, as in the case of recorded history.

2. THE ORIGIN OF MAN

MAN'S PLACE AMONG THE ANIMALS. The various living and extinct species of Man are assigned by zoologists to the family *Hominidae*, which belongs to the sub-order *Anthropoidea* (containing monkeys, apes, and baboons), of the order **Primates** (containing also *Tarsius* and the lemurs), of the class **Mammalia**. His nearest living relatives are the four genera of the family *Simiidae* (the so-called Anthropoid Apes): the gorilla and chimpanzee of equatorial Africa and the orang-utan and gibbon of southeastern Asia and the East Indies. Man is distinguished from the higher apes by the greater size of his brain (especially the fore-brain), his fully erect position in walking, the better adaptation of his hands for grasping and holding, and his use of language for communication.

MAN'S ANIMAL ANCESTORS. No remains have yet been found of Man's immediate precursor, the primitive and more ape-like animal from which he is supposed to be descended. Neither have we yet found any certain traces of the postulated animal (often popularly termed the *Missing Link*) from which both Man and the anthropoid apes are descended. Several forms of fossil apes have been found, however, which show a kinship to Man in some particulars and help to bridge over this gap: notably *Propliopithecus*, from the Lower Oligocene of Egypt; *Sivapithecus*, from Miocene India; *Dryopithecus*, from Miocene France; and *Australopithecus* (the "Taungs skull"), from the Pliocene or Pleistocene of South Africa.

DATE OF MAN'S ORIGIN. This has not yet been definitely established. The ancestors of the great apes and the ancestor of Man probably diverged from one another as early as the Miocene period, and Man acquired certain essentially human characteristics probably in the

Pliocene period. The earliest known skeletal remains that are accepted as human are believed to date from the early or middle part of the Pleistocene period. For the purposes of the prehistorian, who has to rely largely on archaeological evidence, the record of Man may be said to begin at the moment when he was able to fashion the first stone tools which can be unmistakably recognized to be of human workmanship. This was early in the Pleistocene, or possibly in the very late Pliocene.

PLACE OF MAN'S ORIGIN. This is still entirely a matter of speculation. The old theory of Central Asia as the "Cradle of Mankind" was based on false premises, which have been abandoned. From the distribution of the living and fossil great apes, it is thought that Man's divergence from the general anthropoid stem is likely to have taken place somewhere in the area comprising western Europe, the northern half of Africa, and southern Asia, with the preference perhaps slightly in favor of Africa or Asia, but there is no real evidence at present to warrant a final conclusion.

3. CULTURES AND THEIR DATING

a. CULTURES AND PERIODS

Archaeological investigation of the material remains of prehistoric Man has shown that a wide variety of cultures flourished in different parts of the world and at different times. For convenience these have been grouped into a series of major cultures based primarily on the nature of the principal material used for implements (whether stone or one of the metals), and sometimes on the technique used in fashioning these implements. The oldest culture in the world was characterized by the use of chipped stone for implements and has been named Palaeolithic culture. Neolithic culture, on the other hand, was characterized by the use of polished stone implements; Bronze culture, by the use of bronze implements, and so forth.

In most parts of the world the discovery and use of these different materials and techniques took place in a regular sequence in time. In the absence of fixed dates, it was thus found convenient to use these cultural terms in a chronological sense. Accordingly prehistoric times have usually been divided into the following series of periods or ages (beginning with the oldest): **Palaeolithic** (Old Stone), characterized by chipped stone implements; **Mesolithic** (Intermediate Stone), a transitional period; **Neolithic** (New Stone), with polished stone implements; **Chalcolithic** (Stone and Copper), characterized by the first tentative use of copper implements; **Bronze Age,** with full development of copper and bronze implements; and **Iron Age,** with iron implements.

These names are excellent to identify cultures, but their use to designate periods of time has led to much inaccuracy and confusion, as the dates of the cultures to which they refer differ widely in different parts of the world. It is proper, for example, to speak of the Bronze Age of Hungary or some other limited area, where the beginning and end of the bronze culture can be fairly accurately dated. But it is quite impossible to speak with any meaning of the Bronze Age of the Old World, for this period began some thousand or fifteen hundred years earlier in Mesopotamia, for instance, than it did in western Europe, and it gave way to the Iron Age one or two thousand years earlier in Asia Minor than it did in some parts of Siberia; while in Japan there was no true Bronze Age and in Australia no Bronze Age at all. The names of these periods are, however, too well established to be abandoned and are often useful, if employed with caution.

DATING. As there are no written documents, a variety of other means have been employed to determine the duration and dates of prehistoric cultures.

b. RELATIVE DATING

This is established by the following methods:

(1) **Stratigraphy.** When there is accurate excavation of a site, the undisturbed remains in any given level may fairly safely be assumed to be earlier than the remains in the levels that overlie it.

(2) **Typology.** The age of a given culture may sometimes be determined approximately when most of the objects representing it appear to be identical in type with objects found elsewhere in a culture which has been dated by other means.

(3) **Geology.** The relative age of different remains can often be ascertained by finding the relative age of the geological strata in which the remains occur, as in the case of a series of sedimentary deposits, or river terraces and raised beaches, marking former shorelines or flood levels in valleys at times when the mutual rela-

tion of land and water was different from that of the present.

(4) **Palaeontology.** The presence (with the human remains) of extinct or still existing species of animals (including marine and lacustrine fauna) frequently provides a fairly exact basis for dating the human remains, in terms of geological periods.

(5) **Palaeobotany.** The presence of plant remains furnishes a further basis for assigning associated human remains to certain geological periods.

(6) **Climatic evidence.** When the past record of major climatic sequences in an area is known, human remains can often be dated in terms of glacial advances and retreats or pluvial and dry periods, if the remains are found in deposits characteristic of such periods. The kinds of animals and plants found in association with the human remains frequently show whether the climate of the period in question was wet or dry or warm or cold. Thanks to the great progress which has recently been made in palaeobotany it is now possible to trace climatic fluctuations (as reflected by the immigration of new forest forms) through microscopic examination of pollen grains preserved intact for thousands of years in peat beds and elsewhere. Associated archaeological remains can thus often be referred with great accuracy to a given climatic phase.

There is considerable room for error in the use of each of these methods, unless the greatest care is exercised, but they are all sound in principle and in general they may be relied upon, particularly when one confirms another. The ideal system would make use of all the methods listed above, establishing for any area the sequence of climatic changes, earth movements and deposits, and using this as a chronological framework into which to fit the successive cultures, reconstructed on the basis of the stratigraphy of the archaeological remains. For very few regions has this been done.

c. ABSOLUTE DATING

This is more difficult, but several methods have been used.

(1) **Estimate of the time needed to produce observed changes in culture.** There is no exact basis for such estimates, and this method, though often the only one available, is extremely inaccurate and inadequate.

(2) **Estimate of the time necessary for the performance of certain geological work.** This is used to date geological horizons in which human remains occur. For example, the date of a high river terrace may be given if it is estimated that it must have taken the river at least one hundred thousand years to cut down its bed to the present level. Such estimates are almost equally uncertain and inadequate for the purposes of the prehistorian.

(3) **Extent of the breakdown of radioactive minerals in certain rocks.** This method is based on a process that can be measured with some exactness and has been used to determine the age of the great geological epochs but cannot yet be applied accurately to any period that is much under half a million years.

(4) **Geochronology;** that is, the counting of the annual layers (varves) of sediment deposited by the melt-waters of a retreating ice-sheet. This method, first devised by the Swedish scientist, De Geer, has been applied to the Scandinavian region as the basis of an absolute system of chronology covering the last twelve thousand years. Owing to the scarcity of archaeological remains found *in situ* in dated varves, this system is of value principally in correlating and dating the different stages of the retreat of the last ice-sheet and the major fluctuations in sea-level in the Baltic area. These in turn serve to date many deposits which, by pollen analysis, can be assigned to the various post-glacial climatic cycles. Thus indirectly the archaeological remains found in these deposits can be tentatively dated.

(5) **Dendrochronology.** This method, devised by Douglass and applied first in the southwestern United States, is based on the fact that certain species of trees, especially in arid regions, show by the thickness of their annual rings of growth the alternation of relatively wet or dry years. By matching many specimens from trees of various ages it has been possible to construct a time scale by which to date timbers found in prehistoric ruins.

(6) **Historical evidence.** Late prehistoric cultures in backward areas can sometimes be dated in a general way by the presence of imported objects from a known historical culture in some more advanced area, where written documents already exist.

It is thus seen that dates assigned to prehistoric periods are, for the present at least, almost entirely a matter of estimate. In some cases the estimates of most experts are in more or less general agreement, but often they vary widely, depending upon the person who makes them and the particular methods he relies upon as a basis for his dating.

B. THE PALAEOLITHIC PERIOD

(Probably over one million years in duration, ending about 8000 B.C.)

1. CULTURE AND INDUSTRIES

THE word *Palaeolithic* is used to describe a stage of human culture, the earliest of which we have sure evidence. Although this culture persisted longer in some parts of the world than in others, we can use the term with reasonable accuracy to characterize a period of time. This period includes probably 99 per cent of Man's life on earth (at least since he became a tool-using animal), all the other periods down to the present covering the remaining 1 per cent.

Our knowledge of Palaeolithic culture is based principally on implements and animal and human bones found in the gravels of old river terraces, in open camp sites, and in caves. Disregarding the variations of time and place, one may say in general that Palaeolithic men knew the use of fire and lived by hunting and collecting vegetable foods, as the Australian natives and the Bushmen of South Africa do today. They had no agriculture and no domestic animals, excepting possibly the dog. For shelter they probably made wind-breaks and crude huts of branches, occasionally occupying caves. Their clothing was undoubtedly of skins (no textiles). Their tools and utensils were of stone, bone, and undoubtedly also of wood and basketry (no metal and no pottery). We know almost nothing of their social organization, religion, and intellectual life, except that late cave paintings and burials indicate belief in magic (in connection with hunting) and in some kind of existence of the individual after death. It is fairly safe to assume, however, that a large part of the fundamental institutions and beliefs of modern primitive peoples and of our own early historical ancestors had their origin and first development in this period.

The **stone tools,** which are such important criteria for this period, were usually made of flint or other hard rock by a process of chipping. They are classified as **core tools,** when the basis of the implement was a piece of rock, improved by chipping, or **flake tools,** when one of the flakes knocked off from a core (which is then termed a nucleus) was used as the basis for the implement. Sometimes the core was made ready for flaking by first creating a flat surface or striking-platform. Chips were removed by striking with another stone (hammer stone) or by pressure (pressure flaking). Sometimes the edges of a flake were improved by secondary chipping or flaking (retouching). The principal types of implements were hand-axes or *coups de poing* (large pear-shaped or almond-shaped cores, chipped on both sides); scrapers of various shapes; points; awls (borers); and, in late times, long blades with roughly parallel edges, and gravers (small tools of many shapes improved for use as chisels or gouges by striking a special blow near the point).

2. EUROPE

The **Pleistocene period,** or Ice Age, in which Palaeolithic culture developed and flourished, was marked, at least in the Alpine regions, by four major glacial advances (Günz, Mindel, Riss, and Würm), separated by three warmer interglacial periods. The last glaciation had two maxima (Würm I and II), during which much of northern Europe was covered by a sheet of ice, but between them was a comparatively warm period, the Laufen oscillation.

PRE-PALAEOLITHIC. Assigned to this period, at the end of the Pliocene and early part of the Pleistocene, are certain occasional finds of crude, shapeless stones, called *eoliths*, which are supposed by some archaeologists to show traces of Man's first attempts at chipping, but this is still a matter of dispute. Here also come three so-called industries of Reid Moir: the Iceian industry, characterized by rostrocarinate tools; the Darmsdenian, a pebble industry; and the Harrisonian, an industry of so-called utilized flakes.

LOWER PALAEOLITHIC. This period covers the greater part of the Pleistocene. Almost our only information about the peoples and movements of this time consists of what may be inferred from the stone implements, which show, according to Breuil, the contemporary but more or less independent development and mutual inter-influence in western Europe of four separate techniques of manufacture (industries): (1) **Hand-axe** industry (French *biface*), developing through Pre-Chellean (Abbevillian) to Acheulean types; (2) **Clactonian** industry, characterized by rough flakes with an unfaceted striking-platform inclined at a high angle to the main flake surface; (3) **Levalloisean** industry, characterized by large flakes struck from a previously prepared core (tortoise core) and retaining a faceted striking-platform; and (4) **Mousterian** industry, consisting of smaller flakes of various forms, usually exhibiting a characteristic technique of retouching the edges (stepped retouch). These industries are found both separate and mixed, and there are additional intermediate forms. Chronologically they have been grouped into four periods: (1) **Pre-Chellean** (Abbevillian) period, characterized by extremely crude hand-axes; (2) **Chellean** period (now usually included with Acheulean), having hand-axes somewhat less crude than the Abbevillian, as well as some Clactonian tools; (3) **Acheulean** period, marked by more highly evolved hand-axes and, particularly in its later stages, by Levallois flakes; and (4) **Mousterian** period (sometimes designated as Middle Palaeolithic), with typical flake tools (points and scrapers) and a continuation in some places of Levallois flakes. The Mousterian industry proper (which has Pre-Mousterian or Proto-Mousterian forerunners in northern and eastern Europe) is found particularly in the caves of central France, associated with bones of mammoth and reindeer and of Neanderthal Man.

UPPER PALAEOLITHIC. This is a relatively short period, coinciding with the last part of the Ice Age and marked by the appearance of new flint industries and men of modern type (*Homo sapiens*). Three principal cultures are noted: (1) **Aurignacian** culture. This was the earliest. Evidence shows that the climate was comparatively warm. The people were nomadic hunters, living in open camps and caves. The stone industry was marked by great use of the blade and included a variety of characteristic scrapers, gravers, points (Châtelperron, Gravette, Font Robert types), and beginning of very small tools (*microliths*); also bone implements and ornaments of shell and bone. Aurignacian remains are found widely through central and western Europe and the Mediterranean region. (2) **Solutrean** culture. This is distributed from eastern and central Europe as far as France, intruding on the Aurignacian. The climate was cold. The Solutreans lived in open camps and rock shelters, were great hunters of horses, and introduced the technique of pressure flaking (willow-leaf and laurel-leaf points). (3) **Magdalenian** culture, the latest to develop, flourished in northern and central Europe and southern France. The climate was somewhat colder and the Magdalenians lived frequently in caves, where they made remarkable rock-carvings and paintings, representing animals and men. Besides stone tools there was a high development of bone carving (spearheads, harpoons, *bâtons de commande*, and representations of animals).

The Palaeolithic period in Europe ended with the great changes in climate, fauna, and flora that marked the termination of the Pleistocene or Ice Age.

3. AFRICA

The Palaeolithic of Africa is characterized by a variety of stone industries, some of which are purely local, while others are similar to or practically identical with certain of the industries of Europe. Geological investigation, which has only recently been undertaken on an adequate basis, indicates that owing to fluctuations in rainfall the Pleistocene period throughout most of Africa can perhaps be divided into a succession of pluvial and interpluvial periods, which it is hoped may eventually be correlated in some way with the glacial and interglacial periods of Europe. The succession of cultures is well established for certain areas, but not yet for the continent as a whole.

NORTHWEST AFRICA. Heavily patinated hand-axes of definitely Chellean and Acheulean types together with an early fauna have been found, usually without stratigraphy, in Tunisia, Algeria, Morocco, and to the south in the Sahara region, which was apparently once less arid than now. A so-called Mousterian industry (accompanied by a later fauna) is also represented, and excavations show an evolution from Levalloisean types, without typical Mousterian, to a special development known as the **Aterian** industry, characterized by small, tanged leaf-shaped points, delicately trimmed all over both faces. This was succeeded by two contemporary cultures, the early **Capsian** and the **Oranian**

(Ibero-Maurusian), which were Upper Palaeolithic in date and marked by blades, gravers, and microlithic forms, the earliest phases of which bear a fundamental though distant relationship to the early Aurignacian of Europe.

EGYPT. The presence of Palaeolithic Man is shown by discoveries of the following succession of industries, all *in situ*, in the terraces of the Nile Valley: Chellean, a primitive Acheulean and an Egyptian form of the Clactonian, in the 100-foot terrace (no human implements were found in the 150-foot terrace); developed Acheulean in the 50-foot terrace; Levalloisean (first reported as Early Mousterian) in the 30-foot terrace; and developed Levalloisean (reported as Egyptian Mousterian) in the 15- to 10-foot terrace. These were followed, in deposits of later age, by an Egyptian version of the Aterian and a local industry, the Sebilian.

EAST AFRICA. According to Leakey, who has done the most work in this area, there is an early series of industries in Kenya, Uganda, and Tanganyika, which apparently evolved from simple pebbles, roughly chipped to an edge on one side (**Kafuan** industry), through pebbles chipped to an edge on both sides (**Oldowan** industry) and through other intermediate forms to the true hand-axe types (Chellean and Acheulean industries). In higher geological horizons, and thought to be partly contemporary with one another, are found two series of industries, Aurignacian and a sparsely represented Levalloisean (followed by the Stillbay) — both with many stages. Leakey assigns the Kafuan to the First Pluvial period of East Africa (Lower Pleistocene), the Chellean and Acheulean to the Second or Kamasian Pluvial period (Middle Pleistocene), and the Aurignacian and Levalloisean-Stillbay to the Third or Gamblian Pluvial period (Upper Pleistocene).

SOUTH AFRICA. Here the **Stellenbosch** culture, containing Chellean and Acheulean types (hand-axes and cleavers and Victoria West cores), was followed, stratigraphically, by the **Fauresmith** culture (hand-axes and also flakes with faceted striking-platform, suggesting Levalloisean influence), which together form the so-called Older Stone Age. The Middle Stone Age was marked by a series of more or less contemporary flake industries (Mossel-bay, Glen Grey Falls, Howieson's Poort, Bambata Cave, Stillbay, etc.), suggesting by the shapes and technique of their implements a combination of Levalloisean and Aurignacian influences, together with pressure-flaking in one case (Stillbay).

OTHER AREAS. Occasional finds of implements similar to those of some of the industries already described have been reported from Nigeria, the Sudan, Abyssinia, Somaliland, the Congo region, and northern Rhodesia

4. ASIA AND OCEANIA

WESTERN ASIA. A remarkably complete sequence of stone industries, paralleling quite closely those of Europe, has been established for the Palestine-Syria region. Surface finds of Chellean implements are supplemented (in three caves in the Wady-el-Mughara, near Mt. Carmel) by the following stratigraphic series: Tayacian, Upper Acheulean, Levalloiseo-Mousterian (with skeletons of Neanderthaloid type), Aurignacian, and Natufian (a Mesolithic industry). Occasional sites with implements of one or another of these types have been reported from northern Arabia, Asia Minor, Armenia, Transcaucasia, Mesopotamia, and Persia.

INDIA. Many implements of Chellean type, as well as Acheulean hand-axes and cleavers, have been reported in northern, central, and southern India. In the Punjab, De Terra found Acheulean hand-axes in a deposit contemporary with the second Himalayan glaciation or somewhat later. These were succeeded by a crude pebble industry (Soan industry) in strata contemporary with the third Himalayan glaciation. A few Upper Palaeolithic types, with some suggestions of Aurignacian, have also been found in central and northwestern India, as well as cave sites with rock paintings of uncertain age.

CHINA. Skulls of Peking Man (*Sinanthropus pekinensis*), together with traces of fire and very shapeless stone tools, have been excavated in Middle Pleistocene deposits at Chou-kou-tien, southwest of Peiping. Implements of general Upper Palaeolithic type were found in the Ordos region, accompanied by remains of animals related to those associated with the last glacial advance in Europe. Other finds of a similar nature have been reported from Mongolia and Manchuria, but none to date from Japan.

SIBERIA. Hearth sites, Palaeolithic implements and remains of extinct animals have been found in southwestern and central Siberia, especially in the basin of the Ob River and its tributaries, the valleys of the Upper Yenisei (Minusinsk region) and Angara Rivers and around Lake Baikal. Some of the implements resemble quite closely certain Mousterian, Aurignacian, and Magdalenian forms of western Europe. The deposits in which they occur and the fauna suggest that they belong to the Upper Palaeolithic period.

SOUTHEASTERN ASIA AND OCEANIA. The occurrence of a Palaeolithic culture in parts of this region has been reported, as evidenced by crude chipped stone tools unaccompanied by polished stone or pottery, and (in Tonkin) these actually occur below levels containing polished stone tools and pottery. Many of the familiar types of Palaeolithic tools are lacking, however, and recent investigation has revealed that these industries definitely date from the New Stone Age or at earliest from the Mesolithic. In Burma, however, a new Lower Palaeolithic culture (Anyathian), associated with extinct fauna, has been discovered in the Middle Pleistocene terraces of the Irrawaddy River. In Java an important series of remains of early Man has been found, including *Homo modjokertensis*, in a Lower Pleistocene horizon; the famous *Pithecanthropus erectus*, which is now shown by the associated fauna to be Middle Pleistocene in date; and Solo Man, belonging to the Upper Pleistocene. Surface finds of implements of Lower Palaeolithic type and points and scrapers of general Upper Palaeolithic appearance have also been reported from Java. No Palaeolithic remains have been found in Polynesia.

5. AMERICA

For an account of alleged Palaeolithic cultures in America, see below.

6. INTERRELATIONSHIP OF PALAEOLITHIC CULTURES

It should be clear from the foregoing that at present we know a great deal more about Palaeolithic stone implements than we do about the Palaeolithic people who made them. Our data are still too insufficient to warrant any sure account of the way in which the various elements of Palaeolithic culture were developed by different groups of mankind and spread by them throughout the world. However, three fundamental facts relating to this problem may be regarded as reasonably well established:

First, some of the more highly evolved implements and groups of implements found in widely different areas are so similar in shape and technique that we are forced to infer that the cultures in which they occur bear some time-relationship to one another, i.e. the art of making the typical implements in question (such as the hand-axe, the Levallois flake and the Aurignacian blade, to name three fundamental examples) was not evolved independently at different times and in different places but was spread from some original center, either by actual migrations of people or by cultural diffusion.

Second, the geographical distribution of these various type implements, although very wide, is not haphazard, but each one of the fundamental industries has its own distinct area of major development, with outliers along natural routes of migration. For example, the industry characterized by core implements of hand-axe type is found in one continuous area, comprising southwestern Asia, eastern and northern Africa, and southern and western Europe, with outliers in South Africa and India. A less sharply definable industry, characterized by the use of flake implements in preference to cores and (in its most developed form) by the use of flake implements of Levalloisean type with a faceted striking-platform, has its home in the same area, with addition of a broad belt stretching through central and eastern Europe and northern Asia. Finally the blade industry has a distribution which is practically identical with that last described, though with a less characteristic development in South Africa and India. The southeastern part of Asia, from the North China plain to Indonesia, seems to form a separate culture province, with an almost entirely independent development throughout Palaeolithic times.

Third, the three major industries just referred to had their principal development at different periods of time, as is shown by the fact that wherever there is stratigraphic evidence they occur in the same order of succession, with the hand-axe industry the earliest, succeeded in turn by the Levalloisean flake industry and that by the blade industry, the latest of all. The foregoing outline is, of course, oversimplified and disregards many problems of local development and relations, but it is based on a mass of evidence, it represents the best opinion of archae-ologists today, and it may be accepted provisionally as a true interpretation of the facts.

7. THE DATES OF PALAEOLITHIC CULTURES

The Palaeolithic period of Man's development is considered to be roughly contemporary with the Pleistocene period of the earth's history and has to be dated in geological terms. The Pleistocene may be broadly divided, on the basis of faunal remains, into Lower, Middle, and Upper or (in Europe at least), on the basis of Alpine glacial deposits, into four major periods of glacial advance (Günz, Mindel, Riss, and Würm) with three corresponding interglacial periods. The dating of Palaeolithic industries in terms of Alpine glacial and interglacial periods is still, however, a highly speculative affair, owing to the fact, which is not always properly appreciated, that almost no archaeological remains have yet been found in actual glacial deposits of the Alpine region. Attempts have been made to correlate glaciations in Asia and Africa with these Alpine glaciations and to correlate with both the series of implement-bearing river terraces (especially of the Thames, Somme, and Nile) and implement-bearing deposits of so-called Pluvial periods in non-glaciated regions (notably in East Africa), but only preliminary work has yet been done on this large and complicated problem. Hence statements of experts regarding the age of the earlier Palaeolithic cultures differ greatly and should be regarded as opinions or theories only, which require further evidence before they can be accepted as established fact.

That tool-making man existed as early as the Lower Pleistocene period has been contended by a number of authorities. Teilhard de Chardin has dated the Sinanthropus finds at Chou-kou-tien as possibly Lower Pleistocene, and Breuil considers that deposits containing his Abbevillian (Pre-Chellean) industry and the earliest Clactonian industry belong to the First (Günz-Mindel) Interglacial period. Various alleged implements of a very primitive nature (including the so-called *eoliths*) found in Europe and Africa have been ascribed to this period and Reid Moir claims to have found tools of primitive types in deposits that are presumably of pre-Günz age. Such early dates are not yet universally accepted by archaeologists and geologists.

When we come to the Middle Pleistocene, however, there is a more general agreement that the early phases of the hand-axe and flake industries (Chellean, Clactonian, etc.) in Europe and Africa probably existed in the Second (Mindel-Riss) Interglacial period. De Terra has found similar implements in India in deposits contemporary with the end of his Second Himalayan Glacial Advance or the following interglacial period (which may be contemporary respectively with the Second or Mindel Glaciation of Europe and the Mindel-Riss Interglacial).

Furthermore, it is thought very probable that in Europe the fully developed Acheulean and associated Levalloisean industries belong to the Third (Riss-Würm) Interglacial period, the typical Mousterian to the end of this period and the first maximum of the Fourth Glacial period (Würm I), the Aurignacian to the time of the Laufen oscillation, the Solutrean to the second maximum of the Fourth Glacial (Würm II), and the Magdalenian to the last stages and retreat of Würm II. African and Asiatic implements that show relationship to some of the above industries are probably roughly contemporary with them.

It is impossible to give an absolute date to these periods in years. Most recent geological opinion assigns a duration of one and one half to two million years for the Pleistocene. This would mean that the earliest man whose tools we have found and certainly identified lived perhaps as much as a million years ago. It is estimated (largely on the basis of De Geer's studies of varves in the Scandinavian area) that for Europe the Pleistocene period ended (and with it the Palaeolithic Age) circa 8000 B.C.

8. PHYSICAL TYPES OF PALAEOLITHIC MAN

Very few human skeletal remains have been found which can be assigned with any certainty to the Lower or Middle Pleistocene or which are so primitive in type that they are assumed to belong to these early periods. The principal ones are *Homo modjokertensis*, from the Lower Pleistocene of Java; *Pithecanthropus erectus*, from the Middle Pleistocene of Java; *Sinan-*

thropus pekinensis (**Peking Man**), from the Middle Pleistocene of China; *Eoanthropus dawsoni* (**Piltdown Man**), found in England and generally thought to belong to the Lower Pleistocene; *Homo heidelbergensis*, from an early interglacial deposit of Germany; and **Rhodesian Man** (Broken Hill skull), from South Africa, of very uncertain age.

For succeeding periods we have more satisfactory data. Belonging to the latter part of the Pleistocene, and mostly to the time of the first maximum of the last ice (Würm I) are many remains of **Neanderthal Man** (*Homo neanderthalensis*), a type which has been found, with many variations, from western Europe to Palestine (usually associated with Mousterian implements). All the primitive types so far mentioned differ greatly in their physical characteristics, and their exact relationship to one another and to modern races of men is still a subject of discussion, but it is questionable whether any one of them was a direct ancestor of *Homo sapiens* (modern or **Neanthropic Man**), the species to which all present races of men belong.

Alleged early occurrences of individuals of this Neanthropic type (e.g. Foxhall, Galley Hill, Olmo, and Castenedolo Man) are not accepted as valid by most anthropologists, but beginning with Upper Palaeolithic times, contemporary with the Laufen oscillation and the Würm II glacial maximum — in other words with the Aurignacian, Solutrean, and Magdalenian periods of Europe — representatives of modern man appear on the scene. Some of these, such as the men of **Cro-Magnon, Combe-Capelle, Chancelade,** and **Grimaldi** in France, are generally long-headed (*dolichocephalic*) and on the whole like present-day long-headed peoples of the White or European group, though some of the Grimaldi skeletons have been claimed to show slight Negroid characteristics. Others, like **Boskop Man,** of South Africa, are more definitely related to present Negroid types. Still others, such as **Wadjak Man** (Java) and **Talgai Man** (Queensland), show relationships to the present Australian natives (Australoid type). Remains of a few round-headed (*brachycephalic*) individuals of the White group, apparently dating near the very close of the Palaeolithic, have been found in Europe — at Solutré, for example. No remains of Palaeolithic men of Mongoloid type have yet been reported.

C. THE POST–PALAEOLITHIC PERIOD

1. NATURE AND SEQUENCE OF POST-PALAEOLITHIC CULTURES

In the absence of exact dates, archaeologists have divided the time from the end of the Palaeolithic to the present into the following major periods: Mesolithic period, Neolithic period, Chalcolithic period, Bronze Age, Iron Age, and Modern Age. As has been previously pointed out, this nomenclature has many disadvantages, since the names refer really to cultural stages rather than to periods of time. The words were first employed in the description of cultures as observed in Europe and the order of succession is not always the same for other continents. Furthermore, it is impossible to assign even estimated dates to these so-called periods, for each one began and ended at a different time in different parts of the world. On the whole, however, this chronological division does represent the general progress of culture, in the Old World at least, and although it often leads to confusion, unless applied with the greatest care, still it has the advantage of convenience and almost universal usage. The dividing line between prehistory and history comes at no particular place in this series, but varies in different areas. Following is a brief definition of the different periods, after which the Post-Palaeolithic cultures of the world will be described by geographical areas.

a. MESOLITHIC PERIOD

The disappearance of the last ice-sheet, which marked the end of the Pleistocene period and, with it, the end of the Palaeolithic, led to the rise of a new culture, generally referred to as the Mesolithic, in which the Palaeolithic economy of food-gathering, though basically unchanged, was partly modified in some parts of the world under the influence of new climatic conditions. The big animals of the Pleistocene, on which the Palaeolithic hunters had largely depended for their food, disappeared everywhere except in parts of Africa, and their place was taken by the present-day fauna. Also with the ice retreat new regions were opened to settlement. The stone implements of the Mesolithic cultures were still produced by chipping, but a preference was shown for extremely small forms (*microliths*), often of geometric shapes. Some

of these forms had a wide distribution in Asia, Africa, and Europe, showing that there were certain cultural relations and also actual movements of peoples — the latter probably connected to some extent with the drying up of the Sahara and Central Asiatic regions. The Mesolithic period is usually considered to have begun (in northern Europe at least) circa 8000 B.C., and Mesolithic cultures lasted for several thousand years until supplanted (at different dates in different areas) by the food-producing economy of the Neolithic peoples.

b. NEOLITHIC PERIOD

The next stage of development, the Neolithic, is marked by the invention and almost universal adoption of four important new features: **agriculture, domesticated animals, pottery,** and **polished** (instead of chipped) **stone tools.** These changes and the results which flowed from them were revolutionary. Man ceased being a nomad, eternally following his food supply, and became a sedentary being, residing and growing his food in one spot. He now had an assured food supply to carry over lean seasons and this led to a great increase in the population, in most of the formerly inhabited areas, and the opening to settlement of new areas, such as loess lands of Asia and Europe. The altered conditions likewise made possible the accumulation of possessions, the creation and satisfaction of new needs, the leisure for invention and speculation, the growth of large communities and cities, the development of more complex social organization, and in fact all the progress that has taken place since that time.

The four new culture traits which characterize the Neolithic were not necessarily originated at the same time and in the same place, and there is some evidence to indicate that there may have been an early stage, with primitive hoe agriculture and the pig as a domestic animal, before the advent of the Full Neolithic, with oxen, sheep, and plow agriculture. However, there is good reason to believe that Neolithic culture as a whole was developed in one general center and spread from there in successive waves to the ends of Asia, Africa, and Europe, but not, in any significant sense, to the New World. This original center was probably western Asia, for the wild relatives of the cereals and animals that were first domesticated have their home there, and it was the region in which the higher culture or civilization which the Neolithic discoveries made possible was first developed. The earliest remains of Neolithic culture which have yet been found are in Mesopotamia, Syria, Palestine, and Egypt. They represent a fully developed stage of the culture, with wheat and barley in cultivation and cattle, sheep, goats, and pigs as domesticated animals. The date of these remains is considered to be about 4000 B.C. — a period immediately prior to the first use of copper.

Neolithic remains of a much more primitive character have been found in other parts of the Old World, but they are all apparently later than this in date. The first traces of the Neolithic that have been found in Europe are apparently not older than 3000 or 2500 B.C., and Neolithic culture did not begin in many parts of Asia and Africa until much later still.

c. CHALCOLITHIC PERIOD

In a strict sense this is not a true period at all. The word *Chalcolithic* is a term conveniently but loosely used to describe a culture which is still essentially Neolithic in character, but in which the metal **copper** is just beginning to be used, without, however, replacing stone as the principal material for implements. Chalcolithic cultures are thus transitional. People in many areas of the world did not pass through this intermediate stage, but obtained their first knowledge of copper directly from other peoples who had already fully developed the art of copper metallurgy. The dates of Chalcolithic cultures differ everywhere, depending upon the time which it took for the knowledge of metal-working to spread. The earliest cultures in which copper has been found are in the Near East, and their estimated date is somewhere between 4000 and 3500 B.C. Copper did not appear in Europe much before 2000 B.C.

d. BRONZE AGE

In most regions of the Old World (but not in all of them) there was a period in which copper or bronze came into general use as a material for tools and weapons, but iron was still practically unknown. This period is for convenience termed the **Bronze Age** (although strictly speaking the word *bronze* should refer only to true bronze, a mixed metal composed of copper, alloyed with a certain percentage of tin). The date and duration of the Bronze Age in different parts of the Old World vary greatly. As has already been stated, the earliest known use of copper was in the Near East — in Mesopotamia and Egypt — toward the middle of the 4th millennium B.C. Considerable evidence points to the mountainous ore-bearing regions of Asia Minor, Armenia, and Caucasia as the probable area in which copper metallurgy was first discovered and developed. Copper was in widespread use in the Near East by 3000 B.C. and this may be considered a good rough date for the beginning of the Bronze Age in western Asia, although the general use of true bronze itself did not begin until six or seven centuries later.

The Bronze Age in Europe did not begin until 2000 B.C. or later, and it was more retarded or entirely absent in parts of Asia, most of Africa, and all of Oceania. The first use of iron for implements brought the Bronze Age everywhere to a close.

e. IRON AGE

The **Iron Age** is usually considered by archaeologists to be the period of some centuries immediately following the time when iron began to replace bronze as the principal material for implements and weapons. In one sense, we are still living in the Iron Age, but the term is actually seldom used in connection with any specific culture which is later in date than the beginning of the Christian Era, except in referring to primitive peoples, living in remote regions. Rare examples of early ornaments made of meteoric iron are known, and at least two cases of objects made of iron that was not meteoric (and hence may have been smelted) have been reported in Mesopotamia from levels dating before 2500 B.C. The first certain development of iron metallurgy on any scale, however, began in Asia Minor about the 14th century B.C. and in Europe in the Hallstatt region of Austria in the 11th or 10th century B.C. Iron did not penetrate to large parts of Asia and Africa until many centuries later and did not form part of any culture in the New World until introduced from Europe in the 15th and 16th centuries A.D.

2. MODERN RACES OF MAN

Although the various physical types of modern man began to develop and differentiate in the Palaeolithic period, they assumed their present shape in Post-Palaeolithic times and such tentative conclusions as can be established regarding their major migrations, distribution, and mixture form an essential part of any reconstruction of later prehistoric times.

Unfortunately the task is complicated by two factors: first, that we are still largely in ignorance of the exact ways in which biological processes work to form new physical types, and, second, that all groups of mankind can interbreed and have interbred in varying combinations over an immensely long period of time. Thus such things as pure racial types cannot truthfully be said to exist. Rather one must consider that the population of the world is made up of an almost infinite number of physical types which grade imperceptibly into one another. For this reason attempted classifications of races differ widely and the lack of a standard nomenclature is the cause of much confusion.

In spite of all these difficulties, most anthropologists believe that, on the whole, biological and historical considerations justify a division of modern man into three major groups — the **White** (or European) group, **Negroid** group, and **Mongoloid** group — and the establishment of certain sub-groups or races within each of these larger divisions. Making use provisionally of such a classification, it is possible to trace in a general way the more important movements of peoples in the prehistoric and early historic periods.

THE WHITE GROUP. Representatives of this group have had a primary distribution over the western and northern portions of the Old World. In a series of migrations — some of them clearly known to us and some of them still only guessed at — the blond and slightly long-headed **Nordics** occupied the northern third of Europe; the round-headed **Alpines** took possession of a central zone stretching from Russia to France, and one branch of the dark, long-headed **Mediterraneans,** with their relatives, the Arabs, Berbers, etc., spread through southern Europe, northern Africa, and the Near East, while another, it is believed, thrust down into India and Indonesia and the easternmost islands of the Pacific. Vaguely identified remnants of archaic White strains have been traced in various points in Siberia and Japan (Ainus) and are thought to be the basis of the Veddoid type (Ceylon and southern India) and the Australoid type (Australia). Other alleged races or sub-races, such as the prominent-nosed Armenoid, in the Near East, the blond but round-headed East Baltic type in northern Europe and the tall, round-headed Dinaric type of the Balkans, were apparently the result of local specialization and had a more limited distribution.

THE NEGROID GROUP without much question developed in the southern half of the Old World and its representatives stretched in an uninterrupted belt across Africa and southern Asia. Today we find two fundamental Negroid types: the short-statured, somewhat round-headed Negrito (Pygmy) in Africa and in Southeastern Asia and Indonesia; and a second type, with normal stature and long head, occupying much the same areas, the True or Forest Negro branch living in central and western Africa and the Oceanic Negroes (Papuans and Melanesians) in the island world to the southeast of Asia.

THE MONGOLOID GROUP quite evidently had its center in eastern central Asia, and from there its various representatives spread northeast to Siberia, east to China and Japan, southeast to Malaysia and Polynesia, and west in a long series of migrations through the Near East and Russia.

Many special races or sub-races developed which may have been the result of crosses between these three major groups. Notable among these are the Australian (Archaic White and Negroid), Bushman-Hottentot (Mongoloid and Negrito), Dravidian (Mediterranean, Australoid, and Melanesian), and Indonesian, Malay, and Polynesian (which seem to be mixtures in varying proportions of Mediterranean and Mongoloid with some Negroid strains).

The American Indians do not form a single race, but consist of many types, most of them Mongoloid in their principal characteristics, but many of them, like the long-headed Eskimo and the tall, long-headed type of the eastern Woodlands, suggest the presence of other than Mongoloid strains in their makeup.

3. REGIONAL DISTRIBUTION OF POST-PALAEOLITHIC CULTURES

a. ASIA

MESOPOTAMIA.　Excavations at Warka, Ur, Kish, Tello, Fara, and other sites reveal the existence of a Late Neolithic and Chalcolithic culture in southern Mesopotamia during the 4th millennium B.C.　It has been divided into four periods:

c. 4000 B.C.　The **Al Ubaid period** began probably shortly before 4000 B.C. and was characterized by a simple agricultural economy and the use of painted pottery with geometric designs.　The **Uruk period,** which followed, saw the first development of monumental architecture, copper, seals, and pictographic writing.

c. 3200-3000 B.C. The **Jemdet Nasr** period marked the culmination of the prehistoric culture and led up to the **Early Dynastic (Sumerian) period** and the beginning of recorded history.　A similar progress can be traced in northern Mesopotamia, though the lowest levels at Nineveh, Gawra, and Arpachiyah show a somewhat different culture, marked by the brilliant Tell Halaf pottery.

PALESTINE AND SYRIA.　A Mesolithic culture, the **Natufian,** followed the end of the Upper Palaeolithic in Palestine and lasted until perhaps 5000 B.C.

c. 5000–　It was succeeded later by the **Tahunian** and (at Jericho) by a so-called Neolithic culture, at first without pottery and later with pottery, but without polished stone implements.

c. 3000-2000.　With the **Early Bronze Age** recorded history begins in this area, although our information for many centuries comes from Egyptian sources, supplemented by the results of excavations at Beisan, Megiddo, Jericho, etc.　An Early Bronze Age culture in Phoenicia has been revealed at Ras Shamra and Byblos, while Late Neolithic or Chalcolithic levels have been unearthed in northern Syria, at Sakje-Geuzi, Carchemish, Tell Judeideh, and Chagar Bazar.

ARABIA.　Practically nothing is known of this area before the time of the historical Minaean and Sabaean kingdoms of southern Arabia in the 1st millennium B.C.

ASIA MINOR.　A prehistoric culture, of Chalcolithic type, flourished in Asia Minor at the beginning of the 3d millennium B.C., as shown by excavations at the famous site of Troy (Troy I, 3000–2400 B.C.; Troy II, 2400–2000 B.C.) and Alishar Hüyük (Chalcolithic Age, 3000–2800 B.C.; Copper Age, 2800–2300 B.C.; Early Bronze Age, 2300 B.C. on).　The historical period begins with the founding of the first Hittite kingdom about 1900 B.C.

ARMENIA AND TRANSCAUCASIA.　Almost nothing is known of this region before the 1st millennium B.C.　A Chalcolithic culture has been discovered at Shamiramalti, on Lake Van, and there are dubious Neolithic and Bronze Age finds south of the Caucasus.　During the Early Iron Age, however, Georgia and Russian Armenia were occupied by a people who buried their dead in megalithic graves and had an advanced metallurgy.

PERSIA AND RUSSIAN TURKESTAN.　During the 4th millennium B.C. a highly developed Chalcolithic culture, comparable in some respects to that of Mesopotamia and characterized by fine painted pottery, flourished in many parts of this area, notably at Anau, Tepe Hissar, and Rayy in the north, at Tepe Giyan (Nihavand) in the west, and at Susa, Tepe Mussian, and Persepolis in the southwest.　This was followed by the Full Bronze Age in the 3d millennium B.C.　In the latter part of the 2d millennium B.C. a new people, who buried their dead in megalithic graves, appeared in the mountain region of western Persia and the ancestors of the Indo-European Medes and Persians probably entered Persia at about the same time.

INDIA.　Scattered finds of microlithic implements and polished stone celts attest the probable existence of Mesolithic and Neolithic cultures in India, but practically nothing is known about them.　In the middle of the 3d millennium B.C., the remarkable **Indus culture** flourished in the northwest.　The excavations at Mohenjo-daro and Harappa reveal a civilization that rivaled that of Egypt and Mesopotamia.　This was followed at a slightly later date by the so-called **Jhukar and Jhangar cultures** in the same region, but little that represents a real Bronze Age has been found outside the Indus Valley.　History begins for northern India shortly after the invasion of the Indo-Aryans toward the end of the 2d millennium B.C., but no archaeological remains have been found there dating much before 500 B.C.　The rest of India is largely a blank to us until a century or two before the Christian Era, although in central and southern India there are a great number of Iron Age cemeteries (with burials in cists, cairns, stone circles, urns, etc.), some of which are prehistoric and others probably date to some time well within the Christian Era.

SIBERIA AND MANCHURIA. This is a marginal area, which apparently retained a Mesolithic and later a Neolithic culture longer than other parts of the continent. The Bronze Age is represented in a few places, particularly the Minusinsk region of the Upper Yenisei Valley and the region from the western slopes of the Altai Mountains to the upper courses of the Ob and Irtish Rivers. Iron was introduced late in most parts of Siberia and in the extreme north and east many of the tribes were living in a Neolithic stage of culture until the Russian explorations and colonization in the 17th century A.D.

CENTRAL ASIA. Mesolithic and Neolithic cultures existed in Mongolia, but archaeologically we know little about them and practically nothing about Chinese Turkestan and Tibet before the opening centuries of the Christian Era. Such information as we have about this area from Chinese records does not run much before the beginning of Han times (3d cent. B.C.).

CHINA. Implements of Neolithic type but of uncertain date have been found in many parts of China. The **Yang-shao culture,** characterized by the absence of metal and the presence of painted pottery suggesting that of western Asia, existed in Honan and neighboring provinces of northern China at about 2000 B.C. This was succeeded by a culture characterized by black pottery (in lower levels at Cheng-tzu-yai and An-yang), which was followed in turn shortly after 1400 B.C. by the rich Bronze Age culture of the Shang Dynasty and the first written documents (as found at An-yang). In the western province of Kansu interesting but undated archaeological remains, with some suggestion of western influences, have been ascribed to the Neolithic and Bronze Ages.

JAPAN AND KOREA. The **Jomonshiki culture** (Neolithic) flourished in the northern half of the Main Island of Japan (Earlier period, before 200 B.C.; Middle period, 200 B.C.–200 A.D.; Later period, 200 A.D.–600 A.D. and even later). In the southern half of the Main Island and Kyushu there was a somewhat different Neolithic culture, represented by scattered finds dating before 200 B.C. This was followed by the **Yayoishiki culture** (200 B.C.–200 A.D.), which was essentially Neolithic and had its nearest relationships with Korea, from which there were occasional imports of bronze implements. Last

of all was the **Yamato culture** (200 A.D.–600 A.D.), of Korean origin, which introduced iron implements and megalithic burials and which spread gradually through the whole of the Main Island.

SOUTHEASTERN ASIA. A series of prehistoric cultures has been reported from Indo-China, especially from the Hoabinhian and Bacsonian areas in Tonkin. The earliest are Mesolithic, with Palaeolithic survivals (Archaic period and Intermediate period of Hoabinhian and Keo-Phay period of Bacsonian), and possibly belong to the 3d millennium B.C. They were followed by certain Proto-Neolithic cultures (Latest period of Hoabinhian and Early and Late Bacsonian). The full Neolithic is represented by the **Somrong-Sen culture,** which spread through all parts of Indo-China in the 2d millennium B.C. and lasted until the beginning of the Bronze Age, about 500 B.C. Cultures somewhat similar to those of Indo-China have been reported from Burma and the Malay Peninsula.

b. EUROPE

In its broad outlines the prehistory of Europe from the close of the Palaeolithic Age is a record of (1) a series of profound climatic changes, producing modifications of culture and the settlement of new areas; (2) a series of cultural influences coming in from Asia and Africa; (3) a series of invasions of new peoples from Asia and Africa; and (4) the formation of new peoples and the development of new cultures as a result of the interaction of these major factors.

(1) *Climatic Changes and Time-Scale*

By counting and comparing the varves, or annual layers of gravel and clay laid down in post-glacial lakes in many parts of the Baltic area, archaeologists have been able tentatively to tell the year in which each layer was formed over a period covering the past 10,000 years. The thickness of the varves and an analysis of the pollen contained in them and other deposits furnish a record of the progressive climatic changes year by year and date with reasonable accuracy typical archaeological remains found in some clear relation to these deposits. This gives a basic time-scale for northern Europe, which can be applied (in a general way and with modifications) to the rest of Europe, and can be checked, for the later periods, against tentative dates determined archaeologically on the basis of contacts with the historical cultures of Mesopotamia, Egypt, Greece, and Rome.

Following is the sequence of climatic periods in the Baltic region:

-8300 B.C. Sub-Arctic period. Contemporary with the Götiglacial stage of the ice retreat and end of the Palaeolithic period. Very cold and characterized by *Dryas* flora, dwarf birch, willow, and tundra and steppe types of animals.

8300-6800. Pre-Boreal period. Contemporary with the Finiglacial stage of the ice retreat, the Yoldia Sea and first half of the Ancylus Lake phase of the Baltic and the beginning of the Mesolithic period. Less cold, and characterized by birch, pine, and willow trees and mixed tundra and forest types of animals.

6800-5600. Boreal period. Post-glacial and contemporary with the last half of the Ancylus Lake phase of the Baltic. Rise in sea-level. Cool, dry "continental" climate, with birch and pine dominant, but alder and oak-mixed forest coming in and animals mostly of forest and lake type.

5600-2500. Atlantic period. Contemporary with the transgression of the Litorina Sea in the Baltic. Sea-level still high. Warm and moist "oceanic" climate (the so-called *period of climatic optimum*), with alder and oak-mixed forest (oak, elm, and lime) dominant, and forest, lake, and sea types of animals.

2500-700. Sub-Boreal period. Land relatively stable with relation to the sea and the Baltic Sea largely landlocked as at present. Dry, warm climate.

700- Sub-Atlantic period. Wet, cold climate.

(2) *Cultural Changes and Periods*

The principal outside cultural influences which came into Europe at different times followed four main routes: (1) from western Asia through Russia to central and western Europe; (2) from Asia Minor through the Aegean to Greece and also through Thrace to central Europe; (3) from the Near East and the Aegean by sea to the western Mediterranean; and (4) from North Africa to Spain and western Europe. Thus the general direction of cultural movement was from south to north and from east to west; hence at any given moment in time the southern and eastern areas were apt to be enjoying a more advanced form of culture than were the more peripheral regions to the northwest. This is well illustrated by the course which developments took in each of the principal periods.

c. 8000- In the Mesolithic period, lasting for several thousand years, the **Tardenoi-** sian culture, which was most closely related to cultures in Africa and Spain and which was characterized by microlithic implements, spread from the south over most of Europe. At the same time, with the amelioration of the climate, there was a northward movement of peoples following the forests that gradually occupied the steppes and tundras of the North European plain and a forest culture was developed, characterized by the use of the chipped stone axe (Maglemosean and Ertebølle cultures).

c. 4000-3000. The Neolithic period had a similar gradual development. **Neolithic culture** appeared for the first time in Crete in the 4th millennium B.C. By 3000 B.C. some slight Neolithic influences had penetrated as far as western Europe from the east, via Russia, and from the south, via Spain. The earliest full-fledged Neolithic culture in Europe proper appeared in the Danube area of central Europe in the 3d millennium B.C., and spread from there to the Rhine Valley and throughout western Europe. Somewhat later the Megalithic culture, characterized by dolmens, passage graves, cists, and other rough stone monuments, spread along the coastal regions of western Europe from Spain to the Baltic.

c. 3000- The **Bronze Age culture** began, for Europe, in the Aegean and Greece shortly after 3000 B.C. and copper axes appeared in Hungary a little before 2000 B.C. — in both cases due to Asiatic influence. Other copper influences came into Europe by way of Spain about 2000 B.C. and diffused widely, apparently in association with the Bell Beaker culture. At the same time there were further developments of the Megalithic culture throughout its area. The Bronze Age for Europe as a whole is usually considered to cover the period from about 2000 to 1000 B.C. and is divided into three sub-periods: Early, Middle, and Late Bronze Age (or Bronze I, II, and III).

c. 1000- The **Iron Age** began not long after 1000 B.C. with the development of iron metallurgy in Austria and its spread through the rest of Europe. The first part of the Iron Age is usually referred to as the **Hallstatt period** (about 1000 B.C. to 500 B.C.), the second part as the **La Tène period** (500 B.C. to 1 A.D.).

(3) *Movements of Peoples*

It is still uncertain to what extent the spread of all the various cultures was due to trade and borrowing, and to what extent it involved wholesale movements of peoples. The population of Europe in the early part of the Mesolithic period probably consisted largely of the descendants of the food-gathering Upper Palaeolithic peoples and was predominantly of the long-headed, White or European stock, sometimes called Atlanto-Mediterranean. Round-headed peoples began to crowd in early in Mesolithic and Neolithic times, from the east (as shown at the site of Offnet in Bavaria) and possibly from Africa (as shown in certain sites in Portugal and Spain). During the succeeding millennia the three fundamental modern European types became established in their respective areas: the Mediterraneans in southern Europe, the Alpines in central and western Europe, and the Nordics in northern Europe. During the latter part of the Bronze Age and especially in the Iron Age we have further witness to great movements of peoples in the spread of Indo-European languages over the larger part of Europe. Greek-speaking and Illyrian-speaking peoples came down through the Balkans into Greece, and Italic-speaking peoples into Italy; Celtic-speaking peoples moved west through central and northern Europe as far as France and the British Isles, and were followed over much the same route by Teutonic-speaking and, for part of the way, by Slavic-speaking peoples. We know that these groups were of mixed types, but we still have insufficient information about their physical characteristics.

(4) *Regional Distribution of Cultures*

AEGEAN AREA AND GREECE. In Crete a Neolithic culture, related to that of Asia Minor, flourished for at least several centuries in the 4th millennium B.C. This was followed by a high Bronze Age civilization (with its center at Knossos), which has been divided into three major periods: Early **Minoan**, 3000–2200 B.C.; Middle Minoan, 2200–1600 B.C.; and Late Minoan, 1600–1100 B.C. Similar Bronze Age cultures have been reported from Melos and other islands of the Cyclades, namely: Early Cycladic, 2800–2200 B.C.; Middle Cycladic, 2200–1650 B.C.; and Late Cycladic, 1650–1300 B.C. On the mainland of Greece a third series of related cultures flourished in central Greece and the Peloponnesus: Neolithic, shortly before 2800 B.C.; Early Helladic, 2800–2100 B.C.; Middle Helladic, 2100–1600 B.C.; and Late Helladic, 1600–1100 B.C. In Thessaly were two Neolithic cultures, with northern affinities: Thessalian I, before 2600 B.C., and Thessalian II, 2600–2400 B.C., followed by two of the Bronze Age cultures: Thessalian III, 2400–1800 B.C.; and Thessalian IV, 1800–1200 B.C. In Cyprus the

Neolithic began before 3000 B.C., after which developed a series of Bronze Age cultures. During the latter half of the 2d millennium B.C. the so-called **Mycenaean culture** (Late Helladic), with its center in Mycenae in the Peloponnesus, spread throughout Greece and the whole Aegean area, with extensions to western Asia Minor, Cyprus, and Syria. The Iron Age in Greece began about 1000 B.C. with the Geometric period, the close of which marked the beginning of history in this area.

RUSSIA. A Mesolithic culture, related to Tardenoisian, developed in southern Russia before 3000 B.C. and was followed by an Early Neolithic, resembling the Campignian. A rich Late Neolithic and Bronze Age development, related in some details to that of northern Persia, had its center in the Kuban area in the 3d millennium B.C. From 2500 to 1500 B.C. the Late Neolithic and Bronze Age were represented by two distinct series: Tripolye A and B, in the Ukraine, and the Red Ochre Graves, in the steppe region between the Volga and the Dnieper. The most important later culture was that of the Scythians, beginning in the 6th century B.C. In northern and central Russia a version of Mesolithic, with Baltic affinities, survived late and, with influences from the so-called Battle-Axe People, developed in the 2d millennium B.C. into the Fatyanovo culture of central Russia.

CENTRAL EUROPE. In Mesolithic times the principal culture in this region was Tardenoisian, with Azilian influences in the extreme western part. A full-fledged Neolithic, Danubian I, appeared in the Danubian area about 2700 B.C., having come presumably from the east and south. It was succeeded by a second phase, Danubian II (2400–2200 B.C.). Contemporary Neolithic cultures, characterized by painted pottery, have been found at Erösd, Cucuteni, and other places in the Balkans. In the next few centuries there was a further development of the Danubian, with influences from the Corded Ware of Poland and Russia and the Bell Beaker culture. This extended into the Alpine region (Swiss Lake Dwellings), eastern Germany, and the Rhine Valley. With the Bronze Age (about 2000–1000 B.C. or later) there were distinctive local developments in Hungary, Bohemia, Austria, Switzerland, and other sub-areas and several important cultures with wider distribution, of which the principal ones were the Aunjetitz, Knoviz, Tumulus, Urnfield, and Lausitz. The Iron Age began here shortly after 1000 B.C., with the development of the **Hallstatt culture,** followed by the La Tène, which continued to Roman times.

ITALY. Until late prehistoric times Italy was divided into two rather distinct provinces. In southern Italy and Sicily the Tardenoisian persisted until the introduction of the Neolithic in the 3d millennium B.C. This in turn gave way to Chalcolithic in Sicily (Siculan I, 2000–1500 B.C.), with a similar development on the mainland, and a Bronze Age culture in Sicily (Siculan II, 1500–1000 B.C.), also with connections on the mainland. The relations of these were with the Aegean area and the Balkans. They were followed by Siculan III and the Punic Early Iron Age. In northern Italy there were traces of Tardenoisian, then a Neolithic culture, succeeded by Bell Beaker influences and a Chalcolithic culture (Remedello and Italian Lake Dwellers). The Full Bronze Age in this area began about 1600 B.C., and a century or two later the **Terramare culture** appeared in the Po Valley and spread as far as southern Italy. This was followed in the Iron Age by the **Villanova culture** (1000–600 B.C.) with Hallstatt affinities, and the settlement of the Etruscans (800–400 B.C.) in central Italy.

ISLANDS OF THE WESTERN MEDITERRANEAN. A remarkable Neolithic development, characterized by massive stone temples and underground structures, took place in Malta. In Sardinia there was a distinctive Chalcolithic culture (Anghelu Ruju) shortly after 2000 B.C., followed by various phases of Megalithic (Giants' Tombs, dolmens, and Nuraghis), much of which dates to the early half of the 1st millennium B.C. There was a related Bronze Age culture, with stone constructions (Navetas and Talayots) in the Balearic Islands.

SPAIN. There were several cultures in the Iberian peninsula in the Mesolithic period: Final Capsian in the south and center, Tardenoisian and Azilian in the north and two special developments, the Portuguese Kitchen Middens in the west and the Asturian culture in the northwest. Some of these lasted well into the 3d millennium B.C. and were succeeded by various Neolithic cultures of which the most important developments were in the southeast (Almerian culture) and in Portugal and Galicia (Megalithic). The **Bell Beaker culture** (about 2000 B.C.) ushered in the Bronze Age, which was marked by a continuation of the Megalithic and, in the southeast, by the development of the **El Argar culture** (middle of 2d millennium B.C.) in southeastern Spain. In the early part of

the 1st millennium B.C. there was a local Iron Age culture, with Hallstatt affinities, which lasted until the time of the first Punic and Greek colonies (about 500 B.C.).

WESTERN EUROPE. Two cultures, the Tardenoisian and the Azilian, were dominant in western Europe during the Early Mesolithic period, with the Asturian (late Mesolithic) partially represented in southern France and the Maglemosean (Early Mesolithic) in northern France and Belgium. Neolithic influences were late in arriving, but by the middle of the 3d millennium B.C. there was a Neolithic culture, of Mediterranean origin, in the south, and the Campignian and Omalian cultures, of central European origin, in the north. The Bell Beaker culture appeared here shortly after 2000 B.C., while the Megalithic culture spread through the coastal region (especially in Brittany), and influences from central Europe and the Rhine contributed to the development of the Bronze Age in France. Well along in the 1st millennium B.C. this gave way to a western version of the Hallstatt culture, which was followed, as elsewhere in Europe, by the La Tène.

The **British Isles** had a somewhat similar but still more retarded development. In the Mesolithic period a survival of the Upper Palaeolithic Creswellian culture was modified in certain areas by the introduction of Azilian influences into southwestern Scotland, Maglemosean in southern and eastern England, and Tardenoisian more or less generally. About 2500 B.C. or a little later, Neolithic features first appeared, in connection with the Windmill Hill culture and the Long Barrows. Bronze came into England some time after 2000 B.C. (Beaker culture, Long Barrows, and Round Barrows). About 1000 B.C. new bronze-using peoples from the continent invaded England, bringing some iron with them. The true Iron Age began about 400 B.C. with an invasion of continental peoples enjoying a predominantly Hallstatt culture (Iron Age A). They were followed, in the 1st century B.C., by La Tène peoples (Iron Age B), the Belgae (Iron Age C), and the Romans. Modified forms of some of these cultures reached Scotland and Ireland but at considerably later dates.

BALTIC REGION. In the early part of the Mesolithic, which corresponds to the Pre-Boreal period (8300–6800 B.C.), Tanged-point cultures (Remouchamps, Ahrensburg-Lavenstadt, and Swiderian) occupied the North European plain from Belgium to Poland, with outliers in northern and western Norway

(Komsa and Fosna cultures), but there were traces of an early Tardenoisian and the beginning of the new forest or axe cultures (Lyngby). In the Boreal period (6800–5600 B.C.), a Mesolithic axe culture, the Maglemosean, with many local variants, spread widely over the whole area from Yorkshire to Estonia. The Komsa and Fosna cultures continued in Norway, and Tardenoisian developed further at various points on the North German plain. In the Atlantic period (5600–2500 B.C.) the Ertebølle culture developed out of the Maglemosean, while the Komsa, Fosna, Tardenoisian, and a late version of Maglemosean survived in marginal areas. The beginning of the Neolithic period is synchronous with the beginning of the Sub-Boreal phase, circa 2500 B.C. At about 2000 B.C. the Early Neolithic elements, of eastern origin, were profoundly modified by the introduction of the Megalithic civilization, which had spread along the Atlantic seaboard. Several distinct but contemporary cultures developed, viz.: Megalithic (in three phases, characterized respectively by dolmens, passage graves, and stone cists), Battle-Axe, Separate Graves, Arctic, and Dwelling-Place cultures. In 1500 B.C. or thereabouts the Scandinavian Bronze Age began, which was followed later by the Iron Age.

c. AFRICA

EGYPT. The Mesolithic period witnessed the final stages of the Sebilian culture. The Neolithic period began early in the Nile Valley (probably before 4000 B.C.) and is represented by the Fayum, Merimdean, Tasian, and Badarian cultures. During the 4th millenniu.n B.C., under combined African and Asiatic influences, the important **Predynastic culture** developed (Amratian, Gerzean, and Semainian phases), and ended about 3000 B.C. with the establishment of the First Dynasty and the beginning of the historical period.

NORTHWESTERN AFRICA. Mesolithic cultures (final stages of Capsian and Oranian) were, at dates as yet undetermined, modified and transformed by the infiltration of Neolithic influences, which spread gradually through Tunisia, Algeria, and Morocco and south across the Sahara. Bronze was late in reaching most parts of this area, and generally stone did not give way to metal until the Punic Iron Age in the 1st millennium B.C.

EAST AFRICA. Following the close of the Upper Palaeolithic period in this area two Microlithic cultures developed (Wilton A and B) and another culture (Elmenteitan), but the dates of all three may be somewhat late as pottery was already present in Elmenteitan. The succeeding cultures (Gumban A and B, Njoroan, Wilton C, and Tumbian) were clearly Early Neolithic in character but not necessarily in date. There was apparently no true Bronze Age in this part of Africa and iron gradually replaced stone during the Christian Era.

SOUTH AFRICA. In what is termed the Later Stone Age of this area, two Mesolithic cultures, Wilton and Smithfield, spread through the greater part of South Africa, beginning at some time after the close of the Pleistocene and continuing with modifications until the Bantu invasions brought iron to the region at a comparatively recent date. South Africa had no true Neolithic period or Bronze Age, although some traces of agriculture and occasional polished stone implements have been found.

CENTRAL AND WEST AFRICA. This also was a marginal region. Mesolithic implements have been found in parts of the Sudan. The Tumbian culture (Mesolithic) was represented in the Congo Basin and persisted after the introduction of polished stone. Various other Neolithic cultures of more fully developed form but uncertain date have been reported from the Sudan and Nigeria. A true Bronze Age is not found here, and iron was late in arriving, but during the Christian Era iron metallurgy received a special development, notably in Benin.

d. OCEANIA

The prehistory of this area is still very obscure, but it is believed that it was peopled by a series of migrations from southeastern Asia. Certain groups of people occupied first the nearer islands (Indonesia), then New Guinea, Australia, and Melanesia and finally the far islands of the Pacific (Micronesia and Polynesia). The Negritos (pygmies), remnants of whom are now found in remote inland districts of New Guinea and the Philippines, were perhaps the first to enter this region. They were either followed or preceded by some of the ancestors of the Australians and the now-extinct Tasmanians. At a later but undetermined date the Papuans pushed out and occupied New Guinea and they were followed by the Melanesians, who settled largely in the islands to the east of New Guinea. Lastly, the Malays and the Polynesians entered the area, the Polynesians apparently for the most part passing by the already occupied regions and pressing east across the Pacific to Micronesia and Polynesia.

It is debatable whether the Polynesians had already assumed their present racial type before the great migrations began or whether the different groups of peoples (Mongoloid, White, Negroid, etc.) which seem to form their ancestry moved east at different times and by different routes and interbred after their arrival in the islands. In any case the date of these movements was comparatively recent. Navigation received its real development in this part of the world in the 1st millennium B.C. The first long voyages into Micronesia and Polynesia probably did not begin until the 4th century A.D., and the farther islands were not settled until some centuries later.

The majority of the peoples who took part in the settlement of Oceania were in a Neolithic stage of culture, although the Australians and Negritos still practiced a Palaeolithic economy of hunting and food-gathering when the European colonization began.

e. AMERICA

North and South America were peopled from Asia, at a relatively recent date. The immigrants apparently came from Siberia, across Bering Strait to Alaska. Many of them probably followed a route which led up the Yukon Valley, over the divide into the Mackenzie River Basin and down the eastern foothills of the Rockies to Central and South America. Theories that some groups of people may have come from a more southern part of Asia or Oceania directly across the Pacific, bringing elements of a high culture with them, are based on very unsatisfactory evidence and are generally considered to be unproved.

There is difference of opinion on the date when the first immigrants reached America. The majority of American archaeologists have held that this was some time after the close of the last glaciation. Suggestions of Palaeolithic types have been found among the stone implements in various regions, but no complete industry that is closely related to any Palaeolithic industry of the Old World has yet been reported, and no skeletal remains have been found which are appreciably outside the range of modern American Indians. However, recent excavations from California to Texas and as far north as Colorado (Mojave Desert, Lake Cochise, Clovis, Silver Lake, and the Lindenmeier site) have brought to light implements (Folsom point, Yuma point, Abilene flints, etc.)

found in deposits which were laid down at a time when the climate was considerably colder and wetter than it is today. In some cases the implements were discovered in association with the bones of mammoth, camel, ground sloth, and other extinct animals. Accordingly there is a growing tendency to consider that man may have made his appearance in America soon after the close of the last (Wisconsin) glaciation, if not actually in the Glacial Age itself.

Studies of the physical characteristics of American Indians show these to be predominantly Mongoloid, but also reveal the presence, in mixture, of other types, some of which are European or even Negroid in their suggestions, while there seems to be in both continents a marginal distribution of a long-headed stock which may represent the descendants of a group of very early arrivals.

At the time of the first European contact with America in the 16th and 17th centuries A.D., some Indians were still hunters and food-gatherers, like their Palaeolithic ancestors, but the great majority were in a Neolithic stage of culture. The fact that they had no cereals that were cultivated in the Old World and no Old World domestic animals except the dog has led to the general opinion that agriculture and the domestication of animals were in this case independent developments after arrival in the New World. Certain polished stone tools, however, and even certain types of pottery show relationship to forms found in northeastern Asia. So two of the four main elements of Neolithic culture may show some evidence of a continuation of Asiatic tradition. In a few cases American Indian groups passed beyond the Neolithic stage, as is indicated by the use of metal.

The first advanced culture in the western hemisphere is believed to have had its origin about two thousand years ago in the Andean region of South America and in the highland region of Central America and Mexico. Here grew up a high civilization, parallel in many striking ways to that of the Old World but probably entirely independent of it. The cultivation of Indian corn (*Zea mais*) was the basis of the new economy. Rich textiles, fine pottery, and magnificent ornaments of gold, silver, and copper were produced. Great city centers arose, with canals and gardens and monumental temples on lofty pyramids. A highly complex social organization was developed, with priest-emperors, standing armies, schools, courts, and systematized religions. Intellectual progress was marked by astronomical research, the invention of accurate calendars, and — in Yucatan and Mexico — an elaborate hieroglyphic writing.

In the Peruvian area the early Nasca and Chimu cultures were followed by Tiahuanacan and, in immediately pre-Columbian times, by the **Inca civilization.** Influences spread from this center across the Andes into the Amazon Basin and down the Andes to the Argentine region. Farther north, the Chibchan and Chorotegan cultures occupied the intervening area between Peru and Yucatan, where the **Maya civilization,** the climax of native American achievement, developed during the 1st millennium B.C. and reached its culmination shortly before the Spanish Conquest. Similarly, in the Valley of Mexico the Archaic and Toltec cultures culminated in the **Aztec civilization,** discovered by the Spaniards. The effect of these powerful centers of influence must have been felt in lessening degree throughout much of North America, especially in the advanced cultures of the Pueblo area of the southwest, the southeast, and the Mound Builder area in the Mississippi drainage. Simpler cultures occupied the Woodlands area of the northeastern United States and Canada and the Central Plains. California was a marginal region, occupied largely by food-gatherers of a low stage of culture, while the Indians of the Northwest coast and the Eskimos of Alaska and northern Canada had, each in their own way, developed highly specialized cultures, which suggest to some extent Asiatic relationships.

II. Ancient History

A. EARLY EMPIRES OF AFRICA AND ASIA

1. EGYPT

GEOGRAPHY. Egypt (in ancient Egyptian: *Kemet, the black* [*land*]) is the valley of the Nile, from the Delta to the first cataract at Assuan. The valley, extending for about 550 miles, has an average width, south of the Delta, c⁴ 12 miles, and comprises only about 13,000 square miles of cultivable ground (less than the area of Switzerland). Before Menes, the Delta (Lower Egypt) and the valley (Upper Egypt) formed two distinct kingdoms. The principal cities of Lower Egypt were: Tanis, Bubastis (i.e. *house of Bast*), Busiris (*house of Osiris*), Saïs, On (Greek: *Heliopolis*), and Memphis (near Cairo). Those of Upper Egypt, south of the Fayum (with Lake Moëris), were: Heracleopolis, Siut, Abydos, Thebes, Jeb (Greek: *Elephantine*), Philae. Egypt was divided into 42 provinces (*nomes*), 20 in Lower Egypt and 22 in Upper Egypt. Egypt was "the gift of the Nile" (Herodotus): its fertility depended on the overflow of the river (June–October) which has deposited, in the course of centuries, 30 to 40 feet of rich black soil in the valley; laborious irrigation was, however, indispensable.

POPULATION. The estimates of the population given by Diodorus (7,000,000) and by Josephus (7,500,000) are slightly exaggerated. Racially the Egyptians are a mixture of several stocks and are ascribed to the Mediterranean race; their anthropological characters have hardly changed to the present day. Ancient Egyptian is related to the Semitic and to the Berber languages; in a lesser degree to the Galla and Somali dialects.

CIVILIZATION. The basic economic, social, and political institutions of ancient Egypt were developed in the pre-dynastic period: agriculture was, and remained, the foundation of the economic life. A calendar with a solar year of 365 days, according to Edw. Meyer and others, was introduced in 4241 (more probably in 2781). The writing went through pictographic, symbolic, syllabic, and alphabetic stages before Dynasty IV, but retained them all to Roman times; it had a monumental (hieroglyphic) and a cursive (hieratic) form from earliest times; a simpler cursive, called demotic, was introduced in the 7th century. During the Old Kingdom the Pharaoh (*Per-o*, "Great House") was deified in life and in death, and exercised despotic authority, ruling through an elaborate, carefully trained bureaucracy; architects erected colossal pyramids and magnificent columned palaces and temples; sculptors and painters portrayed gods, humans, and animals with admirable realism and grace; literature began to flourish; some rudimentary sciences were cultivated for practical purposes; industrial crafts reached a high degree of perfection. This culture of the Old Kingdom remained the ideal of later epochs.

RELIGION. In the earliest period each town had its own deity: **Ptah** was worshiped at Memphis, **Atum** at Heliopolis, **Horus** at Edfu, **Amon** at Thebes, **Osiris** at Busiris, etc. Most of the gods were conceived as animals: Ptah and Atum as bulls, the goddess Hathor of Dendera as a cow, the goddess Bast of Bubastis as a cat, Anubis as a jackal, Thoth as an ibis, Amon as a ram, etc. **Horus** was the god of the kings of Upper Egypt, **Set** of those of Lower Egypt, but later Horus became the royal god of both kingdoms. Horus (the hawk) was at first the god of heaven, then of the sun; however, the solar religion that ultimately prevailed in Egypt originated at Heliopolis, where the priests of Atum-Re developed the first theological system of Egypt and made of the worship of **Re** (whose symbols are obelisks) the state religion (Dynasty V): Re was accordingly identified with many local gods, particularly with Amon. In the pyramid texts (Dynasties V and VI) the deceased king sails over the sky in the ship of Re. Another conception of life after death in the same texts is connected with the myth of Osiris, who was killed by his brother Set, but was restored to life by his son Horus or, in later versions, by his wife Isis, and became at first the king of the underworld, and later the judge of the deceased (see the *Book of the Dead*). Corpses were embalmed (mummies) and buried under pyramids or in rock-hewn chambers; magical and religious texts were inscribed inside the tombs and the departed were provided with food and drink, furniture, statuary, and paintings.

CHRONOLOGY. Manetho, an Egyptian priest (c. 280 B.C.), wrote a history of his country

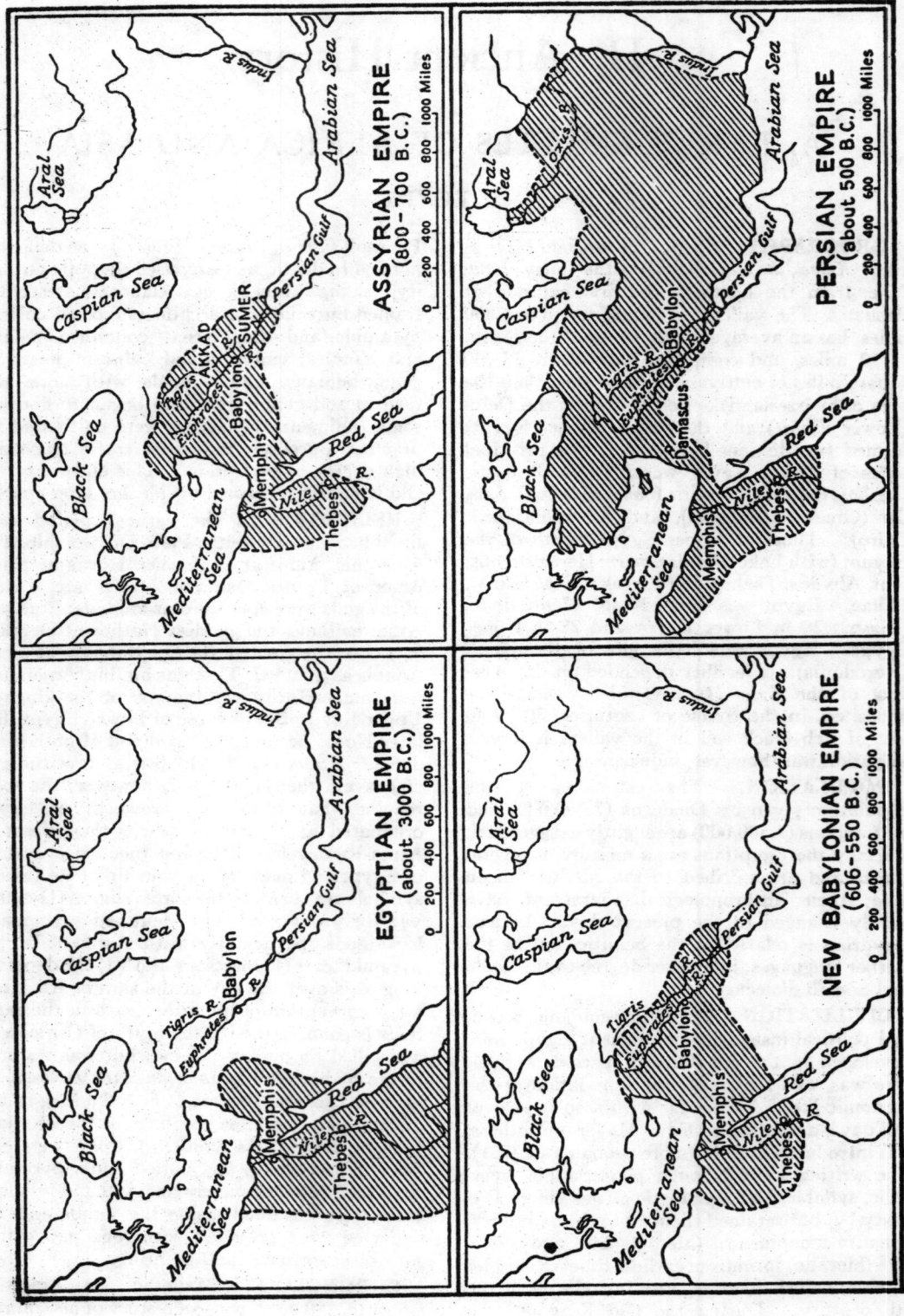

in Greek, of which fragments have been preserved by Josephus, Julius Africanus, and Eusebius. He grouped the kings of Egypt from Menes to Artaxerxes III (343 B.C.) into 30 dynasties. Although his chronology is far from accurate, his dynastic arrangement is still used. The most valuable ancient sources are the **Palermo stone** (a chronicle written in the 5th Dynasty) and the **Turin papyrus** (a list of kings, arranged by dynasties, dating from the 19th Dynasty: it reckons 955 years for the first 8 dynasties and 213 for the 12th). Extant data furnish a fairly accurate chronology, based on "dead reckoning" and astronomical data, for the period after 2000 B.C.; all earlier dates, anywhere, are uncertain.

c. 3200-2780. Dynasties I-II (capital: Thinis). The two kingdoms of Upper and Lower Egypt were united under the rule of **Menes** and his successors.

2780-2270. THE OLD KINGDOM: Dynasties III-VI (capital: Memphis). **Zoser,** the founder of Dynasty III (2780-2720), built the step pyramid of Sakkara. **Snefru** (Dynasty IV, 2720-2560) built the pyramid of Medum and developed navigation; his three successors, **Cheops, Chephren,** and **Mycerinus,** erected the three colossal pyramids at Gizeh. The first pyramid texts appear under Unis, the last king of Dynasty V (2560-2420), and continue under Dynasty VI (2420-2270); Egyptian art reached its culmination during Dynasty V.

2270-2100. Dynasties VII-X. The dissolution of the power of the Pharaohs allowed the nomes to become autonomous.

2100-1788. THE MIDDLE KINGDOM: Dynasties XI (2100-2000), with the capital at Thebes, and XII (2000-1788), with the capital at Lisht (near Memphis) or (with Amenemhet III) in the Fayum. Dynasty XII marks the classical age of Egyptian literature, which was no longer purely religious (fiction begins with the story of Sinuhet); architecture and the plastic arts flourished as well. **Amenemhet I** (2000-1970) curbed the power of the provincial barons and began the wars of conquest continued by Sesostris I (1980-1935), Amenemhet II (1938-1903), Sesostris II (1906-1887), Sesostris III (1887-1849); the latter conquered Nubia and made a campaign in Palestine. Amenemhet III (1849-1801) reorganized the mining operations in Sinai, carried out hydraulic works in the Fayum (Lake Moëris) and built there the great group of palaces known as the *Labyrinth.*

1788-1580. A period of usurpation (Dynasty XIII; capital: Thebes), of shadowy vassal rulers (Dynasty XIV; capital: Xois), and of foreign domination (Dynasties XV–XVI [Hyksos], 1680-1580; capital: Avaris in the Delta). The **Hyksos** (*Rulers of Countries*) were a mixed horde consisting chiefly of Semites and Hurrians from Palestine, Syria, and farther north; they introduced the horse into Egypt. Objects inscribed with the name of the Hyksos king Chian have been found in Crete, Palestine, and Babylonia. Dynasty XVII (1600-1580) began the war against the Hyksos.

1580-1090. THE EMPIRE (New Kingdom).

1580-1350. Dynasty XVIII (Capital: Thebes). **Amosis** (1580-1557) drove out the Hyksos, reconquered northern Nubia, and put an end to the authority of the local nobles. Amenophis I (1557-1536) and Thutmosis I (*Thothmes*) (1536-1520) fought in Palestine and Syria, reaching the Euphrates. The real ruler, from 1520 to her death in 1480, was **Hatshepsut,** the half-sister and the wife first of Thutmosis II, then of Thutmosis III. The great **Thutmosis III** (1501-1447) in 19 years (17 campaigns) conquered Palestine (through the victory at Megiddo in 1479), Phoenicia, and Syria (Kadesh on the Orontes was taken in 1471), to the 36th parallel; although he reached Carchemish, this city and Aleppo remained under the rule of Mitanni. Obelisks of his stand in Stambul, Rome, London, and New York. **Amenophis III** (1411-1375) preserved the integrity of the Asiatic Empire through diplomacy; the *Tell-el-Amarna letters*, written in Assyrian on cuneiform tablets, preserve much of the international correspondence during his and his son's reign. His rule marks a time of great prosperity and cultural refinement. **Amenophis IV** (Ikhnaton) (1375-1358) envisioned a single god of the whole world, Aton (the sun disk and its life-giving rays), but his religious reformation, owing to the opposition of the priests of Amon-Re at Thebes, did not survive him. Meanwhile, with few exceptions, the cities of Palestine, Phoenicia, and Syria, through internal disaffection and outside pressure (Hittites and Amorites in the north, Habiru-Hebrews in the east), were slipping away from Egyptian control. Ikhnaton built a new capital at Tell-el-Amarna, where a new style in painting and sculpture made its appearance. He was followed on the throne by two sons-in-law: the second was **Tutankhamen,** whose richly furnished unviolated tomb was discovered by Carnarvon and Carter in 1922.

1350-1200. Dynasty XIX (capital: Thebes). **Haremhab** (1350-1315) was a general, but devoted himself chiefly to internal reorganization. Seti (Sethos) I (1313–1292) and **Ramses II** (1292–1225) fought against the Hittites for the restoration of Egypt's Asiatic empire. The war ended with a treaty of peace and alliance between Ramses II and Hattushilish (1271); only southern Palestine, however, was incorporated into the Egyptian Empire. During the remaining 46 years of his reign Ramses built prodigiously from the Delta (Pithom and Raamses; Ex. 1 : 11) to Abu Simbel in Nubia. **Merneptah** (1225–1215) (under whom, probably, Moses led the Israelites out of Egypt) quelled a rebellion of Palestine (1223) and repelled the combined attack on Egypt of the Libyans and of the *Peoples of the Sea* (Sardinians, Sicilians, Achaeans, Lycians) (1221). The movement of these Aegean peoples is connected with the Homeric war against Troy and brought about the end of the Hittite Kingdom.

1200–1090. Dynasty XX (capital: Thebes). **Ramses III** (1198–1167) defeated on land and water another wave of the *Peoples of the Sea,* now including also the Danaï, the Philistines, and others (1190); the Philistines (whose culture was Aegean) settled on the Palestinian coast and probably introduced iron there. Ramses' feeble successors (Ramses IV–XII, 1167–1090) were unable to check the growing power of the high priests of Amon. Egyptian authority in Asia became purely nominal (cf. the *Story of Wen-Amon*).

1090–945. Dynasty XXI. The high priests of Amon at Thebes (**Hrihor** and his line) and the nobles of Tanis (**Smendes** and his line) strove for the royal authority.

945–712. Dynasties XXII–XXIV. Shoshenk (later Sheshonk; *Shishak* in 1 Kings 11 : 40; 14 : 25) (945–924), one of the Libyan chiefs who had for some time played a considerable rôle in the Delta, founded a Libyan dynasty (XXII, 945–745) with capital at Bubastis. The high-priestly family of Amon at Thebes founded the independent southern Nubian kingdom with capital at Napata (c. 850); Libyan princes became high priests of Amon at Thebes. Anarchy and civil war prevailed during Dynasties XXIII (745–718) and XXIV (718–712).

712–663. Dynasty XXV (**Ethiopian**) founded by Shabaka, King of Napata, who con-

quered Egypt. After defeating Taharka (*Tirhakah*, 2 Kings 19 : 9) (688–663), Essarhaddon made of Egypt, as far as Thebes, an Assyrian province (671), but Ashurbanipal was forced to undertake two more campaigns into Egypt (668 and 661), during the second of which Thebes was sacked.

663–525. Dynasty XXVI (capital: Saïs). **Psamtik** (Psammetichus) (663–609), son of Necho, the governor of Saïs under Essarhaddon, was appointed governor of Saïs and Memphis by Ashurbanipal (663), but, allying himself with Gyges, King of Lydia, he soon rebelled, and by 652 he was master of Egypt and inaugurated the **Saïtic revival** not only in the applied arts but also in sculpture, painting, architecture, literature, and religion — a renaissance deliberately imitating the masterpieces of the Old and Middle Kingdoms. Greek mercenaries and merchants were encouraged to come to Egypt. **Necho** (609–593), according to Herodotus, failed in his attempt to connect the Nile with the Red Sea by means of a canal, but Africa was successfully circumnavigated in three years by Phoenician sailors at his orders. He attempted to regain Egypt's lost Asiatic empire: he conquered Judea through his victory over Josiah at Megiddo (609), but he was ignominiously driven out of Asia after being completely routed at Carchemish (605) by **Nebuchadrezzar**, the crown prince of Babylon. Necho's successors were likewise unsuccessful in their military campaigns: Psamtik II (593–588) in lower Nubia (Ethiopia), Apries (588–569) against Nebuchadrezzar at the siege of Jerusalem and against the Greeks of Cyrene. Amasis (569–525), while apparently curtailing the privileges of the Greek merchants, allowed them to make of Naukratis a purely Greek city and the most important commercial center of the kingdom.

525–404. Egypt under Persian rule after Cambyses defeated Psamtik III at Pelusium in 525 (Dynasty XXVII).

404–332. Dynasties XXVIII–XXX comprised ephemeral native rulers under whom Egypt was in some degree independent from the Persian kings.

332–323. Egypt under **Alexander the Great.**

323–30. Egypt under the **Ptolemies.**

(*Cont. p.* 83.)

2. MESOPOTAMIA

GEOGRAPHY. The Mesopotamian plain (modern Iraq), extending for 600 miles from the southern slopes of the Armenian plateau, from which spring the Euphrates and the Tigris, to the Persian Gulf, which in antiquity reached the vicinity of Ur (60 miles north of the present shore), was divided into **Assyria** in the north and **Babylonia** in the south: the line of demarcation was roughly the 34th parallel. The principal cities of Assyria (so named after its god and its oldest capital) were its four royal cities on or near the Tigris: Ashshur, Calah, Nineveh, and Dur-Sharrukin (*Sargonburg*, now Khorsabad); also Arbela (Sumerian: *Urbillum*, now *Erbil*, the oldest living city in the world). The principal cities of northern Babylonia, or Akkad, were Babylon (*Bab-ili: Gate of God*), Borsippa, Dilbat, Kish, Kuthah, Opis, Sippar, Akkad; those of southern Babylonia, or Sumer (Hebrew: *Shinar*), were Nippur, Adab, Lagash, Umma, Larsa, Erech (Uruk), Ur, Eridu. Most of the cities of Babylonia were on or near the Euphrates.

RACES. Little is known of the race of the earliest inhabitants of Babylonia; the few known skulls are not unlike those of modern Arabs. During the 4th millennium the Sumerians occupied the southern country (Sumer) and "Semitic" Akkadians the northern part. The race and place of origin of the Sumerians are disputed; their language, which is agglutinative, has no close connections with any other linguistic group. Other "Semites," the Amorites from northern Syria, entered Babylonia at the end of the 3d millennium and founded the Hammurabi dynasty. From the northeast, uncultured mountaineers invaded the country about 2400 (the Gutium) and 1750 (the Kassites). Finally the "Semitic" Arameans overran the country-side along the course of the Euphrates (beginning about 1100); one of their tribes, the Chaldeans, produced the dynasty of Nebuchadrezzar. Although Assyrian is a dialect of Akkadian, the Assyrians were not Akkadians, but probably a mixture of Proto-Arameans and Hurrians. It should always be kept in mind that the term "Semites" does not refer to a race but to a group of peoples speaking "Semitic" languages (Akkadian, Hebrew, Phoenician, Aramaic, Arabic, etc.).

a. SUMER AND AKKAD

SUMERIAN CIVILIZATION AND RELIGION. Sumer was divided into city-states ruled by a "tenant farmer" (*ishak*) of the city-god. These cities were in frequent conflict over border lines and water rights and fought for the hegemony of the country, which passed from one to the other. As a result of these wars the Sumerians were superior to the contemporary Egyptians in military equipment (they had a war chariot, drawn by donkeys, 1200 years before the Egyptians) and organization (the phalanx of Alexander is pictured on the *Stela of the Vultures* of Eannatum). Although agriculture was the chief industry, commerce with distant lands flourished: the Sumerians were influential in establishing commercial and banking practices, standard weights and measures, forms of written contracts, etc., in western Asia and were the first to codify civil law in writing; prices and wages were sometimes fixed by law. Their sexagesimal system (soon combined with the decimal) still survives in the divisions of the day (24 hours, 60 minutes, 60 seconds) and of the circle (360 degrees). Out of pictographs they developed a **cuneiform writing** suitable for clay tablets. Sumerian sculpture, even in the time of Gudea, was stiff and crude in comparison with that of the Old Kingdom in Egypt. Sumerian buildings, with monotonous windowless walls of unbaked (or rarely baked) bricks, were ephemeral and purely practical. Originally each city had its own god and goddess; eventually a pantheon was developed with the triad **Anu** (the sky), **Enlil** (the atmosphere and the earth), and **Ea** (the waters) at its head; Enlil, the god of Nippur, became the supreme god. The temples usually had an irregular three-stepped pyramid (*ziggurat*) surmounted by a small shrine. Myths related the creation of the world, the deluge, the fruitless search for eternal life. Life after death was conceived as a shadowy existence in the subterranean *land of no return*, the *Hades* of Homer and the *Sheol* of the Old Testament.

c. 3000-c. 2600. First dynasty of Ur (Mes-anni-padda, A-anni-padda); "royal tombs" of Ur. Mesilim, King of Kish. The **First Dynasty of Lagash** was founded by Ur-Nina (*Ur-Nanshe*): Eannatum defeated Umma (*Stela of the Vultures*). Urukagina instituted social reforms, but was defeated by Lugalzaggisi, King of Erech.

c. 2600-c. 2420. The Akkadian Empire. Sargon and Naram-Sin ruled over Akkad, Sumer, Elam, Assyria, and northern Syria. The Sumerian culture was adopted and modified by the Akkadians, who made notable progress in sculpture.

c. 2420-c. 2300. The barbaric Gutium from the eastern hills conquered Babylonia and ruled it for 125 years. Lagash, however, flourished under **Gudea** (c. 2350), whose reign marked the classical period of Sumerian sculpture and literature. Utu-hegal, King of Erech, drove out the Gutium.

c. 2300-c. 2200. The Empire of Ur, under the Third Dynasty of Ur (Ur-Nammu [*Ur-*

Engur], Dungi [*Shulgi*], Bur-Sin, Gimil-Sin, Ibi-Sin), extended from Ashshur and Arbela to the Persian Gulf, from Susa to the Lebanon. Commerce thrived, as shown by the thousands of business contracts of the time.

c. 2200–c. 1950. The **Sumerians,** under the mutually hostile dynasties of Isin and Larsa, declined and lost their national identity.

b. BABYLONIA

CIVILIZATION AND RELIGION. In all its manifestations, Babylonian culture represents a development of the Sumerian. The foundations for Babylonia's great commercial expansion, for the elaborate government administration, for the admirable code of laws promulgated by Hammurabi, for the architectural and artistic works, for the literature and religion, were laid by the Sumerians, particularly during the time of the 3d Dynasty of Ur. When Babylon became a great metropolis and the capital of an empire, its god **Marduk** acquired a new importance and, by being identified with Enlil and assuming his functions, such as the creation of the world, he became the supreme god of the pantheon and was later called **Bel,** *Lord,* a Semitic designation of Enlil. The most characteristic and influential features of Babylonian religion, aside from its mythology, were the elaborate systems of magical practices (incantations) and the interpretation of omens (divination), particularly the movements and position of the heavenly bodies (astrology), the actions of animals, and the characteristics of the liver of sacrificial victims.

c. 2050–1750. The **First Dynasty of Babylon** (Amoritic). Its sixth king, the great **Hammurabi** (about 1950), defeated Rim-Sin of Larsa, conquered all of Mesopotamia, carried out extensive public works, and introduced an excellent administration and a code of laws unsurpassed before Roman times. After his death a dynasty arose in the Sea Land, on the Persian Gulf (c. 1890–1520).

1750–1180. After a Hittite raid, the Kassites conquered Babylonia and ruled it for 570 years. The horse became common in Egypt and western Asia after 1600. Diplomatic intrigues in 14th century (*Tell-el-Amarna letters*).

1146–1123. **Nebuchadrezzar I** defeated the Elamites but was routed by the Assyrians.

c. 1100–900. Invasion of Aramaic tribes into Babylonia.

900–625. The wars with Assyria were disastrous for Babylonia. In 729 **Tiglath-pileser III** of Assyria became King of Babylon (with the name of *Pul*), and from then to 625, except for occasional periods of open insurrection, Babylon remained a part of the Assyrian Empire.

625–538. **THE NEO-BABYLONIAN (CHALDEAN) EMPIRE.**

625–605. **Nabopolassar** and his ally Cyaxares, King of Media, destroyed Nineveh (612) and divided between themselves the Assyrian Empire. Through the victory of Nebuchadrezzar over Pharaoh Necho at Carchemish (605), Judea became subject to Babylonia.

605–561. **Nebuchadrezzar** took Jerusalem twice (597, 586), but failed to capture Tyre, which he besieged for 13 years (585–573). The buildings and city walls of Babylon, admired by Greek historians, were erected by Nebuchadrezzar.

555–538. **Nabonidus** (reigning in conjunction with Belshazzar) devoted his time to archaeological excavations and restorations of temples.

538. **Gobryas,** a general of Cyrus, King of Persia, took Babylon.

538–332. Babylonia under **Persian rule.**

332–323. Babylonia under **Alexander the Great.**

312–171. The dynasty of the **Seleucids** ruled Babylonia.

171 B.C.–226 A.D. Babylonia under the **Parthians** (Arsacid Dynasty).

226–641, A.D. The **Sassanian Dynasty.**

c. ASSYRIA

CIVILIZATION AND RELIGION. Assyrian culture was deeply indebted to the Babylonian, to the Hittite, and to the Hurrian. Except for the Assyrian royal annals, which are historical sources of the greatest value and are inspired by Hittite models, for the most part Assyrian literature consisted in new editions of the ancient Babylonian works. **Ashurbanipal** took special pains to collect in his library copies of the ancient writings. In sculpture (particularly in the bas-reliefs depicting realistically religious scenes, hunts, and military operations) and in architecture (influenced by the Hittite styles) the Assyrians surpassed the Babylonians, as also in the fields in which they made their greatest contributions, military equipment and imperial administration. Their fragmentary codes of law (c. 1350) are, however, decidedly inferior to the Code of Hammurabi, although the latter was not unknown among the Assyrians. In religion the Assyrians contributed only the worship of their national god, Ashur, and of Ishtar of Nineveh.

c. 2700–c. 2100. The city Ashshur, at first Sumerian in culture, became part of the Akkadian Empire; rebuilt after a destruction (probably by the Gutium), it was subject to the Third Dynasty of Ur.

c. 2050–c. 1950. Under native rulers (**Sargon I**), Assyrian merchants established a prosperous colony in Cappadocia.

c. 1950–c. 1850. Assyria under **Babylonian rule.**

c. 1850. **Shamshi-Adad** made Assyria independent and extended its territory.

c. 1800–1380. Assyria was hard pressed by the Hittites, the Egyptians (Thutmosis III), and the Hurrians of Mitanni.

1380–1341. **Ashur-uballit** restored the fortunes of Assyria.

1341–1232. Through campaigns in all directions, Assyria consolidated its position.

1232–1116. After a period of weakness due to the fall of the Hittite Kingdom (which seriously affected Assyrian trade) and a revival of Babylonian power, Assyria slowly recovered and began to work iron.

1116–1093. **Tiglath-pileser I** through successful campaigns gained control of the main trade routes of western Asia.

1093–933. Hard pressed by Aramean nomads, Assyria was barely able to survive.

933–782. **THE FIRST PHASE OF THE ASSYRIAN EMPIRE.**

883–859. **Ashur-nasir-pal II** campaigned successfully in the northeast and in the northwest and reached the Mediterranean, where the Phoenician cities paid him tribute. He improved the provincial administration and the military equipment, particularly the battering-rams and the siege engines, adorned his palace at Calah with remarkable bas-reliefs, but was ruthless in war.

859–824. **Shalmaneser III** fought against the kingdom of Urartu (Van) and against Ben-Hadad of Damascus and his allies, including Ahab of Israel, at Qarqar (854); he conquered Carchemish (849), defeated Hazael of Damascus without taking his capital (841), received the tribute of Tyre, Sidon, and of Jehu of Israel, and thus gained control of the Mediterranean trade routes.

810–806. **Semiramis** (*Shammu-ramat*) was the widow of Shamshi-Adad V (824–810) and the mother of Adad-nirari III (806–782).

782–745. Assyria, ruled by incompetent rulers, was unable to check the growing power of the kingdom of Urartu (Van).

745–625. **THE SECOND PHASE OF THE ASSYRIAN EMPIRE.**

745–727. **Tiglath-pileser III** restrained the expansion of Urartu, conquered Arpad, receiving the tribute of Menaheni of Israel and of other Syrian princes; in 734 he forced the submission of Israel, in 732 he took Damascus, in 729 he became King of Babylon (with the name of *Pul*). He consolidated his conquests by deporting entire populations.

727–722. **Shalmaneser V** besieged Samaria for three years.

722–705. **Sargon II** (*Sharrukin*) took Samaria (722), took Carchemish, and raided Urartu (717–714). He then reconquered Babylonia (710–709), where Merodach-baladan had become king in 721. He built a new capital (Dur-Sharrukin) near Nineveh.

705–681. **Sennacherib** (*Sin-ahê-erba*), faced with a general insurrection, fomented by Egypt and Babylonia, in Palestine and Syria, took Sidon and Ashkalon, defeated the Egyptians at Eltekeh, devastated Judah but failed to take Jerusalem (701): all rebellious vassals were forced into submission. In 689 he destroyed Babylon.

681–668. **Essarhaddon** (*Ashur-ah-iddin*) had difficulty in holding back the hordes of the Cimmerians in the north. He permitted the rebuilding of Babylon, directed a campaign against Tyre and Sidon (676), and conquered Egypt (671).

668–625. **Ashurbanipal** (*Sardanapalos* in Greek) made two successful campaigns into Egypt (668, 661), but he could not prevent Psamtik from becoming master of that country (652). Palestine and Syria, however, remained submissive. His half-brother Shamash-shum-ukin, who had been appointed by Essarhaddon viceroy of Babylonia, rebelled: the resulting civil war lasted from 652 to 648 (when Shamash-shum-ukin committed suicide), but operations were continued against the Chaldeans, the Arabs, and Elam (completely devastated in the course of two campaigns in 646 and 640). Ashurbanipal was a patron of arts and letters, and assembled a great library of cuneiform tablets at Nineveh.

625–605. Rapid disintegration of the Assyrian Empire. Nineveh was destroyed by Cyaxares, King of Media, and Nabopolassar, King of Babylonia (612). For a few years an Assyrian general, **Ashur-uballit,** attempted to save a remnant of the Assyrian Empire with Harran as its capital, but he failed dismally (605) and the Assyrian nation ceased to exist.

3. UPPER MESOPOTAMIA (MITANNI)

GEOGRAPHY. The homeland of the **Hurrians** was probably in the Nairi lands, as the Assyrians called the region east and north of Lake Van where the original nucleus of the Kingdom of Van was later located. From there, early in the 19th century B.C., the Hurrians moved southward, east and west of Assyria, founding a number of principalities that were eventually joined together under the rule of the kings of Mitanni. The Kingdom of Mitanni extended from Carchemish on the Euphrates to the vicinity of the upper Tigris, comprising the valleys of the Balich, of the Habur, and the province of Nisibis, and, east of the Tigris, it included also the region of Arrapkha (modern Kirkuk), which had previously been a separate Hurrian kingdom. Whether Arbela was also included is not known. The Hurrians overran also parts of Asia Minor, Syria, and Palestine, without, however, organizing permanent kingdoms: their presence is attested about the middle of the 2d millennium at Boghaz Keui (the Hittite capital), at Ras Shamra (northern Phoenicia), at Jerusalem and Taanach, and in the land of Edom (the Horites); the Hyksos probably included Hurrian contingents.

CIVILIZATION AND RELIGION. The Hurrian language is imperfectly known through the letter of Tushratta, King of Mitanni, to Amenophis III of Egypt, through some tablets in a cuneiform alphabet found at Ras Shamra, through some records from the Hittite archives at Boghaz Keui, and from occasional words in the cuneiform tablets from Nuzi (near Kirkuk). It was probably related to Vannic and Elamitic, but it cannot be classed within any well-known linguistic group. The racial connections of the Hurrians are unknown. The royal dynasty and the nobility of Mitanni were of Indo-Iranian extraction: they took their oaths by the Indian-Iranian deities Indra, Mithra, Varuna, and the Nasatya. The greatest contribution of the Hurrians, or rather of their Indo-Iranian leaders, was the introduction of the two-wheeled horse-drawn war chariot into Egypt and western Asia, where it became common after 1600. A treatise on horse-training written by a Hurrian named Kikkuli, found in the archives of Boghaz Keui, contains many Indian technical terms. The so-called *Hittite* bas-reliefs from northern Syria (Carchemish, Senjirli, Tell Ahmar) and Upper Mesopotamia (Tell Halaf), dating from the middle of the 2d millennium to the 9th century, are probably Hurrian in style if not in origin, as

can be verified by comparison with Hurrian seal impressions. The chief deities of the Hurrian pantheon are **Teshub,** the storm-god, and **Hepa** (*Hepat*), a sun-goddess; of several other deities nothing is known but the name.

c. 1900. Beginning of the Hurrian migration.

c. 1800–1500. The Hurrians organized principalities such as the little Kingdom of Arrapkha (including Nuzi) of which we know three kings: Itkhi-Teshub (son of Kibi-Teshub), Itkhiya, and Kirenzi.

c. 1475–1275. THE KINGDOM OF MITANNI (capital: Washshukanni on the upper Habur).

c. 1475. Saushshattar, the son of Parsashatar, conquered Aleppo and held it, with northern Syria, in spite of the victorious campaigns of Thothmes III; Assyria was reduced to vassalage and, to judge from a letter of Saushshattar found at Nuzi, the Hurrian principality of Arrapkha was incorporated into the kingdom.

c. 1440. Artatama preserved the integrity of the kingdom, if he did not extend it. A friendly policy toward Egypt prevailed.

c. 1410. Shutarna was on friendly relations with Pharaoh Amenophis III, to whom he gave his daughter Giluhepa in marriage.

c. 1390. Tuhi, the leader of the anti-Egyptian party, slew the legitimate heir (Artashuwara) and crowned his brother **Tushratta;** the latter executed the rebels, but lost part of his kingdom (Hanigalbat), where the anti-Egyptians made his brother **Artatama II** king. Tushratta was allied with Pharaoh Amenophis III, Artatama with Shubbiluliu, King of the Hittites, who conquered Tushratta's vassal principalities west of the Euphrates.

c. 1370. Shutarna II was appointed by his father Artatama II as regent, after the assassination of Tushratta and of his supporters; only Mattiwaza, a young son of Tushratta, was saved from the slaughter.

c. 1360. Mattiwaza was placed on the throne by Shubbiluliu, King of the Hittites, his father-in-law. Assyria under Ashur-uballit became independent of Mitanni and began its wars against it.

c. 1350–1300. Decadence of Mitanni. Adadnirari I of Assyria conquered Mitanni as far as the Euphrates, sacking the capital Washshukanni (c. 1300).

c. 1275. Shalmaneser I of Assyria defeated Shattuara, King of Hanigalbat, and devastated his kingdom. Thus the Kingdom of Mitanni disappeared from history.

4. PALESTINE

GEOGRAPHY. Palestine is the southern part of Syria, extending between the Mediterranean and the Syrian Desert, from Mt. Hermon to the southern end of the Dead Sea, or "from Dan to Beersheba." West of the Jordan its length is about 150 miles; its width in the north 23 miles, in the south about 80 miles. The term *Palestine*, derived from the name of the Philistines, was first used by Herodotus; the Hebrew name for the land west of the Jordan was *Canaan*. The country is divided into four zones, running parallel to the coast: the maritime plain (Philistia and the plain of Sharon, south of Mt. Carmel); the western plateau, divided by the plain of Jezreel (the strategic key to the conquest of Canaan) into Galilee in the north and the mountains of Ephraim and of Judah in the south; the Jordan Valley, lying below sea-level (the Lake of Galilee lies 600 feet below sea-level, the Dead Sea 1300 feet), tropical in climate; the plateau of Transjordania, cut by numerous valleys (the three important rivers are the Jarmuk, the Jabbok, and the Arnon) and occupied, from north to south, by the Arameans, the Ammonites, and the Moabites (the occupation of some regions by the Israelitic tribes of Reuben, Gad, and part of Manasseh was precarious). The Kingdom of Edom extended from the southern end of the Dead Sea to the Gulf of Elath on the Red Sea; the list of the eight Kings of Edom that ruled about 1200-1000 is found in Genesis 36: 31-39.

POPULATION. Nations of Semitic speech, commonly called *Semites*, occupied the land in successive waves since the beginning of the Bronze Age (c. 3000 B.C.): the 'amw (= Hebrew *'am,* nation) of the Egyptian records dating from about 2500; the **Amorites** from the Lebanon (c. 2000); the Hebrews (*Habiru* in the *Tell-el-Amarna letters*) in the early 14th century; the Israelites (c. 1200); the Arabs (c. 500). The term *Hebrews* includes, in the *Old Testament*, the nations tracing their ancestry to Abraham (Ishmael and the sons of Isaac, i.e. Israel and Edom) and his brother Harran (sons of Lot: Moab and Ammon); the Arameans were said to be the sons of Nahor, brother of Abraham. The most important non-Semitic invaders of Palestine were the Hurrians (presumably the Horites that occupied the land of Edom before the Edomites), the Hittites, and the Philistines, a contingent of the Aegean *Peoples of the Sea* (c. 1200).

CIVILIZATION AND RELIGION (1600-1200). The language of Canaan was Hebrew (as known from the Old Testament), a northwestern Semitic dialect akin to Phoenician, Moabitic, Amoritic, etc. The civilization was deeply influenced by Babylonia, particularly in commercial terms and practices, and Egypt, whence amulets and religious objects were imported. The influence of the Mycenaean culture antedates the coming of the Philistines. Each locality worshiped its local **Baal** (master), usually at an open-air sanctuary on top of a hill called "high place." **Astarte** was the goddess most commonly worshiped.

c. 3200-2100. **Early Bronze Age** (I: 3200-2900; II: 2900-2700; III: 2700-2300; IV: 2300-2100).

c. 2100-1500. **Middle Bronze Age** (I: 2100-1900; II: 1900-1500). Relations with Egypt (story of Sinuhet; expedition of Sesostris III, c. 1870). Hyksos period (1680-1580).

c. 1500-1400. **Late Bronze Age I.** Thutmosis III of Egypt (1501-1447) conquered Palestine (**battle of Megiddo**, 1479).

c. 1400-1200. **Late Bronze Age II.** Egyptian control of the country began to relax in the Amarna period, particularly during the reign of Amenophis IV or Ikhnaton (1375-1358), when the *Habiru* (Hebrews) from the east and the Amorites and Hittites from the north were intriguing with vassal princes or attacking them. Palestine was reconquered through the campaigns of the Pharaohs of the 19th Dynasty (1350-1200), particularly Haremhab, Sethos I, Ramses II, and Merneptah.

c. 1200-900. **Early Iron I.** The Israelites occupied the Mountain of Ephraim, the Philistines the coastal plain, where they organized five city kingdoms (Ascalon, Ashdod, Ekron, Gath, and Gaza).

a. ISRAEL AND JUDAH

RELIGION. Through Moses, **Jehovah** (Hebrew: *Yahweh*) became the god of Israel after the deliverance from Egyptian bondage. Jehovah was originally the god of a sacred mountain (Sinai or Horeb). As national god, Jehovah led the Israelites into Canaan and after assuming the functions of the *Baals* and taking over their sanctuaries, he became the god of Canaan as well as of Israel. By declaring that Jehovah was an international god of justice, Amos (c. 750) paved the way to the recognition of Jehovah as the only god in existence, in Isaiah 40–55 (c. 550). The combination of this prophetic theology with the elaborate temple worship proposed by Ezekiel at that time produced a new religion, **Judaism,** a revealed religion of salvation possessing a body of inspired scriptures that grew from the **Law of Moses** in Deuteronomy (published in 621) to the *Old Testament* (without the *Apocrypha*), the canon of which was closed about 90 A.D.

LITERATURE. The **Old Testament** was written and edited in the course of the millennium that elapsed from the *Song of Deborah* in *Judges* 5 (c. 1150) to the *Book of Esther* (c. 130). The **Pentateuch,** published in its final edition about 400, embodies writings dated in the six preceding centuries. The *historical books* (Joshua, Judges, Samuel, and Kings) were edited as religious works about 550 and were canonized about 200, but the admirable biographies of Saul and David in the most ancient parts of the *Books of Samuel* date back to about 950. The great prophets (Amos, Hosea, Isaiah, Micah, Jeremiah, Ezekiel, Isaiah 40–55) were active between 750 and 550; their writings and those of the others of later date were canonized (with the exception of Daniel, dating from 164) about 200, together with the historical books. Some *Psalms, Proverbs,* and perhaps the *Book of Job* are earlier than the downfall of the state in 586; the rest of the *Old Testament* belongs to Persian and Hellenistic periods. The **Apocrypha** range in date from about 180 B.C. (*Ecclesiasticus*) to the beginning of our era. The **Apocalypses,** dating from the beginnings of Christianity, were not recognized by official Judaism, but they were influential in oriental Christianity. The legalistic literature of Judaism was collected in the *Mishna* (about 200 A.D.) and in the *Talmud* (about 500 A.D.).

c. 2000-1225. The patriarchs of the sagas in *Genesis* are legendary heroes, artificially connected with Israel. Some of the Hebrew clans entered Canaan in the Amarna period (14th cent.); others roamed in the wilderness. The Joseph tribes settled at Goshen, in the eastern delta of the Nile.

c. 1225-1200. Moses (whose name is Egyptian and means *son*) led a revolt of the Joseph clans in Egypt, after they had been enslaved by Ramses II and brought them to the oasis of Kadesh.

c. 1200. The tribe of Reuben settled east of the Jordan, where the tribe of Gad was already living. The tribe of Judah began to move northward from the wilderness south of the Dead Sea. The Joseph tribes, under Joshua, crossed the Jordan and occupied the Mountain of Ephraim. The other tribes of Israel were already in Canaan, where Merneptah attacked them in 1223.

c. 1200-1028. Living among the Canaanites, ten tribes, without central government, worshiped Jehovah and regarded themselves as parts of Israel. Three other tribes (Simeon, Levi, Judah), living in the extreme south of Palestine, became part of Israel later, through David. Six of the ten tribes answered the summons of Deborah and fought victoriously against the Canaanites of the Valley of Jezreel. Victorious tribal leaders (**Judges**) ruled over their tribes, but, with the exception of Gideon, who was followed by seventy sons ruling jointly, and by Abimelech, they founded no dynasty. Ehud killed Eglon, King of Moab; Jephtah, a Gileadite, defeated the Ammonites. The tribe of Benjamin was nearly exterminated in a civil war. Samson of Dan is a figure of legend, symbolizing the beginning of the conflict with the Philistines, as a result of which the tribe of Dan moved to the extreme north of Palestine.

1028-1013. Under the pressure of the Philistine domination (c. 1080–1028), the Israelites made **Saul** their king, after his spectacular deliverance of Jabesh in Gilead. He defeated the Philistines at Michmash, but took his life after their victory at Gilboa.

1013-973. For seven years after the death of Saul, Ishbaal, his son, ruled in Mahanaim, east of the Jordan, while **David,** a Philistine vassal, was King of Judah at Hebron. As King of all Israel, David conquered Jerusalem and made it his capital. Breaking the power of the Philistines, David fought successfully against the Moabites, the Ammonites, and the Edomites; however, the jealousy between Judah and Israel provoked the rebellions of Absalom and of Sheba.

973-933. In alliance with the Pharaoh of Egypt and with Hiram, King of Tyre, **Solomon** undertook far-reaching trading operations by land and sea. He introduced taxation and forced labor, built the temple, the royal palace, and the city wall at Jerusalem, and public buildings elsewhere. The magnificence of his reign became proverbial.

933. Solomon's son, **Rehoboam**, refused the demand of the northern tribes for relief from taxation and they seceded, making Jeroboam their king.

933-722. KINGDOM OF ISRAEL.

933-887. Jeroboam I chose Shechem as his capital. His son Nadab (912) was slain by Baasha (911), who resided at Tirzah. Elah (888) was killed by Zimri (887).

887-843. Omri (887) overcame Tibni and built a new capital, Samaria: he inaugurated the period of expansion and power of the northern kingdom. He placed northern Moab under tribute, but failed to subdue the Arameans of Damascus. **Ahab** (875) allowed his wife Jezebel, the daughter of Ethbaal, King of Tyre, to spread the worship of Melqarth, her *Baal*, in Samaria, provoking the reaction of **Elijah** and **Elisha**, which eventually wiped out Omri's dynasty. Ahab failed against Mesha, King of Moab, but imposed his peace terms on Ben-Hadad II of Damascus and fought with him at Qarqar (854) against Shalmaneser III of Assyria. Ahaziah (853) and Joram (852) were the last kings of Omri's dynasty.

843-744. Jehu (843) exterminated the princes of Israel and Judah within reach and the worshipers of the Tyrian *Baal* in Samaria. He paid tribute to Shalmaneser III. Hazael of Damascus, in revenge, raided his Transjordanian provinces. Under Jehoahaz (816) and Joash (800) Israel was likewise helpless against Damascus, but **Jeroboam II** (785) reconquered the lost provinces while Damascus was attacked by Assyria (773), and ruled over a kingdom at the height of its power and prosperity. However, Amos and Hosea foresaw the impending ruin of Israel. The last king of the dynasty of Jehu, Zechariah (744), was assassinated by Shallum (744).

744-722. Tiglath-pileser III of Assyria (745–727) forced Menahem (744) and Pekahiah (738) to pay tribute. Pekah (737) allied himself with Damascus (taken by Tiglath-pileser in 732) and his kingdom was devastated. Hoshea (732) refused to pay tribute to Shalmaneser V (727–722) and was deposed; after a siege of three years (725–722) Samaria was taken by Sargon (722–705), who exiled 27,290 Israelites. The Kingdom of Israel ceased to exist.

933-586. THE KINGDOM OF JUDAH.

933-780. Rehoboam (933), Abijah (917), and Asa (915) fought against the Kings of Israel with small success; Jehoshaphat (875) made an alliance with Ahab. Edom rebelled against Jehoram (851). Ahaziah (844) was killed by Jehu, and his mother Athaliah, a daughter of Jezebel (843), ruled until a palace revolution placed Jehoash (837) on the throne; the latter paid tribute to Hazael of Damascus. Amaziah (798) defeated the Edomites but was taken prisoner by Joash, King of Israel.

780-586. Azariah (Uzziah) (780) enjoyed a prosperous reign owing to Israel's revival under Jeroboam II. Jotham (740) was attacked by Pekah and Rezin (last King of Damascus); Ahaz (735), contrary to the advice of Isaiah, called Tiglath-pileser to his help. Hezekiah (720), however, defied Sennacherib, but after a disastrous war (701) he came to terms. Manasseh (692) remained a faithful vassal of Assyria and encouraged the worship of its gods, as also Amon (639). **Josiah** (638) reformed the worship, centralizing it in the temple at Jerusalem, and fell at Megiddo (609) fighting against Pharaoh Necho, who deposed Jehoahaz (607) and placed Jehoiakim (607) on the throne. Through Nebuchadrezzar's victory over Necho at Carchemish (605), Judah passed under Babylonian rule. Jehoiakim rebelled in 598, dying soon after; Jehoiachin (598–597) was taken captive to Babylonia, together with the Judean leaders (among them Ezekiel). Zedekiah (597), against the advice of Jeremiah, defied Nebuchadrezzar, who destroyed Jerusalem (586) **and** brought to an end the Kingdom of Judah.

b. THE JEWS

586-538. The Jews under Babylonian Rule. In Judea the Jews were poor and hard pressed between the Edomites and the Samaritans; in Babylonia they were prosperous and progressive.

538-332. The Jews under Persian Rule. The temple in Jerusalem was rebuilt (520–516), but conditions remained wretched until **Nehemiah** (445 and 433) came to rebuild the walls of Jerusalem and enforce the observance of the Law, thus precipitating the Samaritan schism.

332-198. The Jews under the Rule of Alexander (332–323) and of the Ptolemies of Egypt (323–198).

198-168. The Jews under the Seleucids.

168-63. Led by **Judas Maccabeus** and his brothers, the Jews rebelled against Antiochus IV (Epiphanes) (175–164), who had declared Judaism illegal (168). Religious freedom was achieved in 164, and, after wars under the leadership of Jonathan (161) and Simon (143), political freedom was attained (142). John Hyrcanus (135), Aristobulus I (104), Alexander Jannaeus (103), and Alexandra (76–67) continued the struggle for conquest until the rivalry between Aristobulus II (67–63) and his brother Hyrcanus II forced Pompey to place the Jews under Roman rule.

63 B.C.–395 A.D. Palestine under Roman Rule. Under Hyrcanus II (63–40) the real ruler was his prime minister Antipater, who appointed his own sons Herod and Phasael as governors. A Parthian expedition placed Antigonus, the son of Aristobulus II, on the throne (40–37). **Herod the Great** (37–4 B.C.) ruled as King of Judea by appointment of the Roman Senate. He began the rebuilding of the temple in Jerusalem, erected a temple of Augustus in Samaria (renamed Sebaste in honor of Augustus), and improved the harbor of Caesarea; he was, however, hated by Sadducees, Pharisees, and Zealots. **Jesus of Nazareth** was born in the latter part of his reign (between 6 and 4 B.C.). Herod's three sons succeeded him:

Archelaus as ethnarch of Judea and Samaria (4 B.C.–6 A.D.), Antipas as tetrarch of Galilee and Peraea (4 B.C.–39 A.D.), and Philip as tetrarch of Batanaea, northeast of the Lake of Galilee (4 B.C.–34 A.D.). After their death, except for Herod Agrippa's brief rule over the combined territory (41–44) and his son's (Herod Agrippa II, 50–100) interrupted rule over parts of it, Palestine was placed under the administration of Roman procurators. During the war of the Jews against Rome (66–73), Jerusalem was destroyed by Titus (70). After another war under Trajan (115–117), the Jews, led by Bar Cocheba, rebelled in the time of Hadrian (132–135). After the devastation of Judea, Jerusalem was made into a Roman colony (*Aelia Capitolina*) and was barred to the Jews. Henceforth the centers of Jewish learning were in Galilee (Tiberias) and in Babylonia; the two great editions of the *Talmud* were prepared there at the end of the 5th century.

5. PHOENICIA

GEOGRAPHY. The Phoenician cities lie along the coast of the Mediterranean, west of the Lebanon, and, except for Dor, north of Mt. Carmel. From south to north the most important ones, already mentioned in the *Tell-el-Amarna letters* of the 14th century B.C., are: Acco, Tyre (*Sôr*, "the rock"), Sidon, Beirut, Byblos (*Gebal*), Symira, Arwad, Ugarit (the present Ras Shamra, near Laodicea).

CIVILIZATION. The Phoenicians (called *Sidonians* in Homer and the *Old Testament*) were a branch of the Canaanites, if we may judge from their language, which is one of the western Semitic dialects, closely akin to the Hebrew spoken in Canaan. The greatest contribution of the Phoenicians to civilization was the invention, in the 14th century or earlier, of the alphabet (22 consonants, no vowels) from which the principal ancient and modern alphabets are derived. A cuneiform alphabet of 29 letters, whose existence was unknown before 1929 A.D., was used at Ugarit (Ras Shamra), in the extreme north of Phoenicia, in the 14th century or earlier. After the decay of the Minoan and Mycenaean seapower, the Phoenicians became great sea-traders and after the 12th century established thriving colonies in Cyprus, northern Africa (Utica; Carthage, founded in 814), southern Spain (Tarshish), and, later, in other regions. The main industries, according to the Greeks, were purple dye, weaving, and glass-making. Phoenician art lacks originality: Egyptian and Babylonian motifs prevail.

RELIGION. It is only in the mythological poems of the 14th century, recently found at Ugarit (Ras Shamra), that a real Phoenician pantheon appears: **El,** "the king, father of years," was the supreme god, the creator, the father of **Mot** (the rival of **Aleyan Baal**) and of **Shepesh** (the sun-goddess); **Ashera** "of the sea" (probably his consort) was the mother of the gods and had seventy sons; the virgin **Anat** searched for her dead brother Aleyan and presumably restored him to life; other gods are also mentioned. For the rest, each Phoenician city had its local *Baal* (master), who seldom had a personal name (even the name *Melqarth*, the Baal of Tyre, means simply "king of the city," *malk-qart*; the Greeks identified him with Heracles); **Baal Hammon** was the god of Carthage. The chief goddess was **Astarte** (*Aphrodite* for the Greeks), whose great sanctuaries were at Sidon and at Byblos (where she was called *Baalath*, or lady, of Byblos); at Carthage she was usually called *Tanit*. **Adon** ("Lord," *Adonis* in Greek) at Byblos, the Babylonian **Tammuz,** and **Eshmun** (Greek *Asklepios*) at Sidon and Beirut were gods of vegetation, dying and coming back to life (in Egypt Adonis was identified with Osiris).

c. 2900–2000. Egyptian expeditions went to Byblos to obtain cedar of Lebanon logs. Byblos and other cities were occasionally under Egyptian rule. Sumerian and Akkadian raids reached the Mediterranean.

c. 2000-1500. Practically nothing is known of Phoenicia. Byblos was subject to Egypt.

1500-1447. **Thutmosis III** of Egypt conquered most of Phoenicia.

1411-1358. **The Amarna period** (Pharaohs Amenophis III and IV). The Amorites, under Abd-Ashirta and his son Aziru, in alliance with the Hittites, defeated the Egyptian vassal princes in Phoenicia, particularly Ribaddi of Byblos and Abimelek of Tyre; Zimrida of Sidon joined the ranks of the enemies of Egypt.

1350-1300. Egypt reconquered Phoenicia.

c. 1300-1200. Mycenaean culture at Ugarit. Close contacts with Egypt.

c. 1200-1000. After the Aegean migration, the great cities of Phoenicia, with the exception of Beirut (subject to the Amorites) and Ugarit (permanently destroyed), flourished as independent kingdoms. The oldest inscription in the Phoenician alphabet is on the sarcophagus prepared by King Ittobaal of Byblos for his father Ahiram (c. 1200?). Tiglath-pileser of Assyria (c. 1100) visited Arwad.

c. 1000-774. **Hegemony of Tyre.** Hiram I, son of Abibaal (969–936), provided Solomon with craftsmen and materials for his building operations and equipped for him a fleet on the Red Sea. He subjected the colony of Utica, which had rebelled. Abd-Ashtart (918–909), his grandson, was assassinated by the four sons of his nurse, three of whom ruled in succession (909–887). **Ittobaal** (*Ethbaal*) (887–856), priest of Astarte, founded a new dynasty and ruled over Phoenicia as far north as Beirut and part of Cyprus. Under Pygmalion (820–774) Carthage was founded (814).

774-625. **Assyrian period.** Ashur-nasir-pal II (883–859) and Shalmaneser III (859–824) received tribute from Phoenician cities, without subjecting them. Tiglath-pileser III (745–727) received the tribute of Matanbaal of Arwad, Sibittibaal of Byblos, and Hiram II of Tyre (738); a greater levy was paid to him by Metinna (Mattan) of Tyre in 730; the Valley of the Eleutheros (subject to Hamath) became an Assyrian province. Elulaios (Assyrian *Lule*) of Tyre (c. 725–690) reconquered Cyprus, that had been occupied by Sargon (722–705), and fled there when Sennacherib (705–681) conquered Phoenicia, with the exception of Tyre, in 701; Urumilki was then King of Byblos and Abdiliti of Arwad. Phoenicia and Cyprus were subject to Essarhaddon (681–668) and Ashurbanipal (668–625), who mention Matanbaal and Yakinlu of Arwad and Milkiasaph (followed by Yehawmelek) of Byblos, in addition to three kings of Cyprus. Essarhaddon defeated Abdimilkat of Sidon and destroyed the city (675) Tyre was not conquered, but its king Baal sent his son Yehawmelek with heavy tribute to Ashurbanipal.

625-586. Temporary independence of Phoenicia.

586-538. **Chaldean period.** Nebuchadrezzar (605–561) subjected Phoenicia (586) but besieged Tyre, under Ittobaal II, for 13 years (585–573) without success; Tyre asserted its independence under Baal II (572–563), under judges (563–556), and under Balatoros (556–555), Marbaal (555–552), **Hiram II** (552–532).

538-332. **Persian period.** Phoenicia was divided into four vassal kingdoms (Sidon, Tyre, Arwad, Byblos, in the order of their importance) and prospered; it furnished fleets to the Persian kings. A rebellion of Sidon led by Tennes in 350 was crushed with a great loss of life by Artaxerxes III.

332-323. **Alexander the Great** took Tyre by connecting this island city with the mainland (332) and gained control of the other Phoenician cities by peaceful means.

323-286. Phoenicia was ruled in succession by Laomedon (323), Ptolemy I (320), Antigonus (315), Demetrius (301), and Seleucus (296).

286-197. Phoenicia was under the Ptolemies of Egypt. Sidon's vassal rulers were high priests of Astarte (Eshmunazar I, Tabnit, Eshmunazar II).

197-82. Phoenicia was part of Kingdom of Syria under the Seleucids. Tyre became autonomous in 126, Sidon in 111. Phoenicia was increasingly Hellenized.

82-69. Rule of Tigranes, King of Armenia, over the Kingdom of the Seleucids.

64. Pompey organized the Roman province of Syria, including Phoenicia.

a. CARTHAGE

814. **Carthage** ("New City") was founded, according to tradition, by Tyrian colonists in the time of Pygmalion (820–774); according to legend, by Elissa or by Dido (a sister of Pygmalion who became the tutelar deity of the city). The language of Carthage (*Punic*) is a Phoenician dialect. Its two chief magistrates (*suffetes*) were elected annually by the Senate; the popular assembly, in cases of conflict, had the final decision.

600-480. Under the successive commands of Malchus (executed about 535), Mago (who died about 500), and Hasdrubal (who died in Sardinia about 485), the Carthaginians waged wars of conquest in Africa, Sicily, and Sardinia.

480-405. After **Hamilcar** had been defeated and slain at the **battle of Himera** (Sicily) (480) against Gelo of Syracuse, Carthage developed its sea-power and gained control of the western Mediterranean, including the Straits of Gibraltar. The sons of Hamilcar, Himilko and Hanno, explored the Atlantic coasts of Europe (Himilko) and of Africa (Hanno) about 450. As a result of imperial and commercial expansion Carthage flourished greatly. In 409 **Hannibal** avenged his grandfather Hamilkar by storming Selinus and Himera; three years later Hannibal and Himilko took Agrigentum, and western Sicily became subject to Carthage.

405-367. The Carthaginians fought four wars against **Dionysius I of Syracuse** (405-367). In the first one Himilko besieged Syracuse but was utterly defeated (398-397); in the second Mago was equally unsuccessful and Dionysius gained control of five-sixths of the island (392); the third war was undecisive (383-376); and the fourth (368-367), ending with the death of Dionysius, was inconclusive.

367-268. **The wars in Sicily** were continued intermittently. Timoleon defeated the Carthaginians at Crimissus (340) and Agathocles invaded Africa (310-307), besieging Carthage. Soon afterward the Carthaginians regained control of most of Sicily and Pyrrhus, King of Epirus, could not drive them out (278-276).

268-146. **WARS WITH ROME.** After the **First Punic War** (268-241) (see p. 86), Hamilcar conquered Spain to the Ebro (237-228). In the **Second Punic War** (219-202) Hannibal, in a brilliant campaign, marched from Spain to Italy, defeating the Romans at **Cannae** (216); but after his disastrous defeat at **Zama** in Africa (202), Carthage was forced to accept humiliating terms of peace. The **Third Punic War** (149-146) ended with the destruction of Carthage.

122-B.C.-439 A.D. Carthage under Roman rule.

6. SYRIA

GEOGRAPHY. The term *Syria* (used for the first time by Herodotus) in its wider sense indicates the whole region between the Euphrates and the eastern Mediterranean south of the Taurus range (so Strabo: this corresponds to the Roman province of Syria); in a narrower sense it includes only the northeastern part of this territory with the exclusion of Palestine and Phoenicia; since Hadrian divided the province into Palestine, Phoenicia, and Syria, the term is generally employed in its narrower sense. Syria's principal ancient cities, moving southward, were Sam'al, Carchemish, Arpad, Aleppo, Antioch, Kadesh, Hamath, Palmyra, Damascus. Syria has never been an independent political unity; it was merely at one time, in a general way, the land of the Arameans.

The **ARAMEANS** appear as "Semitic" Bedouins out of the Syrian Desert in the 14th century under the names of *Ahlame* and *Suti*; the name *Arameans* is used about 1100 for the first time. The movement of the Arameans may have been provoked by the expulsion of the Hyksos from Egypt (1580). In the 13th century they threatened to invade the Tigris Valley, but owing to the pressure from the Hittites and the Assyrians they were pushed back into the Syrian Desert, where they remained in the following century after the great Aegean migration of the

Peoples of the Sea. Important trading centers, like **Palmyra,** were developed in the 11th century. In the 10th century powerful **Aramaic kingdoms** were organized in Syria (Damascus) and uncultured Aramaic tribesmen from the desert were invading Mesopotamia: Assyria withstood the pressure, but in Babylonia Aramaic tribes occupied the valleys of the Euphrates and the Tigris and became the basic population of the countryside after the 9th century: the most important among them were the **Chaldeans.** The Arameans were the international traders on land from the 10th century to the 4th; their language became the *lingua franca* of western Asia during the Persian period and was not displaced as the vernacular until the Moslem conquest; much of the religious literature of the Jews and Christians (Syriac) is in Aramaic.

c. 2600-2500. **Sargon of Akkad** and Naram-Sin led campaigns into northern Syria; the reference to *Aram* in the latter's inscriptions is puzzling.

c. 2300-2200. Syria under the **Third Dynasty of Ur.**

c. 1950. Syria probably subject to **Hammurabi** of Babylon.

c. 1900. Beginning of the Hurrian invasion.

c. 1750. Aleppo was conquered by Murshilish I, King of the Hittites.

1680-1580. Probable Hyksos domination in Syria.

1580-1375. Syria subject to the **Pharaohs** of the 18th Dynasty. Thutmosis III (1501–1447) conquered Syria with the exception of Carchemish and Aleppo, which were subject to the Kings of Mitanni.

1375-1350. During the reign of Amenophis IV (Ikhnaton) the Amorites under Abd-Ashirta and his son Aziru, the Hittites under Shubbiluliu, and local rulers ended Egyptian control in Syria.

1350-1200. Syria remained under Hittite rule in spite of the campaigns of Ramses II.

c. 1200. The great Aegean migrations of the *Peoples of the Sea*.

c. 1200-1000. Some Hittite principalities in Syria continued to preserve their identity after the fall of the Hittite Kingdom in the midst of the flood of Aramaic migrations: **Carchemish,** where Shubbiluliu had appointed his son Biyushshilish as king before 1350, was the most important of these kingdoms and lasted until 717, when it was conquered by Sargon of Assyria. **Aleppo,** where Shubbiluliu had made his son Telipinush king, surrendered in 853 to Shalmaneser III of Assyria. The culture of these kingdoms remained Hurrian-Hittite even after they became Aramean.

c. 1000-700. **Aramean kingdoms in Syria and in Upper Mesopotamia.** East of the Euphrates: Beth-Eden (Bit-Adini), with Til Barsip as its capital, paid tribute to Ashurnasir-pal II (883–859) and was devastated by Shalmaneser III (857); Gozan (Tell Halaf); Hadippe (capital: Suru), and other principalities paid tribute to Adad-nirari II in 894. West of the Euphrates: Gurgum (capital: Marqash, now Mar'ash), Sam'al or Ya'udi (now Senjirli), Hattin (including probably Arpad), Hamath, Damascus, and the Aramean (Syrian) kingdoms named in *II Samuel* 10:6. The kings of Sam'al were Haian, son of Gabbar (c. 858), Sha'ul (*Saul*), Kalamu (c. 800), Panammu I, Barsur,

Azariah (d. 740), Panammu II (740–732), Barrekeb (d. c. 725). The last of the Aramean kingdoms of Syria were conquered by Sargon II of Assyria in 720 and in 709.

a. DAMASCUS

c. 1450-1350. Damascus under Egyptian rule.

c. 1350-1200. Damascus under Hittite rule.

1198-1167. **Ramses III** conquered Damascus.

c. 1000-732. **Aramean Kingdom of Damascus.**
The dynasty was founded about 970 by Rezon (Hezion?), son of Eliada, a general of Hadadezer, King of Zobah. He was followed by Tabrimmon (c. 916), Ben-Hadad I (c. 900), Ben-Hadad II (Hadadezer), who was defeated by Ahab but led the coalition against Shalmaneser III of Assyria (**battle of Qarqar,** 854), Hazael (842–c. 810), Mari (Ben-Hadad III), who was besieged in his capital by Adad-nirari III in 805 and was prevented by the successful resistance of Zakir (King of Hamath) from extending his power to northern Syria, Tabeel (c. 772), and Rezin, who was executed by Tiglath-pileser III after the fall of Damascus in 732.

732-538. Damascus, which had lost all importance, was subject to the Kings of Assyria (732–625) and Babylonia (625–538).

538-332. Revival of Damascus under the Persian kings.

332-85. **Hellenistic period:** Antioch took the place of Damascus as the most important city of Syria.

333-323. Syria was conquered and ruled by Alexander the Great.

323-301. **Ptolemy I** conquered Syria for Egypt in 320, but lost it to Antigonus in 315; through his victory at Gaza against Demetrius, son of Antigonus (312), he took possession of southern Syria; northern Syria remained under Antigonus until his death at the **battle of Ipsus** (301).

301. Northern Syria passed under the rule of Seleucus. (*Cont. p.* 80.)

7. ASIA MINOR

GEOGRAPHY. Asia Minor or Anatolia is a bridge between Asia and Europe, easily accessible by sea from the west and by land from the east. The great Taurus range in the south and a series of mountains in the north constitute powerful barriers to population movements, except for such strategically important passes as the Cilician Gates. The high central plateau

(Cappadocia, Lycaonia, Phrygia) is surrounded by mountains and sinks in its central part around a salt-water lake (Tatta) in the midst of a desert.

RACE. The basic population of Anatolia today as in antiquity has the characteristics of the "Armenoid" type, such as a very prominent nose in line with a receding high forehead. These features are intensified in the representation of Hittites on native bas-reliefs and on Egyptian monuments of the 19th Dynasty. Other racial types (particularly the "Mediterranean") are also represented in Asia Minor.

a. HITTITES

CIVILIZATION. The cuneiform tablets from royal archives at Hattushash (now Boghaz Keui) date for the most part from the 13th century and are generally written in the "Hittite" (*nashili*) language (Indo-European in grammatical structure); however, these archives yield information on archaic languages (proto-Hattic and Balaic), on Luvian (a dialect of "Hittite"), and on Hurrian. The decipherment of Hittite hieroglyphics is still in its initial stages. The Hittite kingdom was essentially a feudal aristocracy: the king was crowned by the nobles during the Old Kingdom (1900–1650), but the monarchy became hereditary during the New Kingdom (1450–1200), although the feudal organization persisted to the end. A late fragmentary copy of a code of laws, based on an earlier codification, is characterized by the humaneness of the punishments. Agriculture and shepherding were the chief industries. In literature, impartial historical narratives appear first among the Hittites. The so-called *Hittite* bas-reliefs in Asia Minor and in Syria are apparently Hurrian in style, if not in origin.

RELIGION. The Hittite pantheon included archaic native deities, some of which were worshiped in languages no longer in ordinary use. At the head of the "proto-Hattic" deities was the sun-goddess of **Arinna** (the supreme deity of the kingdom). There are also "Hittite," Hurrian (Teshub and his consort Hepa or Hepat), and even Babylonian-Assyrian deities.

c. 1900-1650. THE OLD KINGDOM.

c. 1900. **Anitta,** King of Kushshar (Cappadocia), defeated Bijustis, King of Hatti (capital Hattushash, now Boghaz Keui).

c. 1800. Under **Labarnash** (or Tabarnash), the founder of the Old Kingdom, and his son Hattushilish I, the capital was Kushshar.

c. 1750. **Murshilish I** captured Aleppo and raided Babylon. He moved the capital to Hattushash (Boghaz Keui).

c. 1650. **Telepinush** came to the throne after three usurpers and fixed the royal succession on a hereditary basis.

c. 1650-1430. Obscure period in which the Hur-

rians probably dominated. Tribute was paid to Thutmosis III of Egypt.

c. 1430-1200. **THE NEW KINGDOM.**

c. 1430-1390. During the reigns of Tudkhaliash II, Hattushilish II, and Tudkhaliash III, the Hurrian Kingdom of Mitanni grew in power at the cost of the Hittite Kingdom.

c. 1390-1350. **SHUBBILULIU,** the greatest of the Hittite kings, reconquered Anatolia, subjected northern Syria, and reduced Mitanni to the position of a small vassal kingdom.

c. 1350-1320. Arnuandash I (1350) and Murshilish II preserved the integrity of the empire.

c. 1320-1287. **Muwatallish** defeated Ramses II at Kadesh on the Orontes.

c. 1287-1281. **Urkhiteshub.**

c. 1281-1260. **Hattushilish III** made a treaty of peace and of alliance with Ramses II (1271), in which the Syrian possessions of the Hittites were recognized by the Egyptians.

c. 1260-1230. **Tudkhaliash IV** was forced to undertake military operations in western Anatolia.

c. 1230-1215. **Arnuandash II** was confronted with general unrest and insurrections.

c. 1200. The Hittite Kingdom came to an end as a result of the great Aegean migrations (the *Peoples of the Sea* of Egyptian records), of which the Homeric war against Troy was an incident.

b. PHRYGIANS

CIVILIZATION. The Phrygians (as well as the Mysians) came from Thrace with the great Aegean migrations about 1200 B.C. and occupied central Anatolia, west of the Halys. Their language belonged to the Indo-European group. Their capital was Gordion. Tumuli (sepulchral mounds) are typical of the Phrygians, although graves cut into the rock also occur.

RELIGION. The chief deities of the Phrygians were **Cybele** (*Ma*, the Great Mother riding in a chariot drawn by lions), whose orgiastic cult was introduced into Rome in 191 B.C., and **Attis**, the god who died as a result of castration but came back to life; his priests, Galli, were eunuchs.

c. 1000-700. **The Kingdom of Phrygia,** the history of which is not known, was organized and grew in power. **Midas** (*Mita* of

Mushku in the inscriptions of Sargon II of Assyria) ruled about 715.

696. The **Cimmerian invasion** devastated the kingdom; somehow the Phrygian nation survived until the time of Cyrus (547).

c. LYDIANS

GEOGRAPHY. Lydia, whose capital was Sardis, lies in western Asia Minor, between the Ionian cities on the coast and Phrygia; it borders on Mysia in the north and Caria in the south.

CIVILIZATION AND RELIGION. Whereas Phrygia constituted a barrier between Greece and the Orient, Lydia became the link between east and west, culturally and commercially; if the Etruscans, or at least their nobility, came from Lydia (according to a classical tradition going back to Herodotus which modern scholarship is inclined to accept), the Lydians contributed materially to the civilization of ancient Italy. The Lydians were great merchants and expert craftsmen; they probably invented coinage. They were fond of horsemanship in the early period, and later contributed to the development of music and the dance; according to Greek tradition, Aesop was a Lydian. Little is known about the religion of the Lydians: the gods **Santas** (*Sandon*) and **Baki** (*Bacchus, Dionysos*) were named in their inscriptions.

670-652. **Gyges,** founder of the dynasty of the Mermnadae, in alliance with Ashurbanipal of Assyria, defeated the Cimmerians and extended the borders of the kingdom. But after sending Carian and Ionian mercenaries to the help of Psamtik, who drove the Assyrians out of Egypt, Gyges fell in battle against the Cimmerians.

652-547. **Dynasty of the Mermnadae:** Ardys, Sadyattes, Alyattes, Croesus. After overcoming the Cimmerian menace, Ardys and his successors carried out the conquest of the Greek cities on the coast (begun by Gyges), except Miletus, and of the interior of Asia Minor as far as the Halys, with the exception of Lycia. Lydia reached the zenith of her power under Croesus, who attacked the Persian Empire, but was defeated and taken prisoner by Cyrus in 547.

547-333. Asia Minor under Persian rule.

d. HELLENISTIC MONARCHIES

333-323. **Antigonus Cyclops** was appointed governor of Greater Phrygia by Alexander the Great.

323-25. After the death of Alexander, Antigonus, who assumed the title of king in 306, extended his dominions to cover most of Asia Minor. He died at the **battle of Ipsus** in 301. The coastal regions of Asia Minor were soon divided between the Ptolemies and Seleucids (p. 77).

The following kingdoms arose in Asia Minor during this period: **Pergamum:** Philetarus (d. c. 263), a steward of Lysimachus, made Pergamum an independent principality (283); Eumenes I (263–241) withstood Antiochus II; Attalus I (241–197) defeated the Galatians and assumed the title of king; Eumenes II (197–159) extended his kingdom over most of western Asia Minor; Attalus III (138–133) bequeathed his kingdom to Rome. **Bithynia:** an independent principality before Alexander's conquests, it became a kingdom with Ziboetes in 297; Nicomedes I (278–250) and his successors increased the power of the kingdom until Nicomedes III (91–74) bequeathed it to the Romans. **Cappadocia:** Ariarathes I was an independent king in the time of Alexander, but he was crucified in 322 by Perdiccas; after passing successively under the rule of Eumenes, Antigonus, Lysimachus, and Seleucus, it became again a separate kingdom under Ariarathes II (c. 260) and his successors until Tiberius reduced it to the status of a province in 17 A.D. **Pontus** (including Paphlagonia): Mithridates I after the battle of Ipsus (301) founded a dynasty that came to its end with the great Mithridates VI Eupator (120–64), the implacable enemy of the Romans. **Galatia:** 20,000 Celts from among those that had invaded Greece with Brennus (279) crossed over to Asia Minor (278–277) at the invitation of Nicomedes I of Bithynia; in 232, after they had ravaged western Asia Minor for 46 years, Attalus I of Pergamum confined them to the territory called from their name (*Galli*, Gauls) Galatia: the tribal organization was retained until 63, when Pompey made Deiotarus king; after the death of its third king (25 B.C.), Galatia became a Roman province.

8. ARMENIA

a. THE KINGDOM OF VAN (URARTU)

GEOGRAPHY. The borders of Urartu (Ararat) cannot be fixed exactly: in a general way the kingdom was located between the Caucasus and Lake Van.

POPULATION. The basic population seems to have been Hurrian; the Hurrian and Vannic languages seem to be related.

CIVILIZATION AND RELIGION. The Vannic inscriptions, written in Assyrian cuneiform characters but still very obscure, were chiefly annals recording wars and building operations, particularly hydraulic works (the irrigation canal of Menuas is still in use). The Vannic people showed special aptitude in industrial arts, particularly metallurgy. At the head of the pantheon, which included numerous deities, stood a triad: **Haldi,** the national god, **Tesheba** (the Hurrian storm-god Teshub), and **Ardini** (a god or goddess of the sun). The temple of Haldi and his consort Bagbartu at Musasir, pictured on a bas-relief of Sargon II of Assyria at Khorsabad, is surprisingly similar to the Greek temples in the Doric style.

c. 1270–850. The Assyrian name for the **Kingdom of Van** (*Uruatri,* later *Urartu*) occurs for the first time in the inscriptions of Shalmaneser I (c. 1270). The lands of the Nairi (east and north of Lake Van) were divided into numerous Hurrian principalities and subject to repeated attacks by the Assyrian kings, particularly by Tukulti-Ninurta I (c. 1250), Tiglath-pileser I (c. 1100), Ashurbelkala (c. 1070), Adad-nirari II (c. 900), Tukulti-Ninurta II (c. 890), and Ashur-nasir-pal II (883–859).

c. 860–843. **Arame,** first known King of Urartu, was defeated by Shalmaneser III (859–824), who captured his capital Arzashkun.

c. 832–820. **Sardur I,** son of Lutipri, was probably a usurper; he chose Tushpa (Assyrian *Turushpa,* the present Van) as his capital and fortified it. He founded the principal dynasty.

c. 820–800. **Ispuini** conquered Musasir, appointing his son Sardur II viceroy there, and was attacked by Shamshi-Adad V of Assyria.

c. 800–785. **Menua,** who was at first co-regent with his father Ispuini, enlarged the kingdom considerably, leaving inscriptions over a vast area.

c. 785–760. **Argishtish I** annexed the territory along the Araxes and around the Lake of Erivan. Shalmaneser IV of Assyria had no success in his campaigns against Urartu.

c. 760–733. **Sardur III** preserved the integrity of the kingdom.

c. 733–612. The last kings of Urartu, Rusas I (c. 733–714) (probably the founder of a new dynasty), Argishtish II (c. 714–685), Rusas II (c. 685–650), Sardur IV (c. 650–625), and Rusas III (c. 625–612), ruled over a much restricted territory. The Cimmerian invasion and the raid of Sargon II of Assyria (714) weakened the kingdom, which met its doom after the Scythian invasion, when the Medes conquered the country (612). The Vannic nation ceased to exist.

b. ARMENIA

The Armenians are mentioned for the first time by Darius (519). They were probably a Phrygian tribe and they gradually occupied the territory of Urartu after 612. They adopted the religion of the Persians.

612–549. Armenia under the Kings of Media.

549–331. Under the Persian kings, Armenia was a satrapy administered by a member of the royal family.

331–317. Under Alexander and his immediate successors, Armenia continued to be ruled by Persian satraps.

317–211. **Ardvates** (317–284), one of these Persian satraps, made the country independent of the Seleucids and founded a dynasty that ruled until 211.

211–190. **Antiochus III,** after removing Xerxes, the Armenian king, by treachery, divided the country into two satrapies, giving the western one (*Armenia Minor*) to Zadriades and the eastern one (*Armenia Major*) to Artaxias.

190–94. After Antiochus was defeated at Magnesia (190), Zadriades and Artaxias made themselves independent rulers, founding two separate dynasties.

94–56. **Tigranes,** a descendant of Artaxias, deposed Artanes, the last king of Armenia Minor, and united the two countries under his rule. From 83 to 69 he was the most powerful king in Asia, ruling over northern Mesopotamia, Syria, and parts of Asia Minor. Defeated by Lucullus in 69, he was stripped of his conquests, but was allowed by Pompey to rule over Armenia as a vassal of Rome.

9. IRAN

GEOGRAPHY. The Iranian plateau extends from the mountains east of the Tigris to the Indus Valley, and from the Persian Gulf and the Indian Ocean to the Caspian Sea and the Jaxartes River. Media (capitals: Ecbatana and Rhagae), Elam (capital: Susa), and Persia (capital: Persepolis) in the west played a much more important historical rôle than Sogdiana, Bactria, Aria, Drangiana, and Arachosia in the east. In the north-central region, the Parthians became Rome's rivals in the Near East.

POPULATION. In the 4th and possibly the 5th millennium B.C., a population of unknown race living at Susa used copper and made pottery decorated with realistic and conventionalized animals. The mountaineers of the Zagros range (Gutium, Lullubu) and the Elamites predominated in the 3d millennium. The Kassites, who ruled Babylonia from 1750 to 1180, were quite distinct from the Elamites. The Aryans, the Indo-European ancestors of the Indo-Iranians, invaded Iran from the northeast (probably about 2000) and became its basic population.

RELIGION. The religion of the early Iranians was similar to that of Vedic Indians: the worship of **Mithra** and **Varuna**, of the Asuras (Iranian *Ahura*), and of the Devas (degraded to demons by Zarathustra), the myths about the first man Yama (Iranian *Yima*) and about the killing of the dragon, and the conception of *rita* (Iranian *asha* or *urta*) or the inflexible order of the world, and the preparation, offering, and divinization of the sacred drink *soma* (Iranian *haoma*) are common to the Aryans of India and Iran and must date back to the time preceding their separation. **Zoroastrianism** was a reform of this ancient Aryan religion and preserved some of its elements even though it took issue with its naturalistic polytheism. **Zarathustra** (*Zoroaster:* "rich in camels.") may have been born in Media about 660 B.C., but seems to have been active in Bactria, where according to tradition he converted King Vishtasp (*Hystaspes*). His teaching is preserved in the *Gathas*, the oldest hymns in the **Avesta.** The *Avesta* is divided into five parts: the *Yasna* (liturgical hymns including the *Gathas*), the *Vispered* (another liturgical book), the *Vendidad* (a code of ritual and ethical laws), the *Yasht* (mythological hymns in praise of the gods), and the *Khorda Avesta* (a prayer book for private devotions). The great doctrines of the finished Zoroastrian system, monotheism, dualism, individual and universal salvation, are present in germ in the *Gathas*. In the cosmic battle between good and evil each person should contribute to his own salvation and to that of the world by obeying the will of the good god **Ahura Mazda** (*Ormuzd:* "Lord Wisdom"). In the later parts of the *Avesta* the god of evil or supreme devil is called *Angro-mainyu* or **Ahriman** (the evil spirit). After death the pious cross the Cinvat bridge to their reward, whereas the wicked fall from it and suffer in the *House of Lies.*

a. ELAMITES

c. 3000-2300. Sumerians and Akkadians frequently defeated and subjected the Elamites, whose civilization was fundamentally Sumerian. **Dynasty of Awan** (c. 2600-2300).

c. 2280. Kudur-nahunte of Elam plundered the temples of Akkad.

c. 2070-1950. Kudur-mabug of Elam placed his son Warad-Sin on the throne of Larsa. The latter's brother and successor, Rim-Sin, was deposed by Hammurabi.

c. 1176. Shutruk-nahunte raided Babylonia taking to Susa the stela of Hammurabi and other monuments.

c. 1130. Nebuchadrezzar I of Babylon defeated the Elamites.

721-640. Merodach-baladan of Babylon and Humbanigash of Elam joined forces against Sargon of Assyria, who was defeated at Der by the Elamites (721). Shutruk-nahunte II allowed Sargon to depose Merodach-baladan (709). Hallushu (699-693) carried into captivity Sennacherib's son, who was ruling Babylonia (694). Umman-menanu (693-689) (who succeeded Kudur-nahunte) fought at Halule against Sennacherib (691). Umman-haldash I (689-681). Umman-haldash II (681-674) raided Sippar during Essarhaddon's Egyptian campaign. Urtaku (674-664) ruled peacefully. Teumman (664-655) was defeated by Ashurbanipal and his kingdom was occupied by the Assyrians. Ummanigash (655-651) sent his forces to the help of Shamash-shum-ukin, King of Babylon, who had rebelled against his brother Ashurbanipal. Ummanigash was assassinated by his cousin Tammaritu. Tammaritu (651-649) was deposed by Indabigash and sought refuge in Nineveh. Umman-haldash III (648-

646) was defeated by Ashurbanipal, who conquered Susa, and was deposed by Tammaritu II. Tammaritu II was taken prisoner by the Assyrians (646). Umman-haldash III (646–640) returned to the throne, but was taken prisoner by Ashurbanipal, who completely devastated the land of Elam and destroyed Susa. The elimination of the Kingdom of Elam facilitated the task of Cyrus, who a century later founded the Persian Empire, with Susa as one of its capitals.

b. MEDES

835–705. **Media,** divided into small principalities, was attacked successively by Assyrian kings, from Shalmaneser III (in whose inscriptions the Medes are mentioned for the first time) to Sargon II.

705–625. Media under **Assyrian rule.** The two kings Dejoces (708–655) and Phraortes (655–633) mentioned by Herodotus were probably local chieftains.

625–593. **Cyaxares** was the founder of the Median Empire and of its dynasty. In alliance with Nabopolassar of Babylon (a daughter of Cyaxares was given in marriage to Nebuchadrezzar), Cyaxares destroyed Nineveh (612) and conquered the Assyrian territory east of the Tigris, as also Urartu (Armenia) and eastern Iran.

593–550. **Astyages** was deposed by Cyrus and Media became part of the Persian Empire (550).

c. PERSIANS

c. 600–550. Achaemenian kings of Anzan (in Elam): Teispes, Cyrus (I), Cambyses, Cyrus (II) the Great.

550–530. **Cyrus the Great** deposed his sovereign Astyages of Media (550), conquered Lydia (546) and Babylonia (538), and founded the Persian Empire, which extended from the Indus to the Mediterranean, from the Caucasus to the Indian Ocean.

530–521. **Cambyses,** son of Cyrus, conquered Egypt (525).

521–485. **Darius I,** son of Hystaspes, after pacifying the empire torn by revolts, notably that of Gaumata or Smerdis, and extending its borders beyond the Indus (521–519), divided it into 20 satrapies. His royal residences were Susa, Persepolis, Ecbatana (Hamadan), and Babylon. Darius was a Zoroastrian. Good roads, with stations for royal messengers, made possible regular communications within the empire. A canal was dug from the Nile to the Red Sea. A general revolt of the Ionian Greeks in Asia ended with the fall of Miletus (500–494), but the war against the European Greeks was unsuccessful (**battle of Marathon, 490**).

485–465. After **Xerxes I** (*Ahasuerus*) was defeated by the Greeks on the sea at Salamis (480), and on land at Plataea and Mycale (479), Persia abandoned her plans for conquering Greece.

465–424. Athens took the offensive against **Artaxerxes I Longimanus,** by sending troops to aid a revolt in Egypt (456–454) and by attacking Cyprus (450), but finally signed a peace treaty (446). The Persian Empire began to decline.

424–404. **Xerxes II** was assassinated by his brother Sogdianus (424), who in turn fell at the hands of his brother Ochus or Darius II Nothus (424–404).

404–358. **Artaxerxes II Mnemon** defeated his rebellious brother Cyrus, the satrap of Anatolia, near Babylon at Cunaxa (401); Cyrus lost his life in the battle and his "ten thousand" Greek mercenaries, after great hardships, reached the Black Sea (Xenophon's *Anabasis*) in March of the year 400. Another insurrection broke out in Asia Minor under the leadership of Datames, the governor of Cappadocia, and spread to the western satrapies (366–360). Egypt became more or less independent after 404.

358–338. **Artaxerxes III Ochus** succeeded, through energetic measures, in asserting the royal authority over the satraps. He was followed by **Arses** (338–336).

336–330. **Darius III Codomannus** was killed after Alexander the Great, through the victories at Granicus (334), Issus (333), and Gaugamela, near Arbela (331), conquered the Persian Empire.

10. INDIA

An early urban civilization in the Indus Valley produced the polished stone, metals, incised seals, and pictographs excavated since 1920 at Harappa and Mohenjo Daro. Not yet known is its relationship to Mesopotamian culture of c. 3000 B.C., and to the much later historic civilization of India. Indian history begins with invasion from the Iranian plateau by **Aryans** of uncertain antecedents, who gradually conquered or pushed back from the rich plains of northern India the earlier black Dravidian and Austro-Asiatic Munda populations. The conquest is variously placed at 2000–1200 B.C.

c. 1200–c. 800 B.C. The Indian Aryans worshiped nature-gods similar to those of Greece and Rome but less personified. The chief were **Indra,** god of the air and of the storm, with **Agni,** the sacrificial fire, and **Soma,** the intoxicant used for libations. Interesting, among many others, was **Varuna,** guardian of cosmic regularity, including individual human acts. The oldest sacrificial hymns, composed in northern India west of the Ganges (perhaps c. 1200–1000), are contained in the *Rigveda*, which dates from c. 1000 B.C., possibly two centuries prior to the related Gathas in the *Avesta* of Iran, and to the *Samaveda*, antiphonal selections from the *Rig;* to the *Yajurveda*, hymns and sacrificial prose; and to the *Atharvaveda*, a repertory of relatively late magical formulae. The *Rigveda* reveals an Indo-European hieratic literary language remarkable for clarity of structure and wealth of inflection which was, however, probably not written until the 5th century. It depicts a wholesome patriarchal society, engaged in cattle-raising and agriculture, characterized by usual monogamy, adult marriage, and normal widowhood. The Aryan tribes were frequently at war among themselves and with surrounding indigenous tribes. The attitude toward life was vigorous and objective, with none of the pessimism and subjective traits characteristic of later India.

c. 800–c. 550 B.C. A transition period during which the Aryans expanded eastward through Magadha (modern Bihar) is known chiefly from the *Brahmanas*, commentaries upon the *Vedas* (c. 800–600), and the earlier *Upanishads* or confidential teachings (c. 600–300). The Vedic division of Aryan society into three honorable classes: priests (*brahman*), noble warriors (*kshatriya*), and commonalty (*vaisya*), including both farmers and artisans, began gradually to crystallize into a **caste system,** augmented by a fourth group, the slaves (*sudra*), who were the first to be segregated because of their black color. Progressive evolution of caste may be traced to desire of priest and noble to perpetuate supremacy, to diversification of specialized occupation, and to indigenous rules of endogamy absorbed through the sudras, many of whom improved their servile status. Continual elaboration by the priesthood of an already exaggerated ritual had become devoid of religious significance. The doctrine of continuous rebirth (*samsara*), conditioned by the inescapable results of former acts (*karma*), which may be derived from indigenous animism, was first expressed in the early *Upanishads* (c. 600–550). The *Upanishads*, too, teach that the soul may escape from the suffering inherent in individual existence only by the realization of its identity with an impersonal cosmic soul. Union with the latter is possible through knowledge, but not through Brahman ritual.

c. 550–321. The Aryan area was divided among many petty states. Sixteen are enumerated in an early list. Kosala (King Prasenajit, contemporary of the Buddha) was the largest, extending from Nepal to the Ganges, including modern Oudh. Magadha was its small neighbor on the east, south of the Ganges. The King of Avanti ruled at Ujjain. The capital of the Vamsas (King Udena) was at Kosambi (on the Jumna below Agra). Ten tribal republics are named in the oldest Pali records.

Dissent from Brahmanism, to abolish authority of its scriptures and rites, was undertaken by many schools, among them the **Jains,** followers of the Jina ("Victorious"), Vardhamana Mahavira (?540–468?), who elaborated the doctrines of an earlier prophet **Parsva,** and in Magadha under Kings Bimbisara (?543–491?) and his parricide son Ajatasatru (?491–459?). Parsva had enjoined four vows: to injure no life, to be truthful, not to steal, to possess no property. **Mahavira** added chastity and rigid asceticism as means to free man's immortal soul from bondage to the material world. He set the example by personal attainment of omniscience and freedom through twelve years of austerities.

BUDDHISM was founded in the same period and region by **Siddhartha** (?563–483?) of the clan of Gautama and the hill tribe of Sakya, who attained "illumination" (*bodhi*) at Bodh-Gaya after he had convinced himself that Brahman doctrine and asceticism were alike ineffective. He accepted rebirth to the recurrent suffering of life in accordance with fate (*karma*), which depends on individual effort, and extended reward and punishment to heavens and hells. He taught the means of escape to **Nirvana,** a state of peaceful release from rebirth, through a twofold way of life, withdrawal for meditation and personal religious experience, combined with strict morality and self-sacrificial altruism. Shortly after the Buddha's death 500 disciples met at Rajagriha to rehearse together his doctrine (*dharma*) and his code of discipline (*vinaya*) for the monastic community (*sangha*) which he founded. That community served as the instrument for propagation of his religion, which, like Christianity, offers salvation to all who accept simple doctrine and ethics and seek for personal religious experience. A second council at Vaisali a century after the Buddha's death was concerned with the *vinaya*, but may have begun the schism between conservative **Sthaviravadins** (Pali Theravadins) and liberal **Mahasanghikas**. About this time were formed the four *Nikayas*, earliest extant anthologies from more primitive collections (*Pratimoksa*, etc.).

517-509 B.C. Darius I of Achaemenid Persia seized Gandhara from the disunited Aryans and sent his Greek admiral Skylax to explore the Indus. *Kharoshthi* script used in northwestern India (5th cent.) is based on Aramaic of the Persian scribes. It was confined to the northwest, doubtless because *Brahmi*, a script which was probably derived from some Semitic alphabet of c. 800 B.C., and ancestor of later Indian writing, was already current in the Jumna basin. The *Sutras* (c. 6th–2d cent. B.C.), "Threads" through the *Brahmanas*, prescribe rules of conduct of various Vedic schools, regions, and periods, for sacrifice and, incidentally, for life. They describe a society in which plural marriage is permitted, child marriage recommended, while numerous taboos mark the beginning of an elaborate theory of caste defilement. **Panini** (? c. 350–300) gives in his *Sutra* the earliest extant Sanskrit grammar, with a wealth of illustration which is augmented by the *Varttikas* or supplementary rules of Katyayana (c. 180) and the rich *Mahabhashya* (Great Commentary) of Patanjali (c. 150 B.C. or later).

327-325. Alexander the Great invaded the Punjab, crossed the Indus (Feb. 326), was welcomed to the rich and cultured city of Takshasila (Taxila), won a battle on the banks of the Jhelum, and withdrew on demand of his troops, sending Nearchus with a fleet by sea.

c. 321–c. 184. THE MAURYA DYNASTY was founded by **Chandragupta** (c. 321–c. 297), who first united northern India from Herat to the Ganges delta, with his capital at Pataliputra (Patna), and who defended it against Seleucus Nicator (c. 305). Megasthenes, a Seleucid envoy, wrote a detailed account of India, now lost. The emperor ruled with aid of a privy council and an elaborate official hierarchy, paid army, and secret service. Administration of public works embraced highways and irrigation.

A Jain high-priest **Bhadrabahu** led a portion of his community south into the Carnatic to escape a 12-year famine in Bengal. On their return (c. 300) the still resident monks in church council at Pataliputra undertook to collect the Jain scriptures, but were unable to record some of the older *purvas*. The canon of the Svetambara sect, the *Siddhanta*, written in its present form at the council of Valabhi (5th or early 6th cent. A.D.), is consequently incomplete. The returning monks maintained a stricter rule, avoided the council, and, as the **Digambara sect,** have steadily maintained that the true canon is lost. The Jain community had then already begun a westward migration to Ujjain and Mathura.

c. 274–c. 236. ASOKA'S EMPIRE, extended by conquest of Kalinga (Orissa with the Circars, c. 262), embraced two-thirds of the peninsula. As a devout convert he ruled at home and abroad in accordance with Buddhist law. Besides many pious foundations, he engraved on rocks and pillars throughout his empire in true Achaemenid style edicts in vernacular Prakrit exhorting respect for animal life, reverence, and truth, and appointed censors to enforce these injunctions. He sent Buddhist missions to Syria, Egypt, Cyrene, Macedonia, and Epirus, and with much greater success to Burma and Ceylon (c. 251–246; Aryan conquest of Ceylon, traditional date 483 B.C.). The Punjab and Gandhara became a stronghold of the liberal Mahasanghikas, who developed a canonical tradition enriched by legends to bring the life of the Buddha into that region. The canon was then or in the 2d century in Kausambhi, Sañchi, and Malwa expanded and fixed in Pali to form the *Tripitaka* ("Three Baskets"): *sutra* (doctrine), *vinaya* (monastic code), and *abhidharma* (philosophical discussion). The Pali tradition, which was carried to Ceylon and there preserved intact, says a third church council was held at Pataliputra under Asoka, but since his inscriptions ignore it, it probably was restricted to the conservative Theravadin of Magadha and vicinity.

Asoka's pillar at Sarnath near Benares is in form and finish Persian. It is surmounted by four lions facing outward which, with a frieze of animals in low relief, may well have been executed by a Hellenistic sculptor, perhaps from Bactria.

The west remained the chief stronghold of **Brahman doctrine** which now underwent a counter-reformation. Efforts by the priesthood to syncretize popular native gods with the Vedic pantheon, and so retain for themselves religious leadership, led to emergence of cults which constitute a new religion. Rudra, a minor Vedic divinity, was exalted as **Siva**, personification of cosmic forces of destruction and reproduction implicit in all change. **Vishnu,** god of the sacrifice, was recognized as incarnate in **Krishna,** a hero presented by popular legend at Mathura as romantic lover of 1000 herd-girls, and on the west coast as a somber warrior. A second avatar of Vishnu was **Rama,** symbol of conjugal devotion. Siva and Vishnu were linked as one Hari-Hara and were equated with a newly personified god Brahma as elements of a *Trimurti* or trinity.

The *Mahabharata*, an epic poem composed by several generations of bards, seems to have taken form about the 2d century B.C., although probably revised early in our era. The original 9000 verses were swelled to 100,000 by later accretions, largely from the *Puranas* (disordered genealogies of kings compounded with legends, put in present form 4th cent. A.D. and later). It recounts a feud between the wily and aristocratic Kurus and the fierce Pandus, a family who are unknown in early literature. Krishna takes prominent part in the struggle in unscrupulous aid of Arjuna, the Pandu chief. Noteworthy within the epic is the *Bhagavadgita* ("Song of the Lord"), which first urges personal love and devotion (*bhakti*) to Krishna. The *Ramayana*, although traditionally ascribed to Valmiki (?6th cent. B.C.), is in its present form later than the *Mahabharata*. It recounts the trials of Rama in rescuing with an army of apes his wife Sita from a fiend. Both epics are composed in a popular form of Sanskrit.

206. **Antiochus III** of Syria occupied Gandhara, but shortly lost it to the Greek (Yavana) King Demetrius of Bactria, who (c. 185) seized the Punjab also. Eastward expansion of the Yavanas was halted (after c. 162) by civil war between the houses of Euthydemus, represented especially by the warrior-philosopher Menander, and Eucratides.

c. 184–c. 72. **THE SUNGA DYNASTY** was founded in the Ganges Valley and in Malwa by **Pushyamitra,** who overthrew the Maurya, repulsed the Yavanas under Menander, and by a Brahman reaction may have stimulated Buddhist emigration to Bharhut, Sañchi, and Mathura. The dynasty in its later years was overshadowed if not actually displaced by its line of Brahman advisers, the Kanvas.

A brilliant flowering of **Buddhist sculpture** is chiefly represented by railings and gates about stupas at Bharhut, Bodh-gaya, and Sañchi. The railing at Bharhut (c. 150 B.C.) is almost purely Indian in design and relatively primitive in execution. A Garuda pillar at Besnagar proves by inscription of a Greek envoy from Taxila contact of central India with the northwest, which is evidenced also by technical progress and by the west Asiatic motifs of the rails at Bodh-gaya and the opulent gates at Sañchi (1st cent. B.C.). Narrative is surrounded with a festive naturalism which is wholly Indian. Presence of the Buddha in these sculptures is suggested solely by symbols (the elephant of his conception, the lotus of birth, the stupa of consecration, the tree of deliverance, or the wheel of the law). At the same time (c. 100 B.C.–50 A.D.) flourished in Gandhara a school of sculpture which created a Buddha image by adding to the Greek Apollo some of the 32 marks of a Buddha specified in Indian texts. Only a few decadent monuments (mostly 1st cent. A.D.) bear dates (318, 356, 384 with coin of Kadphises, 399) by reference to a Mauryan era (? of 322 B.C.) or more probably the Seleucid era of 312 B.C. Stylistic influence of the art of Gandhara was exerted chiefly in Afghanistan (frescoes of Bamiyan and Dukhtar-i-Nushirwan), where it was fused with Sassanian influences; eastern Turkestan; China of the North Wei dynasty; and Japan. But its iconographic formulae were accepted by the entire Buddhist world. Meanwhile, in western India (near Bombay) were cut in rocky cliffs Buddhist *chaityas* or temple halls, of which the earliest (c. 125–100 B.C.) are at Bhaja, Kondane, Pitalkhora, and Ajanta (cave 10); the largest, finest, and latest (1st cent. A.D.) at Karli. Jain caves in the Udayagiri hills of Orissa are of similar date.

Scythian **Sakas** who, dislodged by the Yüeh-chih from the Jaxartes, had overwhelmed the Greeks in Bactria (c. 135 B.C.), only to be expelled thence also by the Yüeh-chih (shortly after 128), invaded the Punjab from Baluchistan and Sind (Greek Indo-Scythia). (*Cont. p.* 128.)

11. CHINA

Present information indicates that the Chinese parent people, their language, and their civilization are alike native to North China. It seems probable that, at a primitive stage, they diverged from the Miao-tzu, who now find refuge in the southern mountains, the various T'ai peoples (Dioi, Laotians, Siamese) of Kwangsi and Indo-China, and the Tibeto-Burman peoples (Lolo, Mosso, Shan, and Tibetans) of southwestern China. **Peking Man,** who had some Chinese characteristics, lived in the Tertiary Pleistocene epoch. Palaeolithic culture deposits (without skeletal material as yet) are known. Three independent Neolithic cultures are found, characterized by: (1) crude gray pottery with pointed foot; (2) red and black painted pottery similar to that found near Odessa and at Susa; (3) thin black pottery tentatively attributed to a Pacific civilization. The latter is linked with historic China through use of tripod vessels with hollow legs, and bone divination.

Two literary sources contain genealogies of **the early dynasties,** with chronologies which diverge prior to 841 B.C. Neither earlier chronology has any authority whatever. Nor can historical value be attached to legends which describe a pre-dynastic golden age of fabulous culture-heroes and model rulers. Of the **Hsia Dynasty** we have only the calendar, honorific use of the name, and the putative genealogy of seventeen kings. It was followed by the **Shang** or **Yin Dynasty** of thirty kings, who practiced fraternal succession and who were masters of the Yellow River plain from the mountains of Shansi and the Mongolian plateau to the Shantung massif. Probably the last twelve ruled at An-yang from about the 12th century. The names of twenty-eight kings are found in oracular inscriptions from this site. Advanced pictographic and ideographic script; conventional decoration and perfect casting of bronze vessels; reliance upon ancestral guidance through divination.

c. 1000-950 B.C. THE WESTERN CHOU DYNASTY established its capital at Hao in the Wei Valley. It exercised actual control over its feudatories only until the murder of King Yu in 771. The king was responsible for sacrifices to his ancestors and to gods of the soil, and for the agricultural calendar, as well as for administration. Tenure of land and office was restricted to a pedigreed aristocracy, whose clan names suggest a possible early matriarchate. The peasantry lived a communal life in the summer fields and winter villages, tilled common land for their prince, and practiced exogamic group betrothals and marriages. The Chinese communities were still surrounded and interspersed with "barbarian," i.e. less cultured, tribes.

770-256. THE EASTERN CHOU DYNASTY reigned powerless at Loyang with diminishing moral authority over the frequently warring princes of surrounding (nominally) feudal states.

722-481. "Annals" period of loose confederation. The chief states were Ch'i and Lu, which divided modern Shantung; Sung, west of Lu; Yen, on the northeast; Chin, in modern Shansi; Ch'in, in the former Chou lands to the west; and Ch'u, in the middle Long River Valley.

458-424. Partition of Chin among three vassal houses: Han, Chao, and Wei.

412. Institution of **ever-normal granary** by Marquis Wen of Wei.

403-221. Epoch of the Warring States, opened by royal recognition of the partition of Chin.

391. Change of dynasty in Ch'i, which, with Chin, had been a chief bulwark of the "middle kingdoms" against the largely non-Chinese states of Ch'u and Ch'in.

334. Ch'u expanded eastward, annexing the coastal state of Yüeh.

333. "Vertical" (i.e. north and south) **alliance of six states,** arranged by Su Ch'in, failed to restrain Ch'in, which conquered Shu (in modern Szechuan) in 316.

307. Prince Wu-ling of Chao gained military advantage for his state by adoption of Tatar dress (Iranian trousers, belt, and boots, which now gradually displaced the loose Chinese costume) and enlistment of cavalry archers, but the continual wars of the eastern states weakened them all, paving the way for

230-221. CONQUEST BY CH'IN OF ALL ITS RIVALS. Golden age of philosophy in China, as in Greece. Four major **schools of ethics,** which absorbed the practical Chinese to the exclusion of abstract speculation: (1) Coherent teaching embodied in *The Canon of the Way and of Virtue* (5th cent. or later?), attributed to **Lao-tzu,** of whom nothing is known: Man is part of an harmonious universe governed by transcendent law, and finds his best ethical guide in his own nature. **Yang**

Chu, an individualist, sought self-expression in harmless hedonism. **Chuang Chou** (fl. 339–329), the most brilliantly imaginative and subtle of all literary stylists, through parables taught *laissez faire*, mysticism, and relativity of truth. (2) **Mo Ti** (5th–4th cent.?) taught universal love, pacifism, economy, and the duty of the wise to set up standards. New dialectic method borrowed by all later writers. From him stem the schools of pacifists and sophists. (3) **K'ung Ch'iu** or **Confucius** (551–479 or later?) taught that clear thinking and self-discipline lead the superior man to correct action in all his relationships. Through moral influence and education he should lead the common herd with kindliness and justice; paternalism; golden rule. Having failed as minister of justice in Lu (500–496) to secure co-operation of his prince, he edited the *Annals* of that state (722–481) to illustrate his monarchical doctrine of political morality. (A much richer chronicle of the feudal states, composed c. 300, is now appended to these *Annals* as part of the *Tso Commentary*.) His precepts were gathered a century later. **Meng K'o** or **Mencius** (fl 324–314) urged the now independent princes to win the world, i.e. North China, by exemplary conduct, declaring popular welfare to be the objective and condition of royal authority. A humanitarian, he elaborated the moral code to assure proper development of man's beneficent nature. **Hsün K'uang** or **Hsün-tzu** (c. 300–235) taught that man requires education and formation of correct habit to realize his capacity to order nature. He suggested forced conformity to standards. He synthesized earlier doctrines, and, although a muddy writer, so impressed his students that even mutually opposed thinkers for a century claimed succession from him. (4) **Shang Yang,** minister of Ch'in, 359–338, organized strong centralized government, created an official hierarchy, and encouraged agriculture in that state under a severe legal code. His reforms paved the way for the triumph of Ch'in. **Han-Fei-tzu** (d. 233) and **Li Ssu** (d. 208), disciples of Hsün-tzu, developed further the legalist doctrine of compulsion to justify Ch'in's use of military force to unify the warring states.

Greek influence, probably traceable to Alexander's invasion of Sogdiana (c. 327), is seen in correct statement of the intervals of the Pythagorean musical scale by **Lü Pu-wei,** prime minister of Ch'in (c. 250), and in diagrammatic illustration of the Pythagorean theorem.

(*Cont. p.* 132.)

B. GREECE

1. THE EARLY PERIOD, TO C. 500 B.C.

a. GEOGRAPHICAL FACTORS

Greece proper forms a southward extension of the Balkan Mountains. It lies between two seas, the Aegean, which separates it on the east from Asia Minor, and the Adriatic and Ionian Seas, which separate it on the west from Italy and Sicily. Greece itself is almost split in two by the Gulf of Corinth, which runs in from the west, and the Saronic Gulf on the east. These are separated by the narrow Isthmus of Corinth, which connects the southern part, the Peloponnese, with the northern. Thus Corinth, which portaged the sea-trade from gulf to gulf and which controlled land communications between south and north, played an important rôle in Greek history from an early date.

The Greeks were forced to become sailors by the mountainous character of their country, a factor which also conditioned the eventual rise of hundreds of small, autonomous, self-centered states, scattered throughout most Greek lands. The Greek name for such a state was πόλις (*polis*), usually translated *city-state*, but including an area of countryside in addition to the city proper. This area was usually small; Sparta (c. 3000 square miles) and Athens (c. 1000 square miles) were exceptionally large *poleis*. Since the best harbors lie on the east coast of Greece and since the Aegean is full of islands, which made primitive navigation easy, the earliest expansion of the Greeks was to the Asia Minor coast, similar in aspect but more fertile than Greece proper. Later they penetrated into the Euxine (*hospitable*) Sea, so-called by an apotropaic euphemism because of its inhospitable character. The closeness of southern Italy to the island of Corcyra also drew them west to the Gulf of Tarentum and Sicily, where again they found a familiar but more smiling landscape.

Some parts of Greece, like Attica and Corinth, were early in the historical period deforested. The resultant soil erosion and rapid off-flow of water made agriculture difficult and unremunerative. The inhabitants, therefore, unable themselves to grow enough grain, imported it from Euboea, Thessaly, the Euxine, or Sicily. They in turn cultivated the olive and vine, to export oil and wine, or developed manufactures, particularly that of pottery. Thus not only geography but economic need encouraged them to become seafarers and individualists.

b. THE AEGEAN CIVILIZATION

The pre-Hellenic inhabitants of Crete early developed an elaborate Bronze Age civilization which spread gradually to the Aegean islands and the surrounding coasts. Its effects were felt throughout the eastern Mediterranean Basin, and it, in turn, was considerably influenced from Egypt. But it made little direct contribution to later Greek civilization, save perhaps in religion and myth (Hera, Athena, Minos, the Idaean Zeus).

c. 4000 B.C. **The Bronze Age** began in Crete with an increased skill in crafts, especially pottery.

c. 2300. A hieroglyphic writing came into use.

c. 2000. The island was unified under one or two dynasties, notably those at Cnossus and Phaestus. There was at **Cnossus** an elaborate palace, with storehouses for taxes in kind and room for a large administrative staff. The palace seems also to have been the religious center, with a priest-king. The inhabitants lived in cities built closely round the palaces. While the basis of economy was agriculture (cereals, olive, vine), handicrafts and trade (especially with Egypt) flourished.

c. 1600. The palaces at Cnossus and Phaestus were destroyed and rebuilt, perhaps in consequence of a revolution. There followed the height of Cretan prosperity. A **linear script** replaced the hieroglyphic. The Cretan civilization spread to Greece proper, notably to Mycenae, Tiryns, Argos, Sparta, Orchomenus, and, in a lesser degree, to Athens. The princes of this Mycenaean civilization were native Greek tribal chiefs who adopted the higher Cretan culture. They built strongly fortified cities as places of refuge for their subjects. Their supreme power was limited by the traditional custom of consulting their nobles and of obtaining the approval of a popular assembly in important matters. This civilization is portrayed in the *Iliad* and the *Odyssey*.

c. 1400. The palaces of Cnossus and Phaestus were destroyed a second time, by sea-raiders who were either the revolting lords of Mycenae or the Achaeans, who had occupied the mainland cities. Cretan civilization rapidly declined and during the succeeding two centuries its Mycenaean derivative, deprived of its source and subject to increasing pressure from northern barbarians, followed suit. By 1250, if not before, the Achaeans occupied Crete, and by 1100 the Dorians overran it and introduced the Iron Age.

c. THE INVASIONS

Greece was apparently uninhabited in Palaeolithic times, but the remains of Neolithic peoples occur throughout the Aegean area. Their ethnic character remains unknown, though they presumably did not speak an Indo-European tongue and were related among themselves. In later times such isolated tribes as the Leleges in Greece, the Carians in Asia Minor, or the Eteocretans in Crete probably represented their survivors.

c. 3000-2000. THE GREEKS, speaking a language belonging to the western (*centum*) division of the Indo-European family, began to spread southward from the northwestern corner of the Balkans.

c. 1300. The Arcadians had already settled in the central Peloponnese and the Achaeans, who had migrated from Thessaly to occupy Mycenae, raided throughout the eastern Mediterranean. With the aid of their Thessalian kin (Achilles) they sacked Ilium (Troy), traditionally after a ten years' war (c. 1184). Their migration may have been due to pressure from new invaders, since the Ionians appear to have occupied Attica and the Boeotians central Greece, while a backward group in Epirus were the original Dorians. Farther north, two peoples of the eastern (*satem*) division of the Indo-European family had settled, the Illyrians along the east coast of the Adriatic and the Thracians north of the Aegean.

c. 1100. The Dorian invasion began. One branch, the Phocians, thrust east to the Euripus; another south to the Gulf of Corinth, whence they crossed into the Peloponnese and drove out or subdued and enserfed the previous inhabitants (later known in Lacedaemon as *helots*, in Thessaly as *penestae*). The Dorians finally mastered Megara, the Argolid, and Laconia.

c. 1000. The Greeks, who had learned seamanship from the Cretans, had long been migrating to Asia Minor for a number of reasons: the adventurous spirit, increase of population, and the Dorian pressure. Some reached Cyprus, though they never fully displaced the Phoenicians. The Dorians occupied Crete. On the Asia Minor coast three distinct groups emerged: Aeolians from Thessaly in the north, with a religious center at Gryneium and the cities of Mytilene on Lesbos, Cyme, Magnesia on the Hermus, and Smyrna (which later became Ionian); Ionians from Attica and Euboea in the middle, with a religious center at Mycale and the cities of Phocaea, Colophon, Ephesus, and Miletus and the islands Chios and Samos; and Dorians from the Peloponnese in the south, with a religious center at Cnidus and the cities of Halicarnassus and the islands Cos, Rhodes, and Crete.

d. ARISTOCRACY AND TYRANNY; COLONIZATION AND TRADE

c. 900-600. Monarchies were replaced throughout Greece by **aristocracies,** and the kings vanished or were reduced to a titular office (the *archon basileus* at Athens) save in Sparta, where they retained considerable power, especially in warfare. The nobles became the dominant power in the state through the possession of good iron arms and the acquisition of property at the expense of poorer farmers. It was for such nobles that the *Iliad*, on the Trojan War, and the *Odyssey*, on the wanderings of Odysseus (Ulysses), were composed, probably gradually and orally out of traditional material by a series of bards in Asia Minor, though the final form is possibly due to a single **Homer** (c. 800?). Slightly later came the *Homeric Hymns*, really introductions to epic recitations, and **Hesiod** (c. 700?) of Boeotia, whose *Works and Days*, a farmer's almanac, voiced the distress of the poor and whose *Theogony* canonized Greek mythology. This was the period of the **geometric style** in vase-painting.

c. 800-600. Distress and food shortage, due to monopolization of the land by the nobles, led to **colonization,** encouraged first by the aristocrats to get rid of discontent and then by the tyrants for political and commercial advantages. The traditional dates of the more important colonies in east and west, which were entered almost simultaneously, follow: Miletus colonized Cyzicus (757), and Abydus (756) on the Euxine. But through friendship with Psammetichus I of Egypt, Miletus also founded the important trading post of Naucratis on the Nile (640). Phocaea settled Massalia (Marseilles) in Gaul (600). Rhodes settled Gela (688) and Gela founded Acragas (580), both in Sicily. Thera colonized Cyrene in North Africa (630). Chalcis and Eretria in Euboea sent colonies to the Chalcidice (northern Aegean) and to Sicily, notably Catana and Leontini (728), Rhegium (730); also Cumae (Bay of Naples, 760). Megara controlled the Hellespont with Chalcedon (660) and Byzantium, as well as settling the Sicilian Megara Hyblaea (728). Corinth occupied the strategic Potidaea (northern Aegean, 609), Corcyra (735), and Syracuse in Sicily (735). In southern Italy (Magna Graecia) Achaea settled Sybaris (721) and Croton (710); while Sparta, occupied with the conquest of Messenia, founded only Taras (Tarentum, 705).

Trade had preceded colonization and in turn colonization encouraged **trade,** since not only the settlers but the peoples among whom they settled desired luxury products (oil, wine, and manufactures) from Greece, which they repaid with raw materials. Greater skill in technical processes like metallurgy and pottery allowed the Greeks to compete favorably with the Phoenicians and encouraged the growth of an industrial population, as well as a trading one, in the cities. Slavery increased and coined money was introduced from Lydia into Ionia and thence into Greece, traditionally by King Pheidon of Argos (c. 680). The two prominent standards of currency were the Euboean and the Aeginetan.

c. 650–500. Tyrannies arose in Greece, for a variety of causes. The aristocracies refused political equality to the landless traders and manufacturers, the peasants were oppressed by the rich and encouraged to get into debt and then were reduced to slavery or exile; slaves began to compete with free labor. Ambitious individuals capitalized this discontent to overthrow the constituted governments and establish themselves as tyrants in almost all the Greek cities, with the notable exception of Sparta, whose landlocked situation, agricultural character, and entrenched ruling class enabled it to preserve its aristocratic form. The tyrants were on the whole popular and successful; they kept the people happy with festivals and public works, they diminished the power of the nobles, and they abolished class or racial distinctions. They fostered, especially, the **artistic and intellectual** life. **Lyric poetry**

flourished; **Archilochus** the father of **satire** (c. 700); the individual lyric of the Aeolians, **Alcaeus** and **Sappho** of Lesbos (c. 600); the choral lyric of the Dorians, **Stesichorus** (c. 650) and **Arion** (c. 600). Contact with Lydia led to the replacing of the geometric style in art by the **oriental** (animal) **style. Philosophy** began with the Milesian School: **Thales** (predicted an eclipse in 585), **Anaximenes,** and **Anaximander.** Among the important tyrants were: **Thrasybulus** of Miletus (c. 620); **Polycrates** of Samos (c. 530), noted for his navy, with which he almost dominated the Aegean, his building, and his alliance with Amasis of Egypt; **Cleisthenes** of Sicyon (c. 600); **Theagenes** of Megara (c. 640); **Periander** of Corinth (c. 600), patron of poetry, who recovered control of Corcyra from the oligarchs; and the **Peisistratids** in Athens. The tyrannies generally were overthrown in the second generation, since they had served their purpose, and the tyrants' sons, born to power, tended to become oppressive. Moreover, Sparta consistently opposed them.

e. FORMATION OF THE GREEK STATES

(1) *Asia Minor*

c. 705. The **Kingdom of Phrygia** (traditional kings Midas and Gordius), which had considerably influenced the Asiatic Greeks, was destroyed by the **Cimmerians,** invaders from southern Russia. Its place was taken by the **Kingdom of Lydia,** in which Gyges founded the active Mermnad Dynasty (c. 685). He and his successors raided the Greek cities, but were prevented from conquest by further incursions of the Cimmerians, who sacked Sardis and slew Gyges (c. 652).

585, May 28. Alyattes, third King of Lydia, and **Cyaxares,** King of Media, ended their war by a treaty defining their boundary at the river Halys. Thales is said to have predicted the eclipse which induced them to treat and which, therefore, determines the date. **Croesus** acceded to the Lydian throne (c. 560) and began to reduce the Ionian cities to a tributary condition, save for Miletus. His mild rule, however, did not check their political growth (tyrannies) but stimulated their economic and intellectual life.

546 (539?). CYRUS, who had united his Persian kingdom with the Median by his defeat of Astyages (550), now defeated Croesus, crossed the Halys, sacked Sardis, and captured Croesus himself. His general, Harpagus, subdued the Ionian cities, save Miletus, which

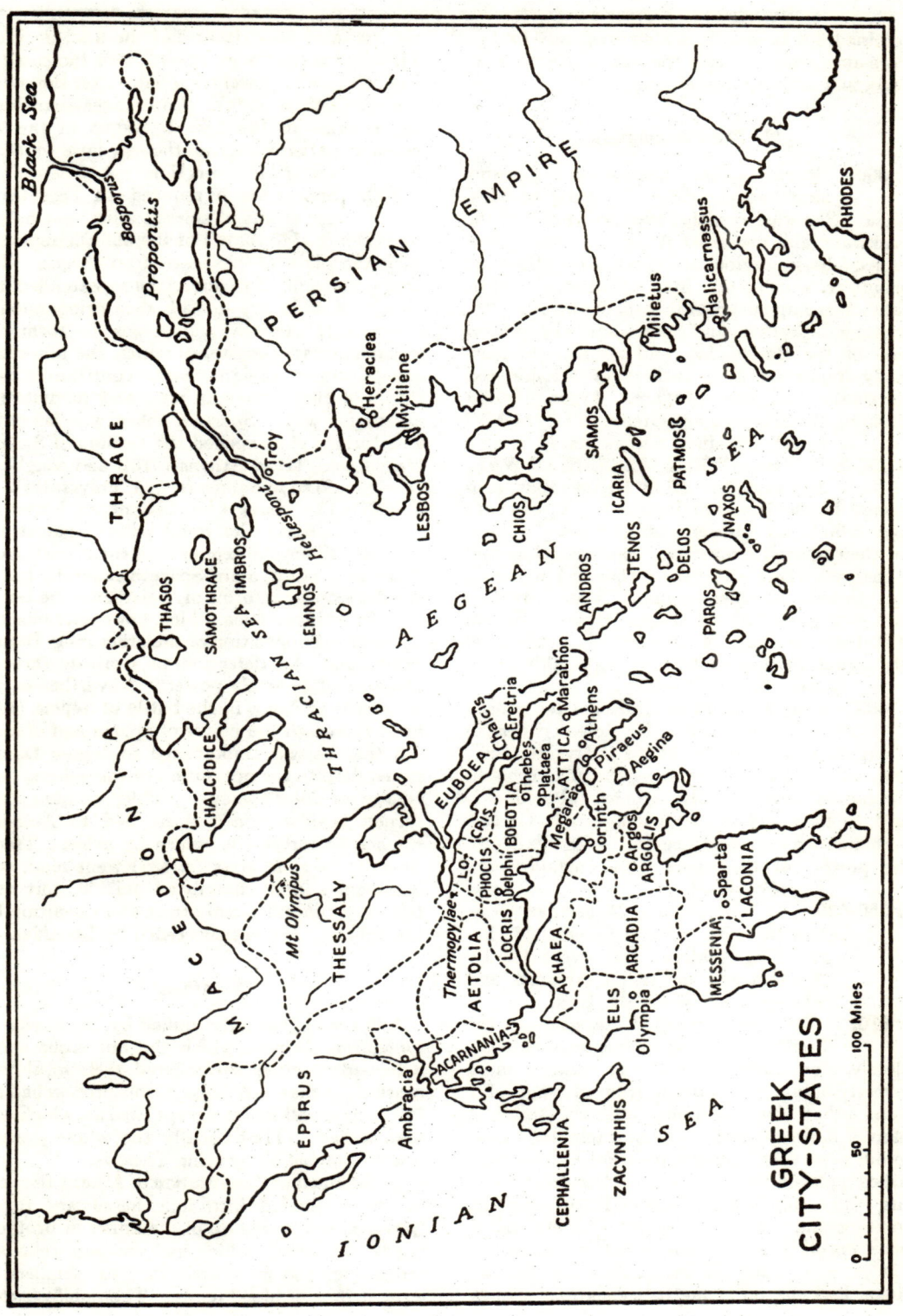

GREEK
CITY-STATES

retained its favorable status, and put in pro-Persian tyrants. With the loss of freedom intellectual activity diminished.

(2) The Peloponnese

c. 800. **Sparta** had become mistress of Laconia and had colonized the coast of Messenia. She warred with **Tegea**, chief city of the backward and disunited Arcadians, who maintained a loose religious union centering about the primitive worship on Mt. Lycaeum. Politically, kingship survived in Arcadia into the 5th century. **Corinth**, under the close oligarchical rule of the Bacchiadae, had become commercially important and, until c. 720, dominated its smaller neighbor **Megara**. **Argos**, though claiming the hegemony of Greece as heir of Mycenae, remained a weak state.

c. 736-716. In the **FIRST MESSENIAN WAR,** Sparta, led by **King Theopompus**, conquered Messenia and divided the rich plain into lots, which the Messenians, as helots, worked for their Spartiate masters. Besides helots and Spartiates, there was a third class of Laconians, the *perioeci* (dwellers-around), who were free but not possessed of citizen rights. Sparta still, however, had an artistic and intellectual life equal to any in Greece, especially in respect to choral poetry.

c. 680. **King Pheidon** made Argos for a brief space powerful. He defeated Sparta allied with Tegea in the **battle of Hysiae** (669), and, in support of revolting Aegina, crushed Epidaurus and her ally Athens. Pheidon is said to have introduced coinage into Greece, perhaps with a mint on Aegina. After his death, the powers of the rulers were curtailed and Argos declined.

c. 650-630. In the **Second Messenian War,** Sparta with difficulty crushed her revolting subjects, who were led by Aristomenes, master of Arcadia, and who took refuge on Mt. Eira.

c. 610. By the so-called *Eunomia*, the Spartans, fearing further revolts, completely reorganized the state to make it more severely military. Youths from the age of 7 were taken for continual military training. Men of military age lived in barracks and ate at common messes (*syssitia, phiditia*). Five local tribes replaced the three Dorian hereditary ones and the army was correspondingly divided, creating the *Dorian phalanx*. In the tribes were enrolled as citizens many non-citizens. The *gerousia*, comprising 28 elders and the two kings, had the initiative in legislation, though

the *apella* of all citizens had the final decision. The chief magistrates, *ephors*, were increased to five, with wider powers especially after the ephorate of **Cheilon** (556). Later ages attributed the reforms to the hero **Lycurgus** in the 9th century, perhaps because the new laws were put under his protection.

c. 560. Sparta finally reduced the Tegeates to the status of subject allies, not helots. She then (c. 546, **battle of the 300 Champions**), took the plain of Thyreatis from Argos. The kings Anaxandridas and Ariston extended the policy of alliances to all the Peloponnesian states save Achaea and Argos to form the **Peloponnesian League,** in which the allies had equal votes on foreign policies, contributed two-thirds of their forces in war, and paid no tax except for war. Sparta's policy was hereafter anti-tyrant; she expelled the tyrants of Sicyon, Naxos, and, later, Athens (510), and sought to do so in Samos (c. 524, Polycrates).

c. 520. The young king **Cleomenes I** tried to reassert the royal power against the ephors. When the expulsion of the tyrants from Athens led not to a pro-Spartan oligarchy but to the democratic reforms of Cleisthenes, he led an expedition into Attica, which, however, failed because of the opposition of the other king, **Damaratus,** and the defection of Corinth through jealousy of Sparta's power. Nevertheless, by his defeat of Argos in the **battle of Sepeia** (494) he so increased the power of Sparta and of himself that he was emboldened to depose Damaratus, despite the opposition of the ephors, on a charge of illegitimacy. Public opinion then turned against him and he fled to Arcadia, whence he forced his return by arms. Traditionally, he soon after (c. 489) went mad, was imprisoned, and committed suicide, but this tale may conceal a real arrest and execution by the ephors. He was succeeded by **Leonidas.**

(3) Athens

Attica was gradually unified by the device of *synoecism*, through which the numerous small independent cities surrendered their local citizenship for that of Athens. This process had by 700 taken in all Attica except Eleusis, which was soon added. Traditionally the whole process was accomplished by King Theseus.

In the **Ancient Constitution of Athens** the people were divided into four hereditary tribes (*phylai*), each made up of a number of brotherhoods (*phratriai*), which had common religious ceremonies and gave assistance to members in legal strife and blood feuds. The nobles (*eupa-*

tridai) formed smaller associations of clans (*genê*); the *phratriai* contained eventually both members of these clans (*gennetai*) and common people (*orgeones*), although at first perhaps only the former. Each tribe was divided for administrative purposes into 12 *naucrariai*, which handled the revenue and cared for the navy. The people were grouped, chiefly for military purposes, into three classes: *hippeis* (knights), *zeugitai* (those with a yoke of oxen), and *thetes* (laborers). The nobles gradually restricted the power of the king by giving first his military functions to a *polemarch* and then his civil functions to an *archon*.

683. The hereditary kingship was abolished and made into an annual office (*archon basileus*) like the archon and polemarch. Six *thesmothetai* were created to determine the customary law. These, with the archon basileus, the polemarch, and the *archon eponymous* (civil archon), were known as the **nine archons.** They were chosen from the nobles by the **areopagus,** a council of nobles which was the greatest power in the state. The **ecclesia** (assembly of all the freemen) had either gone out of use or was completely without power. •

632. Cylon, a noble related to Theagenes, tyrant of Megara, attempted to establish a tyranny, but was foiled. Many of his followers were tricked into surrendering and then slaughtered by Megacles of the Alcmaeonid clan ("Curse of the Alcmaeonids").

621. Publication of the law by **Draco,** the unfairness of the nobles in administering the traditional law having led to a demand for its publication.

c. 600. Athens seized Sigeum from Mytilene; the resulting war was arbitrated (c. 590) in favor of Athens by Periander of Corinth.

594. SOLON was made sole archon to remedy the distress caused by the introduction of coined money and high rates of interest (usually 18 per cent); all parties agreed to give this man of the middle class complete powers of reform. By the **Seisachtheia** (shaking-off-of-burdens) all debts on land were cancelled; all debt slaves in Attica were freed; those sold abroad were redeemed at state expense; securing of debts by the person was forbidden. By his **judicial reforms** a new and milder code of laws replaced all of Draco's except the laws on homicide; a court of all the citizens, the *Heliaea*, was created and a right of appeal to it from decisions of the magistrates was granted. By his constitutional reforms election of magistrates was given to the **ecclesia** of all freemen; a council (**boulê**) of 400

(100 from each tribe) was created as a deliberative body which had the initiative in all legislation: the assembly could only accept or reject its proposals. The areopagus, hereafter composed of ex-archons, continued as guardian of the laws to have large supervisory powers over the magistrates. Four classes of citizens were defined: *pentacosiomedimnoi* (who had revenues of 500 medimni of corn and/or metretai of wine or oil); the *hippeis* (300); the *zeugitai* (200); and the *thetes* (all the rest). Some time later these classes were redefined in terms of money, and based on property rather than income. Only the first two classes were eligible to the archonship; the first three to the lower offices; the fourth could participate only in the heliaea and the ecclesia. By his economic reforms, Solon devalued the drachma by about a quarter; weights and measures were increased in size; the exportation of all agricultural produce except oil was forbidden; and immigration of artisans was encouraged by ready grants of citizenship. •

Solon's reforms were inadequate, chiefly because no provision was made to supply the freed slaves with land or to relieve the *hectemoroi* (share-croppers), who received only one-sixth of the produce of the land for themselves. Besides, the rising class of artisans and traders was deprived of political power by the assessment of the classes on an agricultural basis. Violent party strife continued immediately after Solon's archonship. The rich nobles of the plain (*pediakoi*) were led by **Lycurgus,** the middle class (*paralioi*) by **Megacles** the Alcmaeonid.

c. 565. Peisistratus acquired fame as the successful general in the **conquest of Salamis** from Megara. He organized a new party, the *diakrioi*, of the small artisans, shepherds, and other poor folk.

561-527. PEISISTRATUS made himself tyrant, but was almost immediately driven out by Megacles and Lycurgus. In 560–559 he won Megacles over and was restored. About 556 he was again expelled after a break with Megacles. After he had spent some years in gaining wealth from his mines in Thrace, he was restored with aid from Thessaly and Lygdamis of Naxos, whom he had made tyrant (c. 546). Peisistratus' opponents were now exiled and their confiscated lands used to provide for the poor. The *hectemoroi* were made landowners. Peisistratus encouraged industry and trade, and introduced the popular **cult of Dionysius,** in order to break down the power held by the nobles through their hereditary priesthoods. Miltiades and a few Athenians, with Peisistratus' encouragement, set up a tyranny over the Thracians of the Chersonese. Delos was purified. Abroad, Peisistratus pursued a policy of friendship with all near neighbors; at home, he ruled without abolishing existing forms.

527. On the death of Peisistratus his sons **Hippias and Hipparchus** succeeded to the tyranny. Athens protected Plataea against Thebes (519), which was trying to force her into the Boeotian League.

514. An attempt was made by **Harmodius and Aristogeiton** to overthrow the tyranny, but only Hipparchus was killed. Hippias was finally expelled by the exiled Alcmaeonids with Spartan aid (510). Party strife followed between the nobles led by Isagoras and the commons led by the Alcmaeonid **Cleisthenes**, who was finally victorious and inaugurated a

508. **Democratic reform of the Constitution.** In order to merge the new citizens completely with the old, *demes* (townships) were created to a number of over 150, and citzenship was made dependent on membership in one of these rather than as before in a *phratria*. To break the power of the noble clans, which were connected with the old hereditary tribes, a new system of 10 local tribes (*phylai*) was created: Attica was divided into three sections: Athens and its vicinity, the coast, and the interior. The *demes* in each section were associated in ten *trittyes*, and each tribe was composed of one *trittys* from each section, not always contiguous. A new council (*boulê*) of 500 replaced the Solonian 400; its members were chosen by lot, 50 from each tribe and from each *deme* in proportion to its population. The army was reorganized into ten tribal regiments, each of which in 501 was put under an elective general (*strategos*).

507. At the appeal of Isagoras, **Cleomenes** of Sparta invaded Attica, expelled Cleisthenes, and tried to restore the aristocracy. The Athenians rose, expelled the Spartans, and recalled Cleisthenes.

506. A second expedition of Cleomenes was prevented by King Damaratus and by Corinth. The Athenians crushed the Boeotians and Euboeans and annexed part of Chalcis' territory. They disregarded an ultimatum from Darius of Persia that they restore Hippias, whom Darius had made tyrant of Sigeum.

498. The Athenians sent 20 ships to the aid of the revolting Ionians, but after one campaign withdrew and tried to conciliate Persia by electing Hipparchus, a Peisistratid, to the archonship (496).

493/2. **Themistocles** was elected archon by the anti-Persian party and commenced the fortification of the Piraeus, but his naval policy was opposed by Miltiades, also anti-Persian, who had fled the Chersonese after the failure of the Ionian revolt.

(4) *Central and Northern Greece*

Some time before 700 the cities of Thessaly had been grouped in four *tetrads*, each under a *tetrarch*. Now they were organized into a loose **Thessalian League,** which elected, when common action was necessary, a general (*tagos*). There was a federal assembly which levied taxes and troops on the members. Until the 6th century this league possessed the strongest army in Greece; Thessalian cavalry was always unsurpassed. The looseness of the organization, however, prevented Thessaly from playing a leading rôle in Greece. Thessaly dominated the **Amphictyony of Anthela,** a religious league which by 600 included all the states of central Greece.

c. 590. In the **FIRST SACRED WAR,** under the leadership of Thessaly, and with help from Sicyon and Athens, the Amphictyony of Anthela defeated and demolished Crisa (Cirrha), in whose territory the shrine of Delphi lay. The pretext was the tolls levied by Crisa on pilgrims to Delphi. Delphi was put under the administration of the Amphictyones and their headquarters were transferred thither; Athens and the Dorians of the Peloponnese were admitted to membership.

c. 570. In **Euboea** the two states of importance, Chalcis and Eretria, had been very active in colonization and industry (c. 800–650). The Euboean coinage and weights and measures spread through the Greek world.

c. 570. Chalcis, supported by Corinth, Samos, and Thessaly, now became engaged in the **Lelantine War** with Eretria, aided by Aegina, Miletus, and Megara, over the possession of the rich Lelantine plain. Chalcis was victorious.

c. 600–550. Thebes formed a **Boeotian League** by bringing pressure on the other states of Boeotia. After a long struggle the powerful Orchomenus was reduced.

519–506. Plataea refused to join the league and entered into alliance with Athens. In the ensuing conflict, the Boeotians and Euboeans were defeated by the Athenians.

(5) *Sicily and Magna Graecia*

The original people of Sicily were Sicans; these were displaced by the Sicels from southern Italy. Before 800 the Elymians entered, probably from Spain, and occupied the western corner of Sicily. The Phoenician trading posts in Sicily (p. 31), which had covered the coast, were gradually driven out after 735 (foundation of Naxis) by the Greek colonization, except for Motya, Panormus, and Solus, in the west. Meanwhile **Carthage** (p. 32) had grown into an imperial power by founding colonies of her own and by protecting the older settlements after Tyre and Sidon were weakened by foreign domination after 669.

c. 580. An attempt of the Spartan Pentathlus to colonize western Sicily was defeated by the Elymians.

c. 570-554. **Phalaris,** tyrant of Acragas, pursued a policy of energetic and ruthless expansion, with extreme cruelty at home.

c. 550. The Carthaginian **Malchus** campaigned successfully in Sicily.

535. In the naval **battle of Alalia,** off Corsica, the Carthaginians and Etruscans defeated the Phocaean settlers and forced the abandonment of their colony. Shortly after this Massilia defeated Carthage and imposed a treaty limiting Carthaginian influence in the north and west.

510. **Sybaris** was destroyed by Croton, which was at this time ruled by the sect of the **Pythagoreans.** An attempt of the Spartan Dorieus to colonize western Sicily was prevented by the Carthaginians.

The conquest of Ionia by Persia led to a shift of intellectual and artistic effort to Greece proper and, thanks to their wealth, to the western colonies. **Tragedy** began at Athens with **Thespis** (539); the poets **Pindar, Simonides,** and **Anacreon** flourished c. 500. Attic black-figured vases gave way to red (c. 525). **Sculpture** became more common, in the archaic style (Athens, Delphi). **Heraclitus of Ephesus,** last of the Ionian physicists, advocated "change" against the "one" of **Parmenides of Elea** (*Eleatic School*) in southern Italy. **Pythagoras** founded his sect of mystic philosophers in Croton.

2. THE PERSIAN WARS

499-494. The Ionians revolted under the leadership of **Aristagoras** of Miletus, against the Persians and the pro-Persian tyrants. Aristagoras made a trip to Greece to solicit aid; Sparta refused, but Athens responded with 20 ships (498) and Eretria with five. The rebels made a dash on Sardis, burned it, and retired to Ephesus. Greek disunion and the desertion of the Samians and Lesbians led to the defeat of the Greek fleet in a **battle off the island of Lade** (494). Darius' control of the sea now enabled him to take and sack Miletus. This practically ended the revolt. Darius subdued all the Greek cities, but did not again force tyrants upon them.

490. BATTLE OF MARATHON. To punish Athens and Eretria for their aid to the rebels Darius sent an expedition across the Aegean under the command of Datis and Artaphernes. The Athenian ex-tyrant, Hippias, accompanied the expedition. Athens called for the aid of Sparta, but it came too late because of the festival of the Carneia. Artaphernes besieged Eretria on Euboea with part of the Persian forces, while Datis landed with another part at **Marathon,** the center of Peisistratid strength. When Eretria fell through treachery, **Miltiades,** one of the ten generals, persuaded the Athenians to attack, lest Artaphernes sail round Sunium to Athens while Datis held them at bay. The Athenians won a complete victory and marched back to Athens in time to prevent its betrayal to Artaphernes by the now pro-Peisistratid Alcmaeonids. The Persians returned to Asia.

Miltiades failed to capture Paros and was condemned to a heavy fine. He died soon.

489. Athens waged an indecisive **war with Aegina** until c. 483.

488-482. By a **reform of the Athenian constitution** (488/7), the nine archons were hereafter chosen by lot from 500 candidates elected by the demes; at some later time this was changed to 10 preliminary candidates elected from each tribe, and still later the preliminary candidates also were chosen by lot. This change naturally reduced the power of the polemarch in favor of the 10 elected generals, of whom one might be selected by the people at large as general-in-chief (*strategos autocrator*). To guard against tyranny, the device of *ostracism* was devised. In a meeting in which not less than 6000 votes were cast (*ostraka* were potsherds used for voting), the man with the greatest number was obliged to leave Athens for ten years; he remained a citizen, however, and his property was not confiscated. Hipparchus was ostracized in 487/6; Megacles the Alcmaeonid in 486/5; Xanthippus of the same party in 484/3. The anti-Persian party, of which the noble faction was led by **Aristides** and the commons by **Themistocles,** regained power. Themistocles prevailed upon the people to use a rich new vein of silver found in the state mine at Laurium for the building of 200 **triremes,** a newly invented type of warship. Aristides was ostracized due to his opposition to this measure, and from now on ostracism was used as a measure of party government. By 480 Themistocles headed the state as *strategos autocrator.*

480.   CAMPAIGN OF THERMOPYLAE.
        Xerxes, who had succeeded Darius in 486, demanded earth and water (submission) from all the Greek states, most of which refused. Xerxes thereupon led a carefully prepared expedition of about 180,000 men (not the traditional 900,000) into Greece through Thrace and Macedonia. A Greek force sent to hold the pass of Tempe retired when it was found untenable; the Greek army then occupied the **pass of Thermopylae,** and the fleet the Gulf of Artemisium: the plan was for the army to hold the Persians while the fleet won a victory and thus compelled retreat. The naval fighting, however, was indecisive. Under the guidance of the Greek Ephialtes, a Persian company traversed a side path, routed a small Phocian outpost, and turned the Greek position at Thermopylae. Most of the Greeks withdrew, but **Leonidas,** with 300 Spartans and 700 Thespians, refused to retire and they were annihilated. The Boeotians, Phocians, and Locrians immediately "medized"; the Greek army retreated behind a wall built across the Isthmus of Corinth, and the fleet moved to the Saronic Gulf between Athens and Salamis. The Persians occupied Attica and destroyed Athens, whence the citizens had fled to Salamis and the Peloponnese.

BATTLE OF SALAMIS. The Greek fleet was bottled up in the Saronic Gulf by the superior Persian forces. Themistocles craftily warned Xerxes that the Greeks were about to escape by night, and the Persians thereupon rushed into the narrows, became entangled, and were thoroughly defeated. Since it was impossible to force the isthmus merely by assault, this meant the end of the year's campaign. Xerxes returned to Sardis with a third of the army, Artabazus to Thrace with another third, and Mardonius wintered in Boeotia with the rest.

479.   BATTLE OF PLATAEA. After unsuccessfully trying to detach the Athenians from the Greek cause, Mardonius again invaded Attica. The Peloponnesians, urged by the Athenians, advanced to Plataea under the Spartan **Pausanias.** Mardonius attacked them as they were confusedly shifting their position, but the day was won by the superiority of the heavy-armed Greek *hoplites* and the discipline and bravery of the Spartans. Mardonius was killed, his camp plundered, and the Persian army routed. The Greeks then took Thebes by siege, and abolished the medizing oligarchy in favor of a democracy. In the meantime, the Spartan **Leotychidas** had sailed with a small fleet to guard the Cyclades against Persia. The Samians and Chians prevailed upon him to attack the Persians, who were at Samos. The Persians, fearing to meet him on the open sea, drew up their ships on land at **Mycale** near Samos. Leotychidas stormed their position, but the Persians succeeded in burning their ships before the Greeks could seize them. The Ionians and several of the island cities (Samos, Lesbos, Chios) now revolted from Persia and joined the Greek fleet, which laid siege to Sestos in the Thracian Chersonese. The Spartans returned home in the fall, but the Athenians and Ionians succeeded during the winter in reducing Sestos (478).

3. THE FIFTH CENTURY

a. THE PELOPONNESE, 479–461

479.   Pausanias, in command of the allied fleet, reduced Cyprus and Byzantium. By his domineering he alienated the Ionians and caused the ephors to fear lest his power become excessive; they recalled him and after a first acquittal he was later (c. 471) starved to death in the temple of Athena of the Brazen House. The

Ionians refused to recognize his successor Dorcis and went over to Athenian leadership. Thus Sparta's prestige in the Peloponnese fell very low. In 471 Elis united herself under a democratic government by *synoecism* and Tegea deserted Sparta to form an alliance with Argos, probably fostered by Themistocles.

470.   After a drawn **battle at Tegea** all of Arcadia except Mantinea joined the anti-Spartan alliance. While Argos was occupied in reducing Tiryns and Mycenae (c. 469), however, Sparta crushed the allies at Dipaea and restored her hegemony.

464. An earthquake in Sparta gave the helots of Messenia a chance to revolt (**Third Messenian War**); after a defeat they retired to Mt. Ithome, where the Spartans besieged them. Unable to take the place, the Spartans called on the aid of their allies, including Athens. Athens sent a force under Cimon which was shortly dismissed (462), probably because many of its members were really hostile to Sparta; this marked the end of the Spartan-Athenian alliance. The fall of Ithome ended the revolt (461), and the Messenians were given safe-conduct to Naupactus, which Athens had just acquired from the Ozolian Locrians.

461. **Megara,** involved in a border war with Corinth, appealed unsuccessfully to Sparta and then made an alliance with Athens.

b. ATHENS AND THE DELIAN LEAGUE, 479-461

479. Athens and the Piraeus were fortified by Themistocles, despite the opposition of Sparta.

478-477. **The Ionians,** disgusted with Spartan leadership, made an alliance with Athens for the expulsion of the Persians from all Greek territory. Each ally was to contribute either a quota of ships, or money in lieu of this: the smaller states chose the latter. **Aristides** ("The Just") assessed the tribute, using the old Persian tribute as a guide: the total was probably about 200 talents at first. The league had a general assembly (*synedrion*) on Delos, which at first controlled league policy, although it was soon dominated by Athens.

476. **Cimon** made an expedition to Thrace and captured the Persian forts along the coast except Doriscus; the siege of Eion occupied the winter. Some time later Carystus in Euboea was compelled to join the league. These successes enabled Cimon to procure the ostracism of Themistocles (471), probably because the latter wished to follow an anti-Spartan policy. Themistocles went to Argos, where he conspired against Sparta; he was later (467) outlawed by Athens and fled to Persia, where Artaxerxes gave him a refuge (464).

467. When **Naxos** attempted to withdraw from the Delian League, though the treaty of alliance made no provision for withdrawal, Athens forced the city to raze its walls, surrender its fleet, and henceforth pay tribute. Athens after this often interfered in the internal affairs

of the tributary states, which were soon considered subjects and not equal allies. Commercial disputes between citizens of two subject states or between those of a subject state and Athens, as well as capital criminal cases, were tried in the Athenian courts. Part of the rebels' lands were often taken, especially during Pericles' supremacy, to establish an Athenian *cleruchy* (colony), serving a military purpose as well as relieving unemployment in Athens. Garrisons were left under military captains (*phrourarchoi*) if necessary; sometimes only civil commissioners (*episkopoi*) were sent. Athenian surveyors (*taktai*) reassessed the tribute, and the Athenian people controlled its use, as well as the use of the contingents of the autonomous allies.

466. **Cimon** defeated the Persians in a great naval victory at the **Eurymedon River** on the south coast of Asia Minor. He then crushed a revolt of Thasos (465–463). Under the leadership of **Ephialtes,** a man of great probity and ability, the popular party was rising against the domination of Cimon. He was charged with having accepted a bribe from Alexander of Macedon, but was acquitted and prevailed over Ephialtes in having a force sent to Sparta against the helots (462). When the Spartans dismissed Cimon, the strong anti-Spartan feeling in Athens caused him to be ostracized (461). Ephialtes then succeeded in depriving the areopagus of all its powers except the jurisdiction in homicide cases; the other powers were distributed among the ecclesia, the council of 500, and the popular courts, which by this time, owing to the press of imperial business, had been changed from one panel of 6000 to several panels of from 201 up. Ephialtes was murdered shortly afterwards, and **Pericles,** on his mother's side an Alcmaeonid, took his place in the leadership of the popular party.

c. THE FIRST PELOPONNESIAN WAR

460. **Inaros,** who had previously raised a revolt in Egypt and defeated a Persian force, appealed to Athens for aid and was sent a fleet (probably not of 200 sail), which took Memphis. Simultaneously war broke out between the Athenians and the Peloponnesians, caused in part by the Megarian alliance of 462, which the Athenians had followed with alliances with Argos and Thessaly.

459. The Athenians were defeated at **Halieis** by the Corinthians and Epidaurians, but their fleet won a victory at **Cecryphaleia.** The Aeginetans joined the Peloponnesians (458), but their combined fleet was defeated by the

Athenians in a battle off Aegina and the island was invested by a force of Athenians under Leosthenes. The Corinthians raided the Megarid to create a diversion but were defeated by the Athenian old men and boys under Myronides.

457. The Aeginetans were forced to surrender, join the Delian League as tributaries, and surrender their fleet.

Sparta then entered the war, sent an army across the Corinthian Gulf, and restored the Boeotian League under the hegemony of Thebes. Athens was defeated at Tanagra, but the Spartans returned home, leaving the Athenians to defeat the Boeotians at Oenophyta and enroll all the cities except Thebes in her league; Phocis and Opuntian Locris also entered. The Athenians connected the Piraeus with Athens by two long walls.

456. A Persian force under Megabyzus defeated the Athenians, who were besieging Leukon Teichos, the citadel of Memphis. The Athenians were in turn besieged on the Nile island Prosopitis.

455. The Athenian Tolmides sailed around the Peloponnese, raiding the coast, burning the Spartan shipyard at Gytheum, and gaining Achaea for the Athenian League.

454. Pericles crossed the Isthmus and made an unsuccessful campaign in the Corinthian Gulf. But meanwhile the Athenians in Egypt were defeated and slaughtered, and a relief squadron met the same fate. As a result the treasury of the Delian League was moved to Athens.

451. After three years of inactivity Cimon returned from exile and negotiated a five years' truce with Sparta. Thus, being unprotected, Argos had to make a thirty years' peace with Sparta. Cimon then took a large force to Cyprus (450) but a plague (famine?) caused his death and necessitated the return of the force to Athens. As it was departing, the fleet won a great victory off Salamis, a town of Cyprus. An understanding was then reached with Persia (the so-called Peace of Callias).

449-448. THE SECOND SACRED WAR was begun when Sparta took Delphi from Phocis and made it independent; Athens immediately restored it to the Phocians.

447. Boeotia revolted and an inadequate Athenian force under Tolmides was crushed at Coronea. Moderate oligarchies were set up in all the Boeotian cities. The Boeotian League was re-established on a federal principle: a total of 11 Boeotarchs were sent by the cities in proportion to their sizes; for each Boeotarch a city was entitled to 60 seats on the federal council. Both local and federal councils were divided into four sections, of which each in turn served as council, while the four together constituted a plenary assembly. There was a federal treasury and coinage. Troops were levied in proportion to population. Phocis and Locris followed Boeotia in quitting the Athenian League.

446. Euboea revolted and Pericles crossed over with an army. Simultaneously the Peloponnesians invaded the Megarid and drove out the Athenian garrison. Pericles returned, but not daring a battle retired to Athens and when the Peloponnesians reached Eleusis came to terms satisfactory to the enemy, who withdrew. Pericles then crushed the revolt in Euboea, and established a cleruchy on the territory of Histiaea. Negotiations with the Spartans continued, and during the winter

446/5. THE THIRTY YEARS' PEACE was concluded: Megara returned to the Peloponnesian League; Troezen and Achaea became independent; Aegina was to be tributary but autonomous; disputes were to be settled by arbitration. Disgust among the Athenian conservatives at the failure of the anti-Spartan policy led to an attempt to ostracize Pericles, but it resulted in the ostracism (445) of their leader Thucydides, son of Melesias (not the historian). Pericles enjoyed undisputed control until 430.

d. ATHENS, 460-431

457. Pericles made the *zeugitae* eligible to the archonship; the *thetes* were never legally eligible, but in fact were soon permitted to hold the office. Athenian imperialism was extended to the far west by an alliance with Segesta and Halicyae in Sicily (453). An extremely important measure for the development of the democracy was the institution (451) of pay for the *dicasts* (jurors) of the popular courts, which made it possible for the poorest citizens to serve. At the same time Pericles carried a bill restricting Athenian citizenship to those both of whose parents were Athenians (repealed 429, re-enacted 403), and when Athens received a gift of free corn from Psammetichus of Egypt in 446/5 the lists were revised and 5000 citizens removed. The western policy was continued with the foundation of Thurii (443) and the alliances made with several Ionic cities of Sicily.

441. Miletus, involved in a war with Samos,

appealed to Athens, which replaced the oligarchy in Samos with a democracy.

440. **Samos** revolted and threw out the democracy, but the Athenians after a long siege took the city (439) which lost its fleet, its walls, and its autonomy, being made tributary. Chios and Lesbos were now the only autonomous allies in the league.

437. A policy of expansion in the north was begun with the foundation of **Amphipolis** in Thrace, controlling the mines of Pangaeus; it also relieved unemployment and served as a garrison against disaffected allies. Perhaps in the same year Pericles made an expedition into the Euxine and established good relations with the princes of Panticapaeum, who exported the grain badly needed by Athens. Athenian settlers were sent to various Pontic cities. In the Corinthian Gulf about this time Phormio made an alliance with some of the Acarnanians.

e. SICILY, 499–409

The first decades of the fifth century witnessed the rise of tyrants in the Sicilian cities, of whom the most important were **Theron of Acragas** (488–472) and **Gelon of Gela,** later of Syracuse (485–478). Gelon made Syracuse the first city of Sicily, largely by transporting thither populations from conquered neighbors. He differed from the usual tyrant in favoring the landed nobles (*gamoroi*) at the expense of the commons.

480. **Terillus,** tyrant of Himera until Theron conquered that city, appealed for Carthaginian help. Carthage, fearing the alliance of Gelon and Theron, responded with a force under Hamilcar, which was utterly defeated at Himera by the allies. Hamilcar was killed and Carthage forced to pay an indemnity.

478–466. **Hieron I,** brother of Gelon, marks the height of the first Syracusan tyranny. He moved the citizens of Catana to Leontini and resettled Catana with his mercenaries under the name Aetna. In alliance with Aristodemus of Cumae he defeated the Etruscans in a naval **battle off Cumae** (474).

472. **Thrasydaeus,** a cruel and hated ruler, succeeded his father Theron at Acragas. He immediately became involved in a war with Hieron and was decisively defeated. The people of Acragas and Himera expelled him and set up a democracy.

466. **Thrasybulus** succeeded his brother Hieron at Syracuse, but was expelled directly; a democracy was established. The attempted tyranny of **Tyndaridas** (Tyndarion) led to the introduction of *petalism,* like Athenian ostracism.

467./6. **Rhegium and Taras** were defeated with heavy losses by the native Italian Iapyges. A democracy was established in Taras and the Pythagoreans were expelled from the Italian cities generally.

463–460. After a series of conflicts the mercenaries of the deposed Sicilian tyrants were left in possession of **Messana** (formerly Zancle).

459/8. The Sicels united under **Ducetius** and founded a capital at Palice.

453. The Elymian towns of Segesta and Halicyae became involved in a war with Selinus and made an alliance with the aid of Athens.

450. Syracuse and Acragas finally succeeded in defeating Ducetius at Noae; he was exiled to Corinth and the Sicel federation fell apart. As a result of this victory Syracuse and Acragas fell out over the division of territory (c. 445). Syracuse was finally victorious and became the recognized leader of Sicily. In fear of her, Rhegium, Leontini, Catana (?), and Naxos (?) made alliances with Athens (443). Athens at the same time refounded the site of Sybaris as Thurii, calling in colonists from all of Greece.

440/39. **Ducetius,** who had returned in 446, restored the Sicel federation, and after founding Cale Acte, died; his federation was completely ended; Syracuse destroyed Palice.

427–424. **A general war** broke out in Sicily. Naxos, Catana, Leontini, Rhegium, Camarina, and most of the Sicels opposed Syracuse, which was supported by Gela, Messana, Himera, Lipara, and Locri. Gorgias of Leontini went to Athens and made an appeal for aid, which was granted. After indecisive fighting the aristocrat Hermocrates of Syracuse persuaded the warring cities, which had assembled in the **Conference of Gela,** to make peace and cease to call in the Athenians.

416. **Segesta,** at war with Selinus, again obtained Athenian aid under the treaty of 453.

415–413. The **Athenian expedition** against Syracuse, during the Peloponnesian War. The Athenians were finally defeated at the Assinarus. A democratic reform was instituted in Syracuse by Diocles (412): privileges of the lower classes were extended and many offices were made elective by lot. Hermocrates, who had commanded a naval squadron in aid of

Sparta, was banished after the **battle of Cyzicus** (410).

f. THE GREAT PELOPONNESIAN WAR

Thucydides considered the war of 431–421 (the **Archidamian War**) and that of 414–404 (the **Decelean** or **Ionian War**) to be in reality one, and together they are called the **Peloponnesian War**. Thucydides' incomplete history covers the period to 410. The basic cause of the war was the fact that there existed in Greece two great rival systems of alliances, comprising practically all of continental and Anatolian Greece, each of which was deemed essential by its leader. Thus neither leader could afford to tolerate any action threatening the solidity of its league, nor could it afford to allow the other to attain power appreciably superior to its own. Hence any minor conflict was bound to involve all Greece, and such a conflict was sure to arise.

435. Corcyra, quarreling with Corinth over the latter's interference in their joint colony Epidamnus, defeated the Corinthian fleet in the **battle of Leucimne.** Corinth began preparation of a great expedition, and the Corcyreans in fear appealed (433) to Athens for an alliance, which was granted, since Athens desired a station on the route to the west (to a small degree for commercial reasons), and especially since she feared Corinth's prospective naval power should the latter acquire the Corcyrean fleet. Ten ships were dispatched to Corcyra. The Corinthians attacked at Sybota, but when it was clear they were winning, the Athenians entered the battle, and the arrival of 20 more ships caused the Corinthians to return home. Athens then demanded that her subject Potidaea, a Corinthian colony, cease to receive her annual magistrate from Corinth, and raze her seaward walls.

432. Assured of Peloponnesian aid, the **Potidaeans** revolted in the spring. An Athenian force won a battle before Potidaea in the fall. Pericles passed a bill barring the Megarians from all the harbors of the Athenian Empire, ruining them economically; the Peloponnesians alleged that this was contrary to the Thirty Years' Peace, but the truth is uncertain. The Corinthians, Megarians, and Aeginetans forced the Spartans to take action and, although opposed by King Archidamus, the ephor Sthenelaïdas persuaded the Spartan assembly to declare the peace broken. The **Peloponnesian League** was then assembled and declared war. The winter was taken up by fruitless negotiations.

431. The war began when a band of Thebans by treachery entered Athens' ally Plataea; the Thebans were induced to surrender and were then killed.

The strategy of the Athenians, devised by Pericles, was to refuse a land battle, in which they would almost certainly be defeated, remain within their walls, and let their country be ravaged; they could support themselves through their control of the sea, and hoped 'to wear down the Peloponnesians by coastal raids and destruction of their commerce. They also ravaged the Megarid twice annually, when the Peloponnesian army was not assembled. The strategy of the Peloponnesians was to ravage the land of Attica annually and, if possible, lure the Athenians into battle; they also gave encouragement and support to revolting allies of Athens.

431. The Athenians expelled the inhabitants of Aegina and replaced them with Athenian cleruchs. Thucydides put in Pericles' mouth the famous *Funeral Oration* for the war dead of this year.

430. A great plague broke out at Athens. When an Athenian expedition against Epidaurus failed, it was sent to Potidaea, but returned after infecting the troops there with the plague. Disgusted, the Athenians deposed Pericles. During the winter Potidaea surrendered.

429. The plague continued. Pericles was reelected *strategos* in the spring, but died soon after. Instead of invading Attica, the Peloponnesians laid siege to Plataea. The Athenians sent Phormio to block the Corinthian Gulf. Off **Naupactus** he won two battles against superior forces.

428. Cleon succeeded to the leadership of the radical party in Athens, which favored war; the conservatives, opposed to war, were led by **Nicias.** All Lesbos except Methymna revolted on the promise of Spartan aid. To meet this emergency the Athenians levied the first direct property tax (*eisphora*) since 510 and sent out a large fleet under Paches.

427. Mytilene fell before the dilatory Spartan admiral, Alcidas, arrived. The leaders were executed and Athenian cleruchs were sent to the island. Plataea was finally taken by the Spartans; half the garrison had previously escaped; those who remained were executed. The oligarchs in Corcyra, wishing to end the alliance with Athens, opened civil war on the democrats, but the latter, with Athenian help, put down the rebellion; many oligarchs fled to the mainland opposite.

426. The Spartans offered peace to Athens, but it was refused.

425. The Athenian general, **Demosthenes,** in co-operation with the Acarnanians, took Anactorium. He was then sent to reinforce a fleet in Sicily but on the way seized **Pylos,** on the west coast of the Peloponnesus. Demosthenes was left with five ships, to use this station to stir up the Messenian helots against Sparta. But the Spartans besieged this force on Pylos by landing a force on Sphacteria, an island in the bay. The Athenian fleet returned, defeated the Peloponnesians, and blockaded Pylos. Cleon, in Athens, accused Demosthenes of dilatoriness and, on the motion of Nicias, was sent himself to do better. To everyone's surprise, Cleon and Demosthenes captured the 120 Spartiates on Sphacteria. These were held as hostages to prevent another invasion of Attica.

424. Nicias seized **Cythera.** Cleon almost tripled the tribute assessment; pay for the dicasts was raised from 2 to 3 obols a day. Demosthenes and Hippocrates seized Nisaea but were prevented by Brasidas, on his way to Thrace, from taking Megara. **Brasidas,** with 700 helot hoplites and 1000 Argive mercenaries, continued to Thrace, Athens' only vulnerable point, and raised rebellion in several cities. Demosthenes and Hippocrates planned a synchronized invasion of Boeotia from the west and east respectively, to be aided by Boeotian democrats. The Thebans prevented Demosthenes from invading Boeotia from Acarnania and inflicted a heavy defeat on his colleague Hippocrates at Delium. Brasidas took Amphipolis. Thucydides, the historian, commanded a fleet near-by and was exiled at Cleon's instance on a charge of negligence. The fleet in Sicily returned after the **Conference of Gela.**

423. The Athenians made a year's truce with Sparta. Brasidas, however, continued to raise rebellions in the Thracian cities, so the Athenians broke off negotiations.

422. **Cleon** took a force to Thrace, but was routed and killed before **Amphipolis;** Brasidas also killed: thus the leaders of the war parties on both sides were eliminated and negotiations reopened. Sparta's position in the Peloponnese was being shaken by trouble with Mantinea and Elis, the imminent expiration of the peace with Argos, and the Athenian possession of Pylos, Cythera, and the 120 captives. Athens had exhausted her reserves, which had amounted to 6000 talents in 431.

421. **THE PEACE OF NICIAS** was negotiated, to last for 50 years. The Athenians were to keep Nisaea until the Boeotians restored Plataea; the Chalcidian cities were to be autonomous but tributary; Amphipolis was to be restored; the captives on both sides were to be freed. The Spartans restored the Athenian prisoners, but Brasidas' successor Clearidas refused to give over Amphipolis. The Corinthians, Megarians, Eleans, and Boeotians refused to sign the treaty: the former two because they received no benefits from the whole struggle, the Eleans because of a private quarrel over Lepreum, and the Boeotians because they did not wish to restore Plataea. To protect herself, Sparta made an alliance with Athens for 50 years. Thereupon, Elis, Mantinea, Corinth, and the Chalcidian cities made an alliance with Argos, whose treaty with Sparta had expired. Megara and Boeotia delayed action.

420. Sparta broke the terms of the Athenian alliance by making a separate treaty with Boeotia, whereby Boeotia was to restore Panactum to Athens. The Boeotians, however, first razed Panactum, and the Athenians continued to hold Pylos. The action of Boeotia caused Corinth to quit the Argive League. Athens formed **the Quadruple Alliance** with Argos, Mantinea, and Elis, for 100 years. The two latter states at this time were already at war with Sparta.

418. The Spartans under **Agis** invaded Argos and, after considerable delay, the Athenians sent troops to Argos' support. Agis decisively defeated the Athenians, Argives, and Mantineans (the Eleans dropped out) in the **battle of Mantinea** and restored Sparta's hegemony in the Peloponnese. The Spartans then sent an ultimatum to Argos, which proceeded to repudiate the quadruple alliance and make a 50 years' alliance with Sparta. In the spring of 417, the Spartans put an oligarchic government into Argos, but it fell immediately and the democrats renewed the treaty with Athens for 50 years. During the next two years various Spartan armies raided Argos; the Athenians each time sent troops which arrived too late to encounter the Spartans.

416. Athens took by siege the island of Melos, which had refused to join the empire. The men were killed, the women and children enslaved; a cleruchy was established.

Selinus attacked Segesta, which appealed to Athens. Athens had by now a reserve of 3000 talents; the industrial and trading elements desired westward expansion. Against Nicias' opposition an expedition to Sicily was voted, to be commanded by Nicias, Alcibiades (the prime mover), and Lamachus.

415-413. **The Sicilian expedition** set out with a

fleet of 134 triremes, carrying 4000 hoplites. Nicias refused Lamachus' proposal to attack Syracuse immediately. Alcibiades was recalled on charges of sacrilege, mutilating the *Hermae* and profaning the Eleusinian Mysteries. He fled to Sparta. The Athenians won over Naxos and Catana, but accomplished nothing more.

414. Hermocrates was elected to command the defense of Syracuse. The Athenians almost succeeded in enclosing the city by a wall, but were prevented by the arrival of the Spartan Gylippus with a small force; his seizure of the heights called *Epipolae* permanently prevented circumvallation.

413. Reinforcements were sent under Demosthenes. His night attack on Epipolae failed and he advocated immediate return, but was prevented by Nicias' superstitious fear of an eclipse (Aug. 27). When the Athenians finally attempted to leave, the Syracusans, who had strengthened their fleet, defeated them in two naval battles. The Athenians withdrew by land; the rear under Demosthenes lagged behind and was defeated; the van under Nicias was crushed at the **Assinarus.** The generals were executed; the prisoners were kept for a time in the stone quarries and then sold into slavery.

414. The Athenians sent a fleet against the coasts of Sparta. The Spartans declared the peace broken.

413. The Spartans seized **Decelea** in Attica. This post was fortified and a garrison kept there continually; the Athenians were thus absolutely prevented from using their own land. The radical party in Athens, led by Peisander and Androcles, fell after the Sicilian defeat and a conservative reform took place. A college of 10 "deliberators" (*probouloi*) received many of the functions of the old council. The imperial tribute was replaced by a 5 per cent import and export levy in all harbors of the empire.

412. A small Spartan squadron stirred up revolts along the coast of Ionia. The Athenians voted to use their last 1000 talents, laid away for extreme emergency, and built rapidly a large fleet, which recovered Lesbos and Clazomenae. The **Treaty of Miletus** was negotiated by Alcibiades between Sparta and Tissaphernes, satrap of Sardis. Sparta recognized the Persian king's rights to all lands ever belonging to any of his ancestors, while Persia was to furnish the money to maintain the Peloponnesian fleet.

The Athenians laid siege to **Miletus,** but were forced to withdraw by the arrival of the Peloponnesian fleet. The Athenian fleet at Samos received reinforcements and sent a detachment to blockade Chios. During the winter the Peloponnesian fleet was united at Caunus, but had difficulty in paying its crews, since Tissaphernes' policy, suggested by Alcibiades, was to wear out both sides and let neither win a real victory. The Peloponnesians took Rhodes, where they obtained supplies and money.

411. Sparta made a new treaty with Persia, signed by both Tissaphernes and Pharnabazus, satrap of Phrygia. The king's claims were limited to Ionia.

Alcibiades claimed that he could win Tissaphernes to the Athenians if the democracy were abolished. The oligarchic clubs in Athens (*hetairai*) by terrorism carried a motion to restrict citizenship to about 5000 of the wealthiest Athenians. Pay for public offices was abolished; all citizens except the 5000 were to be completely without political rights. A provisional committee of 400 was to rule until the 5000 had been chosen. The 400, however, continued to rule without choosing the 5000. The crews at Samos, who refused to recognize the new government and constituted themselves as the Athenian people, elected new generals, notably Thrasybulus and Thrasyllus. They forcibly prevented an attempt by Athenian and Samian oligarchs to restore the oligarchy in Samos which had been put down the year before. Alcibiades was recalled and made commander-in-chief; he demanded the abolition of the 400 in Athens, although he approved of the 5000. When the extremists among the 400 seemed ready to surrender to Sparta after four months of rule, the moderates, led by Theramenes, secured their deposition. Nine thousand citizens were enrolled as councilors, to serve in four sections as in Boeotia (so-called **Government of the 5000**). Pay for civic offices was not restored. This government fell before the beginning of the civil year 410/9, and the democracy was restored, with pay for the dicasts.

Meanwhile the Spartans raised revolts in many Hellespontine and Thracian cities and especially in Euboea. The Athenians under Alcibiades defeated the Spartans at Cynossema and Abydos.

410. In the **battle of Cyzicus,** Alcibiades annihilated the Peloponnesian fleet. Sparta offered peace on the *status quo*, but the radical party in Athens, which had risen again under the leadership of **Cleophon**, rejected the offer. Pharnabazus paid for the building of a new Peloponnesian fleet.

409. An Athenian expedition under Thrasyllus failed to take Ephesus. Sparta recovered Pylos; Megara had already recovered Nisaea.

408. The Athenians made a truce with Pharnabazus and sent ambassadors to the king, but before they arrived the king had received a Spartan embassy and decided to help Sparta energetically. He sent his son **Cyrus** to replace Tissaphernes. Alcibiades recovered Byzantium.

407. **Thrasybulus** recovered Abdera and Thasos. Alcibiades was elected general and commander-in-chief at Athens and returned to the city in triumph. Cyrus arrived in Asia Minor and formed cordial relations with Lysander, the able Spartan admiral (*nauarchos*).

406. When **Alcibiades** went off to collect money, his guard squadron at Ephesus was **defeated off Notium** by Lysander. Alcibiades lost all influence and fled to the Hellespont. Callicratidas replaced Lysander, but could not get along with Cyrus. The Athenian Conon was defeated at **Mytilene**. The Athenians with a great effort built another fleet.

406. In the **battle of Arginusae,** Conon won a decisive victory over the Spartan fleet. Eight of the Athenian generals, however, were later tried and, despite Socrates' opposition, sentenced to death for not rescuing the shipwrecked sailors; two fled. The Spartans again offered peace on the *status quo,* but Cleophon again had the offer rejected. On Cyrus' demand, Lysander was sent with the Peloponnesian fleet, nominally as secretary, in reality to command.

405. The Athenians followed Lysander to the Hellespont and, through the gross carelessness of the commanders, the fleet was annihilated while drawn up on the shore at **Aegospotami.** Oligarchies of 10 (*decarchiai*) under Spartan harmosts were set up in all the Athenian subject states.

404. **Theramenes** negotiated peace after Cleophon, who held out against surrender to the last, was finally tried and executed. **Athens was to raze her long walls and the fortifications of the Piraeus, surrender her navy, and make an alliance with Sparta.**

404. The Athenian oligarchs, supported by Lysander and led by Theramenes, set up a commission of thirty which was to make a few immediate reforms and devise a new constitution. Instead of this, the Thirty with Critias at their head seized power and ruled as the **Thirty Tyrants.** They executed Theramenes, when he advocated a more moderate course. Finally 3000 of the richest citizens

were nominally enfranchised, but never exercised any real power. Many citizens were exiled or fled, and these were supported by Argos and by Thebes, who feared the excessive power of Sparta. In the autumn of 404 Thrasybulus led back some exiles, who occupied Phyle and then the Piraeus. In the beginning of 403, the Athenians deposed the Thirty, who fled to Eleusis, and elected a **government of Ten.** These, instead of bringing in the democrats from the Piraeus, asked help from Sparta, which sent Lysander. Then the anti-Lysander party in Sparta replaced Lysander with King Pausanias, who brought about a settlement by which the democracy was restored, and a general amnesty with few exceptions decreed. The decarchies in the former Athenian dependencies were soon abolished.

g. ECONOMIC AND SOCIAL CONDITIONS

The decline of Ionia and the growing prosperity of the western Greeks led, after the Persian Wars, to a shift of trade and industry to Greece proper, toward which converged the routes from both west and east, where the Greeks now sought an outlet for manufactures and a source of raw materials. Corinth and Aegina were the leading commercial states in Greece at the beginning of the 5th century, but they were soon outstripped by Athens. This growth of industry caused a rapid rise in the number of slaves, and many **metics** (*metoikoia,* resident aliens) migrated to the commercial states of Greece, where they were well treated: Athens especially was liberal in granting citizenship from Solon's time until 451. The industrial states were all dependent on the **importation** of food. In Greece itself, only Thessaly, Macedonia, and Sicily exported grain: Sparta, Boeotia, and the backward states of the west and north were self-sufficing. Athens exported wine and oil. The economy of almost all Greek states was now on a **money basis** (e.g. at Athens the Solonian classes had been converted into a money assessment of all property). The Athenian coinage became the predominant medium of exchange. **Prices** had risen tremendously since the 6th century. **Wages** were on a bare subsistence level, and the large number of slaves prevented any increase.

Shipping and agriculture remained very primitive. In Sparta and Thessaly great estates existed, but elsewhere ownership of land was much divided, and even in an industrial state like Athens the large majority of the citizens remained landowners. Foreigners were usually prohibited by law from owning land.

Public finance was simple, with no public debt and few surpluses. The chief source of revenue was indirect taxation; Athens profited greatly from her state-owned mines and depended on semi-compulsory contributions by wealthy citizens (*liturgiae*) for such expenses as the equipment of triremes or production of plays. Direct property taxes were used only in case of extreme need. Expenses in most states were correspondingly low; Athens used the revenues from the empire for extensive public works, and also had a large number of citizens on the public pay-roll. The Peloponnesian War, however, not only exhausted the public finances throughout Greece, but also created economic dislocation, and impoverishment among individuals. These losses must, nevertheless, have been made good rapidly, as the 4th century witnessed a high level of prosperity.

During the 5th century **art and poetry** attained their finest expression in Greece, especially in Athens, whose prosperity favored an artistic life. This was fostered by **Pericles**, who herein, as in other policies, resembled the 6th-century tyrants. In the choral ode, **Pindar** of Thebes (518–442) and **Bacchylides** (c. 480), in the epigram, **Simonides** (556–468), distinguished the early part of the century. At Athens the three great dramatists, **Aeschylus** (525–456), **Sophocles** (495–405), and **Euripides** (480–406) developed tragedy from a crude choral performance to unsurpassed perfection.

Aristophanes (c. 448–385), who overlapped into the 4th century, was the acknowledged master of the **Old Comedy**. Prose lagged behind verse, but the Ionian **Herodotus,** writing at Athens (484–428?), made the Persian Wars the motif of a delightfully discursive history. **Thucydides** (471–c. 400) perfected history in his account of the Peloponnesian War. In philosophy the conflict of unity against multiplicity was solved by the atomic theories advanced by **Empedocles** in Sicily (c. 444), by **Anaxagoras**, an Ionian at Athens (500–425? mind or *nous*), and by **Leucippus** (c. 450?). But philosophy turned from physics to ethics and the **Sophists** became the teachers of Greece and advocates of the subjectivity of standards (*nomos*, convention, against *phusis*, nature). The leading Sophists were **Protagoras, Prodicus, Hippias,** and **Gorgias,** the last of whom came from **Leontini** in Sicily to Athens in 427.

In **architecture,** the heavy and luxurious temples of the early part of the century in Sicily, especially at Acragas (Agrigentum), were succeeded by the perfection of Pericles' Doric and Ionic buildings on the **Acropolis** at Athens, the **Parthenon,** or temple of Athens (447–432), the **Propylaea,** or entrance gate (437–432), and the **Erechtheum** (420–408), or temple of the hero Erectheus. **Sculpture** reached its height in the works of **Myron** (c. 450) and **Polycleitus** (c. 430) of the Argive School and **Pheidias** (500–431) the Athenian. Attic red-figured vase-painters developed line-drawing in a series of exquisite styles (to 415), and **Polygnotus** (c. 480) mastered the technique of large-scale painting.

4. THE RISE OF MACEDON

a. SPARTAN HEGEMONY

401–400. Darius II of Persia had been succeeded in 404 by his eldest son, **Artaxerxes II.** A younger son, **Cyrus,** collected a Greek mercenary force in Asia Minor and marched against his brothers (the *anabasis* or "going up") in 401; he was killed in the battle of **Cunaxa,** and with great difficulty the Greeks, one of whose leaders was the Athenian **Xenophon,** made their way back to the Euxine by 400.

400–394. When **Tissaphernes** besieged Cyme in 400, Sparta sent Thibron to hire a mercenary army and to liberate the Ionians from Persia. Dercyllidas took over the command in 399 and ravaged some Persian territory.

A truce was maintained (398–397) while Artaxerxes prepared his fleet and put the Athenian Conon in command. In 396/5 King Agesilaus, succeeding Dercyllidas, ravaged Persian territory. In 394 Agesilaus returned to Greece with most of the troops.

395–387. The Corinthian War. In the winter of 396/5 Persia sent Timocrates of Rhodes to bribe the leaders of Athens, Thebes, Corinth, and Argos to attack Sparta. Athens made a defensive alliance with Boeotia which Corinth, Argos, Megara, Euboea, and other states joined. In 394, the Spartans won battles at **Nemea** and at **Coronea,** but their fleet, under Peisander, was annihilated by the Persian fleet, under Conon, at **Cnidus.** Persia granted autonomy to the Asiatic Greek cities and withdrew her garrisons. The Ionians revolted from Sparta and established democracies; the Cyclades followed in 393. Conon returned to Greece, and rebuilt the Athenian long walls. Athens recovered Lemnos, Imbros, Scyrus, and Delos; and made alliances with Chios, Mitylene, Rhodes, Cos, and Cnidus. In 392, an attempt at a general settlement was rejected by the Athenian imperialists, who had just come to power. The Persians deposed Conon, who soon died. In 390, Evagoras of Cyprus revolted from Persia. In 389, the Athenian navy under Thrasybulus recovered Thasos, Samothrace, Tenos, the Chersonese, Byzantium, Chalcedon, *et al.*; garrisons were placed in the more important towns, and 5 per cent harbor tolls levied, which really constituted a **revival of the Athenian naval league.** Thrasybulus was killed in action (388).

387-386. THE KING'S PEACE. In 387, the Spartan Antalcidas negotiated with Persia a general Greek settlement. All Greek cities were to be autonomous except those in Asia, which were to belong to Persia. In 386, the Spartan navy forced Athens to accept by blockading the Hellespont; Thebes was frightened into acceptance. Thus the Boeotian and the new Athenian leagues were dissolved.

385-379. Sparta broke Mantinea up into villages (385), seized the citadel, or Cadmeia, of Thebes (382), and captured Olynthus and dissolved its Chalcidian League (379).

379-378. The Theban democratic exiles led by Pelopidas recovered the Cadmeia by a *coup* and established a democracy in Thebes. The raid of the Spartan Sphodrias on the Piraeus caused an Athenian alliance with Thebes (378). Sparta raided Boeotia in 378 and 377.

377. SECOND ATHENIAN LEAGUE AGAINST SPARTA. Shortly after 386, Athens had renewed her alliances with several naval powers. In 377, these, Thebes, and many others united in the "second" (really third) league against Sparta. All decisions were to be made jointly by a council (*synedrion*) of the allies, excluding Athens, and the Athenian *ecclesia*; funds were to be derived from contributions levied by the *synedrion* and handled by Athens; Athens was to command in war; Athens gave up all claims to its former cleruchies. A fleet was quickly built up. In 376 Chabrias crushed the Spartan fleet off **Naxos,** and gave Athens control of the sea. Meanwhile, Thebes restored the Boeotian League on a democratic basis.

372. Jason, who succeeded his father Lycophron in the tyranny of Pherae, unified

Thessaly by having himself made perpetual commander (*tagos*) until his murder in 370.

371. A general peace settlement was reached with Sparta in the summer of 371; but when he was not permitted to sign for all Boeotia, the Theban **Epaminondas** withdrew. Sparta immediately sent King Cleombrotus to chastise Thebes, but he was decisively defeated at **Leuctra** by Epaminondas. This shattered Spartan prestige and ended her chance of hegemony over Greece. Thebes withdrew from the Athenian League, and with her Acarnania, Euboea, and the Chalcidian cities.

b. THEBAN HEGEMONY

370. An Arcadian League was formed under Theban protection as counterweight to Sparta. Mantinea was restored as a city. The government of the league comprised a general assembly (**the Ten Thousand**) of all free-born citizens, with sovereignty in matters of war, peace, etc.; a council of *damiurgoi*, which gave proportional representation to the member cities; a college of generals (*strategoi*) as civil and military executive; a standing mercenary army (*eparitoi*). The Theban army, under **Epaminondas,** liberated Messenia from Sparta and the city **Messene** was built. In 369 Athens and Sparta made an alliance on equal terms. The Arcadians founded **Megalopolis** as a federal capital. In the following years, Thebes secured the union of all of Thessaly save Pherae under a single ruler (*archon*). The pro-Spartan party of Callistratus in Athens was replaced in power by the party of Timotheus, and peace was made with Thebes on the basis of the *status quo* (365). Pelopidas was killed in battle against Alexander of Pherae (364), whom Epaminondas then defeated (363).

362. Because of financial difficulties, the federal army of Arcadia was disbanded. The oligarchs, who could serve at their own expense, came into control of many cities, which then made peace with Elis. The radicals appealed to Epaminondas, and the league broke up: Tegea and Megalopolis remained pro-Theban, while the others made an alliance with Elis and Achaea; all these jointly made an alliance with Athens; Mantinea was allied with Sparta. Epaminondas faced this coalition at Mantinea, but was killed in battle. A general peace was made on the basis of the *status quo*, but it was not accepted by Sparta, which refused to recognize the independence of Messenia.

359. PHILIP II became regent and, in 356, by the deposition of his ward, **King of**

Macedon. Since he was troubled by his unruly barbarian subjects and Athens was involved in war with the Thracian Odrysae, both were glad in 358 to make a treaty by which Philip gave up his claim to Amphipolis and Athens promised to surrender Pydna. Philip now thoroughly reorganized his army, placing more importance on the **phalanx** of infantry, and with it subdued the rebellious barbarians. By agreement with Athens, he conquered Amphipolis (357) to exchange it for Pydna, since Athens was occupied in recovering Euboea from Thebes and the Chersonese from the Thracians.

357-355. The Athenian allies were angry at Athenian policy, e.g. the sending of cleruchies to Samos (365) and Potidaea (361), the subjection of Ceos and Naxos to Athenian jurisdiction (363/2), and especially the arbitrary financial exactions of Athenian generals; further, the decline of Spartan power had removed the league's *raison d'être*. Under encouragement from **Mausolus** (Mausollos, 377-353), who had succeeded Hecatomnus (395-377) as ruler of Caria, Chios, Rhodes, Cos, and Byzantium joined in revolt, known as the **Social War,** i.e. "War of the Allies." After the defeat and death of Chabrias at Chios, the Athenians, under the incompetent Chares, finally withdrew from Ionia and recognized the independence of many of their allies (355). Mausolus in 353 annexed Rhodes and Cos.

c. MACEDON UNDER PHILIP AND ALEXANDER THE GREAT

355-346. THE THIRD SACRED WAR began when the Phocians refused to pay a fine levied on certain of their people by the Amphictyonic Council at the instigation of Thebes (355). The Phocians seized Delphi and made alliances with Athens and Sparta. When the Amphictyons declared war, the Phocians used the sacred money of Delphi to recruit a very large mercenary army. Though they were defeated by the Boeotians at **Neon** (354), they seized Thermopylae and Orchomenus (353). When Philip attempted to oppose them in Thessaly, their general Onomarchus twice defeated him, but in 352 Philip defeated and killed Onomarchus. Philip then united Thessaly, which continued loyal to him. His march south was stopped by Athenians, Achaeans, and Spartans, at Thermopylae. The war continued indecisively in Phocis until Athens made the **Peace of Philocrates** with Philip (346). Philip then conquered Phocis, prohibited the carrying of arms, and spread the Amphictyonic fine in installments.

356-346. When Athens refused to surrender Pydna to Philip in return for Amphipolis, he conquered the former, kept the latter, made a treaty against Athens with Olynthus, and took Crenides, renamed **Philippi,** from the Odrysae. After the end of the **War of the Allies** (355), Athens was financially exhausted and the imperialist party of Chares and Aristophon was replaced by the pacifists under Eubulus. All financial surpluses were put into a **theoric fund** and used for the entertainment of the citizens. Athens allowed Philip to expand eastward almost unchecked. But in 351 Olynthus, suspicious of Philip, appealed to her for aid. **Demosthenes** appeared as the leader of the anti-Macedonian party, urging action in his three *Olynthiac orations.* An alliance was made with Olynthus (349), but an attempt to divert the surplus from the theoric to the military fund failed. Philip induced Euboea to revolt from Athens and the latter, against Demosthenes' advice, divided its efforts by sending a force there as well as to Olynthus (348). Phocion was successful in Euboea, but his successor, Molossus, lost the country. Philip took Olynthus, which he razed, and enslaved the citizens (348). Athens could secure no help from the Greeks, and even Demosthenes favored peace.

346. PEACE OF PHILOCRATES. On the motion of Philocrates, ten ambassadors, including himself, Aeschines, and Demosthenes, were sent at Philip's invitation to negotiate a peace: the terms restored the Chersonese, except Cardia, to Athens, cancelled Athens' claim to Amphipolis, and left other possessions as they should be when the peace was sworn. Athens could not secure the inclusion of her ally Phocis in the terms. On the return of the ambassadors, the assembly accepted the terms and sent them back to swear the oaths; they delayed on the way and Philip profited by this to conquer more of Thrace. After the conclusion of the peace, Philip conquered the Phocians, took their seat in the Amphictyonic League, and, as its chairman, presided over the Pythian games; Athens refused to send a delegation until Philip's threats forced her to recognize his membership in the league.

344-339. Despite the friendly attitude of Philip, Demosthenes persuaded the Athenians to make alliances against him in Euboea (341) and the Peloponnese (340), and to help Byzantium to repel him (339). Demosthenes, now in control in Athens, urged opposition to Philip in his *Philippic orations.* He reformed the system of paying for the navy by replacing the individual liturgy (*trierarchia*) with more equitable and efficient groups of contributors (*symmoriae*). He devoted surplus income to the war fund instead of to the theoric. Philip tried to get the Amphictyons to fine Athens for insulting Thebes, but Aeschines cleverly diverted them against Amphissa.

339-338. When this caused the **Fourth Sacred War,** the Amphictyons called in Philip. Athens, terrified at this, made an alliance with Thebes on terms very favorable to the latter. The allies won some minor successes. But Philip annihilated their mercenaries near Amphissa.

338. In the **BATTLE OF CHAERONEA,** Philip crushed the allied citizen armies. He garrisoned Thebes, but let Athens go free. Philip called a **congress at Corinth,** and all states, except Sparta, entered a **Hellenic League.** There was proportional representation in the league council, which was presided over by the king in wartime, otherwise by a chairman; autonomy of the members was guaranteed; existing constitutions were not to be altered and no private property confiscated; no tribute was required and no garrisons left, except in a few places; the king had the military command; the Amphictyonic Council served as a supreme court. Philip announced plans for an Asiatic campaign.

337. A second congress at Corinth (337) declared war on Persia, and Philip sent an army under his general, Parmenio, to Asia Minor (336).

336. **Philip was assassinated,** allegedly at the instigation of his recently divorced wife Olympias.

337-323. ALEXANDER III, THE GREAT (b. 356), succeeded.

On a rumor that Alexander had died, Thebes revolted with Athens, Arcadia, Elis, and Aetolia, but Alexander swiftly took Thebes, destroyed it, and enslaved the inhabitants. The others submitted (335).

334-331. Alexander, leaving Antipater behind as his governor in Greece, crossed the Hellespont in the spring of 334 with an army of 32,000 infantry and 5000 cavalry, supported by a navy of 160 ships, mostly allied. Memnon of Rhodes, commander of Darius' Greek mercenaries, wished to retreat, laying waste the country, but the satraps, hoping to protect their provinces, forced him to take a stand at the river **Granicus,** where he was completely defeated by Alexander (334).

Most of the Greek cities revolted from Persia. Alexander subdued Caria and (spring, 333) Cilicia. Meanwhile, Memnon died and Darius summoned the mercenaries to Syria. Alexander went on to Myriandrus, where he faced Darius, who had raised a large but motley army. Since Alexander feared to come on to the open plain, Darius went behind him to the plain of Issus.

333. BATTLE OF ISSUS. Alexander attacked and completely defeated Darius. Darius offered to give up all Asia west of the Euphrates and pay 10,000 talents, but Alexander demanded unconditional surrender. All Phoenicia, except Tyre, submitted after Issus, and, by a difficult siege of seven months, Tyre was reduced (332).

332-331. Alexander's **expedition to Egypt** was unopposed; while in Egypt, he founded **Alexandria** and visited the oracle of Ammon.

331. Leaving Egypt in the spring, Alexander met and defeated the Persian army at **Gaugamela** (Oct. 1) and went on to Arbela, where he seized much Persian treasure. Babylonia and Susa surrendered, but at Persepolis resistance was offered, so that the place was looted and burned and immense treasure was taken.

331. Sparta under King Agis III, aided by Persian money and in alliance with Elis, Achaea, and part of Arcadia, defeated a Macedonian force and besieged Megalopolis, but was crushed when Antipater arrived with a greatly superior force.

330. In the spring of 330, Alexander pursued Darius through Media, where Darius was murdered by the satrap Bessus. Alexander subdued the Caspian region and marched southward. When Parmenio's son Philotas had been executed for complicity in a plot, Alexander sent messengers who murdered Parmenio in Media: Alexander feared a revolt and Parmenio was too powerful to be discharged.

329. Alexander went on into Bactria and overcame the Iranians under Spitamenes only with a great deal of trouble (328). Alexander now commenced **the adoption of Persian dress** and court etiquette. In a drunken fury, he murdered his friend Cleitus who had reproached him. He had 30,000 natives trained in Macedonian fashion for the army. He married the Persian **Roxana.** He began to foster **a belief in his divinity** as the best means of dealing with the Greeks as an absolute ruler and yet without offending their sentiments of liberty. Though the Greeks had deified living men before this, Alexander's move met so much opposition that he dropped it temporarily.

327-324. Alexander was invited into **India** by Taxiles against Porus. In the **battle of the Hydaspes** (326), he defeated Porus and advanced as far as the Hyphasis. Here the army refused to go farther. Alexander, therefore, returned via the Hydaspes and Indus to the Indian Ocean (325). Thence **Nearchus** went back with the fleet to explore the Indian Ocean and Alexander returned through the desert of Gedrosia. They met in Caramania and, after a rest, went on to Susa (324).

324-323. In his policy of fusion of the Greek and Asiatic peoples, Alexander had left in office many of the native governors (satraps); most of these, and many of the Macedonian satraps, were now found to have ruled badly; some had enlisted private mercenary armies. These satraps were replaced, usually with Macedonians; the private armies were ordered disbanded. Pursuing the policy of fusion, Alexander, 80 officers, and 10,000 men married native women. Alexander paid all debts of his men. He ordered all exiles recalled by the Greek cities; to give himself a basis for this interference, contrary to the constitution of the Hellenic League, he ordered the Greek states to recognize him as **son of Zeus Ammon.** At Ecbatana Alexander's closest friend, Hephaestion, died.

323, June 13. Alexander died at Babylon. His exploration had fostered commerce; over 25 cities which he had founded served to Hellenize the east, although his policy of direct fusion failed. The organization of his complex empire he left much as he found it, differing in each area. The officers wished to make the unborn son of Alexander and Roxana king, but the privates preferred a Macedonian, the imbecile **Philip III Arrhidaeus,** son of Philip II. When a son, **Alexander IV,** was born to Roxana, a joint rule was established under the regents Craterus and Perdiccas.

330-322. Athens had recouped her strength under the financier **Lycurgus,** who, among other reforms, established compulsory military training for all young men (*epheboi*). In 330, Demosthenes had been acquitted in the trial brought by Aeschines on the justness of the award to Demosthenes of a civic crown. In 326 Lycurgus fell from power, and in 324, **Demosthenes** was exiled for embezzling some of the money which Alexander's treasurer, Harpalus, brought to Athens. On the report of Alexander's death, Athens, led by the radical orator **Hypereides,** organized a new Hellenic League in central Greece and the Peloponnese. The allies under Leosthenes besieged Antipater in Lamia (winter, 323), and eventually forced his retirement to Macedonia. There Craterus joined him from Asia (322).

322. The Athenian fleet was wiped out forever at **Amorgos.** When the allied army was indecisively defeated at **Crannon** the league broke up. Athens received a Macedonian garrison, took back her exiles, and accepted an oligarchic constitution by which only those possessing 2000 drachmas had the franchise, perhaps 9000 out of 31,000 free citizens. Demosthenes, who had been recalled, fled but was caught and committed suicide.

d. THE WEST DURING THE FOURTH CENTURY

413-405. After the defeat of the Athenian expedition, **Syracuse** made democratic reforms. In 410 many oligarchs, including Hermocrates, were banished. Then Segesta, warring with Selinus (409), called in the **Carthaginians,** who, despite Syracusan opposition, sacked Selinus and Himera (408) and, in a second expedition, Acragas (406).

405-367. Dionysius I secured his election as one of the ten generals in Syracuse and then made himself tyrant. He made peace with the Carthaginian forces, who were suffering from a plague. He distributed the confiscated land of the oligarchs to the poor and enfranchised the serfs. He conquered Catana (403), Naxos, and Leontini (400). In a **first war with Carthage** (398-392), he attempted to drive the Carthaginians out, but failed. However, he reduced the Sicels, and then began the conquest of southern Italy (390-379), where he crushed the Italiote League at the **battle of the Elleporus** (389). But he suffered a severe defeat in a **second war with Carthage** (383-381?), which he failed to retrieve in a third (368).

366-344. On the death of Dionysius, his weak son, **Dionysius II,** succeeded under the regency of his uncle **Dion.** Dion brought in Plato to educate Dionysius, but both were forced out (366). Dion regained Syracuse in 357 and ruled tyrannically until his murder in 354. After two more sons of Dionysius I had seized the power and fallen, Dionysius II returned (347), but the Syracusans called in first **Hicetas,** tyrant of Leontini (345), and then **Timoleon** of Corinth.

344-337. Timoleon defeated the Carthaginians at the **Crimissus** (341) and made peace, with the Halycus River as the boundary (339). The tyrants were expelled from the Greek cities, which formed a military league against Carthage.   Timoleon established a moderate oligarchy in Syracuse, with the priest (*amphipolos*) of Zeus as chief magistrate and a council of 600 composed of rich citizens.   He then retired (337).

338-330.   The Greeks in Italy (Italiotes), hard pressed by the natives, called in first **Archidamus of Sparta** (338), who was killed, and then **Alexander of Epirus** (334).   The latter defeated the natives and made an alliance with Rome, but was finally assassinated during a battle (330).

e. GREEK CULTURE IN THE FOURTH CENTURY

The death of Alexander the Great marked the end of the great age of Greece in literature, philosophy, and art.   **Xenophon** (431–354), though a writer far inferior to Thucydides, wrote an able continuation of his history from 410 to 362, as well as other historical works. The lesser writers of **Middle Comedy** were followed by **Menander** (343–c. 280), the most outstanding of the writers of **New Comedy**, or comedy of manners.   But it was in **oratory and philosophy** that the 4th century was most distinguished.   Of the ten Attic orators the best known were **Lysias** (445–c. 380), **Demosthenes** (384–322), and the advocate of pan-Hellenism, **Isocrates** (436–338).   Philosophy was dominated by the figure of **Socrates** (469–399), executed by the Athenians for atheism.   His greatest pupil, **Plato** (429–347), founded the **Academy** in the grove of the hero Academus, and **Aristotle** (384–321), the pupil of Plato and tutor of Alexander, founded the **Peripatetic** (walking about) school or **Lyceum,** in the grove of the hero Lycus.   In **sculpture** a refined and less vigorous style was preferred by **Praxiteles** (385–c. 320), **Scopas** (400–c. 340), and **Lysippus** (c. 380–c. 318).   The center of activity began to shift to Ionia, as seen in the tomb of Mausolus of Caria (the **Mausoleum**), completed c. 350, and the new **temple of Artemis at Ephesus** (the old one was burned by Herostratus in 356).

(*Cont. p. 75.*)

C. ROME, TO 287 B.C.

1. THE EARLY PERIOD

a. GEOGRAPHICAL FACTORS

Italy is a long, narrow peninsula of which the central portion comprises the mountains and isolated valleys of the Apennines. At the northern end, the Apennines swing west and enclose between themselves and the Alps a wide and fertile valley, Cisalpine Gaul, traversed by the Po, which flows east into the head of the Adriatic. The eastern (Adriatic) coast of Italy is infertile and lacks good harbors, while the Adriatic itself, because of prevailing northerly winds, hindered the penetration of the Greeks. Moreover, the rugged opposing shore of Illyria was occupied by wild and piratic tribes, whose forays constituted a continous threat to commerce. The eastern Italian peoples, therefore, remained backward compared to the western. The western part, though mountainous at the northern end, contains fertile plains in its central portion (Etruria, Latium, and Campania), with good harbors, especially around the Bay of Naples. Its rivers, however (the Arno and the Tiber), are too swift to be readily navigable, so that early civilization sprang up along the coast, while the inland peoples remained rude and simple. The western (Tyrrhenian) Sea is enclosed by the islands of Sardinia and Corsica, the former fertile and rich in metals, the latter a wild seat of pirates. Southern Italy, where the mountains begin to fall away, was a land of pastures where later herds moved seasonably from sea to hills under the charge of slave bands of shepherds, whose brigandage formed a constant threat to travelers. Around the Bay of Tarentum, however, the Greek settlers early found a hospitable welcome, and the western toe of Italy afforded ready access, across the narrow Straits of Messana, to the prosperous island of Sicily, whose rich Greek colonies and lavish crops played an important part in Roman history. The western apex of Sicily in turn led towards Africa and the Phoenician colony of Carthage, which became Rome's chief rival for the control of the western Mediterranean.

b. EARLY POPULATIONS OF ITALY

Traces of Palaeolithic, cave-dwelling Man are found throughout Italy, save in Latium, which was still volcanic. Bones from Liguria, the mountainous area around Genoa, suggest that there were at least two races, a Negroid (Africa) and a later, Cro-Magnon (France). Neolithic Man, after the Ice Age (c. 2500–2000), lived in huts and developed more elaborate stone tombs. He practiced agriculture, and herding, made pots, and eventually used copper. He belonged to the new race (Mediterranean) which occupied the whole Mediterranean Basin at this time and which survived perhaps in the later Ligurians (northwest) and Piceni (east-central), and in the pre-Greek inhabitants of southern Italy (Iapyges) and Sicily (Sicels). During this period Illyrians settled along the east coast, to survive in the Veneti (northeast), the Picentes of central Italy, and the Messapians of Apulia (extreme south).

c. 2000. AN INDO-EUROPEAN PEOPLE of the *centum* branch, closely related to the Greeks, began invading Italy either from Switzerland or from the Danube Valley. They brought with them a type of settlement built on piles, first in the lakes of northern Italy (*palafitte*) and then on dry land (*terramare*), in a regular, rectangular form perpetuated in the Roman camp. They already knew the use of bronze.

c. 1000. THE TERRAMARE PEOPLES had spread their settlements and culture southward through Italy and into Sicily and had come into contact with the maritime peoples of the Aegean world. They probably became the later **Samnite, Sabine,** and **Latin** tribes. In the meantime, perhaps, a related people had entered northeastern Italy from the Danube Valley, bringing with them the use of iron and a more advanced culture known, from the site of the chief excavations, as *Villanovan*. Some archaeologists deny, however, that this advance represented an intrusion of new stock and assume only closer cultural relations with the Danube Valley. These peoples possibly became the **Umbrians** and **Oscans.**

c. 900. THE ETRUSCANS first appeared in Italy, probably by sea from Asia Minor (Lydia?) in consequence of the break-up of the Hittite Empire. They established themselves north of the Tiber in Etruria, probably as a conquering minority among enserfed Villanovan (?) natives. The power was apparently held by an aristocracy of princes (*lucumones*), whose fortified cities (traditionally twelve, though the precise constituents varied from time to time) formed a loose league, and whose elaborate tombs were at first furnished with bronze utensils and armor, then painted and supplied with imported luxuries, notably Greek vases. They extended into the Po Valley and into Latium and Campania until the end of the 6th century, when the pressure of **Celtic invaders** into the Po Valley cut off their northern settlements and the Cumaeans and Hiero of Syracuse broke their control of the sea and Latium revolted. Thereafter they declined until their absorption by Rome during the 4th century. Their culture preserved its identity until the Sullan land distributions in the 1st century so disorganized it that within a century thereafter it had become dead. The Etruscans made no original contribution to Rome save for certain forms (lictors, curule chair, purple-striped toga of office) and a gloomy religion (perhaps the three divinities Latinized as Jupiter, Juno, and Minerva, and certainly the practice of prophesying by consulting the entrails, *haruspicium*), but they first introduced to Rome Greek culture, though in a debased shape, mythology, the heavy Tuscan temple (from the Doric), and perhaps the alphabet.

c. 760. GREEK COLONIZATION began in the Bay of Naples in southern Italy, and in Sicily. The Greeks were prevented from further expansion to the west and north, save for Marseilles (Massilia), by the Phoenicians and the Etruscans. Despite victories over both peoples by the tyrants of Syracuse in the early 5th century, the Greeks never succeeded in dominating all of Sicily or southern Italy. From the 4th century their fortunes declined until their eventual absorption by Rome during the 3d. Nevertheless they not only impregnated these areas with a Greek culture which lasted throughout the Roman period, but, by their contact with Rome during the formative period of her national culture, first through the Etruscans and then directly, so Hellenized the Romans that when the latter conquered the Mediterranean world they respected and extended the Hellenistic civilization and, by absorbing it, preserved for later ages the Greek heritage.

c. THE ROMAN MONARCHY

753. FOUNDATION OF ROME, according to Cicero's contemporary, the antiquarian Varro. Traditionally the founder, Rom-

ulus, was son of a princess of Alba Longa, Rhea Silvia, and the god Mars. The kings of Alba Longa, in turn, were descended from **Aeneas,** a fugitive of the Trojan War and son of the goddess Venus (Aphrodite). This tradition dates, however, from the period when Rome was assimilating Greek culture. Actually during the 8th and following centuries small settlements on the Palatine, Esquiline, Quirinal, and Capitoline Hills united into one, with a common meeting-place in the valley between, the **Forum.** These peoples may have been of different racial stocks, chiefly Latin but partly Sabine, Etruscan, and perhaps pre-Italic. The importance of Rome is less likely to have been economic (trade up the Tiber or across the ford at this point is not attested by archaeology) than military, an outpost of the Latins against the encroaching Etruscans. This would account for the inculcation in the Romans from an early date of habits of obedience, organization, and military drill. The traditions of the four early kings (**Romulus,** 753–715, **Numa Pompilius,** 715–673, **Tullius Hostilius,** 673–641, and **Ancus Marcius,** 641–616) are historically unreliable.

Early government. Rome emerged into history with a king (elective, not hereditary), limited by the existence of a **senate** of 100 elders (*patres*) which was advisory, not compulsory, and by a popular assembly of the clans (*curiae*), the **comitia curiata,** which conferred upon the newly elected king his *imperium* and may have had slight legislative power. There were two classes in the state: **patricians,** who alone could belong to the Senate, and **plebeians.** Most probably the patricians were simply the more prosperous farmers, who for their own advantage organized themselves in *curiae*, set themselves up as a superior class and usurped certain privileges (another theory is that the plebeians were the conquered native people). As a result of the plebeians' lack of power to defend themselves, many attached themselves as clients to patrician patrons, who protected them in return for attendance and service.

The early religion was simple, chiefly the worship of Mars (an agricultural divinity who only later became god of war), and of animistic forces. Religious ceremonies were simple to the point of being magical; by their proper performance the divine power (*numen*) inherent in gods or objects was compelled to act, and failure to get results indicated some fault in the ceremony.

c. 616. Tarquinius Priscus (616–578) and his successors, **Servius Tullius** (578–534) and **Tarquinius Superbus** (the Proud, 534–510), may represent the Etruscan domination in Rome and emerge more clearly than their predecessors. Tarquin the First was a great builder (*Cloaca Maxima*, Temple of Jupiter Capitolinus, *Circus Maximus*). To weaken the patrician influence, he is said to have increased the Senate to 300. He fought successfully against Sabines, Latins, and Etruscans. **Servius Tullius,** traditionally of slave and Latin descent, fought against Veii and brought Rome into the **Latin League.** His chief achievement, traditionally, was to substitute for the hereditary clans a new military division into **classes** and **centuries,** based on wealth and arms (cf. reforms of Solon in Athens). It may be, however, that this reform should really be dated about 450 and, in any case, the surviving (and conflicting) descriptions of his arrangements probably portray them in the state which they reached after the 3d century B.C. Upon this arrangement depended a new assembly, the **comitia centuriata.** Since group voting was taken over from the *comitia curiata*, the wealthy, who though few in numbers constituted the majority of the centuries, controlled this assembly as, presumably, the patricians had the former. The last, **Tarquin the Proud,** was expelled in a revolt which according to tradition was led by **L. Junius Brutus** and was due to the rape of Lucretia by Sextus Tarquinius, son of the king.

2. THE EARLY REPUBLIC

The early constitution: two annual **consuls,** originally called *praetors* (generals), held equally the undivded *imperium* of the king; either could prevent the other from acting, but could not force him to act. They had absolute command of the army in the field, including power over life and death; in the city they were provided with *coercitio*, a sort of summary police power, but with slight civil and no criminal jurisdiction. They were elected by the *comitia centuriata*, but their *imperium* was conferred by the *comitia curiata* (*lex curiata*), later represented by 30 lictors.

The judicial system: cases of high treason were handled by the *duouiri perduellionis*; all other criminal cases of which the state took cognizance were handled by the *quaestores parricidii* (investigators of murder), later known simply as *quaestors*. From their collecting of fines, the quaestors became the main financial officers of the state, and in this capacity they became attached to the consuls as comptrollers; later they lost their judicial functions. Civil cases were usually handled by arbitration, but gradually the consuls came to take a larger part, until in 367 there was created a special officer (*praetor*).

In time of crisis the Senate could restore unity of command by instructing the consuls to appoint a **dictator** (*magister populi*), who appointed as his assistant a master of the horse (*magister equitum*); the dictator had absolute power in all fields, but had to resign when his task was completed, and in no case could remain in office for more than six months.

The plebs seem already to have had an organization of their own, the *concilium plebis*, with its own officers, *tribunes* (? originally commanders of the tribal regiments) and *aediles* (custodians of the temple of Ceres on the Aventine, where were kept the plebeian treasury and archives). When the first 17 rustic tribes were organized shortly after the foundation of the republic (the four urban tribes are ascribed by tradition to Servius Tullius, but may be later), the *concilium plebis* was reorganized on the basis of these; some time later a *comitia tributa* of the whole people was organized on the same basis, perhaps to break up the power of the hereditary clans (cf. Cleisthenes, at Athens). It is uncertain how long the *concilium plebis* remained distinct from the *comitia tributa*; in the later republic the difference was merely technical. A resolution of the plebs alone was called a *plebiscitum*, and was originally binding only on the plebeians, as opposed to a *lex* of the entire *populus*, adopted in a *comitia*.

At the beginning of the republican period, Rome was probably the dominant power in the Latin League, but apparently lost this position because of the continued Etruscan pressure; the next two centuries (to c. 280) were characterized externally by Rome's conquest of the primacy in Italy and internally by the struggle of the oppressed plebs, of which the richer members desired social and political equality with the patricians, while the poorer wanted simply protection from unjust treatment at the hands of the patrician magistrates.

509. TRADITIONAL DATE OF THE FOUNDING OF THE REPUBLIC. L. Junius Brutus and L. Tarquinius Collatinus (husband of Lucretia) became consuls. Almost all of the history of the first century of the republic, including the names of the first two or three decades of consuls, is unreliable, but it is not yet possible to establish the truth. The dates given here are those of Cicero's contemporary Varro, adopted by Livy. They are subject to errors of up to ten years in the 1st century of the republic, gradually decreasing to become practically certain from c. 300.

A **lex Valeria de prouocatione** is said to have been passed by the *consul suffectus* (filling another's unexpired term), L. Valerius Poplicola, guaranteeing citizens in Rome (not on military service) the right of appeal to the *comitia centuriata* from a consul who proposed to execute or flog them; probably a retrojection of later legislation, but such a right was recognized by the **Twelve Tables.**

508. A Treaty with the Carthaginians recognized Carthage's exclusive interests in Africa and Rome's in Latium. Doubt has been cast on the genuineness of this treaty, but probably unjustly.

Lars Porsena of the Etruscan Clusium attacked Rome and probably restored the Etruscan domination for a short time, although Roman tradition claimed he had been turned back by the exploits of **Horatius Cocles** (defense of the *pons sublicius*, or wooden Tiber bridge), Cloelia, and Q. Mucius Scaevola.

496. The dictator A. Postumius, in the **battle of Lake Regillus,** defeated the Latins, who, with the help of Aristodemus of Cumae, had some time before freed themselves from Etruscan rule by the **battle of Aricia.**

494. The plebeians, oppressed by debt, seceded to the **Sacred Mount** (probably the Aventine). The patricians were forced to make some concessions before the plebs would return. The latter further protected themselves by swearing to the *leges sacrae*, by which they bound themselves to avenge any injury done to their officials, the **tribunes,** the aediles, and the *decemuiri stlitibus iudicandis*. These officials were therefore called *sacrosanct*. They were not officials of the state, but officers of a corporate group within the state. But because of the unanimous support of the plebs they had *de facto* great powers, which were never legalized but became gradually respected by custom. The basis of the tribunes' powers was the *ius auxilii*, by which they could intervene to save anyone threatened by the action of a magistrate. This *intercessio* against a specific act of a magistrate developed later (when the tribunes secured admission to the Senate) into the right of interposing a veto against any proposed law or decree. They presided over the *concilium plebis*. The original number of the tribunes was 2 or 4; it eventually became

10. The **aediles** handed the fines imposed by the tribunes or the *concilium*, and through the use of this money came to have control of the free distributions of corn to the poor and over the repair of public buildings, etc., which was later extended into a general police power. The *decemuiri stlitibus iudicandis* conducted trials in which the status of persons as slaves or freedmen was in question.

493. A Treaty of Sp. Cassius with the Latin League provided that booty was to be equally divided; new territory to be colonized in common; the rights of *connubium* and *commercium* (to contract valid marriages between members of different states and to carry on commerce with full legal protection) were restored as they had been before Rome's break with the league (c. 508). The reason for this peace was certainly the increasing pressure of the attacks of the neighboring Volsci and Aequi. The Hernici were later admitted to the alliance on terms of equality with the other two members (486).

491. Gn. Marcius Coriolanus traditionally tried to bribe the plebeians with free grain into giving up the tribunate; when he failed and was summoned to trial, he fled to the Volsci and led them against Rome, but was finally turned back by the prayers of his mother and wife.

486. The consul Sp. Cassius attempted to make himself tyrant but was executed. This much may be true, but the story that his method was a proposed division of the public land, which was of insignificant extent for a long time, is probably a retrojection from the Gracchan era.

477. Battle of the Cremera. War had broken out with the Etruscan Veii (483), which was supported by Fidenae, a town controlling the upper Tiber and thus essential to Rome. A large number of Fabii took up a position on the Cremera to prevent the two cities from joining their forces, but were annihilated by the Veientines. Traditionally, only one of 300 escaped. A peace was made in 474.

458. L. Quinctius Cincinnatus, called from his field to assume the dictatorship, rescued a Roman army and defeated the Aequi, who had pressed into the valley of the Algidus.

451. Agitation of the plebs for codification of the law to curb the arbitrariness of the patrician magistrates led to the creation of **ten patrician decemvirs** in place of consuls. According to legend, an embassy had been sent to Athens in 454 to procure the laws of Solon for study. The first decemvirs published ten tables, but since these proved insufficient new decemvirs were created in 450 and drew up two additional tables. Thenceforth the **Twelve Tables** constituted the fundamental law of Rome until the 2d century. Tradition alleges that this decemviral board continued illegally in office in 449 under the extreme patrician **Appius Claudius.** When he attempted to get for himself by false legal process the maiden Virginia, her father Virginius stabbed her and the plebeians seceded to the Aventine and Sacred Mounts. The decemvirs had to abdicate and Appius committed suicide.

448. The moderate patrician consuls Valerius and Horatius passed a series of **Valerio-Horatian laws** weakening the patrician power. Traditionally, these (1) made the *plebiscita* as valid as *leges*; (2) compelled all magistrates, including the dictator, to allow appeals from their decisions; and (3) affirmed the inviolability of the tribunes and also the aediles. All these changes are probably mere retrojections of later reforms. Two more quaestors were added specially for the military treasury, making a total of four. Though patricians, they were elected in the *comitia tributa*, and in 421 the quaestorship was opened to the plebeians. The tribunes acquired the right of taking auspices (necessary before any public business and later convenient as a means of blocking action) and the privilege of sitting on a bench inside the senate, though near the door.

445. A law (plebiscite?) of the tribune Canuleius allowed marriage between patricians and plebeians, the children to inherit the father's rank.

444. As a compromise in the face of agitation that the consulate be opened to plebeians, **6 (?3) military tribunes with consular power,** who might be plebeians, were substituted for the consuls. Two patrician *censors* were also created to hold office for 5 (4?) years, later reduced to 18 months every 5th year. They had no *imperium*, but only a *potestas*, but because usually older and distinguished ex-consuls, they came to outrank even consuls. Their tasks gave them importance, since they made up the citizen lists for tax and military purposes (the *census*), enrolled senators (*lectio senatus*) and knights (*recognitio equitum*), and examined into public morals (*regimen morum*), so that at the end of their term they could perform the ceremony of purification for the state, the *lustrum*, a word which came to be applied to their five-year cycle. They also

made up the state budget, handled its property, and let out contracts for public works.

439. Traditionally, Sp. Maelius was put to death by Servius Ahala, master of the horse for the dictator Cincinnatus, because his free distribution of grain to the people seemed an attempt at a tyranny.

431. The dictator A. Postumius Tubertus decisively defeated the Aequi at the Algidus and drove them out of the valley. The Volsci were then continually driven back and are said to have made peace in 396.

426. Fidenae, which, with Veii, had declared war in 438, was destroyed by the dictator Mamercus Aemilius and the master of the horse A. Cornelius Cossus; thus Veii was forced to make peace for 20 years (425).

405-396. In the **siege of Veii,** tradition alleged that, because the army had to be kept in the field all winter, pay for the troops was introduced. The dictator M. Furius Camillus finally took the town; it was destroyed, and, since the Latins had not contributed to the siege, the territory was annexed directly to Rome and organized in four new tribes. From this time on Rome really outweighed its ally, the Latin League; the Hernici had long been inferior to the other two.

390. **Rome was sacked by the Gauls** under Brennus, who defeated the defending army at the **Allia** on July 18. According to tradition the Gauls held all of Rome except the Capitol, which was only saved by the geese. Their withdrawal after seven months is attributed to Camillus, but they were probably bought off. The Latins and Hernici took advantage of Rome's plight to break off their alliance.

384. The patrician M. Manlius Capitolinus was, according to tradition, convicted of aspiring to a tyranny by releasing plebeian debtors at his own expense, and was executed by being thrown from the Tarpeian Rock.

367. **Licinio-Sextian Laws.** After ten years of agitation the tribunes C. Licinius and L. Sextius secured the passage of reform measures: (1) some sort of relief was granted to debtors; (2) the amount of public land which one person could hold was limited to 500 iugera (1 iugum = ⅝ acre). This provision is almost certainly a retrojection from the Gracchan era. (3) The practice of giving a consular *imperium* to military tribunes was abolished, and one consulship was opened to the plebs. Tradition incorrectly states that both consulships were opened to the plebs, and that one of them had to be filled by a plebeian. At the same time a third *praetor* was created, to handle the judicial functions of the other two chief magistrates, who thenceforth were usually known as consuls. Two patrician *curule aediles* were created, with functions much like the plebeian aediles. The plebeians were soon admitted to all offices, the last being the religious colleges of *pontifices* and *augures*, by the **lex Ogulnia** of 300. As a result of these changes, a new nobility of office-holding families, both patrician and plebeian, grew up, and the patriciate lost all significance. This nobility soon became quite exclusive, so that a *novus homo* (a man without office-holding ancestors) had great difficulty in obtaining an office.

367-349. Four wars were waged against the Gauls, who made incursions from Cisalpine Gaul into central Italy. In them are supposed to have been fought the single combats against Gallic champions of T. Manlius Torquatus (361) and M. Valerius Corvus (349). Peace was finally concluded c. 334.

362-345. Wars with the peoples immediately around Rome. The Hernici and the revolting Latin cities were forced to rejoin the Latin League on severer terms; southern Etruria was brought under Roman supremacy; and the Volsci and Aurunci were reduced, thus putting Rome in contact with the Samnites.

348. Second treaty between Rome and Carthage; some sources and some modern authorities call this the first treaty.

343-341. THE FIRST SAMNITE WAR was started by a request for aid from the Samnite tribes in the Campanian plain against the hill tribes. After minor Roman victories the war ended in a draw.

340-338. THE LATIN WAR began with the revolt of the Latin cities from the league and their demand for complete equality. In the course of the war, P. Decius Mus sacrificed himself for the victory of his army. The consul T. Manlius brought the war to a close by the **victory of Trifanum.** The Latin League was dissolved and its members made dependent on Rome without even *commercium* and *connubium* among themselves. In Rome their inhabitants received private rights but not the vote (*ciuitas sine suffragio*, later called *latinitas*). Some cities ceded land for settlement of Romans, some were made into Roman colonies, others were made dependent states.

339. **Leges Publiliae,** passed by the plebeian dictator Q. Publilius Philo, gave *plebiscita* the force of law provided they obtained the subsequent consent of the senate (*auctoritas patrum*); for regular *leges* it was provided that this consent should now be given in advance, as a pure formality.

326-304. **THE SECOND SAMNITE WAR** began when Rome made Fregellae a colony and the first pro-consul (an ex-consul whose *imperium* was extended for carrying on a military command), Q. Publilius Philo, captured Naples (327). The Romans had the support of the Apulians and Lucanians, and later of certain Sabellian cities. After initial successes the consuls Sp. Postumius and T. Veturius were surrounded in the **Caudine Forks** and forced to surrender with their whole army. The Romans only slowly recovered Campania, but in 312 the censor Ap. Claudius began the great military road, the **Via Appia,** from Rome to Capua to secure Campania. The northern Etruscans joined Rome's enemies but were defeated at **Lake Vadimo** in 310. In 308 the peoples of central Italy, Umbrians, Picentini, Marsians, etc., attacked Rome. The Romans countered by using their first war-fleet in the Adriatic. The Samnites were defeated by M. Fulvius and L. Postumius in 305. In 304 peace was made, slightly to Rome's advantage in that she secured undisputed hegemony of Campania.

313. A law of the consul Poetilius (*lex Poetilia*) secured insolvent debtors against personal imprisonment if they surrendered their property entirely to their creditors.

312. **Appius Claudius** (later Caecus, "the blind"), as censor, is said to have distributed freedmen not holding land among all the tribes, but in 304 they, and freedmen of small landed property, were confined to the four urban tribes. This may reflect later debates as to the disposition of freedmen. In 304 a freedman of Appius, Gnaeus Flavius, is said to have made public the rules of legal procedure (*legis actiones*), to which he had access as clerk to the magistrates. This completed the work begun by the decemvirs in protecting the poor from manipulation of the law by the rich.

At about this time (or perhaps earlier, after the Gallic sack), the Roman army was reorganized so that in place of a solid phalanx with the long thrusting spear (*hasta*) the legion consisted of small groups, maniples of 120 men in two centuries (now purely titular), arranged in echelon in three lines (*hastati* and *principes* with the throwing javelin, *pilum*, and only the rearmost *triarii* with the spear) for greater mobility in mountainous areas.

During the ensuing years, Rome secured the Apennines by colonies, Sora, Alba Fucens, Carsioli, and Narnia, and built the *Via Flaminia* north to Narnia and the *Via Valeria* to Alba Fucens.

298-290. THE THIRD SAMNITE WAR was a final effort of the Samnites, aided by the Lucanians, Gauls, and Etruscans, to break the power of Rome. Their capital, Bovianum, was taken in 298, but their army managed to combine with the Gauls, only to be defeated in 295 at **Sentinum,** where a second Decius Mus secured a Roman victory by self-sacrifice, perhaps in fact the only instance. The Gauls scattered, the Etruscans sued for peace in 294, and the Samnites finally made peace as autonomous allies, though the colony of Venusia was planted in the south to watch them, as well as Minturnae, Sinuessa, and Haria farther north. The Sabines, northeast of Rome, were annexed and given Latin rights.

285-282. The Romans, despite defeats, annihilated the Gallic Senones, crushed the Etruscans at Lake Vadimo and Populonia, and occupied the Greek cities in Lucania: Locri, Croton, and Thurii. This advance brought on the war with Tarentum and Pyrrhus.

287. The **lex Hortensia,** passed by the dictator Q. Hortensius, fully equated *plebiscita* with *leges* by requiring the *auctoritas patrum* for the former to be given in advance as well as for the latter; its passage was brought about by another secession of the plebs, this time to the Janiculum. The plebs had thus achieved complete legal equality with the patricians, but the old problem remained in the oppression of the poor by the rich patricio-plebeian nobility, which was in full control of the *concilium plebis* and the *comitia tributa* because, since the voting was by tribes, only the rich members of the more distant tribes could afford to come to the meetings in Rome. Further, in the assemblies all initiative was in the hands of the presiding magistrates, and these were now almost always from the nobility and under the control of the Senate. As the problems of government became more complex with the expansion of Rome the control of the Senate became still more effective.

Rome had now established her supremacy throughout central Italy. Her relations with the other communities may be summarized as follows:

(1) *Municipia* retained their own municipal administration and enjoyed only the private rights (*connubium* and *commercium*) of Roman citizenship, not the franchise or right of holding office (*ciuitas sine suffragio*).

(2) *Coloniae* were settlements established by Rome for military purposes, usually on land taken from the conquered peoples. Smaller ones, Roman, were real garrisons and their settlers retained full citizenship. At first they may have been administered directly from Rome. Larger ones reflected real attempts to relieve surplus population and included both Latins and Romans, the latter accepting only Latin citizenship, or *ciuitas sine suffragio*. They may have had some local government from the beginning. Ultimately colonies came to have administrations closely modeled on the Roman, with two executive magistrates (*duumuiri*) and a senate or *curia* whose members were called *decuriones*.

Whatever the original form of government of the various *municipia* may have been, it tended to approximate the oligarchical model of Rome and the *coloniae*, with a small executive, often four (*quattuoruiri*), and a *curia*. Moreover, recent study suggests that this general pattern of municipality may not be at all early, may, in fact, date only from Caesar's municipal reforms, and that before that both *municipia* and *coloniae* were governed by officials sent out from Rome, as was certainly the case with *municipia* which, by revolt, were deprived of self-government (e.g. Capua later).

(3) *Ciuitates foederatae* were independent allies (*socii*) of Rome, whose obligations were regulated by treaty. They enjoyed freedom from direct interference in their affairs and from taxation (*libertas et immunitas*) and usually provided auxiliary troops or ships rather than legionaries. But their foreign relations were determined by Rome and, in fact, they suffered considerable control.

(4) There were, in addition, groups or communities which did not have a civic organization and which, consequently, were administered under various names (*fora, conciliabula, uici, pagi*) either directly from Rome, by *praefecti*, or by neighboring cities to which they were attached as *attributi*. (*Cont. p.* 85.)

D. THE HELLENISTIC WORLD

1. CULTURAL DEVELOPMENT

The Hellenistic Age was characterized politically by the **atrophy of the city-state.** The cities of Greece were dominated increasingly by their richer or better educated members and the mass of the population lost power. In their external relations the cities either passed under the control of the various monarchs or joined together in leagues, whose attempts at representative federal government marked an advance in government which unfortunately bore no further fruit during the Roman period. Athens was a university town, respected for its past grandeur but of little political weight after 262. Sparta, however, played a lone and considerable hand in the Peloponnese. To offset the decay of Greece itself, the Hellenistic Age witnessed the **spread of Greek culture** by the conquests of Alexander and his successors as far as the Indus Valley, the creation of Greek cities throughout Asia, and the development of monarchical governments. In the new Greek cities, municipal administration and public building reached a high level, as at Priene (Asia Minor) or Alexandria (Egypt). **Social experiments** ranged from state control of the grain supply (Athens) or distribution of grain to citizens (Samos) to extreme agrarian reforms at Sparta. Private or royal munificence benefited the cities on a grand scale, and the cities themselves substituted for political rivalry that of the splendor of games, buildings, and honors. The administration of the three chief kingdoms was conditioned by their background. In **Macedon** the army, representing the Macedonian people, retained considerable influence, and the king was never so absolute as his Asiatic *confrères.* The **Seleucids** developed a system of provincial administration and of communications based on the Persian satrapies; but their capital, Antioch, never attained the excellence of Egypt's Alexandria and its Hellenism was strongly affected by Syrian emotionalism. The **Ptolemies** administered Egypt as had the Pharaohs, as a state monopoly. They granted a privileged position, however, to Macedonian settlers and to the city of Alexandria, which was kept apart from the rest of Egypt as a Greek city, though it contained also a large Jewish population, for whom, during the 3d century, a Greek translation was made of the Hebrew *Bible,* called the *Septuagint* from the 70 elders traditionally responsible for it. Alexandria was distinguished by its excellent administration and its magnificent buildings, among which were a lighthouse (*pharos*) and an academy of scholars (*museum,* temple of the Muses) with a magnificent library.

The economic life of the eastern Mediterranean was much stimulated by unification in Greek hands, by the opening of new areas, and by improved navigation and communications. The cities became very rich. In particular, the opening of the treasures of the Near East vastly increased the amount of gold and silver in circulation. Two countries were, however, adversely affected. Greece, naturally poor, was drained of men by the opportunities offered for trade or mercenary soldiering in Asia, and could no longer compete with the more fertile areas now opened for exploitation. Egypt's resources, though ample for her self-contained economy, were exhausted by the expenditures of the Ptolemies in their attempt to create an Aegean empire. Nevertheless, in general, the period was one of complacent prosperity throughout the eastern Mediterranean.

Under the great librarians of Alexandria, **Zenodotus** (c. 280), **Aristophanes** of Byzantium (257–180), and **Aristarchus** (217–145), philology, textual criticism, and kindred subjects replaced creative writing. But great advances were attained in science by such men as **Euclid** the geometrician (c. 300), **Eratosthenes** the astronomer and geographer (c. 240), and **Archimedes** the physicist (287–212, in Syracuse). **Literature** became imitative, artificial, and overburdened with learning, as in the poetry of **Callimachus** (c. 260), or the epic *Argonautica* of **Apollonius Rhodius** (295–214). Only the pastoral achieved a delicate and spontaneous freshness in the poems of **Theocritus** (c. 270, from Syracuse). The Attalids, notably Eumenes II, tried to make Pergamum into an intellectual rival of Alexandria, but their capital became famous chiefly for its **Pergamene school of art,** whose exaggerated style is best seen in the friezes of the Altar of Pergamum. Another school flourished in the prosperous island of Rhodes. Much of Hellenistic art dealt with simple subjects of

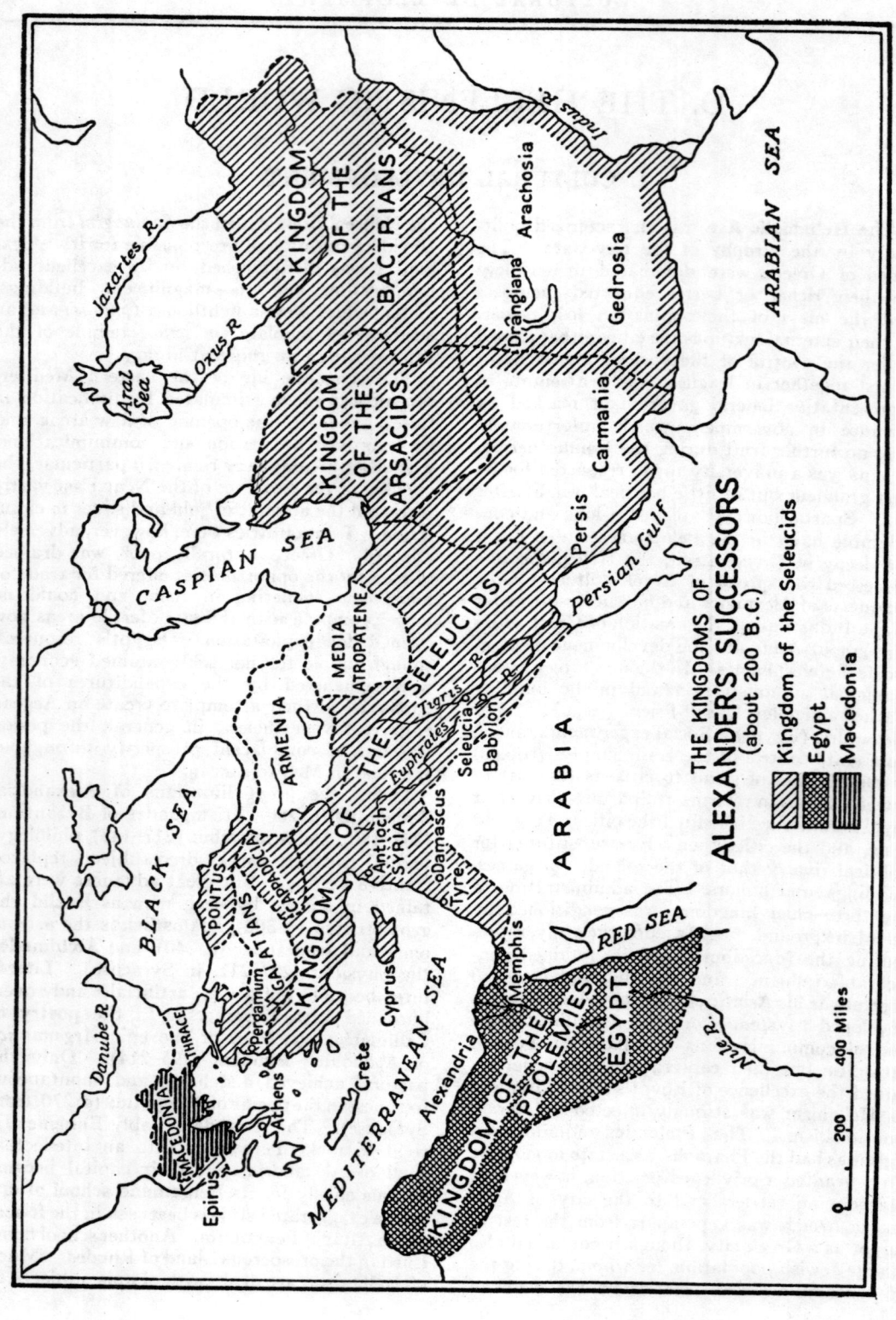

THE KINGDOMS OF
ALEXANDER'S SUCCESSORS
(about 200 B.C.)

Kingdom of the Seleucids
Egypt
Macedonia

0   200   400 Miles

daily life in a realistic fashion, as in the charming pottery figurines from Tanagra, in Greece.

In **philosophy,** the Academy continued the Platonic tradition but with increasing skepticism about the possibility of attaining truth. The **Peripatetics** devoted themselves almost wholly to scientific and historical studies. Two new schools, however, answered the spiritual needs of the time. **Stoicism** was founded by **Zeno** (336–264), a half-Phoenician from Cyprus, who taught in the Painted Porch (*stoa poikile*) at Athens, and **Epicureanism** by **Epicurus** (342–270), who withdrew from the world into his garden. Both sought the same end, a mind which would be so self-sufficient through inner discipline and its own resources that it would not be disturbed by external accidents. The Stoics sought this undisturbed state of mind (*ataraxia*) by modifying the Cynic asceticism to a doctrine of neglect of outward honors and wealth and devotion to duty. A belief that the world was ruled by a universal reason in which all shared led them to a humanitarian view of the brotherhood of men which transcended national, racial, or social differences. This in-ternationalism and the doctrine that the ruler should embody divine reason allowed them to support monarchical government. The Epicureans sought the same end by following the Cyrenaics in advocating an inactive life (*apraxia*) and a moderate, not an excessive, self-indulgence. To free the mind from wrong, they attacked religion and superstition and adopted the atomic metaphysics as a mechanical explanation of the universe.

In **religion,** the Hellenistic Age witnessed a loss of belief in the simple Greek pantheon and a turning to more emotional oriental worships, like those of **Cybele,** the Great Mother of Asia Minor, the Persian **Mithra,** or the Egyptian **Isis.** A fatalistic view of external events led to the personification of Fortune (*tyche*) as a goddess. And a combination of flattery, legalism (since a god could always rule a city without changes in the constitution), skepticism (since many considered that the gods were originally famous men), and real gratitude for the benefits of government introduced the worship of rulers, both dead and living, which the Macedonian monarchs alone refused.

2. THE WARS OF THE DIADOCHI

322–315. When **Perdiccas** became regent for Philip III Arrhidaeus, the other generals, Antipater, Antigonus, Craterus, and Ptolemy, refused obedience. Perdiccas was murdered when he attempted to dislodge Ptolemy from Egypt, but his general **Eumenes** defeated and slew Craterus in Asia Minor (321). Antipater and Ptolemy at Triparadeisus in Syria agreed that Antipater should be regent. Antipater sent Antigonus to dislodge Eumenes, who took refuge in the hills (320). When Antipater died (319), he left **Polyperchon** as regent, but Ptolemy defied him and annexed Syria. Antigonus seized Phrygia and Lydia. Polyperchon gave Eumenes command of the troops in Cilicia. Antipater's son, **Cassander,** seized the Piraeus, garrisoned it, and left Demetrius of Phalerum as virtual dictator of Athens (317). Cassander took Macedon from Polyperchon (317), executed Olympias and Philip Arrhidaeus, when they attacked him, and imprisoned Roxana with her son Alexander IV, both of whom he put to death in 310. In the meantime, Antigonus, after a drawn **battle at Paraetacene** (317), had defeated Eumenes in Gabiene (316) and executed him. Ptolemy in Egypt, Antipater, and Lysimachus in Thrace formed a coalition against Antigonus (315).

315–307. **Antigonus** seized Syria, but his son, Demetrius, was defeated at Gaza (312) by Ptolemy, who had already occupied the Cyclades (314) and the Peloponnese (313). Ptolemy then sent **Seleucus** to capture Babylon from Antigonus. An attempted settlement in 311 merely allowed Antigonus to continue fighting Seleucus, Cassander to secure the throne of Macedon (above), and Ptolemy to continue his expansion in the Aegean. Antigonus sent Demetrius to Athens, whence he expelled Demetrius of Phalerum and restored the democracy (307).

307. ANTIGONUS I, MONOPHTHALMOS ("one-eyed") or Cyclops, and **Demetrius I Poliorcetes** ("besieger") took the title of king, whereupon Ptolemy and Seleucus, Cassander, and Lysimachus did the same. The unity of Alexander's empire was thus openly ended.

306. Demetrius crushed Ptolemy in a naval battle off Cyprian Salamis but Ptolemy repelled a land attack by Antigonus. Demetrius failed to reduce Rhodes by a year's siege (305–304), but relieved Athens from the **Four Years' War** waged by Cassander (307–304). He then revived the **Hellenic League** of Philip (303).

301. BATTLE OF IPSUS (in Phrygia). The allies, Cassander, Lysimachus, and Seleucus, but not Ptolemy, finally crushed and slew Antigonus. Demetrius, who had been recalled by Antigonus, escaped to Corinth. By the division of spoils, Seleucus was given Syria, Lysimachus western and central Asia Minor, Cassander kept Macedon, but his brother Pleistarchus received southern Asia Minor. Ptolemy, however, seized Coele-Syria.

299. Pleistarchus was driven out by Demetrius, and Cassander himself died in 298. His eldest son, Philip IV, died also, so that two younger sons, Antipater and Alexander V, divided his realm.

295. Demetrius, after a bitter siege, recovered Athens, where one Lachares had made himself tyrant. He then murdered Alexander V (294) and took Macedon. He mastered northern and central Greece save for Aetolia.

288. A coalition was formed against Deme-trius, and Lysimachus and King Pyrrhus of Epirus drove him out of Macedon. He attempted a campaign in Asia Minor, but finally Seleucus captured him in Cilicia (285).

283. Demetrius died in captivity, leaving a son in Greece, Antigonus.

281. Seleucus defeated and slew Lysimachus at the **battle of Corupedium** and became master of Asia Minor. When he tried to seize Macedon, however, he was assassinated by Ptolemy Ceraunus, who acquired control of Macedon. Ptolemy, in turn, was slain in an invasion of Celts (279).

279. The **Celts** ravaged Macedon, defeated the Greeks at Thermopylae, and reached Delphi. A second band ruled Thrace until 210, while a third crossed to central Asia Minor and established the **Kingdom of Galatia.**

276-275. Meanwhile, Antigonus recovered Macedon for himself, founding a dynasty that lasted till 168.

3. SICILY TO THE ROMAN CONQUEST

317-289. AGATHOCLES made himself tyrant of Syracuse in consequence of a civil war (c. 323–317) in which he, as democratic leader, expelled the oligarchs with Carthaginian aid and divided their property among the poor. He successfully defended himself against the neighboring cities and the exiled oligarchs until these appealed to Carthage.

311. The Carthaginian general **Hamilcar** defeated Agathocles at the **Himera River** and besieged Syracuse. In 310, Agathocles slipped across to Africa, where he maintained himself until 307. But his army, under his son, was annihilated during his absence.

305. Agathocles came to terms with Carthage and the oligarchs, and took the title of king. In the meantime the Tarentines had made peace with the Samnites (c. 320) and Rome (304), but were hard pressed by the Lucanians.

302. When a Spartan commander, Cleonymus, failed to relieve them, the Tarentines called in Agathocles. He also failed to accomplish much and died at Syracuse in 289, bequeathing their freedom to the Syracusans, who restored the democracy. Certain of the Campanian mercenaries of Agathocles, calling themselves **Mamertines** ("sons of Mars"), seized Messana.

282-275. The **Tarentines,** angered by Roman occupation of towns in southern Italy, destroyed a Roman fleet which, in violation of the treaty of 304, had passed the Lacinian promontory. They then drove the Romans from Thurii. When Rome declared war, they called in Pyrrhus. Upon his departure in 275, the Greeks of southern Italy remained under Rome, while those of Sicily passed under Carthaginian power, save for Syracuse.

269-216. Hiero II made himself tyrant of Syracuse and defeated the Mamertines at Mylae. He took the title of king (265), and joined the Carthaginians in besieging the Roman force which occupied Messana in 264. But when he was defeated and besieged in Syracuse, he made peace with Rome (263). At the end of the First Punic War all Sicily save Syracuse and a few other pro-Roman cities passed into Rome's possession. Syracuse was reduced in 211 during the Second Punic War.

4. MACEDON AND GREECE TO THE ROMAN CONQUEST

290. Emergence of the **Aetolian League,** a military federation in western Greece.

It had a council with proportional representation and a semi-annual assembly. Affairs were handled by a committee of 100 *apokletoi* and a single general (*strategos*) in wartime. The league expanded into Phocis (254) and Boeotia (245) and dominated Greece from sea to sea. It also included Elis and part of Arcadia (245) and made an alliance with Messene, thus separating Sparta from the Achaean League.

280. Formation of the **Achaean League,** consisting of twelve towns in the northern Peloponnese. It had a general (two until 255), a board of ten *demiourgoi*, a federal council with proportional representation of members. There was also an annual assembly of all free citizens. After 251, Aratus of Sicyon dominated its policy and was *strategos* (general) in alternate years. He extended it to include many non-Achaean cities, especially Corinth (243).

276-239. ANTIGONUS II GONATAS ("knock-kneed"?) had to repel an invasion by **Pyrrhus of Epirus** (274-273). Pyrrhus was then called into Greece by the pretender Cleonymus, who sought to oust King Areus (309-265) from Sparta. Pyrrhus was slain at Argos by the Argives and Antigonus (272). Antigonus established tyrants in several cities of the Peloponnese and made peace with the Aetolian League.

266-262. Ptolemy I of Egypt stirred up Athens and Sparta to wage the **Chremonidean War** (from Chremonides, an Athenian leader) against Antigonus. Areus of Sparta was defeated and killed at the Isthmus (265) and, when Ptolemy failed to give energetic aid, Athens was obliged to surrender after a two-year siege (262). Antigonus garrisoned several strong points of Attica and imposed a moderate oligarchy on Athens.

258 (?256). Antigonus defeated Ptolemy in a naval **battle off Cos** and took the Cyclades, though he had to reconquer them later in the **battle of Andros** (245).

c. 252. Antigonus' governor of the Peloponnese, Alexander, revolted and held the peninsula until his death (c. 246).

251. Aratus of Sicyon recovered that city from Antigonus' tyrant, and then joined the Achaean League, which he soon dominated.

245-235. Sparta had fallen into a serious economic crisis because of the excessive concentration of land and wealth in the hands of a few. Coined money had been introduced by King Areus. The number of full citizens who could contribute to their mess-tables (*syssitia*) had fallen to 700. When **King Agis IV** (244-240) tried to redistribute the land into 4500 equal lots, the great landowners executed him.

Cleomenes III, who had married Agis' widow, became king (235).

241. Antigonus sent the Aetolian League to ravage the Isthmus.

239-229. Demetrius II succeeded his father, Antigonus. He protected · Epirus against Aetolia, so that the latter broke with Macedon and made an alliance with Achaea. Demetrius attacked it in the **War of Demetrius** (238-229), but was recalled by invasions from the north (233). Argos expelled the pro-Macedonian tyrant Aristomachus and joined the Achaean League (229), while Athens asserted her independence.

229-221. Antigonus III Doson ("going to give," i.e. always promising) succeeded his cousin Demetrius as guardian of the latter's nine-year-old son, Philip, whom he deposed in 227 to become king himself. He made peace with Aetolia and drove the barbarians out of Macedon.

228-227. Cleomenes defeated the Achaeans under Aratus. He then seized the power in Sparta, redivided the land, and enfranchised 4000 *perioikoi* and abolished the *ephorate*. With an increased citizen army, he reduced Aratus to appeal to Antigonus (225).

222. Antigonus formed a new Hellenic League and crushed Cleomenes at the **battle of Sellasia** (222). Cleomenes fled to Egypt. Antigonus abolished the Spartan kingship, restored the ephors, and forced Sparta into his league.

221-178. Philip V, son of Demetrius II, succeeded Antigonus III. At his instigation the Hellenic League assembled at Corinth to declare

219-217. The War of the Allies, or Social War, against the Aetolians because of the latter's piracy. The Aetolians allied with Elis and Sparta, where an anti-Macedonian faction tried to recall Cleomenes. When he was slain in Egypt, the Spartans nevertheless restored the dual kingship. Philip ravaged Elis (219-218), molested the Aetolian sanctuary of Thermum, and laid waste Laconia.

217. Rhodes and Egypt negotiated the **Peace of Naupactus** between the discouraged Aetolians and Philip, who wanted freedom to act against Rome.

215-205. In the **FIRST MACEDONIAN WAR** Philip V of Macedon attempted to help Hannibal and the Carthaginians against Rome, but a Roman fleet in the Adriatic prevented him from crossing to Italy and the Romans secured the support of the Aetolian League and Pergamum (212), as well as of Elis,

Mantinea, and Sparta (210). Sparta in particular, after a period of attempted social reform under King Cheilon (219), had risen to power under Machanidas, regent for the young King Pelops. When the Achaean League under Philopoemen (since the murder of Aratus in 213) slew Machanidas at Mantinea (207), Nabis became regent and soon, by deposing Pelops, king. The Greeks came to terms with Philip in 206 and Rome accepted the settlement by the **Peace of Phoenice** (205).

203-200.   Philip, allied with Antiochus III against Egypt (203), began operations in the Aegean, but was defeated by Rhodes and Attalus of Pergamum in the **battle of Chios** (201).

200-196.   The **SECOND MACEDONIAN WAR** arose from an appeal by Attalus and Rhodes to Rome (201). When Philip refused to keep the peace, all the Greeks joined Rome (200-198), and Flamininus defeated Philip at **Cynoscephalae** (197), and proclaimed the freedom of Greece at the Isthmian Games (196). Flamininus was forced to check Nabis of Sparta (above), who had carried through agrarian reforms (207-204) and expanded his power in the Peloponnese, especially by acquiring Argos (198). He now lost Argos and much of Laconia, and gave control of his foreign policy to Rome (195). Upon the murder of Nabis (192), Sparta was forced into the Achaean League by Rome, and Messene and Elis soon joined, so that the league controlled all the Peloponnese.

192-189.   The **Aetolians declared war on Rome** and secured the support of Antiochus III with a small force. The Achaeans and Philip supported Rome. The Romans drove Antiochus back to Asia in the **battle of Thermopylae** (191), and the Aetolians were finally made subject allies of Rome by M. Fulvius Nobilior (189).

189-181.   Philopoemen humbled Sparta but lost his life in suppressing a revolt in Messenia (183). His successor in the Achaean League, Callicrates, was subservient to Rome and allowed Sparta to revive.

179-167.   **Perseus** became King of Macedon on the death of his father Philip V. He had already persuaded Philip to execute his pro-Roman brother Demetrius, and now Eumenes II of Pergamum laid charges against him at Rome.

171-167.   In the **THIRD MACEDONIAN WAR** Perseus was crushed by Aemilius Paullus at **Pydna** (168). He later died in captivity in Italy and the Antigonids came to an end. Rome made Macedon into four unrelated republics, paying a moderate yearly tribute (167). In Aetolia, 500 anti-Romans were slain. One thousand hostages, including the historian Polybius, were taken from Achaea to Italy.

149-148.   The **FOURTH MACEDONIAN WAR** was begun by Andriscus, who pretended to be a son of Perseus. On his defeat, Macedon became a Roman province (148).

146.   When the Achaean hostages had returned (151) and Callicrates had died (149), the Achaean League attacked Sparta, but was crushed by the Roman general Mummius (146). The Roman Senate ordered Mummius to abolish the leagues, substitute oligarchies for all democracies, sack Corinth, and place Greece under the supervision of the governor of Macedon. This marked the end of Greek and Macedonian independence, though some Greek states retained autonomy for a long time.

5. THE SELEUCID EMPIRE AND PERGAMUM

305-280.   **SELEUCUS I NICATOR** ("conqueror"), after securing his position against Antigonus (310-306) and assuming the royal title (305), ceded India to **Sandracottus** (Chandragupta) for 500 elephants (304-303). Though Ptolemy took Coele-Syria (301), Seleucus secured Cilicia from Demetrius (296-295). Seleucus failed to reduce **Mithridates I of Pontus,** but got control of western Asia Minor on the defeat of Lysimachus (281).

280-261.   Antiochus I Soter ("saviour") succeeded upon the murder of Seleucus. He fought and finally defeated the Galatians (279-275) by terrifying them with his elephants.

In the **Damascene** (280-279) and **First Syrian** (276-272) **Wars** he lost, to Ptolemy II, Miletus, Phoenicia, and western Cilicia.

263-241.   **Eumenes I** made himself virtually independent of Antiochus as ruler of Pergamum, where his uncle, Philetarus, had ruled as governor first for Lysimachus and then for the Seleucids.

261-246.   **Antiochus II Theos** ("god"), son of Antiochus I, secured the support of Antigonus II and Rhodes against Egypt in the **Second Syrian War** (260-255). The succeeding peace restored to Antiochus: Ionia (including Miletus), Coele-Syria, and western Cilicia (255).

250-230. Diodotus I declared himself independent King of Bactria. In 248-247, Arsaces I of the nomad Parni established himself in the province of Parthia.

246-226. SELEUCUS II CALLINICUS ("gloriously victorious"), son of Antiochus II by his divorced wife, Laodice I, succeeded. Berenice II, daughter of Ptolemy II, whom Antiochus had married in 252, provoked the

246-241. Third Syrian War ("Laodicean War" or "War of Berenice") in favor of her infant son. Though she and her son were murdered in Antioch, her brother, Ptolemy III, invaded Asia and ultimately forced Seleucus to surrender the coasts of Syria and southern Asia Minor (241).

241-197. Attalus I, Soter ("saviour"), who succeeded his father's cousin, Eumenes I, as ruler of Pergamum, took advantage of Seleucus' difficulties to secure for himself western Asia Minor by crushing the Galatians near Pergamum (230), after which he took the title king and received the surname *Soter*.

237. Seleucus attacked Antiochus Hierax ("falcon"), a younger son of Laodice, whom Seleucus in 241 had recognized as ruler of Asia Minor. Hierax secured the aid of Mithridates II of Pontus and the Galatians. The Galatians crushed Seleucus at Ancyra (236).

c. 235. Arsaces II (Tiridates), second ruler of the Parni (246-c. 211), also seized the opportunity to conquer Parthia and Hyrcania and found the Parthian kingdom (p. 82). He made peace with Diodotus II of Bactria (c. 230) and an expedition of Seleucus against him was ineffective. Arsaces likewise converted Armenia into an independent kingdom.

229-226. Attalus I of Pergamum drove Hierax out of Asia Minor (229-228), after which Seleucus drove him out of Syria (227) to Thrace, where he died (226).

226-223. Seleucus III Soter or Ceraunus ("thunderbolt"), son of Seleucus II, was murdered during a war with Attalus I (224-221).

223-187. ANTIOCHUS III, THE GREAT, brother of Seleucus III, regained from Attalus most of the territory lost since 241. He recovered the Mesopotamian provinces from the revolting governor, Molon (221). But in the

221-217. Fourth Syrian War, despite initial successes, he finally retained on the Syrian coast only Seleucia, the port of Antioch.

209-204. In a number of campaigns, Antiochus reduced the Parthian Arsaces III Priapatius to vassalship, made an alliance with Euthydemus, who had usurped the Bactrian throne of Diodotus II, and even secured the submission of the Indian rajah Sophagasenus. Thus he restored the Seleucid Kingdom to its former extent.

201-195. The Fifth Syrian War resulted from the treaty which Antiochus III had made with Philip V of Macedon in 203. The war was decided in 200 by Antiochus' victory of Panium. After several campaigns in Anatolia, Antiochus secured from Egypt most of Coele-Syria and southern Asia Minor (save Cyprus). Although Eumenes II Soter of Pergamum (197-159), son of Attalus I, induced Flamininus to order Antiochus out of Asia Minor, Antiochus did not heed, but confirmed his conquests by a peace with Egypt (195).

192-189. WAR WITH ROME. Antiochus' continued disregard of the Senate led to a war in which he was driven from Greece (191) and his fleet was defeated at Myonnesus (190). The Roman army entered Asia Minor and defeated Antiochus himself at Magnesia (190). In the peace (189), Antiochus paid a large indemnity, lost his fleet, and surrendered Asia Minor, which was divided between Rhodes and Pergamum. This defeat led to the complete breaking away of Armenia (under Artaxias) and of Bactria, where a succession of Greek rulers preserved Hellenism until the invasions of the Sacae (c. 150-125). An offshoot of the Bactrian Kingdom flourished in the Punjab (c. 175-c. 40), and though its rulers adopted Buddhism (c. 150) it introduced Hellenistic art and ideas into India.

187-175. Seleucus IV Philopater ("loving his father") succeeded his father Antiochus, and during his reign the empire gradually recovered strength. Meanwhile Eumenes II of Pergamum fought against Prusias I of Bithynia (186) and Pharnaces I of Pontus (183-179).

175-163. Antiochus IV Epiphanes ("god manifest") succeeded upon the murder of his brother Seleucus. Though friendly to Rome, he was prevented by the Romans from concluding successfully his war against Egypt (171-168). The Romans also weakened Rhodes by making Delos a free port (167). Insurrection of the Jews under Judas Maccabeus, after Judaism had been declared illegal (168). The Jews attained religious freedom in 164 and, after a series of wars, established political independence in 142 (p. 31). Upon his death, Antiochus left as king his young son **Antiochus V Eupater** ("of a noble father"), under the regent Lysias (163–162).

162–150.   Demetrius I Soter ("saviour"), son of Seleucus IV, returned from Rome to eject Antiochus V, but was slain in 150 by a pretender, **Alexander Balas** (150–145), who claimed to be the son of Antiochus IV and was supported by Attalus II Philadelphus ("loving his brother") of Pergamum (159–138) (who had succeeded his brother Eumenes II), by Ptolemy VI of Egypt, and by Rome. Ptolemy, however, soon invaded Syria in favor of Demetrius II, the son of Demetrius I, who slew Balas in 145.

145–139.   Demetrius II Nicator ("conqueror") won several victories (140) over Mithridates I of Parthia, who had seized Media (c. 150) and Babylon (c. 141). Mithridates, however, captured Demetrius by treachery in 139. In the meantime, a son of Alexander Balas, Antiochus VI Epiphanes Dionysus ("god manifest"), had held Antioch from 145 to 142, when he was expelled by the mercenary leader Diodotus, who took the title of King Tryphon (142–139). He was expelled by a brother of Demetrius II.

139–127.   Antiochus VII Euergetes Eusebes Soter Sidetes ("benefactor, pious, savior") did much to restore the Seleucid power. However, after several victories over Phraates II of Parthia, he was finally defeated and killed at Ecbatana (127).

138–133.   Attalus III Philomater ("loving his mother") **of Pergamum,** a son of Eumenes II, succeeded his uncle, Attalus II. In his will, he bequeathed his kingdom to Rome, apparently in order to protect his subjects from absorption by their neighbors. Rome had to suppress the pretender Aristonicus before it could make the Kingdom of Pergamum into the Province of Asia (129).

129–125.   Demetrius II was sent back to Syria

by Phraates II in 129 and was slain in 125 by a pretender with Egyptian support, Alexander Zabinas. Demetrius' son, **Seleucus V,** assumed the diadem but was put to death at once by his mother Cleopatra Thea.

125–96.   Antiochus VIII Epiphanes Philomater Callinicus "Grypus" ("god manifest, loving his mother, gloriously victorious, hooknosed"), a younger son of Demetrius II, reigned with Cleopatra until her death (c. 120). The pretender, Alexander Zabinas, was killed in 123. In 117 Antiochus was forced into retirement by a half-brother, **Antiochus IX Philopater, "Cyzicenus"** ("loving his father, of Cyzicus"), son of Cleopatra and Antiochus VII. After an indecisive series of battles (113–112), they divided the realm in 111 and both reigned until Antiochus VIII was murdered in 96 by his favorite, Heracleon.

95–64.   Seleucus VI, son of Antiochus VIII, defeated and killed Antiochus IX (95). The son of the latter, **Antiochus X,** defeated and killed Seleucus VI, but the latter's brother, Demetrius III, seized Damascus. Another son of Antiochus VIII, **Antiochus XI,** was defeated and killed, but his brother Philip I continued the war with Antiochus X. The latter was killed in 93 fighting the Parthians in Commagene. Demetrius III and Philip I engaged in civil war until Demetrius was captured by the Parthians in 88. **Antiochus XII,** another son of Antiochus VIII, seized Damascus, which he held until he was killed on an expedition against the Nabataeans in 84. An insurrection expelled Philip I from Antioch, and Tigranes of Armenia seized Syria and held it until he was defeated by Lucullus in 69. **Antiochus XIII,** son of Antiochus X, was installed at Antioch (68) and soon had to fight with Philip II, son of Philip I. The Arabian prince of Emesa slew Antiochus XIII by treachery in 67; Philip was unable to secure his rule. In 64 Pompey made Syria a Roman province.

6. PARTHIA

331–323.   Rule of Alexander the Great.

312–282.   Seleucus I founded the dynasty of the Seleucids, ruling over Babylonia and Syria; he built the city of Seleucia near Ctesiphon on the Tigris.

249–247.   Arsaces I founded the Kingdom of **Parthia,** including at first only Parthia and Hyrcania, between the Seleucid Kingdom in the west and the Bactrian Kingdom in the east.

247–212.   Arsaces II (Tiridates I), though defeated by Seleucus II (238), was able to establish the independence of Parthia.

212–171.   Arsaces III withstood the attacks of Antiochus III the Great in 209; he was followed by Arsaces IV (Priapatius) and Arsaces V (Phraates I).

171–138.   Mithridates I conquered Babylonia and Media from the Seleucids; later he added to his kingdom Elam, Persia, and parts of Bactria, thus founding the Parthian Empire. Ctesiphon-Seleucia became the capital.

138-124. **Phraates II** (138–127) defeated Antiochus VII in Media (129), and as a result the Seleucids were permanently excluded from the lands east of the Euphrates; but he died in battle fighting the Tochari (the *Scythians* or *Sacae* of the Greeks), a tribe driven forth from Central Asia by the Yue-chi. The kingdom was devastated and Artabanus I (127–124) fell likewise fighting against the Tochari.

124-88. **MITHRIDATES II, THE GREAT,** defeated the Scythians and also Artavasdes, King of Armenia Major. In 92 he made a treaty with Rome.

88-70. Parthia suffered a collapse and was greatly reduced in territory by Tigranes of Armenia.

70-57. **Phraates III** restored order, but was not strong enough to resist the Roman advance, led by Lucullus and Pompey.

57-37. **Orodes I** defeated Crassus at **Carrhae** (53) and regained Mesopotamia.

37-32. **Phraates IV** defeated Antony in 36, but could not prevent him from conquering Armenia in 34. After a period of dynastic disturbances

A.D. 51-77. **Vologesus I,** after a war with Rome, obtained recognition of his brother Tiridates as King of Armenia (63), thus establishing an Arsacid dynasty in that country. In Parthia itself the utmost confusion prevailed after 77, with two or more kings (all of them little known) ruling at the same time and constantly challenged by other claimants.

(*Cont. p.* 124.)

7. BACTRIA

328-323 B.C. **Bactria under the rule of Alexander.** A mutiny of Greek auxiliaries after Alexander's death was crushed at once by Perdiccas.

323-302. **Bactria under Perdiccas** (d. 321), Antipater (d. 319), Eumenes (d. 316), Antigonus (d. 301). In his wars against Antigonus, Seleucus I conquered the eastern provinces (311–302).

302-c. 250. **Bactria under the Seleucids.**

c. 250-c. 139. **Diodotus,** the satrap of Bactria, made himself an independent ruler and conquered Sogdiana. He founded a dynasty that withstood the attacks of the Seleucids.

After the defeat of Antiochus III at Magnesia (190), Euthydemus and his son Demetrius began the conquest of the Indus Valley. But Eucratides made himself King of Bactria (c. 170) while Demetrius was founding a kingdom in the Punjab. About 150 the Tochari (*Scythians* or *Sacae*) occupied Sogdiana, and about 139 Bactria. The line of Eucratides maintained itself in Kabul until about 40 B.C., but most of the region was ruled by Scythian dynasties.

8. PTOLEMAIC EGYPT, TO THE ROMAN CONQUEST

305-283. **PTOLEMY I SOTER** ("saviour"), the son of Lagus (hence the "Lagid" house), had been governor of Egypt since 323 and king since 305. He had seized Coele-Syria in 301, and acquired from Demetrius, Pamphylia and Lycia (296–295) and Caria and the island of Cos (286). Founding of the Museum at Alexandria.

285-246. **PTOLEMY II PHILADELPHUS** ("lover of his sister") adopted a Pharaonic practice by marrying his sister Arsinoe II (276). He explored the upper Nile and extended his power along the Red Sea and into northern Arabia (278) for commercial purposes.

280-272. In the **Damascene War** (280–279) and **First Syrian War** (276–272), he suffered initial defeat from Antiochus I and the revolt of his half-brother Magas in Cyrene. But he finally defeated both and secured Miletus, Phoenicia, and western Cilicia. He subsidized Pyrrhus against Antigonus (274), aided Athens and Sparta in the Chremonidean War (266–262), and incited Alexander II of Epirus to attack Macedon (264). He likewise incited Eumenes of Pergamum to revolt from Antiochus (262) and supported the seizure of Ephesus (262–259) by his own son, Ptolemy "the Son." These activities brought Antiochus II, Antigonus II, and Rhodes together to wage

260-255. The **Second Syrian War** (260–255), in which Antigonus defeated Ptolemy in the **battle of Cos** (258 or 256). Though by the resulting peace he lost Cilicia and western Pamphylia (255), he later recovered the Cyclades (250) and also Cyrene (c. 248), which had become independent in 258.

246-221. Ptolemy III Euergetes ("benefactor") supported his sister Berenice II in the **Third Syrian War** (246–241) and acquired the coasts of Syria and southern Asia Minor, as well as some Aegean ports, including Ephesus. But he lost the Cyclades to Antigonus through the **battle of Andros** (245). Height of the Ptolemaic power.

221-203. Ptolemy IV Philopater ("loving his father") was a weak monarch, dominated by his minister, Sosibius. In the **Fourth Syrian War** (221–217) he at first lost much of the Syrian coast to Antiochus III, but the victory of **Raphia** (217) brought the recovery of all save the port of Seleucia.

203-181. Ptolemy V Epiphanes ("god manifest"), a young boy, succeeded his father. While the Egyptian natives revolted in the Delta (201–200) Antiochus III attacked him in

201-195. The **Fifth Syrian War**, as a result of which Ptolemy retained only Cyprus of his Asiatic possessions. When he came of age (195), he succeeded in suppressing the native revolts.

181-145. Ptolemy VI Philomater ("loving his mother") followed Ptolemy V under the regency of his mother, Cleopatra I. In consequence of Ptolemy's cowardice during the war with Antiochus (171–168), the people of Alexandria forced him to associate his brother, **Ptolemy VII** in the rule. Rome prevented Antiochus from capturing Alexandria (168). When Ptolemy VI was expelled by his brother (164), the Roman Senate restored him and gave Cyrene and Cyprus to Ptolemy VII, who, however, secured only Cyrene (163). Ptolemy VI expelled Demetrius I from Syria (152–151) and supported Demetrius II against Alexander Balas (147–145), but was slain in the war.

145-116. Ptolemy VII Euergetes II ("benefactor") or Physcon ("fat-bellied") reunited the empire after his brother's death and restored order. At his death, he left Cyrene separately to his son Apion, who willed it to Rome in 96, though it was not actually annexed until 75. Another son, Ptolemy IX, received Cyprus, which was ultimately bequeathed to Rome and annexed in 58.

116-47. Ptolemy VIII Soter II ("savior") or Lathyrus, son of Ptolemy VII, was eventually expelled by his brother **Ptolemy IX Alexander I** (108–88). The people of Alexandria, however, slew Ptolemy IX and restored Ptolemy VIII (88–80). **Ptolemy X Alexander II,** son of Ptolemy IX, succeeded but was at once slain by the people of Alexandria (80), who set up an illegitimate son of Ptolemy VIII, **Ptolemy XI Auletes ("flute-player")** or **Neos ("new") Dionysos.** Though expelled in 58, he bribed the "first triumvirate" (p. 96) to send Gabinus to restore him (55). On his death in 51, he left his throne jointly to his children, **Cleopatra VII** and **Ptolemy XII** (51–47). When Ptolemy expelled his sister, Caesar forced her restoration (48) and, since Ptolemy died during the fighting about Alexandria (48–47), Caesar joined with Cleopatra a younger brother, **Ptolemy XIII** (47–44), whom Cleopatra murdered on Caesar's death (44).

47-30. Cleopatra VII sought to restore the Ptolemaic Empire by winning to her support Caesar and later Antony (41), with whom she sought to establish a Hellenistic monarchy (36). Upon Antony's suicide after Actium (31), she sought to fascinate the young Octavian, but failed and committed suicide rather than adorn his triumph (30). This brought to an end the last of the Hellenistic monarchies.

E. ROME, THE MIDDLE AND LATER REPUBLIC

1. THE PUNIC AND MACEDONIAN WARS

During the 3d and 2d centuries B.C. Rome's internal history was marked by the consolidation of the rule of the patricio-plebeian aristocracy. The extension of Rome's external relations and the consequent complexity of her internal problems raised questions impossible of settlement in the unwieldy and uninformed *comitia*, which came more and more to surrender the initiative in government to the Senate, composed as it was of ex-magistrates, urban, military, and provincial, who had the necessary background and experience. They, in their turn, had come to regard government and office as a prerogative of themselves and their children. This distinction was furthered by the increased opportunities for wealth opened to the ruling group through conquest and provincial government. Since custom, confirmed by a *lex Claudia* of 218, forced senators to invest chiefly in land, they built up large estates, partly by renting public land, which through long tenure they came to regard as their own, and partly by acquiring the holdings of poorer farmers. The poorer farmers, in turn, subjected to the devastations of the Hannibalic Wars, and to the demands of long-term military service abroad, found it difficult to exist, and tended either to emigrate, remain in the army, or congregate as an idle mob in Rome. The political, social, and economic problems thus raised finally caused the ruin of the senatorial republic by the Gracchan troubles.

Rome's position in Italy became increasingly strong during these centuries. In consequence, the senatorial class began to act with increasing arbitrariness toward Rome's Italian allies and to impose on them the burdens of conquest while reserving the rewards for themselves or using them as sops to the Roman citizens. The citizens, who found that citizenship paid in privilege, in some share in the public land, in free entertainment at Rome, eventually in a government-controlled food supply, and probably in the indirect benefits of bribery and corruption, became unwilling to extend the franchise. The discontent of the Italians found ultimate expression in the Social War, which won for them Roman citizenship.

In the Mediterranean, Rome, without really so desiring, was forced to extend her sway, *imperium*, more and more widely. The Senate, like such landed aristocracies as Sparta or the English Tories, was not imperialistic. Nor, on the whole, was the *populus*. But the fear of attack from strong powers led Rome to attack such as might threaten her, and experiments in allowing her rivals a feeble and divided independence (*diuide et impera*, divide and rule) proved unsatisfactory. Either her creations quarreled among themselves and forced her to intervene, or they became the willing or unwilling prey of stronger powers. Hence Rome was forced into annexation. But conquest led ultimately to the corruption of both Senate and people, to the creation of a financial group, the *equites*, interested in imperialism, and to opportunities for self-aggrandizement on the part of generals and governors. In consequence, the discontented peoples of Asia supported Mithridates, the equestrian class became a possible rival to the Senate, and the way was opened for the domination of the state by military commanders.

282-272. WAR WITH PYRRHUS arose from an attack by the Tarentines on Thurii and their destruction of a Roman fleet which entered the harbor in violation of a treaty forbidding Roman warships from sailing east of the western promontory of the Gulf of Tarentum. Tarentum called in **Pyrrhus of Epirus** (p. 79). In 280, with an army of 25,000 men and 20 elephants, he won a hard-fought victory over the Romans at **Heraclea.** Though the Bruttians, Lucanians, and Samnites then joined Pyrrhus, the Senate, instigated by Ap. Claudius, the blind ex-censor, rejected the peace offers of Pyrrhus' ambassador Cineas. In 279 Pyrrhus won his second victory at **Ausculum,** but with losses so great that he exclaimed, "Another such victory and we are lost" (a "Pyrrhic victory"). Pyrrhus then crossed to Sicily. Rome rejected peace with Pyrrhus and made one with his enemy, Carthage. Pyrrhus returned to Italy after two years but was defeated at **Beneventum** in 275 and returned to Greece. His general, Milo, then surrendered Tarentum to the Romans (272), who destroyed its military resources, but left it its own municipal administration. Rome rounded out her subjugation of Italy by the recapture in 270 of Rhegium from the Mamertines and the reduction of the Bruttians, Lucanians, Calabrians, and Samnites.

264-241. THE FIRST PUNIC WAR arose from the fact that certain of the Campanian mercenaries, or Mamertines who were holding Messana against Hiero II of Syracuse (p. 78), appealed to Rome while others appealed to Carthage. The Roman assembly, though the Senate hesitated, sent a fleet and army which found the Carthaginians already in possession. The Romans drove them out and were in turn besieged by the Carthaginians. In 264 the consul Ap. Claudius Pulcher relieved them, but failed to take Syracuse. During the following year two Roman armies invaded Sicily and Hiero shifted to a Roman alliance.

262. The Romans defeated the Carthaginian general Hanno and took Agrigentum (Acragas).

260. After losing the consul Cn. Cornelius Scipio with 17 ships off the Lipara Islands, the Romans under C. Duilius won the naval victory of Mylae, west of Messana.

257. The Romans sent 330 ships under the consuls M. Atilius Regulus and L. Manlius Vulso to carry troops from Sicily and effect a landing in Africa. This fleet defeated the Carthaginians off the south coast of Sicily at **Ecnomus** (256) and landed just east of Carthage. Regulus, left with half the troops, offered such stringent terms that Carthage continued her resistance under the leadership of the Spartan mercenary Xanthippus.

255. **Xanthippus captured Regulus** and part of his army. The Romans sent a fleet which took off the remainder, but was lost in a storm, as happened again two years later.

254. Rome seized Panormus and, in 251, defeated the new Carthaginian general, **Hasdrubal,** son of Hanno. On the advice, traditionally, of Regulus, who had been sent to negotiate an exchange of prisoners with the Carthaginians, they refused to do so and Regulus returned to die in Carthage.

249. The consul Claudius Pulcher, after throwing the sacred chickens overboard because they refused to give a good omen by eating grain, lost his fleet at **Drepana.** The Romans were unable to dislodge the Carthaginian **Hamilcar Barcas** ("lightning") from the strong promontory of Eryx, whence his ships harried their coasts.

241. At the **Aegates Islands,** off Lilybaeum, the Romans annihilated the Carthaginian fleet. Carthage received peace on condition of the surrender of Sicily and the payment of 3200 talents in ten years. Rome left eastern Sicily to Hiero of Syracuse but undertook to govern the remainder herself as her **first province,** regularly constituted in 227.

241-217. Some time during this period the *comitia centuriata* suffered a radical reform, probably because the centuries had lost their military significance. The centuries of *equites* lost the right of first vote, which was hereafter determined by lot among the centuries of the first class. The number of centuries was increased to harmonize in some way with the tribal divisions and divided into seniors and juniors. Perhaps there was one century each of seniors (over 46) and juniors from each of the five classes in each of the 35 tribes, i.e. $2 \times 5 \times 35 = 350$, $+ 18$ of knights and 5 of propertyless persons $= 373$. Though the reform passed for democratic, its basis remained one of property and age, since the first class (wealthy) probably had a proportion of centuries (almost one fifth) in excess of its proportion of population and since the elders, naturally fewer than the younger, had nearly half of the centuries. At the same time (241) the final two tribes were added, making a total of 35. Thereafter new citizens were enrolled in the existing tribes, so that these lost their geographical significance.

238. **Rome seized Sardinia,** rich in minerals, during a revolt of the mercenaries in Carthage. It later (227) formed a province with Corsica.

235. The first recorded closing of the temple of Janus since its foundation by Numa indicated that Rome was at peace with all nations.

229-228. **The first Illyrian War.** Rome sent a fleet of 200 vessels to suppress the pirates of Queen Teuta. The grateful Hellenes admitted the Romans to the Isthmian Games and the Eleusinian Mysteries and thus recognized her as a civilized power. In a second war (219), Rome defeated Teuta's successor, Scerdilaidas.

225-222. Large hordes of **Celts** moved from the Po Valley to Etruria. The Romans surrounded and slew a considerable body at **Telamon** (225) and gradually reduced the Insubres, around Milan. In the **battle of Clastidium** (222) M. Claudius Marcellus slew a Gallic chief in single combat. The Romans founded the fortress colonies of Placentia, Cremona, and Mutina, and extended the *Via Flaminia* from Spoletum to Ariminum.

218. A **lex Claudia** forbade senators to own a

ship of more than 300 *amphorae* (225 bushels), only enough to care for their farm produce; they were thus forced to invest in land rather than in industry or commerce.

218-201. THE SECOND PUNIC WAR arose from Rome's jealousy of Carthaginian expansion in Spain, where Hamilcar Barcas (236–228) and, after his death, his son-in-law Hasdrubal (228–221) had established themselves. Rome made Carthage promise not to attack Saguntum or Emporiae, Greek foundations south of the Ebro, or to cross that river. After the assassination of Hasdrubal, his twenty-five-year-old successor **Hannibal** destroyed Saguntum in 219 (perhaps without the full support of his home government), the conservative element in which was jealous of the power and independence of the Barcids. Carthage, however, refused to disown him.

218. Hannibal executed a daring land march through southern France and by an undetermined Alpine pass advanced into the Po Valley. The Roman consul **P. Cornelius Scipio** reached Marseilles with his fleet too late to stop Hannibal. He therefore sent his brother Cnaeus with most of the fleet to Spain and returned himself to meet Hannibal, who had perhaps 26,000 men and a few elephants, at the **Ticinus,** a branch of the Po. He was defeated, as was his colleague soon after at the **battle of the Trebia,** another branch of the Po. As the Romans took refuge in Placentia and Cremona, the Gauls rallied to Hannibal.

217. Hannibal crossed the **Apennines** west of two new Roman armies posted at Ariminum and Arretium. The consul C. Flaminius followed him from the latter place and was led into an ambush and annihilated at **Lake Trasimene.** The Romans, terrified, appointed **Quintus Fabius Maximus** dictator. Hannibal moved east again to the Adriatic and then south, in hopes of a general Italian rising. The cities, however, refused to receive him and Fabius, without joining battle (hence his title *Cunctator*), harried his army. The Romans were dissatisfied with this policy.

216. The consuls L. Aemilius Paullus (conservative) and C. Terentius Varro (popular) led an army of 86,000 Romans and Italians against Hannibal. Consuls, when together, now commanded on alternate days, and Varro, on his day, unwisely attacked Hannibal at **Cannae,** in Apulia. The Romans, including Paullus, were practically annihilated, though Varro escaped. When, during the same year, a legion was destroyed in Cisalpine Gaul, a rift appeared in the allegiance of Italy to Rome.

Capua deserted, along with the Samnites, Lucanians, and other peoples of southern Italy. The Romans checked all public grief, refused Hannibal's terms, and sent out an army under M. Claudius Marcellus. Carthage made alliances with Philip V of Macedon, and Hieronymus, grandson of the lately deceased (217) Hiero of Syracuse. Hannibal wintered at Capua.

215. **Marcellus,** now pro-consul, defeated Hannibal at **Nola** and forced him into Apulia. The government at Carthage gave Hannibal almost no support and he was unable to receive aid from his brother Hasdrubal in Spain.

218-211. **Publius Scipio** had rejoined his brother Cnaeus in Spain and between them, with varying fortune, they kept Hasdrubal busy and stirred up Syphax, King of western Numidia, against Carthage.

215-205. By using a few troops for the **First Macedonian War** (p. 81), the Romans prevented the irresolute Philip from helping Hannibal. In 211 they organized a Greek alliance, under the lead of the Aetolians (**Treaty of Naupactus**) including even Thracians, Illyrians, and Pergamum, against him. After her Greek allies quit in 206, Rome was forced to make the disadvantageous **Peace of Phoenice.**

214-210. Marcellus carried the war into Sicily, where he defeated a Carthaginian army and sacked Leontini. Though Hieronymus had been murdered, the Syracusans renewed their alliance with Carthage (213), but, despite the ingenious defensive machinery devised by Archimedes, **Marcellus reduced Syracuse** in 211. The rest of Sicily quickly fell again under Roman control.

212. Hannibal seized **Tarentum,** save for the citadel. He compelled the Romans to raise the siege of Capua, defeated two armies, but retired again to Tarentum. Both Scipios were slain in Spain by the Carthaginians, who drove the Romans to the Ebro.

211. Hannibal returned to relieve Capua. The Romans this time refused to abandon the siege, so he marched to within a mile of Rome, but as they did not falter, he again had to retire. Capua surrendered to Rome and was deprived of all self-government. As Hannibal seemed unable to weaken Rome or reduce the citadel of Tarentum, his prestige sank and his Italian allies went back to Rome.

210. **P. Cornelius Scipio,** son of the late general, was sent to Spain with proconsular powers, though only 25 and a mere exaedile. In Sicily, the Romans reduced Agrigentum.

209. Scipio captured New Carthage in Spain. Marcellus defeated Hannibal and Fabius reduced Tarentum. In the following year, Hasdrubal evaded Scipio and reached the Po Valley.

207. In the **battle of the Metaurus River** (Sena Gallica), the consul M. Livius Salinator, supported by his colleague C. Claudius Nero, who had made forced marches from the south, where he was holding Hannibal in check, defeated and slew Hasdrubal. Hannibal withdrew to Bruttium.

206. Scipio drove the Carthaginians out of Spain and made a secret treaty with their ally Massinissa, King (in 208) of eastern Numidia. He returned to Italy and was elected consul under age, for 205.

204. Scipio took a force to Africa and, with Massinissa's help, defeated the Carthaginians and Syphax (203). Carthage was forced to recall Hannibal, who attempted in vain to negotiate.

202. In the **battle of Zama,** Scipio annihilated the Carthaginian army, though Hannibal escaped.

201. Carthage accepted Rome's terms: surrender of Spain and all other Mediterranean islands; transfer of the kingdom of Syphax to Massinissa; payment of 200 talents a year for 50 years; destruction of all except ten warships; promise not to make war without Rome's permission. Scipio, now entitled *Africanus*, celebrated a splendid triumph. The unfaithful Italian allies were in part forced to cede land, in part deprived of independence. Rome founded many colonies in southern Italy.

205-178. **Spain was divided into two provinces** (197), Hither Spain (*Hispania Citerior*) in the Ebro Valley, and Farther Spain (*Hispania Ulterior*) in the south around Gibraltar and the Guadalquivir River. Constant warfare, however, was necessary to subdue the Lusitanians.

200-191. The resubjugation of the Po Valley required considerable effort. Rome founded colonies and built the *Via Aemilia* as a continuation of the *Via Flaminia* from Ariminum to Placentia.

The newly acquired overseas territories could not be governed either from Rome or, as had been just possible in Sicily, by creating new praetors. This last method was tried in Spain, but it became more economical to retain the governors there for two years so that their

imperia were "prorogued" for another year. The device of extending an *imperium* without renewing the corresponding magistracy was apparently first employed to keep the experienced commander Philo in command against Naples. As the number of provinces grew, this custom was regularly applied to the consuls and praetors, who came to expect a profitable year (for governorships were reduced to this) in a province to recoup themselves for the heavy expenses entailed in securing election (bribery) or incident to the tenure of office (games, etc.). A further effect of the transmarine provinces was that it became necessary to maintain a standing army. In the second and first centuries B.C. the soldier not only could not return to his farm for harvest or the winter — that had long been impossible — but he could not look for a discharge at the end of a year of service, for the government could not afford to send new armies each year across the sea. Though the fiction of annual re-enlistment and the requirement of a property qualification were maintained, the soldiers became in fact professional and served for 20 years or more. They could not then return to farms which would have passed into other hands or fallen into decay, and so they had either to be settled in colonies or allowed to congregate in Rome. As they looked to their commander for rewards in war and protection of their interests at home, they shifted their loyalty, and oath (*sacramentum*), from the state to him. It is therefore extraordinary that for nearly a century the corporate class consciousness of the *nobiles* was sufficient to prevent disloyalty to the senatorial government.

200-197. Rome was drawn into the **SECOND MACEDONIAN WAR** by an appeal from Pergamum, Rhodes, and Athens, which were harried by Philip and Antiochus III of Syria. The Senate, fearful of Philip's growing power, frightened an unwilling *comitia centuriata* into declaring war by visions of a renewed invasion of Italy. T. Quinctius Flamininus, supported by both the Aetolian and Achaean Leagues, finally (197) defeated Philip at **Cynoscephalae** in Thessaly and forced him to make peace (196) on the following terms: surrender of Greece; payment of 1000 talents in 10 years; reduction of his forces to 5000 men and 5 ships; promise not to declare war without permission of Rome. At the ensuing Isthmian Games, Flamininus proclaimed the independence of the Greek cities. Rome sought to balance the Achaean League by curtailing but not destroying the power of King Nabis of Sparta.

192-189. **THE SYRIAN WAR** (p. 81). Antiochus III, invited by the Aetolians, invaded Greece, but the consul M. Acilius Glabrio landed in Epirus, moved into Thessaly and, with M. Porcius Cato, repeated the maneuver of Xerxes at Thermopylae to rout Antiochus (191).

190. The Roman fleet, helped by the Rhodians, won two victories. The Roman army, under **L. Cornelius Scipio** (later *Asiaticus*) and his brother Scipio Africanus, crossed the Hellespont and defeated Antiochus in the **battle of Magnesia**, near Smyrna. Antiochus was obliged to make peace on the following terms: surrender of all European and Asiatic possessions as far as the Taurus Mountains; payment of 15,000 talents in 12 years; surrender of Hannibal, who had fled from his enemies at Carthage (195). Though Hannibal escaped, he finally poisoned himself (183) at the court of Prusias I of Bithynia, who was about to betray him. Rome divided the Anatolian territory of Antiochus between Pergamum and Rhodes and aided Eumenes II of Pergamum against the Galatians (189). In Greece, Rome subjected the Aetolians, but left the other cities free. Philip was not rewarded as he had hoped.

171-168. THE THIRD MACEDONIAN WAR was waged against Rome by Perseus, the successor of Philip V. After several unsuccessful campaigns, the Romans sent L. Aemilius Paullus.

168. Battle of Pydna. Paullus utterly defeated Perseus and brought him back in his triumphal procession. So much booty accrued from his victory that Roman citizens were thereafter relieved of direct taxation, the *tributum*. Macedonia was broken up into four wholly distinct confederacies. Illyria was reduced to three tributary confederacies, and Epirus was devastated. From the Achaean cities 1000 of the chief citizens were taken as hostages and kept in Italy for 16 years. Rome likewise dictated to Eumenes of Pergamum, to Rhodes and to Antiochus IV, who was prevented by the ambassador C. Popilius Laenas from making war on the Ptolemies of Egypt.

153. On account of an uprising in Spain, the consuls entered office on Jan. 1 instead of Mar. 15. Thus Jan. 1 became established as the beginning of the civil year.

151. A law forbidding re-election to the consulship superseded an earlier one of 342 which had imposed a ten-year interval between two tenures. It lasted, with some exceptions, until Sulla revived the older law. Possibly the same law raised the minimum ages for the tenure

of all magistracies from those established by a *lex annalis* of the tribune Villius (180) to those of Cicero's time: quaestorship after the thirtieth year, aedileship after the thirty-sixth, praetorship after the thirty-ninth, and consulship after the forty-second.

149. The tribune L. Calpurnius Piso enacted a *lex Calpurnia* which set up a permanent commission to hear the suits of provincials to recover from governors money unjustly collected (*quaestio de rebus repetundis*). This commission differed from previous specially created boards of investigation (*quaestiones*) or panels of special judges (*reciperatores* or *iudices*) in being made always available (*perpetua*) without special legislation. Like its predecessors, the membership for different cases was drawn by lot from a panel of senators and the board met under the presidency of a praetor. The new court soon became an instrument whereby the Senate could discipline governors. Decisions were motivated not by justice but by class selfishness. It is probable that further courts of this type were established before the revision of the system by Sulla.

149-146. THE THIRD PUNIC WAR arose from alarm among conservative Romans over Carthage's revival, typified in the phrase with which Cato expressed his opinion on any question which was discussed in the Senate: *ceterum censeo Carthaginem esse delendam* ("but I declare that Carthage must be destroyed"). The occasion was an attack by Carthage (150) on Rome's ally, the now aged Massinissa. When a Roman army landed in Africa, the Carthaginians offered submission, but refused to vacate the city. With almost no resources they withstood a siege until **Scipio Aemilianus** captured and destroyed Carthage (146). The Romans organized a small area around Carthage as the Province of Africa, but left the rest to the sons of Massinissa (d. 149).

149-148. THE FOURTH MACEDONIAN WAR. A pretended son of Perseus, Andriscus, who called himself Philip, provoked the war, but was defeated by Q. Caecilius Metellus. In 146 Macedonia became a Roman province.

146. When the 300 surviving hostages returned to Achaea, the Achaeans made war on Sparta. Their leaders, Critolaus and Diaeus, were defeated by Metellus and L. Mummius. The latter took Corinth, sent its art treasures to Rome, sold its inhabitants into slavery, and burned the city (at the order of the Roman Senate). The territory of Corinth passed in part to Sicyon, in part became Roman public land. The remaining Greek cities retained a certain measure of autonomy under the governor of Macedonia, though they paid tribute. Not until later (127) did they become organized as the Province of Achaea.

143-133. Continuous unrest in Spain grew into **a war in Lusitania,** led by Viriathus (assassinated 139, thanks to Roman bribery), and in northern Spain, where the city of Numantia took the lead. Numantia fell in 133 and all Spain, except the northwestern part, passed under Roman domination.

135-132. The First Servile War broke out when the ill-treated slaves of the large Sicilian estates revolted under the Syrian Eunus, who called himself King Antiochus. Eunus held Henna and Tauromenium against Roman armies, but was finally captured and his supporters brutally executed.

Rome now possessed **eight provinces:** Sicilia (241), Sardinia (238) with Corsica (c. 230?), Hispania Citerior (205), Hispania Ulterior (205), Gallia Cisalpina (191?), Illyricum (168), Africa (146), Macedonia and Achaea (146). The first four were at first governed by praetors and then, as these became useful at Rome for the new standing courts and as the system of proroguing *imperia* became regular, they were governed by pro-praetors (in the less important or "praetorian" provinces) or pro-consuls (in the more important or "consular"). After the middle of the 2d century, consuls and praetors less frequently took command of a province or army while in office, though this was probably never forbidden by law. Wars were conducted either by the governors or by commanders specially endowed with an *imperium* and ranking usually as pro-consuls, even though they had not held the consulship.

Provinces were generally organized by their conqueror with the aid of a commission of ten senators sent out by Rome. The charter of organization was called a *lex data*, as it was authorized in advance by the *comitia* but not brought before it (*rogata*). Usually the Senate rather than the *comitia* confirmed such arrangements. The Romans tended to leave undisturbed existing arrangements where they could; e.g. the charter of Sicily incorporated the usages of Hiero of Syracuse, the *lex Hieronica*. Moreover, organized cities were left to themselves for purposes of local government. The Roman governor was chiefly concerned with warfare and general police duties, with settlement of disputes between cities, of important native trials, of all cases involving Roman citizens, and with the public land and tax-collections. Since, however, Rome had no elaborate administrative organization, the actual management of such lands (when not distributed to Roman citizens) and the collection of taxes were auctioned off at Rome (but not the taxes of Sicily), as were contracts for public works, every fifth year by the censors to companies of private capitalists (*publicani*), whose members came to be called *equites* because they had the census requisite for membership in the centuries of knights. (The actual cavalry, composed usually of sons of senators and distinguished by the grant from the state of a horse, the *equus publicus*, had been abolished by Scipio Aemilianus at the siege of Numantia.) The evils of the publican system lay not so much in extortionate collections, since the rates were laid down in the contract, as in the fact that on the one hand, a bad year might endanger the revenues, except in Sicily, and lead to undue hardship in the collection and that on the other the municipalities, who were responsible to the *publicani* for the payments, might fall into arrears and have to borrow, which they did from the same *publicani* (acting as bankers, *negotiatores*) at very high rates. Once behindhand, they found it hard to get out of debt. The rates on such loans were in time laid down by law, but the governor, who was often a silent partner in the company (a senator could openly invest only in land), would connive at illegal practices, especially since for a time after the Gracchi, and again after 70 he would be likely to be called to account for his own administration before a court composed of *equites*.

Roman literature began with the production in 241 of a translation of a Greek play by **Livius Andronicus,** who had been captured at Tarentum in 272. The most important early writers, all strongly under Greek influence, were: for verse, **Naevius** (269–199), who wrote plays and an epic on the First Punic War (*Bellum Punicum*); **Plautus** (254–184), writer of comedies; **Ennius,** who dabbled in many fields and produced in quantitative (Greek) dactylic hexameters (instead of the old, native, accentual "Saturnians") an epic on all Roman history, the *Annales*; **Pacuvius** (220–130), a tragedian; **Caecilius** (d. 166) and **Terence** (190–159), authors of comedy; and **Lucilius** (180–103) the "inventor" of satire; for prose, a number of historians who wrote in Greek, like **Fabius Pictor** (c. 200), on the Second Punic War, and **Polybius;** **Cato** (234–149), "founder" of Latin prose with his *Origines* (Italian history) and his work on agriculture. Despite the conservative opposition, Greek rhetoric and philosophy were studied by the liberals who gathered about Scipio Aemilianus, whose "Scipionic circle" included Polybius, Terence, Laelius, and the Stoic Panaetius of Rhodes.

2. DOMESTIC STRIFE AND EASTERN CONQUEST

133. **Ti. Sempronius Gracchus,** a noble, was elected tribune on a platform of social reform. Traditionally his motive was to stop the spread of great estates (*latifundia*) at the expense of the small peasants, but since this tendency was restricted to Etruria and Campania, he was more probably motivated by the problem of the proletariat in Rome. He proposed **an agrarian law** (perhaps only a re-enactment of a law of 367) limiting holdings of public land to 500 iugera (312 acres) per person, with an additional 250 for each of two sons. This measure hurt both the great nobles and certain Italian cities. The Senate persuaded a tribune, M. Octavius, to veto the measure, but Gracchus violated custom and had the assembly depose Octavius; the bill was then passed. A commission of three (Tiberius Gracchus, his brother Gaius, and his father-in-law Ap. Claudius) was appointed to recover land held in violation of this law and distribute it in inalienable lots of 30 iugera. To obtain funds for the new settlers Gracchus again violated custom, which left provincial affairs to the Senate, and proposed that the people accept Attalus' legacy of the Kingdom of Pergamum; probably this measure was not passed. Again contrary to custom, Tiberius stood for a second tribunate, on an even more radical program. The *optimates* (reactionary party of the nobles, contrasted with the democratic *populares*), led by **P. Cornelius Scipio Nasica,** murdered him and 300 of his followers during the election, and afterwards the Senate had more of his partisans executed as public enemies without the right of appeal.

133-129. Apparently the commission carried out in part the redistribution of the public land. In 129, Scipio Aemilianus, who had married a sister of Tiberius and, espousing a middle course, perhaps favored some concession to the increasing bitterness of the Italians, was found dead with suspicions of murder.

129. After the defeat of the pretender Aristonicus, Pergamum became the **Province of Asia.**

125. The Senate balked the attempt of the democratic consul **M. Fulvius Flaccus** to extend the franchise to all Italians and sent him to Liguria, where, by helping Marseilles against the Gauls, he began the conquest of southern Gaul. The **revolt of Fregellae,** a town which despaired of peaceful means, was ruthlessly suppressed. In 123 the **Balearic Islands** were conquered and in 121 southern Gaul became the province of **Gallia Narbonensis,** so-called from the newly established colony of Narbo Martius (Narbonne).

123. **Gaius Gracchus,** the more forceful brother of Tiberius, became tribune. To the motive of social reform was added that of revenge, and in this and the following year, when he secured a second tribunate, he put through a far more extreme program than Tiberius had envisaged. The precise order and interrelation of his measures is uncertain, but the most important were the following: by a *lex iudiciaria* (probably the surviving *lex Acilia repetundarum*) he transferred membership in the court on extortion (*quaestio de rebus repetundis,* and any others that existed) from senators to equestrians. He also passed a law reorganizing the Province of Asia, and particularly changing the tax rate into a tithe on produce, as in Sicily. The collection was to be auctioned off to the *publicani,* as heretofore. The two measures were probably intended to relieve the provincials, but they only served to separate the equestrians from the Senate; the former were now able to avenge themselves on a governor who sought to check their rapacity or divert the profits to his own account.

In behalf of the proletariat Gaius passed three measures: (1) a revival of his brother's **land law;** (2) the foundation of **three commercial colonies** (Capua, Tarentum, and Carthage) to take care of veterans and Oriental freedmen, who comprised the majority of the Roman proletariat and who, it was recognized, would not make good farmers; (3) **a law obliging the government to provide grain at a fair price** (probably not below the average market level) to protect the poor against famine and speculation. The transmarine colonies failed because the proletarians preferred the pleasures of Rome to life in remote provinces. The state control of the grain supply became a means whereby demagogues could win popular support (by reducing the price and by increasing the number of eligible beneficiaries). Less important bills mitigated the conditions of military service and reaffirmed the laws against execution without appeal to the people.   Finally, Gracchus planned to extend the full franchise to Latin cities and to grant Latin rights to all other Italians.   This measure was naturally unpopular with the Roman *populus*, now fully conscious of the advantages of citizenship.   The Senate took advantage of Gracchus' absence in Africa to undermine his influence, and he was defeated in the election for his third tribunate.   When a riot ensued over the repeal of his colonization bill, the Senate invoked a right based on recent custom and of dubious validity, to declare a state of emergency and to call upon the consuls and other magistrates to see to it, even by use of force, that the state suffered no harm (*senatus consultum ultimum*: *ut consules ... opera dent ne quid res publica detrimenti capiat*).   This was a substitute for the dictatorship, the last effective use of which had been made in 216.   In the ensuing struggles, Gaius Gracchus and many of his supporters were slain.

121-111.   A series of measures, ending with the *lex agraria* of 111, recognized the failure of the land distributions by discontinuing them, by relieving the lots of rent and by making them alienable.   After various experiments, the courts also were completely restored to the control of the Senate.

111-105.   The **Jugurthine War** resulted from the usurpation of the African Kingdom of Massinissa's descendants by King Micipsa's nephew, **Jugurtha.**   The latter murdered one rival, bribed a senatorial commission to support his claim, and captured Cirta (Constantine), capital of the surviving son of the king.   The death of some Italians at Cirta led Rome to declare war, but Jugurtha again bought peace.   A second murder led to hostilities, waged with varying success by Q. Caecilius Metellus.

107.   **Gaius Marius,** a self-made man and legionary commander (*legatus*) of Metellus, appealed to the Roman people over the head of a hostile Senate and secured the consulship, with command in the war.   Since the Senate refused to grant him an army, he called for volunteers and took men without the requisite property qualification.   There resulted a thorough **reform of the military system,** carried through by P. Rutilius Rufus in 105: for the manipular system with its three ranks was substituted a division of the legion (6000 men, gradually sinking to about 4500 during the first century) into 10 cohorts, each composed of three maniples; the old military tribunes lost their importance and the command was held by a delegate of the general (*legatus*);

the backbone of the legion became the centurions (commanders of the maniples); to each legion was attached an equal number of auxiliary troops, levied from the subject peoples and usually organized in their own fashion; about 300 professional cavalry replaced the old noble *equites*, abolished by Scipio Aemilianus; from the time of Scipio the general had also a special bodyguard (called from his headquarters *praetorium*), the *cohors praetoria* or praetorian guard.

107-105.   Marius' aristocratic quaestor, **L. Cornelius Sulla,** secured the surrender of Jugurtha by the latter's ally and father-in-law, Bocchus, King of Mauretania.   Marius triumphed in 105, Jugurtha died in prison, and his kingdom was divided between Bocchus and a grandson of Massinissa.

105.   **THE CIMBRI,** a German (or Celtic) people originally located east of the Rhine, who in 113 had moved into the Alpine regions and across the Rhone, ravaged Gaul and defeated two Roman armies at Arausio, on the Rhone.

Marius was elected consul for the second time, and then continuously for four more annual terms (contrary to the law of 151).

The Cimbri, defeated in Spain and again in northern France by native tribes, joined with the Germanic Teutones and other peoples.   Most of the Cimbri then moved on Italy, while the Teutones, some Cimbri, and others advanced into southern Gaul to approach Italy from the west.

104.   By a *lex Domitia* the pontiffs and augurs were made elective, but by a minority (17) of the 35 tribes, chosen by lot so that the gods might exercise their influence.   This law was repealed by Sulla but revived by Caesar in 63 to secure his election as chief priest (*pontifex maximus*).

103-99.   A Second Servile War in Sicily, under Tryphon and Athenion, was suppressed with difficulty by the consul, M. Aquillius.

102.   **Marius,** having deflected the invading barbarians from the Little St. Bernhard Pass and having followed them to Aquae Sextae (Aix in Provence), annihilated them there.   He then returned to the support of Catulus in northern Italy, which had been invaded by the main body of Cimbri coming over the Brenner Pass.

101.   **Marius and Catulus** defeated the Cimbri at **Vercellae** (Campi Raudii).   Marius became the national hero.

100.   **Marius,** consul for the sixth time, but

despised by the Senate, turned to the demagogues C. Servilius Glaucia (a praetor) and L. Appuleius Saturninus (a tribune) to secure land with which to reward his veterans. A number of extreme bills were passed, including one which defined treason no longer as internal revolt (*perduellio*) but as impairing the "majesty" of the Roman people (*lex Appuleia de maiestate imminuta* — later *laesa*). When Glaucia secured the murder of his rival for the consulship, the Senate passed the *senatus consultum ultimum* and Marius was obliged to besiege and kill his former supporters on the Capitoline. Marius then left for a tour of the east.

91. The tribune, **M. Livius Drusus,** son of an opponent of the Gracchi, brought forward several liberal bills: to compromise the problem of the courts by adding 300 *equites* to the Senate; to distribute land; to cheapen the price of grain; and to extend the citizenship to all Italians. The first three measures were passed as one bill, whereupon the Senate, in virtue of a recent law against such omnibus bills (*lex Caecilia Didia* of 98), declared them void.

91-88. The Social War (i.e. War of the Allies.) The disappointed Italians, save for Latins, Etruscans, Umbrians, and some southern cities, flared into open revolt. They formed a republic, **Italia,** with a capital at Corfinium. Though Marius and Gn. Pompeius Strabo succeeded in suppressing it in the north, the consul **L. Julius Caesar** suffered reverses in the south.

90. The danger of the secession of the Etruscans and Umbrians led to the passage by Caesar of a *lex Iulia* by which citizenship was granted to all Italians who had remained faithful.

89. The war in the north was concluded and L. Cornelius Sulla won successes in the south. The two new consuls moved a *lex Plautia Papiria* which extended citizenship to all Italians who applied for it within 60 days, but enrolled them in only eight designated tribes, to prevent them from dominating the assemblies. Cities in Cisalpine Gaul received Latin rights by a *lex Pompeia*, though the precise status of the region between the Po and the Alps, the Transpadanes, remained a matter of dispute until 49. This concession brought the war to a close in 88 and showed that the Italians preferred to remain with Rome rather than to be independent. It also frankly recognized that citizenship was no longer a right, since personal participation in the assemblies at Rome was impossible for most Italians and no system of representation was devised, but a privilege which ensured to its possessors the special protection of Rome, favored treatment in the provinces, and a share in the profits of conquest.

88-84. FIRST MITHRIDATIC WAR. Contemporaneously with the Social War, **Mithridates VI Eupator,** ambitious King of Pontus since 120, made war on Rome. He had absorbed Colchis at the east end of the Pontus (Euxine, Black Sea), the Kingdom of the Bosporus in the Tauric Chersonese (Crimea), Paphlagonia, and Cappadocia. He then came into conflict with Nicomedes of Bithynia, in northwestern Asia Minor, who was supported by the Romans. Mithridates routed both Nicomedes and the Romans, overran the province of Asia, and is said to have commanded the natives to put to death 80,000 "Romans" (Italian traders?) in a single day. Sulla, consul for 88, joined his army at Nola to start for Asia.

88-82. But civil war broke out in Rome. The demagogue **P. Sulpicius Rufus** carried several measures by violence, notably one distributing the new Italian citizens among all the tribes, and another conferring the eastern command on Marius. Sulla marched his troops to Rome, stormed the city, and slew Sulpicius and others. Marius fled to Africa. Sulla put through conservative reforms, which did not last, and went as proconsul to Asia in 87.

87-84. The demagogic consul **L. Cornelius Cinna** turned to violence against the optimates under the other consul, Cn. Octavius. He was driven from the city, raised an army, and secured the support of Marius, who returned from Africa. They seized Rome, instituted a reign of terror, a "proscription" of the optimates, who were either slain or, if they escaped, lost their property. Cinna and Marius became consuls for 86 (Marius' seventh consulship). Marius soon died and his successor, **L. Valerius Flaccus,** went out to command in the east. Cinna tyrannized at Rome until his death in a mutiny in 84.

87-84. In the meantime, Sulla, in Greece, drove the generals of Mithridates, Archelaus and Aristion, back into the Piraeus and Athens respectively. When, in 86, Athens fell, Archelaus retired from the Piraeus by sea to Boeotia, where he was defeated by Sulla at **Chaeronea** and, in 85, at **Orchomenos.**

84. Sulla, supported by a fleet collected in Asia and Syria by **L. Licinius Lucullus,** moved around the Aegean into Asia, where Mithridates made peace on the following terms: evacuation of all his conquests, surrender of 80 warships, and an indemnity of 3000 talents. Sulla then won over the troops of the democratic general C. Fimbria, who had secured command by murdering Flaccus and now committed suicide. Sulla left these two legions to police Asia and to help Lucullus collect an immense fine of 20,000 talents from the Asiatic cities, while he himself returned to Italy.

83-79. Sulla made a cautious advance from Brundisium against the successors of Cinna, in the course of which the army of the consul Lucius Scipio deserted to him after the defeat of the other consul, C. Norbanus. After wintering at Capua, Sulla conducted a brilliant campaign against the various opposing forces which culminated in the **battle of the Colline Gate** (Nov., 82), when he repulsed from Rome a large force of Samnites, who had taken advantage of the civil war to revolt. Sulla punished severely the cities that had sided with his opponents, and then had himself appointed dictator for the purpose of restoring the state (*rei publicae constituendae*).

Sulla's dictatorship was only in name a revival of the old institution. It was not an "emergency" office and was not limited in time, so that actually it was a tyranny. Sulla's objective was to restore the old senatorial system. To this end he sought, by a series of laws (*leges Corneliae*) to subordinate to the Senate all those powers which had been set up against it: magistrates, governors, knights, and people. The size of the Senate was increased from 300 to 600 by the addition of new members, probably equestrians; admission became automatic for those who held the quaestorship, whose numbers had increased to 20. Thus the censors lost the control which they had hitherto had over admissions to the Senate, though probably Sulla only confirmed what had already become a general practice. But he also deprived the censors of the right to remove unworthy members. The *lex annalis* was revived, with permission for re-election to the consulship after ten years. The number of praetors was increased to eight. Governors were forbidden to take troops outside their province by a law which made such action treason. The number of **standing courts** (*quaestiones perpetuae*) was increased to at least seven: *de rebus repetundis*, *de maiestate*, *de ui* (violence), *de peculatu* (embezzlement), *de ambitu* (corrupt electioneering), *de falsis* (fraud) and *inter sicarios* (assassination). Membership was definitely restricted to senators, thus depriving both magistrates and people of judicial power. The **tribunes' veto** was confined to the protection of individuals (*auxilium*)

and they were probably forbidden to bring any measure before the people without previous approval of the Senate. Moreover, election to the tribunate disqualified a man for further political office, so that men of ambition would avoid it. The public distribution of grain, an instrument of demagoguery, was perhaps abolished.

Of these reforms, the only one of enduring importance was that of the **judicial system.** Though sentimentally the Laws of the Twelve Tables continued to be regarded as the fountainhead of the Roman Law, in actual fact the *leges Corneliae* laid the foundations of Roman criminal law by defining the types of crime (which had naturally increased as Rome grew) and by providing a more expeditious system of court trial than the hearings before the *populus*. The importance of the praetors, who (except the *urbanus* and *peregrinus*) normally presided over the courts, was thus vastly increased. During this same period, by the *lex Aebutia* (probably c. 150), the civil law was liberated from the restraints of the old, ritualistic, narrow "actions at law" (*legis actiones*) by the recognition of the praetor's *formulae*. The *formulae*, borrowed by the urban praetor from the peregrine (i.e. praetor for foreigners) were general definitions of civil wrongs not covered by specific laws, for which remedies would be granted. Such formulas were published by the praetor either on special occasions (*edicta repentina*) or in the edict with which he assumed office (*edictum perpetuum*). A large body of such material was naturally passed on from praetor to praetor and became "tralatician" (*edictum tralaticium*). Thus the praetors, until the time of Hadrian, could widen the scope of civil law to meet new needs, and the praetor's edict became the chief authority for civil law.

As soon as his reforms were completed, Sulla voluntarily retired from public life (79). He died in the following year.

83-81. THE SECOND MITHRIDATIC WAR, resulted from a Roman invasion of Cappadocia and Pontus. After victory, peace was renewed on the terms of 84.

80-72. Q. Sertorius, the democratic governor of Hither Spain (83) was expelled by Sullan troops. When the Lusitanians invited him back in 80, he established an independent state modeled on Rome. He soon extended his sway over much of Spain and held the Romans at bay until he was murdered in 72 by a jealous subordinate, M. Perperna. Pompey, who had been sent to Spain in 77, quickly defeated and executed Perperna.

78-77. The democratic consul **M. Aemilius Lepidus** sought to undo Sulla's work. When he was blocked, he raised in Etruria an army of the discontented. He was defeated before Rome by his colleague Q. Lutatius Catulus and the remnant of his army was wiped out in northern Italy in 77 by the brilliant young Roman commander **Gnaeus Pompeius** (Pompey), son of a general in the Social War and a protégé of Sulla.

74. **Cyrene,** which had been tentatively bequeathed to Rome in 154 and again in 96, finally became a province.

73-71. **Third Servile War.** The Thracian gladiator **Spartacus** and other gladiators started a war by seizing Mt. Vesuvius, to which rallied many fugitive slaves. The praetor **M. Licinius Crassus** (b. 112), a favorite of Sulla who had enriched himself by buying the property of the proscribed, defeated Spartacus twice, and Pompey, returning from Spain, finished off the stragglers. For his achievements during this period, Pompey became known as "the Great" (*Magnus*).

70. **Crassus and Pompey** openly deserted the optimate cause and used their troops to win for themselves the consulship for 70, though both were under the age set in 151. As consuls, they secured the restoration to the tribunate of the privileges of which Sulla had deprived it. Already, in 75, the disqualification of tribunes for higher office had been abolished and, in 72, the censors had recovered the privilege of removing unworthy senators. Thus Sulla's restoration of the Senate was largely undone. The prosecution of the corrupt propraetor of Sicily, Verres, by Cicero in 70 brought to a head discontent with the senatorial courts and the praetor L. Aurelius Cotta introduced a *lex Aurelia* under which the senators retained only one third membership on the juries and the other two thirds were filled from the *equites* and a group of slightly lower property census, the *tribuni aerarii*, whose origin is uncertain but whose sympathies were equestrian.

68-67. **Defeat of the Mediterranean pirates** by Q. Caecilius Metellus Pius. There had been a rapid increase of piracy (especially kidnapping for the slave market at Delos) in the eastern Mediterranean after the defeat of Carthage, Rhodes, and Syria and during the civil wars in Italy. The centers were Crete and Cilicia and the situation began to interfere seriously with Rome's grain supply. Efforts to suppress the pirates met with little success until Metellus took Crete (68). It was made a province (67) and later joined to Cyrene.

67. The tribune A. Gabinius secured the passage of the *lex Gabinia*, which conferred upon Pompey for three years the command of the Mediterranean and its coasts for 50 miles inland, equal to that of the governors in each province (*imperium aequum*). Thus enabled to mobilize all available resources, Pompey in three months cleared the sea of pirates and pacified Cilicia.

74-64. **THE THIRD MITHRIDATIC WAR.** Mithridates, encouraged by Rome's troubles at home, supported his son-in-law, **Tigranes of Armenia,** in the annexation of Cappadocia and Syria.

74. **Nicomedes III** of Bithynia bequeathed his kingdom to Rome, presumably to protect it against Mithridates, who nevertheless occupied it. The consul for 74, **L. Licinius Lucullus,** gradually drove Mithridates back and occupied Pontus (73). Mithridates fled to the court of Tigranes.

69. **Lucullus** defeated Tigranes at Tigranocerta and started to push on into the mountains of Armenia. His troops, many of them brought out twenty years before by Flaccus, mutinied and forced him to retire to Asia (68). This failure and his efforts to relieve Asia by wholesale reduction of the indebtedness of the *publicani*, to say nothing of his optimate sympathies, made him unpopular at Rome.

66. The tribune C. Manilius, moved a bill (*lex Manilia*), which was supported by the rising orator, **M. Tullius Cicero** (b. 106), which gave Pompey a command over all Asia equal to that of the governors and valid until the conclusion of the war (*imperium aequum infinitum*, i.e. without time limit). Pompey quickly drove Mithridates to the east end of the Black Sea, after which he captured Tigranes at Artaxata and deprived him of all territories save Armenia, besides imposing a fine of 6000 talents.

65. Pompey pursued Mithridates until the latter fled to the Crimea, where he committed suicide on hearing of the revolt of his son (63).

65-62. **Reorganization of Asia and Syria by Pompey.** He formed four provinces: Bithynia-Pontus (excluding eastern Pontus), which became a client kingdom; Asia, the old province, which was again heavily taxed; Cilicia, including Pamphylia and Isauria; and Syria, the region about Antioch. As client kingdoms he left eastern Pontus, Cappadocia,

Galatia (under King Deiotarus), Lycia, and Judaea.

64. Pompey took **Jerusalem,** in order to pacify Judea. He left in charge the Maccabean high-priest Hyrcanus and a civil adviser, Antipater, from the non-Jewish district of Idumaea. Judea was under the supervision of the governor of Syria and was subjected to a light tax.

Pompey's reorganization of Asia had enduring significance. He followed the Roman practice of making cities the responsible agencies of local government and founding new ones wherever advisable. In order to keep the support of the equestrian class, he extended the pernicious publican system throughout the east. The Senate was loath to confirm his arrangements or look after his veterans, but he did not turn against the government. Instead, he dismissed his army at Brundisium (61) and entered Rome as a private citizen.

64-63. Conspiracy of Catiline. The discontented classes at Rome (debtors, veterans, ruined nobles, those proscribed by Sulla, etc.) found a leader in **L. Sergius Catilina.** He may at first have had the support of Crassus and of Crassus' demagogic agent, **C. Julius Caesar** (b. 102 or 101). Caesar belonged to a poor branch of the patrician *gens Iulia*, but his aunt had been the wife of Marius and his (Caesar's) wife was a daughter of Cinna. Catiline tried to run for the consulship on a radical program in 66, but could not get his name presented to the *comitia centuriata*, as he was threatened with prosecution for extortion while pro-praetor in Africa. After a plot to murder the consuls had failed (65), he ran again in 64, but was defeated by Cicero. Catiline turned to even more extreme methods (sedition in Rome and levying a force in Etruria. Then, if not before, Crassus and Caesar abandoned him. The plot was detected, and Cicero, in virtue of a *senatus consultum ultimum*, arrested the conspirators. With the Senate's approval he had them put to death as *hostes* without appeal, despite the law of Tiberius Gracchus. The forces in Etruria were dispersed. Cicero's famous *Orations against Catiline*.

60. THE FIRST TRIUMVIRATE. Caesar returned from a pro-praetorship in Spain and brought his master Crassus into alliance with Pompey, who had fallen out with the Senate because of the unwillingness of the latter to confirm his eastern arrangements. This informal union became known as the first triumvirate.

59. Caesar, as consul, put through the program of the trio: distribution of the **Campanian** land to Pompey's veterans; confirmation of Pompey's eastern settlement; grant to himself (*lex Vatinia*) for the unprecedented period of five years of the province of Cisalpine Gaul, with Illyria. To this was added later Gallia Narbonensis, with the possibility of action throughout Transalpine Gaul. The political union was cemented by the marriage of Caesar's daughter Julia to Pompey.

58-51. CONQUEST OF GAUL by Caesar, both to enrich himself and to forge for himself an army and a military reputation to rival Pompey's. He used as an excuse the attempt of the Helvetii to move from Switzerland into Gaul. His plan of campaign was to move down the Rhine, separate the Gauls from the Germans, and then turn back on the Gauls. In 58 he defeated the **Helvetii** at **Bibracte** (Autun) and the German Ariovistus near Vesontio (Besançon). He then reduced the **Belgii** (57), including the stubborn Nervii, in northwestern Gaul. He defeated the **Veneti** on the southern coast of Brittany and the Aquitani in southwestern Gaul (56). After he had repulsed the Germanic Usipetes and Tencteri, Caesar built a wooden bridge over the Rhine near Coblenz to make a two weeks' demonstration in Germany (55). He also tried with little success to invade Britain.

58. To remove opposition at Rome, the triumvirs secured the mission of the irreconcilable **M. Porcius Cato** (the younger) to investigate the affairs of Cyprus, and allowed the violent demagogue and tribune **P. Clodius** to move a bill against Cicero for the execution of Roman citizens without appeal. Cicero voluntarily withdrew to Epirus, the bill was passed, and his property was confiscated. Clodius also made the distribution of grain free to a large number of poor, perhaps 300,000.

57. An optimate tribune, **T. Annius Milo,** secured the recall of Cicero, and organized a following to oppose that of Clodius. The optimates summoned up enough courage to attack Caesar's land bill.

In consequence of the shortage of grain, the Senate conferred on Pompey the supervision of the grain supply (*cura annonae*) and an *imperium aequum* over the areas concerned, but without what he really wanted, viz. military force.

56. Worried by the revival of opposition, Caesar, Pompey, and Crassus met at Luca, on the southern boundary of Caesar's province, and laid plans for the future.

55. In pursuance of these plans, Pompey and

Crassus became consuls. By a consular *lex Pompeia Licinia*, Caesar's command in Gaul was prolonged for five years. By a tribunician law (*lex Trebonia*), Crassus was given Syria and Pompey both Spains for the same period. Crassus hurried east, but Pompey, contrary to custom, remained near Rome and governed Spain through his *legati*.

54. INVASION OF BRITAIN. Caesar was more successful than in 55 and defeated King Cassivellaunus somewhere north of the Thames, perhaps at Wheathampstead near Verulamium (St. Albans). Nevertheless, he withdrew to Gaul without any permanent result save to open Britain somewhat to the penetration of trade and Roman influence. In 53 he made a second demonstration across the Rhine.

54-51. Breakup of the Triumvirate. This began with the death of Julia in 54.

53. Crassus was utterly defeated and slain by the Parthians at Carrhae in Mesopotamia.

52. All Gaul flared into revolt under **Vercingetorix.** Caesar failed to take Gergovia (Clermont in Auvergne) and was himself surrounded while besieging Vercingetorix in Alesia (Alise near Dijon), but finally won a complete victory and captured Vercingetorix. He spent the year 51 ruthlessly suppressing the remaining insurgents.

52. Milo's ruffians killed Clodius in a street fight at Bovillae.

As it had not yet been possible to elect magistrates for this year, the Senate passed a *senatus consultum ultimum* and illegally appointed **Pompey sole consul**, i.e. in fact dictator. Milo, tried in a special court under Pompey's presidency, was condemned despite Cicero's faltering defense. Pompey then made the optimate Metellus Scipio, father of his new wife, Crassus' widow, his colleague, thus openly returning to the side of the Senate. Afraid, however, of a decisive break with Caesar, he tried, by a series of indirect moves, to jockey him out of office long enough to leave him open for prosecution in the courts. Since prosecutions could not be brought against one in office, Caesar had so arranged his tenure of Gaul (the details are uncertain) that, by being allowed to canvas in absence during 49, he could proceed direct to the consulship in 48.

49. The Senate finally passed a *senatus consultum ultimum* which declared Caesar a public enemy unless he should disband his army (Jan. 7). The tribunes favorable to him

fled to Ravenna, where he was waiting. During the night of Jan. 10–11, Caesar with one legion crossed the **Rubicon** (*alea iacta est*, "the die is cast"), the brook south of Ravenna on the Adriatic which marked the limit of his province. He thus broke not only Sulla's law on treason, but also an old custom by which a general could bring armed forces into Italy only for a triumph. He justified his action as aimed to protect the sacrosanct tribunes.

49-46. Pompey, fearful of the legions in Gaul, left Italy for Greece, where he might have the resources of the east behind him. Most of the Senate went with him. Caesar, after failing to trap Pompey at Brundisium, turned to Spain, where he defeated the latter's commanders at **Ilerda** (Lerida) north of the Ebro. Marseilles surrendered to him on his way back to Italy.

48. Caesar landed in Epirus and defeated Pompey at **Pharsalus.** Pompey fled to Egypt, where he was treacherously slain by order of the minister of the young king, Ptolemy XII.

48-47. When Caesar reached Alexandria in pursuit of Pompey, he was besieged by Ptolemy and the natives during the winter, until he was rescued by an army from Asia. Since Ptolemy perished, Caesar made his sister **Cleopatra** and a younger brother, Ptolemy XIII, joint rulers of Egypt. Cleopatra soon disposed of her brother and set herself to restore the power of the Ptolemies with Roman aid. She charmed Caesar into remaining three months with her and perhaps siring her son Caesarion.

47. Caesar advanced into Syria to meet a son of the great Mithridates, Pharnaces, who had invaded Pontus. On Aug. 2 Caesar defeated him at **Zela** (*ueni, uidi, uici*).

46. On his return to Rome Caesar subdued a mutiny of his devoted Tenth Legion. He then crossed to Africa and defeated the Pompeians, led by Pompey the Great's son Sextus, at **Thapsus** (Apr.). Cato committed suicide at Utica (hence called *Uti censis*). A part of Numidia, whose Pompeian king, Juba, had committed suicide, was added to the province of Africa; the rest was left to the king of eastern Mauretania. After four simultaneous triumphs in Rome (July) Caesar went to Spain, where Sex. Pompey had joined his brother Gnaeus.

45. Caesar utterly routed them at **Munda** (Mar.). He then returned to Rome (Sept.).

Caesar's position was that of an absolute monarch. In 49 he had been dictator for 11 days to hold elections. In 48 he was consul for the second time. After Pharsalus he was given the consulship for a five-year term and was given the dictatorship annually; perhaps also some of the tribunician powers (*tribunicia potestas*), since being a patrician he could not be tribune. In 46 he was consul for the third time with Lepidus. After Thapsus he was made dictator for ten years and *praefectus morum* (supervisor of morals). In 45 he was sole consul. After Munda he was made consul for ten years; in 44, dictator and *praefectus morum* for life; his tribunician power was extended to include *sacrosanctitas*. Thus his position was essentially a revival of the Sullan dictatorship. His plans for the future are not definitely known, but while he certainly planned to continue as monarch, it is doubtful that he planned to take the crown or move the capital to Ilium.

The **Senate was increased to 900** by enrolling ex-centurions and provincials, as much to weaken it as to make it representative of the empire. To provide for its maintenance at this size Caesar doubled the number of quaestors and praetors (to 40 and 16 respectively); the quaestors were later reduced. His agrarian and colonization program was like that of all reformers since the Gracchi. The citizenship was considerably extended, beginning in 49 with the confirmation of the Transpadanes' long disputed claim. The *lex Iulia municipalis* may perhaps have been a measure to give to the cities in the west something of the autonomy enjoyed by those in the east. The **calendar was reformed** in the light of Egyptian knowledge on the nearly correct basis of 365¼ days per year; this system continued in use in some countries into the 20th century. The number of those receiving free grain was reduced from 320,000 to 150,000. The publican system was somewhat restricted, since Caesar had considerable concern for the provinces and none for the *equites*.

44. ASSASSINATION OF CAESAR. Caesar's greatest weakness was an inability to choose trustworthy subordinates. A conspiracy of such people, together with the high-minded patriots and disgruntled optimates, led by M. Junius Brutus, Decimus Brutus, and G. Cassius Longinus, assassinated him in the Senate on the Ides (15th) of March. The famous *Et tu Brute* ("Thou too, Brutus") may have been addressed to Decimus, not Marcus.

The conspirators had no organization ready to take charge. **M. Antonius** (Mark Antony), formerly Caesar's master of horse, got control, in part by appealing to the sympathies of the proletariat by his funeral oration and in part by seizing Caesar's papers and treasure. The conspirators fled, Decimus Brutus to Cisalpine Gaul, Marcus Brutus to Macedonia, and Cassius to Syria, provinces already assigned to them, and over which the Senate now gave them commands superior (not equal) to those of other governors (*imperia maiora*), so that they could raise armies against Antony. Antony secured from the people the transfer of Cisalpine Gaul and Macedonia to himself and Syria to his colleague, P. Cornelius Dolabella. In the meantime, Caesar's eighteen-year-old great-nephew, **Gaius Octavius**, whose mother, Atia, was daughter of Caesar's sister, Julia, and who had been named as heir and adopted in the will of Caesar, came to Rome to claim his inheritance. Antony refused to give him the money and prevented the passing of the *lex curiata* necessary to ratify his adoption. Octavius nevertheless called himself **Gaius Julius Caesar Octavianus**. He borrowed money and, illegally, as a private citizen, levied a force among Caesar's veterans in Campania.

43. Antony marched north to dislodge Decimus Brutus from Mutina (Modena). The Senate sent the new consuls Hirtius and Pansa to relieve Decimus and joined to them Octavian with the command (*imperium*) of a pro-praetor. In two battles, **Forum Gallorum and Mutina,** Antony was forced to retire westward toward Gaul. But the consuls were killed. Octavian, marching to Rome (July), forced the Senate to hold special elections in which he and Pedius were elected to replace the dead consuls. He had his adoption duly confirmed. By a *lex Pedia* vengeance was declared on the conspirators who had assassinated Caesar. In the meantime, **Marcus Lepidus**, governor of Transalpine Gaul, had allied with Antony and Decimus had been slain. Octavian thereupon changed his support from the Senate to Antony in a meeting at Bononia (Bologna).

43, Nov. SECOND TRIUMVIRATE. A tribunician *lex Titia* confirmed their arrangements: Antony, Lepidus, and Octavian were appointed a commission of three to establish the state (*triumuiri rei publicae constituendae*), which amounted to a Sullan dictatorship in commission and differentiated this second triumvirate from the first by recognizing it legally. The triumvirs proceeded with a widespread proscription inspired both by political hatred and by the need for money and lands with which to reward their troops. Octavian acquiesced in the **execution of Cicero** by Antony's agents (Dec. 7).

42. The triumvirs secured the erection of a temple to Caesar in the Forum, where he had been burnt, and his deification. The magistrates were forced to take an oath to support all Caesar's arrangements (*acta*). Antony and Octavian then crossed to Thrace, where they met the combined forces of Cassius and Brutus at **Philippi.** Cassius, defeated by Antony and misled by a false report of Brutus' defeat, committed suicide. Brutus, though actually victorious over Octavian, was finally defeated twenty days later and also killed himself. Antony betook himself to the eastern provinces, where he met Cleopatra at Tarsus in the summer of 41. Either fascinated by her charms or desiring to get control of her resources, he remained with her in Egypt for a year.

41-40. **Octavian,** who shared the western provinces with Lepidus, had a difficult war against Antony's wife Fulvia and brother Lucius Antonius before finally reducing them at **Perusia** (Perugia) in 40.

40. By a **pact made at Brundisium,** Antony married Octavian's sister, Octavia (since Fulvia had recently died). Octavian took Gaul from Lepidus, who was left only Africa.

39. **Sextus Pompey,** who had conducted a piratical career since Munda, was now a power to be reckoned with, as he controlled Sicily and his fleet could interrupt Rome's grain supply. His possession of Sicily, Sardinia, Corsica, and the Peloponnese was recognized by the triumvirs in the **pact of Misenum.** Octavian divorced his second wife, Scribonia, and married **Livia,** previously wife of Tib. Claudius Nero.

37. Octavia engineered a **second pact at Tarentum.** Octavian gave troops to Antony for his Parthian War and Antony supplied ships for use against Pompey. The triumvirate was renewed for five years more, though the precise date set for its termination is uncertain.

36. Octavian's fleet, under his general **M. Vipsanius Agrippa,** defeated Pompey, who fled to Miletus, where he died. Lepidus, after landing in Sicily ostensibly to help Octavian, tried to secure the island. When, however, his troops deserted to Octavian, the latter annexed his rival's territory but, because Lepidus himself had become chief pontiff

(*pontifex maximus*) on the death of Caesar, kept him in honorable captivity at Circeii until his death in 13. Octavian spent the following years consolidating Roman power in the Alps and Illyria.

36. Antony suffered a severe defeat from the Parthians in 36, but managed to retreat to Armenia. He openly married Cleopatra (though already married to Octavia).

34. At Alexandria he established her as a Hellenistic monarch and distributed Roman provinces to her children as subordinate rulers. How far he intended to be her consort cannot be determined, but Octavian made the most of such a probability.

32. When Antony prepared to attack Octavian, the latter had the support of the west, which was both terrified by fear of an oriental domination under Cleopatra and angry at Antony's high-handed disposition of Roman territory. After the consuls, friends of Antony, fled to him, Octavian had the *imperium* of Antony under the triumvirate annulled by the *comitia*. He published a will purporting to be Antony's in which the Roman possessions in the east were bequeathed to Cleopatra. Italy, and perhaps all the western provinces, took a military oath (*coniuratio Italiae*) to support Octavian. In virtue of this, since he no longer had any legal *imperium* himself if the triumvirate was at an end, he levied troops, outwardly to meet Cleopatra. Antony formally divorced Octavia.

31, Sept. 2. BATTLE OF ACTIUM. The rival fleets met outside the bay. The course of the battle is uncertain, but Cleopatra fled to Egypt, followed by Antony, whose army then surrendered to Octavian. In the following year,

30. Antony, on hearing a false report of Cleopatra's suicide, killed himself. Upon Octavian's arrival at Alexandria, Cleopatra tried to win him as she had his predecessors. When she failed, she committed suicide (the story of the asp is perhaps false) lest she have to grace his triumph. Egypt passed finally into Rome's possession.

29. Octavian celebrated three triumphs and by closing the temple of Janus, something recorded only twice before (by Numa and in 235), signalized the restoration of peace throughout the Roman world.

If the crossing of the Rubicon marked the final fall of the republic, the battle of Actium signalized the final triumph of the empire. The last century of the republic was characterized by the collapse of popular government because of the wide extension of citizenship, the considerable adulteration of the citizen body at Rome by the introduction of un-Romanized Orientals, chiefly through the manumission of slaves, the growth in Rome of an unemployed proletariat, the rise of demagogues, and the complexity of the problems of government. The increasingly corrupt Senate had lost control of the assemblies, the armies, and the generals. The financiers, as well as the governors, saw in the provinces only a field for exploitation. Italy had been exhausted by civil war, proscriptions (which especially reduced the upper classes), recruitment, and land confiscations.

The last century of the republic witnessed a vigorous literary activity at Rome. Hellenism, thoroughly absorbed into Roman education, formed a constituent element in thought rather than something imposed from without. At the same time the native talent of the Romans adapted Hellenism to their own particular needs. Lyric poetry found expression in **Catullus** (87–54) from Verona, who, besides his imitations of the Alexandrine poets, produced strongly personal and intense lyrics on his hates and loves. The Epicurean **Lucretius** (99–55) wrote his epic "On the Nature of Things" (*de Rerum Natura*) to expound a materialistic atomism. Caesar's (102–44) *Commentaries* on the Gallic

Wars, continued by his officers for the other campaigns, are, despite their apologetic purpose, admirably clear and impartial. Minor writings which have survived are the historical monographs on Catiline and the Jugurthine War by **Sallust** (86–35) and the *Lives* by **Nepos** (100–29). Outstanding among antiquarians was **Varro** (116–27), while the **Scaevolae,** father and son, in the Sullan period, were outstanding students of jurisprudence. But the figure who gave his name to the age was **Cicero** (106–43). In spite of his active public life, he not only published his forensic and judicial speeches but wrote extensively on philosophy, rhetoric, and politics. He passed on to the Middle Ages much of value from Greek thought, especially from Plato, the Stoics, and the New (Skeptic) Academy. But he added thereto a Roman color and much of his own thought and experience. Finally, his correspondence, published after his death, gives a deep insight into both the writer and his times.

Roman art began during this century to emerge with a definite character. Though buildings still preserved the heavy lines and ornament of the Etruscans, they acquired majesty and splendor under direct Greek influence. Portrait sculpture, though executed by Greeks, portrayed the individual to a degree unknown in idealizing Hellenic art.

F. THE ROMAN EMPIRE

1. THE EARLY EMPIRE (31 B.C.-192 A.D.)

31 B.C.-14 A.D. IMPERATOR CAESAR OC-TAVIANUS (b. Sept. 23, 63), later called **Augustus,** established his government in 27 (Jan. 23), with some modifications later, especially after a serious illness in 23. He proclaimed that he would "restore the republic," i.e. resign his extraordinary powers and put the Senate and Roman people again at the head of the state. He held the consulship annually until 23, but only twice thereafter for a short part of the year. He also received, and retained after 23, a proconsular command superior to those of other senatorial proconsuls and unlimited in time, though actually renewed at intervals (*imperium proconsulare maius infinitum*). Although he received a special dispensation to retain his *imperium* within the *pomoerium*, it is uncertain to what extent he could actually exercise it over Rome or even Italy, the sphere of the consuls. However, in virtue of the *imperium*, he controlled all the armed forces of the state and appointed as legionary commanders his own senatorial delegates (*legati*). He also divided the provinces between the emperor and the Senate. Augustus himself took charge of all provinces in which the presence of troops was required and appointed to govern them other senatorial delegates, called in this case *legati pro praetore*. The Senate sent proconsuls to the pacified provinces where troops were no longer needed. Thus Augustus hoped to prevent that rivalry of independent commanders which had brought about the downfall of the republic. He also sought to assure better government in the provinces by the payment of salaries to all governors, senatorial and imperial. Two major districts received special treatment. The command of the legions on the Rhine was given to a special legate, independent of the imperial government of the Gallic provinces, and only later did this command develop into two territorial provinces. Egypt was administered by Augustus as a private estate under an equestrian praefect (*praefectus Aegypti*) appointed by himself, who directed the elaborate machinery inherited from the Pharaohs and Ptolemies for the benefit of the new imperial treasury (*fiscus*), which was distinct from the old senatorial treasury (*aerarium Saturni*). Smaller districts were governed, not by senatorial *legati*, but by equestrian procurators or praefects. Imperial governors of all sorts tended to have longer terms than the senatorial and thus to perform their task better. Since, however, the imperial *legati*, in both provinces and the army, were drawn from the Senate and usually held proconsulships later, no sharp distinction was drawn between the republican and imperial administration in the upper ranks.

A distinct **imperial civil service** did, however, grow up among the equestrians, partly in the provinces where, besides the minor governorships above mentioned, they held financial posts as stewards (*procuratores*) of the emperor or of his treasury (*fiscus*) and partly in various administrative posts in Rome and Italy, of which the chief were those with which Augustus supplemented the inadequate republican administration of the city of Rome. The most important officer was a consular senator, the *praefectus urbi* who had general supervision of the city with three "urban cohorts" of soldiers for police. This office, however, may have become permanent only under Tiberius. The other three major officials were equestrian. A *praefectus annonae* had charge of the grain supply for Rome. A *praefectus uigilum* had seven cohorts of freedmen as firemen, one for every two of the 14 regions into which Augustus divided the city. And a *praefectus praetorio* had charge of the nine cohorts of the imperial or "praetorian" guard (praetor-general), which Augustus kept scattered through Italy, but which Sejanus later concentrated in a camp at Rome. Because of the importance of this post, later emperors frequently divided it between two incumbents.

In 23, Augustus secured the consolidation and extension of certain tribunician privileges which had been granted to him because, as a patrician, he could not be a tribune. The value of this tribunician power (*tribunicia potestas*) was in part its traditionally popular appeal and in part the privileges of sacrosanctity, *auxilium*, veto, direct jurisdiction in Rome, consultation of the Senate, and, most important, the initiation of legislation. Augustus, during his reign, initiated a series of far-reaching laws (*leges Iuliae*) in an attempt to reform the criminal law, regulate social classes, and revive morality and family life. With respect to the social order, he purified the Senate of Caesarian intruders by a series of "selections" (*lectiones*); he restricted severely the freeing of slaves and the attainment of full citizenship by freedmen; and he bestowed the citizenship on provincials very grudgingly. However, he did increase the recipients of free grain from Caesar's 150,000 to 200,000. The final law in his effort to restore morality was the consular *lex Papia Poppaea* of 9 A.D., which supplemented his own *lex Iulia de maritandis ordinibus* of 18 B.C. These laws encouraged marriage in the senatorial and equestrian orders by penalizing the unmarried and offering privileges to the fathers of children, especially of three (*ius trium liberorum*).

Augustus likewise held a number of minor offices or titles. Though he did not become chief priest (*pontifex maximus*) until after the death of Lepidus in 13, he undertook to revivify the old Roman religion in the face of an influx of exotic eastern cults. He also allowed the worship of his genius, allied often with the goddess Roma, in Italy and the provinces. After his death he, like Caesar, was deified and temples were erected to him as *diuus Augustus*; but the official worship of living emperors during the early empire is questionable. Besides revising the rolls of Senate, knights, and people either as censor or with censorial powers, he controlled admission to the Senate by various methods. He alone could grant the wide stripe (*latus clauus*), the sign of a senatorial career, to those who did not inherit it as sons of senators. He appointed to the minor military posts which were a necessary qualification for the republican magistracies. And the privilege of either recommending (*nominatio*) or requiring (*commendatio*) the election of certain candidates for office allowed him to advance those whom he thought most fit. The republican magistracies continued with only minor changes save that the term of the consulship suffered progressive diminution until it averaged two months. When the opening pair of consuls (*consules ordinarii*) left office, there followed a succession of *consules suffecti*. Finally, in virtue either of specific enactments or of his general authority (*auctoritas*), Augustus undertook many improvements throughout the empire: roads, buildings, colonies, etc.

The title by which he is best known, **Augustus,** was bestowed on him by the Senate in 27 (Jan. 16) and expressed a semi-religious feeling of gratitude for his achievements. He did not, however, set himself up outwardly as a monarch, and the term which he himself used informally, though not as an official title, to describe himself was **princeps,** chief among equals.

29. The closing of the temple of Janus for the first time since 235 signified the achievement of longed-for peace throughout the empire (cf. year 9, below).

20. By a **treaty with Parthia,** Augustus recovered the standards lost by Crassus and Antony and thereby vindicated Roman honor.

17. A celebration of the *Ludi Saeculares*, religious ceremonies, concluded the fifth era (*saeculum*) since the founding of Rome.

16-15. The **defeat of Lollius** by the Germans necessitated the presence of Augustus in Gaul and Tiberius in Germany. Rhaetia, Noricum, and Vindelicia were annexed so that the frontier reached the upper Danube.

12-9. **Tiberius** was summoned to Pannonia by a severe revolt. Drusus fought against the Germans until his death in 9.

9. The **altar of Peace** (*ara Pacis*), voted by the Senate four years before, was dedicated (cf. year 29, above).

9-7. Tiberius carried on the conquest of Germany, but was sent to Armenia in 6. For some reason now unknown, he retired to Rhodes until the death of the sons of Agrippa and Augustus' daughter, Julia, made him the only possible successor to Augustus. He returned to Rome in 2 A.D., on the death of Lucius Caesar at Marseilles, and was adopted in 4 A.D., after the death of Gaius Caesar in Asia.

4 B.C. **THE BIRTH OF JESUS** (p. 31) probably occurred not in the traditional year, but shortly before the death of Herod the Great, son of Antipater the Idumaean, who had obtained the Kingdom of Judea from the triumvirs in 40. In 6 A.D. some of his territories were distributed among his sons, but Judea itself was placed in charge of an imperial procurator.

The **Christian Era** begins with the year 1 A.D., which follows directly on the year 1 B.C., since no year is numbered 0. Hereafter dates A.D. (*anno Domini*, "year of our Lord") will appear without designation and dates B.C. (before Christ) will be indicated as such.

4-6. Upon his adoption, Tiberius was sent again to Germany. From there he was recalled to suppress revolts in Pannonia and Dalmatia until 9. He finally established the frontier on the middle Danube. At the same time (6) the creation of the Province of Moesia and the reduction of Thrace to a client state advanced the frontier to the lower Danube.

6. Augustus set up a special treasury, the *aerarium militare*, to pay bonuses to retiring legionary veterans. Though land grants to veterans occurred thereafter, this bonus system finally solved the problem of caring for veterans. Augustus reduced the number of legions from 70 or more to 27 or 28 at his death. These, with about an equal number of auxiliary troops, gave a total army of some 300,000 men.

9. The legate, **P. Quinctilius Varus,** with three legions, was annihilated by the German Arminius in **the battle of the Teutoberg Forest,** perhaps near Paderborn. This defeat put an end to Augustus' plans for the conquest of Germany to the Elbe and established the Rhine as the future border between Latin and German territory. Augustus discontinued his conquest because of the financial difficulties involved in replacing the lost legions and levying enough additional forces to subdue Germany permanently.

14. AUGUSTUS DIED at Nola on Aug. 19. Legally, his position could not be inherited, since the various powers and offices composing it ceased with his death and could be received by another only from the Senate and Roman people. In fact, however, Augustus had throughout his life sought so to indicate a successor as to insure the perpetuation of the principate. In this attempt he tried to combine inheritance, by either blood, marriage, or adoption, with selection of the best available man, through the bestowal of a secondary proconsular *imperium* and the tribunician power. After several possible successors had predeceased him, he selected **Tiberius,** son of his wife Livia by her first husband. Though, at the death of Augustus, Tiberius held the tribunician power and an unusually extensive *imperium*, he perhaps sincerely laid before the Senate the option of restoring the republic. The Senate, however, realized the impossibility of such a step or, according to ancient authori ies, found its freedom of action impeded by the hypocrisy of Tiberius. Revolts of the legions in Pannonia and Germany showed the need of a single strong commander to prevent a recurrence of the civil wars of the later republic. Tiberius already occupied too strong a position for anyone else to be chosen. The Senate therefore conferred on him the powers and titles of Augustus.

14-37. TIBERIUS Claudius Nero (b. 42 B.C.), emperor. He transferred the elections from the assemblies to the Senate. Already the passage of laws in the assemblies had become a formality and, though continued until the time of Nerva, the assemblies hereafter had no official share in the government save to confirm the grant of the *imperium* and *tribunicia potestas* to a new emperor. The Roman mob, however, continued by its frequent riots to exert a pressure upon the government out of proportion to its importance.

14-16. The revolt of the Pannonian legions was suppressed by Tiberius' son, the younger Drusus. The son of Tiberius' brother Drusus, who is known by his father's title, **Germanicus,** and whom Augustus had forced Tiberius to adopt as a possible successor, suppressed the German mutiny and campaigned in Germany with some successes. He defeated Arminius, whose kingdom then broke up, and recovered the eagles of Varus' legions. He was, however, recalled, probably not because Tiberius begrudged his victories, but because he found them too costly.

17. On the death of their kings, Cappadocia and Commagene became a province.

17-19. **Germanicus,** sent to install a king in Armenia, conducted himself in a high-handed manner both in Syria and in Egypt. When, however, he died in Syria the enemies of Tiberius rallied about his wife Agrippina, and charged the legate of Syria, Piso, before the Senate with having poisoned him. Piso's consequent suicide gave color to the probably unjust suspicion that Tiberius, or even Livia, had encouraged the supposed poisoning.

19. **Maroboduus,** who had built up a strong kingdom in Bohemia, was forced by internal dissensions to take refuge with the Romans. Thereafter, the Romans were not seriously threatened on the Rhine or upper Danube until the time of Marcus Aurelius.

21. **A revolt broke out in Gaul** among the Treveri, led by Julius Florus, and the Aedui, led by Julius Sacrovir. Though soon suppressed by the commander in upper Germany, Gaius Silius, it showed that anti-Roman feeling was still strong in Gaul, even among the chiefs who had received Roman citizenship, as these Julii from Caesar or Augustus.

23-31. Tiberius fell increasingly under the influence of the ambitious and treacherous equestrian praefect of the guard, **Sejanus,** who quartered the praetorian cohorts in one camp outside Rome. He encouraged the gather-

The Julian-Claudian House

Gaius Octavius == Atia, niece of Julius Caesar

Octavia (1) == (2) Mark Antony   Scribonia (1) == Augustus == (2) Livia Drusilla == (1) Tiberius Claudius Nero

Drusus == Antonia the Younger

Gaius Marcellus == (1) Octavia == (2) Mark Antony

Marcus Marcellus m. Julia, d. of Augustus

Marcella m. Marcus Agrippa

Antonia the Elder m. Lucius Domitius

Antonia the Younger m. Drusus s. of Livia Drusilla

Marcus Agrippa == Julia

Tiberius (adopted by Augustus) == Vipsania d. of Agrippa

Germanicus m. Agrippina   Livilla m. Drusus   Claudius m. Messalina

Gnaeus Domitius m. Agrippina, d. of Germanicus

Domitia Lepida d. of Claudius

Gaius Caesar d. 4 A.D.   Julia   Lucius Caesar d. 2 A.D.   Agrippina m. Germanicus   Agrippa Posthumus

Drusus m. Livilla d. of Drusus

Tiberius

Julia, m. Nero s. of Germanicus

Nero m. Julia d. of Drusus   Drusus   Caligula   Agrippina m. Gnaeus Domitius   Drusilla m. Aemilius Lepidus   Julia

Poppaea Sabina (2) == Nero == (1) Octavia d. of Claudius (adopted by Claudius) m. Octavia d. of Claudius

Octavia m. Nero   Britannicus

ing of information against those hostile to Tiberius by unscrupulous informers (*delatores*, many of whom were of the nobility) and the prosecution of the accused under the law of treason (*lex de maiestate imminuta*), since actions against the person of the emperor were regarded as harmful to the majesty of the state. When such trials involved senators or important equestrians, they were heard by the Senate, which came increasingly to act as a court under the presidency of the emperor or the consuls. Ancient writers have, however, much exaggerated the abuse of this law under Tiberius. In 23, Sejanus probably poisoned Tiberius' son, Drusus, in order to intrigue for his own succession.

26. Sejanus persuaded Tiberius to retire from the annoyances of an increasingly hostile Rome. Tiberius eventually settled on **Capreae** (Capri), an island in the Bay of Naples, where the popular imagination, probably wrongly, imagined him as giving way to the most abominable vices. Actually, Tiberius was of rigid morality and of the utmost conscientiousness in governing the empire and in carrying out the policies of Augustus.

29. **Livia,** accused of attempting to dominate the empire after Augustus' death, died. Sejanus secured the exile of **Agrippina,** wife of Germanicus (she died in 33), and the arrest of his two eldest sons, Nero (d. 31) and a third Drusus (d. 33).

31. The plots of Sejanus finally came to the notice of Tiberius, who engineered his arrest and execution. Tiberius remained in rigid seclusion in Capreae.

33 (?). **PONTIUS PILATE,** procurator of Judea, allowed the Jewish Sanhedrin (national council) to crucify **Jesus,** called the "Anointed" (in Greek, *Christos*), because of his Messianic claims, which seemed seditious.

36. **Artabanus, King of Parthia,** made peace with Rome. Rome was saved from a serious Parthian threat throughout this period by dynastic quarrels within Parthia and by disputes over the possession of Armenia.

37. **Tiberius,** dying at Misenum (Mar. 16), indicated as his successors his young grandson, **Tiberius Gemellus,** and the surviving son of Germanicus, **Gaius Caesar** nicknamed *Caligula* ("Little Boot"). Gaius at first favored Tiberius Gemellus, but soon put him to death.

37-41. **Caius CALIGULA** (b. 12), emperor. If not insane at his accession, Caligula

was at least a megalomaniac and soon became unbalanced. Though the follies ascribed to him may be exaggerated, his conduct was extremely irrational. Behind it may have lain the desire for an absolute monarchy after the pattern of his great-grandfather, Antony. He established many client kings, including Julius Agrippa I, wrongly called Herod Agrippa, a grandson of Herod the Great. He had himself worshiped as a god, though his attempt to erect a statue of himself in the temple at Jerusalem was blocked by the legate of Syria, Petronius.

39. Caligula's **campaign into Germany** was stopped by a conspiracy led by Gaetulicus.

40. A campaign against Britain was also a fiasco.

41, Jan. 24. **Caligula was assassinated** by conspirators led by Cassius Chaerea.

An attempt by the Senate to revive the republic was frustrated when the praetorian guard found in the palace a scholarly, neglected younger brother of Germanicus, Claudius. Being loyal to the family, the guard imposed him upon the Senate as emperor.

41-54. **Tiberius CLAUDIUS Drusus** (b. 10 B.C.), emperor.

He was regarded at Rome as a driveling imbecile, subject to the whims of his wives and freedmen. Of the former he had four. The third, **Messalina** (a great-granddaughter of Antony) used her power to gratify her lusts until her enemies, the freedmen, secured her execution in 48. The last wife was Claudius' niece, Agrippina the Younger. She used her power to insure the succession to Lucius Domitius Ahenobarbus, her son by a former husband. The most prominent of Claudius' freedmen were **Narcissus,** secretary for the imperial correspondence (*ab epistulis*) and **Pallas,** financial secretary (*a rationibus*). Henceforth these secretaryships and others like them, on petitions (*a libellis*), on legal precedents (*a studiis*), etc., which had hitherto been simply posts in the imperial household inherited from the establishments of the republican nobility, became real offices of state, heads of a great bureaucracy. Though they never again conferred such power as they had under Claudius, their administrative importance grew and they were later filled by equestrians. In fact, for all his domestic weaknesses, Claudius took a real and intelligent interest in the administration of the empire. Without departing widely from Augustan precedents, he extended the citizenship and opened the Senate to noble Gauls (48). He incorporated the client provinces of Mauretania Tingitana and Mauretania Caesariensis (42), Lycia with Pamphylia (43), and Thrace (46). Though he made Agrippa king of all Judea in 41, he resumed it as a procuratorial province on Agrippa's death in 44. He restored Macedon and Achaea to the Senate in 44.

43. Aulus Plautius invaded Britain. The precise motives for the Roman conquest are unknown. Claudius himself visited the island to receive the surrender of Camulodunum (Colchester in Essex) in the same year. Thereafter the conquest proceeded slowly north to Lindum (Lincoln) and west to Deva (Chester) and Isca Silurum (Caerlon, i.e. *Castra Legionum*) on the Welsh border. The British leader **Caractacus** was finally captured in 51.

47. Claudius revived the censorship and celebrated secular games (*ludi saeculares*).

48. On the execution of Messalina, Claudius was permitted by a special senatorial enactment to marry his niece Agrippina. In 50, he adopted her son, Lucius Domitius Ahenobarbus who took the name **Nero** and ousted from the succession Claudius' son by Messalina, Britannicus (b. 41 or 42 and inheriting his name from his father's British triumph). In 53, Nero married Claudius' daughter by Messalina, Octavia.

53. Claudius secured a decree of the Senate by which jurisdiction was granted to imperial procurators in financial cases. This marked an important stage in the increase of the importance of imperial officials at the expense of senatorial.

54. Claudius died (Oct. 13), reputedly from poison administered by Agrippina in a dish of mushrooms. When Agrippina secured the recognition of **Claudius Nero Caesar** as successor by the praetorian guard, the Senate had to confer on him the imperial powers.

54-68. NERO (b. 37), emperor. He began his rule well under the guidance of the philosopher **Seneca** and the praefect of the guard Burrus. But in spirit he was an actor and wished to play the monarch in the grand manner. He discharged the freedman financial secretary (*a rationibus*) Pallas and poisoned Britannicus in 55. He deserted Octavia, first for the freedwoman Acte and then for Poppaea Sabina, the wife of his friend Otho. Finally he murdered his mother Agrippina in 59. After the death of Burrus in 62, he divorced, exiled, and murdered Octavia, and married Poppaea.

55-63. The general **Corbulo,** who had been successful under Claudius in Germany, was sent to settle the Parthian problem. After spending three years building up the morale of his troops, Corbulo successfully invaded Armenia and took Artaxata (58) and Tigranocerta (59). In 61, however, Nero replaced him by Paetus, who was thoroughly defeated at **Rhandeia** (62). In 63, therefore, Corbulo's solution, peace without conquest, was accepted by Nero, whose vanity was satisfied when the Parthian Tiridates came to Rome in 66 to receive his crown.

56. By a decree of the Senate, the tribunes were forbidden to usurp the judicial functions of higher magistrates and the power to fine of the tribunes and aediles was limited. At the same time the senatorial treasury (*aerarium Saturni*) was put under special praetorian praefects chosen by the emperor. The senatorial treasury constantly required subventions from the emperor. In 61, there is evidence that the city praefect (*praefectus urbi*), originally a military or police official, had acquired a jurisdiction which was competing with that of the city praetor (*praetor urbanus*). These instances show how even in Rome the imperial officials were gaining power at the expense of the republican.

60. St. Paul, before his conversion to Christianity a Jew of Tarsus named Saul belonging to the rigid sect of the Pharisees, was brought to trial before the procurator of Judea, Felix, and appealed to the emperor.

61. While Suetonius Paulinus, governor of Britain since 59, was engaged in the subjugation of the Druidical center, Mona (Anglesey, an island off northwest Wales), the queen of the Iceni (Norfolk), **Boudicca** (not *Boadicea*, as usually spelled) led a determined revolt and sacked Camulodunum (Colchester), Verulamium (St. Albans) and Londinium (London). Paulinus succeeded in defeating and killing Boudicca.

64. A great fire destroyed most of Rome. Nero's "fiddling," if genuine, was singing to the lyre a poem on the burning of Troy. When suspected of having set the fire himself, Nero found convenient culprits in the new and despised sect of the Christians, already a considerable group in Rome, with their prophecies of an imminent second advent of Christ and a world-wide conflagration. They were put to death with refined tortures.

65. A widespread conspiracy was organized to put **Gaius Calpurnius Piso** into the principate. Its noble leaders conducted it with such pusillanimity that it was discovered and many senators including Seneca, his nephew

Lucan the poet, Faenius Rufus (successor to Burrus as praetorian prefect), and Petronius (the writer and friend of Nero), were executed or forced to commit suicide.

66. Nero's hostility to the opposition culminated in the execution of the irreconcilable Stoics, Thrasea Paetus and Barea Soranus.

66-70. REVOLT IN JUDEA, resulting from misgovernment by a succession of Roman procurators. When the governor of Syria failed to suppress it, **Vespasian** was sent as special legate with three legions (67). He slowly reduced the country, took prisoner the pro-Roman Jewish historian, **Josephus,** and laid siege to Jerusalem (69). After his proclamation as emperor, Vespasian left his son **Titus** to continue the siege against the Zealot leader, John of Giscala, who had removed his rival Eleazar. Jerusalem fell (7 Sept.). Titus celebrated a triumph in 71, which is commemorated on the surviving Arch of Titus at Rome. Some of Judea was given to Marcus Julius ("Herod") Agrippa II, son of Agrippa I, but most of it became imperial domain. The Temple was destroyed, the Sanhedrin (Jewish national council) and high-priesthood abolished, the two-drachma tax paid by Jews to the temple was diverted to a special account in the imperial treasury (*fiscus Iudaicus*), and a legion under a senatorial legate superior to the procurator, was quartered in Jerusalem.

67. Nero undertook an artistic tour in Greece, in the course of which he executed Corbulo, and two ex-legates of Germany.

68. On Nero's return to Italy, he heard that **C. Julius Vindex,** legate of Gallia Lugdunensis, had revolted. Though the revolt was put down by the legate of upper Germany, L. Verginius Rufus, who refused to be saluted as emperor (*imperator*) by his troops, the two legions in Hispania Tarraconensis, on the suggestion of Vindex, had already (March) saluted as emperor their elderly legate, Servius Sulpicius **Galba.** When the praetorian guard, under the praefect Nymphidius Sabinus, recognized Galba, the Senate declared Nero a public enemy (*hostis*). He committed suicide in a villa outside Rome ("*what an artist I perish*") and the Julio-Claudian line came to an end.

68-69. Servius Sulpicius GALBA (b. 5 or 3 B.C.), emperor. By the recognition of Galba, the helpless Senate admitted that, in the words of Tacitus, "emperors could be made elsewhere than at Rome." The success of Augustus' compromise depended on the loyalty of the troops to the person to whom the Senate might grant the powers of the principate. It had already been made clear that the Senate could not resist accepting a candidate of the praetorian guard; now the provincial legions, disabused of their loyalty to the Julio-Claudian house by the unwarlike conduct of Nero, and jealous of the privileges of the praetorians, asserted themselves during this year of the four emperors (Galba, Otho, Vitellius, and Vespasian).

69, Jan. 1. The eight legions on the Rhine refused allegiance to Galba, and on Jan. 3 the four in lower Germany saluted as emperor their legate **Aulus Vitellius** (b. 15). He was also accepted by the four legions of upper Germany under Hordeonius Flaccus. Galba, whom Tacitus called "in the judgment of all, capable of ruling if he had not ruled" (*capax imperii nisi imperasset*), had reached Rome, where he adopted as his successor the aristocrat Piso Licinianus.

Thereupon, Marcus Salvius **Otho** (b. 32), the dissolute friend of Nero, who had been made legate of Lusitania so that Nero could marry his wife Poppaea and had returned with Galba, secured the support of the praetorians and had Galba and Piso murdered (Jan. 15). Otho was then recognized by the helpless Senate.

Meanwhile, the troops of Vitellius approached Italy in two divisions under Valens and Caecina. They met in the plain of the Po and defeated the forces of Otho (Apr. 19) in the **first battle of Bedriacum** (near Cremona), whereupon **Otho** committed suicide. The Senate immediately recognized Vitellius, who presently reached Rome himself.

In the meantime (July 1) the praefect of Egypt, Tiberius Julius Alexander, proclaimed as emperor **Vespasian,** legate in Judea. Mucianus, legate of Syria, lent his support. Antonius Primus, commander of the seventh legion in Pannonia, rallied all the Danubian legions to Vespasian and moved rapidly into northern Italy. There he defeated the forces of Vitellius in the **second battle of Bedriacum** and sacked Cremona (late Oct.). When Antonius approached Rome, Vespasian's brother seized the Capitol, which was burnt in the ensuing struggle. The Vitellians fought bitterly in the city streets, but Vitellius was finally slain (Dec. 20). The Senate immediately recognized Vespasian. When Mucianus reached Rome in Jan. (70), he ruled it until Vespasian arrived during the summer.

69-79. Titus Flavius VESPASIANUS (b. 9), emperor and founder of the Flavian dynasty. He was the son of a humble tax-collector from the Italian municipality of Reate. Vespasian was confronted with the task, not only of restoring the principate, but of equating himself with his aristocratic Roman predecessors. He himself, with his son Titus, held the opening consulship of every year of his reign save 73 and 78. A surviving law (*lex de imperio Vespasiani*) may be part of an inclusive measure whereby all the powers accumulated by preceding emperors were conferred specifically and together on Vespasian. Such events as the restoration of the Capitol (70, dedicated by Domitian in 82), the triumph of Titus (71), the erection of a temple of Peace (71–75), the closing of the temple of Janus (71), the destruction of Nero's extensive "Golden House" and parks, on the site of which a vast public amphitheater, the Coliseum (or Colosseum, *amphitheatrum Flavianum*), was begun, served to surround the new dynasty with material glamor. To reorganize the Senate, Vespasian felt compelled to revive the censorship with Titus in 73, instead of tacitly assuming the right of enrollment (*adlectio*) exercised by his predecessors. In 74 he granted Latin rights to all of Spain. He reorganized and rigidly controlled the finances.

69-71. The revolt of some Batavian auxiliaries under their native commander, Julius Civilis, won the support of some of the legions of Germany. This inflamed the Gallic Treveri under Julius Classicus and Julius Tutor and the Lingones under Julius Sabinus. Hordeonius Flaccus was slain at Novaesium (Neuss) on the lower Rhine. Petillius Cerialis, with six legions, took advantage of disagreements between Gauls and Batavians to crush the revolt piecemeal. The movement, though ostensibly begun in the interests of Vespasian, had in reality aimed at the establishment of an independent Gallic empire; the last instance of dangerous national separatism during the early empire. Thereafter auxiliaries were not employed in the country of their origin and the corps soon came to be composed of recruits of different nationalities. By this time the praetorian guards were alone recruited in Italy; the legions drew from Roman settlers in the provinces or Romanized provincials, to whom citizenship was often granted to secure their enlistment. Thus the army had become less Italian, more provincial in its sympathies. After the revolt, Vespasian disbanded at least four disloyal legions.

70. By putting Cappadocia in charge of the imperial governor of Galatia, by moving the eastern legions from Syria to forts on the upper Euphrates (Satala, Melitene, and Samo-

sata), and by absorbing a number of small native principalities in Asia and Syria, Vespasian consolidated the eastern frontier against Armenia and Parthia and prepared the way for Trajan's expansion.

71. **Titus,** though a senator, was made praetorian praefect, a post hitherto equestrian. He also received both the pro-consular command (*imperium*) and the tribunician power (*tribunicia potestas*), whereby Vespasian made it clear that he would follow the hereditary principle of succession.

73-74. Vespasian began the conquest of the territory east of the upper Rhine and south of the Main, the later *agri decumates* (or *decumathes*; the meaning is uncertain). He furthermore reorganized the defenses of the upper and lower Danube.

73. At about this time Vespasian banished and later executed Helvidius Priscus, son-in-law of Thrasea and his successor as leader of the Stoic opposition to the empire. He also banished the professors of philosophy, perhaps because their doctrines encouraged disloyalty.

77-84. **Conquest of Britain. Cn. Julius Agricola** (40–93) as imperial governor continued the conquest carried on by his predecessors Cerialis (72–74) over the Brigantes around Eboracum (York) and Frontinus (74–77) over the Silures in Wales. In 83 he fought a successful engagement against the Caledonians at **Mt. Graupius** (not *Grampius*), possibly near Aberdeen in Scotland, the farthest point reached by Roman arms. But Domitian recalled him in the following year; due to the fact that troops were needed for the German war. Despite later revolts Romanization progressed rapidly thereafter in Britain.

79-81. **TITUS Flavius Vespasianus** (b. 39) emperor, succeeding on the death of his father, Vespasian (June 24). Though popular, Titus was more concerned with playing the prince charming than with the economical administration of the empire. Public opinion forced him to put away the Jewish princess Berenice, already thrice married sister of Agrippa II.

79. An **eruption of Mt. Vesuvius,** on the Bay of Naples, buried the cities **Pompeii** and **Herculaneum.** In 80, a severe fire occurred in Rome. During this year, however, Titus dedicated magnificently the Coliseum and some elaborate public baths (*Thermae Titianae*).

81-96. **Titus Flavius DOMITIANUS** (b. 65) succeeded upon the death of his older brother, Titus (Sept 13).

Naturally of a suspicious, perhaps cruel, temperament, Domitian had apparently borne with ill grace the favor and preference shown to his brother and came to the throne determined to rule without respect for others, especially the Senate. Nevertheless, despite the hatred which his reign aroused, he appears to have been an able administrator and general. He legislated against immorality and strictly controlled the governors.

83. Domitian crossed the Rhine at Mainz to **campaign against the Chatti.** His victory allowed him to begin the construction of a series of forts connected by a road and later by an earth rampart surmounted by a wooden palisade which served to prevent the infiltration of barbarians into Roman territory and as a base for offensive or defensive operations, though it would not have withstood a full-fledged invasion. This system, which later extended along the central Rhine, then from Mainz outside the *agri decumates* to the upper Danube so as to straighten the dangerous re-entrant angle of the frontier at that point, and along the upper Danube north of Rhaetia, was known as the *limes.*

84. Through his election as consul for ten years and censor for life, Domitian openly subordinated the republican aspect of the state (Senate and magistrates) to the monarchical. By increasing the pay of the troops by one-third (probably in itself a needed reform), he secured their loyalty. And with lavish shows and buildings, he ingratiated himself with the Roman mob. He revived the excessive use of the law of treason with its attendant encouragement of informers. After the abortive **revolt of Saturninus,** legate of upper Germany, in 88, he proceeded bitterly against the opposition; expulsion of the philosophers in 89 was followed in 93 by the execution of Herennius Senecio, Junius Arulenus Rusticus, and Helvidius Priscus. Flavius Clemens, a first cousin of Domitian, was executed in 95 on a charge of atheism (Christianity?), though perhaps the real ground was fear of him as a possible rival. Domitian, besides widening the cult of his deceased father and brother, had himself addressed as "lord and god" (*dominus et deus*), in the tradition of Gaius and perhaps Antony.

85-89. An **invasion of the Dacians** across the Danube into Moesia in 85 was repulsed by Domitian in person. In 89, however, the complete reduction of Dacia was prevented by his defeat at the hands of the Marcomanni and Quadi, who had occupied Bohemia, west of Dacia. Domitian made a somewhat humiliating peace with the Dacian king, **Decebalus,** who retained his independence and defeated, but did not crush, the Marcomanni, Quadi, and Iazyges (a Sarmatian people) in 92. Thus the situation on the middle and lower Danube remained dangerous.

88. In consequence of the revolt of Saturninus, Domitian ceased the quartering of more than one legion in one camp to prevent any commander from gaining excessive power. The individual legions became permanently fixed in separate camps and no longer highly mobile, as they had been meant to be by Augustus.

96. **Assassination of Domitian** (Sept. 18) in a palace plot. The senate decreed the removal of his name from all public inscriptions (*damnatio memoriae*) and cancellation of his arrangements (*rescisio actorum*). Thus ended the Flavian house.

Since the conspirators, wisely, had a candidate ready to receive the Senate's grant of powers, the armies remained quiet and **Nerva,** an elderly and distinguished senator, acceded without difficulty. This marked the last attempt at self-assertion on the part of the old republican element in the principate. Already the old aristocratic families had become exhausted by persecution and race suicide. Their places had been taken by a new nobility of families elevated from the cities of Italy or the provinces through the imperial (equestrian) organization to senatorial rank. Despite a sentimental attachment to the traditions and forms of the Republic, the new generation admitted that the emperor was master, not, as Augustus had pretended, servant of the Senate.

96-98. **Marcus Cocceius NERVA** (b. 35), emperor. He was forced to recognize that the wishes of the army should be consulted by adopting in the autumn of 97 as his successor the successful general **Trajan.** Since Nerva and his three successors had no sons of their own, the principle of adoption, triumphing over heredity, secured a succession of capable rulers known as **the five good emperors** (Nerva, Trajan, Hadrian, Antoninus Pius, Marcus Aurelius). Nerva's two important contributions were to shift from the cities to the imperial treasury the cost of the postal service maintained for government dispatches (*cursus*) and to supplement existing private charity by a system of state aid for orphans (*alimenta*) supported by government grants or, under Trajan, by the interest on permanent loans to small farmers. Both reforms are symptomatic of the gradual breakdown of local economy and the municipal, system. The last reference to legislation in the assemblies is to an agrarian law (*lex agraria*) in his reign. Nerva died Jan. 25, 98.

98–117. Marcus Ulpius TRAIANUS (b. 53), emperor. At the time he was in command in lower Germany, but was accepted at Rome without difficulty, though he was the first provincial emperor (born near Seville) and though he did not visit Rome until 99. On the Rhine frontier, Trajan continued the boundary palisade (*limes*) begun under Domitian.

101–107. In two **Dacian Wars** (101–102, 105–107), whose precise chronology is uncertain, Trajan first seriously exceeded the limits set to the Empire by Augustus. Upon the final death of Decebalus, Dacia, north of the Danube, became a Roman province. The war was commemorated by a column, covered with a spiral band of continuous reliefs in the magnificent Forum of Trajan in Rome. Trajan had many fine buildings and arches erected throughout the empire.

111–112 (?). Pliny the Younger was sent by Trajan as special legate with pro-consular power to reorganize the senatorial province of Bithynia. The appointment of Pliny is symptomatic of a spreading bankruptcy of municipalities, particularly in the Greek east, which necessitated imperial interference. The emperor not only sent special legates to senatorial provinces but appointed special supervisors for cities (*curatores rei publicae*). Extravagance and increased cost of administration, both municipal and imperial, thus started locally the crisis which disrupted the whole empire during the third century. Further indications of financial stringency appear in the enlargement of the alimentary system and in the burning of records of unpaid taxes in the Forum. During his governorship, Pliny corresponded with Trajan on many problems, including the treatment of Christians, toward whom Trajan instructed him to be lenient.

113–117. Parthian War. When the Parthian monarch **Chosroes** set up his puppet in Armenia, thus violating the compromise reached under Nero, Trajan declared war on Parthia. In 114, on the death of the Parthian puppet, he annexed Armenia. As he advanced, he formed the provinces of Mesopotamia (115) and Assyria (116) and made the Tigris the eastern boundary of the empire. He was, however, recalled from the Persian Gulf by a widespread **revolt of the Jews** and of the newly conquered areas. Both were suppressed with great severity. In 117 Trajan was repulsed from the desert town of Hatra. He

died at Selinus in Cilicia (June 22 or July 9) after having adopted on his deathbed (some suspected his wife Plotina of having invented the adoption) his ward and cousin, **Hadrian,** at the time legate of Syria. Trajan's conquests, though spectacular, were of no permanent value and probably hastened the financial collapse by increasing the military expenses.

117–138. Publius Aelius HADRIANUS (b. 75), emperor. He was recognized as emperor by the Senate on Aug. 11. Almost immediately he abandoned the new provinces across the Euphrates. His lack of military ambition may have been responsible for the serious conspiracy, in 118, of four generals of consular rank, whom the Senate put to death. Hadrian then took an oath, which had become a test of constitutionalism, not to execute senators without trial by their peers. Under him the appointment of equestrians rather than freedmen to the important posts in the imperial secretariat became regular. He spent most of his reign (121–126, 129–134) traveling through the provinces, where he erected many buildings. He especially favored the Greek cities, notably Athens. In Britain he built (122–127) the elaborate combination of road, ditches, and stone wall from the Tyne to the Solway which constituted a boundary (*limes*) between the Roman province and the unconquered Caledonians. In Numidia he completed the extensive permanent camp of the Third Augustan Legion at Lambaesis.

In the collection of taxes, the companies of *publicani* had given way to individual collectors (*conductores*) under municipal supervision. Like his predecessors, Hadrian lightened or remitted certain taxes. Yet the economic difficulties continued. He had to deal with the problem of deserted farm lands (*agri deserti*), an indication that peasants were finding agriculture unprofitable, and with complaints from tenants (*coloni*) on the imperial estates in Africa. The replacement of slaves by tenants on large estates had begun when the cessation under Augustus of wars of conquest put an end to large supplies of cheap slaves. The oppression of tenants on both private and imperial estates by rising rents, heavier taxation, and forced labor rendered their lot ever more wretched.

131. The **Praetor's Edict** was definitively codified by the jurist Salvius Julianus under Hadrian's orders. Since no praetor could thereafter alter it, the extension of legal procedure by praetorian *formulae* ended. Senatorial decrees became only a confirmation of the imperial speech (*oratio principis*) which initiated them. The tribunician privilege of introducing business had been extended to the first five motions in any meeting so that the emperor presented all important matters. The only source of law was now **the edicts of the emperor.** The emperor hereafter summoned to his advisory council (*concilium*) distinguished jurists, who profoundly influenced the development of law.

132-135. The **Jews of Judea revolted** upon the founding of a Roman colony (Aelia Capitolina) in Jerusalem and the dedication of a temple to Jupiter Capitolinus on the site of their temple. Their leaders were the priest **Eleazar** and the fanatic **Simon Bar-Cocheba.** The suppression of the revolt all but depopulated Judea and thereafter Jews could enter Jerusalem but once a year. This completed the denationalization of the Jews begun by Vespasian. Until 1919 the Jews of the Dispersion (*Diaspora*), scattered among other peoples and, generally despised, possessed only a racial and religious unity.

138. Upon the death (Jan. 1) of his first choice for successor, **Lucius Ceionius Commodus,** Hadrian adopted (Feb. 25) the competent Titus Aurelius Fulvius Boionius Arrius **Antoninus,** who received the imperial powers and took the name Imperator Titus Aelius Antoninus. He, in his turn, had to adopt the young son of Commodus, Aelius Aurelius Commodus (later Lucius Aurelius Verus) and his own nephew, Marcus Annius Verus, henceforth called Marcus Aurelius Antoninus. Hadrian died on July 10.

138-161. Titus Aurelius **ANTONINUS PIUS** (b. 86) emperor. Warned by Hadrian's unpopularity with the Senate, he spent his reign in Rome. For his filial piety in securing the deification of Hadrian from a hostile Senate, he received the title *Pius*. His uneventful reign marked the culmination of the happy age of the Antonines.

142-143. **Quintus Lollius Urbicus,** legate of Britain, suppressed a revolt of the Brigantes in Yorkshire and, along the temporary line of forts built by Agricola from the Forth to the Clyde, constructed a turf wall north of Hadrian's. This however, was soon abandoned.

147. **Marcus Aurelius,** who had married Faustina, daughter of Antoninus, received the imperial powers. Antoninus apparently passed over the younger and incompetent Verus.

155. A brief **war with Vologesus of Parthia** ended in an inconclusive peace.

161-180. **MARCUS AURELIUS Antoninus** (b. 121) became emperor on the death of Antoninus (Mar. 7). Loyal to the wishes of Hadrian, he shared the imperial powers in full equality with **Lucius Aurelius Verus** (b. 130). This constitutes the first sure instance of complete collegiality in the imperial position, save for the office of chief pontiff (*pontifex maximus*), which remained unshared until Pupienus and Balbinus.

The reign of Marcus represents the triumph of **Stoicism.** Politically, the emperor was regarded as the human counterpart of the guiding reason of the universe and as obliged to rule for the good of his subjects. In law, the doctrine of the universal brotherhood of man, transcending limits of city or station, emphasized the humanizing trend which had long been operative, especially in legislation on slaves and women. Socially, the municipal and provincial aristocracy, which had appeared in the Senate through the imperial service, had wholly replaced the old Roman nobility and worked in complete loyalty with the emperor. Economically, the empire most nearly approximated unification. Italy had yielded her economic supremacy to the increased prosperity of the provinces and was losing its favored political position. It received from the emperor four special judges (created by Hadrian, abolished by Antoninus, revived by Marcus).

162-165. **Verus** was sent by Marcus to command in the east against Parthia, adumbrating the later territorial division of the empire. Though Verus dissipated at Antioch, his generals sacked Artaxata, Seleucia, and Ctesiphon, put a Roman puppet on the throne of Armenia, and made part of Mesopotamia a province.

166-167. The troops of Verus brought from the east a terrible plague, which seriously depopulated the empire.

166-175. The upper Danube was crossed by hordes of **Marcomanni** from Bohemia, with kindred tribes. Marcus created his young sons, Lucius Aelius Aurelius Commodus and Marcus Annius Verus, Caesars. He himself, with his colleague Verus, set out at once for the north. Verus died in 169. Just when Marcus had settled with the Marcomanni and had set an extremely important precedent by importing (172?) considerable numbers of them to occupy areas in the empire which had been depopulated by the plague, the **Sarmatians** attacked the lower Danube frontier.

175. **Avidius Cassius,** a distinguished general and legate of Syria, revolted,

perhaps misled by a false report of Marcus'
death. Though his revolt was crushed before
Marcus could reach the east, it prevented a
final settlement of the Sarmatian war.

177. Marcus' eldest son, **Commodus,** became
Imperator, then Augustus, coequal
with his father. The younger son had died in
169. Marcus is said to have issued a severe
rescript against the Christians. In any case,
they were subjected to increasingly bitter and
far-reaching persecution, probably as fomenters
of trouble by their prophecies of evil, and as
disloyal to the state because they would not
swear oaths to the emperor or offer incense to
his statues or serve in the army.

178-180. The Marcomanni again opened war
so that Marcus and Commodus had
to go to the Danube. The wars of
Marcus were commemorated on a column in Rome. Marcus died at Vindo-
bona (Vienna) (Mar. 17, 180).

**180-192. Marcus Aurelius COMMODUS An-
toninus** (b. 161), as Marcus' son was
now called, was the first emperor since Domitian
to succeed by birth rather than by adoption.
He made a peace with the Marcomanni which,
though temporarily satisfactory, lost him favor
with the troops. He returned to Rome, where
he gave himself up to pleasure. The government
was at first managed by the capable praetorian
praefect **Perennis,** but on his unwarranted execution in 185, at the request of a deputation of
mutinous soldiers from Britain, it fell to the
mercenary freedman **Cleander,** who, in turn,
was sacrificed in 189 to the Roman mob, which
blamed him for a grain shortage. Commodus,
already hostile to the Senate in consequence
of an abortive conspiracy in 182, became ex-
travagantly despotic. He identified himself
with Hercules and lavished wealth acquired
from the treasury or by confiscation on his
favorites, the praetorians, whose pay he increased by a quarter, and on hunts of beasts, in
which he participated. On Dec. 31, 192, his
concubine Marcia, his chamberlain Eclectus,
and the praetorian praefect Laetus had him
strangled by a wrestler named Narcissus. Thus
ended the Antonine line.

The important trends in the early empire
were: **politically,** the transformation of the
princeps, agent of the republican Senate and
Roman people, into a Stoic king, head of a
state in which all good men co-operated for the
common weal; **administratively,** the subordination of the republican magistracies and organs
to the will of the emperor and the growth of
the imperial secretariat and equestrian civil

service; **socially,** the substitution for the irreconcilable republican nobility of a new aristocracy drawn from the better classes throughout the Empire, which, though sentimentally
republican, accepted the Empire if the emperor
was good; **economically,** the financial breakdown of the municipal system, which was accompanied by a loss of local pride, and the increased burdens of the imperial government; and
militarily, greater and more constant pressure on
both frontiers, north and east, at the same time.

The literature of the early empire falls into
two periods; the **Augustan Age,** which, with
the preceding Ciceronian Age, forms the **Golden
Age;** and (after 14) the **Silver Age** of the Julio-
Claudians, Flavians, and Antonines. Under
Augustus, the chief figures gathered around
his friend, their patron **Maecenas: Publius
Vergilius Maro** or Virgil (70–19 B.C.) author of
the *Bucolics, Georgics* and the *Aeneid,* and
Quintus Horatius Flaccus or Horace (65–8 B.C.),
author of *Odes, Epodes, Satires,* and *Epistles.*
Besides these, **Albius Tibullus** (54–19 B.C.) and
Sextus Propertius (50–15 B.C.) wrote erotic
elegies and **Publius Ovidius Naso** or Ovid (43
B.C.–17 A.D.) composed the erotic *Amores,
Heroides, Ars Amatoria,* etc., and the longer
*Metamorphoses, Fasti, Tristia, Letters from
Pontus,* etc. **Titus Livius,** or Livy (59 B.C.–
17 A.D) composed his *History of Rome (Libri
ab urbe condita),* a prose glorification comparable
to the *Aeneid.* The writers of the Silver Age
are numerous and less outstanding: **Aulus
Persius Flaccus** (34–62 A.D.) and **Decimus Iunius
Juvenalis** (55–138) wrote satire, and **Marcus
Valerius Martialis** (40–104) composed satirical
epigrams. **Lucius Annaeus Seneca** the Philosopher (1–65), son of Seneca the Rhetorician
(55 B.C.–40 A.D.), and his nephew, **Marcus Annaeus Lucanus** (39–65), author of the epic
Pharsalia, belong, like Martial, to the Spanish
group of authors prominent in the first century,
as does also **Marcus Fabius Quintilianus** (35–
100), teacher of rhetoric and author of an *Insti-
tutio Oratoria.* **Gaius Petronius Arbiter** (d. 66),
the Epicurean friend of Nero, probably composed
the *Satyricon,* a picaresque novel. **Publius
Cornelius Tacitus** (55–118?), author of the
Dialogue on Oratory, the life of his father-in-
law *Agricola,* the *Germania,* the *Annals,* and the
Histories, **Gaius Plinius Caecilius Secundus**
(61–113?), whose *Letters* are preserved, and
nephew of the erudite Gaius Plinius Secundus
(23–79), the author of the *Natural History* who
died in the eruption of Vesuvius, and the biog-
rapher **Gaius Suetonius Tranquillus** (70–121?),
whose *Lives of the Twelve Caesars* extend from

Caesar through Domitian, belonged to the literary circle which flourished under Trajan. Under Hadrian began a revival of interest in pre-Ciceronian Latin language and literature, while under the Antonines, a school of African writers introduced a florid and exaggerated style. Its chief exponent was **Lucius Apuleius (124–?)**, whose *Metamorphoses* and other writings cast light on the mystery religions and neo-Pythagoreanism. The surviving writings of emperors, apart from administrative edicts, etc., are the succinct account of his life by Augustus, preserved on inscriptions at Ancyra (Ankara, *Monumentum Ancyranum*) and, in fragments, elsewhere; some speeches and letters of Claudius in inscriptions or papyri; and the *Meditations*, in Greek, of Marcus Aurelius.

In **philosophy**, Stoicism remained dominant throughout the period and claimed among its chief exponents the statesman **Seneca** (1–65), the slave **Epictetus** (60–140), and the emperor **Marcus Aurelius**. But it had to compete with mystical tendencies which found expression in astrology, in such **oriental religions** as those of the Egyptian **Isis**, the Persian **Mithras**, and the Jewish **Jesus Christ**, and in a revival of the early Greek mystical philosophy of Pythagoras. **Christianity**, which had begun as a Jewish sect but was universalized and widely spread by the ardent convert, **Paul**, soon developed both an organization and a literature. The organization consisted of independent churches governed by boards of elders (*presbyters*) among whom one frequently secured pre-eminence as bishop (*episcopos*, overseer). Those churches which traced their foundation to the immediate associates of Christ, the **Apostles**, or which arose in big cities, tended to overshadow the less important ones and their bishops, especially, in the west, the Bishop of Rome, became authorities in ecclesiastical quarrels. Heresies appeared from the beginning, like **Gnosticism** and, about 150, **Montanism**. Christian literature commenced with the *Gospels* and *apostolic* (or pseudo-apostolic) *writings*. The early martyrs, **Ignatius of Antioch** (d. 117?) and **Polycarp of Smyrna** (d. 155?), as well as the Greek bishop, **Irenaeus of Lyons** (c. 130–200), who attacked the heretical transcendentalism of the Gnostics, wrote largely for Christians. But the increasing hostility of the public and government occasioned apologetic writings addressed to non-Christians, like those of **Justin Martyr (153?)** and others.

Augustan art, like Augustan literature, achieved a happy blend of native Roman realism and Greek idealism, as best appears in the sculpture of the *Ara Pacis* or the famous " Prima Porta " statue of Augustus. Julio-Claudian art aped the manner without attaining the excellence of Augustan. Under the Flavians, a certain heaviness and materialism, characteristic of the period, appeared. But two relief techniques were perfected, that of illusionism, the attempt to represent space, as on the panels of the Arch of Titus, and the continuous style, by which a series of events was represented in an unbroken sequence, as on the Column of Trajan. Hadrian's reign witnessed a revived interest in and copying of Greek archaic art. Under the Antonines, a crudeness appears on the Column of Marcus, though not in the reliefs from his arch. Mention should be made of the **wall-paintings** of all periods from the 2d century B.C. to 79 A.D. preserved at Pompeii and of the common red pottery with appliqué reliefs known as **Arretine ware** (modeled on the Greek Samian ware) made first in Italy, at Arretium (Arezzo), and then progressively at various places in Gaul and even in Britain.

In **architecture**, the grandeur of the Augustan Age, as in the porch of the Pantheon or the Maison Carrée at Nîmes, gave way to massiveness, as in the temple of Venus at Rome and the Coliseum. But the Roman engineers produced at all periods substantial and useful structures: aqueducts, theaters, circuses, baths, harbors, roads, etc.

2. THE THIRD CENTURY (192-284)

The third century is characterized by the complete collapse of government and economics throughout the Mediterranean. Upon the death of Commodus, the armies asserted themselves against the Senate as they had in 68. The ultimate victor, **Septimius,** finally and frankly unmasked the military basis of the imperial power. After an attempted revival of "**constitutional**" government under Alexander, the imperial position became the reward of successful generals of increasingly provincial and uncultured origins. The one ideal which still dominated the armies was the preservation of the frontiers against the Germans and Persians. Even the separatist movements were aimed, not at independence, but at the preservation of the *imperium Romanum*. To secure this end and their own support, the troops made and unmade emperors and drained the scanty resources of the civilians by taxation, depreciation of coinage, and exactions of food, quarters, etc. The military wholly absorbed the civil administration. Intellectual life ceased, inscriptions became rare, and archaeological finds show a rapid decline in skill and taste.

193. Publius Helvius PERTINAX, emperor. He was chosen by the Senate, but his strict and economical rule led to his murder (Mar. 28) by the praetorian guard, which then auctioned off the empire to him who promised them the highest gift of money, **M. Didius Severus Julianus** (b. 133?). The British legions proclaimed as emperor the legate, **D. Clodius Septimius Albinus;** the Pannonian, the legate of Upper Pannonia **L. Septimius Severus** (April or May); and the Syrian, the legate **C. Pescennius Niger Justus.** Septimius at once seized Rome, where the Senate deposed and executed Julianus (June 1).

193-211. L. SEPTIMIUS SEVERUS (b. 146, at Leptis in Africa), emperor. He dissolved the existing praetorian cohorts, composed of recruits from Italy, and enrolled new ones from deserving legionary veterans. He kept Albinus quiet by recognizing him as Caesar (i.e. heir). He then defeated Niger in **battles at Cyzicus** and **Nicaea** and at Issus (the Cilician Gates), and put him to death near Antioch (194). Byzantium held out until 196, when it was sacked and reduced to the status of a village. Albinus, who now claimed full equality, was defeated and slain (197, Feb. 19) at Lugdunum (Lyons), which was also sacked and never recovered its prosperity.

Severus created three new legions, one of which was quartered on the Alban Lake in Italy, hitherto free from the presence of legionary troops. He appointed equestrians to command these legions contrary to the Augustan rule and also put the new province of Mesopotamia under an equestrian. He thus initiated the replacement of senators by equestrians in military posts which culminated under Gallienus. Military marriages were recognized, since the immobilization of the legions had made these usual. Auxiliaries were settled on public land in return for military service and the legionary pay was raised. Severus humiliated the Senate, which had supported Albinus, and put equestrian deputies to watch senatorial governors. When he closed down the now almost defunct courts (*quaestiones*), he transferred the jurisdiction over Rome and the area within 100 miles to the praefect of the city and over the rest of Italy to the praetorian praefect, who also exercised jurisdiction on appeal from the provinces. After the fall of the single and powerful praetorian praefect Plautianus (205), Severus returned to the practice of having two, one of whom was the distinguished jurist Papinian. In the criminal law, a distinction was drawn between the privileged classes (*honestiores*), who were treated favorably, and the ordinary people (*humiliores*). The emperor began the subdivision of provinces into smaller units, which culminated under Diocletian and extended the organization of municipalities as the basis of tax-collecting even to Egypt, which shows how valueless municipal status had become. He created a new treasury in addition to the *fiscus* (the original imperial treasury) and the *patrimonium Caesaris* (originally the ruler's private property, then crown property), namely the *res privata*, his personal funds. He depreciated the silver content of the denarius to 60%. Despite all of these difficulties, his administration was good.

197-198. In a successful **Parthian war** Severus advanced as far as Ctesiphon and reconstituted the Province of Mesopotamia under an equestrian governor with two legions.

205-211. A recurrence of **troubles in Britain,** which had suffered from invasion in 155 and revolt in 180, required the presence of Septimius himself to fight the Caledonians. He definitely withdrew from the wall of Antoninus to that of Hadrian, which he rebuilt. He died at Eboracum (York) on Feb. 4, 211.

211-217. CARACALLA (properly Caracallus), so named from a Gallic cloak which he wore. He was the oldest son of Septimius and had been associated with him as Augustus (198). To strengthen the bond between the Severi and the Antonines he had changed his name from Septimius Bassianus to Marcus Aurelius (Severus) Antoninus (197). Upon his accession, he murdered his colleague (since 209) and younger brother, P. (originally L.) Septimius (Antoninus) Geta (b. 189), along with the jurist Papinian and many others. He increased the pay of the troops to a ruinous degree and called them all *Antoniniani.* To meet the consequent deficit he issued a new coin, the *Antoninianus*, with a face value of 2 *denarii* but a weight of only one and two thirds. He erected at Rome the vast **Baths of Caracalla** (*thermae Antoninianae*).

212. The **EDICT OF CARACALLA** (*constitutio Antoniniana*) extended Roman citizenship to all free inhabitants of the empire save a limited group, perhaps including the Egyptians. His motive has been much disputed; citizenship now meant so little that this step was a natural culmination of the levelling down of distinctions which had been continuous throughout the empire. Moreover, he may have hoped to extend to all inhabitants the inheritance tax paid by Roman citizens.

213-217. Caracalla successfully defended the northern frontier against the Alamanni in southern Germany and the Goths on the lower Danube (214), and in the east he annexed Armenia (216). But as he was preparing an invasion of Parthia, he was murdered by a group of his officers (217, Apr. 8).

217-218. M. Opellius (Severus) MACRINUS (b. 164?), emperor. He was a Mauretanian who had risen from the ranks to be praetorian praefect, and was the first equestrian emperor. He surrendered Caracalla's eastern gains and sought to reduce the pay of the troops, who set up as a rival (218, May 16) at Emesa in Syria a grandnephew of Julia Domna, the Syrian wife of Septimius. Macrinus fell on June 8, 218.

218-222. ELAGABALUS (Heliogabalus, b. c. 205), emperor. He derived his cognomen from the Emesa god, whose priest he was. To legitimize his rule, he changed his name from (Varius) Avitus to Marcus Aurelius Antoninus and claimed to be a son of Caracalla. While Elagabalus surrendered himself to license and introduced the worship of his god to Rome, the empire was really ruled by his forceful mother, **Julia Maesa.** She obliged him to adopt his cousin (Gessius) Bassianus (Alexianus?), son of her sister, Julia Mamaea. The praetorians murdered Elagabalus (222, Mar. 11).

222-235. Marcus Aurelius SEVERUS ALEXANDER (b. c. 208), emperor. He was the adopted son of Elagabalus and was dominated by his mother, Mamaea. She established a regency committee of senators and used the advice of the jurists Paulus and Ulpian. The new rule was an attempt to revive the Antonine monarchy. It was marked, however, by an extension of governmental control over the trade guilds (*collegia*) and further depreciation of the coinage.

227. The New Persian (Sassanid) Empire (p. 124) was founded by **Ardashir** (Artashatr, Artaxerxes), a Persian who overthrew the Parthian Arsacids, Artabanus V and Vologaesus V. The strength of the new empire lay in a revival of **Zoroastrianism.**

231-233. Persian attacks required the presence of Alexander, who seems to have won some success before his recall to the west.

234-235. Alexander was forced to buy peace from the Alamanni on the Rhine. The disgruntled troops murdered him (235, Mar.). With his death the last attempt to preserve a civil or "constitutional" government came to an end and military anarchy began.

235-238. C. Julius Verus MAXIMINUS "Thrax" (b. c. 172), a Thracian peasant of huge size and no culture, was elevated by the Rhine legions, but was not recognized by the Senate, which put forward the senators **M. Clodius Pupienus Maximus** and **D. Caelius Calvinus Balbinus.** In the meantime, the African legions proclaimed the eighty-year-old pro-consul **Marcus Antonius Gordianus I** and his son **Gordianus II.** Though the praefect of Mauretania defeated and slew them, the populace of Rome forced the Senate to join the grandson, **Gordianus III,** with Pupienus and Albinus. Maximin was slain by his troops while besieging Aquileia (238, June) and the praetorians murdered Pupienus and Balbinus (238, June?).

238-244. Marcus Antonius GORDIANUS III (b. 225) was dominated by the wise praetorian praefect **C. Furius Timesitheus** (Misitheus?), whose daughter he married (241). Timesitheus drove the son of Ardashir, Shapur (Sapor), out of Antioch (241–243) but died himself of disease. The new praetorian praefect, an Arabian, made himself co-Augustus, then murdered Gordian (early in 244).

244-249. M. Julius PHILIPPUS "ARABS" bought peace with the Persians and, at Rome, celebrated the *ludi saeculares* for Rome's thousandth birthday (248). He was killed at Verona (249) in battle against his commander in Dacia, Decius.

249-251. C. Messius Quintus Traianus DECIUS (b. 200?) instituted the first general **persecution of the Christians,** and perhaps of all who would not sacrifice to the emperor. Emperor-worship, though used as early as Pliny as a test against Christians, seems now to have become a requirement of all loyal subjects, which indicates a growing belief in the actual divinity of the emperor. Decius was slain by the Goths in Dacia (251) because of the disloyalty of the legate of Moesia, Gallus.

251-253. C. Vibius Trebonianus GALLUS (b. c. 207) put to death his co-Augustus, **Hostilianus,** son of Decius. In his reign began a fifteen-year plague. When he marched against his successor in Moesia, the Moor M. Aemilius

Aemilianus, his own troops slew him (before Oct., 253).

253-259. P. Licinius VALERIANUS (b. c. 193), commander in Germany, became emperor, with his son Gallienus as co-Augustus. He fought unsuccessfully against the Franks, who crossed the Rhine in 256, the Alamanni, who reached Milan, and the Goths. As the frontiers ceased to hold, cities within the empire began to build walls. Valerian recovered Antioch again from Shapur (256–258) but was treacherously seized at a parley (259?) and died a captive at an uncertain date.

259-268. P. Licinius Egnatius GALLIENUS (b. 218) continued to reign alone, though pretenders appeared throughout the empire and the period has been called that of the "thirty tyrants." He completed the substitution of equestrians for senators as legionary commanders and as governors.

The Goths, who had broken through to the Black Sea, harried Asia and the Aegean area from ships.

258-267. Odenathus, ruler of Palmyra in the Syrian Desert, kept the Persians out of Asia (260), but his queen and successor **Zenobia,** declared her independence (267).

259-268. Postumus set himself up as emperor in Gaul. **Gallienus** was finally murdered by his own troops before Mediolanum (Milan), where he was besieging the pretender **Aureolus** (before Sept., 268). Aureolus in his turn was slain by Claudius II.

268-270. M. Aurelius CLAUDIUS II "Gothicus" (b. ?) was the first of a series of capable Illyrian emperors who prepared the way for Diocletian. He repelled a Gothic invasion of the Balkans (269, whence his title) at **Naissus** (Nisch) and settled numbers of Goths in the vacant lands of the Danubian provinces. Upon his death from plague, the Balkan legions elevated his compatriot and assistant, Aurelian (before July, 270).

270-275. L. Domitius AURELIANUS (b. c. 214?) was rightly entitled "restorer of the world" (*restitutor orbis*). He abandoned trans-Danubian Dacia and settled its Roman inhabitants in a new Dacia carved out of Moesia. He repulsed the Alamanni from Italy (271) and built the existing walls of Rome (271–276) as a protection against future incursions.

271-272. Probus, and then Aurelian himself, defeated and captured Zenobia and, upon a second revolt, sacked Palmyra (273), which remained a ruin.

273 or 274. Aurelian recovered Gaul from the successor of Postumus, Tetricus, in a battle at Châlons. Both Zenobia and Tetricus adorned his magnificent triumph in Rome (274). He was murdered by some officers while preparing to invade Persia (275).

275-276. M. Claudius TACITUS (b. ?), an elderly senator, was appointed emperor against his will by the Senate, to whom the troops left the choice (275, autumn?). Though he defeated the Goths and Alans, who had invaded Asia Minor, the troops slew him and, soon after, his brother M. Annius Florianus.

276-281. M. Aurelius PROBUS (b. ?), an Illyrian, was saluted by the eastern armies (276, early summer?). He repelled from Gaul the Franks and Alamanni and other peoples, who had inflicted great devastation. He also strengthened the Danube frontier, quieted Asia Minor, and suppressed pretenders in Gaul. When he tried to use the troops in works of peace, e.g. clearing the canals in Egypt, they murdered him (281, autumn?).

281-283. M. Aurelius CARUS, an Illyrian (?) and praetorian praefect to Aurelian, succeeded and campaigned successfully against the Persian monarch Varahran. He perished (murder, disease, or lightning? in 283, midsummer?) and his son Marcus Aurelius Numerius Numerianus, co-Augustus with him, was murdered (284, autumn). A second son, M. Aurelius Carinus, tried to hold the west against **Diocletian,** an officer whom the eastern army had elected emperor, but he was slain by his own troops during the battle at the river Margus in Moravia (285, summer?).

The troubles of the third century had two main causes: the increased pressure on the frontiers from the new Germanic tribes and from the vigorous Persian Empire, and the economic collapse within, the causes of which cannot be wholly established. In part, at least, the economic crisis was due to the heavy burdens of government and defense and to the oppressive and erratic system of taxation; in part, perhaps, to a "fatigue of spirit." Literature ceased almost entirely. Of art and building notable examples survive, like the Arch of Septimius, the Baths of Caracalla, and the Walls of Aurelian at Rome, but these are imitative and uninspired. **Roman law,** however, reached its heights under the Antonines and Severi. Though the two great schools of jurisprudence, the **Sabinians** and the **Proculians,** originated under Augustus or Tiberius, the great jurists were **Salvius Julianus** under Hadrian, who dealt with the **Praetor's Edict, Gaius** under the Antonines, whose *Institutes* became a standard textbook, and the triumvirate of **Papinian, Paul, and Ulpian** under the Severi, whose various works provided most of the material for Justinian's *Institutes*. In philosophy, neo-Pythagoreanism gave way to neo-Platonism, whose chief exponents were **Plotinus** (204-207), **Porphyrius** (233-306), and, later, **Iamblichus** (d. 333?).

Despite the persecutions under the Antonines, Severus, Maximin, and Decius, **the Christian Church** grew in numbers and power. Its chief competitor was the cult of the Persian **Mithras,** a god popular with and widely spread by the troops. The major internal problems of the church in the third century were the heresy called Montanism (an extreme asceticism) and the acute question of the treatment of those who lapsed from their faith during persecutions (*lapsi*) or betrayed the sacred books (*traditores*). Those who had confessed their faith in the face of persecution (*confessores*) opposed the readmission of backsliders to full communion, while the church as a whole, led in the west by the Bishop of Carthage, **Cyprian,** and the Bishop of Rome, **Stephen,** advocated a milder policy. The extremists were called **Novatians** in the third century and **Donatists** in the fourth, after a certain Donatus, whose riotous bands of schismatics (*circumcelliones*) terrorized the province of Africa. Christian apologetics gave way to homiletic and theological writings in the hands of the African **Tertullian** (150-225) and **Cyprian** (200-258) and the Alexandrians **Clement** (d. 215) and **Origen** (182-251), the last two of whom combined Platonism with Christianity in the manner of contemporary neo-Platonism.

3. THE LATER EMPIRE (284-527)

284-305. C. Aurelius Valerius DIOCLETIANUS (b. 245, saluted as emperor 284, Nov. 17?), was of humble Illyrian stock. Faced with the task of bringing order out of chaos, he desired to emulate Augustus, to revive the happy days of the early empire, but he succeeded only in creating an oriental despotism.

Since it is difficult to distinguish how far the reorganization of the empire was due to Diocletian and how far to Constantine, a brief outline will be given here. In general, all these reforms were merely a regularization and crystallization of practices developed in the 3d century. Although the Senate continued to meet and the higher republican magistrates survived to varying dates, e.g. the consulship in the east until its abolition by Justinian, and although two provinces, Asia and Africa, still received senatorial pro-consuls, nevertheless the whole administration was organized in a pyramid of interlocking bureaus emanating from the emperor.

According to Diocletian's system, which operated only sporadically, there were to be two coequal emperors (*Augusti*), as in the case of Marcus and Verus. Now, however, the empire was divided for practical administrative purposes into two spheres, eastern and western, the line between which ran from the Danube to the Adriatic south of Dalmatia. Each part was administered by one of the Augusti. But the edicts of the emperors were issued conjointly and they might on occasion command in one another's spheres.

The emperors ruled absolutely, in virtue of selection by the troops and without the consent of the Senate (since 282). Each surrounded himself with the pomp of an oriental court. No longer was he the first citizen among equals (*princeps*), but, since Aurelian, "lord" (*dominus*). All connected with him was "sacred" (the "sacred court," *sacra aula*, appeared under the Severi). Each emperor chose an assistant and successor (*Caesar*).

Under these four rulers, praetorian praefects, now wholly civilian magistrates, administered the four praefectures, Gaul, Italy, Illyrium, and the east. Each praefecture was divided into several dioceses under vicars (*uicarii*) independent of the praefects and directly responsible to the emperor. The dioceses were subdivided into provinces under presidents (*praesides* or *rectores*). These provinces were subdivisions of those of the early empire and their number increased from 60 to 116.

The military power, which during the third century had absorbed all the functions of government, was now wholly separated from the civilian. Each province had a duke (*dux*) or count (*comes*) in charge of its permanent garrison, which was not, as in the early empire, concentrated in large camps, but scattered in smaller posts along the frontier, often in the guise of soldier-peasants (*limitanei, riparienses,* border or riverbank men). In each praefecture, under masters of the infantry and of the horse (*magistri peditum, equitum*), were mobile forces which could be rushed to strengthen threatened points (*comitatenses,* companions of the emperor). The emperors, moreover, had large bodies of special guards (*protectores* or *domestici*). The old legions were split into smaller, more mobile but less highly trained units of about 2000 men. Heavy armed cavalry (*cataphractarii*) played a large part in warfare. The auxiliary troops were mostly mercenary bands of barbarians, whose chiefs became extremely influential. The total forces now numbered about 500,000 men, an increase over the Augustan 300,000 which accounts in part for the financial problems of the later empire.

Besides the separate and elaborate administration for each territorial unit, the emperors had an extensive central bureaucracy, the various "offices" (*officia*) under such officials like the quaestor of the sacred palace (*quaestor sacri palatii*, the chief judicial officer), the chancellor (*magister memoriae*, master of records), and the personnel manager (*magister officiorum*, master of the offices, very powerful because he had a finger in every department). These men automatically belonged to the Senate, and other high officials had the titles of honor formerly reserved for equestrians, who vanished as a class. The senators also now formed a class of dominant and very wealthy landowners throughout the empire, who might seldom actually attend the Senate, but who enjoyed privilege and exemption. The rest of the population were crushed by heavy taxes, which were largely collected in kind (*annona*) after the collapse of the currency, and which were reassessed every fifteenth year by an "indiction" (*indictio*). Both labor and property were evaluated in terms of a unit of wheat-producing land (*iugum*). The taxation bore especially heavily on the members of the municipal senates (*curiales, decuriones*), who continued to be held responsible for the collection of taxes and the payment of arrears, and on the small landowners, who had to provide recruits for the army and see that waste lands (*agri deserti*) were kept under cultivation. Thus freemen found it wisest to flee the country, enter monasteries, or become serfs (*coloni*) on large estates. Craftsmen and tradesmen were rigorously confined to their professions. The whole caste system was arranged to insure the maintenance of the administration and the army. Since, therefore, it benefited no one but the great landlords or imperial officials, the vast majority of the population lost interest and either accepted the barbarian invasions supinely or even welcomed relief from oppression. Whether, however, this lethargy, which pervaded not only the political and economic life but also the

intellectual, save in the Christian Church, resulted from the system or whether the unwieldy and inflexible system indicated the poor mental caliber of the rulers, so many of whom were of peasant or barbarian origin, and the effeteness of the hereditary upper class, cannot be determined.

285. Upon the defeat of Carinus, Diocletian chose as his colleague (Caesar in 285, Augustus in 286) the Illyrian **M. Aurelius Valerius Maximianus** (b. c. 240?), who was a harsh, uneducated man but a competent general. They assumed the titles respectively of *Jovius* and *Herculius*. Diocletian took up his residence in the east, at Nicomedia in Bithynia, from which the main road to the upper Euphrates frontier began, while **Maximian,** in the west, lived mostly at Mediolanum (Milan) in northern Italy, which was a better center for the defense of the northern frontier than Rome. Despite its sentimental pre-eminence, Rome thereafter declined in practical importance. But the departure of the imperial court gave the Bishop of Rome increased scope.

293, Mar. 1. Diocletian chose as Caesar **C. Galerius Valerius Maximianus** (b. c. 250), who became his son-in-law and received the government of Illyricum; Maximian chose **Flavius Valerius Constantius** (misnamed Chlorus) (b. ?) who divorced his wife Helena to marry Maximian's daughter Theodora; he received the praefecture of Gaul. He at once drove out the rebel Carausius from Boulogne and subdued the Franks.

294. A revolt was raised in Egypt by Achilleus, whom Diocletian besieged in Alexandria (295) and captured.

296. **Narses,** King of Persia, invaded Roman Mesopotamia and defeated Galerius, but the latter gathered reinforcements in the winter and returned to defeat Narses (297) and recover Mesopotamia; Roman influence was restored in Armenia, whose king became Christian.

297. Constantius crossed to Britain and his lieutenant defeated and killed Allectus, who had murdered and replaced Carausius.

298. Constantius returned to Gaul and defeated the Alamanni.

301. An edict limiting prices of goods and labor was passed by Diocletian in an attempt to end the economic distress caused by the collapse of the currency; no attempt was made to enforce it in the west, and in the east it soon proved impracticable.

303, Feb. 23. Galerius persuaded Diocletian to

declare a **general persecution of the Christians,** which, however, Constantius did not enforce in his praefecture. The persecution was stopped in the entire west in 306 but raged in the east until 313.

305, May 1. Diocletian and Maximian abdicated; Galerius and Constantius became Augusti; Diocletian and Galerius selected as Caesars **Flavius Valerius Severus** under Constantius, receiving the praefecture of Italy, and for Galerius his own nephew **Galerius Valerius Maximinus Daia,** who received Syria and Egypt. The hereditary claims of Maximian's son Maxentius and Constantius' son Constantine were neglected.

306-337. Flavius Valerius CONSTANTINUS I THE GREAT (b. 288? of Constantius and Helena) fled from Galerius to his father in Britain. On the death of the latter (July) Constantine was saluted as emperor by the troops, but made an agreement with Galerius by which he became Caesar and Severus became Augustus. In Rome the praetorians and the people proclaimed **Maxentius Augustus** (Oct. 28); he called his father Maximian to be Augustus and temporarily took the title of Caesar. When the Emperor Severus came with an army, it deserted and he surrendered to Maximian and was later executed by Maxentius. In fear of Galerius, Maximian went to Constantine in Gaul; Constantine recognized him as senior Augustus and married his daughter, Fausta. Galerius attempted an invasion of Italy (307), but disloyalty in his army forced its abandonment. Maxentius took the title of Augustus (308) and Maximian fled to Constantine; for four years Maxentius ruled in Italy very oppressively. Galerius induced Diocletian to preside over a conference at Carnuntum, where it was decided that Maximian should abdicate, **Valerius Licinianus Licinius** was to be Augustus in the west, and Constantine was to return to the rank of Caesar. Constantine refused and Galerius gave him and Daia the rank of *filius Augusti*; both were still unsatisfied, and were finally given the rank of Augustus (310). Maximian made an attempt to revolt, but was killed by Constantine. When Galerius died of disease (311, May), Daia seized Asia Minor, leaving the Balkans to Licinius.

312. Constantine suddenly invaded Italy and after winning a battle over Maxentius' general at Verona defeated and killed Maxentius himself near Rome at the **Milvian Bridge** (Saxa Rubra) (Oct. 28). Before the battle he is said to have seen in the sky a cross and the device *in hoc signo vinces.* Sometime later he became a Christian. He dissolved the praetorian guard. At a meeting with Licinius in Milan (early 313?) equal rights were proclaimed for all religions and the property confiscated from the Christians was restored by the **Edict of Milan.**

313. Daia crossed to Europe, but was defeated by Licinius at **Tzirallum** and fled to Tarsus, where he died soon after. Licinius now held the entire east and Constantine the west.

314. After a brief war, in which Licinius was defeated at **Cibalae** (Oct. 8), a peace was made giving Constantine all of the Balkans except Thrace.

324. Relations between the two were strained by Licinius' anti-Christian policy, and war finally broke out. Licinius was defeated at **Adrianople** (July 3), his fleet was defeated by Constantine's son Crispus, and Licinius was again defeated at Chrysopolis in Anatolia (Sept. 18). He surrendered and was executed in the next year.

324-337. CONSTANTINE REUNITED THE EMPIRE under his sole rule. He had already interfered in the affairs of the Church (at its invitation) when in 316 he tried to settle the Donatist schism.

325. He now summoned the **first oecumenical** (world-wide) **council of the Church,** to meet at **Nicaea** in Asia Minor. It was to settle a controversy which had arisen in Alexandria between the priest **Arius,** who maintained that Christ was of different substance from God (*heter-ousios*), and the Bishop Alexander (succeeded in 328 by **Athanasius,** who continued his doctrine), who supported the doctrine that they were of the same substance (consubstantiality, *homo-ousios*). The council agreed on a creed favorable to Alexander (not the present "Nicene" creed); in addition it adopted certain canons giving privileges to the Bishops (Patriarchs) of Alexandria, Antioch, and Rome. Constantinople later acquired similar rights. The **primacy of Rome,** although in a very restricted sense, had been generally recognized in the west since the **Council of Arles** in 314. The prominent part taken by Constantine in this council laid the basis for the later supremacy of the emperor in the eastern Church. Though Arius died a horrible death in 336, Constantine and his successors swung the Church increasingly toward Arianism, and strife in the Church on this subject was not ended until the reign of Theodosius I. The west remained firmly Athanasian.

330, May 11. Constantine dedicated as his capital **CONSTANTINOPLE,** which he had spent four years in building on the site of Byzantium, commanding the strategic center of the east, the Bosporus.

337, May 22. Constantine died at Nicomedia. He had been induced (326) by his wife Fausta to execute Crispus, his son by his first wife. His heirs were three sons and two nephews. Of the sons, all Augusti, Constantinus II (b. 317) received the praefectures of Italy and Gaul; Constantius II (b. 317) took the east; and Constans (b. 323?) got Illyricum and part of Africa. The nephews, Dalmatius and Annibalianus, were at once executed by Constantius.

337–361. RULE OF CONSTANTINE'S SONS. While Constantius carried on an indecisive war against Persia, Constantinus attacked Constans, but was slain at Aquileia (340). Constans was killed by the pretender **Magnus Magnentius** (350, Jan.).

351, Sept. 28. Constantius defeated Magnentius at **Mursa,** near the confluence of the Danube and Drave. The latter slew himself at Lugdunum (353) and the empire was once more united.

351, Mar. 15. Constantius chose his cousin Gallus as Caesar, but had him executed in 354.

355, Nov. 6. Constantius chose as Caesar the half-brother of Gallus, **Julian,** who was given command against the Alamanni and Franks.

360. Julian marched against Constantius, who died before Julian reached the east (361).

361–363. JULIANUS, "the Apostate," (b. 332). He is known chiefly for his attempt to substitute paganism for Christianity and to organize a pagan church. After continuing his successes against the Franks, he campaigned against the Persians, but died on his way back from an attack on Ctesiphon (363, Jul. 26). With him ended the line of Constantine.

363–364. JOVIANUS (b. c. 331), was elected by the troops. He surrendered Mesopotamia to the Persians and died soon after (364, Feb. 17).

364–375. FLAVIUS VALENTINIANUS I (b. 321) was the next choice of the troops. He ably defended the west against the barbarians and made his brother **Valens** co-Augustus in the east (364, Mar. 28).

367. Valentinian made his son **Gratian** coemperor in the west. Valentinian died on an expedition against the Quadi and Sarmatians (375, Nov. 17).

375–383. GRATIANUS (b. 359), named his half-brother **Valentinian II** (b. 371) co-Augustus in the west.

376. The Visigoths (West Goths) crossed the Danube. Valens fell in battle against them at **Adrianople** (378, Aug. 9). The Goths continued to ravage the Balkan region.

379, Jan. 19. Gratian appointed as co-Augustus for the east, **Theodosius,** son of a successful general in Britain.

382. Gratian, at the request of Bishop Ambrose, removed from the senate-house the pagan altar of victory and gave up the title of *pontifex maximus.*

379–395. FLAVIUS THEODOSIUS "THE GREAT" (b. 346). He supported orthodoxy (i.e. Athanasianism) in the east, and came to terms with the Goths by settling them as military allies (*foederati*) in the Balkans.

383. The British legions proclaimed **Magnus Maximus,** who seized Gaul. Gratian was slain at Lugdunum (Aug. 25). Theodosius recognized Maximus.

387. When Maximus drove Valentinian II from Italy, Theodosius captured and executed him at Aquileia (388, July 28).

390. Theodosius cruelly massacred 7000 people at Thessalonica in revenge for an insurrection. Bishop Ambrose of Milan forced him to do penance for this act and emphasized thereby the independence of the western church from imperial domination.

392, May 15. The Frankish count (*comes*) **Arbogast,** murdered Valentinian II at Vienne and set up as emperor the pagan rhetorician **Eugenius.**

394, Sept. 5. Theodosius defeated and slew Eugenius and Arbogast at the Frigidus, just east of Aquileia. The empire was reunited for a brief space.

395, Jan. 17. Theodosius died at Milan. The empire was divided between his elder son **Arcadius** (made Augustus in the east in 383) and the younger son **Honorius** (made Augustus in the west in 393). The division proved to be permanent, though at the time the unity of the empire was fully accepted in theory and was always envisaged as a practical possibility. One consul regularly held office in Rome (until 472) and one in Constantinople (until 541).

395–408. ARCADIUS (b. 377), emperor of the east. He married Eudoxia, daughter of the Frank, Bauto (395). The praetorian praefect, Rufinus, managed to check the inroads of the Visigoths in the Balkans until his murder by the troops, but thereafter the eunuch Eutropius failed to prevent the invasions of the Visigoths or of the Huns, who overran Asia.

395-423. HONORIUS (b. 384), emperor of the west. He fell wholly under the influence of the Vandal **Stilicho** who, as master of the troops (*magister militum*), commanded all the forces and married his daughter Maria to Honorius (398).

396-397. Stilicho drove the Visigoths, led by Alaric, out of Greece.

402, Apr. 6. He frustrated their efforts to invade Italy (victory of the Romans at **Pollentia**).

406, Aug. 23. Stilicho at Florence broke up a miscellaneous force of barbarians which Radagaisus had led into Italy.

At about this time Gaul was overrun by Vandals, Alans, Suevi and Burgundians.

407. EVACUATION OF BRITAIN by the Romans. Constantine, whom the troops in Britain had proclaimed emperor, crossed to Gaul with his forces and it is probable that Roman troops were never sent back. The Romanized natives were left to deal as best they could with the inroads of Caledonians (Picts) from the north and of various German tribes coming by sea. The Saxons seem to have secured a permanent footing at the mouth of the Thames about 441.

408, Aug. 22. Murder of Stilicho, at Honorius' order.

408-450. THEODOSIUS II (b. 401), emperor of the east. He was the son of Arcadius and was a weak ruler dominated by his sister Pulcheria. With Valentinian III, Theodosius issued the earliest collection of existing laws, the **Theodosian Code** (438).

The Huns, under Attila, continued to ravage the empire and extort tribute.

409. Alaric again invaded Italy and set up a usurper, **Attalus** (praefect of Rome, the last pagan "emperor"). Alaric soon deposed him again.

410, Aug. 14 or 24. ALARIC SACKED ROME. He died soon after in southern Italy. His brother Ataulf led the Visigoths into Gaul (412) and thence began the conquest of Spain from the Vandals (415). There **Wallia** (416-419), successor of Ataulf, established the first recognized barbarian kingdom (419).

411. Constantine was defeated by Honorius' commander Constantius, near Arles.

423-425. **Johannes** usurped the purple on the death of Honorius at Ravenna (which he had made the capital in place of Milan).

425. Forces sent from the east by Theodosius II captured Johannes and put him to death.

425-454. VALENTINIAN III (b. 419), emperor of the west. He was the son of Honorius' half-sister Galla Placidia and the general Constantius, who had been made Augustus in 409, but had died almost at once. Valentinian was recognized by Theodosius II and married his daughter Eudoxia (437).

429. The general **Bonifatius** tried to set himself up as independent in Africa, with the aid of the Vandals, who crossed from Spain under **Gaiseric** (*Genseric*). But the Vandals seized Africa for themselves after a two-year siege of Hippo Regius (430-431) during which the bishop, **St. Augustine,** died (430, Aug. 28).

430. Aëtius, master of the troops, disposed of his rivals, Felix and Bonifatius (recalled from Africa in 432). He then devoted himself to clearing Gaul of barbarians, which he did by a resounding victory over the Visigoths (436) and by suppressing an uprising of the peasants and slaves (*Bagaudae*, 437).

435. The Vandal Kingdom in Africa was recognized. The Vandals took Carthage in 439.

450-457. MARCIAN, emperor of the east. Pulcheria, sister of Theodosius II (d. 450), had married Marcian, an able general. He allowed the Ostrogoths (east Goths) to settle as military allies (*foederati*) in Pannonia.

450. Attila, leader of the Huns, decided to bring his people from the east into Gaul.

451, June. Aëtius, aided by the Visigothic king, Theodoric I (*Theoderich, Theoderid*), defeated the Huns in the **battle of Châlons** (actually the *campi Catalauni* or Mauriac plain, near Troyes).

452. Attila invaded Italy, but turned back, traditionally because warned by Pope Leo I, but probably because well paid. Attila died in 453 and his hordes broke up.

454, Sept. 21. Valentinian rewarded Aëtius by murdering him with his own hand.

455, Mar. 16. Valentinian was murdered by two of Aëtius' guards. End of the house of Theodosius.

455-472. A succession of puppet rulers in the

west. In 455 Eudoxia, widow of Valentinian, set up **Petronius Maximus** at Rome. On his murder, in the same year, she called the Vandals from Africa.

455, June 2-16. Gaiseric and the Vandals sacked Rome. By the thoroughness of their destruction they attached a permanent stigma to their name.

456. Avitus advanced from southern Gaul to Rome, but was deposed by his able general, the Suevian **Ricimer.** Ricimer retained power by securing the consent of the eastern emperors to his nominees, who were **Majorianus** (457–461), **Severus** (461–465), and after a two-year interregnum, **Anthemius** (467–472), and **Olybrius** (472). When in 472 both Ricimer and Olybrius died, the eastern emperor, Leo I, appointed **Glycerius** (473), and **Julius Nepos** (473–475).

457-474. LEO I (b. ?), a Thracian (?), succeeded Marcian as emperor of the east. To offset his master of the troops, the Alan Aspar, he married his daughter Ariadne to Zeno, an Isaurian from the mountains of southern Asia Minor (467) and made Zeno's son, Leo, his colleague (473).

474. Leo II, who succeeded on the death of Leo I. His father, Zeno, made himself his colleague. Leo died the same year.

474-491. ZENO (b. 426), disposed of the pretender Basiliscus, brother-in-law of Leo I (475). He then tried to control the Goths by setting the rival chiefs, Theodoric, son of Strabo, and Theodoric the Amal, against each other.

475. The master of the troops, **Orestes,** removed Nepos in favor of his own son, whose name combined those of the founder of Rome and of the Empire,

475-476. ROMULUS AUGUSTUS (nicknamed *Augustulus*).

476, Sept. 4. After defeating and killing Orestes at Pavia, the Herulian **Odovacar** (*Odoacer*) deposed Romulus Augustulus, the last emperor of the west, at Ravenna. Traditional end of the Roman Empire.

The eastern emperor, **Zeno,** apparently recognized Odovacar as "patrician" (*patricius* had become the title of honor for barbarian commanders). Nepos retained titular claim as emperor until his death in 480 and after that date the empire was theoretically reunited under the eastern emperors, but actually Odovacar ruled as an independent king in Italy.

481. On the death of Theodoric, the son of Strabo, Zeno recognized his rival as patrician and master of the troops. His people were established in Moesia as *foederati*.

488. Theodoric, ostensibly as Zeno's agent, invaded Italy.

493, Feb. 27. After a three-year siege of Ravenna, Odovacar surrendered. He was soon after murdered by Theodoric. Italy was united under Theodoric the Great (b. c. 455) as the kingdom of the Ostrogoths (p. 145).

491-518. ANASTASIUS I (b. 431) emperor of the east. He married Zeno's widow and removed the Isaurians from power, thus causing a serious revolt in Isauria (suppressed only in 497).

The inroads of the Slavic Getae forced him to protect Constantinople by a wall.

502-506. The emperor waged a long war with the Persians (p. 126).

514-518. Conflict with the pretender Vitalian, commander of the Bulgarian *foederati*. Anastasius died in 518 (July 1).

518-527. JUSTINUS I (b. 450?), a humble Illyrian who had risen to be commander of the imperial bodyguard. He took as his colleague his able nephew Justinian (527) and died the same year.

527-565. JUSTINIAN. (For his reign see Byzantine Empire).

Diocletian and his successors managed to delay, but not to stop the decay which had attacked the empire during the 3d century. The administrative reforms added to the burdens of taxation without stopping the military domination and rivalry for the purple. The army became increasingly barbarized and immobilized by settlement on the land as peasant militia or barbarian *foederati*. The active defense was entrusted to barbarian mercenaries under their powerful chiefs, who came to dominate the state. Thus, the empire in the west did not fall: it petered out; and the establishment of the barbarian kingdoms simply recognized the end of a gradual process. In the east the empire, in Greek garb, maintained itself, at times as a very great and splendid power, until the conquest of Constantinople by the crusaders in 1204 and the definitive fall of the city into the hands of the Turks (1453).

In **architecture,** the later empire continued the able engineering of earlier days, as in the Baths of Diocletian at Rome, his palace at Spalato, or the Basilica of Maxentius and Constantine at Rome. But **art** showed a rapid decline, e.g. in the frieze of the Arch of Constantine at Rome. The second half of the 4th century witnessed a revival of pagan Latin literature in

Symmachus, the praefect of the city who vainly urged Valentinian II to restore the altar of victory (384), the Gallic poet **Ausonius,** consul in 379, and the Alexandrian **Claudius,** court poet of Honorius and Stilicho. **Boethius,** the last classical philosopher, whether he was pagan or Christian, wrote his *Consolation of Philosophy* in prison before his execution by Theodoric the Ostrogoth (524).

Active intellectual life, however, appeared chiefly in the Church. The great Latin fathers were: **Lactantius** (d. c. 325), **Ambrose** (340–397), Bishop of Milan (374), **Jerome** (340–420), who retired from Rome to Bethlehem, where he translated the Bible into Latin (the *Vulgate*), and **Augustine** (354–430), Bishop of Hippo Regius in Africa (395), who founded Christian theology on Platonism. The important Greek fathers were: **Basil** of Caesarea (330–379), his brother **Gregory** of Nyssa (d. c. 394), and **Gregory** of Nazianzus (329–389), all three Cappadocians, and **John Chrysostom** (329–389), Patriarch of Constantinople (381). **Eusebius** (264–340), orthodox Bishop of Caesarea (315), who should be distinguished from the contemporary Arian, Eusebius of Nicomedia, is noted for his *Ecclesiastical History* and other historical works.

During the 5th and 6th centuries the eastern Church was torn by the **monophysite heresy,** whose doctrine was that Christ had a single nature. The orthodox doctrine, that Christ combined divine and human, had the support of Pope Leo of Rome and was approved at the **Council of Chalcedon** (451), but the eastern emperors on the whole were monophysite. In the west, as imperial authority weakened, and as rival bishoprics passed into barbarian hands, the Bishop of Rome — or pope (*papa*) as he came to be known — became supreme, and such great popes as **Damasus** (pope, 366–384) and **Leo I, "the Great"** (pope, 440–461) became temporal as well as spiritual leaders of their people. A claim of territorial sovereignty began to be based on a fictitious **"Donation of Constantine"** to Pope Sylvester of the lands around Rome. A significant missionary effort of the Church was the sending of **Ulfilas to the Goths** (c. 340–348), who converted them to Arianism. But the chief feature of the Church during this period was the introduction of **monasticism.** In the east, the single solitary had long been common and **St. Antony** first gathered some of them together for a common life (*coenobite*) in Egypt in about 285. **Basil of Caesarea** (above) established a monastic rule popular in the east. Monasticism spread to the west under the efforts of **Martin of Tours** (362) and **Jerome** (above). **Cassian of Marseilles** (c. 400) wrote *Institutes* for his monastery, but the rule which became dominant was that of **St. Benedict** (*regula Sancti Benedicti*), who founded his monastery at Monte Cassino, near Naples, in 529. His rule was adopted by Cassiodorus (480–575), secretary to Theodoric the Ostrogoth, who founded a monastery at Beneventum in 540. The closing of the schools at Athens by Justinian, the execution of Boethius, and the founding of Benedict's monastery mark the transition from classical to mediaeval intellectual life. (*Cont. p.* 141.)

G. THE EMPIRES OF ASIA

1. THE NEO-PERSIAN EMPIRE OF THE SASSANIANS
(226-651 A.D.)

226-240 A.D. Ardashir I (*Artaxerxes, Artah-shatr*), son of Papak, a vassal-king of the Parthian Empire ruling in Fars (Persia proper), revolted against Artabanus, last king of the Arsacid dynasty of Parthia, and defeated him finally at **Hormuz** (226–27), where Artabanus was slain.

Merv, Balkh, and Khiva conquered by Ardashir; submission of the kings of Kushan, Turan, and Makran received; India invaded and tribute levied on the Punjab.

229-232. War with Rome (p. 115). Rome summoned to evacuate Syria and the rest of Asia. Defeat of Alexander Severus, peace concluded. Armenia, the real objective of Ardashir's campaign, subjugated after the murder of its Arsacid king, Chosroes.

Under Ardashir a strongly centralized nation supported by the priesthood created; Zoroastrianism revived and the privileges of the Magi restored; collection of the text of the *Zend Avesta* under Arda-Viraf. He was succeeded by

240-271. Shapur I (*Sapor, Shahpuhri*). Revolts in Armenia and Hatra crushed (240).

241-244. FIRST WAR WITH ROME (p. 115). Shapur invaded Mesopotamia and Syria, took Nisibis and Antioch, but was finally driven back across the Euphrates and defeated at Resaina by the Emperor Gordian. Gordian was murdered and peace was concluded by his successor, Philip. In the east, Balkh apparently independent.

258-260. SECOND WAR WITH ROME (p. 116). Shapur again invaded Mesopotamia and Syria, taking Nisibis, Edessa, and Antioch, and defeating and capturing near Edessa the Emperor Valerian, who remained a captive until his death (265–66). Asia Minor also invaded, Caesarea Mazaca in Cappadocia taken, but no attempt made to consolidate and hold the conquered territory.

260-263. Palmyra. In a brilliant campaign **Odenathus,** the Arab prince of Palmyra, drove the Persians back across the Euphrates, defeated Shapur and besieged Ctesiphon, seized and occupied Mesopotamia, Syria, and other provinces west of the Euphrates, and was recognized by Gallienus as co-regent for the east.

Shapur's later years were devoted to public works, of which the greatest was the dam at Shuster. He also founded many cities, among them Nishapur. In his reign appeared Mani (215–273), founder of **Manichaeism,** whom Shapur at first favoured, then banished.

271-293. Shapur was succeeded by his son, **Hormisdas I** (271–272), who was followed by his brother, **Varahran I** (272–275). Mani executed. Insufficient support given to **Zenobia of Palmyra** (p. 116), the widow of Odenathus, against Aurelian, whose Persian expedition came to an end with his murder (275). Varahran succeeded by his son, **Varahran II** (275–282). An eastern campaign, in which the Sakae of Sistan were subdued, was brought to a close by a Roman invasion of Persia under the Emperor Carus, who conquered Mesopotamia and took Ctesiphon (283). The mysterious death of Carus ended the war (284). Armenia seized by Tiridates, the son of the murdered Chosroes, with the help of the Emperor Diocletian (286). **Varahran III,** son of Varahran II, reigned four months, and was succeeded by his brother,

293-301. Narses, who finally worsted his brother and rival, Hormisdas, and drove Tiridates from Armenia (296).

296-297. WAR WITH ROME (p. 118). The Roman army under Galerius routed near **Carrhae** (296). The Persian army surprised by Galerius in the following year and almost annihilated. Peace concluded (297). Terms: 1. Cession to Rome of the five provinces west of the Tigris. 2. The Tigris to be the boundary instead of the Euphrates. 3. Cession to Armenia of Median territory up to the fort of Zentha. 4. Iberia (*Georgia*) to be a Roman protectorate.

Abdication of Narses and accession of his son, **Hormisdas II** (301–309), noted for his activity in building and for setting up a court of justice at which the poor were encouraged to make complaint against the oppression of the rich. Upon his death his natural heir, Hormisdas, was set aside by the nobles, who elected his posthumous son, the famous

309-379. SHAPUR II.

309-337. His minority and early campaigns.

Persia invaded by the Arabs of Bahrain and Mesopotamia; Ctesiphon sacked. At the age of seventeen Shapur grasped the reins of state, adopted an active policy, invaded Arabia and exacted a terrible revenge upon the Arabs.

337-350. FIRST WAR WITH ROME (p. 120).

The Romans were defeated in the field, but Shapur was unable to capture the Roman strongholds. Nisibis invested three times in vain (338, 346, 350). Constantius routed at Singara (348). Persecution of the Persian Christians (from 339 on). **Treaty with Armenia** (341), but in 351 Armenia went over to Rome. Successful campaigns in the east against the Huns, Euseni, and Gilani (350–357).

359-361. SECOND WAR WITH ROME.

Syria invaded, Amida taken after a heroic defense (359). Singara and Bezabde captured (360). Constantius attempted in vain to recapture the latter place, and died in the following year. His successor, Julian, invaded Persia, forced the passage of the Tigris, defeated the Persians north of Ctesiphon, but retreated before investing that city and was mortally wounded in a battle near Samarra (363). His successor, Jovian, concluded peace with Shapur for thirty years. Terms: (1) restoration of the five provinces ceded by Narses; (2) surrender of Nisibis, Singara, and a third fortress in eastern Mesopotamia to Persia; (3) Armenia declared to be outside the Roman sphere of influence. Conquest of Armenia by Shapur and invasion of Iberia.

371-376. THIRD WAR WITH ROME.

No decisive results and an obscure peace. Persian power at its zenith at the death of Shapur II. His immediate successors weak and unenterprising. **Ardeshir II** (379–383) and **Shapur III** (383–388). Shapur concluded a peace with Rome (384) by the terms of which Armenia was partitioned between Rome and Persia. **Varahran IV** (388–399). Khusru (*Chosroes*), the satrap of Persian Armenia, who had revolted, was deposed and succeeded by Varahran's brother. Varahran was killed in a mutiny and succeeded by his son,

399-420. Yezdigird the Wicked.

A peaceful reign. A firman issued permitting Christians to worship openly and rebuild their churches (409), a decree as important to the eastern church as the **Edict of Milan** to the

church of the west. The **Council of Seleucia** adopted the decrees and the creed of the **Council of Nicaea**. Yezdigird possibly contemplated baptism and persecuted the Magians, but returning to his old faith he authorized the destruction of the Christian sect. A terrible persecution for four years. Yezdigird succeeded by his son,

420-440. Varahran V.

Brought up among the desert Arabs who supported him against his cousin, Khusru, the choice of the nobles, who finally accepted him peacefully. He continued persecution of the Christians and declared war on Rome (420), when the Christians crossed the border seeking Rome's protection. Varahran was defeated and peace concluded (422). Christians to be allowed to take refuge in the Roman Empire, persecution of the Christians to cease. Declaration of the independence of the eastern church at the **Council of Dad-Ishu** (424). Persian Armenia reduced to a satrapy (428). Campaigns of Varahran against the White Huns or Ephthalites (*Haytal*), of Turkish stock probably, in Transoxania. They invaded Persia, but were surprised and defeated by Varahran, who crossed the Oxus and forced them to sue for peace. Varahran succeeded by his son,

440-457. Yezdigird II.

War declared upon Rome and peace concluded the same year (440). Successful campaigns against the Ephthalites of Transoxania (443–451). Armenia forcibly converted to Zoroastrianism (455–456), after the defeat of the Christian party at the hands of the Persians and their Armenian supporters. Persecution of Christians spread to Mesopotamia. Khorasan again invaded by the Ephthalites, who inflicted a severe defeat upon Yezdigird, after he had driven them across the Oxus. At his death his younger son, Hormisdas, seized the throne, but the elder son,

459-483. Firuz (Perozes),

defeated and captured Hormisdas with the aid of the Ephthalites. A famine of several years; wise measures adopted by Firuz. Unsuccessful campaigns against the Ephthalites ending in a humiliating peace (464–480?). A further defeat at the hands of the Kushans of the maritime provinces of the Caspian Sea (481) led to the revolt of Iberia and of Armenia under Vahan (481–483). This was still smouldering when Firuz, breaking his troth, attacked the Ephthalites, was defeated and slain. Succeeded by

483-485. Volagases (Balas),

his brother. Tribute paid by Persia to Khush-Newaz, the Ephthalite Khan, for about two years. Conciliation of Armenia. **Edict of toleration granted** Christians, after Vahan aided Volagases in a civil war. Thereupon Armenia and Iberia contented provinces of the empire. Nestorian Christological doctrine of the two natures in Christ established by **Bar-Soma** in the Persian Church with royal authority; the college of Edessa driven out by Zeno and set up at Nisibis by Bar-Soma (489). Repudiation by Armenia of the **Council of Chalcedon** (491). Volagases succeeded by his son,

485–498. Kobad (first reign), who had taken refuge with the Ephthalites after an abortive attempt to seize the throne. Successful campaign against the Khazars, dwelling between the Volga and the Don. Many converts gained for his communistic and ascetic doctrines by **Mazdak,** a high priest of Zoroastrianism, among them the king. Unrest in Armenia and Persia owing to the intolerant proselytism of the Mazdakites, leading to a conspiracy of the Chief Mobed, nobles, and army against Kobad, who was deposed and succeeded by his brother **Zamasp,** who reigned from 498 to 501. Kobad escaped to the Ephthalites, who espoused his cause with vigor. Zamasp resigned the crown voluntarily.

501–531. Kobad (second reign). Official support withdrawn from Mazdak.

503–505. FIRST WAR WITH ROME. Cause: non-fulfillment of the Eastern Empire's agreement to pay a share of the expenses of the defense of the pass of Derbend, the usual route taken by nomadic tribes in their invasions of Persia and the Eastern Empire. Roman Armenia invaded; Theodosiopolis taken; sack of Amida in northern Mesopotamia (502). An Ephthalite raid forced Kobad to conclude peace on the basis of the *status quo ante.*

503–523. Successful and final campaign against the Ephthalites (503–513). Massacre of the Mazdakites (523). Rebellion in Iberia.

524–531. SECOND WAR WITH ROME. Cause: Erection of the fortress of Daras within a day's march of Nisibis by the Emperor Anastasius. The first campaign ended in the defeat of the Romans (526), who were again defeated in 528, but were finally victorious in the **battle of Daras** (528) under Belisarius. An indecisive battle near Callinicum brought the war to a close. Kobad was succeeded by

531–579. ANUSHIRWAN THE JUST (*Chosroes*), his son. The most illustrious member of the Sassanian dynasty. Succession disputed. Execution of all his brothers and their male offspring with one exception. Massacre of Mazdak and his followers. Conclusion of the **Endless Peace with Rome** (533). Terms: (1) Rome to pay 11,000 pounds of gold toward the upkeep of the Caucasian defenses. (2) Rome to keep Daras as a fortress, but not as its headquarters in Mesopotamia; (3) restoration on both sides of captured strongholds in Lazica; (4) eternal friendship and alliance. Within seven years, however, Anushirwan, alarmed at Justinian's successes in Africa and Italy (533–539) and prompted by the Ostrogoths and Armenians, began a defensive war.

540–562. WAR WITH ROME. Syria invaded. Antioch sacked. Terms of peace agreed upon and ratification of the treaty received by Anushirwan at Edessa. He nevertheless extracted ransoms from the cities along the route of his return march, whereupon Justinian denounced the treaty.

540–557. Campaigns in Lazica. Lazica (ancient *Colchis*), a Roman protectorate since 527, appealed to Anushirwan for help to throw off the Roman yoke. Petra taken by the Persians (540). Lazica a Persian province. Petra retaken by the Romans (550), and the Persians driven out of the country (555). A truce agreed upon (557). **Definitive peace with Rome** (562). The terms included: (1) cession of Lazica to Rome; (2) payment by Rome of 30,000 pieces of gold annually; (3) free exercise of their religion guaranteed to the Christians of Persia; (4) commercial intercourse restricted to certain roads and marts; (5) Daras to remain a fortified town; (6) arbitration of all disputes and free diplomatic intercourse; (7) inclusion in the treaty of the allies of either party; (8) the defense of the Caspian gate to be undertaken by Persia alone; (9) the peace to hold for fifty years.

554. Subjugation of the Ephthalites with the aid of the Turks and the division of their territory with the Oxus as boundary. Successful campaign against the Khazars.

572. Declaration of war on Persia by Justin. Syria ravaged by Anushirwan and Daras taken (573). Abdication of Justin. A peace purchased by Tiberius.

576?. Arabian campaign. The Abyssinians driven out of southern Arabia, which became a Persian province.

576–578. Alliance of the Turks with the Eastern Empire. Ill-success of their invasion of Persia. Armenian campaigns. An Indian campaign also reported.

Under Anushirwan the administration was reorganized. The empire was divided into four great satrapies: the east comprising Khorasan and Kerman; the west including Iraq and Meso potamia; the north comprehending Armenia and Azerbaijan; and the south containing Fars and Khuzistan. A fixed land tax was also substituted for the former variable tax on produce, and its collection placed under the supervision of the priests. Irrigation and communications were improved, the army reformed, foreigners protected, agriculture encouraged, laws revised, the Christians granted toleration, learning subsidized, Indian tales and chess introduced. Anushirwan was succeeded by his son,

579-589. Hormisdas IV (*Hormazd*). War with Rome continued. The Persians were defeated at Constantia (581) and again at Arzanene near Martyropolis (588). In 589 the Persians took Martyropolis and defeated the Romans, who, however, gained a signal victory near Nisibis soon thereafter.

589. Invasion of Persia by Arabs, Khazars, and Turks. The advance of the Turks constituted a real danger, but they were defeated by the great Persian general, Varahran (*Bahram*). Bahram was then ordered to invade Lazica, but was met and defeated by the Romans on the Araxes. Superseded and insulted by the king, he rebelled. Hormisdas was deposed, and murdered, and succeeded by his son,

589-628. KHUSRU PARVIZ (*Chosroes II*), the last famous king of the Sassanian dynasty. Under him the Neo-Persian Empire reached its greatest extent and suffered also a sudden downfall. Defied by Bahram, Khusru was forced to flee to Constantinople, whereupon Bahram seized the throne and reigned as Bahram (*Varahran*) VI (590-591). Restoration of Khusru with the aid of the Emperor Maurice. Flight of Bahram to the Turks, by whom he was assassinated.

603-610. A victorious war against Phocas, the murderer of Maurice. Capture of Daras, Amida, Harran, Edessa, Hieropolis, Berhoea (Aleppo), etc. Armenia, Cappadocia, Phrygia, Galatia, and Bithynia ravaged.

610. A Persian force defeated by the Arabs at Dhu-Qar, a famous day in the annals of the tribes.

610-620. Accession of Heraclius as Roman emperor. War with Rome continued. Sack of Antioch and Apamea (611) by the Persians. Invasion of Cappadocia (612). Capture of Damascus (614). Sack of Jerusalem and capture of the *True Cross* (615). Capture of Pelusium and Alexandria by Shahr-Baraz. Subjugation of Egypt (616). Chalcedon taken. The Persians within a mile of Constantinople (617). Ancyra and Rhodes captured (620).

Khusru had now restored the empire of Darius I, and the condition of the Roman Empire was desperate. Thrace was overrun by the Avars. Heraclius decided to flee to Carthage, but was prevented by the citizens of Constantinople. He determined as a forlorn hope to make use of his one great advantage, the possession of sea power, and carry the war to enemy territory.

622-627. The famous campaigns of Heraclius. Disembarkment at Issus and defeat of Shahr-Baraz (622). Expedition to Lazica and invasion of Armenia (623). Retreat of Khusru and wintering of Heraclius in Albania. The second invasion of Armenia. Surprise and defeat of Shahr-Baraz (624). Invasion of Arzanene and the recovery of Amida and Martyropolis. Campaign in Cilicia. Indecisive **battle of the Sarus**. Retreat of Shahr-Baraz (625).

626. THE SIEGE OF CONSTANTINOPLE. Alliance between Khusru and the Avars. Two Persian armies placed in the field, one against Heraclius in Asia Minor, the other to co-operate with the Avars in the siege of Constantinople. The first under Shahen, the captor of Chalcedon, was defeated by the emperor's brother, Theodore. The second was prevented by the Roman command of the sea from assisting the Avar assault on Constantinople, which failed.

627. Invasion of Assyria and Mesopotamia by Heraclius. Defeat of the Persians near Nineveh. Flight of Khusru. Heraclius marched on Ctesiphon, but did not besiege it. His retreat to Canzaca. Mutiny of the Persian troops in Ctesiphon under Gurdanaspa, their commander. Imprisonment and murder of Khusru, he was succeeded by

628-629. Kobad II (*Siroes*), who made peace with Heraclius on the basis of an exchange of conquests and prisoners and the surrender of the "True Cross." The massacre of his brothers and his death by plague (629). The usurpation of Shahr-Baraz and his murder by his own troops (629). The reign of **Purandukht** and that of **Azarmidukht,** daughters of Khusru Parviz, followed by a period of anarchy, in which pretender after pretender aspired to the throne and perished almost immediately (629-634).

634-642. Yezdigird III, grandson of Khusru Parviz, and last Sassanian king of Persia, whose story is that of the expansion of the Muslim Caliphate eastwards.

633-651. Arab invasion of Iraq under Khalid ibn al-Walid. Hira and Obolla taken. The Arab advance checked temporarily at the

Battle of the Bridge. The Persians under Rustam were decisively defeated by the Arabs under Sa'd ibn Abi Waqqas at **Qadisiya** (636). Mesopotamia invaded by Sa'd and Ctesiphon (*Madain*) captured. Defeat of the Persians at Jalula (637). Invasion of Susiana and Fars (639). Defeat of the Persians at Ram Hormuz; Shuster taken; conquest of Khuzistan (640). **Final defeat of the Persians under Firuzan at Nehawand** (642). Conquest of the Persian provinces and their incorporation into the caliphate. Flight of Yezdigird to Balkh; his appeal for help to the Emperor of China; his murder in a miller's hut near Merv (651).

2. INDIA, TO 500 A.D.

a. NORTHERN INDIA

1st cent. B.C. Dating of the known Saka rulers, the **"Great King Moga"** or Maues, Azes, and Azilises, raises a complex chronological problem affecting the whole epoch from 100 B.C. to 200 A.D. It springs from multiplicity of eras, which are hardly ever explicitly identified. The sequence of rulers has been well established by E. J. Rapson, with the aid of numismatic evidence. Moga appears to date an inscription at Taxila ("78" = c. 72 B.C.) with reference to a Scythian era cf c. 150 B.C. Azes seems to have begun a new era, for "136 ayasa" (= AZOY) is identified (although disputed) in the Chir Tope, Taxila. There is no positive evidence that either the "Vikrama" era of 58 B.C. or the Saka era of 78 A.D. originated or was ever used in the Northwest. A Jain text prior to 1428 A.D. purports to explain their origin in Ujjain, but no certain examples of their use are found until 372 A.D. and 578 A.D. respectively. Accession of Azes, however, presumably took place not far from 58 B.C. which may be employed as a working hypothesis.

The Pahlavas (Parthians closely related to the Scythians) under Vonones and his brother Spalirises became independent in eastern Iran with the title of King of Kings sometime (c. 30? B.C.) after the death of Mithradates II (88 B.C., supposed by L. de la Vallée Poussin to begin a Pahlava era; or does such an era begin with appropriation of the imperial title?). **Azes II**, son of Spalirises, succeeded the Sakas in the Punjab. The period of these events depends on the era intended in the Takht-i-Bahi inscription in the 26th year of his successor Gondopharnes, dated "103." He ruled 19–45+ A.D. if the era is that of Azes-Vikrama; c. 11 B.C.–c. 15+ A.D. if it is that of c. 88 B.C. To him St. Thomas was sent according to a legend current by 250. Pacores was the last to rule as suzerain, although others probably continued as satraps.

The Kushana Kujula Kadphises forcibly united the five tribes of Yüeh-chih in Bactria (end 1st cent. B.C.) and seized from the Pahlavas the Kabul Valley and adjacent regions. His son **Vima Kadphises** conquered northwestern India and ruled it by deputy till his death at 80. An inscription near Panjtar speaks of a "Gushana Great King" under date "122" which is 64 or 34 A.D. by the Azes or Pahlava systems. The inscription of "136" similarly belongs to 78 or 48 A.D.

c. 78–176+ A.D. A second **Kushana dynasty** was founded by

c. 78–96+ A.D. KANISHKA, who extended his rule from Benares and Kabul to the Vindhyas, and established his capital at Peshawar. His inscriptions are dated from "3" to "18," and that of "9" is explicitly dated as of his reign. Whether or not the era which he founded is the "Saka" era of 78 A.D., he probably came to the throne near that date. The Chinese *Later Han History* says:

84. A Yüeh-chih king was allied to Sogdiana by marriage, and by presents to him Pan Ch'ao secured the help of the latter against Kashgar.

88. The king presented precious stones and lions with a request for a Chinese princess, peremptorily refused by Pan Ch'ao.

90. A punitive army of 70,000 sent across the Pamirs under the Yüeh-chih viceroy Hsieh was starved into surrender by Pan, the ablest strategist of his time, who exacted payment of annual tribute. Although the king is not named, only a powerful ruler could have played so strong a hand across the mountains. Some scholars identify Kanishka rather with King Chien of Khotan, who was killed in error by a Chinese envoy in 152 A.D. The Chinese source does not, however, suggest any connection of this king with the Yüeh-chih or with India.

Kanishka appears to have been tolerant in religion, and built a great stupa at Peshawar over relics of the Buddha. A fourth church council, unknown to the Pali sources, was apparently convoked at Jalandhara in the Punjab by the powerful Sarvastivadin, a realist sect of the conservative Sthaviravadin. It probably supervised translation into Sanskrit of the canon which had been fixed in Prakrit in Mathura, the Punjab, and Kashmir in the last centuries B.C. The four Sanskrit *Agamas* agree with the earliest Pali *Nikayas*, but the seven *Abhidharma* books contain catechism, comment, and doctrine peculiar to the school. The *Vibhasha* commentary on one of the *Abhidharmas*, completed by Kashmir professors after the death of Kanishka, cites conflicting doctrines of diverse sects.

The earliest and most vigorous classical Sanskrit is found in Asvaghosha's *Saundarananda* ("Conversion of Nanda") and the *Buddhacharita*, an artistic versified life of the Buddha, together with a work long supposed to be his *Sutralamkara*, which is now identified as the *Kalpanamanditika* of Kumaralata, a junior contemporary.

2d cent. A. D. Kanishka's successors with their inscriptions (dated in terms of his reign) are: his son Vasishka (24, 28, 29); the latter's son Kanishka II (41); his younger brother Huvishka (29 or 33–60); Vasushka, son of Kanishka II (68, 74); and Vasudeva (76–98).

Asoka's inscriptions name three **Tamil states** in the Carnatic: Pandya (extreme south), Chola (southeast), and Chera or Kerala (southwest coast, chief port Muziris). These competed with Maesolia at the mouth of the Kistna and especially with the rich western port of Barygaza (Broach) in thriving trade with the Roman Empire. An embassy to Augustus (c. 22 B.C.) was sent by a king "Pandion" who may have been a Pandya. Strabo (d. 21 A.D.) speaks of fleets of 120 ships from Egypt to India, and Pliny (23–79) values annual imports from India at 50 million sesterces.

THE DECCAN was dominated (from c. 100 B.C to c. 225 A.D.) by a dynasty of Dravidian or **Munda kings**, called *Andhra* by the late *Puranas* but *Satavahana* or *Satakani* in their own Prakrit inscriptions. Founded by Simuka on the ruins of the Sunga-Kanva power, with capital at Pratishthana (Paithan) on the upper Godaveri, its early conquests to north and northwest were appropriated by the Saka satraps. A Saka satrap **Bhumaka** established Scythian power on the northwest coast (c. 70 A.D.). Nahapana, junior to him, ruled many years over Surashtra (Kathiawar) and the adjacent coast with capital probably at Junnar, east of Bombay. Named Mambanos in the *Periplus* (c. 89), his inscriptions are dated "41–46" (?119–124 A.D.), probably with reference to the Saka era of 78 which he may have founded.

c. 109-132+. **Gotamiputa Siri Satakani** conquered Surashtra from Nahapana, and in an inscription at Nasik (18th year of his reign, c. 126) claimed not only the Deccan from the Vindhyas to Banavasi, but less probably Malwa as well. Very likely by this epoch the Satakani had extended control over the properly Andhra Telugu (Dravidian) lands of the Godaveri and Kistna deltas. The Prakrit poems of the *Sattasai* "Seven Centuries" in part date from this time. Liberal towards all religions, the Satakani especially exalted the Brahmans. Sculptures about the great Buddhist stupa of Amaravati on the lower Kistna reveal union of Hindu traditional style with its crowding and naturalism, already more refined than at Bharhut and Sañchi, with Greco-Buddhist motifs which were borrowed from Gandhara and in turn transmitted to Malaya, Sumatra-Java, Cambodia, and Champa.

c. 120-c. 395. **A DYNASTY OF WESTERN SATRAPS** of Ujjain in Malwa was founded by Bhumaka's son Chashtana (Tiastanes of Ptolemy, c. 150).

c. 170. **Rudradaman,** Chashtana's grandson, in a Sanskrit inscription at Girnar in Kathiawar, records repair of a dam which broke in 150 A.D., defeat of northern tribesmen, and repeated rout of the southern Satakani.

Ujjain became a center of Sanskrit learning, and was taken as meridian by Indian astronomers. At Mathura, where sculpture early resembled that of Bharhut and Sañchi, and later clumsily imitated the forms of Gandhara, the heavy drapery of the Hellenistic school was rendered transparent, and schematized in decorative ridges, creating the so-called *Udayana Buddha*, carried to China and Japan.

The Buddhist community was now divided between two means to salvation: the **Hinayana** or *Lesser Vehicle*, which retained much of the primitive simplicity of the "Law" *Dharma*, by which "Buddhism" was then named; and the **Mahayana** or *Great Vehicle*, which emphasized personal devotion to Sakyamuni and to a pantheon strange to him. Although practically deified in the *Lalitavistara* (2d cent.?, Chinese trans. 308) and *Saddharma-pundarika-sutra*, "Lotus of the Good Law" (Ch. trans., 265–316), he is regarded as but the human representative (*manushi-buddha*), for the current epoch, of an infinite series of buddhas. Some of these, identified as *dhyani-buddhas*, dwell permanently in various heavens as spiritual guides to more active colleagues. Amitabha, says the longer

Sukhavativyuha (Ch. trans. by a Yüeh-chih before 186), is the Buddha of Boundless Light who reigns in a western paradise (Iranian influence). Maitreya, who is destined to complete human salvation as next manushi-buddha, waits in Tushita heaven as a *bodhisattva*, a being capable of enlightenment (Chinese trans. 265–316). No less popular bodhisattvas are Avalokitesvara (*Lotus Sutra*, ch. 24), Manjusri (*Avatamsaka-sutra*, 2d–3d cent., Chinese trans. 317–420), Samantabhadra, and Kshitigarbha, all of whom have deferred their own illumination to succor struggling mankind. The goal of effort is no longer sainthood or final absorption in nirvana, but direct attainment of buddhahood or rebirth to indefinite residence in a celestial paradise. Nagarjuna (2d cent.), founder of the Madhyamika school, in his *Madhyamika Sutra* teaches that all sensory and mental experience is illusion, and comments on the *Prajñaparamita*, "*Perfect Wisdom*" (Chinese trans. 160) which consists in recognition of the Buddhist law as sole reality.

Already before our era Indian writers recognized and wrote treatises about three phases of human existence: *dharma*, religious and moral duty; *artha*, politics and practical life; and *kama*, love. The *Artha-sastra* (compounded from earlier materials c. 300–330) aims to teach a prince the whole science of successful rule according to accepted principles. It assumes autocratic monarchy, justification of all means by the end (personal aggrandisement), and chronic war. It advocates use of spies in all quarters; deception, intimidation, false witness, and confiscation to obtain money; cunning and assassination. Virtuous rule is described because desirable to win affection of a conquered people. The *Kama-sutra* ("Laws of Love") by Vatsyayana Mallanaga (c. 4th cent. or later) imitates the *Artha-sastra* in both form and morals.

320–c. 535. THE GUPTA DYNASTY united northern India after five centuries' division.

320–c. 330. Chandragupta I ruled from Pataliputra (Patna), having strengthened his position by marriage into the ancient Lichchavi tribe. His son

c. 330–c.375. Samudragupta completed the conquest of the north (Aryavarta) and won glory by traversing Telugu lands to force homage of the Pallava. Claiming to receive tribute from southeastern Bengal, Assam, and Nepal, with presents from the Kushan "son of Heaven and king of kings" (now actually vassal of the Sassanids) in Kabul-Kapisa-Gan-

dhara, the Satrap of Ujjain, and King Meghavanna (352–379) of Ceylon (who founded a monastery at Gaya for his subjects), he revived the Vedic horse-sacrifice which sanctified claim to the title of "universal monarch." He was a patron of poetry and music.

c. 375–c. 413. Chandragupta II Vikramaditya (on throne in 379) ended the Satrapy of Ujjain by conquest of Malwa, Gujerat, and Surashtra (between 388 and 401). He moved his capital to Ayodhya (in Oudh) and then to Kausambi on the Jumna.

c. 413–455. Kumaragupta I probably founded the monastic community at 'Nalanda which was the principal Buddhist seminary till it burned c. 988.

455–c. 467. Skandagupta repulsed the White Huns, as heir apparent and as emperor (455).

477–496+. Budhagupta, last emperor of the dynasty, ruled from northern Bengal to eastern Malwa, perhaps to Surashtra. After c. 500 the chief branch of his house ruled as kings of Magadha till the 8th century.

The **Brahman legal writers** defined the social structure in sloka metre. The *Dharma Sastra* of **Manu** (1st cent. B.C.?) was respected and freely utilized by later writers. The *Dharma Sutra* of **Vishnu** (3d cent. A.D.), like the epics, recognized *suttee*, widow-burning, though it is not yet recommended. The days of the week were named from Greek sources. **Yajnavalkya** (4th cent.) admitted documentary evidence, and recommended use of ordeals of ploughshare, scales, and poison in addition to Manu's fire and water. **Narada** (5th cent.) first omitted religious and moral precepts from legal discussion. **Brihaspati** (c. 600 or 700) cited nine ordeals. Punishments: impalement, hanging, burning, mutilation, fines and outcasting, were adjusted to caste. A plaintiff might enforce justice by fasting to death on a debtor's premises. Fa-hsien, pioneer Chinese Buddhist pilgrim at the height of Gupta power, stated that fines were usually imposed, and that mutilation was reserved for brigands and rebels. He was enthusiastic about the peace and happiness of northern India (401–409) and Ceylon (410–411).

Six **schools of Hindu philosophy** (or rationalized religion) developed during the first centuries before and after Christ. They enjoy orthodox status in that all recognize the primordial and eternal character of the *Veda*, although in fact they do not derive from it. None is concerned primarily with ethics, but all seek freedom from bondage through deeds to rebirth. Escape for the soul is found in knowledge and cessation of thought. The Purvami-mamsa is a systematization of rules for sacrifice. The *Vaiseshika-sutras* are variously dated from the 2d cent. (Masson-Oursel) or 4th–5th cent. (Stcherbatsky). They elaborate an analysis of matter as composed of atoms combined in molecules under influence of time and direction. Souls are bound through linkage to such matter. The Nyaya is a system of logic calculated to attain that knowledge necessary to freedom. The *Yoga-sutras* (5th cent.?) teach rigid concentration of mind and body, a method open to all and regarded as valuable by many diverse religious groups. The *Samkhya-karika* is attributed to Isvarakrishna (3d or 4th cent.? Ch. trans. c. 560). It sets forth a dualistic system teaching that the eternal soul can be freed by realization that it is not material like the world about it. The *Brahma Sutra* (c. 350–400) gives the first clear expression of the Vedanta *darsana* or "point of view," developed continuously from the older *Upanishads*: God is everything, the soul is God, and it is the task of the high-caste Brahman to realize in contemplation this identity.

Vasubandhu (c. 300–350), leading philosopher of Hinayana Buddhism, in his *Abhidharmakosa sastra* gave a classic summary of the Vibhasha and of the Vaibhashika school based upon it, with illuminating comments on the competing Sautrantika school founded by Kumaralabdha (c. 150–200) and developed by Harivarman. Vasubandhu was converted to the Mahayana by his brother Asanga, founder of the Vijñana-vadin (Idealist) or Yogachara (Mystic) school, which explains phenomena as mere reflections of ideas and exalts the bodhisattvas, in particular Maitreya. The active translator to Chinese, **Kumarajiva** (c. 344–413), and the logician **Dignaga** (c. 5th cent.) were both adherents of this school, which developed important branches at Valabhi and Nalanda (6th–7th cent.). Fa-hsien first reported Mahayanist monasteries separate from those of the Hinayana.

Literary studies at Ujjain blossomed under the Guptas into the **golden age of classical Sanskrit**. **Arya Sura** in the *Jatakamala* (Ch. trans. 428) put into elegant *kavya* verse tales of former births of the Buddha which had been best known through the *Divyavadana* (Ch. trans. in part, 265). Secular fables gathered into the *Panchatantra* passed through Pehlvi (531–570), Syriac (570), and Arabic (750) into the languages of Europe. The *Sakuntala* and *Vikramorvasi* of **Kalidasa** (c. 400–455) rank first among Indian dramas (Greek influence), his *Meghaduta* equally high as a lyric poem,

while his *Kumarasambhava*, and *Raghuvamsa* mark the apogee of *Kavya*, scholarly epic poetry. Literary taste survived the Gupta Empire: witness **Sudraka's** drama, *Mrichchakatika* ("Little Clay Cart"), and **Dandin's** romance *Dasaku-maracharita* (both 6th cent.) and **Santideva's** brilliant poem of Mahayanist altruism, *Bodhi-charyavatara* (late 7th cent.).

As in literature, so in **art** the Gupta period is one of dignity, restraint, and refinement: classicism in a land given to exaggeration. Neither the Dhamekh Stupa at Sarnath nor Buddhist sculpture copies the motifs of Gandhara, yet they have assimilated its spirit to chasten the exuberant naturalism of Sañchi and Amaravati. At Ajanta new caves were cut, both *chaitya* halls (nos. 19 and 26) and monasteries (nos. 1 and 2). Many of these were decorated with troweled fresco paintings (still visible in caves 1, 2, and 17), which are impressive in scale, graphic facility, and sensitive naturalism, but marred by crowding and incoherence. Slightly later frescoes survive in caves at Bagh (s.w. Vindhyas), and at Sigiri, the rock fortress of parricide king Kassapa (526–552) of Ceylon.

Indian medicine largely parallels the Greek, but was limited, and surgery atrophied, by objection to dissection. An ethical code like the Hippocratic oath appears in works of Charaka and Susruta (prior to 4th cent., though present texts date from 8th and 11th). Greek origin is clear for many astronomical ideas in the (4th cent.?) treatises summarized in **Vara-hamihira's** *Pañchasiddhantika* (c. 550). Zodiacal division of the ecliptic replaces the (Babylonian?) Nakshatras; planetary motion is explained by epicycles; parallax and eclipses are calculated, etc. But many Indian inconsistencies suggest that Greek astronomy was known imperfectly, perhaps through rule-of-thumb manuals. **Aryabhata** (499) taught rotation of the earth and the value of π as 3.1416 (epic value 3.5). **Brahmagupta** (b. 598) systematized the rules of astronomy, arithmetic, algebra, and geometry. His integral solution of an indeterminate equation, with another method given by **Bhaskara** in his *Siddhantasiromani* (1150) is called by Hankel the finest thing in numerical theory before Lagrange (1736–1813). The abacus was described in the *Abhidharmakosa* from first-century sources long before its use in China (1303–1383). More important, the zero (actually a superscribed dot) is attested in Indian literature (600), and the decimal position in a Sanskrit inscription in Cambodia (604) before they passed to the Arabs of Syria (662), and thence to the Europeans.

b. SOUTHERN INDIA

The whole Indian peninsula south of the Vindhyas, save for a part of Maharashtra (Nasik and Pratishthana) easily accessible from Malwa and already Aryanized before our era, was occupied by **Dravidians**: Canarese on the northwest, Telugu on the east, and Tamil in the Carnatic. Jainism, brought to Sravana Belgola in Mysore under Chandragupta (end 4th cent. B.C.), flourished in the Digambara, "naked clergy," form which the north rejected. Buddhism with its stupas and sculpture was brought to Amaravati and Mysore under Asoka. Sanskrit and Hindu culture were carried from the south to Cambodia about the opening of our era. Sanskrit influence is clear in the early (pre-Christian?) Tamil grammar *Tolkappiyam*, and the *Kural* of Tiruvalluvar, lofty songs of a priest of pariahs (2d–3d cent. A.D.). Brahman colonies with Hinduism and the caste system were at various periods imported from the Ganges Valley and endowed by local rulers, as was done also in Bengal.

The south, however, placed its own impress on what it received, and developed linga-worship, *bhakti* devotion to Vishnu and Siva, organization of Saiva monasteries and laymen, occasional violent religious intolerance, and municipal and corporate life with a sacrificial spirit of personal loyalty.

c. 225. Breakup of the Satakani Empire led to establishment in Maharashtra near Nasik, of a

c. 250–c. 500. **Traikutaka dynasty**, probably founded by chiefs of the pastoral Abhira tribe, which used for dating an era of Aug. 26, 249, possibly based on a usurpation of the throne of Ujjain. Another local dynasty,

c. 300–c. 500. **The Vakatakas**, extended their power from the fortress of Gawilgarh in northern Berar to Nagpur, Bundelkhand, and Kuntala, probably limiting Gupta expansion to the south. At Ajanta caves 16 and probably 17 date from the reign of Harisena (c. 475–500).

Farther south the **Chutu branch of the Satakani**, called *Andhrabhrityas* in the Puranas, ruled at Banavasi (c. 200–c. 250), where they were succeeded by

c. 350–c. 500. **The Kadamba dynasty**, founded by a Brahman rebel from the Pallava. His great-grandson **Kakutsthavarman** (c. 435–475) married his daughters to a Gupta, a Vakataka (445), and a Ganga of Mysore.

In the Telugu lands, the Andhras were succeeded by the **Ikshvaku dynasty** (3d cent.), notable for donations to a Buddhist stupa on the Nagarjunikonda (hill), on the Kistna above Amaravati; by the

c. 300–c. 450. **Salankayana of Vengi**; and by the

c. 400–611. **Vishnukundins**, a dynasty of at least ten kings at the same place.

c. CEYLON

Ceylon traditionally received Buddhism from Asoka under

?247–?207 B.C. **Devanampiya Tissa**, who founded the Mahavihara or Great Monastery at his capital Anuradhapura. The Pali *Tripitaka*, which reflects Theravadin tradition, was written under

89–40 or 29–?17 A.D. **Vattagamani**, who founded the rival Abhayagiri Monastery. His epoch is supported by the geography (c. 90–200 A.D.) of the *Mahaniddesa*, a commentary admitted late to the Canon. Under

412–434. **Mahanaman**, Buddhaghosha of Magadha, author of the *Visuddhimagga* or "Way of Purity," recorded in Pali Singhalese traditions. (*Cont. p.* 345.)

3. CHINA, TO 618 A.D.

221–207 B.C. **THE CH'IN DYNASTY** established by the self-styled *First Emperor* (Shih Huang Ti, b. 259; acceded 247; d. 210), advised by **Li Ssu**. Territorial reorganization into thirty-six *chün*, each under civil, military, and supervisory officials. Disarmament by melting down weapons. Standardization of law, weights and measures, and axle length to facilitate interstate commerce.

214. Earlier ramparts linked by convict labor to form the **Great Wall** against the Turkish Hsiung-nu or Huns. Strategic roads. Wholesale transportation of families, especially criminals, to strengthen defenses and weaken particularism. Central South China conquered, from T'ai and Miao tribes, as far as the Southern Mountains and Canton, with the help of a new canal at Hsing-an, from present-day Hunan into Kwangsi.

213. **Proscription of books** which had been em-

ployed by enemies of the new order. Exception made for all scientific works and for those in the hands of seventy official scholars. Introduction of roll silk as writing material led to improvement of hair brush (attributed to Gen. Meng T'ien, d. 209) and to standardization and simplification of script (attributed to Li Ssu). Old complex characters were quickly forgotten.

206. **Epic struggle of Hsiang Yü against Liu Pang** (posthumous temple name (Han) Kao Tsu), who founded

202 B.C.-9 A.D. **THE FORMER OR WESTERN HAN DYNASTY,** with capital at Ch'ang-an. Classic illustration of the typical Chinese dynastic pattern: foundation by rude warrior and administrator; gradual weakening of ruling line; renaissance under a strong successor whose reign reveals cultural progress; further degeneration of dynasty, weakening of control over officials, oppression, revolts, dissolution. In general the Han continued the Ch'in system of administration, gradually increasing the *chün* from 36 to 108.

200. The emperor was surrounded for seven days by the Hsiung-nu, who had formed the first Turkish Empire in Mongolia during the preceding decade. The gift of an imperial princess as consort (repeated in 173), with other presents, secured peace till 166.

196. **Chao T'o** was recognized as king of Southern Yüeh (the modern Kwang provinces) which he had conquered for the Ch'in in 218–214. An expedition against him in 181 ended in disaster.

191. Withdrawal of proscription of conservative literature permitted private scholars in the cultured East to begin its restoration and (equally vital) to transcribe it into modern characters.

155-130. **Liu Teh,** Prince of Ho-chien, collected a library of archaic texts. His cousin, Liu An, Prince of Huai-nan (d. 122), directed an inclusive compilation of early (especially Taoist) philosophy.

140-87. **The reign of Wu Ti,** *The Martial Emperor,* was notable alike for foreign conquests and for the establishment of Confucian scholarship in control of civil administration.

140. **Tung Chung-shu** advocated Confucian training for a civil service, and urged limitation of private holding of land and slaves to remedy undue concentration of wealth which resulted from commerce and mining on a national scale. As result of his efforts the emperor appointed in

136. **Doctors of the Five Classics.** These were the *I* or Changes (an early divination manual); the *Shih* or Odes; the *Shu* or History (documents compiled in the 6th century); the *Ch'un Ch'iu* or Annals of Confucius; and the *Shih-li* (now *I-li*) or Rituals. All were studied in terms of moralistic and ritual commentaries. The Han had followed the bad precedent of the Chou by granting fiefs to relatives and assistants, and found that direct efforts to weaken them resulted in revolt of seven princes (154).

127. **Chu-fu Yen** solved the problem by suggesting that younger sons should share by inheritance one-half of their father's fief. He thus also demonstrated the utility of the scholars.

126. **Chang Ch'ien** returned empty-handed, but with new knowledge of Central Asia and India, from a mission (138) to secure help against the Hsiung-nu from the **Yüeh-chih,** an Indo-European people who had been driven by the Hsiung-nu west from the Chinese border into Ili, and had thence invaded Hellenistic Bactria.

124. **Creation of a Grand College** to train officials for civil service through study of what was now fast becoming Confucian orthodoxy.

121-119. The Hsiung-nu were driven north of the Gobi by **Ho Ch'ü-ping** (d. 117, aged 22). They then split into northern and southern divisions (54).

111-110. **Subjugation of Eastern Yüeh** and Southern Yüeh (along the coast from modern Chekiang to Tonkin), and of the southwest. These conquests rounded out the frontiers of modern "China proper," and gave the Chinese all the best lands in their known world. During the next century Chinese officials traveled on the coasting vessels of local southern merchants at least as far as the Indian Ocean, exchanging gold and silk for glass and pearls.

110. **Wu Ti inaugurated the sacrifice to Heaven** which has since been the primary prerogative and obligation of imperial office.

108. **Conquest of Ch'ao Hsien,** a border kingdom of Korea.

102. **Conquest of the petty states of the Tarim Basin** and Ferghana (Ta Yüan) by Li Kuang-li and a large army. Indo-European languages were spoken throughout this region: Tokharian and Kuchean in the northern oases, Eastern Iranian or Shaka in those of the south, while Sogdian served as *lingua franca*.

Imperial finances, drained by war, were replenished by sale of military titles (123), monopolies of salt and iron (119), forced contributions by the nobility (112), and commutation by fines of judicial sentences (97). They were inflated by debasement of currency (119). The government, guided by Sang Hung-yang, entered the grain business (110), buying cheap and selling dear until exactions of greedy officials led to repeal under Chao Ti (86–73).

The *Shih Chi* or *Historical Memoirs*, first general history of China and a model for later dynastic histories, was compiled by **Ssu-ma Ch'ien** (d. c. 87). **Tai Teh** and **Tai Sheng** compiled standard repertories of early ritual texts, the *Ta Tai Li-chi* and *Li-chi*. **Liu Hsiang** (79–8) prepared a series of reports on the contents of the imperial library. His son **Liu Hsin** (d. 23 A.D.) digested these to form the first classified inventory of extant literature, and rescued from archaic script several important texts, notably the *Tso-chuan* (cf. supra) and the *Chou-li* or Chou Ritual.

1–8 A.D. **Wang Mang** served as regent for child-emperors.

6. All candidates for office were required to take **civil-service examinations.** Tribute of a live rhinoceros was presented on request by the distant but unidentified southern state of Huang-chih.

9–23. **WANG MANG** reigned as emperor of the **Hsin Dynasty,** and undertook radical reforms: nationalization of land with division of large estates and manumission of slaves had to be repealed (12); a tax on slaveholding was substituted in 17. To monopolies of salt, iron, and coinage was added one on wine, and other mining profits were taxed. Seven regional commissions were directed to establish annual high, low, and mean price levels for staple products; to buy surplus goods at cost; and to peg the market by sales above the seasonal index. To curb usury, loans were offered free up to 90 days for funerals, and at 3 per cent a month or 10 per cent a year for productive purposes. Merchants and capitalists employed as administrators provoked revolts, in one of which Wang was killed.

25–220. **LATER OR EASTERN HAN DYNASTY,** founded by a collateral imperial scion, (Hou Han) Kuang Wu Ti (25–57), reigned at Loyang. **Buddhism** was introduced by missionaries from Central Asia, and later from India, probably about the time of Christ. In 65 A.D. the presence of monks and lay believers at his brother's court was favorably mentioned in a decree by Emperor Ming (58–75). The story of official introduction following a dream of this emperor has been shown by Maspero to be a pious legend, completed in its main outlines by the end of the 2d century.

43. **Ma Yüan** conquered Tonkin and Annam, much of which remained (except for brief revolts) under Chinese control until 939. A few natives adopted the Chinese classics, Confucianism, and Buddhism; but the masses retained their own language and customs. Commercial relations through the southern seas were gradually extended. "Java" (perhaps then Sumatra) sent tribute early in 132, and traders from the Roman Empire reached Cattigara or Chiao-chih (now Tonkin) in 166 and 226. A newly organized Malay people, the Chams, occupied Quang-nam, the region of Tourane, c. 192; but when they came farther north they were repelled (270, 360, and 446).

74–94. **Pan Ch'ao,** by personal diplomacy and strategy, brought into submission all the petty states of Turkestan, opening the way for extensive silk trade with the Roman Orient (Ta Ch'in). His lieutenant Kan Ying penetrated to the Persian Gulf (97). Even the Yüeh-chih, who had recently founded the Kushana Kingdom in the Indian Punjab, sent tribute in 90. The northern Hsiung-nu, as a result of successive defeats by the southern Hsiung-nu (85), by the Mongol Sien-pi (87), and by the Chinese general Tou Hsien (89), in part submitted, in part migrated westward, leaving their lands to the Sien-pi, who in 101 in turn began raiding the frontier. To the west the Ch'iang Tibetans disturbed the peace of modern Kansu for several decades until repulsed by Chao Chung, 141–144.

After only two vigorous reigns the court was dominated by women, by their relatives, and by eunuchs by whom they were surrounded.

82. **Empress Tou** altered the succession, and, with her family, ruled as dowager (88–97).

105–121. **Empress Teng** ruled as dowager for her infant son and his boy successor till her death, when her most prominent relatives chose suicide.

124. A change in succession made by Empress Yen was violently reversed in the same year.

132. **Empress Liang** secured honors for her father, and ruled for three youthful emperors from 144 until her death in 150. A younger empress of the same family survived until 159.

159. **Emperor Huan** finally compassed the death of Liang Chi, brother of the elder empress.

184. Rebellion of the Yellow Turbans, provoked by the rapacity of the eunuchs, against whose influence and ruthless murder of scholars opposed to them there had been vigorous protests in 135–136.

189. Massacre of the eunuchs by Yüan Shao.

190-220. Emperor Hsien, last of the Later Han dynasty, never really governed, the actual power having passed to cõmpeting military dictators.

Insecurity of life and property contributed to the popularity of **religious Taoism,** a cult of mysticism and occultism which promised longevity or even immortality as a reward for support, faith and monastic austerity. Its founders, **Chang Ling** (according to tradition he ascended into heaven in 156 at the age of 123) and his son **Chang Heng,** claimed authority from Lao-tzu and philosophic Taoism, but followed the practices of alchemy, breath-control, and magic inherited from charlatans who had infested the courts of Ch'in Shih Huang Ti and Han Wu Ti. Their successors slavishly imitated Buddhism by creation of a divine hierarchy, a voluminous textual canon, and a monastic community.

Cultural tradition was maintained by **Pan Ku** (32–92), who compiled the dynastic *History of the Former Han,* his sister **Pan Chao,** whose *Lessons for Women* codified the standard of feminine morality, and **Hsü Shen,** who completed in 100 the first lexicon of archaic script, *Shuo wen chieh tzu.* The rhymed and rhythmic prose-form *fu* was developed at this time. In 105 the eunuch **Ts'ai Lun** presented to court **paper** made of vegetable fibers: bark, hemp, fish ·nets, and rags. Paper rolls now rapidly supplanted bamboo or wooden slips strung with cords, and the costly roll silk and silk floss paper. **Ma Jung** invented the device of double-column commentary (138–140). Six classics were first engraved on stone (175–183) to perpetuate the academic victory of the conservative school of commentators, who accepted only the earliest renderings into modern script. Figure painting (portraits of 28 generals) and calligraphy (text for stone classics written by Ts'ai Yung) emerged as fine arts. Mortuary chapel of Wu Liang decorated with stone flat reliefs (151).

220-264. Three kingdoms divided the empire, each claiming imperial status.

220-264. Wei dynasty formally founded by Ts'ao P'ei, son of Ts'ao Ts'ao who had dominated the court since 196. Loyang remained the capital. Eunuchs excluded from government. Families of empresses excluded from future exercise of regency (222). Three classics cut in stone (240–248) to establish versions sponsored by the Archaic Text School, founded by Liu Hsin.

221-264. Shu or Shu-Han dynasty founded in the west by Liu Pei (d. 223), antagonist of Ts'ao Ts'ao since 194. Capital at Ch'eng-tu. Chu-ko Liang chief minister 221–234. Rapid development of Szechuan.

222-280. Wu dynasty founded by Sun Ch'üan in the lower Long River Valley with capital at Chien-K'ang (modern Nanking).

c. 245-250. K'ang T'ai mission to Fu-nan, Khmer state in southern Cambodia (first tribute 243), learned details of southern Asia from the envoy of the Indian king.

265-317. Nominal reunion under weak **western Chin dynasty,** established by rebellion of Ssu-ma Yen against the Wei. Institution of the censorate.

317-589. Southern and Northern dynasties divided the empire. Six dynasties (counting the eastern Wu) ruled at Chien-K'ang. The later five are considered legitimate:

317-420. Eastern Chin dynasty,

420-479. Former (or Liu) Sung dynasty, so called from the eight emperors of the Liu family,

479-502. Southern Ch'i dynasty,

502-557. Southern Liang dynasty,

557-589. Southern Ch'en dynasty.

Meantime a series of barbarian dynasties was established in the north by invasion and infiltration of diverse peoples who avidly sought Chinese culture, followed Chinese precedents, and were rapidly absorbed.

304-439. Sixteen kingdoms established along the northern marches by three Chinese and leaders of five northern peoples: three Turkish Hsiung-nu, five Mongol Sien-pi, three Ti, one Chieh, and one Tibetan Ch'iang.

386-534. Northern Wei dynasty, founded at Ta-t'ung by the Toba Tatars who spoke a Mongol dialect strongly palatalized by contact with the Tungus. In 495 the capital was transferred to Loyang.

534-550. The Eastern Wei dynasty ruled at Ye (present Anyang) as did their successors,

550-577. The Northern Ch'i. Meanwhile at Ch'ang-an

535-556. The Western Wei were succeeded by
557-581. The Northern Chou, who overthrew
the northern Ch'i in 577.

This long epoch of political division retarded
cultural progress. Pseudo-reconstruction of
texts which had been added to the *Canon of
History* by K'ung An-kuo in the 2d cent. B.C.,
but lost in the 1st cent. A.D., was probably carried out c. 250, and was presented to the throne
in 317–322. Thirteen texts, including the *Bamboo Annals*, were recovered (281) from a tomb
which was closed in 299 B.C. Gen. **Wang
Hsi-chih** (321–379) provided the classic models
(cut in stone) for formal and cursive calligraphy. **Ku K'ai-chih** (c. 344–c. 406) perfected
the technical refinement of episodic figure-paint-
ing.

Buddhism flourished in China already by the
close of the Han. The splendor of the Buddhist
pantheon and ritual, with its novel conceptions
which embraced ten heavens, ten hells, re-birth,
and salvation of individual souls of common
men, proved irresistible. Sutras were translated
in terms borrowed from philosophic Taoism
chiefly by Indian and Central Asiatic missionaries among whom the most prolific was **Kumarajiva** (c. 344–413, to China 383), son of an Indian and of a princess of Kucha. Indian sectarian divergencies became reflected especially
in versions of the monastic law (*vinaya*). Desire for direct intelligence of authoritative texts
led at least 82 Chinese pilgrims to visit India
during the period 200–600 (61 in the 5th cent.
alone). Fa-hsien blazed the desert trail across
Central Asia and returned by sea (399–414), and
Sung Yün followed the land route to and from
Udyana and Gandhara (518–522). Most popular text of the 6th century was the *Parinirvana-
sutra*, which recounts the birth, illumination,
first teaching, and death of the Buddha. Un-
favorable Confucian appraisal of Indian asceticism, parasitic practices (celibacy, monasticism, mendicancy), and unrestrained imaginative metaphysical literature, together with
hostility of the competing Taoist priesthood,
led to brief persecution by the Northern Wei
(446) and by the Northern Chou (574).

The Northern Wei cut **cave temples** in the
Yün-kang cliffs near Ta-t'ung and decorated
them with Buddhist sculpture in imitation of
the Caves of a Thousand Buddhas at Tun-
huang, then the point of bifurcation of trade
routes north and south of the Tarim basin.
After 495 new caves were cut at Lung-men
near Loyang. The various Buddhas, Bodhisattvas (future Buddhas), Lohan (Skt. Arhat or
Saints), and militant guardians of the law reflect Indian iconography given form by Greek
artisans in Gandhara, as well as Iranian influence.

In Central Asia the Juan-juan or Avars
founded the **first Mongol empire** throughout
Mongolia (407–553). Revolt by the T'u-
chüeh in the Altai (551) led to establishment
in imitation of it of a Turkish empire which
shortly (572) split into eastern and western
divisions. The Western Turks assailed Sassanian Persia from the east, and by weakening
it contributed to the triumph of Islam a few
decades later.

581-618. The Sui dynasty was founded at
Ch'ang-an by Yang Chien (Wen Ti),
chief minister (580) of the Chou.
585 and 607-608. Reconstruction of the Great
Wall (as in 543 by the Eastern Wei and
in 556 by the Northern Ch'i), against
the Eastern Turks of the Orkhon.
589. REUNION OF THE EMPIRE by conquest of the southern Ch'en dynasty.

Active patronage of Buddhism, the common
religion of north and south, multiplied shrines
and images. Chinese Buddhists increasingly
neglected the intangible goal of Indian theology,
the eventual ending of the perpetual chain of
sentient existences by nihilistic absorption into
nirvana; and stressed more practical objectives:
immediate response to prayer by the protective
Bodhisattva Kuan-yin (Avalokitesvara), direct
rebirth into the Western Happy Heaven (Sukha-
vati) of O-mi-t'o (Amitabha), and salvation by
the coming Buddha Mi-lo-fo (Maitreya). Early
Chinese philosophic divergencies reappeared
within Buddhist sectarian doctrine. Taoist
thought was reflected in the increasingly influential **Ch'an sect** which taught that the Buddha-
nature is in every man, and that illumination is
to be sought solely through meditation, to the
exclusion of prayer, asceticism, and good works.
Confucian reaction was evident in the emphasis
by the **T'ien-t'ai school,** founded (575) in the
mountains of Chekiang by Chih-i (538–597),
upon education as necessary to realization of the
Buddha-nature. Strongly synthetic, approval
was given to ecstasy, ceremonial, discipline, and
to a variety of texts which were interpreted as
corresponding to stages in the Buddha's teaching. Perfection was reached in the Lotus
(*Saddharmapundarika*) Sutra, which thenceforth
surpassed all others in popular favor.
602-605. Liu Fang suppressed rebellion in Annam, repelled the Chams, and sacked
their capital Indrapura (near Tourane). The
Chams now paid tribute for a century and a
half. They controlled (until the 10th cent.) the

trade in spices for China, and in silk and porcelain for the Abbasids, which was largely in the hands of Persian merchants. Probably before this time the Cambodian kingdom of Chen-la overthrew its suzerain Fu-nan, and now resumed tribute missions to China (616 or 617).

605–618. Yang Ti, a parricide (604), was ruined by extravagance at home and fruitless foreign wars.

605. The Grand Canal was formed by linking existing waterways from the sumptuous new capital at Loyang (604) to the Long River. It was extended to Cho-chün (near modern Peking) by a million laborers in 608, and to Hangchou in 610.

606. The National College was enlarged, and the doctoral *chin-shih* degree first awarded. The first Japanese embassy was received from the Empress Suiko.

607. Appointment of P'ei Chü to command in the west led to defeat (608) of the Mongol T'u-yü-hun, who had entered the Koko-nor region in the early 4th century, and submission of minor kingdoms (609), but provoked the Eastern T'u-chüeh, who invested the emperor in Yen-men (615).

610. The king of the Liu-ch'iu Islands (or Formosa?) was killed by Ch'en Leng.

611–614. Disastrous wars with Kao-li in the Liao Basin and Korea completed exhaustion of the empire and provoked

613–618. Domestic revolts which led to murder of Yang Ti.

618–907. The T'ang dynasty was founded.

(*Cont. p.* 345.)

4. KOREA, TO 562 A.D.

Korea is a mountainous peninsula 100 to 150 miles wide and about 400 miles long extending southward from Manchuria towards the western tip of Japan. High mountains and the cold Japan Sea have retarded the development of the east coast, but the milder climate and more suitable terrain of the west coast facing China and the south coast opposite Japan have made these regions the natural centers of Korean history.

The people since prehistoric times seem to have been closely related racially, linguistically and culturally to the ancient peoples of Manchuria and Siberia as well as to the Japanese, but their post-neolithic civilization came largely from China.

c. 300–200 B.C. A semi-Sinicized state called **Chosŏn** (Japanese: Chōsen) developed in the northwest, and other less civilized states appeared in the south and east.

108 B.C. Emperor Wu-ti of the Han dynasty of China conquered Chosŏn and established four prefectures covering central and western Korea and centering around Lo-lang near the modern P'yŏngyang (Ch. P'ing-jang, J. Heijo), where an extensive Chinese colony grew up.

c. 150 A.D. Koguryŏ, founded over 100 years earlier in Manchuria and northern Korea, and other states in the south and east asserted their independence of the Chinese colony.

c. 210. The Kung-sun family of southern Manchuria obtained control of Lo-lang and established Tai-fang to the south of it.

c. 238. The Wei dynasty of China captured Lo-lang and Tai-fang by sea.

c. 250. Northern invaders established the state of **Paekche** in the southwest.

313. The last remnants of the Chinese colonies were extinguished by native states, and Chinese civilization was diffused throughout the peninsula by the dispersed Chinese colonists. This marked the beginning of

313–668. THE THREE KINGDOMS PERIOD. After the elimination of China, Korea remained for several centuries divided between Koguryŏ in the north, Paekche in the southwest and Silla, established probably in the second or third century, in the southeast.

c. 360–390. Period of greatest Japanese influence and activity in Korea through their foothold on the coast between Silla and Paekche.

372. Koguryŏ received Buddhism from China.

413–490. King Changsu brought Koguryŏ to the height of its power and moved the capital from the banks of the Yalu River to P'yŏngyang (427).

528. Silla adopted Buddhism. The last of the Korean states to do so and culturally the most backward, Silla at this time began to make rapid progress and to expand at the expense of the Japanese sphere.

554. Silla won an outlet on the East China Sea in central Korea, giving her easy sea communications with China.

562. Silla destroyed Japan's sphere in Korea.

(*Cont. p.* 354.)

5. JAPAN, TO 645 A.D.

GEOGRAPHY: Jápan proper consists of a group of islands running eastward from the southern tip of the Korean peninsula for some 700 miles and then turning abruptly northward for about the same distance, approaching the Asiatic mainland once more off the coast of the Maritime Province of Siberia. The cold Japan Sea enclosed by this island arc gives the inner side of the archipelago a cold damp climate, but because of the Japan Current the Pacific coast of southwestern Japan enjoys a warm temperate climate. Consequently, here the main centers of civilization have developed. Four main islands account for most of the land area of Japan. Hondō, the largest, extends for the greater part of the arc. The next largest, Hokkaidō or Ezo, ies to the north of Hondō. Kyūshū at the southwestern extremity and Shikoku east of it, together with the westernmost portion of Hondō, almost surround a long narrow strip of water known as the Inland Sea. Among the many lesser islands Tsushima and Iki are of most significance, for they lie in the straits between Korea and Japan.

The two most important areas of Japan are the group of small plains lying in Hondō at the eastern end of the Inland Sea and the great Kantō Plain around Tōkyō Bay in eastern Hondō. The Inland Sea, as an artery of communications, and northern and western Kyūshū, which face the Asiatic mainland, are also important regions.

The rivers are all short and shallow and are consequently of little significance. Mountains cover almost the entire area and are particularly high in central Hondō. Many of them are volcanic, and eruptions and earthquakes are frequent. The climate is temperate throughout the land, and rain is abundant. Since antiquity rice has been the principal crop.

ETHNOLOGY: The origin of the Japanese people is still in question. Archaeology and physical anthropology indicate a close connection with the Koreans and the Tungusic peoples of northeastern Asia. Linguistic evidence, though more hotly disputed, tends to support this. However, ethnographical evidence and mythology suggest South Chinese, Malaysian or even Polynesian origin. Furthermore, the Ainu (also called Ezo and Emishi), possibly a proto-Caucasian people, originally inhabited the northeastern half of Japan and undoubtedly contributed to the racial composition of the Japanese. One may conclude, therefore, that, though the early Japanese seem to have been primarily a Mongolian people, there was probably some admixture of blood from southeastern Asia and from the Ainu.

RELIGION: The primitive religion of Japan was a simple worship of the manifold manifestations of the powers of nature combined with a system of ritualistic observances, notable among which was an insistence on physical and ritual purity. The deities tended to become anthropomorphic and to merge with memories of past heroes. They were also affected by attempts to explain the origins of man and society in mythological terms. This eventually resulted in an organized mythology centering around the sun-goddess (*Amaterasu*) and her descendants, the imperial family. After the introduction of Buddhism this combination of nature-worship, ritualistic observances and ancestor-honoring mythology was given the name of **Shintō** to distinguish it from the Indian religion.

CIVILIZATION: Japan's earliest known civilization was a neolithic shell-mound culture, which before the Christian era gave way to a culture featured by sepulchral mounds over dolmens containing pottery and iron and bronze objects which show a predominantly north Asiatic influence. Prehistoric Japanese civilization seems to have come from what is known linguistically as the Altaic region and seems early to have been influenced strongly by the much higher Chinese civilization.

HISTORY: The first authentic historical accounts of Japan occur in Chinese histories of the 3d century A.D., and picture western Japan, if not all of Japan, as divided among a great number of small political units, among which feminine rule was not uncommon. Some of these petty states had direct relations with the Chinese colonies in Korea, and embassies from Japanese states to the Chinese capital are recorded from 57 to 266.

Japanese historical mythology commences with the accession of the first emperor, **Jimmu**, in 660 B.C., a date arbitrarily chosen, probably over thirteen centuries later. The mythology hints at the migration of the future imperial clan from Kyūshū up the Inland Sea to the plain of Yamato or Nara, and a successful contest for supremacy with another clan in Izumo on the Japan Sea. The Izumo clan seems to have had a rather distinctive culture and to have had close

relations with Korea.   During the first four centuries of the Christian era the imperial clan in
Yamato seems gradually to have established its
suzerainty over most of central and western
Japan in a long series of wars with neighboring
clans and with the Ainu in the east and the Kumaso in the west, a people apparently of alien
and quite possibly of southern origin.

c. 230 A.D.   With the accession of the tenth emperor, **Sujin,** Japanese records begin to
contain some material of probable historical accuracy.   The victories of the half-legendary
Prince Yamatodake over the Kumaso and the
Ainu seem to reflect a period of rapid expansion
in the early decades of the 4th century.

c. 360.   The story of the **conquest of Korea** by
the Empress Jingō, ruling in the name
of her deceased husband and later in the name of
her son, probably refers to Japanese campaigns
in the peninsula.   Korean records mention Japanese inroads during this century, and a Korean
inscription of 391 proves that their armies were
widely active in the peninsula at that time.
From this period probably dates the establishment of a Japanese protectorate over a group of
miniature states in southern Korea known as
Kara or *Imna* (J., *Mimana*), which had for long
constituted a Japanese sphere of influence, and
at the same time a semi-protectorate over Paekche, a larger state in southwestern Korea. Japan
in the 5th century claimed suzerainty over all of
Korea, but in reality her power was on the wane
even in the south, as Silla, a vigorous kingdom in
the southeast, gradually rose to supremacy.   The
chief significance of the Korean contacts was
that Japan through them was able to imbibe
deeply of Chinese civilization and was able to
open the way once more for direct relations with
China, which was accomplished in 413.

About the end of the 4th century or early in
the 5th scribes able to read and write Chinese are
said to have come from Korea.   This implies the
official **adoption of Chinese writing,** but not the
first knowledge of it in Japan.   Writing spread
slowly, but was early used for historical records,
for by the first half of the 6th century the traditional Japanese chronology becomes reasonably
accurate.

Japan's **social organization** as it emerged at
this time was that of a large group of clans (*uji*)
under clan chiefs (*uji-no-kami*).   The members
of a single clan all claimed descent from a common ancestor, often the clan god (*ujigami*).   The
clan chief acted as high priest to the clan god,
and his political rule was tinged throughout with
a sacerdotal flavor.   The chief and his immediate family often had one of several hereditary

titles (*kabane*), which in time came to be grouped
hierarchically.   Below the clans were hereditary
occupational groups (*be* or *tomo*), often called
guilds or corporations.   They were the economic
foundation of the clan system.   Below them in
turn was an inconsiderable number of slaves.

The imperial clan at first was little more than
hegemon among the various clans.   Its chief
was the emperor, and its clan god was made the
national deity.   Its rule over the country was
extremely loose and feeble.   The clans with the
two most important hereditary titles, *Omi* and
Muraji, were controlled through a chief *Omi*
(*Ōomi*) and a chief *Muraji* (*Ōmuraji*).   *Tomo-
no-miyatsuko* were placed over the imperial
clan's hereditary occupational groups and *Kuni-
no-miyatsuko* over its rice lands.   Chieftains of
the Kume, Ōtomo and Mononobe clans served as
imperial generals and those of the Nakatomi and
Imube (also pronounced Imibe and Imbe) clans
were in charge of the court religious ceremonies.

The importation of Chinese civilization and an
influx of Korean immigrants seriously shook the
clan system.   In imitation of China there developed a greater centralization of power in the
hands of the imperial clan and its ministers, who
at times even aspired to the throne themselves.
Imperial lands were gradually extended, and imperial authority grew, eventually leading to a
complete political and economic reorganization
of Japan on the Chinese model.

? 527.   A serious **revolt in Kyūshū** prevented
the crossing of an army to Korea to aid
Imna.   Dissension among the Japanese and the
treason of some of their officers in Korea seriously reduced their prestige in the peninsula and
opened the way for the conquest of Imna by
Silla.

? 552.   The official introduction of **Buddhism**
from Paekche, which itself had re-
ceived it in 384, marked the beginning of a new
epoch in Japan.   There probably were Buddhist
converts in Japan prior to 552, but at this time
Buddhism first began to play a significant rôle
in Japanese history and to stimulate the influx
of Chinese civilization by way of Paekche.   Supported by the powerful Soga clan and strengthened by the arrival of clerics from Korea, Buddhism made headway at court, but soon a temporary proscription of it was brought about by
the Nakatomi and Mononobe clans, the political
rivals of the Soga.   It was presently restored,
and the Emperor Yōmei (585–587 ?) embraced
the faith shortly before his death.

? 562.   Silla drove the Japanese out of Imna,
ending their long direct control of a
portion of Korea.

? 587. The Soga crushed their rivals in a short civil war, thereby establishing their political supremacy and the right of Buddhism to an unhampered development in Japan.

592. **Soga Umako** (d. 626) had his nephew, the Emperor Sushun (587–592), murdered.

593–628. **Suiko,** the first officially recognized empress, ruled over the land at the crucial period when Buddhism was taking root and the importation of Chinese civilization was strongly influencing the basic forms of Japanese government and society. The leading spirit during her reign was the crown prince, **Shōtoku** (d. 621 or 622), who was the real establisher of Buddhism in Japan, the pioneer in laying the foundations for the Sinicized form of government of the next several centuries and the founder of such great monasteries as the Shitennōji (593), the Hōkōji (588–596) and the Hōryūji (607?).

604. **Prince Shōtoku** issued the so-called **Seventeen Article "Constitution,"** a moral code consisting of somewhat vague injunctions imbued with Confucian ethics and the Chinese political theory of a centralized imperial government. Thus it served as an ideological basis for political centralization. The constitution was also strongly influenced by Buddhism and shows that the prince was aware of its moral and philosophical import and not merely of its supposed magical powers, which chiefly attracted the contemporary Japanese. In this same year, in imitation of China, official grades known as "cap ranks" (*kan'i*), an official calendar and regulations for court etiquette were adopted.

607. **Ono Imoko,** the first official envoy from the central government, was dispatched to the Sui court in China. This and a second embassy to the Sui in 608 were followed in the course of the next two and a half centuries by twelve embassies to the T'ang. Since Japanese students, scholars and monks accompanied the envoys to China and sometimes remained there for prolonged periods of study, these embassies were a very important factor in the importation of Chinese civilization to Japan.

630. First embassy to the T'ang.

643. Prince Yamashiro no Ōe, the heir of Prince Shōtoku, was forced to commit suicide by Soga Iruka (d. 645), the son of Emishi (d. 645), the kingmaker of the period. The prince had twice been overlooked in the imperial succession by the Soga, whose obvious imperial aspirations brought about

645. **THE DOWNFALL OF THE SOGA** in a *coup d'état* led by the future Emperor Tenchi (661–672) and by Nakatomi Kamatari (d. 669), the founder of a new clan, the Fujiwara. This incident gave the progressive element at court a chance to begin a series of sweeping reforms along Chinese lines, which mark the beginning of a new era in Japan. (*Cont. p.* 355).

III. The Middle Ages

A. THE EARLY MIDDLE AGES

1. WESTERN EUROPE

a. THE EARLY PAPACY

The Church before the emergence of the Bishops of Rome. The center of gravity was in the east. Possession of the Holy Places and the presence of the emperor gave the east political and ecclesiastical supremacy.

Rise of the episcopate. The bishops, originally overseers (*episcopus*), thanks to their consecration, the tradition of apostolic succession, and their control of the sacraments, were distinguished among the clergy. Each church was originally independent, but the evolution of an ecclesiastical counterpart to the centralized civil state gave the bishop a clearly monarchical quality in the 3d century. The lay and ecclesiastical states met in the person of the emperor, and the original loose autonomy of the independent churches began to be lost in a centralized system. The precedence of **metropolitans** (i.e. the bishops of the great sees) was recognized (341), without reducing the accepted superiority of the **patriarchs.** The five patriarchates (ecclesiastical equivalents of exarchates) were (save for Rome) in the east — Jerusalem, Antioch, Alexandria, Constantinople. The west (including Rome) was either poorly represented or not represented at all at the oecumenical councils in the east. Vague precedence in honor was conceded to Rome, but no more.

Oecumenical councils settled general problems of dogma and discipline. These councils were called by the emperor and presided over by him in person or by legate. Local problems were dealt with in synods.

EMERGENCE OF THE BISHOPS OF ROME.[1] *Papa* was a title applied to all bishops until c. 425, and did not take on its present meaning until the 7th century. **Bishop Victor** of Rome (c. 190) exercised a kind of spiritual sovereignty which was continued in the 3d century. Gradually the recession of the Church of the east, the loss of Africa, and the rise of powerful churches in the east, left Rome isolated in the west. As the sole western apostolic see, the scene of the martyrdom of Peter, and guardian

[1] A complete list of the popes will be found in Appendix IV.

of the tombs of Peter and Paul, Rome enjoyed a unique spiritual prestige, and until the reign of Diocletian (285–305) it was the administrative center of the empire. After that the capital was at Milan, and this see at times was almost equal to Rome in influence. With the removal of the imperial capital to Constantinople (330), Rome lost prestige, especially in the east. On the other hand, between 330 and 395, since there was no emperor permanently resident in the west, the Bishop of Rome had no political rival.

(1) The emperors supported the Roman campaign against paganism and against heresy (e.g. Arians and Donatists) with civil penalties, and confirmed and deprived bishops.

(2) The Roman See as early as the days of Diocletian was rich, and was further enriched by the emperors until it was the wealthiest in the Church; the Bishop of Rome enjoyed the "presidency in charity" throughout Christendom.

(3) Sporadic intervention (usually on appeal) was made outside his direct jurisdiction by the Bishop of Rome, but until after 1000 the Bishop of Rome "never once on his own special authority pronounced upon any doctrinal point addressed to the Catholic world." Nor did he interfere between a bishop and his flock in ordinary diocesan affairs or collect money except within his own immediate episcopal jurisdiction.

(4) **The Petrine theory,** on the basis of Matthew 16: 18, 19, asserts that Peter was designated by Christ as the founder of the Church, and that Christ conferred the "power of the keys," i.e. the "power to bind and loose," upon Peter, who transmitted it to his successor the Bishop of Rome, through whom it passed to all bishops. This theory was given currency by **Pope Celestine I** (422–432). In effect this abandoned the original concept of the Bishop of Rome as *episcopus inter episcopos* for the more radical monarchical concept of the Roman bishop as *episcopus episcoporum.* Early writers give no indication of such interpretations, and Cyprian (d. 258) in a famous passage avers that the Bishop of Rome is no more than a bishop among other bishops.

340. The introduction of **eremitical monasti-**

cism into the west by Athanasius marked the beginning of a strong ascetic reaction against the corruption of western life. Supported by Jerome, Ambrose, and Augustine, this development led to a great growth of monasticism. Bishop Eusebius of Vercelli (d. 371), by insisting that his clergy lead a monastic life, began a practice which led to the general ordination of monks. Martin of Tours founded (c. 362) a cenobitic community of monks near Poitiers.

343. **The Council of Sardika** apparently recognized the right of appeal from a provincial synod to the Bishop of Rome.

The oldest extant decretal dates from the episcopacy of **Siricius** (c. 384–498).

THE LATIN FATHERS OF THE CHURCH: Jerome (c. 340–420), a Dalmatian, devoted to pagan learning despite his keen ascetic convictions. The first great western exponent of monasticism. One of the greatest scholars of the Latin Church, his translation of the *Bible* into Latin (the *Vulgate*) is still authoritative in the Roman Church today. This excellent version exerted stylistic and theological influence throughout the Middle Ages. **Ambrose** (c. 340–397) of Trier, a Roman provincial governor, elected (374) Archbishop of Milan before he was baptized. His *Duties of the Clergy* (based largely on Cicero, *de Officiis*) was for centuries the standard work on ethics, and is probably the chief single source of the Stoic tradition in early western thought. He made Milan almost the equal of Rome in prestige, and forced the Emperor Theodosius to do penance, maintaining that in ecclesiastical matters a bishop was superior to an emperor. **Augustine** (354–430) of Hippo, greatest of the western fathers. Converted to Christianity after ventures in Neo-Platonism and Manichaeism, he was the founder of western theology, the link between the classical tradition and the mediaeval schoolmen. Through him a great stream of Platonic and Neo-Platonic thought came into the Church. For a thousand years all thought was influenced by Augustine, and theology betrays his influence to this day. He gave wide currency to the doctrines of original sin, predestination, salvation through divine grace, and his influence was felt by Calvin and Luther. His *City of God* presents a dualism of the heavenly city (identified with the Christian Church) and the earthly city (Rome), and is written to prove that the misfortunes of Rome (e.g. the sack of 410) were not due to Christianity. The *Confessions* set the fashion in spiritual autobiography.

402-417. **INNOCENT I** asserted that the pope was custodian of apostolic tradition and claimed universal jurisdiction for the Roman Church.

440-461. **LEO THE GREAT,** the first great pope, a highly cultivated Roman, vigorous foe of the Manichaean heresy. He procured an edict from Emperor Valentinian III (445) declaring that papal decisions have the force of law. Leo was probably the first pope to enunciate the theory of the mystical unity of Peter and his successors, and to attribute all their doings and sayings to Peter. Leo, repudiating the decrees of the Robber Council of Ephesus (449) at the Council of Chalcedon (451), dictated without discussion, and with imperial support, his solution of the greatest doctrinal controversy since 325. His *Tome* promulgated the doctrine of the union of the two natures. He refused to accept the decree of the council that the Patriarch of Constantinople was supreme in the Church. The tradition of his miraculous arrest of Attila's advance and his efforts to stop Gaiseric's attack (455) won the papacy tremendous prestige in later days. (*Cont. pp.* 150, 216).

b. INVADERS OF THE WEST

ORIGINS OF THE INVADERS. The Germanic race was established in Scandinavia (Denmark) and between the Elbe and Oder as early as the 2d millennium B.C. Eastward lay the Balts (Letts) and to the west of the Elbe were the Celts.

EXPANSION. (1) The West Germans (Teutons) displaced (c. 1000 B.C.) the Celts, moving up the Elbe and Rhine (the Main reached c. 200 B.C.). South Germany was occupied (c. 100 B.C.); Gaul threatened (cf. Caesar's *Commentaries*). These invaders were a pastoral, agricultural folk, tending to settle down. By the time of Tacitus' (c. 55–c. 117 A.D.) *Germania* they were wholly agricultural. Later new tribal names and a new kind of federated organization appeared. (2) The East Germans (Scandinavians) crossed the Baltic (c. 600–300 B.C.) and pushed up the Vistula to the Carpathians. (3) The North Germans remained in Scandinavia.

NEW GROUPINGS AMONG THE WEST GERMANS. **Alamanni** (of Suevian stock) on the upper Rhine; **Franks** (i.e. "free" of the Romans) and **Saxons** between the Weser and the Elbe, inland to the Harz; **Thuringians**, south of the Saxons.

GOVERNMENT. All were tribal democracies, some under kings, others under *grafs*. In each case the head of the state was elected by the assembly of free men, the kings chosen from a royal house, e.g. Amals (Ostrogoths), Balthas (Visigoths), Mervings (Franks), the *grafs* without such restriction.

PROGRESS OF MIGRATIONS. The East Germans (Alani, Bastarnae, Burgundians, Gepids, Goths, Heruls, Rugians, Sciri) moved toward the Black Sea where they had arrived by 214 A.D. The division of Visigoth (West Goth) and Ostrogoth (East Goth) probably arose after their arrival at the Black Sea.

(1) The Huns

The Huns, nomadic Mongols of the Ural-Altaic race group, probably under pressure from the Zhu-Zhu Empire in Asia, swept into Europe in the 4th century and halted for some 50 years in the valley of the Danube and Theiss.

372. They defeated the Alans and Heruls, destroyed the Ostrogothic empire of Hermanric, absorbed the Ostrogoths for a time in their own empire, routed the Visigoths under Athanaric on the Dniester River, and then began a new thrust to the west.

445-453. Height of the Hun power under **Attila.** Honoria, sister of Valentinian III, to escape an unwelcome marriage, sent her ring to Attila and asked for aid. Attila claimed this to be an offer of marriage. About the same time Gaiseric the Vandal was intriguing to induce Attila to attack the Visigoths. By a clever pretense of friendliness to both sides, Attila kept the Romans and Goths apart, and set out westward with a great force (451) which included Gepids, Ostrogoths, Rugians, Scirians, Heruls, Thuringians, Alans, Burgundians, and Ripuarian Franks. Metz was taken and the Belgic provinces ravaged. To meet Attila the Roman Aëtius mustered a force of Salian Franks, Ripuarians, Burgundians, Celts, and Visigoths under Theodoric I, as well as his own Gallo-Romans. Attila apparently declined battle near Orleans and turned back.

451. Aëtius overtook him at an unknown spot near Troyes, the so-called *Lacus Mauriacus* (Châlons), and a drawn battle was fought. Attila continued his withdrawal. Still claiming Honoria, Attila turned into Italy, razed Aquileia, ravaged the countryside (foundation of Venice) and opened the road to Rome. Pope Leo, one of a commission of three sent by the emperor, appeared before Attila. Attila retreated after plague had broken out in his force, food supply had run low, and reinforcements arrived from the east for the Roman army. Attila's death (453) was followed by a revolt of his German vassals led by the Gepids, and (454) the defeat of the

Huns on the Nedao (in Pannonia). The remnant of the Huns settled on the lower Danube, the Gepids set up a kingdom in Dacia, the Ostrogoths settled in Pannonia.

(2) The Visigoths

After their defeat by the Huns, the Visigoths (perhaps 80,000 in number) sought refuge in the Roman Empire.

376. The **Emperor Valens** ordered them disarmed and allowed to cross the Danube in order to settle in Lower Moesia. Faced with the unprecedented problem of these refugees, the Roman government bungled the administration, failed really to disarm the Goths and ultimately had to fight a two-year war with them.

378. The Visigoths, under **Fritigern,** defeated and killed **Valens** near Adrianople, thereby making the first decisive break in the Rhine-Danube frontier. This defeat of the Roman infantry by mounted warriors forecast the revolution in the art of war which determined the military, social, and political development of Europe throughout the Middle Ages.

Fritigern, hoping to carve a Visigothic empire out of the Roman provinces, ravaged Thrace for two years, but could not take Adrianople. After his death (379), the Emperor **Theodosius** arranged a pacification of the Visigoths as part of a general policy of assimilation. He won over some of the chieftains, including **Alaric** of the royal house of Balthas, who hoped for a career in the Roman service. Alaric, disappointed in his hopes at the death of Theodosius, was elected king by the Visigoths, and ravaged Thrace to the gates of Constantinople. Arcadius, emperor of the east (395–408), was helpless until the arrival of Stilicho, *magister utriusque militiae* (field marshal of both services) in the east.

Stilicho, a Vandal by blood, married to Theodosius' sister, was guardian of Theodosius' sons, Arcadius and Honorius. He faced Alaric in Thessaly and the Peloponnesus, avoiding battle, apparently on orders from Honorius. Alaric was made *magister militum* in Illyricum, and Stilicho, out of favor in Constantinople, was declared a public enemy.

401. Alaric began a thrust into Italy, probably because of the triumph of an anti-German faction in Constantinople, and ravaged Venetia. Simultaneously Radagaisus (an Ostrogoth) began an invasion of Raetia and Italy. Stilicho, firmly against any Germanic invasion of the west, repulsed Radagaisus.

402. Pollentia, a drawn battle between Stilicho and Alaric, was a strategic defeat for

Alaric. Alaric's next advance was stopped, probably through an understanding with Stilicho. Halted again (403) at Verona, the Visigoths withdrew to Epirus.

406. The Rhine frontier, denuded of troops for the defense of Italy, was crossed by a great wave of migrants, chiefly East Germans: Vandals, Sueves, and Alans (non-German). The usurper **Constantine** having crossed from Britain to Gaul, Alaric in Noricum was paid a huge sum of gold by the Senate, as a sort of retainer for his services against Constantine. Stilicho, his popularity undermined by these events and by the hostility of Constantinople, was beheaded. There is no evidence of treason by Stilicho. His execution was followed by a general massacre of the families of the barbarian auxiliaries in Italy, and some 30,000 of them went over to Alaric in Noricum.

410. Alaric took Rome after alternate sieges and negotiations. He sacked it for three days, and then moved south toward Africa, the granary of Italy. Turned back by the loss of his fleet, Alaric died and was buried in the bed of the Busento. His brother-in-law Ataulf was elected to succeed him. Ataulf, originally bent on the destruction of the very name of Rome, now bent his energies to the fusion of Visigothic vigor and Roman tradition.

412. Ataulf led the Visigoths north, ravaged Etruria, crossed the Alps, ravaged Gaul and married (against her brother Honorius' will) Galla Placidia (414) after the Roman ritual. He was forced into Spain (415), where he was murdered. **Wallia** (415–c. 418), after the brief reign of Sigeric, succeeded him.

Ulfilas (311–381), a Gothic bishop of Arian convictions, invented the Gothic alphabet for his translation of the *Bible*. This translation, the first literary monument of the German invaders, had enormous influence, and recalls the wide extent of the **Arian heresy,** which won every important Germanic invader except the Franks, a development with the greatest political consequences, since the lands where the Germans settled were peopled by orthodox Roman Catholics.

Spain had already been overrun by a horde of Vandals, Sueves, and Alans (409), and the Roman blockade made food hard to get. Wallia planned to cross to the African granary, but lost his ships, was forced to make terms with Honorius and restore Galla Placidia to her brother. He agreed to clear Spain of other barbarians. Succeeding in this he received the grant of *Aquitania Secunda* (i.e. the land between the Loire and the Garonne) with Toulouse as a capital. Thus began the

419–507. KINGDOM OF TOULOUSE. The Visigoths received two-thirds of the land, the remainder being left to the Roman proprietors. A Gothic state was created within the Roman state. Honorius, hoping to counteract alien influences, revived a Roman custom of holding provincial councils, decreeing an annual meeting of the leading officials and the chief landowners for discussion of common problems. The most important rulers of Toulouse were

419–451. Theodoric I, who fell in the **battle of Châlons,** and

466–484. Euric, whose reign marked the apogee of the kingdom. He continued the pressure of the Visigoths upon Gaul and Spain, and by 481 extended his domain from the Pyrenees to the Loire and eastward to the Rhone, securing Provence from Odovacar (481). Euric first codified Visigothic law, but the *Breviary of Alaric* (506), a codification of Roman law for Visigothic use, had tremendous influence among the Visigoths and among many other barbarian peoples. Under Visigothic rule the administration in general remained Roman and the language of government continued to be a Latin vernacular. The Gallo-Roman population and clergy were hostile to the Visigoths as Arians, and this hostility opened the way for the **Frankish conquest** (507), which reduced the Visigothic power to its Spanish domains.

507–711. The Visigothic Kingdom of Spain dragged out a miserable existence under more than a score of rulers, some mere phantoms, until the arrival of the Moslems (p. 163).

554. Belisarius' invasion of Spain, part of Justinian's reconstruction of the Roman Empire (p. 172), was a brilliant campaign, but reduced only the southeast corner of Spain, later regained by the Visigoths, who also reduced the Sueves in the north.

(3) *The Vandals*

406. The Vandals (Asding and Siling), allied with the Sciri and Alans, crossed the Rhine near the Main, followed the Moselle and Aisne (sacking Reims, Amiens, Arras, Tournai), then turned southward into Aquitaine, and crossed the Pyrenees into Spain (409).

429–534. THE VANDAL KINGDOM IN AFRICA. The Vandals and Alani had been established in southern Spain under Gunderic. His brother **Gaiseric** received an appeal from Boniface, the revolted Roman governor of Africa, following which the Vandals (perhaps 80,000 in number) crossed into Africa (429).

430. The first siege of Hippo failed, but Boniface, now reconciled to the regency of Galla Placidia, was annihilated, and the city fell (431). **St. Augustine,** Bishop of Hippo, died during the siege. The creation of a great Vandal power in Africa, supported as it soon was by a powerful navy, distracted the attention of the Roman government from the new barbarian kingdoms of the west and had a decisive effect of a negative kind.

In Africa the Vandals spared nobody and nothing and the treaty made with the Romans was no restraint. After the arrival of a fleet from Constantinople, a second treaty was made. Eudocia, daughter of Valentinian, was betrothed to Gaiseric's son, Huneric, and the Vandals received most of the Roman territory except the region about Carthage.

439. Gaiseric took Carthage from the Romans, and made it his capital and naval base.

455. Gaiseric attacked Rome, on the invitation (according to tradition) of Valentinian's widow Eudocia. He took it easily, and for two weeks pillaged the city, scientifically and ruthlessly, but without wanton destruction.

In Africa the Vandals were hated as Arians, and they had to deal with serious Berber revolts, but their power was not broken until the

533-548. Vandalic Wars of Justinian. Belisarius quickly defeated the Carthaginian power of the Vandals; the ensuing Berber revolt was not put down until 548.

(4) The Burgundians

411-532. The Burgundians, arriving from the Oder-Vistula region, moved along the Main athwart the Rhine, entered Gaul under King Gundicar, and finally settled as federates of the Roman Empire in upper Germany (i.e. the lands including Lyons, Vienne, Besançon, Geneva, Autun, Macon). King **Gundibald** (d. 516) codified Burgundian law in the *Lex Gundobada.* The Burgundians were finally conquered by the sons of Clovis (c. 532), but the Burgundian state remained separate under Frankish control with Merovingian princes until 613. After 613 it was a province of the Frankish Empire.

c. THE OSTROGOTHS IN ITALY, 489-554

On the breakup of the Hunnic Empire (after Nedao, 454), the Ostrogoths settled in Pannonia (their first settlement inside the Roman frontier) as federates of the empire. Under the Huns the emergence of a single ruler had been impossible. Thiudareiks (ruler of the people), corrupted into Theodoric, educated as a hostage at Constantinople, was elected (471) merely a *gau* king, but soon became leader of his people on a march into the Balkan Peninsula where he forced the Emperor Leo to grant them lands in Macedonia. His ambition for imperial appointment was realized (483) when he was made *magister militum praesentalis* and (484) *consul.* He quarreled with the emperor and marched on Constantinople. To get rid of him the emperor commissioned him (informally) to expel Odovacar from Italy. Arriving in Italy (489) the Ostrogoths triumphed over Odovacar, but did not reduce Ravenna until 493. Theodoric killed Odovacar with his own hands and had his troops massacred.

489-526. THEODORIC THE GREAT. In general Theodoric continued Odovacar's policy, substituting Ostrogoths for Odovacar's Germans, and assigning one-third of the Roman estates (as Odovacar had probably done) to his people. Theodoric's rule was officially recognized (497) by Constantinople. Together with the emperors he named the consuls in the west, but never named an Ostrogoth. Theodoric was the only member of his people who was a Roman citizen, constitutionally the others were alien soldiers in the service of the empire. No Roman was in military command, no Ostrogoth in the civil service. Imperial legislation and coinage continued. The so-called *Edictum Theodorici* is a codification of Theodoric's administrative decrees rather than a body of legislation, as none of Theodoric's "laws" were anything more than clarifications of imperial legislation. Theodoric's secretary of state was the learned Italian, **Cassiodorus,** and the dual state was paralleled by a dual religious system. Theodoric was tolerant of the orthodox Catholics and a protector of the Jews. His chief aim was to civilize his people under the Roman environment and to keep peace.

Theodoric's co-operation with the other Germanic peoples was close, and he cemented his associations by marriage alliances (one daughter married Alaric II the Visigoth, another in Burgundy, and he himself married Clovis' sister). He intervened to protect the Alamanni from Clovis and tried to save the Visigoths. Provence was acquired from Burgundy and annexed to Italy. He was regent and protector of his grandson Amalaric after Alaric II's death, and virtually ruled the Visigothic Kingdom until his death (526).

To the Italians Ostrogothic rule was alien and

heretical and they resented it. The end of Theodoric's reign was marked by a growing ill-feeling and suspicion which may have been due to this. **Boethius,** the Roman philosopher and commentator on Aristotle, author of the *Consolation of Philosophy,* an official of Theodoric's government, and his father-in-law, the brilliant and polished Roman **Symmachus,** were both executed (c. 524) on a charge of treasonable conspiracy.

535-554. RECONQUEST OF ITALY BY THE EMPEROR. Justinian, as part of his grandiose reconstitution of the Roman Empire, dispatched **Belisarius** and later **Narses** who reduced the stubborn Ostrogoths and drove them over the Alps to an unknown end.

After the expulsion of the Ostrogoths the **Exarchate of Ravenna** was established under the Emperor Maurice (582–602). The exarch had military and civil powers and received full imperial honors. He exercised imperial control over the Church, including the Bishopric of Rome. War and pestilence had completely ruined northern Italy; Rome, in ruins, had sunk from her imperial position to be a provincial town; the way was open for the Lombard invaders.

Ravenna had been the capital of the west (c. 402–476) and was the home of Theodoric's brilliant court. The architecture of the city offers a unique series of examples of Roman and Romano-Byzantine buildings begun under the emperors and continued by Theodoric. The name and glory of Theodoric have survived in German tradition in Dietrich von Bern (i.e. of Verona, where he had a palace).

PROGRESS OF THE PAPACY. Gelasius (492–496) was the first pope to proclaim the independence of the papacy from both emperor and church council in matters of faith. He asserted that two powers rule the world, the *sacerdotium* and the *imperium.* The *sacerdotium,* since it is the instrument of human salvation, is superior to the *imperium.*

As soon as Italy ceased to be a ruling state, there began a long effort to create national unity and to establish national independence. The barbarian invasions had isolated Italy, accentuated the break with the empire and left the pope as the sole native representative of ancient unity and Italian hegemony. At the same time the Ostrogoths (half romanized as they were) did not destroy Italian culture, but allowed the Church to transmit the Greco-Roman tradition (linguistic, social, cultural, administrative, and religious) in the west.

529. Western monasticism, representing a wide ascetic reaction against current corruption in life and supported by Jerome, Ambrose, and Augustine, had expanded rapidly in the 6th century and reached a chaotic condition ranging from extremes of eremitical asceticism to the laxest kind of cenobitic worldliness. **Benedict** of Nursia, scandalized at conditions, withdrew to Monte Cassino where he founded a colony and gave it (traditionally in 529) the famous *Benedictine Rule.* This rule, which dominated western monasticism for centuries, was a remarkable and characteristic Roman compromise adapted to the average man. It placed the monks under the control of an abbot, made each house autonomous in a loose federation (not strictly an order at all), and provided for careful recruiting and probation. Discipline was efficient but not extreme, and great stress was laid on labor, especially in the open air (*laborare est orare*). The individual was merged in an ascetic, self-contained, self-sufficient corporation. The spread of the Benedictines was rapid, and soon the only important survival of eremitical monasticism was in the Irish monks of St. Columban. The order became the chief instrument for the reform of the Frankish (Gallic) Church, and for the conversion and civilization of England and Germany. In the course of history it gave the Church 24 popes, 200 cardinals, 5000 saints, 15,000 writers and scholars.

Ruined by invasion, its aqueducts cut, Rome was reduced in population from a half million to perhaps 50,000. Its aristocracy had fled, and mediaeval decay had replaced pagan grandeur. The city was not revived until the Renaissance.

554. Justinian's Pragmatic Sanction restored the Italian lands taken by the Ostrogoths and made a *pro forma* restoration of government, but agricultural lands were depopulated and grown into wilderness, the rural proprietors were sinking into serfdom. Town decline was similar. The Roman Senate ceased to function after 603 and the local *curiae* disappeared at about the same time.

Duces were appointed, probably over each *civitas,* as part of the imperial administration, but they gradually became great landowners and their military functions dominated their civil duties. A fusion of the ducal title and landownership ensued and a new class of hereditary military proprietors emerged beside the clergy and the old nobles. The details of this process are, of course, hard to determine, the more so as evidence is scant.

d. THE FRANKISH KINGDOM, 481-752

The Franks first appear as settlers on the lower Rhine in two divisions, the Salians (dwellers by the sea, *sal*) and the Ripuarians (dwellers by the riverbank, *ripa*). By the end of the 4th century the Salians were established in the area between the Meuse and the Scheldt as federates of the Roman Empire; the Ripuarians in the tract between the Rhine and Meuse. They formed no permanent confederations, and, unlike the other Germanic peoples, did not migrate as a nation, but expanded.

431-751. THE SALIAN FRANKS UNDER THE MEROVINGIANS.

451. **Chlodio** (son of Merowech) invaded Artois, and was defeated by Aëtius. Salian Franks were in the Roman forces at the **battle of Châlons.** King Childeric (d. 481) fought as a federate of the empire at Orléans when Aëtius defeated the Visigoths, and he later defeated the Saxons on the Loire. His tomb was found (1653) at Tournai, the "capital" of the Salians.

481-511. **CLOVIS** (Chlodovech), son of Childeric, in the service of Julius Nepos and Zeno. He defeated the Gallo-Roman general Syagrius at Soissons (486), expanding Salian power to the Loire. The story of the **Soissons vase** is significant of the friendly relations between Clovis and Bishop Remigius. Siegebert, the Ripuarian, defeated an Alamannic invasion at Tolbiac (496) with Salian support. Clovis in the same year defeated the Alamanni (Strasburg?) and later, after election as King of the Ripuarians, emerged as master of the Franks on both sides of the Rhine.

496. The traditional date of the **conversion of Clovis** to Roman Catholicism is 496. He had previously married a Burgundian, Clotilda, who was of the Roman communion. The Burgundians in general were Arians, and Clovis' choice may have been deliberate. In any case his conversion won him powerful papal and episcopal support and opened the way to wide conquests from the heretic (i.e. Arian) German peoples. Burgundy was conquered (after 500), the Visigoths defeated at Vouillé (507), and their whole kingdom north of the Pyrenees (except Septimania and Provence) was soon subjugated. These conquests were warmly supported by the Gallo-Roman clergy as a religious war. Clovis founded the Church of the Holy Apostles (Ste. Geneviève) at Paris, and shortly moved his "capital" from Soissons to Paris. He was made

an honorary consul by the Emperor Anastasius, a proceeding which brought the Franks technically into the empire.

511-628. **Divisions of the Frankish lands** after the death of Clovis: (1) His four sons established four capitals — Metz, Orléans, Paris, Soissons. Expansion eastward continued along the upper Elbe; Burgundy was added, and the territory of the Ostrogoths north of the Alps. After a period of ruthless conflict, only **Lothair** (Chlothar) survived, and for a brief time (558–561) the Frankish lands were under one head again. (2) Lothair's division of his lands among his four sons led to a great feud from which three kingdoms emerged: Austrasia (capital Metz) lying to the east (Auster) and mostly Teutonic; Neustria (the "new land" as the name implies) (capital Soissons), Gallo-Roman in blood; Burgundy, which had no king of its own but joined Neustria under a common ruler. The Prince of Neustria exterminated the rival house in Austrasia, but the local baronage preserved the kingdom's identity. Under Lothair II all three kingdoms were united again (613) under one ruler.

628-638. **Dagobert** (Lothair's son), the last strong ruler of the Merovingian House, made wide dynastic alliances and found wise advisers in **Bishop Arnulf** and **Pepin of Landen.** His firm rule led to a revolt. Under the *rois fainéants* following Dagobert the **mayors of the palace** emerged from a menial position to a dominant rôle in the government both in Austrasia and Neustria.

Merovingian government retained the Roman *civitas* as a unit of administration and set a count (*comes* or *graf*) over it. The source of law was not the king, but local custom administered by the *graf* with the aid of local landowners. Military leaders of large districts were the *duces* who were over several counts. Land grants were made in lieu of pay to officials.

Gregory, Bishop of Tours (c. 540–594), a Frank, wrote in Latin the *History of the Franks*, the best single source on the history of the Merovingian period.

Decline of the royal power under the last of the Merovingians, and beginning of feudal decentralization. (1) Concentration of landownership in the hands of a few (i.e. a landed aristocracy of which the mayors of the palace were representative). (2) The breakdown of the old clan and tribal organization without an effective state to replace it, leading to personal and economic dependence on private individuals rather than on the state (e.g. commendation, *beneficium*, immunity). (3) Military service on

The Merovingian Kings

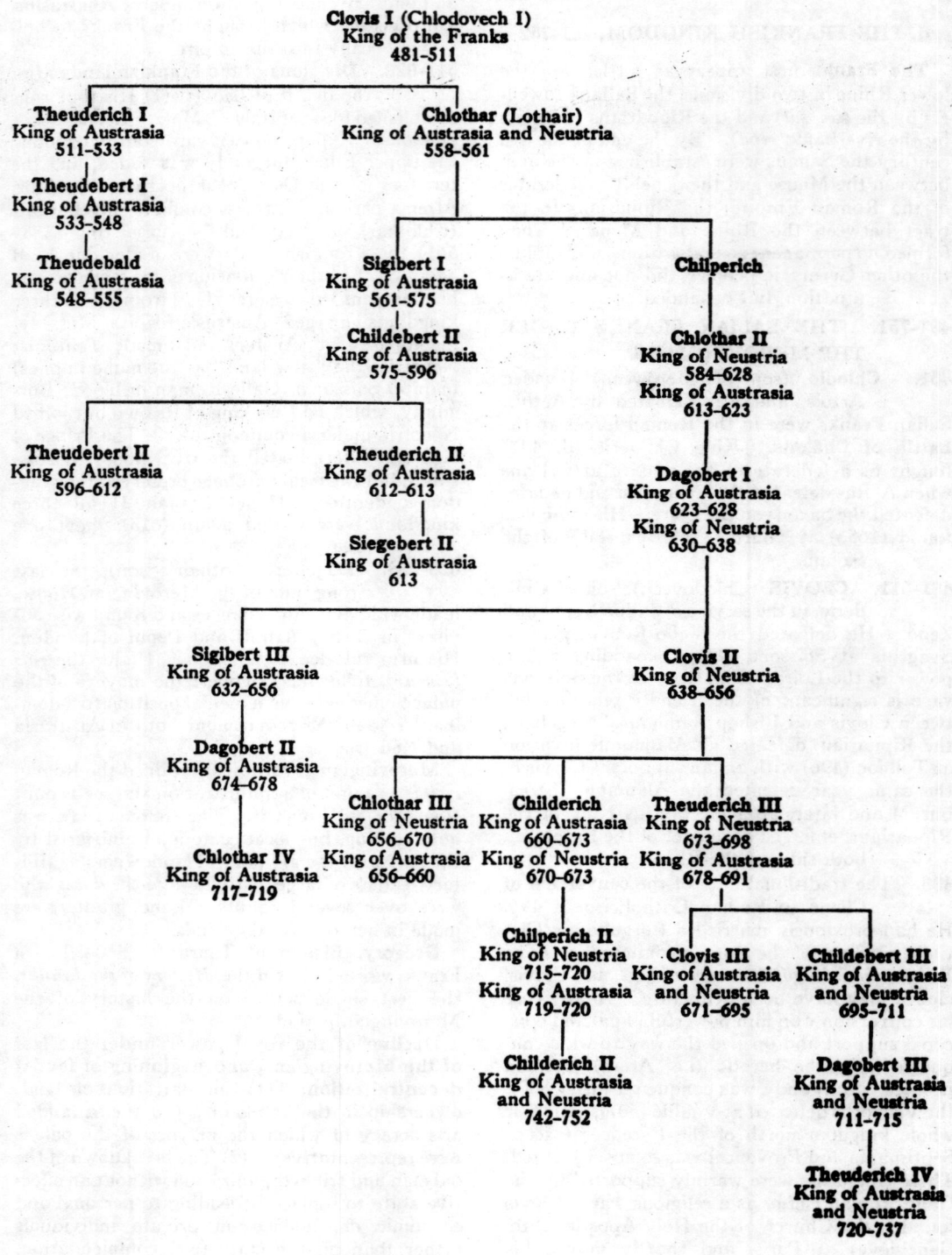

Clovis I (Chlodovech I)
King of the Franks
481–511

Theuderich I
King of Austrasia
511–533

Chlothar (Lothair)
King of Austrasia and Neustria
558–561

Theudebert I
King of Austrasia
533–548

Theudebald
King of Austrasia
548–555

Sigibert I
King of Austrasia
561–575

Chilperich

Childebert II
King of Austrasia
575–596

Chlothar II
King of Neustria
584–628
King of Austrasia
613–623

Theudebert II
King of Austrasia
596–612

Theuderich II
King of Austrasia
612–613

Dagobert I
King of Austrasia
623–628
King of Neustria
630–638

Siegebert II
King of Austrasia
613

Sigibert III
King of Austrasia
632–656

Clovis II
King of Neustria
638–656

Dagobert II
King of Austrasia
674–678

Chlothar III
King of Neustria
656–670
King of Austrasia
656–660

Childerich
King of Austrasia
660–673
King of Neustria
670–673

Theuderich III
King of Neustria
673–698
King of Austrasia
678–691

Chlothar IV
King of Austrasia
717–719

Chilperich II
King of Neustria
715–720
King of Austrasia
719–720

Clovis III
King of Austrasia
and Neustria
671–695

Childebert III
King of Austrasia
and Neustria
695–711

Childerich II
King of Austrasia
and Neustria
742–752

Dagobert III
King of Austrasia
and Neustria
711–715

Theuderich IV
King of Austrasia
and Neustria
720–737

horseback became attached to the benefice as early as the 8th century; for example, Martel's cavalry (see *infra*) for service against the Saracens. Since these grants involved church lands to a considerable degree, Martel in effect compelled the Church to help support national defense. (4) The royal domain was exempt from visitation except by the king's personal administrators. This immunity was extended to royal lands granted to others, and then to lands never in the royal domain. The upshot of the system was complete decentralization by the delegation of the royal powers to local officials who tended to become entirely independent.

The Carolingians

Emergence of the Carolingians in Austrasia. The son of Arnulf married the daughter of Count Pepin I (of Landen, d. 639), mayor of the palace, founding the line later called Carolingian.

656. Pepin's son Grimoald made a premature effort to usurp the crown, which cost him and his son their lives, and led to a reaction in favor of the Merovingians.

678-681. Ebroin, mayor in Neustria, united the mayoralties under one house; he was murdered (681).

687. Pepin II (of Heristal), grandson of Pepin I, gained supremacy in Austrasia and Neustria by his victory at Tertry. The kingdom was on the verge of dissolution (ducal separatism), and Pepin began an effort to reduce the landed aristocracy from which he himself had sprung.

714-741. Charles Martel (i.e. the Hammer), Pepin's son, an ally of the Lombards, supported Boniface's mission in Germany (Bon-

The House of Pepin

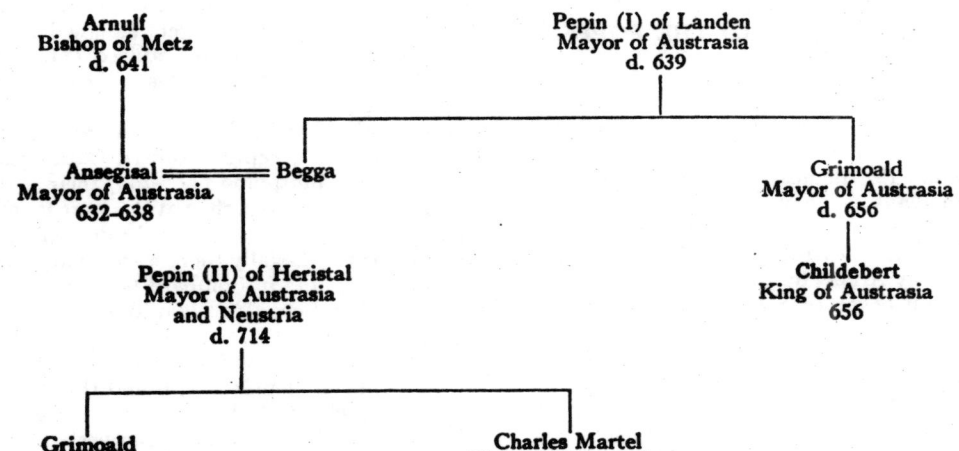
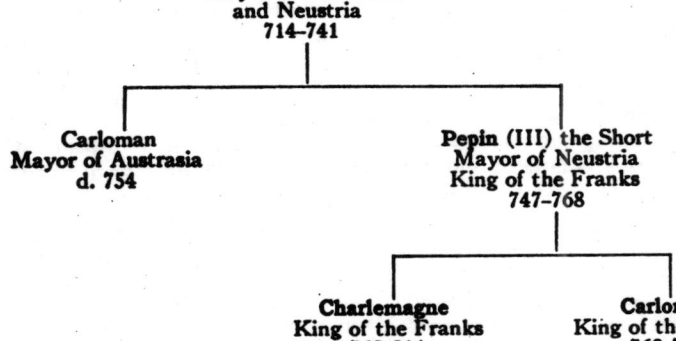

iface testified that his achievements would have been impossible without Martel's aid).

732. Martel's great victory at **Tours** arrested the advance of the Moslems in the west, and was followed by their final retreat over the Pyrenees (759).

Pepin's conquest of the Frisians was continued, five wars were waged against the Saxons, and powerful decentralizing forces (notably in Burgundy and Alamannia) were broken down.

739. Pope Gregory III, threatened by the Lombards, sent an embassy to Martel, and offered the title of *consul* in return for protection against the Lombards. Charles, an ally of the Lombard king, ignored the appeal. At the end of his life Martel, like a true sovereign, divided the Merovingian lands between his sons, Austrasia and the German duchies going to Carloman, Neustria and Burgundy to Pepin. Carloman and Pepin ruled together, 741–747; Pepin ruled alone, 747–768.   (*Cont. p.* 158.)

e. THE LOMBARDS AND THE POPES, 568-774

Under the Emperor Augustus the Lombards were still established on the lower Elbe (Bardengau) and were defeated (5 A.D.) by the Romans. Their history for the next 400 years is confused and often blank. They were members of the Hunnic Empire and were subdued by the Heruls (505), whom they then destroyed (508). They were probably Arians by this time. Resistance to the Gepids began (c. 546). They were given land by Justinian in Noricum and Pannonia and aided (553) the imperial attacks on the Ostrogoths. The Avars arrived (c. 560) from the Volga, entered Thuringia (562), were defeated by the Franks, and allied themselves (c. 565) with the Lombards against the Gepids, who were annihilated. The Lombards moved on toward Italy and the Avars occupied Dacia. Alboin (d. 573), the Lombard king, killed the Gepid king, Cunimund, with his own hand and married his daughter Rosamund (story of Cunimund's skull as a drinking-cup). The Lombards took part in Belisarius' conquest, and soon the nation began to move south toward Italy.

568. THE LOMBARD CONQUEST OF ITALY. Italy, worn out by the Gothic wars, famine and pestilence, offered little resistance. Constantinople was indifferent, and the conquest was easy. The Lombards, always few in numbers, had associated other peoples (including 20,000 Saxons who soon departed, and some Slavs) in their invasion, but even then they

were not numerous enough to occupy the whole peninsula. Rome and Naples were never held, and Ravenna only briefly. The coast was not really mastered. The Lombards (unlike even the Vandals) did not enter into a compact with the empire, and Italian feeling against them was bitter. Pavia became the capital (Italy, until 774, had always two and usually three capitals: Rome, the papal capital; Ravenna, the Byzantine capital; and Pavia the Lombard capital after 573) and the peninsula was a mosaic of Byzantine, papal, and Lombard jurisdictions.

Lombard occupation (virtually military rule at first) covered inland Liguria, inland Tuscany, inland Venetia, the Duchy of Spoleto and the Duchy of Benevento. **Imperial Italy** comprised Venice and the land from north of Ravenna to the south of Ancona, and included the Duchy of Rome and the Duchy of Naples, as well as the toe and heel of Italy. *Hospitalitas* was revived and one-third the produce of the land (not one-third the land) was given to the Lombards. Lombards also took the lands of the dead and the exiled. At first lands were assigned with a full title, but Liutprand introduced (713, 735) leases, and the grant of estates without permanent tenure.

The Lombards took Roman titles and names, and in the end accepted Roman Catholicism. By the time of **Liutprand** (712–744) their speech was clearly Italian, but the natives were loyal to their past, and remained sharply divided from the Lombards. Legally there was a dual system of private law, and in Lombard territories there was a dual episcopal system (i.e. Arian and Roman).

573-584. Alboin's murder was followed by the rule of Cleph (d. 575) and then by ten years of anarchy and private war under a loose federation of dukes (some 36 in number). Roman Catholic opposition and papal negotiations with the Franks alarmed the Lombards, and led to the election of

584-590. Authari, a grandson of Alboin, who was endowed with half the baronial lands as royal domain. The dukedoms were gradually absorbed (the marches like Friuli, Trent, Turin, survived longest).

Authari's widow Theodolinda, a devoted Roman Catholic, bidden to choose a husband who should also be king, selected a Thuringian,

590-615. Duke Agilulf, of Turin, who was friendly to the Roman Church and the true founder of the Lombard state. Gregory the Great blocked an Italian conspiracy against the Lombards. **Rothari** (636–652) became a Roman

Catholic. He collected Lombard customary law in Latin and began the consolidation of Lombard power. Eventually Roman law triumphed and Lombard law survived only in the schools (e.g. Pavia).

The Italian bishops since 476 had been the leaders of the peaceful civilians in the cities, the protectors of the oppressed, and the dispensers of charity. Under the Lombards a system of **episcopal immunities** emerged which made the bishops virtually local temporal sovereigns and enabled them to preserve the local spirit of municipal independence and organization (e.g. consuls, guilds). The urban population was free of feudal bonds, and the town walls (often built by the bishops) were refuges. Milan resumed her greatness and almost equaled Rome. These developments prepared the way for the great assertion of Italian town independence against Roman clerical and German feudal encroachments. **Paul the Deacon** (c. 720–c. 800) the first important mediaeval historian, wrote the *History of the Lombards*.

590-604. GREGORY THE GREAT. Of medium height, good figure, large, bald head, brown eyes, aquiline nose, thick red lips, prominent bearded chin, with exquisite tapering hands. His family was a rich senatorial house and Gregory was prefect of Rome (573). He founded (c. 574) six monasteries in Sicily and one at Rome (St. Andrews) into which he immediately retired as a monk. Embassy to Constantinople (c. 579–586). As Abbot of St. Andrews (586) his rule was severe. Elected pope (590) against his will, he began a vigorous administration. Discipline within his patriarchate was rigorous (stress on celibacy, close watch on elections, insistence on exclusive clerical jurisdiction over clerical offenders). Church revenue was divided into four shares for the bishop, the clergy, the poor, and church buildings. His administration of the wide estates of the Church was honest and brilliant, and the revenue was expanded to meet the tremendous demands on Rome for charity. The pope continued the old imperial corn doles in Rome and elsewhere, aqueducts were repaired, urban administration, especially in Rome, reformed.

Outside his immediate patriarchal jurisdiction Gregory expanded the influence and prestige of the pope, maintaining that the pope was by divine designation head of all churches. Appeals to Rome were heard even against the Patriarch of Constantinople, whose claim to the title of universal bishop was denied. Gregory boldly assumed the rôle of the emperor in the west, and the powers of a temporal prince,

counterbalancing the prestige of Constantinople. From his administration date the foundations of later **claims to papal absolutism**. Gregory was the real leader against the Lombards, appointing governors of cities, directing the generals in war, and receiving from Constantinople pay for the army.

As the first monk to become pope, Gregory made a close alliance between the Benedictines and the papacy (at the expense of the bishops). The monks were given charters and protected from the bishops, the Benedictine Rule was imposed, and a great missionary campaign was begun with monkish aid: (1) The mission to Britain (596) under **Augustine of Canterbury** and the conversion of England provided a base from which the Frankish (Gallic) Church was later reformed and the German people converted; (2) campaigns against paganism in Gaul, Italy, and Sicily, and against heresy in Africa and Sicily.

Gregory was the last of the four great Latin Fathers, and first of the mediaeval prelates, a link between the classical Greco-Roman tradition and the mediaeval Romano-German. Not a great scholar, he was a great popularizer, and spread the doctrines of Augustine of Hippo throughout the west. At the same time he gave wide currency through his *Dialogues* to the popular (often originally pagan) ideas of angels, demons, devils, relic worship, miracles, the doctrine of purgatory and the use of allegory. Gregory reveals the clerical contempt for classical Latin which profoundly influenced the Latin of the Middle Ages. His *Pastoral* remained for centuries an essential in the education of the clergy. There was a school of music at Rome, but how much Gregory had to do with it, and how much with the introduction of the Gregorian Chant, is doubtful.

Gregory introduced the papal style, *Servus Servorum Dei*.

CONTINUED ALIENATION OF ITALY FROM THE EAST. (1) The **Monothelete controversy**: condemnation by the **Lateran Synod** (649) of Emperor Heraclius' *Ecthesis* (of 638) and Emperor Constans II's *Typos* of 648. Arrest (653) by the exarch of Pope Martin I (649–655), who died in exile in the east. **The Council of Constantinople** (680–681) compromised on the controversy, taking a position in favor of Rome. The Council of Constantinople (692) reasserted the equality of the Patriarchates of Constantinople and Rome. (2) **Emperor Leo the Isaurian's** (717–740) attempt to bring Italy back to obedience: heavy taxation to reduce the great landowners angered Pope

Gregory II (the largest landowner in Italy) and Leo's iconoclastic decree (726) aroused all Italy. Gregory III excommunicated all Iconoclasts (731). Gregory's defeat and final humiliation weakened the pope and opened the way for the final Lombard advance.

712-744. DESTRUCTION OF THE LOM-BARD KINGDOM. Liutprand, fearing Frankish, Slavic, Hungarian, Byzantine, and papal hostility, began to consolidate his kingdom, reducing the duchies of Benevento and Spoleto. Ravenna was taken temporarily. During the Iconoclastic controversy Liutprand's sincere efforts at rapprochement with the papacy met a brief success.

749-756. Aistulf continued Liutprand's policy of consolidation. The pope, alarmed at Lombard progress, had already (741) made overtures to Charles Martel. Martel, busy with the Moslems, remained faithful to his alliance with the Lombards, but Aistulf's continued advance brought a visit (753) from Pope Stephen II. Stephen had already begun negotiations with Pepin, and the mutual needs of the rising papacy and the upstart Carolingian dynasty drew them into alliance.

754, 756. Pepin in two expeditions forced Aistulf to abandon the Pentapolis and Ravenna (bringing the Lombards virtually to their holdings of 681). Legally the lands involved in the **Donation of Pepin** (756) belonged to the Eastern Empire. The Donation was a tacit recognition of implicit claims of the popes to be the heirs of the empire in Italy. Most important from the papal point of view was the fact that the Church had won a powerful military ally outside Italy. Henceforth the Carolingians maintained a protectorate over the papacy in Italy.

774. Charlemagne, heir to the traditions of Pepin, having repudiated the daughter of the Lombard king, Desiderius, appeared in Italy to protect the pope. After a nine-month siege Pavia was taken, Spoleto and Benevento were conquered, Charles absorbed the Lombard Kingdom into the rising Frankish Empire, and assumed the crown of the Lombards. On a visit (774) to Rome (the first of any Frankish monarch), Charlemagne confirmed the Donation of Pepin, but made it plain that he was sovereign even in the papal lands. At no time did Charlemagne allow the pope any but a primacy in honor (in this respect following the strict Byzantine tradition). The Donation of Pepin was the **foundation of the Papal States** and the true beginning of the temporal power of the papacy. Henceforth there was neither the

Lombard menace nor the overlordship of the exarch to interfere with the rising papal monarchy. In this sense the fall of the Lombard Kingdom was decisive in papal history. It was equally decisive in Italian history, for the papal victory over the Lombards terminated the last effective effort to establish national unity and a national government until the end of the 19th century. For the Carolingian monarchy the episode was equally significant.

Under the successors of Charlemagne the emperors continued to participate in the papal elections and did what they could to protect Italy against the attacks of the Moslems from Africa.

827-831. The Moslems conquered Sicily.

837. They attacked Naples, pillaged Ancona (839) and captured Bari (840).

846. In the battle of **Licosa,** Duke Sergius of Naples defeated the Moslems at sea.

847-848. Construction of the **Leonine Wall** by Pope Leo IV (847–855) to defend St. Peter's from the Moslems.

875-877. The Emperor **Charles the Bald** continued to support the papacy against the invader and came to Rome (875) to be crowned, having forced Charles the Fat to retreat and having induced his brother Carloman to sign a truce and withdraw. He was then elected King of Italy by the local magnates.

888. Berengar of Friuli was crowned emperor at Pavia.

891. Guido of Spoleto was consecrated emperor with his son Lambert as co-emperor and co-king.

893. Zwentibold (illegitimate son of Arnulf) was sent to Italy in response to an appeal from Pope Formosus (891–896), but he accomplished nothing. Arnulf then came in person (894) and received an oath of fealty from the Italian magnates, but Guido continued as emperor and was succeeded by

892-899. Lambert. Arnulf embarked upon a second expedition, took Rome and was formally crowned (896).

The Papacy in the Carolingian Period

POPE NICHOLAS I (858–867), one of the few great popes between Gregory I and Gregory VII, was the arbiter of western Christendom. Elected by the favor of Louis II. Three great controversies: (1) **Support of Ignatius,** Patriarch of Constantinople, resulting in the excommunication (863) of Ignatius' rival, Photius. Photius' futile deposition (867) of Nicholas. This controversy brought the Eastern and Western Churches closer to the final rupture (1054). (2) **Discipline of King Lothair** of Lorraine because of the divorce of his wife Theutberga. Lothair had been allowed (Synod of Aix) by his pliant bishops to remarry, and Nicholas reopened the case at the Synod of Metz (863), which found for Lothair. Nicholas (supported by Charles the Bald) quashed the entire proceeding, disciplined the bishops, and, despite the invasion (864) of the Leonine City by Louis II, compelled Lothair to submit. (3) **Vindication of the right of appeal to Rome** by a bishop against his metropolitan — humiliation of the powerful Archbishop Hincmar of Reims. First papal citation (865) of the *Forged Decretals* (brought to Rome, 864). Emergence of the theory that no bishop may be deposed or elected without papal approval.

867- **Decline of the papacy,** after the pontificate of Nicholas and the death of Louis II. As the popes had no powerful protectors outside Italy until 961, they fell increasingly under the dominance of the Roman and Italian feudal aristocracy. The lapse of the imperial power left room for the insinuation of a new **doctrine of papal autonomy,** well formulated in the *False Decretals.* Outside Italy the relaxation of papal control and the decline of papal prestige, accompanied by the rise of dominant local feudal lords, accentuated the power of the bishops and made the unity of the western Church a mere shadow until the papacy, having learned to cope with feudalism in the second half of the 11th century, once again made its supremacy felt in the Church. (*Cont. p.* 216.)

f. THE EMPIRE OF CHARLEMAGNE AND ITS DISINTEGRATION

747-768. **PEPIN THE SHORT,** who attempted to conciliate the Church by granting and restoring lands to it.

752. **Pepin was elected king** by the Frankish magnates. Both the house of Pepin and the papacy (in the act of usurping political control from the emperor at Constantinople, needed each other's support. The immediate need of the popes was protection against the expanding Lombard monarchy. Aistulf, King of the Lombards, had taken Ravenna (751), the seat of the exarch, besieged Rome, and exacted tribute.

754. **Pope Stephen II** arrived in Gaul, anointed Pepin, and by conferring the title *Patricius* (which could legally come only from Constantinople) designated him in a sense *regent and protector of Italy.* The net result was to give some shadow of authority to Pepin's new title as King of the Franks.

754. Pepin marched into Italy, defeated the Lombards, and required them to hand over the exarchate and Pentapolis to the pope. The Lombards failed to do so.

756. Pepin returned and, after defeating the Lombards again, made his famous Donation. The **Donation of Pepin** (which Pepin had no legal right to make) established the Papal States (*Patrimonium Patri*) and began the temporal power of the papacy. It also established the Franks, a distant, non-Italian power, as the allies and defenders of the papacy.

759. Pepin conquered Septimania, disciplined Aquitaine, and so brought effective Frankish rule to the Pyrenees. On his death his lands were given to his sons: Charles receiving Austrasia, Neustria, and northern Aquitaine; Carloman, southern Aquitaine, Burgundy, Provence, Septimania. The brothers ruled together, 768–771; Charles alone, 771–814.

771-814. **CHARLES THE GREAT** (Charlemagne), a reign of the first magnitude in European history. Charles was a typical German, six feet in height, a superb swimmer, of athletic frame, with large, expressive eyes and merry disposition. He understood Greek, spoke Latin, but could not learn to write. He preferred the Frankish dress. In general he continued the Frankish policy: (1) expansion of Frankish rule to include all the Germans was completed (omitting only Scandinavia and Britain); (2) close understanding with the papacy; (3) support of church reform (which settled the foundations of mediaeval Christian unity).

Italian conquest and reduction of German tribes: Already overlord of the Lombards, Charles married King Desiderius' daughter, soon repudiate: her, conquered

773-774. Lombard Italy, and became King of the Lombards, whose kingdom was absorbed into the Frankish Empire. Charlemagne also established his rule in Venetia, Istria, Dalmatia, and Corsica.

787-788. Bavaria was incorporated, its Duke Tassilo first made a vassal and then deposed.

785. Saxony, after a costly and bitter struggle of thirty years, involving eighteen campaigns, was conquered, and Christianity forcibly introduced despite stubborn pagan resistance. Foundation of the Bishopric of Bremen (781).

795-796. The Avars (on the lower Danube) were reduced.

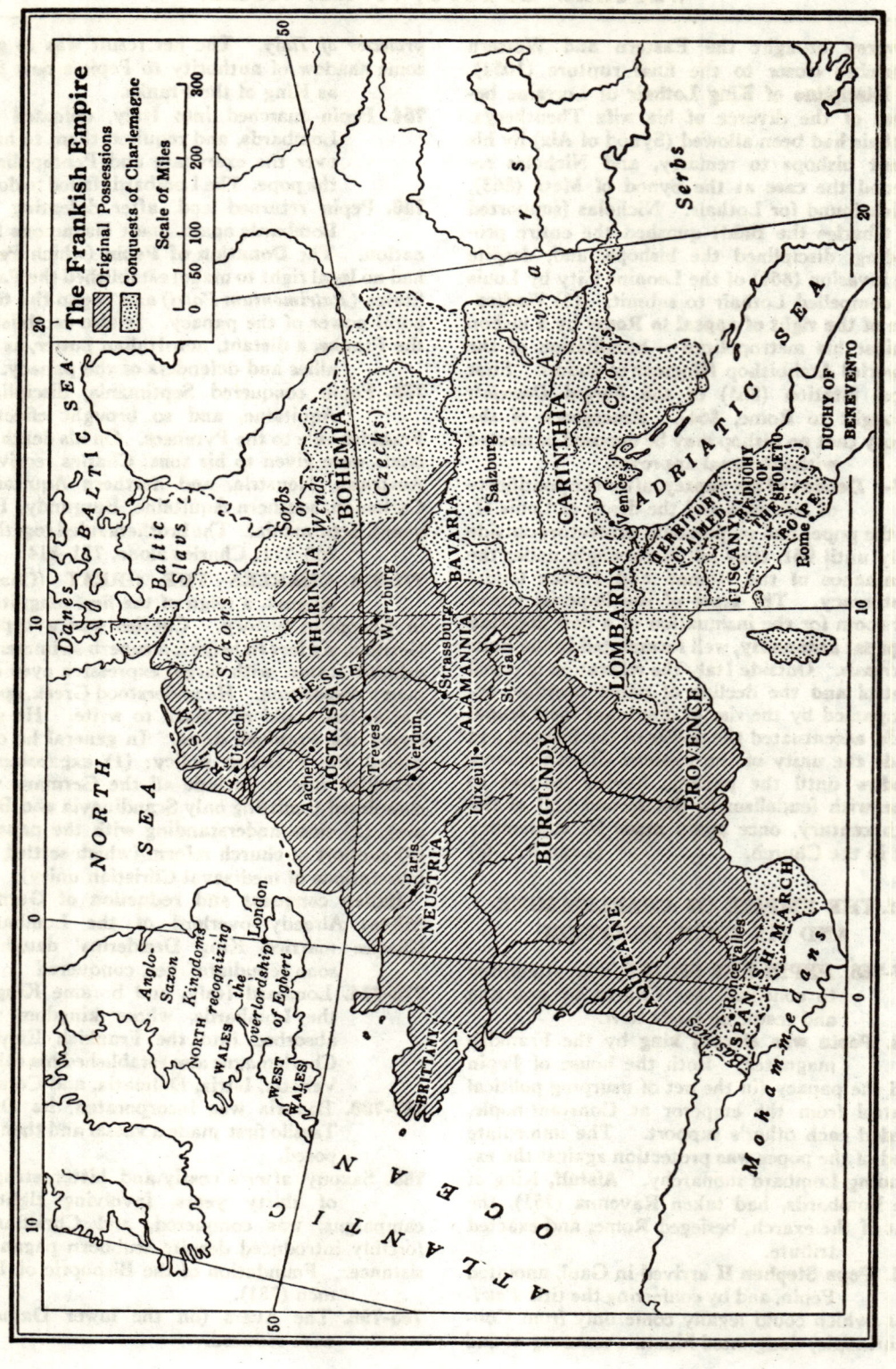

The Frankish Empire

Original Possessions

Conquests of Charlemagne

Scale of Miles

0   50   100   200   300

801. After the Frankish defeat at **Roncesvalles** (778), the Moslems in northeastern Spain were gradually reduced (Barcelona taken, 801), and the **Spanish March** created.

Establishment of marks (after c. 782) to hold the conquests: Dane Mark, the Altmark (against the Wends), Thuringian Mark, Bohemian Mark, Ostmark (against the Avars), Friulian Mark (on the Italian border), and the Spanish Mark. These marks were also centers of colonization and germanization.

Relation to the Church and to Constantinople. Charlemagne held it to be his duty to defend the Church and the pope, and to maintain the faith. He treated the pope like any Frankish bishop, but recognized his unique spiritual prestige. His visit (774) to Rome was the first of a Frankish sovereign: the Donation of Pepin was confirmed, but the terms are not clear. The pope crowned Charles' son, Pepin, King of Italy (781), his son Louis, King of Aquitaine.

REVIVAL OF THE ROMAN EMPIRE IN THE WEST. Pope Leo III, a submissive pontiff, notified Charlemagne of his election to the Holy See, and dated his pontificate by Charlemagne's regnal years. Driven from Rome (799) by a conspiracy and riot, he sought refuge at Charlemagne's court and was restored by Frankish troops.

800. Charlemagne arrived in Rome, allowed Leo to clear himself of a series of charges by oath (avoiding the trial of a pope), and was crowned emperor in St. Peter's on Christmas Day. According to Einhard, Charlemagne avowed his regret at the coronation. He cannot have been unaware of the general plan, and his feeling may have been due to modesty or concern at Byzantine reactions or hostility to papal pretensions. Charlemagne disregarded the imperial title in a partition of the empire (806), and arranged to have his son Louis crown himself (813). Theoretically the coronation of 800 marked a return to the dualism of Theodosius I (i.e. two emperors over an undivided empire). In fact the Frankish Empire was more German than Roman in population and institutions. Byzantium regarded Charlemagne as a usurper; Charlemagne seems to have meditated a marriage with the Empress Irene as one solution of the difficulty. The papal coronation, an act of rebellion in Byzantine eyes, marked a definite break between Rome and Constantinople. The Emperor Michael I recognized (812) Charlemagne's title in the west in return for sovereignty in Venice, Istria, Dalmatia.

GOVERNMENT: (1) **In the Church:** Charlemagne's rule was a theocracy, and he insisted on supremacy over the Frankish Church, legislating on all subjects, settling dogmatic questions, deciding appointments, presiding at synods. (2) **In the Frankish state:** centralization continued; taxation in the Roman sense (which survived only under local and private auspices) was replaced by services in return for land grants (the economic basis of Carolingian society). Such services included forced labor on public works among the lower ranks, the provision of food for the court and public officials on duty, and judicial and military obligations (primarily among the upper ranks). Charlemagne's continuous campaigns reduced the small farmers, accentuating the tendency to serfdom. Charlemagne tried to offset this tendency by allowing groups of poorer farmers to co-operate in sending a single soldier, and by excusing the poorest from ordinary field service. Systematization of the army and of military service was also begun. Commendation and immunity continued, and the basis of later feudal development was firmly established.

Administration: The tribal dukes were largely eliminated and government was carried on by counts, appointed for life, but frequently removed. This system was extended to Italy, Bavaria, and Saxony. To prevent the counts establishing an hereditary tenure, and to limit local abuses, the *missi dominici* (usually a bishop and count) were introduced (802) as officers on circuit in a given district. The *missi* held their own courts, had power to remove a count for cause, and were charged with the supervision of financial, judicial, and clerical administration. They formed an essential link between the local and central government. Under the counts were viscounts and vicars (*centenarii*). Margraves (*Mark grafen*) were set over the marks with extended powers to meet the needs of their position. Local administration of justice was reformed by the introduction of *scabini*, local landowners appointed by the counts to sit as permanent judiciary officers.

The Carolingian revival of learning: Charlemagne, perhaps out of concern for the improvement of ecclesiastical education, set up the Palace School under **Alcuin** from the School of York, later Abbot of Tours. Various clerics were also given liberal grants that they might establish local schools, though no general system of education was introduced in the Frankish Empire. In general, the source of inspiration was Latin rather than Greek. **Einhard, for example,** who came to the Palace School from Fulda, wrote his biography of Charlemagne in

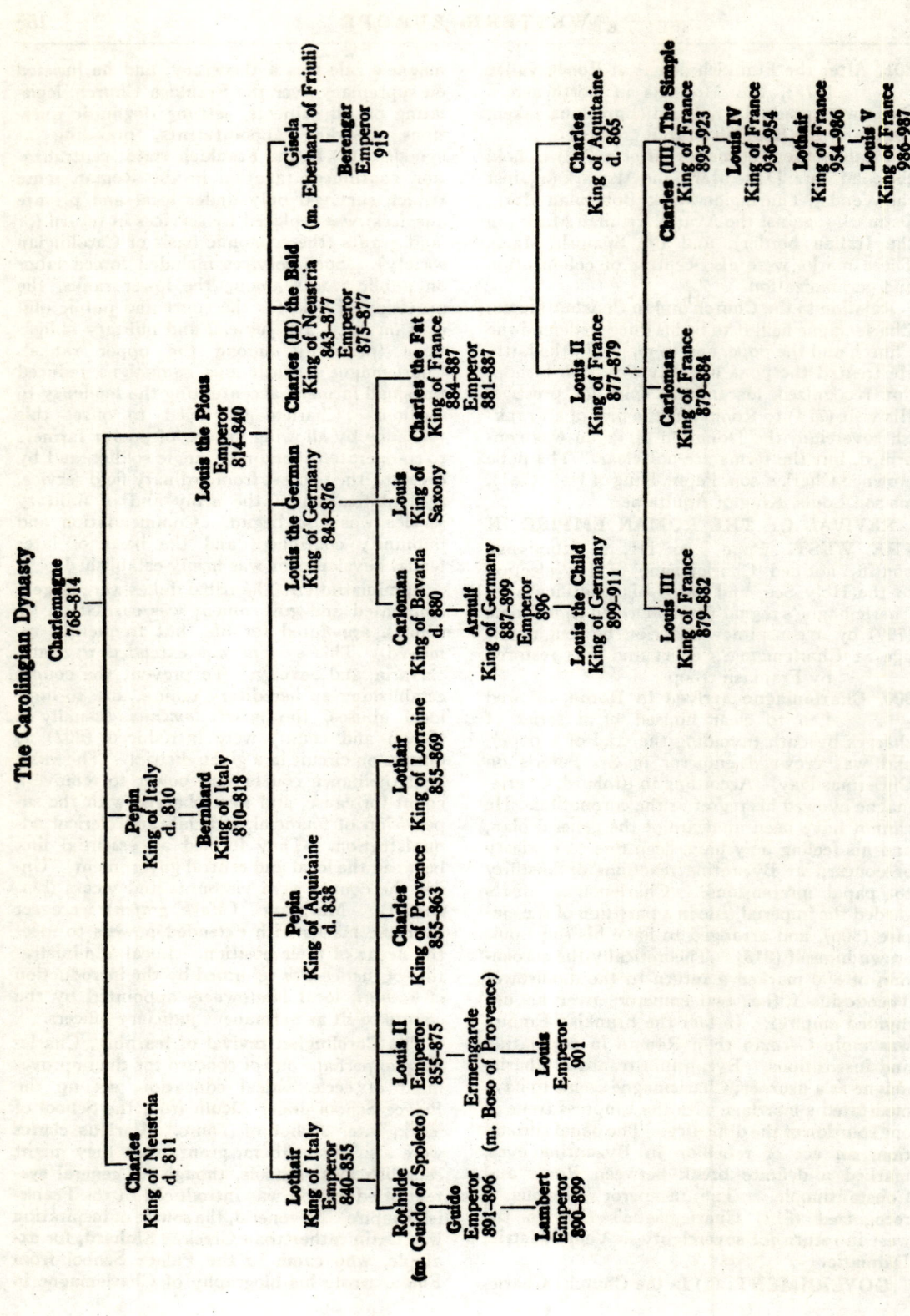

The Carolingian Dynasty

Charlemagne
768–814

Pepin
King of Italy
d. 810

Bernhard
King of Italy
810–818

Charles
King of Neustria
d. 811

Louis the Pious
Emperor
814–840

Lothair
King of Italy
Emperor
840–855

Pepin
King of Aquitaine
d. 838

Charles (II) the Bald
King of Neustria
843–877
Emperor
875–877

Louis the German
King of Germany
843–876

Gisela
(m. Eberhard of Friuli)

Berengar
Emperor
915

Charles the Fat
King of France
884–887
Emperor
881–887

Louis
King of Saxony

Carloman
King of Bavaria
d. 880

Arnulf
King of Germany
887–899
Emperor
896

Louis the Child
King of Germany
899–911

Louis II
King of France
877–879

Charles
King of Aquitaine
d. 865

Louis III
King of France
879–882

Carloman
King of France
879–884

Charles (III) The Simple
King of France
893–923

Louis IV
King of France
936–954

Lothair
King of France
954–986

Louis V
King of France
986–987

Louis II
Emperor
855–875

Charles
King of Provence
855–863

Lothair
King of Lorraine
855–869

Rothilde
(m. Guido of Spoleto)

Ermengarde
(m. Boso of Provence)

Guido
Emperor
891–896

Louis
Emperor
901

Lambert
Emperor
890–899

the manner of Suetonius. At Charlemagne's court were gathered scholars and literary men of almost every nationality, including **Peter of Pisa**, the grammarian, the Visigothic poet **Theodulf**, the Lombard historian, **Paul the Deacon** (*History of the Lombards*). Great care was given to the copying of texts, and the refined Carolingian minuscule was evolved.

814-887. THE DISINTEGRATION OF THE CAROLINGIAN EMPIRE.

Such efficiency as the Carolingian government possessed under Charlemagne derived rather from his personality than from permanent institutions. Local administration was carried on by unpaid officials whose compensation was a share of the revenue. Local offices tended to become hereditary. The tentative partitions of the empire in Charlemagne's lifetime followed Frankish tradition, and had no relation to any racial or national elements. One son, Louis the Pious, survived, and the empire was passed on to him (quite by accident) undivided. The decisive stage in the partition of the empire came under Louis and his heirs.

814-840. LOUIS the Pious (emperor), educated at the Palace School, crowned in his father's lifetime. Sincerely religious, a reformer of his court, the Frankish Church, and the monasteries, he allowed himself to be crowned again by the pope (816). Ineffectual as a soldier and ruler. Louis and his heirs concentrated on a long struggle (leading to civil war) over territorial questions, to the neglect of government, foreign policy, and defense, a program which hastened the breakup of the empire.

817-838. A significant series of **partitions** involving Louis' sons: Lothair (d. 855), Louis the German (d. 876), Pepin (d. 838), and their half-brother, Charles the Bald (d. 877).

The division of 817: Aquitaine and parts of Septimania and Burgundy went to Pepin as sub-king; Bavaria and the marches to the east were assigned to Louis the German as sub-king undivided; Francia, German and Gallic, and most of Burgundy were retained by Louis and his eldest son Lothair. Italy went to a third sub-king.

The division of 838: Charles the Bald was assigned Neustria and to this was added Aquitaine on the death of Pepin. Charles' holding, which had no name, approximated (accidentally) mediaeval France, and was mainly Romance in speech.

840-855. LOTHAIR I (emperor). On the death of Louis the Pious the three

heirs continued their struggle, and after the indecisive **battle of Fontenay** (841) Carolingian prestige sank to a new depth. Charles the Bald and Louis the German formed an alliance against Lothair (who was supported by the clergy in the interests of unity) in the bilingual (Teutonic and Romance) **Oaths of Strassburg** (842), sworn by the rulers and their armies, each in their own vernacular. They then forced a family compact upon Lothair at Verdun.

843. THE TREATY OF VERDUN divided the administration and control of the Carolingian Empire as follows: (1) **Lothair** kept the (empty) title of emperor, and was King of Italy and of an amorphous territory (the "middle kingdom") which was bounded roughly by the Scheldt, the upper Meuse, Saône, and Rhone on the west, and by the Rhine and Frisia on the east (i.e. the territory of Provence, Burgundy, and what was later called *Lotharingia*). (2) **Louis the German**, as King of the (East) Franks, ruled a realm essentially Teutonic in blood, speech, and geography, extending from the Rhine (except Frisia) to the eastern frontier of the empire. (3) **Charles the Bald**, as King of the (West) Franks, received a realm (loosely called Karolingia for a time) made up of West Francia and Aquitaine, Gascony, Septimania, etc., mainly Romance in speech, approximating mediaeval France in general outline.

855-875. LOUIS II (emperor). At Lothair I's death his lands were divided as follows among his sons: Louis II received Italy, Charles (d. 863) the newly formed Kingdom of Provence (centered around the city of Arles), and Lothair II the inchoate aggregate (from Frisia to the Alps and from the Rhine to Scheldt) which began to be called *Lotharii regnum* or *Lotharingia* (modern Lorraine).

870. Treaty of Mersen, following the death (869) of Lothair II, King of Lorraine. Louis the German forced Charles the Bald (crowned King of Lorraine, 869) to divide equally and solely on the basis of revenue the lands of Lothair outside of Italy. Thus Louis gained a strip of land which brought his frontier west of the Rhine.

875-877. CHARLES THE BALD, emperor.

877-881. Anarchy and interregnum in the empire.

879. The **Kingdom of Burgundy** (Cisjuran Burgundy) was established by Boso of Provence.

888. The **Kingdom of Juran Burgundy** (i.e. Besançon, Basel, Lausanne, Geneva, etc.) was erected by Rudolf I. It **passed to**

the empire by bequest in the time of Conrad II.

c. 787-925. THE NINTH CENTURY INVASIONS:

(1) **In the North.** Bands of Northmen (Scandinavians, p. 170), under pressure of population and resentful at the rise of local kings, pushed outward from Scandinavia. The Swedes penetrated into Russia, the Norwegians and Danes moved into the northern islands (including the British Isles) and south to the Continent. Within a half century of the first raid (c. 787) on England, the British Isles had been flooded. Masters of the sea in the west, the Northmen pushed inland from the mouths of the great rivers (e.g. Rhine, Scheldt, Somme, Seine, Loire), sacking the cities (e.g. Utrecht, Paris, Nantes, Bordeaux, Hamburg, Seville). "Normandy" was invaded (841) and a simultaneous attack made (845) on all three Frankish kingdoms. The Mediterranean was entered (843). In the east Constantinople was attacked by Swedes (*Rus*), who came down from Russia. A great attack on Paris (885) was heroically met by Count Odo (Eudes), son of Robert the Strong. Raids were pushed farther into France and the Mediterranean in the course of the 9th century.

(2) **In the East.** Bulgarian expansion produced a great Bulgar state between the Frankish and Byzantine Empires. The Bulgars were converted to the Greek communion (870). Hungarians (Magyars), closely followed by Petchenegs, crossed the Carpathians and the lower Danube, pushing into Venetia, Lombardy, Bavaria, Thuringia, Saxony, the Rhineland, Lorraine, and Burgundy (925).

(3) **In the Mediterranean.** Moslem domination of Sicily, Corsica, Sardinia, and the Balearic Islands made the Mediterranean virtually a Moslem lake. Raids were almost continuous, Rome was attacked (846) and later Monte Cassino.

852-886. Under the combined influence of the disruption of the Carolingian Empire and the pressure of the 9th-century invasions, the great fiefs of France began to appear as the only effective centers of local resistance to invasion, and feudalism may be said to have struck root.

Feudalism. Its origins may be traced to the German *comitatus* and the proprietary system of the later Roman Empire. Essentially it was an informal system of contracts for the disposal of land and honorable services, and was in no sense a form of government. Inseparable from it was the agricultural organization (*manorialism*) which rested on servile tenures and contracts for manual labor and services. Antedating feudalism, manorialism was also derived from the Roman proprietary system. The feudal system evolved in each country under local conditions and followed a different development. The feudalism of France is ordinarily regarded as typical.

g. THE WEST FRANKS UNDER THE CAROLINGIAN KINGS, 843-987

843-877. CHARLES THE BALD (emperor, 875-877). His kingdom under the Treaty of Verdun was roughly equivalent to modern France with additions in the north and south and a restricted frontier on the east. Charles was effective master of Laon, but his sway over Neustria was nominal, his control sporadically maintained by war and intrigue. Charles granted three great fiefs as a buffer for his frontiers: The County of Flanders to his son-in-law, Baldwin Iron-Arm (862); Neustria to Robert the Strong as "Duke between Seine and Loire"; the French Duchy of Burgundy to Richard, Count of Autun. Brittany (Armorica) was semi-independent under its own dukes and counts in the 9th century and continued so virtually to the end of the Middle Ages. Aquitaine, joined to Neustria for Charles (838), soon emerged as a duchy and was consistently hostile. The Duchy of Gascony was joined to Aquitaine in 1052. From Neustria were carved the Counties of Anjou (870) and Champagne. Septimania remained refractory.

870. Carloman, Charles' son, emerged from monastic retirement and led a series of intrigues which ended when he was blinded and fled to his uncle, Louis the German. He died in 874. Charles was further weakened by his intrigues in Lorraine and Italy, and by his efforts to win the imperial crown, leaving France open to invasion, anarchy, and brigandage.

The crown, impotent and virtually bankrupt, commanded no respect from magnates or prelates, and the **Capitulary of Mersen** (847) shows clear evidence of the progress of essentially feudal ideas: every free man is to choose a lord; none may quit his lord; each must follow his lord in battle. It must be noted that this was purely a military measure. France was already divided into *comtés* under counts theoretically removable by the king.

875. Expedition of Charles to Italy and imperial coronation.

877. The Capitulary of Kiersy made honors hereditary, but lands were still granted only for life.

877-879. **LOUIS II** (*the Stammerer*), son of Charles the Bald, maintained himself with difficulty despite the support of the Church. His sons

879-882. **LOUIS III** and

879-884. **CARLOMAN** divided their heritage, Louis taking Neustria, Carloman Aquitaine, Septimania, and Burgundy, and reduced their rivals to impotence. Louis' victory over the Northmen (Saucourt, 881) did not stop their raids.

884-887. **CHARLES THE FAT,** son of Louis the German, already King of the East Franks (879) and emperor (881-887), was chosen King of the West Franks instead of Charles the Simple, the five-year-old brother of Louis and Carloman. Charles the Fat, having failed (886) to aid the gallant Odo (Eudes) against the Northmen, was deposed (887).

888-898. **Odo** (Eudes), Count of Paris, Marquis of Neustria (son of Count Robert the Strong, whence the name *Robertians* for the line before Hugh Capet) was elected King of the West Franks by one faction of magnates to avoid a minority on the deposition (887) of Charles the Fat. Another faction chose Charles III, the Simple, son of Louis II (Carolingian). Despite five years of civil war

893-923. **CHARLES III** ruled from Laon, the last Carolingian with any real authority in France. Charles, unable to expel the Northmen from the mouth of the Seine, granted (911) **Rollo** (Hrolf the Ganger, d. 931), a large part of what was later Normandy, for which Rollo did homage.

Formation of Normandy. Rollo was baptized (912) under the name **Robert,** acquired middle Normandy (the Bessin, 924) and the western part of the duchy (Cotentin and Avranche, 933). The colony was recruited with fresh settlers from Scandinavia for the best part of a century, and was able to retain a strong local individuality. Yet soon after 1000 the duchy was French in both speech and law. Between this period and the accession of Duke William I (the Conqueror) Norman history is fragmentary.

923-987. **The French kingship.** Robert, Count of Paris, *Duke between the Seine and Loire,* won the West Frankish crown with the aid of his sons-in-law, Herbert, Count of Vermandois, and Rudolf, Duke of Burgundy, but was killed (923), leaving a son (later Hugh the Great) too young to rule.

929-936. **RUDOLF** followed Robert as the foe of Charles the Simple, and ruled with no opposition after Charles' death. **Hugh the Great,** master of Burgundy and Neustria, declined the crown, preferring to rule through the young Carolingian heir,

936-954. **LOUIS IV,** a son of Charles the Simple. Hugh's title, *Duke of the French,* seems to have implied governmental functions as much as territorial sovereignty, and he held most of the northern barons under his suzerainty.

954-986. **LOTHAIR** succeeded his father Louis IV. On the death of Hugh the Great, his son Hugh, known as *Capet,* succeeded him (956).

978. Lothair's effort to gain Lorraine led to an invasion by Emperor Otto II to the walls of Paris. Hugh Capet, in alliance with Emperor Otto III, and aided by Gerbert of Reims, reduced Lothair's rule at Laon to a nullity. Lothair's son

986-987. **LOUIS V** was the last Carolingian ruler of France.

987. **ELECTION OF HUGH CAPET,** engineered by Adalbero, Bishop of Reims, and by Gerbert. Hugh was crowned at Noyon with the support of the Duke of Normandy and the Count of Anjou. His title was recognized by the Emperor Otto III in exchange for Hugh's claims to Lorraine. The emergence of the new house of Capet was not the victory of a race, a nationality, or a principle, but the triumph of a family, already distinguished, over a decadent rival. (*Cont. p.* 226.)

h. GERMANY UNDER THE CAROLINGIAN AND SAXON EMPERORS, 843-1024

843-876. **LOUIS THE GERMAN.** Increasing Slavic and Norse pressure (general Norse attack, 845, on Carolingian lands). Louis had three sons: Carloman (d. 880), Louis (d. 882), and Charles the Fat. Carloman was assigned Bavaria and the East Mark; Louis, Saxony and Franconia; Charles, Alamannia. Contest with Charles the Bald for Lorraine. By the **Treaty of Mersen** (870) Louis added a strip of land west of the Rhine.

876-887. **CHARLES THE FAT.** He blocked Charles the Bald's advance toward the Rhine. Emergence of the Kingdom of Cisjuran Burgundy (i.e. Dauphiné, Provence, part of Languedoc) under Boso (879). Expedition to Italy and coronation by John VIII (881). Negotiations (882) with the Northmen, now permanently established in Flanders. While Charles was in Italy settling a papal election, a great Norse invasion burst on France (Odo's defense of Paris, 886). **Deposition of Charles** by the Franconian, Saxon, Bavarian, Thuringian, and Swabian magnates at Tribur (887).

887 (896)–899. ARNULF (illegitimate son of Carloman, grandson of Louis the German).   A certain supremacy was conceded to Arnulf by the various rulers of Germany and Italy who rendered a kind of homage to him. Victory over the Norse on the Dyle (Löwen, 891); resistance to the Slavic (Moravian) advance (893), with Magyar aid.   Magyar raids after 900.   Arnulf dared not leave Germany to answer the appeal of Pope Stephen V (885–891) for aid.   His illegitimate son Zwentibold was sent on the call of Pope Formosus (891–896), but accomplished nothing (893).   Arnulf went to Italy in person (894), was crowned king and received an oath from most of the magnates. On another appeal from Formosus (895) he took Rome and was crowned emperor (896).

900–911. LOUIS THE CHILD (born 893), last of the Carolingians, elected king by the magnates at Forcheim (900).   Increasing Norse, Slavic, and Magyar pressure and devastation.

The weakening of the royal power as the East Frankish Kingdom of the Carolingians declined, and the survival of tribal consciousness, left the way open for the emergence of the Stem (German *Stamm*, a tribe) duchies.   These duchies preserved the traditions of ancient tribal culture, and their independent development under semi-royal dukes (beginning in the 9th century) ensured the disruption of German unity for a thousand years.   These Stem duchies were: Franconia (the Babenbergers ultimately drove the Conradiners into the East Mark, later Austria); Lorraine (not strictly a stem duchy but with a tradition of unity); Swabia (the early ducal history is obscure); Bavaria (under the Arnulfings; repulse of the Magyars, acquisition of the Mark of Carinthia); Saxony (under the Liudolfingers; repulse of the Danes and Wends, addition of Thuringia); the Frisians (no tribal duke appeared).

911.   End of the East Frankish line of the Carolingians, with the death of Louis the Child (899–911); the German magnates, to avoid accepting a ruler of the West Frankish (French) line, elected Conrad, Duke of Franconia.

911–918.   CONRAD I. Magyar raids and ducal rebellions in Saxony, Bavaria, and Swabia met vigorous but futile resistance from Conrad. Lorraine passed (911) temporarily under the suzerainty of the West Frankish ruler, Charles the Simple.   Conrad nominated his strongest foe, Henry, Duke of Saxony, as his successor, and he was elected.

919–1024.   THE SAXON (OR OTTONIAN) HOUSE.

919–936.   KING HENRY I (called *the Fowler*, supposedly because the messengers announcing his election found him hawking). Tolerant of the dukes, he forced recognition of his authority; cool to the Church, he avoided ecclesiastical coronation.

920–921.   Reduction of the Duke of Bavaria; alliance with Charles the Simple.

923–925.   Lorraine restored to the German Kingdom and unified into the **Duchy of Lorraine,** a center of spiritual and intellectual ferment.   Henry's daughter married the Duke of Lorraine (928).

924–933.   Truce (and tribute) **with the Magyars,** fortification of the Elbe and Weser Valleys (Saxony and Thuringia), palisading of towns, villas, monasteries, etc., establishment of *Burgwarde,* i.e. garrisons (which later often became towns like Naumburg, Quedlinburg), where one-ninth of the Saxon effectives were on duty and trained as horsemen each year.

928.   Saxon expedition across the frozen Havel River **against the Wends:** Branibor (Brandenburg) stormed; the Wends driven up the Elbe; creation of the Marks of Branibor, Meissen, and (later) Lusatia as guardians of the middle Elbe.

933.   Henry ended the Magyar truce with his **victory at Riade** on the Unstrut River, the first great defeat of the Magyars.   Occupation of the land between the Schlei and the Eider (Charlemagne's Dane Mark), and erection of the Mark of Schleswig, guardian of the Elbe mouth; the Danish king was made tributary and forced to receive Christian missionaries. Henry had prepared the way for his son whose election was a formality, the succession becoming virtually hereditary.

936–973.   KING OTTO I (*the Great*).   Otto revived the policy of Arnulf, was crowned and anointed at Aachen, Charlemagne's capital; his coronation banquet revived the Carolingian coronation banquet (of Roman origin) at which the Duke of Franconia served ceremonially as steward, the Duke of Swabia as cup-bearer, the Duke of Lorraine as chamberlain, and the Duke of Bavaria as marshal.

Otto's vigorous assertion of royal authority (a three-year war reduced the Dukes of Bavaria, Franconia, Lorraine, and Saxony).   He followed the policy of keeping the great duchies (except

The Saxon Emperors

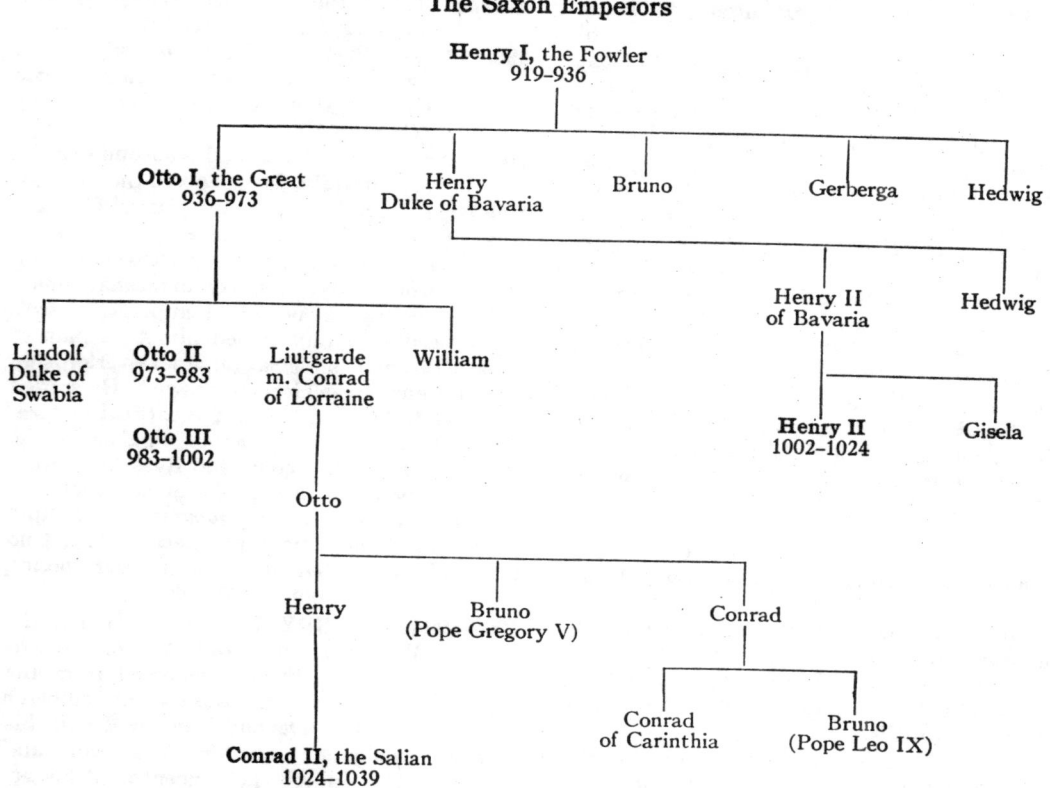

Saxony) in his own hands or those of his family. Taking Conrad, the boy King of Arles (Provence and Burgundy), under his protection (937), Otto forced the recognition of his overlordship (forestalling Hugh of Provence); Conrad's sister, Adelheid, married Lothair, one of the claimants to the crown of Italy, and later Otto himself. The Bavarians defeated Otto (944) at Wels, but Otto conquered (950) Duke Boleslav of Bohemia and put the duchy under the suzerainty of Bavaria.

951-952. **Otto's first expedition to Italy** to keep the passes through the mountains open. Marriage to Adelheid and assumption of the crown of Italy; the pope refused him imperial coronation; Berengar of Ivrea, forced into vassalage, ceded the Marks of Verona, Friuli, Istria (the keys to the passes), to Otto's son Henry, Duke of Bavaria.

953. Revolt of Otto's son (Liudolf, Duke of Swabia, son-in-law of Conrad, Duke of Lorraine) and others (suppressed, 955).

955. **BATTLE OF THE LECHFELD.** Otto, with an army recruited from all the duchies, ended the Magyar menace by a great victory. Defeat of the Wends on the river Rechnitz. Re-establishment and colonization with Bavarians of Charlemagne's East Mark (Austria).

968. The bishoprics established among the Slavs (e.g. Brandenburg, Merseburg, Meissen, Zeiz) were consolidated under the new **Archbishopric of Magdeburg.** German bishoprics were everywhere filled with bishops loyal to the monarchy, marking the alliance of the king and the Church against feudal opposition.

961-964. **Otto's second expedition to Italy** on the appeal of Pope John XII for protection. Assumption of the crown of Italy at Pavia.

962. **IMPERIAL CORONATION BY THE POPE: REVIVAL OF THE ROMAN EMPIRE IN THE WEST.** Otto put a temporary end to feudal anarchy in Rome, deposed one pope and nominated another, and compelled the pope to recognize the emperor's right to approve or reject papal elections.

966-972. **Otto's third expedition to Italy:** deposition of one pope, restoration of another; nomination of a new pope; punishment of the Romans. Imperial coronation (967) of the future Otto II and assertion of suzerainty over Capua and Benevento (967). Betrothal of **Theophano** (daughter of the Greek emperor, Romanus I) to the future Otto II (969); coronation of Theophano (972) and marriage to Otto (supposedly bringing Greek Italy as her portion).

Otto, with the able assistance of his brother Bruno, Archbishop of Cologne, began a cultural revival (the so-called *Ottonian Renaissance*) in the manner of Charlemagne; late in life, he learned to read, but not to speak, Latin; Bruno knew Greek. The cosmopolitan court literary circle included Irish and English monks, and learned Greeks and Italians, notably **Liutprand of Cremona** (*Historia Ottonis; Legatio Constantinopolitana*). Great literary activity of the monasteries: **Widukind of Corvey** (*Res Gestae Saxonicae*); **Roswitha,** the nun of Gandersheim, author of the *Carmen de gestis Ottonis* and of learned Latin comedies in a bowdlerized Terentine style, celebrating saintly virginity; the vernacular *Heliand* (9th century), a Christian epic; **Ekkekard of St. Gall's** *Waltherius*, inspired by German legends.

The German rulers and nobles of the 9th century had regarded the monasteries as their personal property and prepared the way for a strong clerical reaction toward reform supported by the regular clergy (e.g. Cluny), opposed by the seculars who were rapidly passing under feudal influences.

973-983. **OTTO II.** The revolt of Henry the Wrangler, Duke of Bavaria, in alliance with Boleslav of Bohemia, and others, required five years to put down; Henry was banished (978). Repulse of a Danish incursion.

978. **Lothair,** King of the West Franks, invaded Lorraine and was forced to abandon his claims by Otto's invasion of France (980).

981-982. **Otto's campaign in southern Italy,** to expel the Saracens and reduce the Byzantine power, ended in defeat.

983-1002. **OTTO III** (an infant of three years). Rule of his brilliant mother Theophano (983-991), his grandmother Adelheid, and Archbishop Willigis of Mainz (991-996). Under Theophano's influence his education was in the Byzantine tradition; his tutor Gerbert of Aurillac, one of the most learned men of his day, whose brilliance won him the nickname *Stupor Mundi*. Henry the Wrangler proclaimed himself king, but was forced to submit.

996. **Otto's first expedition to Italy** ended Crescentius II's sway in Rome; Otto designated his cousin Bruno as pope (Gregory V).

998. Returning to Rome on his **second expedition to Italy,** Otto deposed the Crescentine pope, John XVI, and decapitated Crescentius. Otto made Gerbert of Aurillac pope, as Sylvester II. Sylvester shared Otto's devotion to the Carolingian tradition of an intimate union and co-operation of pope and emperor. Otto's romantic antiquarianism led him to a plan of reform through universal imperial overlordship independent of the German crown. He settled down at Rome and began a theatrical restoration of the splendors of the city: palace on the Aventine, Byzantine court and Byzantine titles, futile revival of ancient formulae (seals inscribed *Renovatio imperii romani*, etc.); rapid alienation of the Roman populace. He left no heir and was buried by his own orders beside Charlemagne at Aachen.

1002-1024. **HENRY II** (son of Henry the Wrangler, cousin of Otto, great-grandson of Henry the Fowler) emerged from the contest for the throne, and was crowned emperor at Rome (1014). Devout (canonized with his wife, St. Kunigunde), but a political realist and firm with the Church, he concentrated his attention on Germany. Against episcopal objections he founded (1007) the great Bishopric of Bamberg, endowed it richly as an outpost of German culture against Slavdom; the cathedral, one of the glories of German architecture, contains his tomb. Vigorous (Gorzian) monastic reform with many confiscations.

1002. Successful **revolt of Ardoin** in Lombardy (reduced temporarily in 1004, and finally in 1014).

1003-1017. A long, unsuccessful struggle with Boleslav Chrobry (992-1018) of Poland, Duke of Bohemia, who had acquired Lusatia and Silesia.

1006-1007. Unrest in Burgundy and **revolt of Baldwin of Flanders** (suppressed, 1007).

In practice Henry had no choice but to allow the great fiefs to become hereditary. He relied heavily on the clergy to supply advisers and administrators, and looked to the Church also for military and financial support, but he dominated the Church in Germany through his control of the episcopal appointments. Extensive secularization and reform of the monasteries of the Church resulted.

(*Cont. p. 205.*)

i. SPAIN

(1) *The Visigothic Kingdom,* 466-711

In the time of **Euric** (466–484) the Visigothic rule extended from the Loire to Gibraltar and from the Bay of Biscay to the Rhone. The capital was Toulouse.

507. Clovis' victory in the **battle of Vouillé** obliged the Visigoths to withdraw over the Pyrenees, retaining only Septimania north of the mountains. The new capital was Toledo.

The Visigoths in Spain were a small minority (about one in five) and were rapidly romanized (e.g. the *Breviary of Alaric*). The conversion of King Reccared (587) from Arianism to Roman orthodoxy brought an end to their religious separateness, accelerated the process of romanization and initiated the domination of the clergy over the monarchy. The **Synod of Toledo** (633) assumed the right to confirm elections to the crown. After 600 the Jews were forced to accept baptism, for which reason they later on welcomed the Moslem invasion. Visigothic speech gradually disappeared and the current vernacular was of Latin origin. Roman organization and tradition survived to a marked degree. **Isidore of Seville** (c. 560–636), a bishop, theologian, historian, man of letters, and scientist, produced in his *Etymologiae* a general reference work which remained a standard manual for 500 years and served as a medium for the transmission of much ancient knowledge to the mediaeval world.

(2) *Moslem Spain,* 711-1031

711-715. THE MOSLEM CONQUEST. In 711 a mixed force of Arabs and Berbers, led by the Berber **Tariq** (whence Gibraltar — *Gebel al-Tariq*) crossed from Africa. Roderick, the last Visigothic king, was completely defeated in the **battle on the Guadalete** (Rio Barbate), whereupon his kingdom collapsed. The Moslems took Cordova and the capital, Toledo. Tariq was followed (712) by his master, **Musa,** who took Medina Sidonia, Seville, Merida, and Saragossa. The Moslems soon reached the Pyrenees (719), having driven the remnants of the Christians into the mountains of the north and west.

732. In the **battle of Tours** the Moslems, having crossed into France, were decisively defeated by Charles Martel and the Franks. By 759 they had been entirely expelled from France.

756-1031. THE OMAYYAD DYNASTY OF CORDOVA.

756-788. Abdurrahman, emir. He was the grandson of the Omayyad Caliph of Damascus, and was the founder of the Moorish state in Spain. Christians were given toleration in return for payment of a poll tax. The Jews were very well treated. But Abdurrahman met with vigorous opposition from the Arab nobility, which was supported from abroad by Pepin and Charlemagne.

777. Invasion of Spain by Charlemagne, checked by the heroic defense of Saragossa. Annihilation of his rear-guard at Roncesvalles (778 — *Song of Roland*). Wars with the Franks continued throughout the rest of the century, Charlemagne ultimately conquering northeastern Spain as far as the Ebro River (capture of Barcelona, 801).

788-796. Hisham, son of Abdurrahman, emir, during whose reign Malikite doctrines were introduced in Spain.

796-822. Hakim, son of Hisham, emir. Revolts in Cordova (805, 814) and Toledo (814). The Toledan rebels, expelled from Spain, went to Alexandria and thence to Crete, which they reconquered.

822-852. Abdurrahman II, son of Hakim. During his reign Alfonso II of Leon invaded Aragon. He was defeated and his kingdom destroyed. The Franks too were driven back in Catalonia. The Normans first appeared on the coasts. In 837 a revolt of Christians and Jews in Toledo was suppressed, but Christian fanatics continued to be active, especially in Cordova.

852-886. Mohammed I. He put down another Christian uprising in Cordova, and carried on extensive operations against the Christian states of Leon, Galicia, and Navarre (Pampeluna taken 861).

886-888. Mundhir.

888-912. Abdullah, brother of Mundhir.

912-961. ABDURRAHMAN III. The ablest and most gifted of the Omayyads of Spain, who assumed the titles of *Caliph* and *Amir al-Mu'minin* in 929, thus asserting supremacy in Islam as against the Abbasid Caliphs of Bagdad. Abdurrahman's reign was marked by the pacification of the country, by completion of governmental organization (centralization), by naval activity, by agricultural advance and by industrial progress. **Cordova** (population c. 500,000) became the greatest intellectual center of Europe, with a huge paper trade, great libraries, and pre-eminent schools (medicine, mathematics, philosophy, poetry, music; much translation from Greek and Latin).

The height of **Moslem learning** was reached by **Averroës** (ibn Rochd, c. 1126–1198), philosopher, physician and commentator on Plato and Aristotle, master of the Christian schoolmen.

The aristocracy, by this time almost extinguished, was replaced by a rich middle class and feudal soldiery. The Christians and Jews continued to enjoy wide toleration.

Abdurrahman continued the wars with Leon and Navarre, which extended over most of his long reign. By the **Peace of 955** with Ordono III of Leon, the independence of Leon and Navarre was recognized and the Moslem frontier withdrawn to the Ebro; on the other hand, Leon and Navarre recognized the suzerainty of the caliph and paid tribute. This peace was soon broken by Ordono's brother Sancho (957) who, after his defeat, was expelled by his subjects but restored by the caliph (959).

961-976. Hakim II. He continued the wars against Castile, Leon, and Navarre and forced their rulers to sue for peace (962–970). At the same time he waged successful war against the Fatimid dynasty in Morocco, which was brought to an end (973) and replaced by the Omayyad power.

976-1009. Hisham II, whose reign marked the decline of the Omayyad dynasty. Power was seized by Mohammed ibn Abi 'Amir, with the title of *Hajib al-Mansur* (European: *Almansor* = the Victorious Chamberlain), a brilliant reforming minister (army and administration). He carried on successful campaigns against Leon, Navarre, Catalonia, and Mauretania, and temporarily checked the religious and racial separatism which later on brought about the collapse of the Omayyad Caliphate. On his death in 1002 he was succeeded by his son, Abdulmalik al-Muzaffar (the Victorious), who several times defeated the Christians and was followed by his brother, Abdurrahman, named Sanchol. The latter obliged Hisham to proclaim him his heir, whereupon a revolt took place in Cordova under the leadership of Mohammed, a member of the royal family. Hisham was compelled to abdicate in favor of Mohammed, and Sanchol was executed. In the meanwhile the Berbers nominated Sulayman as caliph. Civil war ensued, reducing Spain to more than a score of petty kingships (*taifas*) and making easier the Christian reconquest.

1027-1031. Hisham III, the last Omayyad caliph.

(3) Christian Spain

CASTILE AND LEON, 718-1065

718-737. Pelayo, successor to Roderick the Visigoth, created the **Kingdom of the Asturias,** a theocratic elective monarchy in the Visigothic tradition. Beginning of the reciprocal alliance of kings and clergy under

739-757. Alfonso I, who assigned to the Church a generous share of the lands conquered from the Moslems and used the clergy as a counterweight to the aristocracy.

899. Miraculous discovery of the bones of **St. John the Greater** and erection of the first church of Santiago de Campostella, which became the center of the Spanish national cult and one of the most influential shrines in Europe.

910-914. Garcia, King of Leon, began a rapid expansion of his domain to the east (construction of numerous castles, hence the name *Castile*).

c. 930-970. Count Fernán Gonzalez, Count of Burgos (later Castile), marked the rise of the Counts of Burgos. By intrigue and alliance with the Moslems he expanded his domains at the expense of Leon, and made the country of Castile autonomous and hereditary. His progress was arrested by Sancho the Fat of Leon (d. 966), who was in alliance with Abdurrahman III.

970-1035. Sancho the Great of Navarre effected a close union of Castile and Navarre and began the conquest of Leon.

1035-1065. Ferdinand I, of Castile, completed the work by conquering Leon (1037) and assuming the title of *King of Leon*.

(Cont. p. 234.)

j. THE BRITISH ISLES

(1) England to 1066

Prehistoric Britain. The prehistoric inhabitants of Britain (called *Celts* on the basis of language) were apparently a fusion of Mediterranean, Alpine, and Nordic strains which included a dark Iberian and a light-haired stock. Archaeological evidence points to contacts with the Iberian Peninsula (2500 B.C.) and Egypt (1300 B.C.).

1200-600 B.C. The true **Celts** are represented by two stocks: Goidels (*Gaels*), surviv-

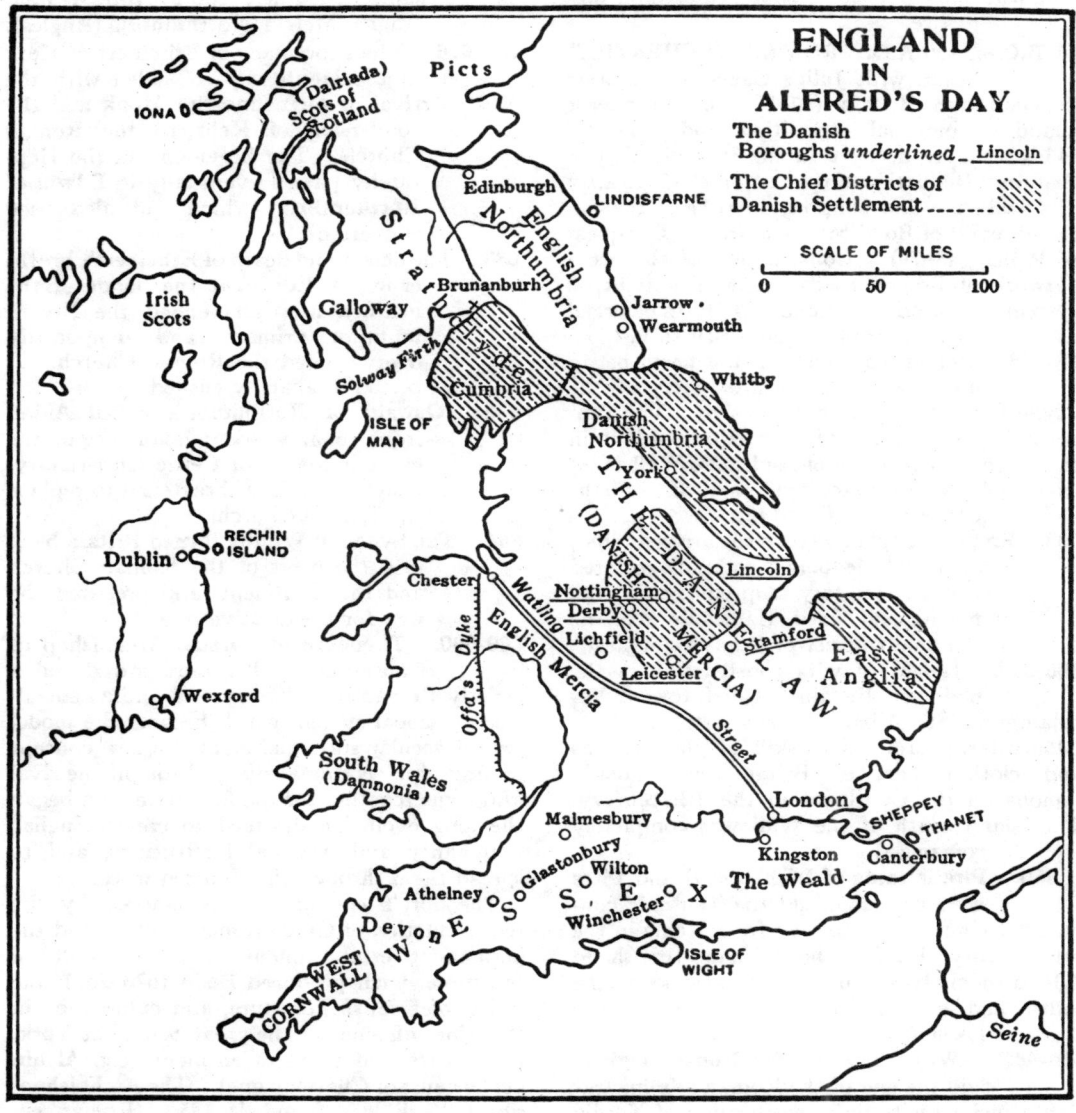

ENGLAND
IN
ALFRED'S DAY

The Danish
Boroughs *underlined* _ Lincoln
The Chief Districts of
Danish Settlement _____

SCALE OF MILES

0   50   100

ing in northern Ireland and high Scotland, and Cymri and Brythons (*Britons*) still represented in Wales. The Brythons were close kin to the Gauls, particularly the Belgi. Their religion was dominated by a powerful, organized, priestly caste, the Druids of Gaul and Britain, who monopolized religion, education, and justice.

57 B.C.–c. 450 A.D. ROMAN OCCUPATION began with Julius Caesar's conquests in Gaul and Britain (57–50 B.C.); Emperor Claudius' personal expedition and conquest (43 A.D.) were decisive in the romanization of Britain. Reduction of the "empire" (5–40 A.D.) of Cymbeline and suppression (61) of the national revolt of Boudicca (*Boadicea*). Conquest of Wales (48–79). Construction of the great network of Roman roads began (eventually 5 systems, 4 centering on London). Bath emerged as a center of Romano-British fashion.

78–142. Roman conquests in the north began under Agricola; results north of the Clyde-Forth line were not decisive. The Emperor Hadrian completed the conquest of Britain in person: construction of **Hadrian's Wall** (123) from Solway Firth to Tyne mouth. Firth-Clyde rampart (c. 142).

208. Emperor Septimius Severus arrived (208), invaded Caledonia (Scotland), restored Roman military supremacy in the north, and fixed Hadrian's Wall as the final frontier of Roman conquest.

300–350. Height of villa construction in the plain of Britain. Chief towns: Verulamium (St. Albans), Colchester, Lincoln, Gloucester, York. The skill of the artisans and cloth-workers of Britain was already famous on the Continent in the 4th century. The island south of the Wall was completely romanized.

c. 350. Piratic raids of Irish (*Scoti*) and Picts were common, and the Teutonic conquest of Gaul cut Britain off from Rome in the 5th century, leaving the Romano-British to defend themselves against Saxon attacks on the south and east which soon penetrated the lowlands.

410–442. Withdrawal of the Roman legions and the end of the Roman administration coincided with an intensification of Nordic pressure and the influx of **Jutes, Angles, and Saxons,** which permanently altered the racial base of the island. By c. 615 the Angles and Jutes had reached the Irish Channel and were masters of what is virtually modern England. A Celtic recrudescence appeared in the highlands of the west and northwest. The history of Britain for two centuries (c. 350–597) is obscure. Christianity had not made much progress under the Romans.

Seven Anglo-Saxon kingdoms, the *Heptarchy*, emerged after the Teutonic conquest: Essex, Wessex, Sussex (probably prevailingly Saxon as the names suggest); Kent (Jutes); East Anglia, Mercia, Northumbria (Angles).

560–616. The supremacy of **Ethelbert of Kent** in the Heptarchy coincided with the

597. Arrival of **Augustine the Monk** and the conversion of Kent to the Roman Church. The hegemony in the Heptarchy passed eventually to **Edwin of Northumbria** (which had also been converted).

633. The defeat and death of Ethelbert's brother-in-law Edwin at the hands of the heathen Mercians ended the Northumbrian primacy and temporarily overwhelmed the Roman Church. A period of anarchy ensued.

633. Oswald of Northumbria called Aidan from Iona, whose mission began the great influence of Celtic Christianity, which for a time threatened to replace the Roman Church.

664. The Synod of **Whitby** turned Britain back into the orbit of the Roman Church and the Continent, and prepared the way for the decisive rôle of

669–690. Theodore of Tarsus, Archbishop of Canterbury. Theodore introduced a strictly Roman parochial system and a centralized episcopal system which became the model for the secular state and created a new concept of kingship. National synods brought the rival kingdoms together for the first time, and began the long evolution destined to create English nationality and national institutions, and to spread them through the civilized world.

Theodore's episcopate was marked by the reintroduction of Greco-Roman culture and the permanent establishment of a new cultural tradition which produced **Bede** (673–735), the father of English literature, and culminated in the wide influence of the great School at York, which extended to the Continent (e.g. **Alcuin** at the court of Charlemagne). The Archbishopric of York was founded, 735. Roman ecclesiastical architecture and church music flourished.

757–796. Under Offa II the Kingdom of Mercia, supreme south of the Humber, reached its maximum power, after which it broke up.

787. The first recorded raid of the **Danes** in

England was followed by the Danish inundation of Ireland. In the pause before the great wave of Viking advance, Wessex under

802-839. **Egbert,** who had been in Charlemagne's service, emerged supreme (conquering Mercia), exercised a vague suzerainty over Northumbria, and received the homage of all the English kinglets.

856-875. Full tide of the first Viking assault. Wessex was the spearhead of resistance.

871-899. **ALFRED THE GREAT** purchased peace until he could organize his forces and build up a navy. Almost overwhelmed by the winter invasion of 878, he finally defeated the Danes and forced the **Peace of Wedmore,** whereby Guthrun the Dane became a Christian and divided England with Alfred. The *Danelaw,* north of the Thames-Lea line, went to Guthrun; the south, together with London, went to Alfred.

878-900. The Danes were masters of the northeast, and under Danish pressure **Scotland** began to take on shape and unity.

Alfred proceeded to organize the defense of his kingdom. London was walled and garrisoned with burghers charged with its defense. Earth forts (*burhs*) of the Viking type were thrown up and garrisoned. The *fyrd* and the fleet were reorganized, the army increased, the *thegns* began to be used as a mounted infantry. Henceforth all citizens of the requisite wealth were forced to thegnhood, i.e. to join the military class attached to the royal household. A Danish reaction (892-896) was firmly put down.

Alfred's patronage of **learning.** Foreign scholars and learned refugees were welcomed at court. Alfred translated Bede's *History,* Orosius, and Boethius' *Consolatio* into the vernacular. To provide trained administrators, Alfred established schools for the sons of thegns and nobles. The Anglo-Saxon *Chronicle* was started.

899-924. **Edward,** Alfred's son, succeeded him, and with his sister, Ethelfreda of Mercia, began the conquest of the Danelaw, which was completed under

924-939. **Ethelstan,** Edward's son. The sons of Alfred were the first true kings of England; his grandson **Edgar** (959-975) was recognized as such. Archbishop Dunstan, Edgar's chief counselor, was a great ecclesiastical reformer (simony and morals) of the Church and the people. He followed a policy of fusion and conciliation toward the Danes, and Oda, a full-blooded Dane, became (942) Archbishop

of Canterbury. The absorption of the Danelaw by Wessex left the Celtic fringe in Scotland and Wales independent under a vague kind of vassalage to the king.

As the Danelaw was absorbed, the shire system was extended to it with the old Danish boroughs as a nucleus. The administration was often in the hands of men of Danish blood. The Anglo-Saxon farmers had no love for war, and the thegns began to emerge as a professional soldier class. The old tribal and clan organization was superseded by a system of quasi-feudal form whereby each man had a lord who was responsible for him at law. The great earldoms were beginning to emerge.

No common law existed; shire and hundred courts administered local custom with the freeman suitors under the king's representative-ealdorman, shire-reeve, or hundred-reeve. From the days of Edgar, the feudal element tended to encroach on royal authority, especially in the hundred courts. The old monasticism had been destroyed by the invasions, and the Church in England fell into corruption and decadence, only reformed by the influence of Cluny and Fleury and the Norman Conquest.

991. An ebb in Viking raids was followed by a fresh onset during the reign of **Ethelred the Redeless** (978-1016), led by Sven I (*Forked Beard*), King of Denmark. *Danegeld* had been sporadically collected under Alfred; now it was regularly levied and used as tribute to buy off the invaders. This tax, and the invasions, led to a rapid decline of the freeholders to a servile status. Under Canute, the Danegeld was transformed into a regular tax for defense. Collection of the Danegeld, originally in the hands of the towns, fell increasingly to the lord of the manor, and it was only a step from holding him for the tax to making him lord of the land from which the tax came.

1013-1014. Sven I (d. 1014) was acknowledged by the English, and Ethelred fled to Normandy, the home of his second wife, Emma.

1017-1035. **King Canute,** one of the two sons of Sven, elected by the Witan. The Witan was a heterogeneous body of prelates, magnates, and officials without any precise constitutional status. Canute was "emperor," on the model of Charlemagne, over a northern empire which included Denmark, Norway, and England, and, but for his early death, might have played a more important rôle. His reign was marked by conciliation and fusion. The Church was under Anglo-Saxon clergy. Canute maintained a good navy, and his standing army included the famous *housecarls*, which soon had an Anglo-Saxon contingent. The four great earldoms, Wessex, East Anglia, Mercia, Northumbria, and seven lesser earldoms can be distinguished in this period. The greatest of the earls was **Godwin of Wessex.** Canute's sons were incompetent, and his line ended, 1042.

Godwin was chiefly responsible for the election of the successor to Canute's line, Edward, son of Emma and Ethelred, who married (1045) Godwin's daughter.

1042-1066. EDWARD THE CONFESSOR, of the line of Alfred, was under Godwin's domination. Brought up at the Norman court, speaking French, he tried to Normanize the English court. Godwin's influence led to the deposition of the Norman Archbishop of Canterbury and the selection of the Saxon Stigand by the Witan. As Stigand had supported an antipope, Alexander II favored the Normans, as did Hildebrand, the power behind the papal throne. Godwin's son, **Harold,** succeeded (1053) him as Earl of Wessex, and dominated Edward as his father had. Another son of Godwin, Tostig, became Earl of Northumbria. Harold (c. 1064) was driven ashore on the Channel, fell into the hands of William, Duke of Normandy, a cousin of Edward the Confessor, and was forced to take an oath to aid William to attain the crown of England, which William declared Edward had promised him.

1066. Tostig, exiled after the Northumbrian revolt (1065), returned with Harold Hardrada to attack Northumbria. The Confessor died in January (1066) and William at once began vigorous preparations for the conquest of England.

1066. On Edward's death **Harold** was chosen king by the Witan and was guarding the coasts of England against William when Tostig and Hardrada appeared in the north. After a brilliant dash northward, Harold defeated them at **Stamford Bridge** in September, at the very moment that the Norman invaders arrived in the Channel. Rushing southward after his victory, Harold confronted the Normans, who had already landed, with a reduced, wearied, and shaken force, and was beaten and killed in the

OCT. 14. Battle of Hastings, or Senlac.

(*Cont. p.* 191.)

(2) *Scotland to* 1034

Racial origins obscure. A wave of Neolithic peoples from the Mediterranean was followed by Celts, Goidels, Brythons, Saxons in the 6th century B.C., and then by Picts. The Romans arrived at the end of the first century, A.D., but made no permanent impression.

450-600. Four political nuclei: Picts (Pentland Firth to the central plain); **Dalriada** (Argyllshire and the islands of Jura and Islay); **"Welsh" refugees** in Strathclyde; **Ida of Bernicia's realm** (from the Tweed to the Firth of Forth).

c. 565. COLUMBA arrived from Iona and converted the King of the Picts to the Celtic Church, giving Scotland her first cultural contact with the civilized world.

664. The Synod of Whitby turned England to the Roman Church and temporarily isolated Scotland. The Picts ultimately went into the Roman communion (c. 700) and Iona itself followed (716).

685. The English power was broken on the southern frontier, and Scotland began her independent evolution. Under **Kenneth I** (d. 858) began the first Scottish union.

794. Arrival of the Norse. Iona burned (802); a series of devastations followed.

921. Edward, son of Alfred the Great, was acknowledged lord of Scotland. Ethelstan enforced the bond in arms (934) and a Scottish effort to revolt was crushed. (937).

1005-1034. Under **Malcolm II,** Lothian was added to the Scottish crown and Strathclyde completed (1034) the union of the four nuclei under

1034-1040. Duncan, but without a homogeneous racial or political basis. The Isles and the north were under Scandinavian dominance, and England aimed to make Scotland her vassal.

(*Cont. p.* 201.)

(3) *Ireland to* 1171

Racial origins. The Neolithic inhabitants, followed by Celts and Goidels (c. 600–500 B.C.). The "fifths" (i.e. Ulster, Leinster, Connaught, East and West Munster) may date from the Goidel arrival. Belgic and other Brythonic migrations (300–150 B.C.) probably in the southeast. Supremacy of the Brythonic **Kingdom of Tara** in the 4th century of the Christian Era. The **Picts** pushed into Antrim and Down. There is an enormous body of legend dealing with the early origins.

431. Traditional date for the arrival of **Bishop Palladius** and his mission.

432. **PATRICK,** a pupil of Germanus of Auxerre, especially trained for this mission, arrived to continue Palladius' work. He founded churches in Meath, Ulster, Connaught, and probably established the Bishopric of Armagh. Chieftains were converted, but much paganism survived. Patrick began the education of the priesthood. Patrick's ecclesiastical organization was probably close to that of Britain and Gaul, but with the withdrawal of the Roman legions the Roman connection was cut, and there was a recrudescence of paganism. The diocesan organization of Patrick apparently slipped back into the native system.

Chieftains, on their conversion, made donations of land to the Church, and at first the ecclesiastical offices seem to have remained in the hands of the sept, with the *coarb* (inheritor) as bishop or abbot. The cenobitic organization of the 5th century was that of a sept, whose chief was a Christian. Later there was a rigorous form which separated the sexes. As the earlier diocesan organization declined, the number of bishops rose to fantastic figures. There was a great exodus of Irish scholars and monks to Europe during the 8th and 9th centuries.

c. 500-800. **The Golden Age of Irish monastic scholarship** occurred in the 6th to the 9th centuries. A great school founded by **Eudo**, Prince of Oriel (c. 450–540), at Aranmore drew scholars from all Europe. Establishment of the monastery of **Clonard** (c. 520) under Welsh inspiration. Here there were said to be 3000 students living in separate, wattled huts under open-air instruction. From Clonard went forth the so-called *Twelve Apostles of Ireland*, founding schools all over Ireland and later the Continent.

c. 533. **True monasticism** began with the work of Columba. Columba founded Iona (563), the mother Church of Scotland, whence Aidan, the apostle to England, founded Lindisfarne (635) for the conversion of Northumbria. The *Book of Kells* and the flowering of Gaelic vernacular poetry date from this period.

590. **Columban of Leinster,** from Bangor, began his mission to Europe, founding Luxeuil and a great series of other foundations (e.g. Gall, Würzburg, Salzburg, Tarantum, Bobbio). The 8th century saw a great wave of missions from the Rhine-Meuse area inland to the Rhone-Alps line. This powerful advance of Celtic Christianity at one time seemed destined to win northern Europe from Rome.

The chief formal differences from Rome were in tonsure, the date of Easter, the consecration of bishops. In the 7th century the Irish Church conformed to Roman usage, but the bond with Rome was not close

723. **Boniface** (Winfred) the Anglo-Saxon, arrived on the Continent to begin the organization on Roman lines of the Celtic establishments among the Franks, Thuringians, Alamanni, and Bavarians.

Between the death of Patrick and the arrival of the Norse at Dublin, Irish history is almost a blank. Before the coming of the Norse there were no cities, no stone bridges in Ireland, and no foreign trade of importance.

795. **The first Norse attack.** Dublin (840), Waterford, and Limerick founded as centers of Norse trade with the Continent. Soon a mixed race, the Gallgoidels (whence Galloway) arose, and a Christian decline set in. The Scandinavians remained chiefly in the ports.

1002-1014. **Brian of Munster** established his supremacy. A period of road- and fort-building. At Clontarf (1014) Brian defeated the Norse, ending the domination of Dublin, though the Norse remained in their cities. Brian fell in the battle and anarchy followed — the struggle of the O'Brians of Munster, the O'Neils of Ulster, the O'Connors of Connaught — which ended in an appeal to King Henry II of England by Dermond Mac-Murrough.

1152. **The Synod of Kells** established the present diocesan system of Ireland, recognized the primacy of Armagh, and the Archbishoprics of Cashel, Tuam, Dublin. Tithes were voted.

1167-1171. **The Norman Conquest.** Henry II, on his accession, had the idea of conquering Ireland. John of Salisbury records that on his request as Henry's envoy (1155), Pope Adrian IV sent Henry a letter granting him lordship of Ireland, and a ring as the symbol of his investiture. Henry seems never to have availed himself of the papal grant.

1167. On the appeal of Dermond MacMurrough, Henry issued a letter allowing Dermond to raise troops in England for his cause. Dermond came to terms with Richard of Clare, a Norman, Earl of Pembroke, and with other Normans, most of whom were related to one another. A series of expeditions to Ireland brought into the island a group of Norman families (e.g. Fitzmaurices, Carews, Gerards, Davids, Barries, *et al.*), who began to establish a powerful colony, which alarmed Henry.

1171. HENRY II, with papal sanction, landed in Ireland to assert his supremacy and to reconcile the natives. The **Synod of Cashel,** at which Henry was not present, acknowledged his sovereignty. *(Cont. p. 201.)*

k. SCANDINAVIA

ORIGINS: References in Pytheas, Pomponius, Mela, Pliny the Elder, Tacitus, Ptolemy, Procopius, Jordanes. Archaelogical remains indicate Roman connections in the 3d century after Christ, but there is no evidence for close continental relations until the Viking period.

VIKING PERIOD. Scandinavia developed in isolation during the barbarian migrations until the 2d century after Christ. The Viking expansion from Scandinavia itself prolonged the period of migrations in Europe for four hundred years. The traditional participation of Scandinavia in the Viking migration through Europe was as follows: (1) **Norwegians** (outer passage): raids in Scotland, Ireland, France (Hrolf the Ganger, i.e. "Rollo"). (2) **Danes** (the middle passage): British Isles, France, the Low Countries. (3) **Swedes** (eastward passage): across Slavdom to Byzantium (foundation of Novgorod 862, Kiev, c. 900). There never was a mass migration, and probably all stocks shared in the various movements to some degree. **Causes:** (1) pagan reaction, including renegade Christians; (2) pressure of population; (3) tribal warfare and vassalage of the defeated, especially after 872 (this is the traditional explanation for Rollo's migration, 911); (4) love of gain; (5) fashion and love of adventure.

NORWEGIAN COLONIZATION. (1) Ireland: the Norwegian conquest began c. 823 and centers were established at Dublin (the kingdom endured until 1014), Waterford, and Limerick. Exodus of learned monks to Europe (**Scotus Erigena?**). Attacks by the Picts and Danes. The subsequent colonization of the Scottish Islands drew Norwegians from Ireland and accelerated the celtization of the colonists who remained there. (2) **The Islands:** Hebrides, Man, Faroes, Orkneys, Shetlands. (3) Iceland: reached by Irish monks c. 790; discovered by the Norsemen in 874 and colonized almost at once; establishment of a *New Norway*, with a high culture. (4) **Greenland:** visited by Eric the Red of Iceland (981) and colonized at once; expeditions from Greenland to the North American Continent (p. 371). The Norse settlements in Greenland continued until the 15th century.

CIVILIZATION. Large coin hoards indicate the profits of raids and trade with the British Isles, Mediterranean, Byzantium, and Moslem Asia. Export of furs, arms (to eastern Europe), and mercenary services to rulers (e.g. bodyguards of Ethelred, Canute, Slavic princes, Byzantine emperors). Trade eastward was cut off by the Huns and Avars (5th and 6th century), but resumed after Rurik's expedition (862) reopened Russia.

Runes (from a Scandinavian root, meaning to inscribe) were already ancient in the Viking period, and probably are modified Roman letters. The *Eddas,* dramatic lays (prose and verse) of the Norwegian aristocracy (especially in Iceland) dealing with gods and heroes (many in the German tradition, e.g. Sigurd and the Nibelungs), are the highest literary production of heathen Scandinavia.

Scandinavian society rested on wealth from raids and commerce and consisted of a landed aristocracy with farmer tenants with the right and obligation to attend local courts; there were few slaves. The only general assembly was the *Allthing* of Iceland (established 930), the oldest continuous parliamentary body in existence.

Mythology and religion. The Norwegians had a more complicated mythology than any other Teutonic people: giants, elves, dwarfs, serpents, succeeded by the triumph of **Odin,** his wife **Friga,** and his son **Thor.**

Conversion to Christianity. The first Christians (probably captives) appeared in the 6th century. The first Christian missionary was the Anglo-Saxon, **Willibord** (c. 700), who accomplished but little. A Carolingian mission (c. 820) was welcomed by King Bjorn of Sweden. A few years later (c. 831) the Archbishopric of Hamburg was established and became at once the center for missionary work in the north. *(Cont. p. 203.)*

2. EASTERN EUROPE

a. THE EASTERN EMPIRE TO 1025

527–565. JUSTINIAN. A Macedonian by birth and the chief adviser of his uncle, Justin, since 518. Justinian was a man of serious and even somber temperament, but of strong, even autocratic character, sober judgment, grandiose conceptions. He was strongly influenced by his wife **Theodora** (d. 548), a

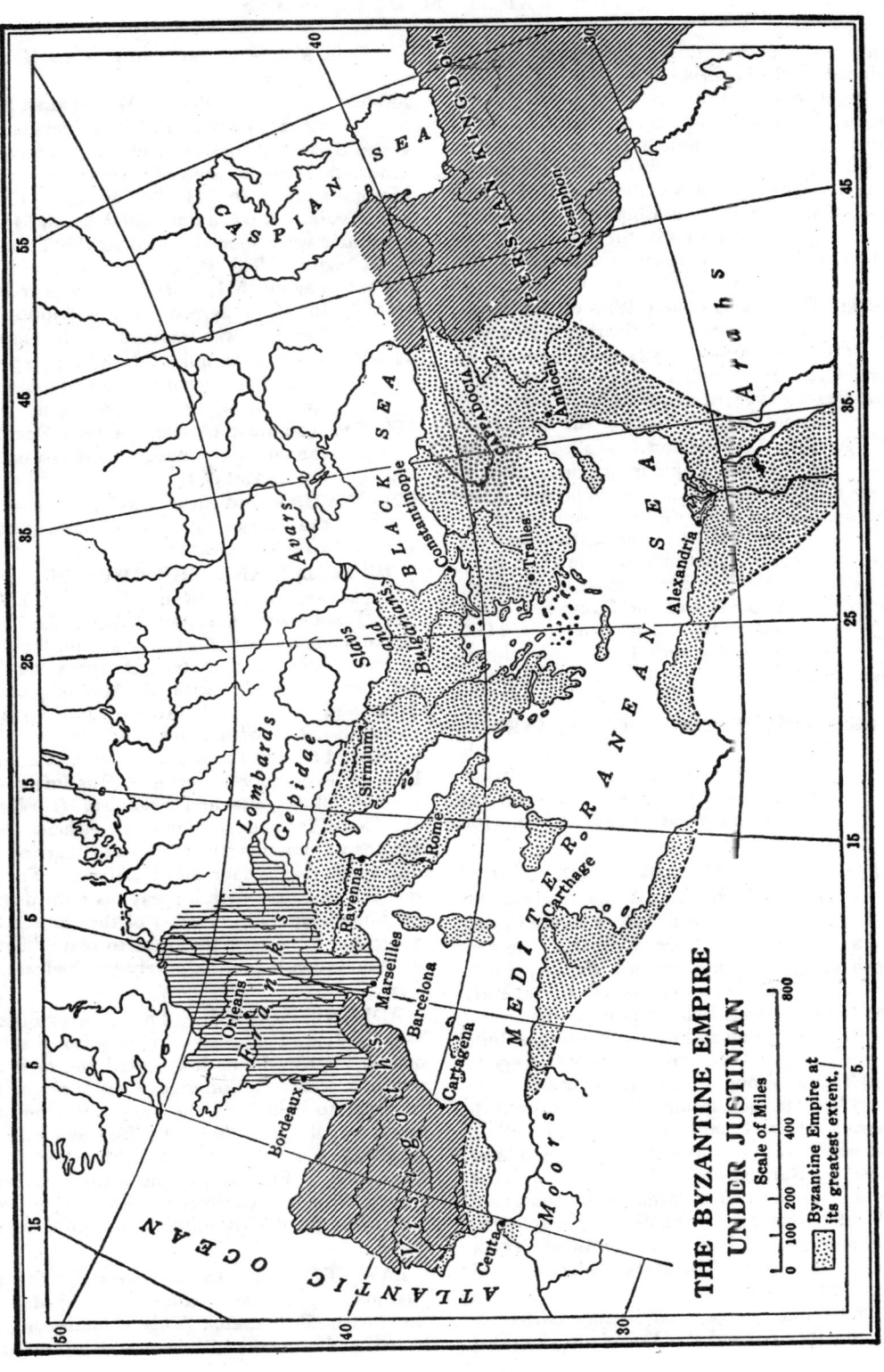

THE BYZANTINE EMPIRE
UNDER JUSTINIAN

Scale of Miles

0 100 200 400 800

Byzantine Empire at
its greatest extent.

CASPIAN SEA

PERSIAN KINGDOM

Ctesiphon

Arabs

BLACK SEA

CAPPADOCIA

Antioch

Tralles

Constantinople

Alexandria

Avars

Slavs and Bulgarians

Gepidae

Lombards

Sirmium

Ravenna

Rome

Marseilles

Barcelona

Carthage

Cartagena

Ceuta

Orleans

Bordeaux

FRANKS

VISIGOTHS

Moors

MEDITERRANEAN SEA

ATLANTIC OCEAN

woman of humble origin, probably unduly maligned by the historian Procopius. Theodora was cruel, deceitful, and avid of power, but a woman of iron will and unusual political judgment. Justinian's whole policy was directed toward the establishment of the absolute power of the emperor and toward the revival of a universal, Christian Roman Empire. The entire reign was filled with wars in the east and in the west, punctuated by constant incursions of the barbarians from the north.

527-532. The first Persian War of Justinian. His commander, **Belisarius,** won a victory at Dara (530), but was then defeated at **Callinicum.** The conflict ended with the **Perpetual Peace of 532,** designed to free the imperial armies for operations in the west.

532. The Nika Insurrection (so-called from the cry of the popular parties, *Nika =* *Victory*). This was the last great uprising of the circus parties and led to great violence and incendiarism. Much of Constantinople was destroyed by fire. Justinian was deterred from flight only through the arguments of Theodora. Ultimately Belisarius and the forces put down the insurrection with much cruelty (30,000 slain). Therewith the period of popular domination came to an end and the epoch of absolutism began.

533-543. CONQUEST OF NORTH AFRICA. Belisarius, with a relatively small force, transported by sea, defeated the Vandal usurper, Gelimer, and recovered the whole of North Africa for the empire.

535-554. THE RECONQUEST OF ITALY. Belisarius landed in Sicily, overran the island, conquered southern Italy from the Ostrogoths and took Rome (Dec. 9, 536). The Ostrogoth king, **Witiges,** besieged the city for a whole year (537-538), but failed to take it. In the following year Belisarius advanced to the north, took Ravenna and captured Witiges, but, after the recall of Belisarius, the new Ostrogoth leader, **Totila,** reconquered Italy as far as Naples (541-543). He took Rome (546) and sacked it. Belisarius returned, captured the city, but then abandoned it to the Goths (549). He was later replaced by **Narses,** who invaded Italy by land from the north with a large army composed chiefly of barbarian mercenaries. He defeated the Ostrogoths decisively in the **battle of Tagina** (552) and brought all of Italy under imperial rule.

540. The Huns, Bulgars, and other barbarian tribes crossed the Danube and raided the Balkan area as far south as the Isthmus of Corinth.

540-562. The great Persian War against Khusru I (*Chosroes*). The Persians invaded Syria and took Antioch, after which they attacked Lazistan and Armenia and raided Mesopotamia. In 544 they besieged Edessa, but in vain. A truce was concluded in 545, but hostilities were soon resumed in the Transcaucasus region. The Persians took Petra (549), but lost it again (551). By the fifty-year **Peace of 562,** Justinian agreed to pay tribute, but Lazistan was retained for the empire.

542-546. Constantinople and the empire were visited by a very severe and disastrous epidemic of the bubonic plague.

554. The conquest of southeastern Spain by the imperial armies. Cordova became the capital of the province.

559. The Huns and Slavs, having advanced to the very gates of Constantinople, were driven off by Belisarius.

JUSTINIAN AND THE CHURCH. Peace had been made with Rome in 519 and Pope John I had visited Constantinople in 525. Justinian made a great effort to maintain the unity of the western and eastern churches, but this led him into trouble with the **Monophysites** of Syria and Egypt. He attempted to reconcile them also, but with indifferent success. The cleavage between Latin and Greek Christianity became ever more marked. Justinian suppressed all heresies and paganism (closing of the Neo-Platonic Academy at Athens, 529). Extensive missionary work was carried on among the barbarians and in Africa. For the rest the emperor, with a great taste for dogma, set himself up as the master of the Church and arrogated to himself the right to make binding pronouncements in even purely theological matters.

ADMINISTRATION. The emperor insisted on honesty and efficiency. He abolished sale of offices, improved salaries, united the civil and military powers of provincial authorities, etc. In order to hold back the barbarians, he built hundreds of forts along the frontiers and established a regular system of frontier forces (*limitanei*). Financially the empire suffered greatly from the extensive military operations and from the great building activities of the court.

LAW REFORM. In order to clarify the law, Justinian appointed a commission headed by the jurist, **Tribonian.** This commission collected and ordered all the constitutions promulgated since the time of Hadrian and published them as the *Codex Justinianus* (529). There followed the collection of opinions of the jurists, the *Digest* or *Pandects* (533), and a general textbook of the law, the *Institutes*. Justinian's own legislation was collected in the *Novellae* (565). By this great work of codification Justinian assured for the Roman Law an immense prestige and far-reaching influence, but at the same time diminished its chances of further development.

BUILDING ACTIVITY. The period was one of unexampled construction, ranging from whole towns to public baths, palaces, bridges, roads and forts, as well as countless churches and cloisters. It was a period of much free experimentation and originality, resulting in unusual variety of types, all of them, however, marked by grandeur and splendor. The **Church of St. Sophia** (constructed between 532–537 by Anthemios of Tralles and Isidoros of Miletus) is the greatest of the many monuments of Justinian's reign.

LITERATURE. An age of revival. The *Secret History* of **Procopius**; the historians **Agathias** and **John of Ephesus**. Renascence of Greek classical poetry; creation of religious poetry by **Romanos**.

565-578. JUSTIN II, nephew of Justinian, who seized the throne with the aid of Tiberius, commander of the guard. Justin was a careful, economical ruler, who continued the policies of his predecessor, but attempted to concentrate attention upon the economic plight of the empire and the growing danger from the barbarians. In 574 he became insane, after which the empire was ruled by Tiberius, in conjunction with the Empress Sophia.

568-571. The Lombard invasion of Italy led to the loss of most of the imperial possessions in the north and center, though Ravenna, Rome, and Naples were retained.

572-591. War with Persia, growing out of an insurrection in Armenia, which was supported by the emperor. The Persians took Dara (573) and devastated Syria. In 575, Khusru ravaged the country as far as Cappadocia, but was finally driven back by the imperial commander, Maurikios.

578-582. TIBERIUS, emperor. His reign was marked by a great inundation of the Slavs, who advanced into Thrace and Greece and settled in large numbers, thus changing profoundly the ethnographic composition of the Balkan populations.

582-602. MAURICE (*Maurikios*), emperor. Like his forerunner, Justin, he pursued a policy of retrenchment, which only made him unpopular in the capital. The reign was marked by constant disturbances and by widespread dissatisfaction.

583. The Avars, grown to be a formidable power, took the forts along the Danube.

589-591. Last phase of the Persian War. Khusru I had died in 579. In 589 a military revolt led to the deposition of Khusru II, who fled to Constantinople. The emperor, espousing his cause, led a great army to the east (591) and restored him to the throne. In return the emperor received Dara and the larger part of Armenia.

591. The Avars raided to the very gates of Constantinople.

593. The imperial armies, under **Priscus,** proceeded against the Avars. The latter were defeated at **Viminacium** (601) after which Priscus pushed on to the Theiss.

602. A mutiny of the troops on the Danube, led by Phocas, resulted in a march to the capital, the outbreak of popular insurrection in the city, and the flight of the emperor.

602-610. PHOCAS, emperor. He was an untutored soldier, cruel and utterly incompetent. Maurice was captured and executed with his sons. All his supporters met with a like fate.

606-608. Resumption of the Persian War. The Persians again captured Dara and overran Syria and Mesopotamia (608) advancing through Anatolia as far as Chalcedon.

610. Conspiracy against Phocas, led by Priscus and supported by the Exarch of Africa. The latter sent an army by land which conquered Egypt, while a fleet from Carthage arrived at Constantinople. The mob thereupon rose, slew Phocas and proclaimed Heraclius, the son of the exarch, as emperor.

610-641. HERACLIUS I, founder of a new dynasty, in whose reign the empire became definitely a Greek (*Byzantine*) monarchy. Heraclius found the empire in a parlous state, threatened from the north by the Avars and from the east by the Persians. But he showed himself an able organizer, general and statesman, and found in the Patriarch Sergius a courageous supporter.

611-622. The Persian advance. They took Antioch, Apameia, Emesa, and Kaisareia; Damascus (613); Jerusalem (614), which was sacked, the inhabitants and the Holy Cross being transferred to Ctesiphon. In 615 the Persians were at Chalcedon. In 619 they conquered Egypt.

616. The imperial possessions in Spain were lost to the Visigoths.

619. The Avars appeared at Constantinople, which was threatened on the Asiatic side by the Persians. Heraclius was deterred from flight to Africa only by the influence of the patriarch.

622–630. DEFEAT OF THE PERSIANS. Heraclius, with a newly organized army and supported by a tremendous outburst of religious enthusiasm (the *Byzantine Crusade*), took the offensive against the Persians and carried on three brilliant campaigns in the Transcaucasian region, refusing to allow himself to be distracted by the constant attacks of the Avars in the Balkans. In the **battle of Nineveh** (Dec. 12, 627) he won a decisive victory, which enabled him to advance to Ctesiphon (628). The **death of Khusrau** (628) and dynastic disorders in Persia made possible the conclusion of a victorious peace. All the Persian conquests were returned and the Holy Cross restored to Jerusalem.

626. The Avars and Slavs attacked Constantinople by land and sea, but were unable to storm the walls. This marked the height of the Avar power.

634–641. The Arab conquests (p. 184). They took Bostra (634); Damascus (635); by the **battle of Yarmuk** (636) gained all Syria; forced the surrender of Jerusalem (637); overran Mesopotamia (639) and conquered Egypt (640–642).

635. Alliance between the emperor and Kuvrat, King of the Bulgars, intended to break the power of the Avars.

638. The *Ecthesis*, a formula elaborated by the Patriarch Sergius and other churchmen in the hope of reconciling the Monophysites, who were welcoming rather than opposing the Islamic advance. The formula recognized one will in the two natures of Christ (*monotheletism*), but failed to win acceptance in Syria and Egypt. On the contrary, it called forth much opposition in the strictly orthodox Italian and African possessions.

641. HERACLIUS CONSTANTINUS, son of Heraclius, became emperor, but died in a few months under suspicious circumstances.

641. HERACLEONAS, younger son of Heraclius, emperor, under his mother's tutelage. He was almost at once overthrown by the army.

641–668. CONSTANS II (*Constantinus*), grandson of Heraclius, emperor. He was an energetic and able ruler, who did his utmost to check the Arab advance. With this object in view he reorganized the provincial administration by establishing **themes** (*themata*) under military governors with wide powers (*strategoi*) and authority over the civil officials. This system greatly strengthened administrative control and was the basis of the imperial organization for centuries.

643. The Arabs took Alexandria, last outpost of the Greeks in Egypt.

647–648. Arab invasion of North Africa.

648. The Arabs, having assembled a fleet, took Cyprus.

649. Pope Martin condemned the teaching of the *Ecthesis*, but was soon arrested by the Exarch of Ravenna (653) and sent to Constantinople.

653. The Arab advance continued. Armenia was conquered (653) and Rhodes plundered (654). In 655 the Arab fleet defeated an imperial armada under the emperor's own command off the Lycian coast. But in 659 a truce was concluded with the Arab commander in Syria.

663–668. Transfer of the court to Italy. Constans was intent on blocking the Arab conquest of Sicily and Italy and had dreams of restoring Rome as the basis of the imperial power. But he failed to make any conquests in Italy at the expense of the Lombards and in his absence the Arabs annually invaded and devastated Anatolia.

668. Constans was murdered in the course of a mutiny at Syracuse.

668–685. CONSTANTINE IV (*Pogonatus*), the son of Constans, a harsh character, but an able soldier. He had been in charge of affairs and had come to Sicily to put down the revolt that had resulted in his father's death. On his return to Constantinople, the troops obliged him to accept his brothers Heraclius and Tiberius as co-rulers, but after 680 Constantine was sole emperor. His reign witnessed the high point of the Arab attack, accompanied, as usual, by repeated incursions of the Slavs in the Balkans.

673–678. The **Arab attacks on Constantinople.** After a siege by land and sea (Apr.–Sept. 673), the assailants blockaded the city and attacked it every year for five years.

The city was saved by the strength of its walls and by the newly invented **Greek fire**, which raised havoc with the Arab fleet. In 677 the Greeks destroyed the Arab fleet at **Syllaeum** and secured a favorable thirty-year peace (678). Never again did the Arab menace become so pressing. The empire had proved itself a formidable bulwark of Europe.

675-681. Repeated assaults of the Slavs on Thessalonica. The city held out, but the settlement of Thrace and Macedonia and northern Greece by Slavic tribes continued uninterruptedly.

679. Appearance of **the Bulgar menace.** The Bulgars, a people of Turkish race, had pressed westward through southern Russia and settled in Bessarabia. The emperor failed in his efforts to defeat them there. They crossed the Danube, settled in the region between the river and the Balkan Mountains, gradually fused with the Slavs and became largely Slavicized, and founded the first coherent Slavic power in the Balkans.

680-681. The sixth oecumenical council at Constantinople condemned the monothelite heresy and returned to pure orthodoxy. Since the loss of Syria and Egypt, there was no longer any need for favoring the monophysite view. The return to orthodoxy was a victory for the papal stand and was probably intended to strengthen the Byzantine hold on Italy. In actual fact the Patriarch of Constantinople (now that the Patriarchs of Antioch, Jerusalem, and Alexandria were under Moslem power) became more and more influential in the east and the primacy of the Roman pope was hardly more than nominal.

685-695. JUSTINIAN II, the son of Constantine and the last of the Heraclian dynasty. He ascended the throne when only sixteen and soon showed himself to be harsh and cruel, though energetic and ambitious like most members of his family.

689. The emperor defeated the Slavs in Thrace and transferred a considerable number of them to Anatolia.

692. The Byzantine forces were severely defeated by the Arabs in the **battle of Sebastopolis.**

695. A revolt against the emperor, led by Leontius and supported by the clergy and people, initiated a period of twenty years of anarchy. Justinian was deposed and exiled to the Crimea (Cherson).

695-698. LEONTIUS, emperor. His reign was marked by the domination of the army.

697-698. The Arabs finally took **Carthage** and brought to an end the Byzantine rule in North Africa.

698-705. TIBERIUS III, made emperor by another revolt in the army. The reign was distinguished by an insurrection against Byzantine rule in Armenia and by constant Arab raids in eastern Anatolia.

705-711. JUSTINIAN II, who returned to the throne with the aid of the Bulgar king. He took an insane revenge on all his enemies and instituted a veritable reign of terror.

711. The emperor failed to suppress a serious **revolt in the Crimea,** supported by the Khazars. The insurgent troops, under Philippicus, marched on Constantinople and finally defeated and killed Justinian in an engagement in northern Anatolia.

711-713. PHILIPPICUS, emperor. He proved himself quite incompetent and was unable to check the raids of the Bulgars (reached Constantinople in 712) or the ravages of the Arabs in Cilicia (they took Amasia, 712).

713-715. ANASTASIUS II, emperor, the creature of the mutinous Thracian army corps. He attempted to reorganize the army, but this led to new outbreaks.

715-717. THEODOSIUS III, an obscure official put on the throne by the army. He was helpless in the face of the Arabs, who in 716 advanced as far as Pergamon. The invaders were finally repulsed by the *strategos* of the Anatolian *theme*, Leo, who forced the abdication of the emperor and was enthusiastically proclaimed by the clergy and populace of the capital.

717-741. LEO III (*the Isaurian*), founder of the Isaurian dynasty, an eminent general and a great organizer. Leo used drastic measures to suppress revolts in the army and reestablished discipline by issuing new regulations. The finances were restored by heavy, systematic taxation, but steps were taken, by an **agrarian code,** to protect freemen and small holders. By the *Ecloga* (739) the empire was given a simplified law code, distinguished by the Christian charity of its provisions. In the administrative sphere Leo completed the **theme organization,** dividing the original units and making seven *themes* in Asia and four in Europe.

717-718. Second great siege of Constantinople by the Arabs. The siege, conducted by land and sea, lasted just a year and ended in failure, due to the energetic conduct of the defense.

726. Beginning of the great iconoclastic controversy. Leo found the empire generally demoralized and a prey to superstition and miracle-mongering. Like many devout persons (especially in the Anatolian regions), he disapproved of the widespread image-worship, which he proceeded to forbid. Behind these measures there undoubtedly lay the desire to check the alarming **spread of monasticism,** which withdrew thousands of men from active economic life and concentrated great wealth in the cloisters, which were free from taxation. The first measures led at once to a revolt in Greece (727), whence a fleet set out for Constantinople with an anti-emperor. This was destroyed by the Greek fire of the imperial fleet. The pope at Rome (Gregory II) likewise declared against the emperor's iconoclasm and the population of the Exarchate of Ravenna rose in revolt and made an alliance with the Lombards. Only with the aid of Venice were a few crucial stations held by the imperial forces. A fleet from the east failed to restore Byzantine authority (731). In revenge the emperor in 733 withdrew Calabria, Sicily, and Illyria from the jurisdiction of the pope and placed them under the Constantinople patriarch.

739. The Byzantine forces won an important victory over the Arab invaders of Anatolia in the **battle of Akroinon.**

741-775. Constantine V (*Kopronymos*), the son of Leo and for years associated with him in the government. Constantine was autocratic, uncompromising, and violent, but withal able and energetic as well as sincere. A revolt of his brother-in-law, Artavasdos, was supported by the idolaters and by part of the army. It took fully two years to suppress it.

745. The emperor, taking the offensive against the Arabs, carried the war into Syria.

746. The Greeks destroyed a great Arab armada and reconquered Cyprus.

746. The empire suffered from the greatest **plague epidemic** since the time of Justinian.

751-752. The emperor led a successful campaign against the Arabs in Armenia. The Arabs were weakened by the fall of the Omayyad Caliphate and the removal of the capital from Damascus to Baghdad (p. 189).

751. The Lombards conquered the Exarchate of Ravenna. The pope thereupon called

in the Franks and was given the former Byzantine territory by Pepin (*Donation of Pepin*) (p. 153).

753. The Church Council of Hieria approved of the emperor's iconoclastic policy. Therewith began the violent phase of the controversy. The monks offered vigorous resistance, but the emperor was unbending. The monks were imprisoned, exiled, and some even executed; monasteries were closed and their properties confiscated; images were destroyed or whitewashed.

755-764. Nine successive **campaigns against the Bulgars.** The emperor won important victories at Marcellae (759) and Anchialus (763), and, despite some reverses, forced the Bulgars to conclude peace (764).

758. The Slavs were defeated in Thrace and a large number of them settled in Asia.

772. Renewal of the **war with the Bulgars,** marked by further victories of the emperor.

775-780. LEO IV, the son of Constantine. In religious matters he simply continued his predecessor's policy.

778-779. Victory over the Arabs at **Germanikeia** (778) and their expulsion from Anatolia.

780-797. CONSTANTINE VI ascended the throne as a child, wholly under the influence of his ambitious, unscrupulous, and scheming mother, **Irene,** and her favorites. Irene, anxious to secure support for her personal power, devoted herself almost exclusively to the religious question. The Arabs, who again advanced to the Bosporus (782), were bought off with heavy tribute (783). On the other hand, the general, Staurakios, carried on a successful campaign against the Slavs in Macedonia and Greece (783).

787. The Council of Nicaea abandoned iconoclasm and ordered the worship of images. Tremendous victory for the monkish party, which soon advanced far-reaching claims to complete freedom for the Church in religious matters.

790. The army, opposed to the monks, mutinied and put Constantine in power. Irene was forced into retirement. The emperor set out on campaigns against the Arabs and Bulgars, but met with indifferent success.

792. Constantine recalled his mother and made her co-ruler. She took a vile advantage of him and, after his divorce and a remarriage arranged by her (795), put herself at the head of a party of the monks in opposing the step. A rising of the army put her in control and she had her son taken and blinded (797).

797-802. IRENE, the first empress. Though supported by able generals (Staurakios and Aëtios), she preferred to buy peace with the Arabs (798) and devote herself to domestic intrigue.

800. Resurrection of the empire in the west, through the coronation of Charlemagne. The Eastern Empire refused all recognition of the claim.

802-811. NICEPHORUS, who was put on the throne by a group of conspiring officials of the government. Irene, deposed, died in 803. Nicephorus was a firm ruler, who carried through a number of much-needed financial reforms.

803. The emperor made **peace with Charlemagne,** the Eastern Empire retaining southern Italy, Venice, and Dalmatia.

804-806. The Arabs resumed their raids in Anatolia and ravaged Cyprus and Rhodes, ultimately forcing the conclusion of a humiliating peace.

809. Banishment of the monks of Studion, who, under **Theodoros of Studion,** took the lead in advancing claims of church freedom. They went so far as to appeal to the Roman pope and offer to recognize his primacy.

809-813. War with Krum, the powerful king of the Bulgars. The emperor was defeated and killed in a great battle (811).

811. STAURAKIOS, son of Nicephorus, was emperor for a few months.

811-813. MICHAEL I (*Rhangabé*), brother-in-law of Staurakios, emperor. He proved himself quite incompetent, being unable to check the advance of Krum to Constantinople, or the success of the party of monks in domestic affairs.

813-820. LEO V (*the Armenian*), called to the throne by the army. Though personally not much moved by the religious controversy, he could not avoid taking up the challenge of the monks.

815. THE COUNCIL OF ST. SOPHIA marked the return to iconoclasm and the beginning of the second period of active and violent persecution of the monks.

817. The emperor won a great victory over the Bulgars at **Mesembria,** Krum having died (814). The Bulgars were obliged to accept a thirty-year peace.

820-829. MICHAEL II (*Phrygian dynasty*), succeeded to the throne after the murder of Leo by conspirators.

822-824. Insurrection of the general, **Thomas,** in Anatolia. This was supported by the lower classes and encouraged by the Arabs. Thomas attempted twice to take Constantinople, but was ultimately defeated and executed in Thrace.

826. Crete was seized by Moslem freebooters from Spain and until 961 remained the headquarters of pirates who ravaged the eastern Mediterranean.

827-878. Conquest of Sicily by Moslems from North Africa.

829-842. THEOPHILUS, emperor. He was an arrogant, theologizing fanatic who promulgated a new edict against idolaters (832) and pushed the persecution to the limit.

837-838. War against the Arabs. The Byzantine armies, after invading the caliphate, were repulsed. After a long siege, Amorion, one of the key positions on the frontier, was taken by the Moslems (838).

842-867. MICHAEL III, for whom his mother Theodora was regent. Advised by her brother, **Bardas,** she decided to end the religious controversy.

843. Image-worship was restored. This was a great victory for the opposition party, but only in the matter of doctrine. Politically the power of the emperor over the Church remained unimpaired, if not strengthened.

849. Reduction of the Slavic populations of the Peloponnesus, followed by their conversion.

856. Theodora was obliged to retire, but her brother Bardas, an able but unprincipled politician, remained the real ruler of the empire by exploiting to the full the weaknesses of the emperor.

860. First appearance of the Russians (*Varangians*) at Constantinople.

863-885. Missionary activity of **Cyril** and **Methodius** of Thessalonica among the Slavs of Moravia and Bohemia. They invented the Glagolitic (i.e. Slavic) **alphabet** and by the use of Slavic in the church service paved the way for the connection of Slavic Christianity with Constantinople.

865. Tsar Boris of Bulgaria (852–889) allowed himself to be baptized. Although Michael III acted as godfather, the Bulgarian ruler was for a time undecided between the claims of Rome and Constantinople to religious jurisdiction in Bulgaria.

866. Bardas was murdered by Michael's favorite, Basil.

867. Michael himself was deposed and done away with at Basil's order.

867. Schism with Rome. The great patriarch, **Photius,** had replaced **Ignatius** in 858, whereupon the latter had appealed to the pope for an inquiry. Photius came to represent the Greek national feeling in opposition to Rome. He took a strong stand towards the papal claims and the **Council of Constantinople** (867) anathematized the pope, accused the papacy of doctrinal aberrations, rejected the idea of Rome's primacy, etc.

867-886. BASIL I, founder of the *Macedonian dynasty* (he was really of Armenian extraction, though born in Macedonia). His reign initiated what was probably the most glorious period of Byzantine history. The empire had by this time become a purely Greek monarchy, under an absolute ruler. Settlement of the iconoclastic controversy released the national energies and there followed a period of brilliant military success, material prosperity, and cultural development. An important departure was the recognition of the idea of legitimacy and of an imperial family. This was paralleled by the gradual emergence of a feudal system.

Basil I was himself an intelligent, firm, and orderly ruler, a good administrator and general, whose ambition was to restore the empire both internally and externally. He rebuilt the army and especially the navy, and did much to revise the legal system: the *Procheiros Nomos* (879), a compilation of the most important parts of the Justinian code; the *Epanagoge* (886), a manual of customary law.

869. The eighth oecumenical synod. Photius had been banished (867) and Ignatius recalled. The latter made peace with Rome on papal terms, but conflict and friction continued.

The Macedonian Emperors

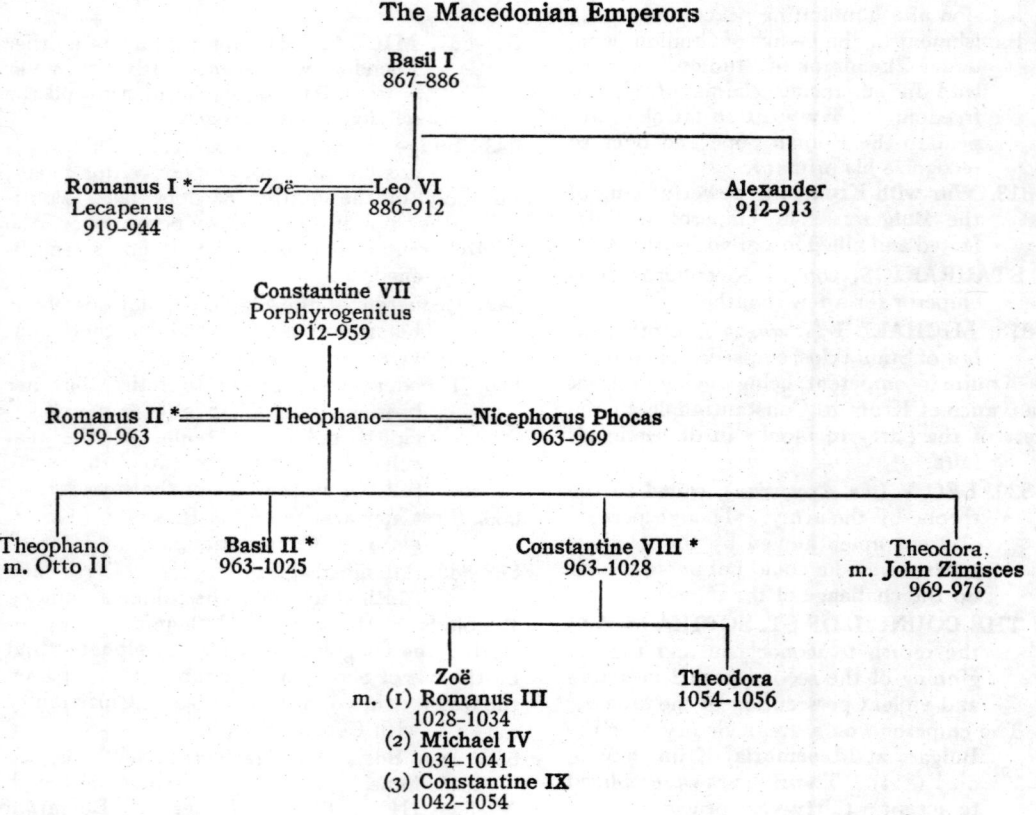

* Died without male issue.

871-879. Campaigns in the east. Border warfare with the Arabs was chronic, but the campaign against the Paulicians (Christian purists hostile to the empire) was a new departure. The imperial armies advanced to the upper Euphrates and took Samosata (873). In 878-879 victorious campaigns were carried through in Cappadocia and Cilicia. By land the Byzantine forces were gradually taking the offensive against the Moslems, wracked by internal dissensions.

875. The Byzantine forces seized **Bari** in southern Italy. Some years later (880) they took Tarentum and then (885) Calabria, establishing two new themes in southern Italy, which became a refuge for Greeks driven from Sicily by the completion of the Saracen conquest (Syracuse taken, 878; Taormina taken, 902).

877. Photius was restored as patriarch and the break with Rome was renewed.

880-881. A number of naval **victories over the Moslem pirates** of the eastern Mediterranean marked the beginning of a long campaign against this scourge.

886-912. LEO VI (*the Wise*), a somewhat pedantic philosopher, but nevertheless a determined ruler with a high sense of his office and obligations. He deposed Photius at once and put the Ignatians back in power. The result was a renewal of the **union with Rome** (900), which, however, could hardly be more than external. The reign of Leo was marked also by further legislative work. The *Basilika* (887-893) provided a series of 60 new law books, consisting largely of a compilation of decrees since the time of Justinian.

889- **War with the Bulgarians,** who now entered the period of greatness under **Tsar Symeon** (893-927). The emperor encouraged the Hungarians to attack by way of diversion and most of Symeon's reign was taken up with continued campaigns against this enemy. Symeon was educated at Constantinople and was deeply impressed with Greek culture, which he introduced in Bulgaria.

904. The Saracen corsair, **Leo of Tripoli,** stormed Thessalonica, plundered it and carried off some 20,000 of the inhabitants.

907. The Russians, under their prince, Oleg, appeared again at Constantinople and secured rights of trade.

912-913. ALEXANDER, the brother of Leo, emperor for less than a year.

913-959. CONSTANTINE VII (*Porphyrogenitus*) ascended the throne as a child, with a regency composed of his mother Zoë, the Patriarch Nikolas, and John Eladas. Constantine was a learned man of artistic tastes. He never really governed, leaving the actual conduct of affairs to strong men who were associated with him.

913-917. The Bulgarian threat. Tsar Symeon, who had established a brilliant capital at Preslav (seat also of the Bulgarian patriarchate), styled himself Emperor of the Romans, and undoubtedly hoped to possess himself of the imperial crown. In 913 he appeared at Constantinople; in 914 he took Adrianople, only to lose it again. But in 917 he defeated a Byzantine army at Anchialus. The war continued, indecisively, for years. In 924 Symeon again appeared at Constantinople.

915. A Byzantine victory over the Arabs at **Garigliano** assured the empire of its possessions in South Italy.

919-944. ROMANUS LECAPENUS, co-emperor with Constantine. He was the emperor's stepfather, an able but ruthless Armenian, whose whole policy was designed to strengthen his own control and establish that of his family.

920-942. Brilliant campaigns of the Byzantine general, **John Kurkuas,** in the east. He took the modern Erzerum (928) and Melitene (934), and extended the imperial power to the Euphrates and Tigris.

920. Official reunion with Rome.

924. The piratical fleets of **Leo of Tripoli** were completely defeated off **Lemnos.** Nevertheless, the Moslem pirates continued to be the scourge of the Mediterranean.

927. The empire suffered from a **great famine,** which probably explains the stringent legislation of the government to prevent the purchase of small holdings by the great landed magnates.

941. A great armada of Russians, under **Prince Igor,** was signally defeated by the Greeks.

944. The Emperor Romanus was seized and imprisoned (d. 948) by the very sons whose interests he had attempted to serve. The Emperor Constantine became officially the sole ruler, but governed with the aid of the great general, **Bardas Phocas,** and under the influence of the Empress Helena and her favorite, Basil.

957. Visit to Constantinople and baptism of **Princess Olga** of Russia.

959-963. ROMANUS II, the young and dissipated son of Constantine.

961. Reconquest of Crete from the Saracen

pirates. A great armada was sent out under Nicephorus Phocas. Candia was stormed, the Moslems expelled from the island or converted to Christianity.

962. Otto I, Roman emperor in the west, claimed suzerainty over the Lombards in southern Italy, initiating a period of friction with Constantinople, which was only temporarily broken by the marriage of Otto II and the Byzantine princess, Theophano (972).

963-1025. BASIL II, an infant at the death of his father. The principle of legitimacy was carefully respected, but before Basil II really assumed power, the empire was governed by two great generals associated with him.

963-969. NICEPHORUS PHOCAS, who had carried on a successful campaign in the east. He seized control and married the widowed Empress Theophano. Never popular, especially with the clergy, Nicephorus, by his victories in the field, helped to raise the empire to its greatest glory.

964-968. Victorious campaign in the east. Adana was taken (964) and then Tarsus (965). Cyprus was reconquered and in 968 northern Syria was invaded. **Aleppo** and even **Antioch** fell into the hands of the Greeks.

966-969. The Bulgarian campaign, carried through with the aid of Sviatoslav and the Russians. The latter, with their fleets, were so successful on the Danube that the Greeks made peace with the Bulgars.

969. Nicephorus Phocas was overthrown by a conspiracy of officers led by his own nephew

969-976. JOHN ZIMISCES, an Armenian by birth and one of the greatest of Byzantine generals.

969. Sviatoslav, the Russian, crossed the Balkan Mountains and took Philippopolis. John Zimisces marched against him, defeated him near Adrianople, and, with the aid of the Byzantine fleet on the Danube, forced him to evacuate Bulgaria (972). John thereupon annexed eastern Bulgaria as far as the Danube to the empire. The Patriarchate of Preslav was abolished.

971. A great feudal insurrection, led by Bardas Phocas, was put down only with difficulty.

972-976. Continuation of the campaigns in the east. John took Edessa and Nezib (974), Damascus and Beyrut (976), and ad-

vanced to the very gates of Jerusalem, where he was halted by the Moslem forces from Egypt.

976. Sudden **death of John Zimisces,** at the early age of 51.

976-1025. BASIL II (*Bulgaroktonos = Slayer of the Bulgarians*) now became sole emperor. He was only 20 years old, but serious and energetic, cynical and cruel. Until 989 he was much influenced by Basil the Eunuch, the illegitimate son of Romanus Lecapenus. The reign of Basil began with another great feudal upheaval, led by Bardas Skleros, who marched his armies from the east through Anatolia and to Constantinople. Basil appealed to Bardas Phocas, defeated leader of the earlier rising, to save the situation, which he did by defeating Skleros at Pankalia (979).

976-1014. Tsar Samuel of Bulgaria. He built up another great Bulgarian empire, with its capital at Ochrid and extending from the Adriatic to the Black Sea and from the Danube to the Peloponnesus. In 981 he defeated Basil near Sofia.

987. Rising of Bardas Phocas and Bardas Skleros against Basil and the imperial authority. The great feudal barons overran Anatolia. In 988 they threatened Constantinople, but the movement collapsed with the defeat of Phocas at Abydos (989) and his subsequent death. Skleros then submitted.

989. Conversion of Prince Vladimir of Russia, at Cherson. This initiated the general conversion of the Russians to eastern Christianity and the close connection between Kiev and Constantinople.

992. Extensive trade privileges in the empire were granted to **Venice,** by this time quite independent of imperial control, but in close co-operation with Constantinople in the Adriatic.

995. Victorious campaigns of the emperor in the east. Aleppo and Homs were taken and Syria incorporated with the empire.

996. Land legislation of Basil II. Many of the great estates were confiscated and divided among the peasants and provision made to prevent the further development of feudalism.

996-1014. THE GREAT BULGARIAN CAMPAIGNS. In 996 Basil defeated Samuel on the Spercheios River and reconquered Greece. In 1002 he overran Macedonia. Samuel recovered, however, reconquered Macedonia and sacked Adrianople (1003). In 1007 Basil subdued Macedonia again and after years of indecisive conflict annihilated the Bulgarian army at **Balathista** (1014). He sent several thousand blinded soldiers back to Samuel, who died of the shock. The Bulgarians finally submitted (1018), but were left their autonomy and an autocephalous church at Ochrid. Many of the Bulgarian noble families settled in Constantinople and merged with the Greek and Armenian aristocracy.

1018. The Byzantine forces won a great victory over the combined Lombards and Normans at **Cannae,** thus assuring continuance of the Greek domination in southern Italy.

1020. The King of Armenia, long in alliance with the Greeks against the Arabs, turned over his kingdom to Basil to escape the new threat from the Seljuk Turks. Thereby the empire became firmly established in Transcaucasia and along the Euphrates.

BYZANTINE CULTURE reached its apogee in the late 10th and early 11th centuries. The empire extended from Italy to Mesopotamia and its influence radiated much farther. Constantinople, indeed, was the economic and artistic center of the Mediterranean world.

Government: The emperor was an absolute ruler, regarded almost as sacred. Under the Macedonian emperors the idea of legitimacy became firmly established. The imperial court reflected the emperor's power and splendor. There was an extensive and elaborate ceremonial (cf. the *Book of Ceremonies* of Constantine Porphyrogenitus); the administration was highly centralized in Constantinople and was unique for its efficiency; the treasury was full and continued to draw a large income from taxes, customs, and monopolies; the army and navy were both at the peak of their development, with excellent organization and leadership; the provinces were governed by the *strategoi*; there were, by this time 30 *themes* (18 in Asia and 12 in Europe), but throughout this period there was a steady growth in the number and power of the provincial magnates (*dunatoi*), feudal barons who acquired more and more of the small holdings and exercised an ever greater influence, even challenging the emperor himself. All the legislation of the Macedonian emperors failed to check this development.

The Church was closely connected with the throne, but during this period it too became more and more wealthy and gradually produced a clerical aristocracy. The union with Rome, when it existed, was a purely formal thing. The Greek patriarchate in practice resented the Roman claim to primacy and the popular dislike of the Latins made any real co-operation impossible.

Economic life. This was closely controlled by the state, which derived much of its income from the customs and monopolies. Yet it was a period of great commercial development, Constantinople serving as the *entrepôt* between east and west. It was also a great center of the industry in luxuries (organization of trades in rigid guilds, etc.).

Learning. The University of Constantinople (opened c. 850) had quickly become a center of philosophical and humanistic study, in which the emperors took a direct interest. In the 11th century there appeared the greatest of the Byzantine scholars, **Psellus,** reviver of the Platonic philosophy and universal genius. In the field of literature there was a conscious return to the great Greek models of the early Byzantine period; historians, **Constantine Porphyrogenitus, Leo the Deacon,** etc. The great popular epic, *Digenis Akritas*, describing the heroic life of the frontier soldiers (*Akritai*), dates from the 10th century.

Art. The period was one of extensive construction, especially in Constantinople; full exploitation of the St. Sophia type in church architecture; mosaics; ikons; gold and silver work. Byzantine influence in this period permeated the entire Mediterranean world, Moslem as well as Christian. (*Cont. p.* 251.)

b. THE FIRST BULGARIAN EMPIRE
TO 1018

The Bulgarians, first mentioned by name in 482 as a people living to the northeast of the Danube, were members of the Finno-Tatar race, probably related to the Huns and at first ruled by princes of Attila's family. They were organized on the clan system, worshiped the sun and moon, practiced human sacrifice, etc.

584-642. KURT, or **KUBRAT,** of the Dulo family, the first authenticated ruler. His dominions lay in the eastern steppes, from the Don to the Caucasus. In 619 he visited Constantinople to secure aid against the Avars, at which time he became converted to Christianity, though this step seems to have had no consequences for his people.

643-701. Isperikh (*Asperich*), the son or grandson of Kurt. The old Great Bulgaria was disrupted by the attacks of Avars and Khazars, and various tribes of Bulgars moved westward into Pannonia and even into Italy. Those under Isperikh crossed the Danube (650-670) and established a capital at Pliska. In 680 they defeated a Byzantine army and occupied the territory between the Danube and the Balkan Mountains. At the same time they still held Wallachia, Moldavia, and Bessarabia. The amalgamation with the Slavic inhabitants was probably very gradual, the upper, military classes remaining strictly Bulgar for a long time.

701-718. **Tervel,** who established friendly relations with the Emperor Justinian II, who paid a subsidy or tribute to the Bulgars, but only after the imperial forces had been defeated at Anchialus (708) and after Tervel had advanced to the very gates of Constantinople (712).

718-724. Ruler unknown.

724-739. **Sevar,** during whose reign the peace with the empire was maintained. The Dulo dynasty came to an end with Sevar, whose death was followed by an obscure struggle of noble factions.

739-756. **Kormisosh,** of the Ukil family. Until the very end of his reign he maintained peace with the empire, until further domestic disorders gave the signal for Byzantine attacks (755 ff.).

756-761. **Vinekh,** who was killed in the course of an uprising.

761-764. **Telets,** of the Ugain family. He was defeated at Anchialus by the Byzantines (763) and put to death by the Bulgarians.

764. **Sabin,** of the family of Kormisosh. He was deposed and fled to Constantinople.

? 764. **Pagan,** who finally concluded peace with the emperor.

766. **Umor,** who was deposed by

766. **Tokt,** who was captured and killed by the Greeks. This entire period is one of deep obscurity, the years 766–773 being a complete blank.

? 773-777. **Telerig,** whose family is unknown. The Greeks renewed their attacks, which were on the whole successful and resulted in the subjugation of Bulgaria.

777-791. Ruler unknown.

? 791-797. **Kardam,** whose reign marked the turning of the tide. He took advantage of the confusion in the empire to defeat the Greeks at **Marcellae** (792) and to relay the foundations of the state. What happened after his death is unknown.

808-814. **KRUM,** one of the greatest Bulgarian rulers. He appears to have been a Pannonian Bulgar, who rose to power as a result of his victories over the Avars. During his short reign he organized the state and encouraged the Slav elements at the expense of the Bulgar aristocracy. His objective seems to have been the establishment of the absolute power of the khan. For five years (808–813) he carried on war with the Byzantine Empire. The Greeks sacked Pliska (809; 811), but Krum defeated and killed the emperor in a battle in the mountains (811). In 812 he took the important fortress of Mesembria and in 813 won another victory at Versinicia. In the same year he appeared at Constantinople. The city was too strong for him, but he retired, devastating Thrace and taking Adrianople.

814-831. **Omortag,** the son of Krum. After a defeat by the Greeks (815), he concluded a thirty-year peace with them (817), returning Mesembria and Adrianople. Construction of the earthwork barrier (the *Great Fence*) on the Thracian frontier. Founding of the new capital, **Great Preslav** (821). During the peace in the east, the Bulgars began systematic raids into Croatia and Pannonia (827–829).

831-852. **Malamir,** the son of Omortag, the period of whose reign is vague, excepting for gradual expansion into upper Macedonia and Serbia (839).

852-889. **BORIS I.** He continued the campaigns in the west, but suffered severe defeats by the Germans (853) and a setback from the Serbs (860). Boris' reign was important chiefly for his

865. **Conversion to Christianity.** The way had undoubtedly been prepared by numerous prisoners of war, but Boris was induced to take the step under pressure from Constantinople, where the government was eager to frustrate a possible German-Roman advance. Boris had all his subjects baptized, which led to a revolt and the execution of a number of noble leaders. For some time Boris was undecided whether to lean toward Rome or toward Constantinople. To counteract the aggressive Greek influence he accepted the primacy of Rome (866), but then turned to Constantinople (870) when the pope refused to appoint an archbishop for Bulgaria. In 885 the Slavonic liturgy was introduced among the Slavs of Bulgaria by the successors of Cyril and Methodius. In 889 Boris voluntarily retired to a monastery.

889-893. **Vladimir,** the son of Boris, who was soon exposed to a violent aristocratic, heathen reaction.

893. **Boris** re-emerged from retirement, put down the revolt, deposed and blinded his son, completed the organization of the Church

and made the Slavonic liturgy general in its application. The capital was definitely moved to Preslav. Boris then returned to his monastery, where he died (907).

893-927. SYMEON, another son of Boris, the first Bulgarian ruler to assume the title *Tsar.* Symeon had been educated at Constantinople, as a monk. He was deeply imbued with Greek culture and did much to encourage translations from the Greek. Splendor of Great Preslav and Symeon's court; development of a second cultural center at Ochrid, under St. Clement and St. Nahum.

894-897. Symeon's reign was filled with **wars against the Byzantine Empire,** which grew originally out of disputes regarding trade rights and ultimately developed into a contest for possession of the imperial throne. The war began in 894, with the defeat of a Greek army. The emperor thereupon induced the Magyars, located on the Pruth River, to attack the Bulgarians in Bessarabia (895). Symeon induced the Greeks by trickery to withdraw and then defeated the Magyars, after which he returned and fell on the Greeks at Bulgarophygon. Peace was made in 897, the emperor paying tribute.

In the meanwhile the **Magyars,** driven westward by the Patzinaks (Pechenegs), advanced into Transylvania and Pannonia, which were lost to the Bulgars.

913. Symeon, taking advantage of the dynastic troubles in the empire, advanced to Constantinople, but withdrew with many presents and the promise that the young emperor, Constantine Porphyrogenitus, should marry one of his daughters. Symeon evidently hoped to attain the crown for himself, but was frustrated by the seizure of power by Zoë. He thereupon made war (914), raiding into Macedonia, Thessaly, and Albania. But the Patzinaks, instigated by the Greeks, invaded and occupied Wallachia (917), while Symeon defeated the Greeks near **Anchialus** (917). In 918 Symeon defeated the Serbs, who had also been aroused by the empress.

919-924. Symeon four times advanced to the Hellespont and Constantinople, but was unable to take the city because of his lack of a fleet. In 924 he had an interview with the Emperor Romanus Lecapenus and finally made peace.

925. Symeon proclaimed himself **Emperor of the Romans and the Bulgars.** The Greek emperor protested, but the pope recognized the title.

926. Symeon set up Leontius of Preslav as a patriarch.

926. Conquest and devastation of Serbia.

927-969. Peter, the son of Symeon, a pious, well-intentioned but weak ruler, who married the granddaughter of Romanus Lecapenus. Peace with Constantinople was maintained, the Greek emperor recognizing the Bulgar ruler as emperor and acknowledging the Bulgarian patriarchate. Bulgaria was, during this period, occupied by the constant threat from the Magyars (raids, 934, 943, 958, 962) and the Patzinaks (great raid of 944). Internally the period seems to have been one of unrest and religious ferment (founding of monasteries; St. John of Rila; beginning of the **Bogomil heresy,** c. 950, a dualistic creed possibly inspired by the Paulicians settled in the Thracian region by the Byzantine emperors).

967. Invasion of Bulgaria by Sviatoslav and the Russians. Tsar Peter roused the Patzinaks, who attacked Kiev in 968 and forced Sviatoslav to withdraw.

969-972. Boris II. The reign was filled with the second invasion of Sviatoslav, who took Preslav and captured Boris and his family (969). The Greeks, in alarm, sent an army against him and defeated him at **Arcadiopolis** (970). In 972 the Emperor John Zimisces attacked the Russians by land and sea. He took Preslav and destroyed it, besieged Sviastoslav at Dristra on the Danube and finally forced him to evacuate Bulgaria. Boris was obliged to abdicate, the patriarchate was abolished, and Bulgaria came to an end as a separate state.

976-1014. SAMUEL, son of a governor of one of the western districts, which had been unaffected by the Russian invasion, set himself up as ruler. He soon expanded his domain to Sofia, and re-established the patriarchate (ultimately fixed at Ochrid, which was the center of the new state).

986-989. Samuel took Larissa after several annual raids into Thessaly and c. 989 took also Dyrrhacium on the Adriatic coast. In the east he extended his power to the Black Sea.

996-1014. The campaigns of Basil II (*Bulgaroktonos = Slayer of the Bulgarians*) against Samuel. Basil proceeded to reduce one stronghold after another. Samuel avoided open battle as much as possible, but throughout suffered from defection of his leaders, who were bribed by attractive offers by the emperor. The crowning defeat of the Bulgarians at Balathista (1014) and the sight of his 15,000 blinded warriors brought on Samuel's death.

1014-1016. Gabriel Radomir (or *Romanus*),

the son of Samuel. He tried to make peace, but was murdered by his cousin

1016-1018. John Vladislav, who continued the war, but was killed in a battle near Dyrrhacium. He left only young sons. The Bulgar leaders thereupon decided to submit. Bulgaria was incorporated into the Byzantine Empire (*themes* of Bulgaria and Paristrium); the patriarchate was abolished, but the Archbishop of Ochrid retained practical autonomy. The Bulgarian aristocracy settled in Constantinople and merged with the leading Greek families.

(*Cont. p.* 250.)

3. THE MOSLEM WORLD

a. MOHAMMED AND ISLAM

Arabia before the time of Mohammed was inhabited by tribes of Semitic race, those in the desert areas (*Bedouins*) of nomadic, pastoral habits, those in the coastal valleys along the Red Sea (Hedjaz, Yemen) much more settled, engaged in agriculture and trade. The towns of Mecca and Medina were centers of considerable commercial and cultural development, in which Greek and Jewish influence was probably quite marked.

570-632. MOHAMMED. He was the posthumous son of Abdullah of the Hashimite sept of Mecca. Having lost his mother when about six, he was brought up by his grandfather, Abdul-Muttalib, and his uncle, Abu Talib. Mohammed became a merchant in the caravan trade, serving Khadija, a widow of means whom he married when he was about 25, thus achieving for himself a modest independence. Given to religious meditation and affected by the Christian and Jewish ideas and practices, he began his prophetic career about 612, preaching the One God, the Last Judgment, Alms, Prayers, and surrender to the will of God (Islam). Gaining a few adherents, but rejected and persecuted by his townsmen, he and his followers fled to Medina, on July 2, 622.

622, July 16. The traditional (though erroneous) date of **Mohammed's flight** (*Hijrah, Hegira*). This date has been adopted as the beginning of the Moslem era.

622-632. In Medina, Mohammed organized the **commonwealth of Islam** by welding together the Meccan fugitives and the Medinan tribes in and around the town (the Aus and the Khazraj), and expelling or devoting the Jewish tribes, into a community based on the will of God as revealed to his prophet, and on the common law of the tribesmen. At the same time he carried on war against the Meccans.

624-630. The Moslems defeated the Meccans at **Badr** (624), but were themselves defeated at Ohod (625). The Meccans thereupon besieged Medina (627), but were repulsed. By the **Treaty of Hudaybiya** (628): Mohammed and his followers were granted permission to make the pilgrimage to Mecca. When the treaty was broken by the allies of the Meccans, the war was resumed and Mohammed took Mecca (630). Many of the Arab tribes were subdued before Mohammed's death (632).

The **six essential articles of the Moslem faith** are: Belief in the One God, **Allah,** in his angels, and in his prophets, of whom Mohammed is the last and greatest; belief in his revealed books, of which the *Koran* is the last and the only one necessary; belief in the Day of Resurrection, and in God's predestination, which determines the fate and the actions of men.

The **five fundamental duties** are: The five daily prayers; the fast in the month of Ramadhan; the Zakāt, or legal alms; the pilgrimage to Mecca; and the Holy War.

632-661. The Orthodox Caliphate, including the first four caliphs.

632-634. Abu Bakr, the first caliph or vicegerent of the Prophet, chosen by acclamation. Defeat of the so-called false prophets, Tulayha and Musaylima; reduction of the rebellious tribes (632).

632-738. EXPANSION BEYOND ARABIA. First incursion into Iraq (Persia) under **Khalid ibn al-Walid** (633). Hira, the ancient Lakhmid capital, and Obolla taken and put to ransom. The main advance, however, was against Syria. Defeat of Theodore, brother of the Emperor Heraclius, at Ajnadayn (*Jannabatayn*) between Gaza and Jerusalem (634). Death of Abu Bakr, who appointed as his successor,

634-644. Omar, who first assumed the title of *Amir al-Mu'minin* (*Prince of the Faithful*) and established the primacy of the Arabs over their taxpaying subjects.

Conquest of Syria. Defeat of the Byzantines under Baanes at Marj al-Saffar, near Damascus,

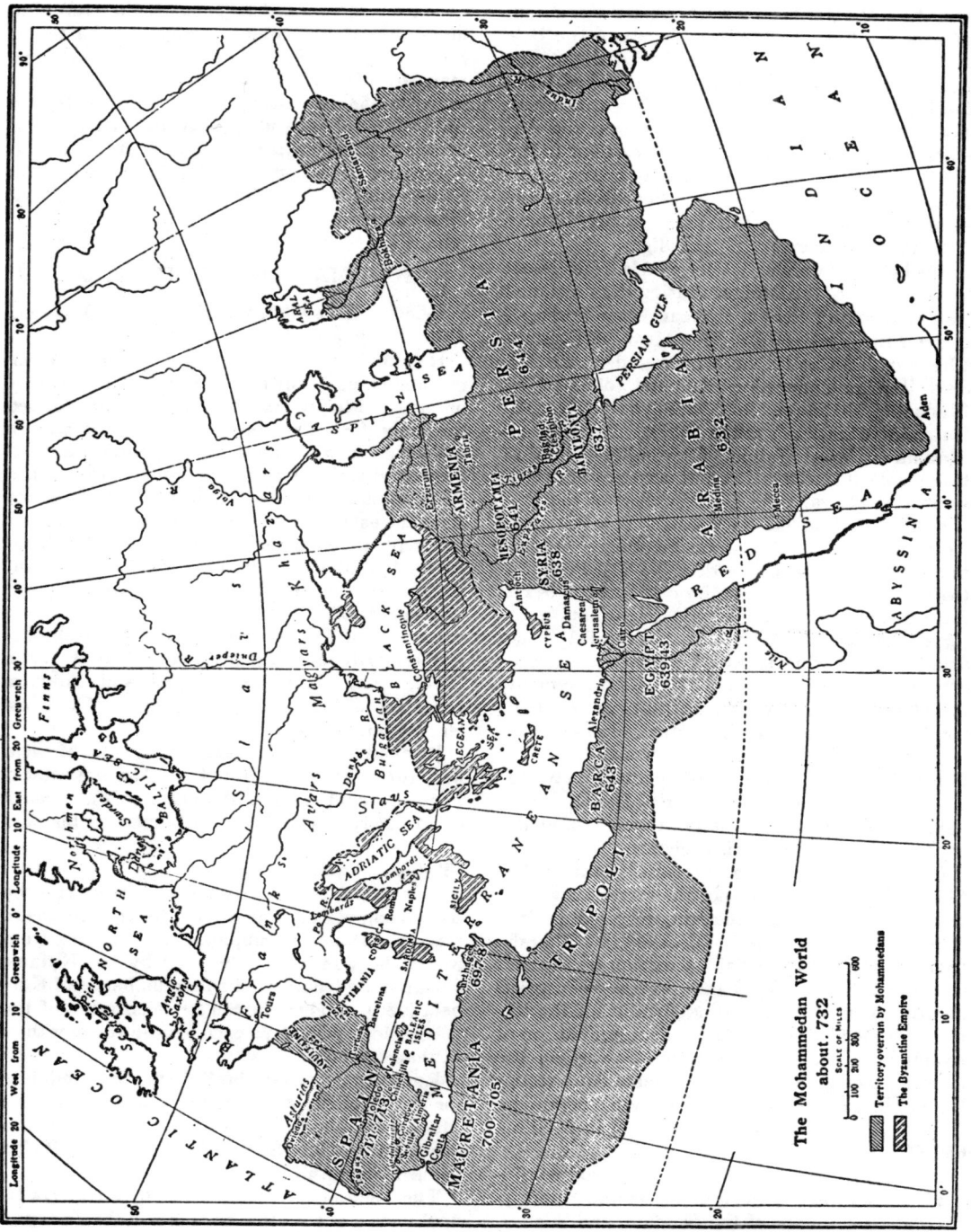

The Mohammedan World
about. 732

SCALE OF MILES

100 200 300   600

☐ Territory overrun by Mohammedans

▨ The Byzantine Empire

by Khalid (635). Damascus and Emessa taken, only to be given up, however, under the pressure of superior forces. Decisive defeat of the Byzantines at **Yarmuk**, south of the Lake of Tiberias (636). Damascus and Emessa retaken. Subjugation of northern Syria, Aleppo and Antioch taken. Capitulation of Jerusalem (638). Caesarea captured (640). The seacoast occupied. Northern boundary of the caliphate the Amanus Mountains. Subjugation of Mesopotamia (639–641).

Conquest of Persia. After a disastrous defeat at the **Battle of the Bridge**, the Moslems resumed their attack on Persia. Invasion and occupation of Iraq (635–637). Defeat of the Persians under Mihran at Buwayb by Muthanna (635). The Persian chancellor, Rustam, defeated by Sa'd ibn al-Waqqas at **Qadisiya** (637). Al-Madain (*Ctesiphon*) taken (637). Persians defeated again at Jalula, fifty miles north of Madain (637). Invasion and occupation of central Persia (638–650). Final defeat of the Persians at Nehawand (641).

Conquest of Egypt. Invasion of Egypt by the Arabs under Amr ibn al-'As (639). Pelusium taken (640). Byzantines defeated at Heliopolis (640). Death of the Emperor Heraclius (641). Capture of Babylon (642). Capitulation of Egypt arranged by Cyrus, Patriarch of Alexandria (642). Terms: security of person and property guaranteed to the inhabitants on payment of a tribute and free exercise of their religion. Omar assassinated (644). His successor was chosen by a body of electors.

644–656. Othman, a member of the Omayyad family of Mecca, notorious for his nepotism. The official redaction of the *Koran* made by Zayd ibn Thabit in this reign.

Occupation of Barqa and the Pentapolis (642–643). Revolt of Alexandria, inspired by the appearance of a Byzantine fleet (645). The city retaken by assault (645). Creation of an Arab fleet by Abdullah ibn Sa'd, governor of Egypt. Capture of Cyprus (649) and Aradus (650). Expedition against Constantinople, annihilation of the Byzantine fleet at Dhat al-Sawari on the Lycian coast (655). Disaffection of Arab troops in Iraq and Egypt owing to Othman's nepotism, led to the assassination of Othman in Medina. He was succeeded by

656–661. Ali, the prophet's cousin and son-in-law, whose succession was disputed.

First civil war. Revolt of Talha and Zobayr, two old companions of the Prophet, and 'Aisha, the Prophet's favorite wife, in Iraq. They seized Basra, but were defeated by Ali in the **Battle of the Camel**, near that town.

Revolt of Mo'awiya, Omayyad governor of Syria, who demanded revenge for the murder of his kinsman, Othman. Indecisive battle at **Siffin** (657). Hostilities suspended by an agreement to arbitrate the dispute. Arbitration of Adhroh (658). Rejection of the decision by Ali, who was deserted and opposed by a party of his followers, the Kharijites, whom he decimated at Nahrawan. Egypt taken for Mo'awiya by its first conqueror, Amr (658). Murder of Ali by a Kharijite.

b. THE OMAYYAD CALIPHATE, 661–750

661–680. Mo'awiya, founder of the Omayyad dynasty.

Hasan, Ali's eldest son, was proclaimed caliph, but abdicated in the face of Mo'awiya's advance on Iraq. Mo'awiya, who had been proclaimed caliph in Jerusalem in 660, moved the seat of government to Damascus. Expedition against Constantinople, Chalcedon taken, Constantinople besieged (669). Ifriqiya (North Africa from the eastern limits of Algeria to the frontiers of Egypt) invaded and the conquest consolidated by the founding of Qairawan by 'Oqba ibn Nafi' (670). In the east under Mo'awiya's brilliant viceregent, Ziyad ibn Abihi, Sind and the lower valley of the Indus were overrun by Mohallib. Eastern Afghanistan invaded. Kabul taken (664). The Oxus was crossed and Bokhara captured (674). Samarcand taken (676). Moslem advance to the Jaxartes.

Blockade of Constantinople by the Moslem fleet (673–678). Failure of the Moslem attack. Peace concluded for thirty years (678). Death of Mo'awiya, who had proclaimed as his successor in 676,

680–682. Yazid I.

The second civil war. Husayn, the second son of Ali, was invited by the Kufans in Iraq to assume the caliphate. Advancing from Mecca he was basely deserted by the Kufans, defeated, and slain at the famous **battle of Kerbela** (680), whence the Shi'ite celebration of the martyrdom of Husayn each year in the month of Muharram.

Revolt of Abdullah ibn Zubayr, the candidate for the caliphate supported by the Meccans and Medinans. Defeat of the Medinans on the Harra near the town. Siege of Mecca; the Ka'ba burned. Death of Yazid.

The son and successor of Yazid, **Mo'awiya II,** died some months after his father. **Ibn Zubayr's** caliphate accepted in Arabia, Iraq, Egypt, and by the adherents of the Qais tribe in Syria. The Omayyad party with its adherents of the Kalb tribe chose **Marwan ibn al-Hakam,** a cousin of Mo'awiya I. The Qais were defeated with great slaughter at Marj Rahit (684), north of Damascus, which began the disastrous feud between the so-called northern and southern Arabs, which was largely responsible for the fall of the Arab kingdom of the Omayyads.

684-750. THE MARWANIDS.

684-685. Marwan I. Proclaimed caliph in Syria. Egypt was recovered from **Ibn Zubayr.** Death of Marwan. He was succeeded by his son,

685-705. Abdulmalik, creator of the Arab administration of the empire.

Inroads of the Mardaites of the Amanus, encouraged by the Byzantines, occupied Abdulmalik's first years. His rival, Ibn Zubayr, was occupied by Shi'ite and Kharijite revolts in Kufa and Basra, Arabia and Persia.

The **Shi'ite sect** were supporters of the claims of the "House of the Prophet," the descendants of the Caliph **Ali,** and of the prophet's daughter, Fatima. Later they developed the dogma of the **Imamate,** that the Imam (the leader of the people) was the representative or incarnation of the deity and the only seat of authority both religious and civil.

The **Kharijites** held that any Moslem in good standing could be elected by the community as caliph. They held that *Works* were an essential part of religion and that those who committed mortal sins were unbelievers. Both sects were bitter opponents of both the Omayyad and the Abbasid dynasties.

Mus'ab, Ibn Zubayr's brother and governor in Iraq, was defeated by Abdulmalik on the Tigris (690). Medina was captured by Abdulmalik's general, Hajjaj, later his governor in Iraq (691). Mecca was besieged and captured (692). Ibn Zubayr was killed and Abdulmalik became undisputed master of the empire. The Kharijites (Azraqites) were crushed in Iraq and Persia by Muhallib (693-698). A rebellion in the east under Ibn al-Ash'ath, who was proclaimed caliph, was put down by Hajjaj (699). Kabul retaken

In Africa **Oqba ibn Nafi,** now a saint, had raided as far as Tangier, but had met death on his return march (683). Carthage, however, was finally taken (698), and peace concluded with the Berbers, after they had defeated the Arabs under Hassan ibn No'man near Mons Aurasius (703). Thereupon the Berbers became allies of the Arabs. Death of Abdulmalik. He was succeeded by his son,

705-715. Walid I, who built the cathedral mosque at Damascus. Conquest of

Transoxania under Qutayba (705-715). Bokhara taken (709), Ferghana (712). It is reported that Qutayba invaded China and reached Kashgar (c. 713). Conquest of Sind and part of the Punjab by Mohammed ibn Qasim (708-715).

Invasion of Cilicia (710-711) **and of Galatia** (714). Preparations for a grand attack on Constantinople by land and sea. Subjugation of the western Berbers and pacification of North Africa by Musa ibn Nusayr (708-711).

711-715. CONQUEST OF SPAIN. Invasion of Spain by a mixed force of Arabs and Berbers under Tariq, a freed slave of Musa (711). The Goths under their king, Roderick, were totally defeated in Wadi Bekka, near Rio Barbate (not at Xeres de la Frontera) (July, 711). Fall of Ecija, Cordova, and the capital, Toledo. Tariq master of half of Spain. The advance of Musa himself (712). Capture of Medina Sidonia, Carmona, Seville (712), Merida (713), and Saragossa. Resistance to Arab arms continued only in the mountains of Asturias. Death of Walid. He was succeeded by his brother,

715-717. Sulayman. Conquest of Jurjan (*Hyrcania*) and Tabaristan by Yazid ibn Mohallib (716). Siege of Constantinople by the caliph's brother, Maslama (717-718), which failed. The crossing of the Pyrenees and invasion of southern France by Hurr, the successor of Musa. Sulayman succeeded by his cousin,

717-720. Omar ibn Abdul-Aziz, who attempted to reorganize the finances of the empire. Members of the subject races, who had become Moslems, were placed on the same footing as the Arabs in respect to taxation. Narbonne in southern France taken by Samh, the successor of Hurr. Omar was succeeded by the third son of Abdulmalik,

720-724. Yazid II. Samh was defeated and killed by the Duke Eudo before Toulouse (721). Revolt of Yazid ibn Muhallib in Iraq. His defeat at Akra on the Euphrates by Maslama. Outbreak of internecine strife between the Yemenites (Kalb) and Modharites (Qais) (the so-called southern and northern Arabs) throughout the empire, especially in Khorasan and Transoxania, where propaganda for the Abbasids (descendants of the prophet's uncle, Abbas) also began. Yazid was succeeded by his brother,

724-743. Hisham. Defeat of the Khazars, conquest of Georgia (727-733).

738. Kharijite revolts in Iraq, insurrection of Sogdians and Arabs in Khorasan supported by the Turkomans of Transoxania, was quelled by Asad al-Kasri, governor of Khorasan.

738. **Invasion of southern France** by Abdurrahman, governor of Spain; his defeat at Poitiers (Tours) by Charles Martel.

740. **Shi'ite revolt in Iraq** under Zayd, grandson of the martyred Husayn; his defeat and death. Hisham was succeeded by his nephew.

741-742. **The Revolt of the Kharijites and Berbers** in North Africa was put down by Hanzala, the viceroy in North Africa.

743-744. **Walid II,** who was killed in a Yemenite revolt led by his cousin, who succeeded him as **Yazid III,** only to die a few months later. He was succeeded by the last Omayyad

744-756. **Marwan II,** the grandson of Marwan I. Insurrections in Syria at Homs and in Palestine. Kharijite revolt in Mesopotamia (745), and in Arabia (745-746). Mecca and Medina seized by the rebels. Shi'ite insurrection in Iraq and Persia under Abdullah, grandson of Ali's brother, Ja'far, which was joined by Kharijites and Abbasids (745-747). The black standard of the Abassids was raised by **Abu Muslim** in Khorasan (747). Marwan's governor of Khorasan, Nasr, was defeated at Nishapur and Jurjan by Abu Muslim's general, Kahtaba, who routed the Omayyad forces again at Nehawand and Kerbela. Marwan himself was defeated at the **battle of the Zab,** and was pursued to Busir, Egypt, and killed (750). Slaughter of the Omayyad princes. Few escaped, but among those was **Abdurrahman,** grandson of Hisham, who later founded the Omayyad Kingdom of Cordova in Spain (755).

c. THE ABBASID CALIPHATE, 750-c. 1100

750-1258. **THE ABBASID CALIPHATE.** Spain never recognized it, nor did Morocco. Abbasid authority was re-established in the Province of Africa as far as Algiers in 761, but only for a short period.

750-754. **Abu-l-Abbas al-Saffah,** the first Abbasid caliph. Omayyad revolts in Syria and Mesopotamia. Byzantine raids into the northern provinces. Abu al-Saffah was succeeded by his brother,

754-775. **AL-MANSUR,** the real founder of the dynasty. The revolt of his uncle, Abdullah, governor of Syria, was crushed by Abu Muslim, who was then murdered at Mansur's orders (754). Revolt of Abu Muslim's followers in Khorasan (755). A Byzantine invasion was repulsed with great slaughter. Cappa-

docia reoccupied; Malitia (*Melitene*), Mopsuestia, and other cities rebuilt and fortified against Byzantine raids (758). Annexation of Tabaristan (759); Shi'ite revolt in Iraq and Medina under the Hasanids, Mohammed and Ibrahim (762). Foundation of Baghdad (762). Khazar invasion of Georgia repelled (762). Insurrection of Ustad Sis in Khorasan and Sistan (767). Rise of the **Barmecides** to power as viziers of the realm (752-803). Mansur was succeeded by his son,

775-785. **AL-MAHDI,** noted for his improvement of the communications of the empire. his fortification of important centers, his founding of towns and schools, and his encouragement of the arts.

Persecution of the Manichaeans. Revolt of the veiled prophet, **Mokanna,** in Khorasan (775-778). Rise of a communistic, nihilistic sect, the Zindiqs, in Khorasan, western Persia, and Iraq. Invasion of the Byzantines, who were routed. Moslem advance against Constantinople; the Empress Irene forced to sue for peace (783-785). Mahdi was succeeded by his son,

785. **Al-Hadi,** who reigned only a year and was succeeded by

785-809. **HARUN AL-RASHID** (of *Arabian Nights'* fame). Kabul and Sanhar were annexed to the empire (787). Khazar invasion of Armenia (799). Fall of the Barmecides (803). Kharijite revolts.

791-809. **War with the Byzantines.** Defeat of the Emperor Nicephorus at Heraclea or Dorylaeum (798). The peace, which was concluded, was broken by Nicephorus, and the Moslems invaded Asia Minor led by the caliph in person. Capture of Tyana (806). Advance to Ancyra. Meanwhile Cyprus (805) and Rhodes (807) were ravaged by the Moslem fleet. Iconium and Ephesus in Lydia captured, Sideropolis, Andrasus, and Nicaea reduced. Heraclea Pontica on the Black Sea taken by storm. Nicephorus again invaded Moslem territory in 808, but troubles in Khorasan compelled Harun to march east, where he died. In his reign the **Hanafite school of law** began to assume a systematic form. He was succeeded by his son,

809-813. **AL-AMIN,** against whom his brother Mamun rebelled and was accepted as caliph in Persia. Siege of Baghdad by Mamun's general, Tahir (813). Amin was murdered after surrendering on terms.

813-833. **MAMUN THE GREAT.** His reign probably the most glorious epoch in the history of the caliphate. The arts and sciences were liberally endowed. Two observatories were built, one near Damascus, the other near Baghdad. A *House of Knowledge*, provided with a rich library, was erected near the Baghdad Observatory. Literary, scientific, and philosophical works were translated from Greek, Syriac, Persian, and Sanscrit. A liberal religious attitude adopted. **Mu'tazilitism** became the established faith. The Mu'tazilites maintained, like the Qadarites of the later Omayyad period, man's free will, also that justice and reason must control God's action toward men, both of which doctrines were repudiated by the later orthodox school of the Ash'arites.

Transference of the capital by Mamun from Merv to Baghdad, owing to Omayyad and Shi'ite revolts in Arabia, Iraq, and Mesopotamia. To meet this crisis he had proclaimed as his heir-apparent, Ali al-Ridha, a descendent of the Caliph Ali (817).

Conquest of Crete (from Egypt) by Arabs who had been expelled from Spain by the Omayyads (825); of Sicily by the Aghlabites of North Africa (827). Palermo taken (831). Only Syracuse and Taormine left in Byzantine hands.

Terrorization of the northern provinces by the Magian, **Babek,** leader of the communistic Khurramites, from his stronghold in Azerbaijan (816-833). Byzantine invasions in his support were repulsed by Mamun in person (829-833). Death of Mamun. In his reign the Tahirids of Khorasan became practically independent (820-872). Mamun was succeeded by his brother,

833-842. Al-Mu'tasim. Transference of the capital to Samarra (836). Formation of a standing military corps composed of Turkish slaves and mercenaries, of whom the later caliphs were the mere puppets.

Revolt of the Jats or **Gypsies** on the lower Tigris (834). Babek was defeated by Afshin and put to death (837-838). **War with Byzantium** (837-842). Defeat of the Byzantines at Anzen on the Halys, Ancyra destroyed; Amorium, the place of origin of the Byzantine dynasty, captured (838). Preparations for the siege of Constantinople. Arab fleet destroyed by a tempest. Death of Mu'tasim (842) and his succession by his son,

842-847. Wathiq, who continued his father's policy of aggrandizing the Turks at the expense of the Arabs and Persians. Interchange of prisoners between the Byzantines and Moslems. Wathiq's reign marks the beginning of the decline of the caliphate. He was succeeded by his brother,

847-861. Mutawakkil, who sought to re-establish the traditional Moslem faith. Mu'tazilite doctrines were abjured, their professors persecuted. Shi'ites, Jews, and Christians also persecuted. The mausoleum of Husayn, the martyr of Kerbela, was razed to the ground. Damietta in Egypt was taken and Cilicia ravaged by the Byzantines. Mutawakkil was murdered by his Turkish guard and was succeeded by his son,

861. Muntasir, who reigned only six months, when he was deposed by the Turkoman chiefs of his guard, who raised to the throne another grandson of Mu'tasim, **Musta'in** (862-866), who escaped from the Turks to Baghdad, but was forced by them to abdicate and was later murdered by an emissary of his successor, **Mu'tazz** (866-869), in whose reign Egypt became virtually independent under **Ahmad ibn Tulun,** founder of the Tulunid dynasty. Mu'tazz was murdered by his mutinous troops and succeeded by **Muqtadi** (869-870), a son of Wathiq, who was compelled to abdicate by the Turks, who chose as his successor the eldest surviving son of Mutawakkil,

870-892. Mu'tamid, who transferred the court to Baghdad; and for this and the next two reigns the power of the Turkish guard was successfully checked.

The Zenj rebellion in Chaldaea (869-883), which devastated this region for fifteen years, was put down finally by the caliph's brother, Muwaffiq. A Byzantine invasion of Syria was repelled by the Tulunid governor of Tarsus.

In this reign the caliphate lost its eastern provinces. The Saffarid dynasty was founded by Ya'qub ibn Layth, who established himself in Sistan, drove out the Tahirids of Khorasan, and became master of the whole of modern Persia. The dynasty lasted from 870 to 903, when it was extinguished by the Samanids of Transoxania, who had succeeded the Tahirids there (872), and who, after the overthrow of the Saffarids, ruled from the borders of India to Baghdad and from the Great Desert to the Persian Gulf. Their power was finally broken by the Ilak Khans of Turkestan (999), who then ruled over Transoxania, Kashgar, and eastern Tatary from Bokhara (932-1165). Under the Samanids, Bokhara was the intellectual center of Islam.

Mu'tamid was succeeded as caliph by his nephew,

892-902. Mu'tadid, who restored Egypt to the caliphate and reformed the law of inheritance. His successor, Muqtafi (902-908), brought Egypt under his direct control and repulsed the Byzantines, storming Adalia.

891-906. The Carmathian revolt. These communistic rebels overran and devastated Arabia, Syria, and Iraq, took Mecca, and carried away the sacred **Black Stone.** Muqtafi was succeeded by

908-932.   Muqtadir, his brother, during whose reign occurred the **conquest of North Africa** by the Fatimid, Obaydullah al-Mahdi, who also drove out the last Aghlabite, Ziyadatullah, from Egypt. Establishment of the Ziyarids in Tabaristan, Jurjan, Ispahan, and Hamadhan as independent sovereigns (928-1042). **Rise of the Buwayhids** (932-1055) under the patronage of the Ziyarids. Conquest and division of Persia and Iraq by the three Buwayhid brothers, Imad al-Dawla, Rukn al-Dawla, and Mu'izz al-Dawla. Mu'izz granted the title of Amir al-Umara (Prince of the Princes) by the Caliph Mustaqfi (945). The caliphs became puppets of the Amir al-Umara. The Buwayhid dominions fell piecemeal to the Ghaznawids, the Kakwayhids of Kurdistan (1007-1057), and the Seljuks, owing to divisions among the Buwayhid rulers.

962-1186.   THE GHAZNAWIDS. Founder of the dynasty was Subaktagin, a Turkish slave of Alptagin, himself slave and commander-in-chief of the Samanids in Khorasan and independent prince of the petty fief of Ghazna in the Sulayman mountains. Subaktagin defeated the Rajputs and received Khorasan from the Samanids (994). His successor, **MAHMUD** (*the Idol-Breaker*), one of the greatest figures in the history of Central Asia, became master of Khorasan (1000) and invaded India several times. His court was the resort of famous scholars and poets, such as Beiruni and Firdausi. The Ghaznawids were overthrown by the Seljuks.

929-1096. Meanwhile in Syria and Mesopotamia four Arab dynasties and one Kurdish dynasty held sway.

929-1003.   The Hamdanids of Mosul and Aleppo, the most famous of whom, **Sayf al-Dawla,** took Aleppo from the Ikhshidids of Egypt (944) and warred successfully against the Byzantines. His court was one of the brilliant centers of Islam in the 10th century. The great Arab poet, **Mutannabi,** was its chief ornament. The Hamdanids were descendants of the Arab tribe of Taghlib. Their dominions were absorbed by the Fatimids and the Buwayhids.

1023-1079.   The Mirdasids of Aleppo, of the Arab tribe of the Banu Kilab, were engaged in continual warfare with the Fatimids and the Buwayhids, and were finally driven out by the

996-1096.   'Uqaylids of Mosul, a division of the Banu Ka'b tribe, who succeeded the Hamdanids in Mosul, and whose dominions under **Muslim ibn Quraysh** extended from the neighborhood of Baghdad to Aleppo. Their domain was ultimately merged in the Seljuk Empire.

990-1096.   The Marwanids of Diyar-Bakr, established by the Kurd, Abu-l Ali ibn Marwan, ruled over Amid, Mayyarfariqun, and Aleppo. They too fell before the Seljuks.

1012-1050.   Mazyadids of Hilla, a tribe of the Banu Asad. The fourth ruler of this dynasty, The Sadaqa, was one of the great heroes of Arab history. The state was ultimately absorbed by the Zanjids.   (*Cont. p.* 257.)

B. THE AGE OF THE CRUSADES

1. WESTERN EUROPE

a. THE BRITISH ISLES

(1) *England*, 1066-1307

1066-1087. WILLIAM I (*the Conqueror*), of medium height, corpulent, but majestic in person, choleric, mendacious, greedy, a great soldier, governor, centralizer, legislator, innovator.

1066-1072. Rapid collapse, speedy submission or reduction of the south and east. The Confessor's bequest, acceptance by the Witan, and coronation " legalized " William's title. Reduction of the southwest (1068). Reduction of the rest of England (1067–1070): a series of local risings leniently dealt with; construction by forced native labor of garrison castles (Norman mounds). Great **rising of the north** (Edwin and Morca's second) with Danish aid (1069) put down by William in person. The "harrying of the north" (1069–1070), a devastation (often depopulation) of a strip from York to Durham (the consequences survived to modern times) ended Scandinavian opposition in England. **Reduction of Hereward's last stand** (the "last of the English") in the Isle of Ely (1070–1071); raid into Scotland (1072).

Norman fusion, conciliation, innovation: (1) Feudalization on centralized Norman lines (on the ruins of the nascent Saxon feudalism) followed military reduction and confiscation of the rebel lands (1066–1070). Theoretically every bit of land in England belonged to the crown; in practice only the great estates changed hands and were assigned to William's followers on Norman tenures. The king retained about one sixth of the land; less than a half of the land went to Normans on feudal tenures. Except on the border few compact holdings survived; the earldoms, reduced in size, became chiefly honorific. Some 170 great tenants-in-chief, and numerous lesser tenants emerged. A direct oath (the *Oath of Salisbury*) of primary vassalage to the crown was exacted from all vassals, making them directly responsible to the crown (1086). Construction of castles (except on the borders) subject to royal license; coinage a royal monopoly; private war prohibited. (2) **The Anglo-Saxon shires** (34) and hundreds continued for local administration and for local justice (bishops no longer sat in the shire courts and the earls were reduced) under the sheriffs (usually of baronial rank), retained from Anglo-Saxon days, but subject to removal by the king. The sheriffs were an essential link between the (native) local machinery and the central (Norman) government. Communities were held responsible for local good order; sporadic visitations of royal commissioners. Anglo-Saxon laws little altered. (3) Early grant of a charter to London guaranteeing local customs. (4) **Innovations of the centralizing monarch:** a royal council, the **Great Council** (*curia regis*), meeting infrequently (three stated meetings annually) replaced the Anglo-Saxon Witan and was of almost the same personnel: tenants-in-chief, the chancellor (introduced from Normandy by Edward the Confessor), a new official, the justiciar (in charge of justice and finance, and William's viceroy during his absences), the heads of the royal household staff. This same body, meeting frequently, and including only such tenants-in-chief as happened to be on hand, constituted the **Small Council,** a body which tended to absorb more and more of the actual administration.

The Church retained its lands (perhaps a fourth of the land in England). Pope Alexander II had blessed William's conquest, and William introduced the (much-needed) Cluniac reforms. Archbishop Stigand and most of the bishops and great abbots were deprived or died, and were replaced by zealous Norman reformers; **Lanfranc** (an Italian lawyer, a former Prior of Bec), as Archbishop of Canterbury, carried through a wide reform: celibacy enforced, chapters reorganized, new discipline in the schools, numerous new monastic foundations. By royal decree episcopal jurisdiction was separated from lay jurisdiction and the bishops given their own courts, a decisive step in the evolution of the common law as an independent force. William refused an oath of fealty to Pope Gregory VII for his English conquests, and (despite the papal decree of 1075) retained control of the appointment of bishops and important abbots, from whom he drew his chief administrators (thereby making the Church, in effect, pay for the administration of the state). No papal bull

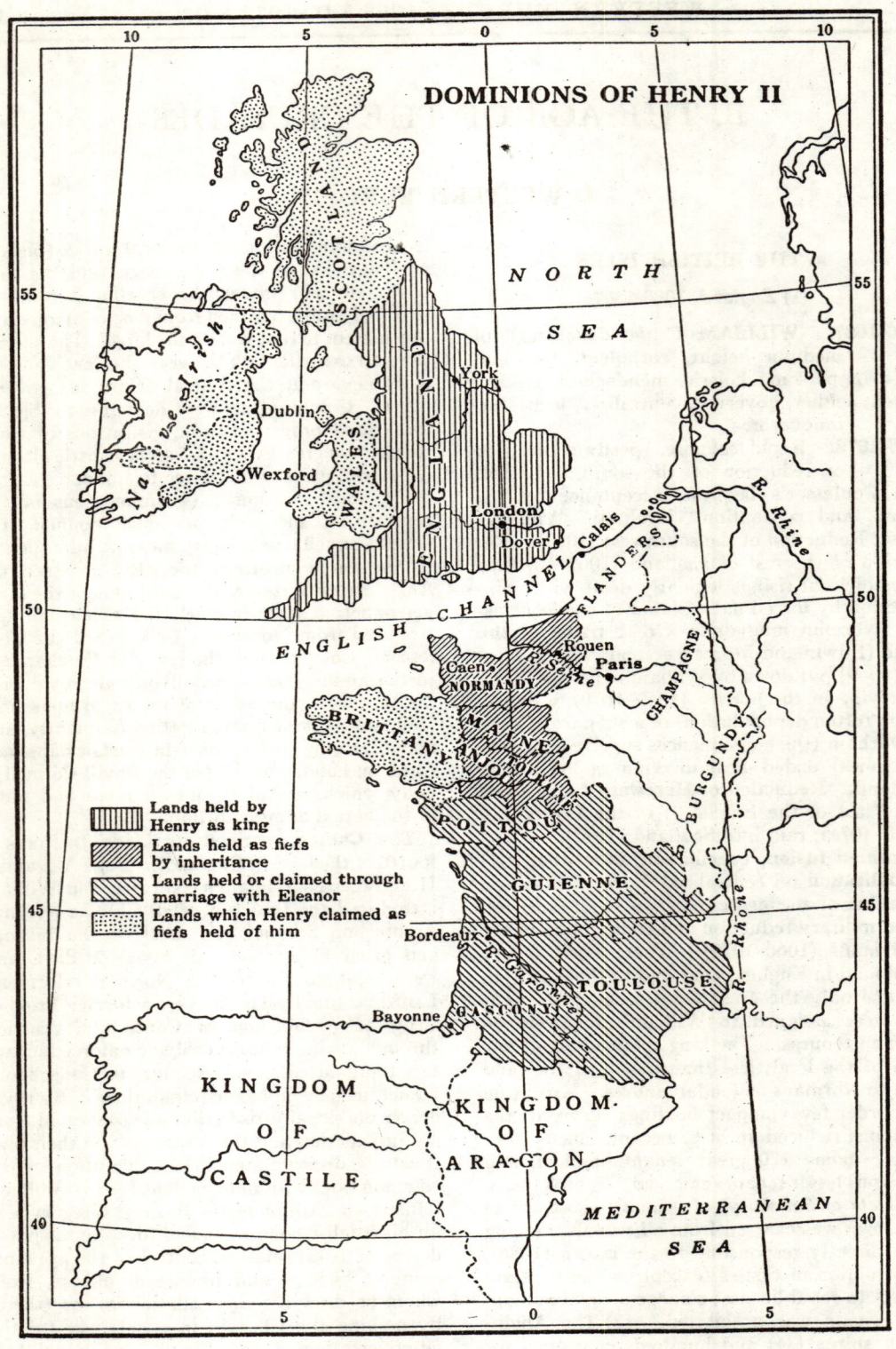

DOMINIONS OF HENRY II

Lands held by Henry as king
Lands held as fiefs by inheritance
Lands held or claimed through marriage with Eleanor
Lands which Henry claimed as fiefs held of him

NORTH SEA

SCOTLAND

Irish Sea

Navarre

Dublin

Wexford

WALES

ENGLAND

York

London

Dover

Calais

ENGLISH CHANNEL

FLANDERS

NORMANDY

Caen

Rouen

Paris

Seine

CHAMPAGNE

R. Rhine

BRITTANY

MAINE

ANJOU

TOURAINE

POITOU

BURGUNDY

GUIENNE

Bordeaux

R. Garonne

TOULOUSE

R. Rhône

Bayonne

GASCONY

KINGDOM OF CASTILE

KINGDOM OF ARAGON

MEDITERRANEAN SEA

or brief, no papal legate might be received without royal approval and no tenant-in-chief or royal officer could be excommunicated without royal permission. The king retained a right of veto on all decrees of local synods. The great prelates were required to attend the Great Council, even to do military service.

1086. The great Domesday survey: royal commissions on circuit collected on oath (sworn inquest) from citizens of the counties and vills full information as to size, resources and present and past ownership of every hide of land. The results, arranged by counties in *Domesday Book*, gave a unique record as a basis for taxation and administration.

Royal finance: (1) non-feudal revenues: Danegeld, shire farms, judicial fines; (2) the usual feudal revenues.

Military resources of the crown: (1) (non-feudal) the old Anglo-Saxon *fyrd* (including *ship fyrd*) was retained (i.e. a national non-feudal militia, loyal to the crown, was used, e.g. against the Norman rebellion of 1075); (2) (feudal) about five thousand knights' fees owing service on the usual feudal terms. The prosperity of England under Norman rule was great and an era of extensive building (largely churches, cathedrals and monasteries) began under the Conqueror and continued even through the anarchy of Stephen and Matilda.

1087–1100. WILLIAM II (*Rufus*), a passionate, greedy ruffian, second son of the Conqueror, designated by his father on his deathbed (Robert, the eldest, received Normandy; Henry, cash). A Norman revolt (1088) was put down, largely with English aid, and William firmly settled on the throne. Justice was venal and expensive, the administration cruel and unpopular, taxation heavy, the Church exploited. On Lanfranc's death (1089), William kept the revenues of the See of Canterbury without appointing a successor until he thought himself dying, when he named (1093) Anselm (an Italian, Abbot of Bec, a most learned man, and a devoted churchman), who clashed with William over the recognition of rival popes; Anselm maintained church law to be above civil law and went into voluntary exile (1097). William, deeply hated, was assassinated (?) in the New Forest.

1100–1135. HENRY I (*Beauclerc, Lion of Justice*), an educated, stubborn, prudent ruler, a good judge of men, won the crown by a dash to the royal treasury at Winchester and a quick appeal to the nation by his so-called *Coronation Charter*, a promise of reform by a return to the good ways of the Conqueror (a promise often broken). Henry married Edith (of the line of Alfred), whose name became Maud out of deference to the Norman's difficulties with Saxon names. Anarchy in Normandy under Robert's slack rule, an invitation from the revolting Norman barons, and the victory of **Tinchebray** (1106), gave Henry Normandy (Robert remained a prisoner until his death), and made a later struggle between the new English kingdom and the rising Capetian power in France inevitable. Anselm, faithful to the reforming program of the revived papacy, on his recall from exile refused homage for the archiepiscopal estates (i.e. he refused to recognize lay investiture) and refused to consecrate the bishops who had rendered such homage. Henry temporized until firmly on the throne, then seized the fiefs and exiled Anselm. Adela, Henry's sister, suggested the **Compromise of 1107** which terminated the struggle by clerical homage for fiefs held of the king, while the king allowed clerical investiture with the spiritual symbols. The crown continued to designate candidates for the great prelacies.

This reign was marked by a notable expansion, specialization, and differentiation of function in the royal administration (e.g. the exchequer, influenced by accounting methods from Lorraine or Laon). Extension of the jurisdiction of royal courts: growing use of royal writs, detailing of members of the Small Council as judges on circuit (hitherto a sporadic, now a regular practice), who not merely did justice but took over increasingly the business formerly done by the sheriffs (e.g. assessment and negotiation of aids and other levies), and brought the *curia regis* into closer contact with shire and hundred courts.

Prosperity was general and trade in London attracted Norman immigrants. The **Cistercians** arrived (1128) and began an extensive program of swamp reclamation, mill and road building, agricultural improvement, and stock-breeding. Henry began the sale of charters to towns on royal domain.

Influence of the Conquest on English culture: (1) **Architecture:** wide introduction of the Norman (Romanesque) style (e.g. St. John's Chapel in the Tower of London, end of the 11th century; Durham Cathedral, c. 1096–1133). (2) **Literary:** Anglo-Saxon, the speech of the conquered, almost ceased to have a literary history, rapidly lost its formality of inflections and terminations, and became flexible and simple if inelegant. Norman French, the tongue of the court, the aristocracy, the schools, the lawyers and judges, drew its inspiration from the Continent until the loss of Normandy (1204). The Normans then began to learn English, and the Anglo-Saxon was enriched with a second vocabulary of Norman words, ideas and refinements.

Anglo-Norman culture: (1) **Historical writing: Geoffrey of Monmouth,** *History of the Kings of Britain* (written in Latin, before 1147), created the tale of Arthur for Europe. **Walter Map** (c. 1140–c. 1200), author of Goliardic verse, welded the Grail story into the Arthurian cycle, giving it a moral and religious slant; **Wace** (c. 1124–c. 1174) *Roman de Brut* and *Roman de Rou*; **Marie de France;** all three were at the court of Henry II. (2) **Science: Walcher of Malvern** observed the eclipse of 1092 and attempted to calculate the difference in time between England and Italy. Walcher began to reckon in degrees, minutes and seconds (1120). **Adelard of Bath,** a student of Arabic science in the service of Henry II, observed and experimented (e.g. the comparative speed of sound and light), translated Al-Khwarizmi's astronomical tables into Latin (1126) and introduced Al-Khwarizmi's trigonometric tables to the west. **Robert of Chester** translated Al-Khwarizmi's algebra into Latin (1145). (3) **Philosophy: John of Salisbury** (d. 1180), pupil of Abélard, the best classical, humanistic scholar of his day, attached to the court of Henry II, and later Bishop of Chartres, wrote the *Policraticus,* etc. **Beginnings of Oxford University** (c. 1167) on the model of Paris, a center of national culture.

1135–1154. STEPHEN. Henry's son drowned on the White Ship (1120), and Henry had had his daughter **Matilda** (widow of the Emperor Henry V) accepted as his heir and married to Geoffrey of Anjou, as protector. Stephen of Blois (son of Henry's sister Adela) asserted and maintained his claim to the throne at the price of a dynastic war (till 1153) with Matilda, the climax of feudal anarchy, and the ruin of English prosperity. Archbishop Theobald finally negotiated a compromise (1153) whereby Matilda's son Henry should succeed to the crown on Stephen's death. The reign was remarkable for a tremendous amount of ecclesiastical building.

1154–1399. THE HOUSE OF PLANTAGENET (Angevin).

1154–1189. HENRY II. Master of a hybrid "empire" (England, Normandy, Anjou, Maine, Touraine, by inheritance; Poitou, Aquitaine, Gascony, by marriage with Eleanor of Aquitaine (1152); Brittany (acquired, 1169), and Wales, Ireland, and Scotland (on a loose bond) without unity save in the person of the ruler. **Dynastic marriages:** daughter Eleanor to the King of Castile, Joan to the King of Sicily, Matilda to Henry the Lion. King Henry was a man of education, exhaustless energy, experience as an administrator, realistic, violent of temper.

Restoration of England to the good order of Henry I: dismissal of mercenaries, razing of unlicensed castles (1000?), reconquest of Northumberland and Cumberland from the Scots, resumption of crown lands and offices alienated under Stephen. Reconstitution of the exchequer and Great Council. After 1155 Henry felt free to leave England, and spent less than half his reign in the realm.

1155–1172. Struggle to reduce clerical encroachment on the royal courts: Under Stephen anarchy and the theories of Roman law had favored the expansion of clerical courts, extending benefit of clergy to include even homicides. **Thomas Becket** (a deacon and crony of Henry's at the time of his elevation to the chancellorship, 1155) resigned as chancellor when he became Archbishop of Canterbury (1162), and clashed at once with Henry over the criminous clerks. The *Constitutions of Clarendon* (1164), largely a restatement of old customs (including the Conqueror's), provided (*inter alia*) for the indictment of clerics in royal courts, their trial in ecclesiastical courts, and their degradation, followed by their sentence and punishment in royal courts. They also extended royal (at the expense of clerical) jurisdiction, and asserted royal rights of control in episcopal elections. Becket yielded, was dispensed from his oath by the pope, violated the *Constitutions,* and fled to France. Reconciled (1170) with Henry, Becket returned, excommunicated certain bishops friendly to Henry, and was murdered in the Cathedral of Canterbury by four knights of Henry's court, spurred by Henry's outbreak of fury against Becket, but not by Henry's orders. Henry escaped excommunication by promising to abide by the papal judgment, and was reconciled with the papacy (1172) after an oath denying all share in the crime. After this incident Henry had no choice but to tolerate benefit of clergy, which continued to be an increasing scandal in England until the reign of Henry VII. Henry retained the right of presentation and virtual control over episcopal elections. The **Assize of Clarendon** (1166) contains the first civil legislation on heresy since Roman days.

1170. Extensive replacement of the (baronial) sheriffs with men of lower rank, trained in the royal service. Henceforth the barons ceased to hold the shrievalty.

1173–1174. Reduction of the last purely feudal

The Norman and Plantagenet Kings

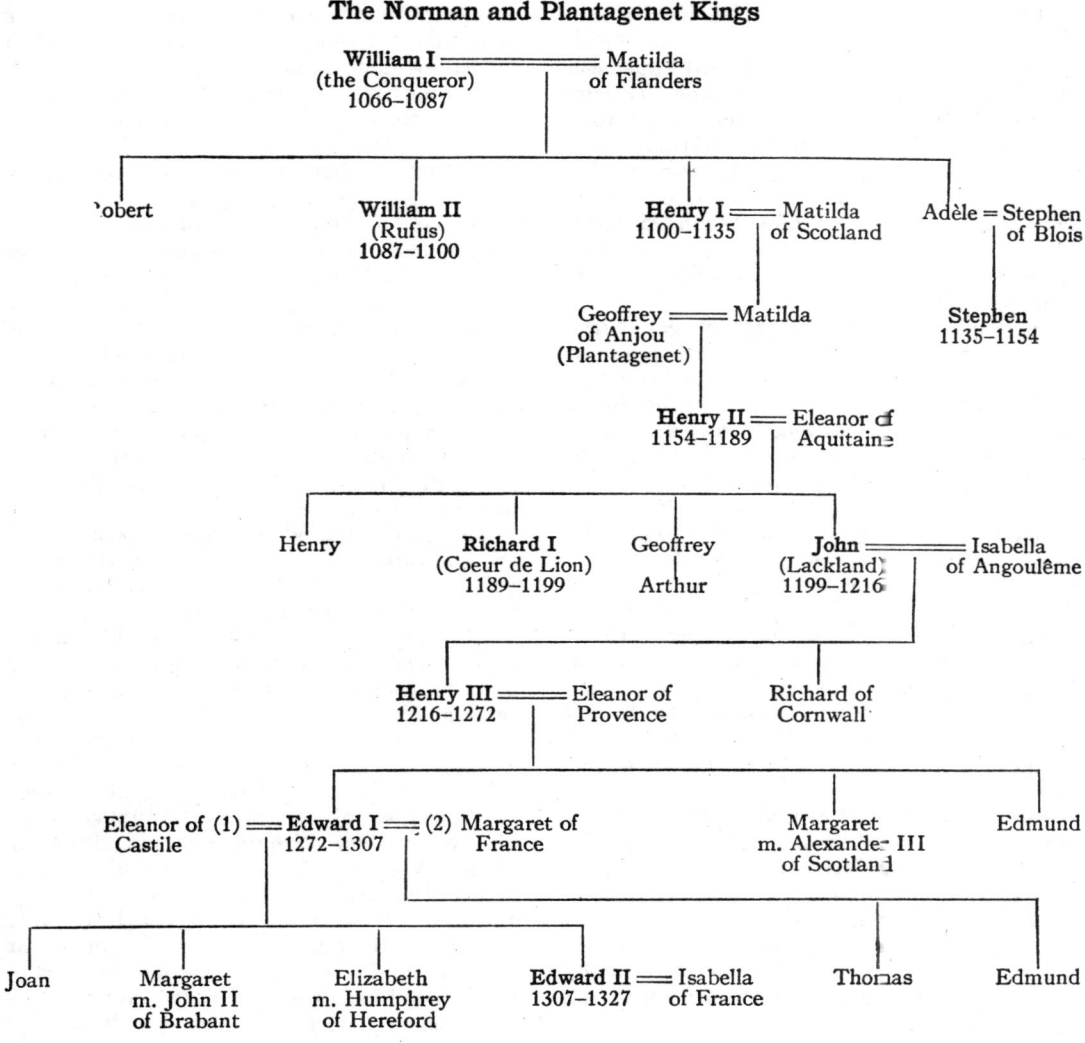

revolt; Henry's only use of mercenary troops in England.

1181. The Assize of Arms: by this reorganization of the old *fyrd* every freeman was made responsible, according to his income, for his proper share in the defense of the realm. The king thus ensured a national militia for the defense against the baronage.

Henry was not a great legislator, but he initiated a remarkable series of innovations in government which fixed the political framework of national unity.

Judicial Reforms: (1) Increasing concentration of judicial business in the Small Council.

(2) Designation (1178) of five professional judges from the Small Council as a **permanent central court**; extension of the transfer of judicial business to royal courts by the increase and specialization of royal writs (the fees a valuable source of revenue); formalization and regularization (c. 1166) of the itinerant justices (*justices in eyre*), the great source of the **Common Law** (a law universal in the realm). One of the judges, **Glanvill**, wrote the *Treatise on the Laws and Customs of the Kingdom of England*, the first serious book on the Common Law revealing the formal influence of Roman Law, but English in substance. The itinerant judges were charged

with cases dealing with crimes like murder, robbery (soon forgery and arson), and with financial business as well as judicial. (3) **Expansion of the sworn inquest** (probably of Roman origin, introduced into England by the Conqueror): statements by neighbors (freeholders) under oath in the shire courts: (a) *jury* (12 members) *of presentment in criminal cases* (Assize of Clarendon, 1166), a process which expanded (after 1219), replacing the ordeal; and (b) the *use of juries* (recognitions) instead of ordeal to determine landownership.

Reorganization of the exchequer: Nigel, Bishop of Ely (nephew of the original organizer, Roger of Salisbury), restored the exchequer to the general form of Henry I. **Innovations in the raising of revenue:** (a) *tallage*, levied by local negotiations (i.e. by the itinerant justices) with boroughs and tenants; (b) *hidage* (*carucage*) replaced the Danegeld; (c) *scutage*, levied by Henry I on the clergy, now extended to knights' fees in lieu of military service (due to Henry's need of non-feudal levies across the Channel); (d) *personal property taxes* (the first, 1166), Saladin tithe (1188), assessed by neighborhood juries. *The Dialogue of the Exchequer* written by one of the officials of the exchequer.

Extension of trade: German merchants well established in London (1157); large Italian business (wool); extensive development of domestic trade.

Foreign affairs: (1) **Norman penetration of Wales** since the Conquest bred a sporadic national resistance; Henry by three expeditions reduced Wales to nominal homage to the English crown. (2) **Ireland,** despite a brilliant native culture, was in political chaos under rival tribal kinglets and economically exhausted. Pope Adrian IV, hoping that Henry would reform the Church in Ireland, "gave" Ireland (1154) to Henry. Richard of Clare's (Strongbow) expedition (1169–1170) established a harsh rule; Henry landed (1171), temporarily reduced the rigors of the baronial administration, and reformed the Irish Church (Synod of Cashel, 1172). **John Lackland** (Henry's son) was appointed Lord of Ireland (1177), arrived (1185) but was soon recalled for incompetence.

Intrigues and revolts (beginning 1173) of Henry's sons, supported by their mother Eleanor, King Louis VII, and later Philip II of France, as well as by disgruntled local barons.

The ruling class continued to speak French during this reign, but the establishment of primogeniture as applied to land inheritance insured that younger sons would mingle with the non-aristocratic sections of society and accelerate the fusion of Norman and native elements. Manor houses began to appear in increasing numbers as domestic peace continued. Numerous Cistercian houses spread new agricultural methods and especially improved wool-raising.

1189–1199. RICHARD I (*Coeur de Lion*). Neither legislator, administrator, nor statesman, but the greatest of knights errant, an absentee ruler who spent less than a year of his reign in England, visiting his realm only twice, to raise money for continental ventures. Taxation was heavy. The government remained in the hands of ministers largely trained by Henry II, but there appeared a tendency toward a common antipathy of barons and people toward the crown. Richard (having taken the Cross, 1188) went on the Third Crusade with Frederick Barbarossa and Philip II, his most dangerous foe. On his return trip Richard was captured by Duke Leopold of Austria and turned over to the Emperor Henry VI, who held him for a staggering ransom. John and Philip bid for the prisoner, but Richard finally bought his freedom (1194) with a ransom raised partly by taxation in England. The crusade gave Englishmen their first taste of eastern adventure, but drew few except the adventurous portion of the baronage. The domestic reflection was a series of anti-Semitic outbreaks. John Lackland (despite his known character) was given charge of several counties; his plot against Richard was put down by **Hubert Walter** with the support of London. Hubert Walter, Archbishop of Canterbury and Justiciar (1194–1198), ruled England well, maintained the king's peace, and began a clear reliance on the support of the middle class in town and shire. Charters were granted towns (London received the right to elect its mayor) — and the knights of the shire were called on to assume a share of county business as a balance to the sheriffs. Knights (elected by the local gentry) served as coroners and chose the local juries, a departure looking to the day when local election and amateur justices of the peace would be the basis of government. The first known merchant guild, 1193.

1194–1199. Richard's continental struggle against Philip II, in which Richard more than held his own. Château Gaillard, a new departure in castle architecture, based on eastern lessons, built by Richard on the Seine, as an outpost against Philip.

1199–1216. JOHN (*Lackland, Softsword*), cruel, mean, licentious, faithless, weak of will, without counterbalancing virtues. Crowned with the support of the Norman barons against his nephew Arthur's claims (by primogeniture), he became Arthur's guardian.

1202-1204.   John's first contest with Philip (to protect his French possessions): struggle over Brittany, Maine, Anjou (temporary acceptance of John's title by Philip, 1200). John's marriage to Isabella of Angoulême (already betrothed to his vassal Hugh of Lusignan), led Hugh to appeal to Philip II as their common overlord.   John ignored Philip's summons to judgment (1202); his French fiefs were declared forfeit, and Philip began a war with rapid successes.   The death of Arthur (1203), possibly by John's own hand, ruined John's cause, and Philip, already master of Anjou, Brittany, and Maine, took Normandy (1204) and soon Touraine.   John's vassals in southern France (preferring an absent Angevin to an encroaching Capetian) resisted Philip's advance south of the Loire.   John's loss of the lands north of the Loire reduced the power and prestige of the English crown, cut the Norman baronage in England from their French connections, and turned their interests back to the island, with decisive constitutional and social consequences.

1205-1213.   John's struggle with Pope Innocent III: after a double election to the See of Canterbury, Innocent rejected both elections (including John's nominee) and named (1207) **Stephen Langton,** a noted scholar and theologian. John refused to accept Langton, confiscated the estates of the see, expelled the monks of Canterbury; Innocent laid an interdict on England (1208).   John confiscated the property of the English clergy who obeyed Innocent's ban without arousing serious public opposition.   Innocent excommunicated John (1209), but John, holding as hostages the children of some of the barons, weathered the storm.   Innocent deposed John (1213) and authorized Philip II to execute the sentence.   John, aware of treason and mounting hostility, promised indemnity to the clergy, did homage to the pope for England and Ireland, agreed to an annual tribute, and was freed of the ban.

1213-1214.   Final contest with Philip II (to regain the lands north of the Loire): John's great coalition (including his nephew, Emperor Otto IV, and the Count of Flanders) against Philip; most of the English baronage held aloof.   Crushing defeat of the coalition at **Bouvines** (1214) ended all hope of regaining the lands north of the Loire (formal renunciation of English claims, 1259).

1215.   MAGNA CARTA. The first politico-constitutional struggle in English history: in origin this struggle resulted from an effort of the feudal barons, supported by Archbishop Langton (notwithstanding papal support of John) and public opinion, to enforce their rights under their feudal contract with the king; it did not aim to destroy the monarchy or the royal administration.   Preliminary demands of the barons (1213); John's concessions to the Church and negotiations with Pope Innocent; civil war.   London opposed John (despite his liberal charter to the city).   John's acceptance of the **Great Charter** at Runnymede.   Magna Carta was essentially a feudal document, exacted by feudal barons from their lord but with national implications in its reforms: (1) concessions to the barons: reform in the exaction of scutage, aid, and reliefs, in the administration of wardship and in the demands for feudal service; writs of summons to the Great Council to be sent individually to the great magnates, collectively proclaimed by the sheriffs to the lesser nobles (i.e. knights): (2) concessions to the agricultural and commercial classes: Mesne tenants granted the privileges of tenants-in-chief; uniform weights and measures; affirmation of the ancient liberties of London and other towns; limitation on royal seizure of private property; reform of the forest law; reform of the courts.   (3) concessions to the Church (in addition to John's charter of 1214): promise of freedom and free elections.

The most significant provisions of the Great Charter: (1) Chapter 12: no scutage or aid (except for the traditional feudal three) to be levied without the consent of the Great Council; (2) Chapter 14: definition of the Great Council and its powers; (3) Chapter 39: "*No freeman shall be arrested and imprisoned, or dispossessed, or outlawed, or banished, or in any way molested; nor will we set forth against him, nor send against him, unless by the lawful judgment of his peers and by the law of the land.*" Even these clauses were feudal and specific in background, but centuries of experience transformed them into a generalized formula of constitutional procedure, making them the basis of the modern English constitution.   At the time their chief significance lay in the assertion of the supremacy of law over the king.   Careful provisions were made for the enforcement of the charter by the barons, even by force of arms, but in practice such enforcement was impossible.   The charter was repeatedly reissued by succeeding rulers.   The pope, as John's feudal suzerain, declared the Great Charter void.   Civil war followed; a Francophil section of the barons called Louis, son of Philip

II, to the throne (1216). John opportunely died; his young son Henry, with the support of the Anglophil barons, succeeded him, and Louis abandoned his pursuit of the crown. (1217).

1216-1272. HENRY III (a boy of nine). Guardianship (1216–1219) of **William Marshal,** Earl of Pembroke; an able, patriotic régime: two reissues (1216, 1217) of the (modified) Great Charter; elimination of French influence and interference, opposition to papal encroachments, reduction of feudal castles. William Marshal had designated the pope as Henry's guardian, and the government passed on his death (1219) to the papal legate Pandulph, the justiciar Hubert de Burgh, and Peter des Roches, tutor to Henry. Arrival of **the Dominicans** (1220) and **the Franciscans** (1224). Henry's personal rule (1227–1258) was marked by a major constitutional crisis.

Growth of national consciousness: After a futile but expensive effort (1229) to recover Aquitaine, Henry, always devoted to the papacy, gave free reign to papal exactions. At the same time the increase of papal provisions filled the English Church with alien (usually absentee Italian) appointees, to the exclusion of natives. A bitter anti-papal outbreak (perhaps supported by De Burgh) drove De Burgh from office; Des Roches succeeded him (1232–1234), filling the civil offices with fellow Poitevins. Henry's French marriage increased the alien influx and public opinion grew bitter. The papal collector was driven out (1244), and the Great Council refused (1242) a grant for Henry's effort to recover Poitou, which failed. Henry's acceptance of the crown of Sicily from the pope for his second son Edmund (1254), and his permission to his brother, Richard of Cornwall, to seek election as emperor (1257), both costly ventures, added to public ill-feeling. Finally, in a period of great economic distress, Richard asked the Great Council for one-third of the revenue of England for the pope. This grant was refused and the barons set out to reform the government with public approval (1258). A committee of 24, representing king and barons equally, brought in a proposal,

1258. THE PROVISIONS OF OXFORD, a baronial effort to restore the charter, with strong clerical and middle-class support: creation of a council of fifteen (containing a baronial majority) with a veto over the king's decisions; the Great Council to be superseded by a committee of twelve, meeting thrice a year with the permanent council of fifteen; the chancellor, justiciar, and treasurer were to be chosen annually by the council. All officials, including the king and his son, took an oath of loyalty to the Provisions.

1260-1264. The knights, alienated by the baronial oligarchy, appealed to Edward (Henry's eldest son). Gradually there emerged a group of progressive reformers (younger barons, many of the clergy and knights, townsmen, notably of London and Oxford); the more conservative barons turned to the king. Henry obtained papal release from his oaths (1261) and replaced the council of fifteen with his own appointees; chaos was followed by civil war (1263). Papal exactions continued. Louis IX (asked to arbitrate the Provisions of Oxford), in the *Mise of Amiens* (1264), decided in favor of the king. This decision was rejected by London and the commercial towns, and civil war soon broke out.

1264. Simon de Montfort (son of Simon of the Albigensian crusade), Henry's brother-in-law, of French blood and education, a friend of Grosseteste, Bishop of Lincoln (a lifelong champion of ecclesiastical and governmental reform), emerged as leader of the reforming group. This group, ahead of its time, manifested strong religious fervor, and even traces of democratic ideas. Simon's victory at **Lewes** (1265), capture of Henry and exaction of the *Mise of Lewes* (a return to the reforms of 1258).

In the course of this reign the Great Council came to be called *Parliament* (c. 1240) and at various times knights of the shire were summoned to share in its deliberations. Parliament was still as much concerned with administration and justice as with "legislation"; its membership, control of finance, and specific functions were by no means precisely defined. The summoning of the knights in effect merely transformed the negotiation of shire business into a collective negotiation by the same men who managed it locally.

1265. De Montfort's parliament: two knights from each shire, and two burgesses from each borough were summoned, probably the first summons to townsmen in parliamentary history.

1265. Edward, now leader of the baronial, conservative opposition, defeated De Montfort at **Evesham** (death of De Montfort).

Henry's return to power was formal, as Edward was the real ruler, and Edward and the barons were aware of the need of reform. Edward, on a crusade with Louis IX when Henry died, was proclaimed king while still absent, spent a year in Gascony on the way back, and was not crowned until 1274.

1272-1307. EDWARD I (*Longshanks*; the *English Justinian*), an able ruler and a great legislator, fit to rank with Frederick II, Louis IX, and Alfonso the Wise. He observed his motto, *Pactum serva* (Keep troth), but tempered it with realism. The first truly English king, he surrounded himself with able ministers and lawyers. The reign was marked by a frequent consultation of the knights and townsmen, not always in Parliament. The institutions of the English state began to take shape.

EXTERNAL AFFAIRS:

1276-1284. Reduction of Wales. Wales during the reign of Henry III had gotten out of hand, and a national revival had set in (bardic poetry and tribal union under the Llewelyns around Snowdon in the north). **Llewelyn,** Prince of Wales, joined De Montfort's opposition, refused homage (1276), and, with his brother David, renewed war with the English (1282). Edward marched into Wales, killed Llewelyn and executed David (1283), asserting the full dominion of the English crown. In these wars Edward became aware of the efficiency of the Welsh longbow. Edward's second son Edward (later Edward II) was born at Carnarvon (1284), and with him began the customary title, **Prince of Wales,** bestowed on the heir to the English throne. Local government was organized in Wales, and the *Statute of Wales* settled the legal status of the newly disciplined Welsh.

1285-1307. Scotland. William the Lion had purchased freedom from homage to the English king from Richard I in 1189, but his successors continued to do homage for their English lands. The Scottish nobility were largely Normanized. Margaret, the *Maid of Norway* (daughter of Eric of Norway) was granddaughter and heir of King Alexander II of Scotland. After Alexander's death (1286), Edward arranged a marriage for her with the Prince of Wales (1290), but she died on her way to England and Edward's hope of a personal union of the two crowns vanished. There were three collateral claimants to the Scottish crown: **John Baliol, Robert Bruce, John Hastings.** Edward, asked to arbitrate, demanded (1291) homage and acknowledgment of paramountcy from the Scots, which was given (the commons protested). He awarded the crown to Baliol (1292), who did homage for Scotland. Edward's insistence on appellate jurisdiction alienated the Scots and disposed them toward France, and an alliance began (1295) which endured intermittently for 300 years. Edward invaded Scotland, defeated Baliol at **Dunbar** (1296), declared himself King of Scotland, received the homage of the nobles, took away the coronation stone of Scone. Oppressive administration by Edward's officials led to the rising of **William Wallace** (1297), who was supported by the gentry and commonalty, but got little aid at first from the nobles. Wallace won a victory at Stirling. Edward, using the longbow to open the way for a cavalry charge, defeated Wallace at **Falkirk** (1298), drove him into exile, and completed his second conquest of Scotland (1304). Wallace was taken (1305) and executed, and Scotland incorporated under the English crown. Scottish law was retained, Scottish representatives sat in Parliament, but the nobles had to yield their fortresses, and an English lieutenant was sent to rule Scotland with a council and with power to amend the laws. Scottish nationalism found a leader in **Robert Bruce** (grandson of the claimant to the crown), who was crowned at Scone. Edward died (1307) on an expedition against Bruce.

1293-1303. France. Ill-feeling between sailors from the Cinque Ports (Sandwich, Dover, Romney, Hythe, Hastings, and [later] Rye and Winchelsea) and the French, culminated in a victory for the Anglo-Gascon fleet (1293) and Edward's summons to the court of his French overlord, King Philip IV. Under a *pro forma* compromise (1294), Edward turned over his Gascon fortresses to Philip, who refused to return them, and declared Gascony forfeited. Futile expeditions of Edward (1294, 1296, and 1297, in alliance with the Count of Flanders) against Philip. Philip, busy with his contest against Boniface VIII and other matters, returned Gascony to Edward (1303).

DOMESTIC AFFAIRS:

1290. Expulsion of the Jews: Hitherto the Jews had been protected by the kings, as they were important sources of loans. By this time public opinion was hostile to the Jews, and the Italian houses, like the Bardi and Peruzzi, were ready to finance royal loans. Foreign trade, like banking, was in the hands of foreigners, and there were few native merchants, except for wool export, where Englishmen did about 35 per cent of the business, Italians 24 per cent. The English wool staple was established in Antwerp under Edward.

1296. The clash with Pope Boniface VIII: Winchelsey, Archbishop of Canterbury, in accordance with the bull *Clericis laicos,* led the clergy in refusing a grant to the crown. Edward, with the general support of public opinion, withdrew the protection of the royal courts, and thus promptly brought the clergy to an evasion of the bull through "presents" to the crown; the lands of recalcitrant clergy were confiscated, the pope soon modified his stand, and the victory of Edward was complete.

Institutional and "legislative" developments: (1) The Parliament of 1275 granted (hitherto permission had not been asked) an increase of the export duty on wool and leather to the king, to meet the rising cost of government. (2) **Distraint of knighthood:** Various enactments (beginning in 1278) to insure that all men with a given income (e.g. £20 a year from land) should assume the duties of knighthood. Probably primarily an effort to raise money, the acts also ensured a militia under royal control. (3) *Statute of Gloucester* (1278), providing for *quo warranto* inquests into the right of feudal magnates to hold public (i.e. not manorial) courts. (4) *Statute de religiosis* (Statute of Mortmain, 1279), forbade gifts of land to the clergy without consent of the overlord (a usual policy elsewhere in Europe). Such consent was often given; the statute frequently evaded. (5) *Second Statute of Westminster* (*De donis conditionalibus*, 1285) perpetuated feudal entail (i.e. conditional grants of lands), and led to the later law of trusts. It also reorganized the militia and provided for care of the roads. (6) *Third Statute of Westminster* (*Quia emptores*, 1290) forbade new sub-infeudations of land. Land could be freely transferred, but the new vassal must hold direct of the king or from a tenant-in-chief.

1295. The Model Parliament. The writs of summons included (probably by accident) the famous phrase, *quod omnes tangit ab omnibus approbetur* (let that which toucheth all be approved by all). Bishops, abbots, earls, barons, knights, burgesses, and representatives of the chapters and parishes were summoned. The clergy did not long continue to attend Parliament, preferring their own assembly (*Convocation*) and left only the great prelates, who sat rather as feudal than ecclesiastical persons.

1297. The Confirmation of Charters (*Confirmatio cartarum*), a document almost as important as *Magna Carta*, extorted by a coalition of the barons (angered by taxation and the Gascon expedition) and the middle classes (irritated by mounting taxes) under the leadership of Archbishop Winchelsey. In effect the Confirmation included *Magna Carta* (and other charters) with the added provision that no non-feudal levy could be laid by the crown without a parliamentary grant. Edward left the actual granting of this concession to his son Edward as regent, and Pope Clement V later dispensed Edward from the promise in exchange for the right to collect (for the first time) annates in England. Edward did not surrender tallage, despite the so-called statute *de tallagio non concedendo*.

1303. The *carta mercatoria* granted the merchants full freedom of trade and safe conduct, in return for a new schedule of customs dues.

1305. The petition from the barons and commonalty of the Parliament of Carlisle to end papal encroachments, notably in provisions and annates. Edward enforced the petition except in the matter of annates.

The reign is remarkable for frequent consultation of the middle class (in Parliament and out), for the encouragement of petition to Parliament (now one of its chief functions), and for frequent meetings of Parliament, which educated the nation not merely in the elements of self-government but in ideas, and kept the crown in close contact with public opinion. The word *statute* as used of this reign means any formal royal regulation intended to be permanent, and does not imply formal parliamentary enactment.

Judicial developments. Under Edward the differentiation of the great common law courts is clear: (1) **Court of King's Bench** (concerned with criminal and crown cases); (2) **Court of Exchequer** (dealing with royal finance); (3) **Court of Common Pleas** (handling cases between subjects). The **King's Council** (Small Council) still remained supreme as a court by virtue of its residual and appellate jurisdiction, and the councillors were expected to take the councillor's oath to the king. Edward began the practice of referring residual cases which did not readily come within the jurisdiction of the common law courts to the chancellor with a committee of assessors from the council. This chancellor's court tended to absorb the judicial business of the council and finally emerged as a court of equity. The **Year Books,** unofficial, verbatim reports in French (the language of the courts) of legal proceedings, a record unique for completeness in the period, began in this reign. Coherence and continuity of tradition among the lawyers was greatly facilitated by the establishment of the **Inns of Court** under the three Edwards. Here the lawyers assembled their libraries, lodged, and studied, transmitting with increasing strength the living force of the Common Law, to the virtual exclusion of Roman Law.

PROGRESS OF ENGLISH CULTURE: Architecture: Early English Gothic (under French influence): Canterbury, begun 1175;

Lincoln, 1185–1200; Salisbury, 1220–1258. Decorated Gothic: Choir of Lincoln, 1255–1280; York, west front, 1261–1324.

Painting and minor arts: St. Albans at the opening of the 13th century was the greatest artistic center in Europe (manuscript painting by Matthew Paris). The court of Henry III was a mecca for European craftsmen, especially Frenchmen.

Literature: Orm's *Ormulum* (early 13th century), a translation into English of portions of the Gospels; the *Ancren Rewle*, rules for the ascetic life tinged with the cult of the Virgin (c. 1200); **Layamon's** *Brut*, an English verse translation of Wace's *Brut*. Political songs and satires of the Barons' War, etc. (e.g. *Song of the Battle of Lewes*; the *Husbandman's Complaint*). **Matthew Paris** (c. 1200–1259), a friend of Henry III, monk of St. Albans, in his compilation, the *Historia Maior*, covered the history of the world, but in the portion dealing with the years 1235–1259 produced a work of original research in which he glorified England and things English.

Foundation of Cambridge University (1209). Foundation of University College (1249); Balliol (1261); Merton (1264) began the collegiate system of Oxford.

Science and learning: Bartholomew Anglicus (c. 1230), *On the Properties of Things*, a popular encyclopedia influenced by Pliny and Isidore, combining accurate observation (e.g. the domestic cat) with discussion of the fantastic (e.g. the griffin).

The English Franciscans at Oxford: Robert Grosseteste (d. 1253), Bishop of Lincoln: insistence on the study of the sources (the Fathers and the Bible); knew Greek and Hebrew, a precursor of the Christian humanists; student of philosophy, mathematics, astronomy, physics, teacher of Roger Bacon. **Roger Bacon** (d. 1292), greatest mediaeval exponent of observation and experiment. Foresaw the application of mediaeval power to transport, including flying; "formula" for gunpowder; author of the *Opus Maius* and *Opus Minus*.

Opponents of the Thomist rationalists: Duns Scotus (c. 1270–1308) and **William of Occam** (c. 1300–1349).   (*Cont. p.* 268.)

(2) *Scotland*, 1034-1304

1034-1286. Racial and political turmoil. Duncan I was followed by his murderer, the usurper

1040-1057. Macbeth, and his son and avenger

1059-1093. MALCOLM CANMORE. Malcolm was forced to do some kind of homage by William the Conqueror (1072) and by William Rufus (1091), and Anglo-Norman penetration began. Malcolm's wife, (Saint) Margaret (sister of Edgar Aetheling, grand-niece of Edward the Confessor), was a masterful and remarkable woman whose Anglicizing influence on Scottish culture, on the national life and the native Church was profound. Her three sons, especially

1124-1153. DAVID I, continued the so-called "bloodless Norman conquest," and the new Anglo-Norman aristocracy (e.g. Baliols, Bruces, Lindsays, Fitz Alans, i.e. Stewarts) became the bulwark of the crown.

1153-1286. The next four reigns were notable for the consolidation of Scotland, and for signs of impending collision with the English monarchy. William the Lion, captured in a raid by the English, accepted (1174) the feudal lordship of the English crown and did ceremonial allegiance at York (1175). Richard I weakened England's position, John tried to restore it.

1249-1286. ALEXANDER III did homage (1278) to the English king for his English lands, "reserving" his Scottish fealty. All of Alexander's issue were dead by 1234, leaving only his granddaughter Margaret, the *Maid of Norway*. Margaret's death (1290) made impossible the personal union of England and Scotland (by Margaret's marriage to Edward I's heir). Thirteen claimants to the Scottish crown were narrowed down to the candidacy of **Robert Bruce** and **John Baliol.** Edward I of England, called upon to arbitrate, awarded the crown to Baliol (1292), but when Baliol ignored a summons to attend Edward and instead embarked upon an alliance with France (1295), the English invaded the country and, after some years of warfare, reduced it in 1304 (p. 199).   (*Cont. p.* 276.)

(3) *Ireland*, 1171-1307

The period following the expedition of Henry I (1171) was marked by a steadily developing conflict between the feudal system of the incoming Normans and the old tribal organization of the Irish. In its later phases this struggle bred centuries of discord and bloodshed. Henry's authority was precariously maintained by a viceroy who had orders to be fair to the natives, a policy which estranged the Norman elements.

1185. Henry's son, John Lackland, returned to England after a short and inglorious

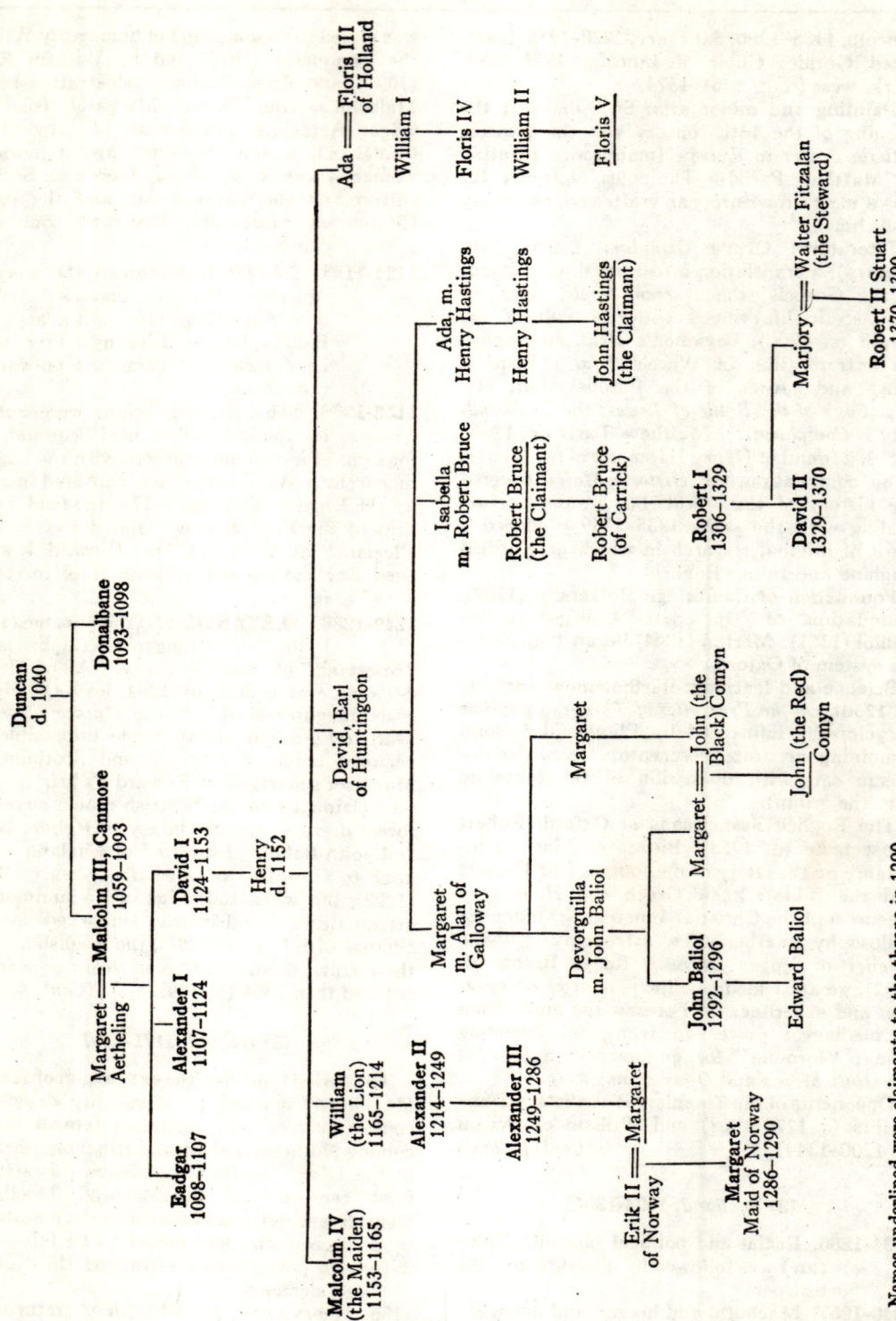

The Scottish Succession

Names underlined were claimants to the throne in 1290.

rule as Lord of Ireland, but his authority was maintained by his representative, **William Marshal,** Earl of Pembroke, who married the daughter of Richard of Clare.

1213. John abandoned Ireland, along with England, to Pope Innocent III.

1216-1272. Under Henry III the power and possessions of the Anglo-Norman colony expanded rapidly: bridges and castles were built, towns prospered and guilds were formed.

1272-1307. Edward I's revolutionary legislation in England was extended to Ireland, which continued to prosper, at least in the Anglo-Norman sections. But the cleavage between the two races had become very marked and the native clans remained restive. (*Cont. p.* 276.)

b. SCANDINAVIA

(1) *Denmark,* 950-1320

c. 950-985. HAROLD BLUETOOTH, whose reign saw a steady advance of Christianity and expansion of Danish power over Schleswig, the Oder mouth, and Norway. But the kingship was of little importance until the reign of

985-1014. SVEN I (*Forked-beard*). He defeated the Norwegians, Swedes, and Wends and conquered England (1013).

1014-1035. KNUT THE GREAT (*Canute*), Sven's son, was King of Denmark, Norway (1028), and England (1016-1035), the first "northern empire." Knut's conversion completed the conversion of his people. He imported priests, architects, and artisans from his English realm, and new influences spread from Denmark to Norway and Sweden. On his death Norway broke away, England passed to Edward the Confessor.

1157-1182. Under **WALDEMAR THE GREAT,** the founder of the **Waldemarian dynasty,** a great expansion eastward took place at the expense of the Wends; Copenhagen was established as the capital.

1182-1202. KNUT VI made conquests in (Slavonic) Mecklenburg and Pomerania.

1202-1241. WALDEMAR II (*the Conqueror*) led crusading expeditions into Livonia, Estonia (Reval founded), and penetrated the Gulf of Finland, making the southern Baltic a Danish lake (the second "northern empire"). This empire collapsed in 1223, and the advance

was in fact more in the nature of a crusade than of permanent imperial expansion. The monarchy was now dominant, the nobles largely feudalized, the clergy (with royal grants) powerful, the bourgeoisie vigorous (fisheries and cattle-raising), the yeoman class strong and independent.

1241-1250. ERIC PLOWPENNY, whose reign was taken up with civil war against his brothers Christopher and

1250-1252. ABEL, who was supported by his brother-in-law, the Count of Holstein, and also by the Swedes and by the city of Lübeck.

1252-1259. CHRISTOPHER. His effort to tax the Church opened a struggle that lasted nearly a century.

1259-1286. ERIC (V) GLIPPING. He was forced by the nobility to sign a charter, the **Danish Magna Carta** (1282), recognizing the national assembly and initiating the subordination of the king to the law. He continued the contest with the clergy, fought against dynastic rivals, planned expansion in Mecklenburg and Pomerania, and lost Scania and North Halland to Sweden

1286-1320. ERIC (VI) MENVED, during whose reign the conflict between the crown and the Church came to a head. By a compromise (1303) the rights of the Church were guaranteed, but the king's right to levy military service on church lands was upheld.

(*Cont. p.* 315.)

(2) *Sweden,* 993-1319

The origins of the Swedish kingship are obscure, but the kingdom may be dated back to the **union of Gothia and Svealand** (prior to 836). The conversion of the country to Christianity took place in the 9th century and

993-1024. OLAF SKUTKONUNG was the first Christian ruler. He was the son of Eric the Conqueror, the founder of the Northern Kingdom, and brought to Sweden many Anglo-Saxon workers. His wars with St. Olaf of Norway led to some conquests, which were soon lost. The century following his death was marked by wars between the Goths and the Swedes and by what appear to have been religious conflicts.

1134-1150. SVERKER. Amalgamation of the Swedes and Goths with alternation of rulers from the two peoples (an arrangement which continued for a century). The monarchy gradually became established on a firm basis and the progress of Christianity was marked by the foundation of many bishoprics (including Uppsala, 1163). The first monasteries also belong to this period.

1150-1160. ERIC IX (*the Saint*), whose reign was a short golden age. He led a crusade into Finland, the first real expansion of Sweden. The line of St. Eric came to an end with

1223-1250. ERIC LAESPE, whose reign was dominated by his brother-in-law, Jarl (i.e. Earl) **Birger Magnusson,** the greatest statesman of mediaeval Sweden. He controlled the government from 1248-1266 and had his son elected king in 1250, thus founding the **Folkung line.**

1250-1275. WALDEMAR. As regent, Jarl Birger abolished judicial ordeal by fire, ended serfdom by choice, encouraged commerce, favored the settlement of German artisans, checked the power of the baronage. He attempted to introduce typical European feudalism, setting up his other sons in quasi-independent duchies.

1279-1290. MAGNUS LADULOS, who had dethroned and imprisoned his brother Waldemar. Magnus continued his father's feudal innovations, extended the powers of the clergy and set up an hereditary nobility. Town charters became numerous as the burghers became prosperous through trade and mining.

1290-1319. BIRGER (son of Magnus). His rule was chaotic, due to civil war with his brothers, whom Birger ultimately captured and executed. This led to a popular uprising and the expulsion of Birger, who was followed by his three-year-old nephew. (*Cont. p. 316.*)

(3) *Norway, 872-1319*

Norway was a region with little natural unity, which in the earlier mediaeval period was ruled by numerous petty kings.

872-930. HAROLD HAARFAGER (*Fairhair*) began the unification of the country by deposing many of the chieftains (traditionally including Hrolf or Rollo). It was in this period that the Norsemen supposedly made their conquests in Iceland, the Faroes, Shetlands, Orkneys, Hebrides, Scotland, and Ireland.

935-961. HAAKON THE GOOD, who attempted, prematurely, to convert the country to Christianity.

995-1000. OLAF (I) TRYGVESSON, who, with the aid of English clergy, converted Norway, Iceland, and Greenland. He was defeated by the Kings of Denmark and Sweden, who supported the Norwegian nobility. There followed a period of feudal disruption.

1016-1028. OLAF II (*St. Olaf*) reunited the country and established Christianity on a firm footing.

1046-1066. HARALD (III) HARDRADA, who was defeated by King Harold of England in the **battle of Stamford Bridge** (p. 168). There followed another period of confusion, marked by constant wars of succession, and by a struggle against the growing power of the clergy. Nevertheless the expansion of trade brought increasing prosperity.

1184-1202. SVERRE. He was able to maintain a strong monarchy in the face of aristocratic and clerical opposition, thanks to support from the small landowners. Nevertheless Norway continued to be troubled with dynastic conflict.

1223-1262. HAAKON IV, a strong king, who temporarily restored order, conquered Iceland, but was defeated in a war with Scotland.

1262-1299. ERIK THE PRIEST-HATER, whose reign was marked by a war with the Hansa towns, in which he suffered a reverse. As a result he was obliged to grant the towns full privileges in Norway and to join the Hanseatic League.

1299-1319. HAAKON V, marking the culmination of decline of the royal power.

The crown in Scandinavia depended on its vassals for soldiers and for administration. The introduction of cavalry (first recorded in Denmark, 1134) accentuated this feudal tendency, and a new nobility emerged. This nobility was a professional military class always ready for war, exempt from taxes; it quickly became a governing class receiving local offices and lands as a reward for military services. From Denmark this new society spread to Norway and Sweden. Henceforth the nobles added a further complication to dynastic wars, causing a series of crises, and restricting the normal evolution of royal power.

German capital and German merchants began to penetrate Scandinavia, achieving by the second half of the 13th century a dominating position. The growth of the Hanseatic League delayed the progress of the native bourgeoisie, but commerce led to the active growth of towns and town life. Population was increasing rapidly, lands were cleared, the arts were advancing in distinction and perfection under the patronage of wealthy kings and prosperous prelates.

The heroic age of the Icelandic *skalds* (court poets) in the 10th and 11th centuries brought the art to an involved perfection and a concentration on war that ultimately killed it. Meantime the kings, interested in politics as well as war (notably Sverre of Norway, c. 1185) began to patronize the Norwegian story-tellers, particularly the Icelanders, and the **Sagas** emerged. The greatest master of the new form was an Icelander, **Snorri Sturleson** (1179–1241), an active political figure in both Iceland and Norway. Snorri's *Younger Edda* in prose and verse, containing the rules of versification, the old myths, and a collection of ancient Icelandic poems, is unique. History was written by **Saxo Grammaticus** (died c. 1208), whose *Historia Danica* is the chief source for the Hamlet story. Both Snorri and Saxo were preoccupied with the ideals of national unity, strong royal power and resistance to baronial particularism.

(*Cont. p. 316.*)

c. GERMANY UNDER THE SALIAN AND HOHENSTAUFEN EMPERORS, 1024-1268

1024-1125. THE FRANCONIAN (or Salian) **HOUSE.** Dawn of the great imperial age.

1024-1039. CONRAD II (the Salian). He continued the general policy of Henry: personally interested only in the churches of Limburg and Speyer, he was firm in his dealings with the Church in general and relied on the lesser nobles to balance the clergy and magnates. The *ministeriales*, laymen of humble or even servile origin, were used to replace the clergy in many administrative posts; regalian rights were retained and exploited. Dukedoms were not regranted as they fell vacant, but were assigned to Conrad's son Henry, who on his accession to the crown held all but the duchies of Lorraine and Saxony. By encouraging the making of fiefs heritable Conrad weakened the dukes and got the support of the lesser nobles, but insured the ultimate feudalization of Germany. Conrad's imperial coronation (1027), one of the most brilliant in mediaeval Rome, was witnessed by two kings, Canute the Great and Rudolf III of Burgundy. Burgundy, willed to Conrad by Rudolf III, guardian of one road to Italy, was reincorporated (1033) in the empire on the death of Rudolf. Failure of an expedition (1030) against Stephen of Hungary; successful disciplinary expedition (1031) against the Poles; recovery of Lusatia; payment of homage by the Poles.

1039-1056. HENRY III (the Black). Imperial authority at its height. A period of great town prosperity, due to development of trade. His wife, Agnes of Poitou, was an ardent devotee of Cluny; Henry, an honest reformer, abandoned simony, purified the court along Cluniac lines, but retained a firm hold on the Church. Strongest of the German emperors, he asserted his mastery in Poland, Bohemia, and Hungary; Saxony was the only duchy to keep a trace of its original independence; resumption of the dan-

The Salian Emperors

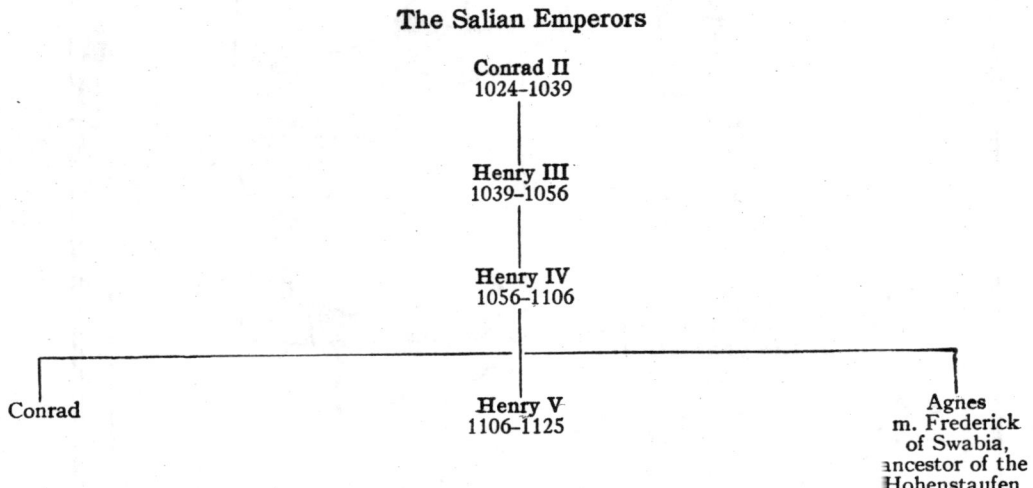

Conrad II
1024–1039

Henry III
1039–1056

Henry IV
1056–1106

Conrad

Henry V
1106–1125

Agnes
m. Frederick
of Swabia,
ancestor of the
Hohenstaufen

HOLY ROMAN EMPIRE
AND SOUTHERN ITALY
about the year 1000

SCALE OF MILES

0   50   100   150   300

Saracen Territory   Holy Roman Empire

Byzantine Territory   Independent or semi-independent
                               Christian principalities

Longitude   East   12°   from   Greenwich   17°

gerous practice of granting duchies outside the royal house made Germany a feudal volcano; use of the *ministeriales* in administration, but retention of the bishops as principal advisers and administrators. Henry's reforms alienated the bishops, the magnates, and the nobles.

1043. Henry proclaimed the "**Day of Indulgence,**" forgiving all his foes and exhorting his subjects to do likewise; Bratislav of Bohemia forced (1041) to do homage; pagan reaction in Hungary put down (1044); final peace in Hungary (1052), which became a fief of the German crown. Homage of Denmark, repudiated soon after.

1046. Synods of Sutri and Rome: deposition at Henry's instigation of three rival popes and election of his nominee, Clement II, the first of a series (Clement, Leo IX, and Nicholas II) of reforming German popes; reaffirmation of the imperial right of nomination to the papacy.

1047. Godfrey the Bearded, Duke of Upper Lorraine, disappointed at Henry's refusal to award him Lower Lorraine, stirred up serious disaffection, and finally joined Baldwin of Flanders in a revolt at first supported by Henry of France (1047); he married (1054) Beatrice, widow of Boniface, Marquis of Tuscany, one of the most powerful Italian supporters of the popes.

1056–1106. HENRY IV. (Aged six at his accession; nine-year regency of his pious, colorless lay and clerical magnates appropriated royal resources and sovereign rights with impunity, and dealt a fatal blow to the German monarchy.

1062. Anno, Archbishop of Cologne, kidnaped the young king and with **Adalbert,** Archbishop of Hamburg-Bremen, governed in his name, dividing the monasteries (one of the chief resources of the crown) between themselves.

1066. The **Diet of Tribur,** thanks to the reaction of the clergy and nobles against Adalbert, freed Henry from Adalbert and his personal government began.

Henry was a remarkable but undisciplined man, intelligent, resolute, ill-balanced, and headlong, with the odds against him from the start; under papal pressure he was reconciled (1069) with his wife Bertha, reformed his personal life, and began a vigorous rule. His policy was a return to the Ottonian habit of using the Church as a major source of revenue; simony was open, and the reforming party appealed to Rome against Henry. Henry began

the recapture, reorganization, and consolidation of royal lands and revenues, especially in Saxony, and probably planned to consolidate the monarchy in the Capetian manner around a compact core of royal domain in the Harz-Goslar region.

1073. A great **conspiracy of the leading princes** led to a rising of virtually all Saxony. Henry came to terms with the pope, played one faction off against the other, won the South German baronage, and finally defeated the rebels (1075).

1074. Charter of Worms, the first imperial charter issued direct to citizens without episcopal intervention.

1075–1122. THE STRUGGLE OVER LAY INVESTITURE. The German bishops, alarmed at Hildebrand's reform policy (p. 219), opposed his confirmation as pope, but Henry, in the midst of the Saxon revolt, sanctioned it, and apparently promised reforms in Germany. The sudden abolition of lay investiture would have reduced the emperor's power in Germany and would have made government impossible. With the end of the Saxon revolt Henry's interest in reform vanished.

1075. Pope Gregory, at the Lenten Synod, issued a rigorous reform program and later sent a stern warning to the emperor and the German episcopate. Henry, under pressure from his bishops, called

1076. The **Synod of Worms:** The bishops repudiated their allegiance to Pope Gregory, addressed a list of (ridiculous) charges to him, and declared him deposed. Henry's letter to the pope associated him with the charges and demanded Gregory's abdication in the most insolent and violent terms. Public opinion was shocked at the letter, but the North Italian bishops at Piacenza supported Henry. Gregory at the Lenten Synod (1076) in Rome, suspended and excommunicated the German and Lombard prelates involved, and deposed and excommunicated Henry, absolving his subjects from allegiance and producing political and ecclesiastical chaos in Germany. Henry was isolated, the Saxon rebellion broke out again, and a powerful coalition of German magnates eager to regain power was formed against him. The **Diet of Tribur** (October) compelled Henry to humble himself and agree to stand trial and clear himself of Gregory's charges before Feb. 22, 1077, on pain of the withdrawal of their allegiance. The princes called a synod to meet at Augsburg, inviting Gregory to preside; Gregory accepted and started for Germany.

1077. Henry, after a midwinter dash across the Alps with his wife, was welcomed by the North Italians and avoided the humiliation of a public trial in Germany by presenting himself as a penitent at Canossa (Jan. 21). Gregory, outmaneuvered, hesitated three days, and finally on the appeals of the Countess Matilda and Abbot Hugh of Cluny (Henry's godfather), accepted Henry's promises and solemn oaths of contrition, and absolved him. **The penance at Canossa** is hardly mentioned by contemporaries, and made much less impression in Germany than the excommunication; the chief source on the episode is Gregory's letter of justification to the disappointed German nobles; Gregory, after some months of waiting for a safe conduct into Germany, turned back.

1077. A faction of the nobles elected an anti-king, **Rudolph of Swabia,** with the approval of Gregory's legates, but without papal confirmation.

1077-1080. Civil war ensued, but Henry, loyally supported by the towns, gained strength steadily; Rudolph of Swabia was defeated and killed (1080); Gregory again excommunicated and deposed Henry, but a synod of German and North Italian prelates then deposed **Gregory,** naming as his successor Guibert of Ravenna, a reforming bishop and former friend of Gregory (1080).

1083. Henry, at the end of a series of expeditions to Italy (1081–1082), besieged Rome; after futile efforts at reconciliation he gained entrance to the city and Gregory called in his Norman allies. Henry, crowned at Rome by his anti-pope, invaded Apulia; **Robert Guiscard** expelled him from Rome and sacked (1084) the city. The horrors of the Norman sack made it impossible for Gregory to remain in Rome and he departed with his allies, dying as their "guest" in Salerno (1085). The papal position was justified by **Manegold of Lautenbach's** theory that an evil ruler violates a contract with his subjects and may therefore be deposed by the pope, who is responsible for the salvation of mankind. Henry's advocate, **Peter Crassus,** based his denial of this right on historical precedent backed by citations of Justinian (one of the earliest examples of such quotations).

1093-1106. Gregory's successors, unbending champions of reform, supported the revolts of Henry's sons in Germany and Italy: **Conrad** (1093), and the future **Henry V** (1104). Henry was elected king, but his father retained the loyalty of the towns to the end. Henry V shamefully entrapped and imprisoned his father, who abdicated, escaped, and was regaining ground when he died.

1106-1125. HENRY V (married to Matilda, daughter of Henry I of England in 1114). A brutal, resourceful, treacherous ruler, Henry continued his father's policies. Skillfully pretending to be dependent on the princes he continued lay investiture, opposed papal interference in Germany, and retained the support of the lay and clerical princes; meantime, relying on the towns and *ministeriales,* he built up the nucleus of a strong power. Wars against Hungary, Poland, and Bohemia (1108–1110).

1110-1111. Imposing expedition to Italy to secure the imperial crown, universally supported in Germany. In Italy the Lombard towns (except Milan) and even the Countess Matilda yielded to Henry. Pope Paschal II (1099–1118) offered to renounce all feudal and secular holdings of the Church (except those of the See of Rome) in return for the concession of free elections and the abandonment of lay investiture, a papal humiliation more than equal to the imperial mortification at Canossa. At Henry's coronation the clergy repudiated Paschal's renunciation, there was a scuffle, Henry took the pope and cardinals prisoners, and forced the pope to acknowledge the imperial powers. The net result was nil, but papal prestige was badly damaged.

1114-1115. A series of revolts (Lorraine, along the lower Rhine, in Westphalia, and soon in East Saxony and Thuringia). Henry was saved by the loyalty of the South Germans.

1115. Matilda, Countess of Tuscany, who had made over all her vast holdings to the papacy, retaining them as fiefs with free right of disposition, willed these lands to Henry on her death, and Henry arrived in Italy to claim them (1116–1118).

Both pope and emperor were weary of the investiture controversy, Europe was preoccupied with the Crusades (p. 258), and the time was ripe for compromise. The first important compromise negotiated by the pope was with Henry I of England (1107) and provided that the king should not invest with the spiritual symbols (the ring and the staff), but that he was to be present or represented at all elections. After due homage the king should then invest with the symbols of temporal authority. In France a similar compromise was reached in practice with Philip I (c. 1108). Pope Calixtus II convinced Henry that neither Henry of England nor Philip of France had suffered by their compromise.

1122. At the **Synod of Worms,** under the presidency of a papal legate, the **Concordat of Worms** was drawn up in two documents of three brief sentences each which provided that: (1) elections in Germany were to be in the presence of the emperor or his representative, without simony or violence; in the event of disagreement the emperor was to decide; the emperor was to invest with the temporalities before the spiritual investiture; (2) in Italy and Burgundy consecration was to follow within six months of election; the emperor to invest with the *regalia* after homage. This concordat ended the investiture struggle, but not the bitter rivalry of pope and emperor, for the papacy, now clearly the independent spiritual leader of Europe, could not long tolerate an imperial rival.

1125. Henry left no direct heir, and at the bitterly fought election of 1125 the Archbishops of Mainz and Cologne, foes of the anti-clerical Salian line, cleverly prevented, with papal aid, the election of the nearest heir, Frederick of Swabia, of the House of Hohenstaufen, on the ground that the hereditary principle was dangerous, and Lothair of Supplinburg, Duke of Saxony, was chosen, opening the great struggle of Welf and Waiblinger (Hohenstaufen) in Germany (**Guelf** and **Ghibelline** in Italy).

1125-1137. LOTHAIR II. Elected by the support of the clergy, he remained loyal to the Church, was the first German king to ask papal approval of his election and did not exercise his rights under the Concordat of Worms for some years. Bitter civil war against the Hohenstaufens (1125–1135); vigorous policy of German expansion among the Wends and Scandinavians; renewal of Wendish conversions (1127).

1133. Influenced by Bernard of Clairvaux, Lothair decided in favor of Pope Innocent II (against Anacletus II) and went to Italy to settle the papal schism; he was crowned; had the Concordat of Worms confirmed, and received the lands of Matilda as fiefs.

1135. The "year of pacification" in Germany — general peace proclaimed. Lothair apparently planned to create a vast dynastic holding for his son-in-law, the Welf Henry the Proud, to include Bavaria, Swabia, Saxony, the allodial lands and fiefs of Matilda of Tuscany, and to secure him the imperial crown. Lothair died suddenly on his return from an expedition against King Roger II of Sicily, and in the election (1138) the clergy, led by Adalbert of Treves, had the Waiblinger, Conrad of Hohenstaufen, chosen. Conrad almost at once put Henry the Proud under the ban, gave Saxony to Albert the Bear, Bavaria to Leopold of Austria, his half-brother, and reopened the civil war.

1138-1268. The HOUSE OF HOHENSTAUFEN (from Staufen, their Swabian castle). The first German dynasty to be conscious of the full historical implications of the imperial tradition and the significance of Roman law for imperial pretensions. Their consequent devotion to a policy of centralization and to the aggrandizement of the lay imperial power in the face of the new spiritual supremacy and political aspirations of the Papacy precipitated a second great struggle between the popes and the emperors, centering in Italy but turning upon a sharp conflict between rival spiritual and political concepts.

1138-1152. CONRAD III, a gallant, knightly, attractive, popular hero, but no statesman. The Welf, **Henry the Lion** (son and successor of Henry the Proud), acknowledged Conrad's title, but regained Saxony by force and was granted it by the peace (1142); the struggle of Welf and Waiblinger reduced Germany to chaos and Conrad left on the Second Crusade. On his return Conrad found Germany in worse confusion.

The most significant development of the reign was the renewal of **expansion against the Slavs and Scandinavians** (chiefly on the initiative of Albert the Bear and Henry the Lion): a regularly authorized German crusade against the Slavs (1147); colorization of eastern Holstein; foundation of Lübeck (1143); conversion of Brandenburg and Pomerania; Albert the Bear began to style himself Margrave of Brandenburg; Henry the Lion began the creation of a principality east of the Elbe. Conrad took no share in these developments; was the only king since Henry the Fowler not to attain the imperial title. Alienated from the Church toward the end of his life, Conrad was preparing a more vigorous assertion of the imperial position, and supported the strong imperialist Frederick of Swabia, his nephew, as candidate for the throne. On Conrad's death anarchy was so prevalent in Germany that even the magnates favored a strong ruler, and Conrad's candidate, Frederick, Duke of Swabia, was unanimously elected.

1152-1190. FREDERICK I (*Barbarossa,* i.e. *Red Beard*), a handsome man with flowing golden hair, who could both frighten and charm, the embodiment of the ideal mediaeval German king. A close student of history and surrounded with Roman legists, he regarded

The Welf and Hohenstaufen Families

Hohenstaufen (Staufer)

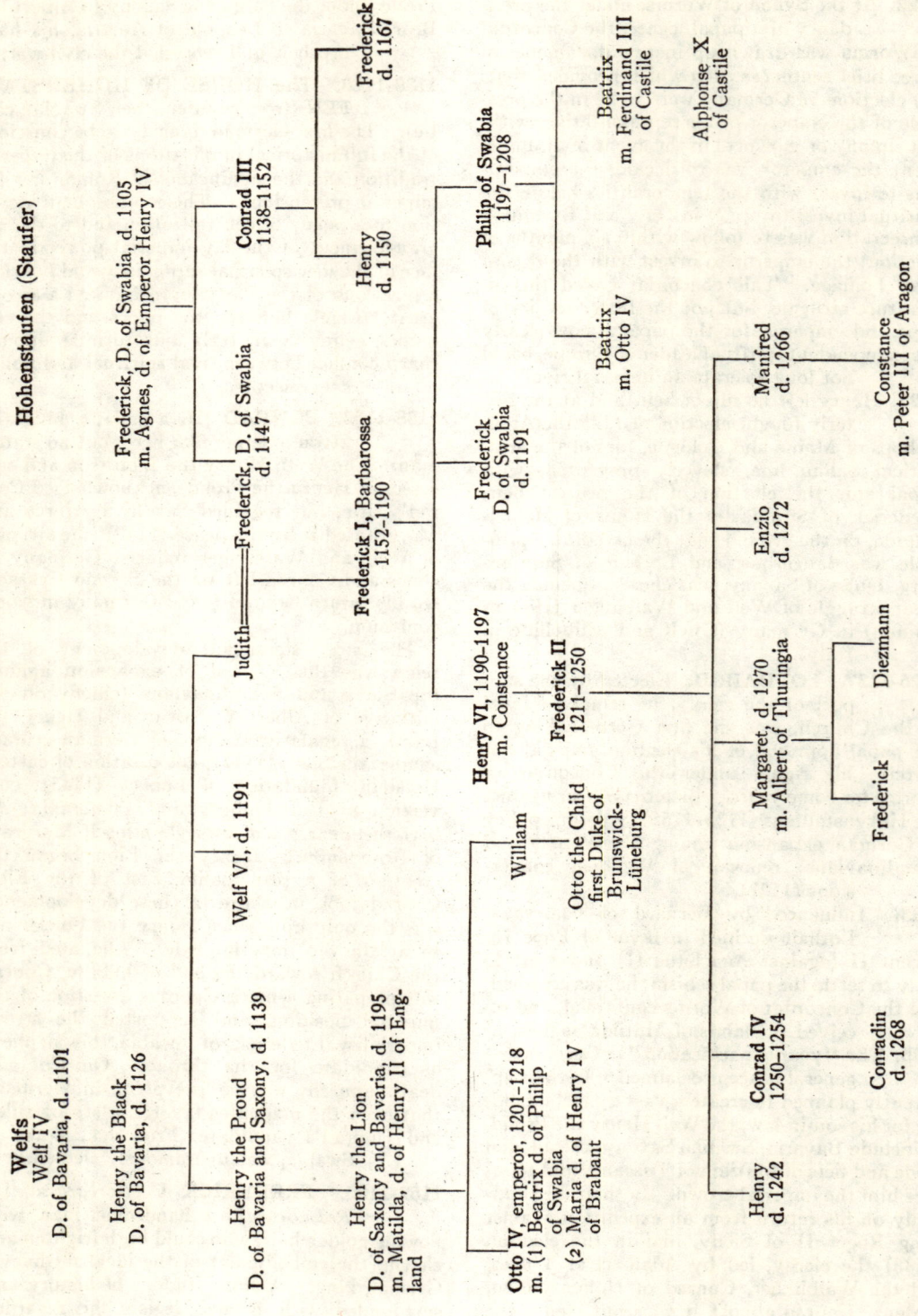

himself as heir to the tradition of Constantine, Justinian, and Charlemagne (whom he had canonized by his anti-pope), and aimed at restoring the glories of the Roman Empire. He began the style *Holy Roman Empire*.

Policy of consolidation and expansion of royal lands: Burgundian lands regained by marriage (1156) with Beatrice, heiress of the County of Burgundy; purchase of lands from the Welfs in Swabia and Italy; exploitation of regalian rights.

Conciliation of the magnates: (1) **Henry the Lion,** recognized as virtually independent beyond the Elbe; confirmed in Saxony; regranted Bavaria (1156). (2) **Austria made an independent duchy** (1156), granted to Henry of Austria in return for Bavaria. (3) **Alliance with the episcopate:** free exercise of rights under the Concordat of Worms; reforming bishops replaced with hard-headed appointees of the old school, loyal to the crown. Administration delegated to the *ministeriales*. Successful maintenance of public order; Frederick won the title *pacificus*.

Expeditions to Italy (*p.* 220, *seq.*): (1) 1154–1155; (2) 1158–1162; (3) 1163–1164; (4) 1166–1168; (5) 1174–1177; (6) 1184–1186.

1156-1180. Henry the Lion's "principality" beyond the Elbe: military progress against the Slavs and colonization (Hollanders, Danes, Flemings); Bremen taken from the archbishop (1156), Lübeck from Adolph of Holstein (1158); commercial relations with Denmark, Sweden, Norway; alliance with Waldemar II of Denmark; reduction of Slavic pirates; colonization of Mecklenburg, extension of Christianity; war with Albert the Bear; refusal of aid to Frederick in Italy (1176); confiscation of Henry's holdings and exile (1180); dismemberment of Saxony.

1156. Diet of Ratisbon: emergence of the *prince electors* as a substantive body in the German state.

1157. Diet of Besançon: emissaries from Rome, France, England, the Spanish princes, Apulia, Tuscany, Venice and the Lombard towns did honor to Frederick. Frederick saved the life of the papal legate, Cardinal Roland, whose statement of papal claims enraged the German nobles (translation of *beneficia* as "fiefs"). Boleslav, Duke of Bohemia, granted the style of "king" (1158).

1174-1177. Frederick's fifth expedition to Italy: vain siege of Alessandria, futile efforts at reconciliation with the pope.

1176. LEGNANO: decisive defeat of Frederick by the Lombard League, the first major defeat of feudal cavalry by infantry, herald of the new rôle of the bourgeoisie.

1183. Final peace of Constance between Frederick, the pope, and the Lombard towns: restoration of all imperial confiscations during the papal schism confirmed, recognition of general imperial suzerainty in Italy; the Lombard towns virtually autonomous city-states under a loose administration by imperial legates and vicars. Frederick retained the Matildan lands without a specific definition of their status. Henceforth there was no shadow of unity in the empire, as Germany and Italy followed a divergent development.

1184. Great Diet of Mainz: a tremendous mediaeval pageant for the knighting of Frederick's two sons in the presence of a great concourse, 70 (?) princes, 70,000 (?) knights.

1186. Marriage of the future Henry VI to Constance (daughter of Roger II of Sicily), heiress of King William II; possibly arranged by the pope in the hope of permanent peace with the empire. The net result of the marriage was the transfer of the center of gravity in the struggle between the popes and the emperors to Sicily, the final destruction of German unity and the ruin of the house of Hohenstaufen. The pope refused imperial coronation to Henry.

1186. Triple coronation at Milan: Frederick as King of Burgundy; Henry as *Caesar* (a deliberate revival of the title), and Constance as Queen of the Germans.

1186. Frederick took the Cross, and until his death led the Third Crusade (p. 260) in the traditional rôle of the emperor as the knightly champion of Christendom.

1190-1197. HENRY VI (already Caesar and regent, crowned emperor, 1191). The Mediaeval Empire at its maximum, ideally and territorially. Henry was not robust, and lacked the usual Hohenstaufen good nature. A good soldier, learned, practical, a shrewd diplomat, stern, cruel, but of heroic and original mind.

1190-1195. Intermittent struggles with the Welfs in Germany under Henry the Lion.

1191-1194. Restoration of order in Sicily: struggle with the Norman anti-king, Tancred of Lecce (d. 1194); coronation of Henry as King of Sicily (1194); birth of Frederick (later Frederick II) at Jesi (1194).

1192-1194. Henry used the captivity of King

Richard I of England to make the crown of England a fief of the empire, and to extort an enormous ransom.

Henry's plans to unite the German and Sicilian crowns, and to crown Frederick without election, thereby establishing the heredity of the German crown, were blocked by powerful German and papal opposition. Frederick was elected King of the Romans (1196). Plans (traditional with the Norman Kings of Sicily) for the foundations of a Mediterranean empire on the ruins of the Byzantine Empire as the basis for a universal dominion; dynastic marriage with the Greek imperial house; active preparations for a crusade; advance in central Italy and conciliation of northern Italy. Sicilian outbreak against the German administration brutally crushed. Henry's sudden death was followed by a bitter anti-imperial reaction in Italy, by fourteen years of civil war in Germany.

1197-1212. Civil war in Germany, chaos in the empire. Rival kings; Henry's brother, the Waiblinger **Philip of Swabia** (supported by King Philip II of France) and the Welf **Otto of Brunswick,** son of Henry the Lion (supported by King Richard I of England). The German nobles played one side off against the other. Chaos in Sicily, where Pope Innocent III acted as guardian of Frederick (after 1198). Otto's title validated by Innocent (1201); assassination of Philip (1208); imperial coronation of Otto (1209); papal break with Otto (1210) and support of Frederick (with Philip II); Frederick's second election (1211) and dash to Germany.

1211-1250. FREDERICK II (*Stupor Mundi*), a valetudinarian of middle height, courteous, amiable, charming, pitiless, arrogant; the most brilliant ruler and one of the most learned men of his day; a legislator of the first order, able soldier, diplomat, skeptic, one of the leading scientific investigators of his time; an astrologer with the mind of a Renaissance rationalist; Sicilian by taste and training, half Norman by blood, with little of the German about him. Crowned: King of the Romans, 1212; King of the Germans, at Aachen, 1215; Emperor, at Rome, 1220.

1212. Alliance with King Philip II of France.

1213. The Golden Bull of Eger: Frederick, who had already sworn an oath to keep his two crowns separate and to support the pope, abandoned the German Church to Innocent (conceding the free election of bishops, the right of appeal to Rome) and undertook to support the pope against heretics.

1214. The battle of Bouvines (p. 231): Frederick and Philip II completed the defeat of Otto and the Welfs. On the death of Innocent III (1216) Frederick's personal rule may be said to have begun.

1216-1227. Frederick on tolerable terms with Pope Honorius III, his old tutor: election (1220) of Frederick's son Henry as King of the Romans (a violation of Frederick's promise); Frederick allowed to retain Sicily during his lifetime; renewal of his crusading oath; grant of generous privileges (1220) to the clergy: exemption of the Church from taxation and of clerics from lay jurisdiction, making clerical princes virtually independent territorial princes; support of the bishops against the towns; promises to suppress heresy. Crusade postponed until 1225.

1222. First appearance of the Mongols in Europe (p. 264); capture of Cracow (1241); defeat of the Hungarians and Silesians.

1226. The conversion of Prussia undertaken by the Teutonic Order (p. 216).

1226-1232. Renewal of the ancient imperial claims in Lombardy, formation of the **Second Lombard League,** and appearance of the **First League of the Rhineland;** town leagues in central Italy; Pope Gregory alienated.

1227-1229. Frederick's crusade (p. 261): return of Frederick due to illness; first excommunication (1227); resumption of crusade (1228); violent papal and imperial propaganda and recrimination; the Teutonic Knights under Hermann of Salza remained faithful to Frederick. Aware of the commercial value of Moslem friendship Frederick negotiated a ten-year truce (1229) with El-Kamil, Sultan of Egypt, which restored Jerusalem, Nazareth, and Bethlehem to Christian hands. Frederick crowned himself King of Jerusalem. Papal war (1228-1229) of devastation in Apulia (first known papal mercenaries, the *soldiers of the keys*); Frederick on his return expelled the papal forces and threatened the *Patrimonium Petri* with invasion.

1230. Hollow peace of San Germano with Pope Gregory IX: Frederick promised to protect the papal domains, confirmed papal rights over Sicily, and was absolved. In preparation for the next struggle Frederick concentrated on Italy, especially Sicily. Frederick's son Henry on his majority (1228) devoted himself to Germany, and favored the towns. Frederick, like Barbarossa, had leaned heavily on the German episcopate, especially Engelbert of Cologne, and had increased the independence of the lay princes and *ministeriales*; administrative offices tended to become hereditary, and after Engelbert's death (1225) the administration had become less efficient. Settlement of the Teutonic Knights in Prussia: union (1237) with the Livonian Brothers of the Sword and eastward expansion: foundation of Thorn (1231), Kulm (1232) and Marienwerder (1233).

1231. Privilege of Worms. Hoping for German support for his Italian policy, Frederick extended to the lay princes his generous grants of 1220 to the clergy; giving them control over local justice, minting rights, roads, and streams, etc. From this grant dates a clear emergence in Germany of the territorial sovereignty of both lay and clerical princes. The **Decree of Ravenna** (1232) allowed expansion of the power of the princes at the expense of the towns. Henry objected, revolted (1234), and tried to win the German and Italian towns to his side.

1231. Completion of the **reorganization of Sicily**: clean sweep of private titles and royal privileges in the Norman manner; resumption of royal domain; destruction of private garrisons and feudal castles; ban on private war; criminal jurisdiction transferred from feudal to royal courts; towns deprived of magistrates and put under royal officers; clergy taxed and excluded from civil office. Sicily reduced to order (1221–1225): feudal revolts put down, towns brought to heel; large Saracen garrison-colonies (loyal to Frederick and indifferent to papal threats) established at Lucera and Nocera. Recognizing in Sicily the true source of his strength in money and men, Frederick aimed to unify Sicily and Italy into a kingdom of the empire. Local risings (1228–1230 and 1232) in Apulia and Sicily; unrest (1234) in southern Italy.

1231. The Constitutions of Melfi, the most conspicuous and constructive single piece of "legislation" in the Middle Ages, completed the Sicilian reorganization: an efficient divine right absolutism (much of it a return to the policy of Roger II) profoundly influenced by Roman law; centralization under an expert departmentalized bureaucracy; clerical jurisdiction limited to ecclesiastical matters; heresy a civil crime; simony in civil office a capital offense; gift or sale of Church land forbidden. Feudal, clerical, and municipal administration replaced by royal officials; supreme court at Capua; justices on annual circuits; careful financial organization. The University of

Naples (the first European university on a royal charter) founded (1224) to train state officials, and given a monopoly of higher education; Salerno revived as a school of medicine.

Advanced economic policy in Sicily based on Arab practice: abolition of internal tolls; mercantilistic regulation, state monopolies. Replacement of feudal dues by fixed payments; direct taxation in crises, efficient customs collection and internal prosperity.

1235-1237. Frederick's last visit to Germany: deposition, arrest, and imprisonment of Henry, who committed suicide in prison (1244) and was succeeded by his brother Conrad (1237); conciliation and peace with the Welfs strengthened Frederick in Germany. Great reform **Diet of Mainz** (the German Melfi, 1235); issue of the model *Landfrieden*. Frederick was unable to stem the steady progress of towns (resting on expanding commerce) in Germany or Italy.

1237. Frederick at **Cortenuova** smashed the Second Lombard League and humiliated Milan.

1239. Pope Gregory's second excommunication of Frederick, followed by a tremendous battle of pamphlets and preaching: Frederick painted as a heretic, rake, anti-Christ. He retorted with a demand for reform of the Church and an appeal to the princes of Europe, proposing a league of monarchs against the papacy.

Beginning of the amalgamation of northern and central Italy with the imperial administration on Sicilian lines: a system of general vicariates under imperial vicars, each city with an imperial *podestà* (generally Apulians, and often relatives of Frederick).

1241. Gregory's call for a synod at Rome to depose Frederick: Frederick ravaged papal territory, almost took Rome, and his fleet captured a large delegation of prelates off Genoa on their way to the synod; annexation of papal Tuscany to the empire. Gregory's death (1241). During the two-year interregnum in the papacy Frederick intrigued for a friendly pope, and welcomed

1243. The election of Sinobaldo Fiesco (*Innocent IV*), who turned out to be the architect of his ruin.

1244. Frederick's invasion of the Campagna and vain efforts at reconciliation with the pope; Innocent's flight to Lyons, and call for a synod.

1245. The Synod of Lyons: appeal to the Germans to revolt and elect a new king; deposition of Frederick; Louis IX's efforts at conciliation and Frederick's offers rebuffed by the pope: Innocent unleashed the Franciscans and Dominicans in a war of propaganda and proclaimed a crusade against Frederick. Henry Raspe, Duke of Thuringia (d. 1247), was set up (1246) as an anti-king in Germany, followed by

1247-1256. William of Holland, who was supported by a newly formed league of Rhenish towns. Innocent's ruthless but vain campaign against Frederick's episcopal allies in Germany; bitter warfare in northern Italy with extreme cruelty on both sides; Italian conspiracy to assassinate Frederick (probably with Innocent's knowledge) put down in cold blood; Piero della Vigne, Frederick's most trusted official, supposedly implicated. He was arrested, blinded, and died a suicide (1249); capture of Frederick's son Enzio (1249) who died in prison (1272).

1248. The defeat of Frederick after a long siege of Parma did not destroy his hold on northern Italy.

1250. Sudden death of Frederick; burial in the cathedral at Palermo, where his sarcophagus still remains.

1254-1273. THE GREAT INTERREGNUM.

1250-1268. Relentless persecution of the Hohenstaufens by the popes:

1250-1254. CONRAD IV, emperor, and King of Sicily by the will of his father, Frederick; Manfred, his illegitimate half-brother, regent of Sicily; Pope Innocent IV.'s offer (1253) of the Sicilian crown under papal suzerainty to Edmund (son of Henry III of England); renewal of Conrad's excommunication and proclamation of a crusade against him; papal invasion of the kingdom (i.e., southern Italy and Sicily).

1255-1261. Manfred regained southern Italy (1255) and Sicily (1256), was crowned King of Sicily (1258), and after the Sienese (Ghibelline) victory over Florence at Montaperto (1260) almost dominated Italy; Alexander V's peace offers were rejected by Manfred (1261).

1257. Double election in Germany of two foreigners: **Richard of Cornwall** (brother of Henry III of England, brother-in-law of Frederick II), and **Alfonso X** of Castile.

1266. Charles of Anjou (brother of Louis IX of France), accepting Urban IV's offer (1262) of the Sicilian crown under papal suzerainty, invaded southern Italy in accordance with papal plans and with his own ambitions to create a Mediterranean empire. He defeated Manfred who fell in the battle (**Benevento,** 1266), ending any hope of a native ruler for Italy.

1268. Conradin (Conrad IV's son, aged 15), called from Germany by the Italian Ghibellines, was defeated at **Tagliacozzo,** betrayed to Charles of Anjou, and beheaded at Naples with, at least, the tacit approval of Pope Clement IV. European public opinion was shocked, and Henry III of England and Louis IX of France were aroused. The heir of the house of Hohenstaufen was Constance, daughter of Manfred, whose husband, Pedro III of Aragon, was destined to become the first Aragonese king of Sicily (1282–1285) (p. 286).

The imperial title remained (1268–1806) an appendage of the German monarchy, but as the Germans were little interested in the title the way to the imperial throne was opened to ambitious foreigners. The bitter struggle of the Hohenstaufens and the popes, followed by removal of the papacy to French soil, alienated the German people from the Roman popes and bred a lasting suspicion of the Latin Church that bore fruit in the nationalism of the Reformation.

The princes of Germany, busy consolidating their own power, were not eager to elect a king, and there was no election until Pope Gregory X, alarmed at the progress of Charles of Anjou and the degeneration of Germany, which reduced papal revenue and indirectly strengthened France, and needing an imperial leader for the crusades, threatened to name an emperor.

The Great Interregnum, an epilogue to the mediaeval struggle of the popes and the emperors, marks the end of the mediaeval Holy Roman Empire and the failure of imperial efforts to establish German unity; it was a prologue to the complete triumph of particularism which dominated German life until well into the 19th century.

SIGNIFICANT ELEMENTS IN 13TH-CENTURY GERMANY:

I. **Great tenants-in-chief:** (1) Four ancient princely houses: the **Ascanians** (Brandenburg and eastern Saxony with the ducal title); the **Welfs** (Brunswick); the **Wittelsbachs** (Upper Bavaria, the County Palatine of the Rhine, Lower Bavaria); the **Wettins** (Saxony after the 15th century); (2) **Ottokar,** King of the Slavic Kingdom of Bohemia (1253–1278), with claims to Austria, Styria, Carinthia, Carniola.

II. **Great ecclesiastical tenants-in-chief:** especially in the Rhineland (notably the Archbishops of **Mainz, Trier,** and **Cologne**).

III. **Three minor houses** about to emerge into importance: (1) **Luxemburgs**, (2) **Hapsburgs**, (3) **Hohenzollerns**.

IV. **Lesser tenants-in-chief** (the so-called *Ritterschaft*), who regarded the central power as their defense against the great princes.

V. **Imperial cities** (*Reichstädte*), growing richer and more powerful and disposed to support the crown against the princes. Tendency of the cities to organize as leagues.

The informal (until the 14th century) constitution of the German monarchy: (1) Election of the king (originally by tribal chieftains) devolved upon the tenants-in-chief, then upon a group of them; election to be followed by ratification by the others. In the 13th century the group election became final election and was confined to a body of seven electors (of varying personnel).

(2) The ancient feudal *Reichstag* (*curia regis*) became (in the 13th century) the German *Diet* (equivalent to Parliament or the Estates-General) divided into two houses: princes and electors. Its functions remained vague and amorphous. Towns were admitted in 1489.

The great ecclesiastical states of the Rhineland and their feudal satellites reached the zenith of their power in the 13th century, and strove to maintain their position in the face of the rising lay states to the east (Saxony, Brandenburg, Austria, and Bohemia) by electing to the monarchy feeble princes who could pay well for election and would remain amenable. The lay states became dynastic principalities primarily concerned with their own fortunes and anticlerical in policy.   (*Cont. p.* 303.)

(1) *The Teutonic Knights*

1190-1191. Crusading origin. Merchants of Lübeck and Bremen founded a hospital at Acre which soon became attached to the German church of Mary the Virgin in Jerusalem.

1198. The brethren of this hospital were raised to a military order of knighthood (as the *Order of the Knights of the Hospital of St. Mary of the Teutons in Jerusalem*) by the Germans gathered for Henry VI's crusade. Henceforth membership in the order was open only to Germans, and knighthood only to nobles. Pope Innocent III gave them the rule of the Templars. Headquarters were successively at Acre (1191–1291), Venice, and (after 1309) Marienburg, clear evidence of the new orientation of the Knights. Intense rivalry existed between the order and the Templars and Hospitalers in the

Holy Land until the failure of the Crusades turned them to other fields of action. The robes of the Teutonic Knights were white with a black cross.

Reconstitution of the order and **transfer to the eastern frontier** of Germany. The eastward advance (*Drang nach Osten*) of the Germans, begun under Charlemagne, had never wholly ceased, and colonization with Netherlandish farmers and German merchants, coupled with Cistercian efforts during the days of Adolf of Holstein, Albert the Bear (self-styled Margrave of Brandenburg), and Henry the Lion of Saxony, established the Germans firmly in Mecklenburg and Brandenburg. Lübeck (founded 1143) early became an important commercial center. The foundation of Riga (1198), as a crusading and missionary center, the establishment of the *Livonian Brothers of the Sword*, and an influx of Westphalian nobles and peasant immigrants insured the continued advance of Germanization and the progress of Christianity (largely under Cistercian auspices) in Livonia. The defeat of the Danes at Bornhörde (1227) by the combined princes of North Germany, cost them Holstein, Lübeck, Mecklenburg, and Pomerania, leaving only Estonia to Denmark. The Poles had already begun the conversion of the Prussians and East Pomeranians.

1210-1239. Under **HERMANN VON SALZA,** the first great grand master, the order, at the invitation of Andrew of Hungary, was established (1221–1224) in Transylvania as a bulwark against the Comans (Cumani) until their progress alarmed the Hungarian monarch.

Hermann was an intimate friend of Emperor Frederick II, and was the real founder of the greatness and prosperity of the (still relatively poor and insignificant) order.

1226. By the **Golden Bull of Rimini,** Frederick laid down the organization of the order (on Sicilian lines) and prepared the Knights for a new career as pioneers of Germanization and as Christian missionaries on the eastern frontier. Frederick repeatedly made them generous gifts, used them for his own crusade, and employed individual knights on important missions. The grand master was given the status of a prince of the empire.

Organization of the order. Districts, each under a commander; a general chapter, acting as advisers to the grand master; five chief officers; the grand master elected for life by the Knights. The order was nominally under the pope and the emperor, but in the days of its might only strong popes exerted any influence.

1229.   The call to Prussia.   (The name *Prussia* is probably derived from a native word *Prusiaskai* and not from *Bo-Russia*.)   An appeal (1225–1226) from Conrad of Masovia, Duke of Poland, for aid, coinciding with Frederick's reorganization, was accepted by Hermann of Salza, and the Knights embarked on a unique crusade comparable only with that in the Iberian Peninsula, as champions of Christianity and Germanism.   Conrad gave (1230) them Kulmerland, and promised them whatever they conquered from the Prussians.   Frederick confirmed their rights.

1234.   The Knights transferred all their holdings to the pope, receiving them back as fiefs of the Church and thus had no other lord than the distant papacy.

1237.   Union with the Livonian Brothers was followed by notable progress in Livonia and plans for the conversion of the Russians from the Greek Church to the Roman, which led to a serious defeat for the order.   Courland was also gained and Memel founded (1252) to hold the conquests.   Eventually the southern Baltic coast from the Elbe to Finland was opened by the order to the missions of the Church and the trade and colonies of the Germans.

A great era of town foundations (some 80 in all) opened under the order: Thorn (castle, 1231), Kulm (castle, 1232), Marienwerder (1233), Elbing (castle, 1237), Memel (1252), Königsberg (1254), *et al.*

1242-1253.   A Prussian revolt was put down, and the conquest of Prussia continued with aid from Ottokar of Bohemia, Rudolf of Hapsburg, Otto of Brandenburg.

1260.   The battle of Durben, a disastrous defeat of the order by the Lithuanians, was followed by another Prussian revolt which had national aspects and was put down with Polish aid.   The suppression was marked by deliberate extermination and the virtually complete Germanization of Prussia ensued.   Castle Brandenburg was built (1266) and the reduction of Prussia completed (1285).

The order allowed great freedom to the towns (especially after 1233); no tolls were collected, only customs dues.   The large commercial towns joined the Hanseatic League (p. 312). The Knights were also generous (after 1236) in charters to German (and Polish) nobles, the peasants were well treated, and mass migrations into territories of the Knights became common.

1263.   The pope granted the order permission to trade, not for profit, a concession later expanded (by devious means) into full commercial freedom.   As a result the order, founded as a semi-monastic crusading society, eventually became a military and commercial corporation of great wealth and selfish aims, and a serious competitor of the very towns it had founded.   The Knights escaped the fate of the Templars, though temporarily on the defensive.

Great state was kept at the headquarters in Marienburg, and under Grand Master Winrich (1351–1382) the order was the school of northern chivalry, just as later it became a great cultural influence through the foundation of schools everywhere in its domains and the maintenance of its houses as centers of learning.

(*Cont. p.* 315.)

d. ITALY AND THE PAPACY, 888-1314.

The papacy was a local and secular institution until 1048; Italy was without effective native rule.

888-924.   **Berengar I,** last of the phantom "emperors" (vacancy in the empire, 924–962), was the grandson of Louis the Pious.   Surviving rival "emperors" were Guido of Spoleto, Lambert his son, and Louis of Provence, who was crowned emperor in 915.   **Raids of Saracens** (c. 889) and **Magyars** (c. 898) into Lombardy; a Saracen stronghold at Freinet controlled the Alpine passes; Saracen settlements in southern Italy, and the **Moslem conquest (917) of Sicily** began the isolation of that area; Italian urban life had become almost extinct; the invasions were checked, not by the shadowy monarchs, but by the rise of feudal defenders.

914-963.   **The nadir of the papacy** (the *pornocracy*): the landed aristocracy of Rome, under the leadership of the Senator Theophylact, his wife Theodora, and his daughter Marozia (mistress of Pope Sergius III, and mother of Sergius' son John, later Pope John XI) dominated the Curia.

928.   **Marozia,** having imprisoned Pope John XI, took control of Rome until her son

932-954.   **Alberic II** assumed power; the *Patrimonium Petri* was a plaything of the Crescentii (Marozia's family), who maintained an intermittent supremacy in Rome during the 10th century.   The papacy was without political power or spiritual prestige and the Western Church for all practical purposes became a loose organism under its bishops, who gave "national churches" such coherence as they had, and acknowledged a vague kind of allegiance to Rome.

924. **Rudolf** of (Juran) Burgundy elected king, followed by

926-945. **Hugh of Provence.**

945. **Lothair II** (d. 950), Hugh's son and co-regent, was declared sole king. Lothair's rival,

950-961. **Berengar II,** imprisoned his widow Adelheid, who appealed (according to tradition) to Otto the Great.

951-952. **Otto the Great's first expedition** to Italy.

961-964. **Otto's second expedition** to Italy, in answer to the appeal of the profligate pope, John XII, for protection against Berengar. Otto's coronation at Pavia as King of Italy and his coronation by the pope as Roman Emperor, marked the

962. **REVIVAL OF THE ROMAN EMPIRE.** Otto confirmed his predecessors' grants in the *Patrimonium Petri* (probably with additions), but made careful reservation of the imperial right to sanction papal elections, and treated the pope like a German bishop (i.e. subject to the state). Otto also exacted a promise from the Romans not to elect a pope without imperial consent. He established a precedent by calling a synod at Rome which deposed (963) Pope John XII for murder and other crimes, and selected a (lay) successor, Leo VIII (963-964). This synod opened a period of about a hundred years when the papacy was dominated by the German emperors and by the Counts of Tusculum, vassals of the emperors, with the title of *patricius* in Rome. In the same period the bishops in the west lost the position they had won in the 9th century, and became increasingly dependent on the kings and feudal nobility, and increasingly secular in outlook. The homage of Paldolf I for Capua and Benevento (967) and his investiture with the Duchy of Spoleto, mark the beginning of the long imperial effort to include southern Italy in the empire.

964. **Leo VIII** was expelled by the Romans shortly after his election, and **Benedict V** was (964-965) elected by the Romans without imperial consent.

966-972. **Otto's third expedition to Italy:** Otto held a synod which deposed Benedict. Pope John XIII (elected with imperial co-operation) was soon expelled by the Romans, and Otto, after a terrible vengeance on Rome, restored him. Imperial coronation of the future Otto II (967) by John XIII, coronation of Theophano and her marriage to Otto in Rome (972).

980-983. **Otto II's expedition to Italy:** Otto crushed Crescentius I, Duke of the Romans, restored the pope (981), and was utterly defeated in his effort to expel the Saracens from southern Italy by a Greco-Moslem alliance (982). Otto nominated **Pope John XIV** (983-984).

983. **Great Diet of Verona:** remarkable unity of the Italian and German magnates; resolve on a holy war against the Moslems; election of the future Otto III as successor to his father. Venice, already profiting by her Moslem trade, refused ships and defied the emperor.

996. **Otto III,** on his first expedition to Italy deposed the *Patricius*, Crescentius II, and (at the request of the Roman people) nominated as pope his cousin Bruno, **Gregory V** (996-999), the first German pope, an ardent Cluniac. Gregory and Otto compelled Gerbert to yield the Archbishopric of Reims to the German Arnulf, and forced the French espiscopate to acquiesce. Gregory censured King Robert of France. As the successor to Pope Gregory, Otto named **Gerbert of Aurillac.**

999-1003. **SYLVESTER II** (Gerbert of Aurillac), the first French pope, a man of humble origin, one of the most learned men of his day (Arabic, mathematics, and science). An intriguer and diplomat who co-operated with Otto in his mystic renewal of the empire; he was a moderate reformer, asserting that simony was the worst evil of the Church.

1012-1046. **The Tusculan popes** were either the relatives or the creatures of the Counts of Tusculum: **Benedict VIII** (1012-1024), something of a reformer; **John XIX** (1024-1032), his brother, and **Benedict IX** (1033-1044), a debauchee who sold the papacy for cash, (i.e. the Peter's Pence from England) to his godfather, a priest, **Gregory VI** (1044-1046), who bought the See of Peter in order to reform it. The emperors, preoccupied with German affairs, made only rare visits to Italy.

Notable local efforts were made by the Church to reform itself and society:

(1) Local synods decreed clerical celibacy (e.g. Augsburg, 952; Poitiers, 1000; Seligenstadt, 1023; Bourges, 1031), and attacked simony.

(2) Foundation (910) of the **Abbey of Cluny** by William the Pious, Duke of Aquitaine, as a reformed Benedictine house, wholly free of feudal control, directly under the Holy See. Centralization of all daughter and affiliated houses (priories) under a single Abbot of Cluny; rapid spread of Cluniac organization (France, Lorraine, Germany) and ideas of reform into western Europe: celibacy of the clergy; abolition of lay investiture; and of simony.

(3) Gerard, Lord of Brogne, founded (923) a monastery on his own estate which became a center of ecclesiastical reforms among existing foundations in Flanders and Lorraine.

(4) Synods in Aquitaine and Burgundy (where monarchical opposition to feudal anarchy was weak) pronounced (c. 989) anathema on ravagers of the Church and despoilers of the poor, initiating a long series of clerical efforts throughout Europe to force feudal self-regulation, which go by the name of the **Peace of God.** These decrees, repeatedly renewed and extended, were supplemented (after c. 1040) by the **Truce of God,** an effort to limit fighting to certain days and seasons of the year.

(5) An effort to restore the central authority of the Church by reference to past decrees, of which the most notable were the so-called *Isidorean* (or Forged) *Decretals,* attributed to Isidorus Mercator, and produced (c. 850) by a Frankish cleric. A combination of authentic and forged papal decrees, they aimed to establish the authority and power of the bishops and the position of the pope as supreme lawgiver and judge, and to make him supreme over councils.

(6) Notable increase in new ascetic orders in Italy and monastic schools north and south of the Alps; outstanding individual reformers (e.g. **Peter Damian,** d. 1072; **Lanfranc,** d. 1089; **Anselm,** d. 1109).

ITALY AT THE OPENING OF THE 11TH CENTURY: Sicily was in the hands of the Saracens; Apulia and Calabria under the feeble rule of Constantinople; Gaeta, Naples, Amalfi, were city republics; Benevento, Capua, and Salerno the capitals of Lombard principalities. Norman pilgrims arriving (1016) at the shrine of St. Michael on Monte Gargano began the penetration of the south by Norman soldiers of fortune in the service of rival states: the first permanent Norman establishment was at Aversa (c. 1029); the sons of the Norman Tancred of Hauteville (including Robert Guiscard) appeared (after c. 1035), and their steady advance at the expense of the Greeks led Benevento to appeal for papal protection (1051). Feudal anarchy prevailed in the north.

1027. **Conrad II,** in Italy for his coronation, restored order in the north, reducing the Lombard nobles.

1037. On a second expedition he disciplined Archbishop Aribert of Milan, restored order in the south; his *constitutio de feudis* made Italian fiefs hereditary.

1044-1046. **GREGORY VI** purchased the papal throne to reform the papacy, but the end of his reign saw three rival popes (Gregory,

Sylvester III, and Benedict IX). All three were deposed by the **Synods of Sutri and of Rome** (1046) under pressure from the reforming emperor, Henry III, who made Suidgar, Bishop of Bamberg, pope as **Clement II** (1046–1047), the first of a series of German pontiffs: Damasus II (1048), Leo IX (1048–1054); Victor II (1055–1057), representing strong Cluniac influences. Henry pacified southern Italy, reaffirmed the imperial right of nomination to the papacy, and left Italy in sound order.

1049-1085. Restoration of the independence of the papacy, resumption of papal leadership in the Church and of spiritual supremacy in the west.

1049-1054. **LEO IX** (Bruno of Toul, a kinsman of Henry III) began the identification of the papacy with Cluniac reforms, and the restoration of the spiritual primacy of the Holy See. He insisted on his own canonical election to the papal throne, reorganized the chancery on the imperial model, reformed the Church by personal or legatine visitation, giving reform reality in the west. The **Synod of Rome** (1047) had issued stern decrees against simony and clerical marriage.

1052. Henry III granted the Duchy of Benevento to the papacy.

1053. Leo, in his personal effort to enforce papal rights in the south, was utterly defeated by the Normans at Civitate.

1054. The long doctrinal controversy with the **Greek Orthodox Church,** which really hinged on fundamental divergences between east and west, ended with the final schism between the eastern (Orthodox) and western (Roman) Church (p. 252).

1054-1057. VICTOR II. Elected at the urging of Hildebrand (later Gregory VII), who dominated this pontificate and the following one and who made the papacy the leader in reform. Beatrice, mother of Matilda, and widow of Count Boniface of Tuscany, married (1054) Godfrey the Bearded, Duke of Upper Lorraine, Henry's most dangerous foe in Germany, as Boniface had been in Italy. Henry arrested Beatrice and her daughter Matilda, Boniface's heiress; Godfrey fled; Matilda remained all her life a powerful ally of the papacy, and kept middle Italy loyal to the popes.

1057-1058. STEPHEN IX (brother of Godfrey the Bearded), a zealous Cluniac. The **Pataria** (c. 1056), a popular movement (the result of a preaching campaign), gained wide currency in the Milan region for its demands of clerical celibacy, the end of simony and for apostolic simplicity among the clergy. It came into sharp conflict with the bishop and clergy. Peter Damian, sent by the pope, maintained the papal position (1059), and brought the archbishop to terms; there was a later outbreak of the Pataria.

1058-1061. NICHOLAS II.

1059. The Synod of the Lateran, by its electoral decree, replaced the vague traditional rights of the Roman clergy in papal elections by an electoral college of cardinals: the prerogative voice in the election went to the seven cardinal bishops; the cardinal clergy represented the clergy and people at large; a Roman prelate (if worthy) was to be preferred; the election to be at Rome if possible. Henry's rights were provided for, but the provision seems to have been personal rather than general.

1059. Under Hildebrand's influence an alliance was made with the Norman, Richard of Aversa, and Nicholas after exacting an oath later invested Robert Guiscard with the Duchy of Apulia and Calabria, and promised him Sicily if he could conquer it, thereby establishing papal suzerainty over southern Italy, the first great expansion of temporal suzerainty by the popes. The **Synod of Melfi** condemned (1059) the marriage of clergy.

1061-1073. ALEXANDER II. His election without consultation of Henry IV created serious tension; the **Synod of Basel** declared the election invalid, and chose an anti-pope. Alexander, on friendly terms with William the Conqueror, blessed the Norman conquest of England.

1071. Robert Guiscard (d. 1085) captured Bari, ending the Greek power in Italy; his capture of Palermo (1072) began the

1072-1091. Norman conquest of Sicily. Roger I (d. 1101) succeeded Guiscard as lord of southern Italy (except Capua, Amalfi, and papal Benevento).

1073-1085. GREGORY VII (*Hildebrand*). Short, corpulent, with glittering eyes, the son of an Italian peasant educated at Rome under strong Cluniac influence. Inspired by Gregory the Great, Gregory VI, and the study of the Decretals, he was neither an original thinker nor a scholar, but was intensely practical and of lofty moral stature. After a brilliant career in the *Curia* he was acclaimed pope by the Romans before his election. German bishops protested the election, and Gregory postponed his consecration, awaiting Henry's decision in a sincere effort to live up to his ideal of perfect co-operation between pope and emperor in the interest of peace, reform, and the universal monarchy of the papacy. His pro-

gram was summed up by his *Dictatus*, an informal memorandum which asserted: (1) The Roman Church has never erred, can never err; (2) the pope is supreme judge, may be judged by none, and there is no appeal from him; (3) no synod may be called a general one without his order; (4) he may depose, transfer, reinstate bishops; (5) he alone is entitled to the homage of all princes; (6) he alone may depose an emperor.

1075-1122. THE INVESTITURE STRUGGLE; vindication of the spiritual supremacy and leadership of the papacy (p. 207).

The Emperor Henry IV after his Saxon victory forgot his promises of reform in Germany. The **Synod of Rome** (1075) passed severe decrees against simony, clerical marriage, and (for the first time) against lay investiture, providing deposition for clerical offenders, excommunication for laymen. Gregory's letter of remonstrance and rebuke to Henry was ignored, and Henry, on the urging of the German bishops, called a **Synod at Worms** (1076). This synod deposed Gregory. Henry's first excommunication and the so-called humiliation at Canossa (1077) profited neither party; Henry's second deposition (1080) was without serious effect. After a series of invasions (1081–1084), Henry entered Rome and was crowned by his anti-pope, only to be expelled by Gregory's Norman ally, Robert Guiscard, with a motley army which included Saracens; the atrocity of the Norman sack made it impossible for Gregory to remain and he died a virtual exile, almost a prisoner of his allies at Salerno, leaving Henry and his anti-pope master of Rome for the time.

Gregory was on excellent terms with William the Conqueror and responsible for Alexander's blessing of the Conquest (1066), but William, true to the Norman conception of strong monarchy, ignored Gregory's pressure to make England a fief of the papacy, and forbade the circulation of papal bulls in England without his permission. Gregory asserted papal suzerainty over Hungary, Spain, Sardinia, and Corsica. After a vacancy of a year, a close friend of Gregory was elected pope, **Victor III** (1086–1087), an aged, unwilling pontiff, soon driven from Rome by Henry's partisans.

1088-1099. URBAN II. A Frenchman of noble blood, long intimate with Gregory; handsome, eloquent, learned, he continued Gregory's policy of maintaining the complete independence of the papacy and vigorous opposition to the emperors. Urban arranged the marriage of Countess Matilda and the son of the (Welf) Duke of Bavaria (1089).

Henry invaded northern Italy successfully, but Matilda held out in the hills; Urban, profiting by the anarchy in Germany, urged Henry's son Conrad to a revolt (1093) which was taken up by half of Lombardy. Urban at the **Synod of Piacenza** (1095) renewed the decrees against simony and clerical marriage, added a ban on clerical homage to laymen, and received the appeal of the Byzantine emperor for help against the Turks at the **Synod of Clermont** (1095) (p. 258). Urban excommunicated King Philip I of France for adultery, and proclaimed the **First Crusade,** directing his appeal to the nobles and peoples rather than the monarchs, most of whom were hostile to the papacy. On a visit to southern Italy, Urban made Roger of Sicily his legate (1098), thus exempting him from the visits of an ordinary legate. At the **Synod of Bari,** Urban was as much interested in keeping the papal leadership in the Crusade as he was in the debates on the procession of the Holy Ghost. The First Crusade was the first great victory for the reformed papacy; the papal dominance of the military effort to defend Christendom is significant of the new prestige of the papacy and the decline of the emperors.

1099-1118. PASCHAL II renewed the excommunication of Henry IV; intrigued with Henry, his son; Anselm waged the investiture battle in England (1103–1107), ending in a compromise (1107), followed almost at once by the lapse of lay investiture in France (formerly one of the worst offenders). Paschal's humiliating renunciation (1111) of papal fiefs and secular revenues, his repudiation by his clergy, and his arrest by Henry V made a much more profound impression in Europe than Canossa. Paschal recalled (1112) his concessions.

1115. The Countess Matilda, having made a donation (1086 and 1102) of her allodial lands (the second great addition to papal holdings) to the papacy (subject to free testamentary disposition), willed them at her death (1115) to Henry V, who came and occupied the Matildine lands (1117), destined to be a bone of contention between the popes and emperors for a century.

1118-1119. GELASIUS II was forced to flee Rome; Henry V appointed his own pope; Gelasius having excommunicated (1118) Henry, was finally driven to France.

1119-1124. CALIXTUS II, a Burgundian, related to half the rulers of Europe and a skilled diplomat, arranged the **Concordat of Worms** (1122) which closed the investiture controversy with a compromise. The **Synod of Reims** (1119) renewed the decrees against simony,

clerical marriage, and lay investiture, as well as the excommunication of Henry V.

1130-1138. Papal schism: precipitated by the corrupt election of the (Cluniac) Cardinal Pierleone (son of a rich converted Jewish banker of Rome), as **Anacletus II** (1130–1138), and the hostility of the rival houses of Corsi and Frangipani. The rival pope, **Innocent II** (1130–1143), supported by Bernard of Clairvaux and most of Europe, was given military support by Lothair in return for confirmation of his rights under the Concordat of 1122, imperial coronation, and investiture with the Matildine lands. Anacletus confirmed Roger II's title as king in return for his support.

1139. The Second Lateran Council (the tenth general council in the west) was attended by a thousand bishops. It marked the end of the schism.

1143. The Commune of Rome: established in opposition to the non-Roman pope, it defied three feeble popes (Celestine II; Lucius II; Eugenius III). **Arnold of Brescia,** pupil of Abélard, emerged as the eloquent leader with bitter denunciations of clerical wealth and papal bloodshed and burning appeals for a return to apostolic poverty and simplicity. Temporary restoration of the ancient Roman state, appeal to the emperor's protection. **Bernard of Clairvaux** agreed with Arnold's indictment (cf. *De Consideratione,* addressed to Pope Eugenius), but saw salvation for the Church in purification from within, not in diminution of its great powers, and opposed Arnold as he had Abélard.

1147-1149. The Second Crusade (p. 260).

1154-1159. Adrian IV (Nicholas Breakspear, the only English pope). Son of a poor man, learned, kindly, of high character, he had risen by his own merits. Roman anarchy ended by a stern interdict; Arnold expelled; alliance with **Frederick Barbarossa** against William, King of Sicily; altercation with Frederick over his haughty refusal of ceremonial service to the pope (stirrup episode). The bitter hostility of the Romans to pope and emperor forced a surreptitious coronation and hurried departure from Rome.

1155. Frederick executed Arnold as a heretic, but abandoned Adrian to the Normans and forced him to an independent Italian policy (i.e. alliance with an anti-Norman league of southern barons and with Constantinople) which brought William of Sicily to his knees as the pope's vassal. Adrian accepted the Roman Commune and returned to Rome.

1158-1162. Frederick's second expedition to Italy: the **League of Pavia** (Brescia,

Cremona, Parma, Piacenza) supported Frederick; Milan and its league were reduced to submission. The great **Diet of Roncaglia:** Frederick, using Roman law to justify an extreme assertion of imperial rights and a brusque resumption of imperial regalia, substituted an imperial *podestà* for the consuls in the Lombard cities, drove Milan into open revolt (1159–1162) and turned the towns to alliance with the pope. Renewal of the papal alliance with Byzantium; formation of an alliance of Lombard towns under papal auspices.

1159-1181. ALEXANDER III (imperialist antipopes: Victor IV, Paschal III, Calixtus III). Frederick, citing precedents from Constantine, Charlemagne, and Otto the Great, held a synod at Pavia to adjudicate the claims of Alexander III and Victor IV. Alexander ignored the synod, Victor was recognized. Alexander, after an exile in France, returned and excommunicated Frederick (1165). Renewal of the town leagues (1164); Milan rebuilt, expulsion of imperial *podestàs*.

1167-1168. Frederick's fourth expedition to Italy: Alexander's flight to the Normans; Frederick's capture of Rome; renewal of the Lombard League (1168): promises of mutual aid; organization for federal administration; erection of Alessandria, a great fortress city (named for the pope), to guard the passes (1168); Italy virtually independent.

1174. Frederick's fifth expedition to Italy: vain siege of Alessandria, complete **defeat at Legnano** (1176); preliminary peace of Venice (1177, the centenary of Canossa).

1179. **The Third Lateran Council** decreed a two-thirds vote of the conclave to be necessary for a valid papal election.

1181-1198. A series of unimportant popes, often exiled from Rome by local anarchy until 1188, when papal recognition of the Commune of Rome made peaceful residence again possible.

1183. **Peace of Constance:** imperial suzerainty in Italy recognized; resumption by the Lombard towns of all *regalia* they had ever enjoyed, including the right to maintain an army, to fortify, to keep the league or expand it, full judicial jurisdiction, control of their own coinage, abolition of the imperial *podestàs*. The only relic of imperial control was the reservation of the emperor's right to confirm elected consuls, the right of appeal to the imperial court, and the retention of the *fodrum* as a contribution to military needs. The Lombard towns were autono-

mous for all practical purposes under a very loose system of imperial legates and vicars.

1184. Frederick's sixth expedition to Italy: utilizing the split in the Lombard League (after 1181) and local feuds in Tuscany and Bologna, Frederick created a strong imperial party in middle Italy and by a liberal charter (1185) even won over Milan.

1189-1192. The Third Crusade (p. 260).

1198-1216. INNOCENT III. A tough-minded Italian patrician of German blood (whose family provided the Church with eight popes), chosen by the cardinals to restore the political power of the papacy. Animated by an historical mysticism, he looked on Christendom as a single community in which he aimed to combine moral unity with a world-state under papal guidance. He deduced the papal powers from the Petrine Theory, the *Old Testament*, the *Donation of Constantine*, and from the duty of the pope to insure justice, maintain peace, prevent and punish sin, and aid the unfortunate. With a clear grasp of essentials, he never lost sight of this concept, but his frequent opportunism destroyed his moral grandeur. Insistence, not on moral or theological, but on historical grounds (i.e. the Translation of the Empire) on the right (claimed by Gregory VII) to pass on imperial elections. A brilliant administrator, he first brought the papal chancery into systematic organization (division into four sections under experts, careful systematized treatment of documents) and made a great collection of canons and decretals. This pontificate was the zenith of the mediaeval papacy.

Restoration of the Papal States (Spoleto, Ancona, Romagna regained); many towns succeeded in escaping and keeping their local autonomy. Tuscany: an anti-imperial league under papal auspices; towns like Florence, Lucca, and Siena retained their appropriations of the Matildine lands (a partial foundation of their later power); the rest of the Matildine lands were regained by the Church. Innocent used his position first as protector, then as guardian of Frederick II, in an attempt to alienate Sicily from the Hohenstaufens.

Steady insistence on a crusade: The Fourth Crusade (p. 260) combined opportunity to attack the infidel with a chance to reunite the Roman and Orthodox Churches; Innocent reconciled himself to the sack of Constantinople by the organization of the new Latin Church of Constantinople. The Albigensian Crusade (p. 230), directed against the spreading heresy of southern France, drenched that region with blood and exterminated one of the most advanced local cultures in Europe, under revolting circumstances of feudal cynicism and clerical intolerance. Simon de Montfort nullified Innocent's efforts to divert the crusaders' ardor to Spain against the Moslems.

Vindication of the political claims of the papacy: (1) Asserting his right to pass on imperial elections, Innocent rejected the Hohenstaufen claimant (Philip of Swabia) to the imperial crown, ignored the undoubted rights of Frederick, crowned and supported Otto (in return for large promises of obedience to papal authority), and then procured (in alliance with King Philip II) the election of Frederick II. (2) By excommunicating Philip II (1198) he forced him to a formal recognition of his wife Ingeborg, but was coldly rebuffed when he intervened in Philip's struggle with the Angevins. (3) Maintaining the rights of his nominee to the See of Canterbury (Langton), Innocent forced King John of England (interdict, 1208) to cede England to the Holy See and receive it back as a fief (1213). (4) Innocent received the homage as papal vassals of the following states: Aragon, Bulgaria, Denmark, Hungary, Poland, Portugal, Serbia, and brought the Roman Church to its closest approximation to an ideal Christian, universal commonwealth.

The struggle against urban heresy: The Church, long organized to deal with a predominantly rural society, was increasingly out of touch with the rising bourgeoisie and urban proletariat as town life revived and expanded; the anti-clericalism of the cities had become a major problem. The Italian, **Francis of Assisi,** and the Spaniard, **Dominic,** organized the spontaneous response within the Church to this crisis: Francis (d. 1226), a converted gilded youth, as the joyous "troubadour of religion" began preaching the beauties of humbleness, poverty, simplicity, and devotion, of the brotherhood of man, of man and the animals, of man and nature. His cheerful vernacular hymns won tremendous success in the towns of Italy. Founded as a brotherhood, whence the name **Friars Minor** (*Minorites, Grey Friars*, also *Cordeliers*), the **Franciscans** won cautious support from Innocent, but not formal ratification as a corporation until 1223.

The second of the Mendicant Orders, the **Dominicans,** born of Dominic's campaign against the Albigensian heresy, was sanctioned by Innocent (1215). Organized as a preaching order, the Dominicans (*Friars Preachers, Black Friars*, or *Jacobins* in Paris) patterned their constitution on the Franciscan. These two mendicant orders were not monastic, rural monks, but town-dwellers devoted to preaching and charity. The conduct of the Inquisition was entrusted to them (1233) and their direct influence on education (especially that of the Dominicans) was enormous.

1215.   The Fourth Lateran Council was the climax of Innocent's pontificate (attended by 400 bishops, 800 abbots and priors, and the representatives of the monarchs of Christendom) and its decrees were of tremendous significance: (1) The Church was pronounced one and universal; (2) the Sacraments were decreed the channel of grace, and the chief sacrament, the Eucharist; (3) the Dogma of transubstantiation was proclaimed; (4) annual confession, penance and communion were enjoined; (5) careful rules were made as to episcopal elections and the qualifications of the clergy, and (6) injunctions for the maintenance of education in each cathedral and for theological instruction were formulated; (7) the Albigensian and Catharist heresies were condemned; (8) trial by ordeal and by battle forbidden; (9) relic worship regulated, and (10) rules of monastic life were made more rigorous. Finally, another crusade was proclaimed.

1216-1227. HONORIUS III, a high-minded noble of conciliatory disposition who managed to keep on relatively good terms with Frederick II.

1227-1241. GREGORY IX, a relative of Innocent III, aged and fiery, he never relaxed his relentless pressure on Frederick. **Canonization of Francis of Assisi** (1228) and **Dominic** (1234).

1243-1254. INNOCENT IV, a canon lawyer. Supposedly friendly to Frederick, he continued the uncompromising attack on the emperor, and encompassed the final ruin of the Hohenstaufen.

1271-1276. GREGORY X (*Visconti*), a high-minded pope with three aims: to pacify Italy; to check Charles of Anjou and the rising power of France; and to pacify Germany. At the **Synod of Lyons** (1274) he provided for the seclusion of conclaves to avoid corruption. His successors were occupied with Italian affairs (the war of Naples and Sicily, baronial anarchy in Rome, etc.), and the advancement of their own houses: **Nicholas III** (*Orsini*) (1277–1280), a foe of Charles of Anjou; **Martin IV** (1281–1285), a puppet of Charles of Anjou; **Honorius IV** (*Savelli*) (1285–1287); **Nicholas IV** (*Colonna*) (1288–1292). The rivalries of the great houses was so close that two years were required to elect Nicholas' successor, a hermit dragged unwilling (as a result of Cardinal Malabranca's dream) to the Holy See, **Celestine V** (1294), who never saw Rome, a puppet of Charles of Anjou and Cardinal Caetani. Induced (probably) by Caetani (the midnight voice, a megaphone over the papal couch) he resigned (*The Great Refusal,* Dante, *Inf.* III, 60) and was kept a prisoner by his successor, Boniface VIII (*Caetani*).

1294–1534. THE SECULARIZED PAPACY: absorption in secular politics to the exclusion of spiritual leadership.

1294–1303. BONIFACE VIII (*Caetani*). Surpassed all his colleagues in the Sacred College as lawyer, diplomat, and man of affairs. A skeptic in religion, but a believer in amulets and magic, well read in the pagan classics, he was the *last mediaeval pope,* and the last pope to claim the universal authority of the papacy as asserted by Gregory VII and maintained by Innocent III. Addicted to low company, he was not as vicious as contemporary propaganda painted him. Handsome and vain, he substituted on occasion imperial dress and regalia for papal vestments (*I am pope, I am Caesar*). Rude beyond belief, domineering and well-hated, his chief aim was the aggrandizement of the Caetani family. An intelligent patron of architecture and art: Giotto in Rome.

1295. Bent on regaining Sicily for the papacy, Boniface continued the support of the Angevin claimant, Charles II of Naples, arranged the **Peace of 1295,** by which James of Aragon exchanged Sicily for the investiture of Sardinia and Corsica, and the extinction of French claims in Aragon.

1296. The Bull *Clericis laicos,* designed to bring the kings of France and England to accept papal intervention, forbade the payment of taxes by the clergy to lay rulers without papal consent (a vain attempt to maintain a mediaeval custom in the face of rising national states). Philip IV of France answered with an embargo on the export of bullion; Edward I of England with outlawry of the clergy; both were supported by public opinion expressed in their national assemblies (pp. 199, 233).

1297. Angered by the Colonna, their insistence on the validity of Celestine V's election, their appeal to a general council, and their support of the Aragonese in Sicily, the pope began a veritable crusade which exiled the Colonna (Palestrina, the family stronghold, razed).

Recognition of the rights of Robert (second son of Charles II) in Naples (exclusion of Carobert of Hungary). Beginning of the formation of a Caetani *state* as a threat to the barons.

1300. THE GREAT JUBILEE, zenith of the pontificate, one of the magnificent pageants of the mediaeval papacy, managed with tremendous pomp by Boniface; huge donations (raked over public tables by papal "croupiers"); the proceeds intended by Boniface for the second Caetani state to be formed in Tuscany and for the subjection of Sicily.

1302. Charles of Valois' failure to dislodge Frederick, the Aragonese claimant in Sicily, forced Boniface to the **Peace of 1302** which ended the War of the Sicilian Vespers, left Frederick king, and provided for the ultimate reunion of Naples and Sicily under the Angevins.

1302–1303. Boniface's defeat and humiliation by the national states.

The **Bull** *Unam sanctam* (1302) marked the climax of papal claims to superiority over national states and lay rulers. Philip IV (his appeal for a compromise rejected) dispatched Nogaret to bring the pope to French soil for trial by a general council called by Philip.

1303. The "Terrible Day at Anagni": Nogaret and Sciarra Colonna penetrated to the papal apartment, found Boniface in bed, threatened him with death, tried to force his resignation, took him prisoner. Faced with a public reaction against them as foreigners, Nogaret and Colonna fled, and Boniface died shortly of humiliation. The papacy, so lately triumphant over the empire, found itself defeated by a new force, national feeling supporting national monarchy, and the defeat vindicated the claim of the new states to tax clerics and to maintain criminal jurisdiction over them.

1303–1304. BENEDICT XI. Exiled to Perugia by the anarchy in Rome, he promulgated a bull condemning the principals in the affair at Anagni, and died almost immediately (reputedly by poison). The cardinals, almost evenly divided for and against Boniface, after a conclave of ten months, chose a compromise candidate, the French Archbishop of Bordeaux, Bertrand de Got (supposed to be a bitter foe of Philip IV), who assumed the name

1305–1314. CLEMENT V (1305–1314). Clement never entered Italy and became friendly (bribed?) to Philip. The **Synod of Vienne** (1311–1312) exonerated Boniface's memory despite Philip's pressure, but Philip had his way with the Templars (1307) (p. 233). Italy was in anarchy, but Clement was bent on returning there as soon as he had made peace between England and France and launched a crusade. To escape Philip, Clement established the papal **court at Avignon.** (Avignon was an enclave in the Venaissin which was papal territory). (*Cont. p.* 290.)

(1) *The Norman Kingdom in South Italy and Sicily*, 1105-1194

1130-1154. The Norman Count **Roger II of Sicily** (1105–1130) succeeded the Norman Duke William of Apulia (1111–1127) and in 1130 assumed the title of King of Sicily, Apulia, and Capua with the approval of anti-Pope Anacletus II. Excommunicated by Pope Innocent II (1139) for his alliance with Anacletus, he defeated Innocent (1140), took him prisoner, and forced recognition of his title. By skillful diplomacy he prevented a joint invasion of Sicily by the Greek and Roman emperors. Planning a Mediterranean commercial empire, Roger established an extensive North African holding (at its maximum, 1153).

1154-1166. **William I,** continuing Roger's policy, defeated (1156) the Byzantine allies of Pope Adrian IV and compelled Adrian to recognize his title in Sicily, Apulia, Naples, Amalfi, and Salerno. He supported Pope Alexander III against Frederick I.

1166-1189. **William II** continued this policy, but as he planned a Mediterranean empire and wished a free hand, he welcomed the marriage (1186) of Constance (Roger II's daughter), his heiress, to the future Emperor Henry VI. He himself married Joan, sister of King Richard I of England, and intended to lead the Third Crusade as part of his imperial plans. On his death,

1190-1194. **Tancred of Lecce** (son of Roger, Duke of Apulia, the brother of Constance) led a vigorous native resistance to the Emperor Henry VI (king, 1194–1197) with the support of the pope and Richard I. Henry reduced Sicily, southern Italy, and part of Tuscany, with the aid of Pisa and Genoa, retained the Matildine lands in central Italy, organized an imperial administration of his holdings, and planned a great empire with Italy as its base. **Purely Norman rule ended with Tancred.**

The Norman kingship in southern Italy and Sicily was theocratic, on Byzantine lines; the administration was an efficient, departmentalized bureaucracy. Tremendous prosperity and efficient taxation made the Sicilian monarchs perhaps the richest in Europe. Dealing with a cosmopolitan kingdom containing Italian, Greek, and Saracen elements, and needing settlers, the Norman rulers practiced a tolerant eclecticism which provided for wide racial divergences in law, religion and culture.

Roger II's cosmopolitan court and generous patronage of the learned produced a brilliant circle including: the Arab geographer **Edrisi, Eugenius** the translator of Ptolemy's *Optics,* and **Henry Aristippus,** translator of Plato's *Phaedo* and Book IV of Aristotle's *Meteorologica.*

(2) *The Development of Italian Towns*

No continuous tradition of mediaeval and classical town government in Italy can be traced. The post-Carolingian anarchy left defense in local hands and rural refuges and town walls were the work of local co-operation. The bishops in Lombardy, traditional guardians of their flocks, with large episcopal and comital powers delegated from the monarchs, played a decisive rôle in communal organization for defense (e.g. Bergamo, 904). The first cases of true urban autonomy were in Amalfi, Benevento, and Naples (1000–1034), a development cut short by the advent of the Normans.

The great urban evolution took place in the north, and particularly in Lombardy, where sworn municipal leagues and urban associations appeared (probably) in the 10th century. In these cities the nobles (since ancient times town-dwellers for at least part of each year) played an important part, though they were always balanced by the bishops. The emperors, busy in Germany or preoccupied with the popes, made wide grants of regalian rights over local coinage, tolls, customs dues, police powers, and justice (diplomas of Henry I, Lothaire III, and Conrad II); there were also considerable delegations of local episcopal powers. Full-fledged communes appeared in the 11th and 12th centuries (e.g. Asti, 1093; Pavia, 1105; Florence, 1138; and Rome itself, by papal charter, 1188). Expansion in the great maritime and commercial republics was rapid (e.g. Pisa's new walls, 1081; Florence's second wall, 1172–1174; Venetian expansion in the Adriatic after the capture of Bari from the Saracens, 1002).

As a result of revolt and negotiation the towns of Lombardy were largely self-governing communes by the opening of the 12th century, and the consulate or its equivalent was in full activity by the end of the century. Typical town organization: an assembly (legislation, declaration of war and peace, etc.); the consuls, core of the magistracy, usually four to twenty in number, serving a one-year term, and chosen from the leading families; the town council and minor magistrates.

The development of the merchant and craft guilds led to a vigorous class warfare as the rising bourgeoisie asserted itself, and brought in the podestate (the *podestà*), a kind of local dictator, during the last quarter of the 12th century.

In Tuscany the towns treated the counts as the Lombards had treated their bishops. Venice, thanks to her peculiar circumstances, evolved a unique commercial oligarchy.

(3) *The Rise of Venice to* 1310

Fugitives from the Huns found refuge among the fishing villages of the lagoons; the permanent establishment of Venice seems to date from the Lombard invasion (568). Venetian aid to Belisarius began the formal connection between Venice and Constantinople and a (largely) theoretical connection with the Eastern Roman Empire. The *tribuni maiores* (a central governing committee of the islands) dated from c. 568.

687. **Election of the first doge.** A salt monopoly and salt-fish trade were the sources of the first prosperity of Venice. Two great parties: (1) pro-Byzantine aristocrats favoring an hereditary doge; (2) democrats friendly to the Roman Church and (later) the Franks. Venice offered asylum to the Exarch of Ravenna fleeing from Liutprand, and gained trading rights with Ravenna. When Charlemagne ordered the pope to expel the Venetians from the Pentapolis and threatened the settlement in the lagoons, Venice turned again to Constantinople, and in a treaty

810. Charlemagne and Nicephorus recognized Venice as Byzantine territory and accepted her mainland trading rights.

1000. After a two-hundred-year expansion in the Adriatic, Venice completely reduced the Dalmatian pirates, and the doge took the title of Duke of Dalmatia. Venice was mistress of the sea road to the Holy Land (commemorated in the wedding of the doge and the sea).

1032. The aristocratic effort to establish an hereditary doge was defeated. Establishment of a council and senate.

1063. The construction of the **Church of St. Mark** begun; one of the most notable and influential examples of Byzantine architecture in the west.

1063. The first three crusades established Venetian trading rights in a number of Levantine ports (e.g. Sidon, 1102, Tyre, 1123) and founded the power of a wealthy ruling class. A war with the Eastern Empire (financed by the first known government bonds) was unsuccess-

ful, and led to the institution of a deliberative assembly of 480 members (the germ of the **Great Council**).

1171. Appointment of the doge was transferred to this council, a complete triumph for the commercial aristocracy.

1198. A coronation oath (in varying terms) began to be exacted of the doge.

1204. **IN THE FOURTH CRUSADE** (p. 260) Venice gained the Cyclades, Sporades, Propontis, the Black Sea coasts, Thessalian littoral, and control of the Morea. She administered this vast empire on a kind of feudal tenure, portioning it out to families charged with defense of the sea-ways. Venice had also gained a further foothold in Syrian ports.

From this period dates a great epoch of building and increasing oligarchic pressure as the government began to become a closed corporation of leading families.

1253-1299. **THE STRUGGLE WITH GENOA** for the Black Sea and Levantine trade. The feud of Genoa and Venice was ancient, and trouble began at Acre (1253). The first war with Genoa ended in the complete defeat (1258) of the Genoese.

1261. The Greeks seized Constantinople during the absence of the Venetian fleet; they favored Genoa, turning over Galata to her.

1264. The Venetians destroyed the Genoese fleet at **Trepani,** and soon returned to their old status in Constantinople.

1289-1299. The **advance of the Turks** (capture of Tripoli, 1289, of Acre, 1291) led Venice to a treaty with the new masters of Asia Minor. Genoa met this by an effort to close the Dardanelles, and won a victory (1294) at Alexandretta; Venice forced the Dardanelles and sacked Galata. The Genoese defeated the Venetians at **Curzola** (1299), but Matteo Visconti negotiated an honorable peace (1299) for them.

1284. The first ducat was coined.

1290-1300. The perfection of the great galleys. Establishment of the **Flanders galleys** (1317).

1297. The **Great Council** was restricted in membership to those who had been members within the preceding four years. A commission added other names and then the council was closed to new members (except by heredity). In effect this excluded a large section of the citizens from any share of the government in favor of a narrow, hereditary, commercial oligarchy. Popular reaction led to a revolt (1300), the leaders of which were hanged.

1310. Tiepolo's rebellion, the only serious uprising in Venetian history, was crushed. This seems to have been a patrician protest against the extreme oligarchy, and led to the creation of an emergency committee of public safety, the **Council of Ten,** which soon became permanent (1335).

The **Venetian government** thus consisted of: The Great Council (i.e. the patrician caste); the Senate (a deliberative and legislative body dealing with foreign affairs, peace, war, finances, trade); the Council of Ten, a secret, rapidly acting body concerned with morals, conspiracy, European affairs, finance, the war department, which could override the Senate; the *Collegio* or Cabinet (the administrative branch); the doge and his council, which, sitting with the Ten, made the Council of Seventeen. (*Cont. p.* 302.)

e. FRANCE, 987-1314

987-1328. DIRECT LINE OF THE CAPE-TIAN HOUSE (the dynasty continued until 1792).

987-996. HUGH (called *Capet,* from the cloak he wore as lay abbot of St. Denis). At Hugh's accession the kingship was at its nadir; such power as Hugh had was feudal; the royal title meant little more than an hegemony over a feudal patchwork, an ill-defined area called France, and the prestige of ancient monarchical tradition sanctified by ecclesiastical consecration. Hugh's own feudal domain consisted of the Île de France (extending from Laon to Orléans, with its center at Paris) and a few scattered holdings. The great barons of the so-called royal fiefs recognized Hugh as their suzerain, but never did homage nor rendered service. Hugh's special interest was to maintain his control over his chief resources, the Archbishopric of Reims and the great bishoprics (Sens, Tours, Bourges) and abbeys of the Île de France, and to wean northeastern France away from the Carolingian and imperial interest. Despite clerical pressure, he avoided submission to imperial suzerainty, a policy which facilitated the demarcation between France and Germany. In defiance of pope and emperor he forced his own candidate into the Archbishopric of Reims. Hugh crowned his son shortly after his own coronation and began a practice (*co-optation*) which the early Capetians continued (until Philip II no longer felt it necessary), thus insuring the succession, and weakening the principle (dear to the feudality) of elective kingship.

996-1031. ROBERT II (*the Pious*), an active, well-educated, polished, amiable ruler, a good soldier, supported by the Duke of Normandy in constant wars against his neighbors, and by the religious houses of Burgundy in attacks on the Dukes of Burgundy. The Duchy of Burgundy escheated to the crown, and was given to Robert, a younger son. Robert the Pious, like his father, supported the Cluniac reformers. Minor territorial additions signify the revival of royal power.

1031-1060. HENRY I, an active, brave, indefatigable ruler, whose reign nevertheless marked the lowest ebb of the Capetian fortunes. The rebellion of his brother Robert, supported by Eudes, Count of Chartres and Troyes, was put down with the aid of the Duke of Normandy, and Robert was pacified by the grant of the Duchy of Burgundy (which continued in his family until 1361). Henry supported the Duke of Normandy (1047), but led a coalition against him two years later, and was defeated. He boycotted the pope and his synod at Reims, and, like his son and successor, opposed the reform movement in the Church. The *prévôts* were introduced to administer justice and taxation in the royal lands. The Kingdom of Burgundy passed (1032) to the empire.

1035-1066. RISE AND EXPANSION OF NORMANDY. William I became duke (1035) and until 1047 faced a series of baronial revolts. With the aid of his feudal suzerain, King Henry of France, William defeated his revolting barons (1047) and razed their castles. The union of Normandy and Maine was completed (1063) against powerful opposition from the Counts of Anjou. William's alliance with Henry was broken (1053), and Henry ravaged the heart of Normandy (1058). Normandy was now a fully developed feudal state under firm ducal control. Military service, assessed in knights' fees, was attached to specific pieces of land, no castles could be built or maintained without ducal license. Private warfare and blood feud were strictly limited. Coinage was a ducal monopoly. The legal jurisdiction of the duke was wide, local government was under the duke's representatives (the *vicomte*) who commanded the local forces, guarded the castles, did justice, collected the revenue (a large part of which was cash). The Church had been revivified, but here too the duke was supreme, naming bishops, most of the abbots, and sitting in provincial synods.

Norman relations with England had grown closer, and this tendency culminated (1002) in the marriage of Duke Robert's sister Emma with

The Capetian Kings

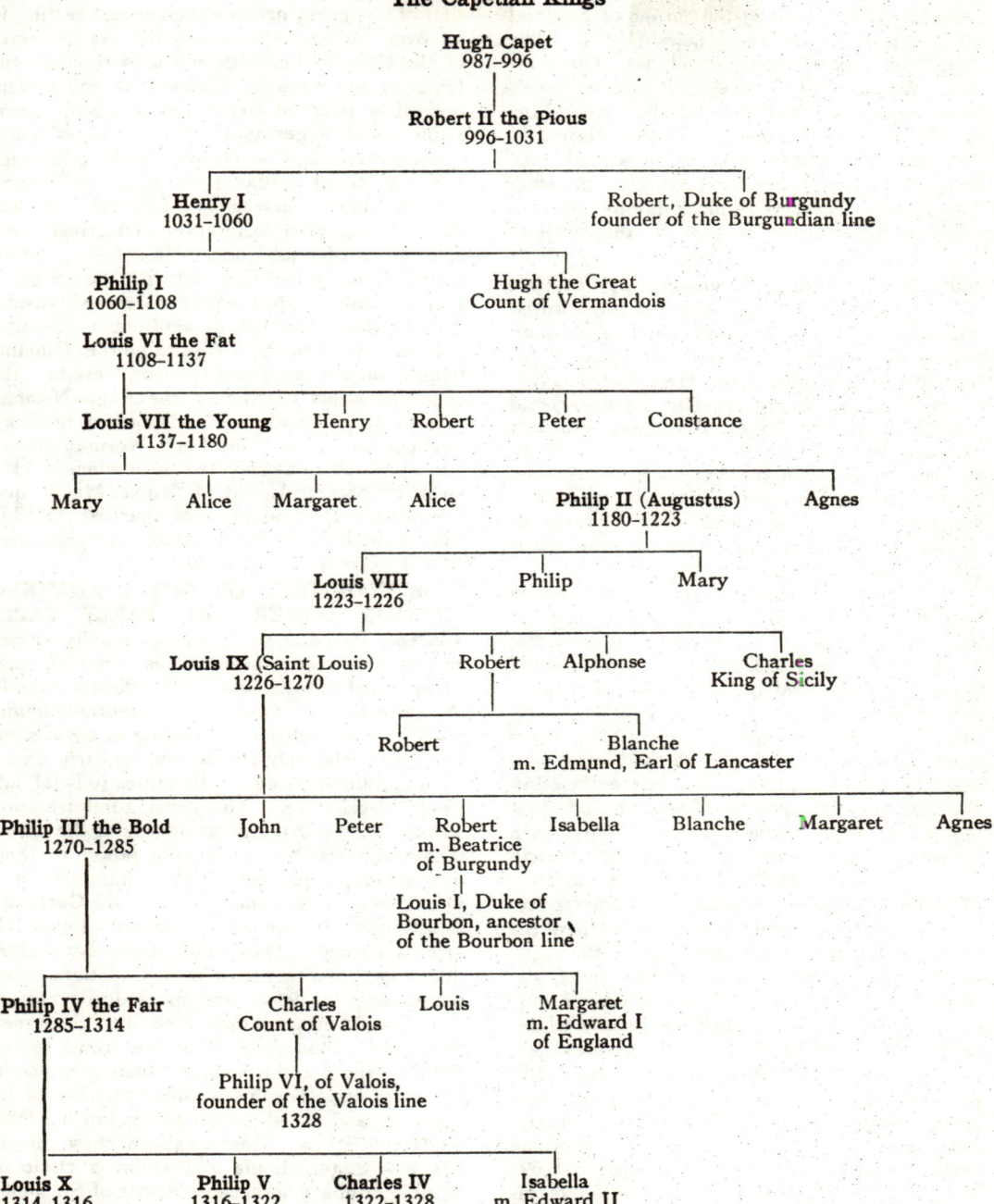

Hugh Capet
987–996

Robert II the Pious
996–1031

Henry I
1031–1060

Robert, Duke of Burgundy
founder of the Burgundian line

Philip I
1060–1108

Hugh the Great
Count of Vermandois

Louis VI the Fat
1108–1137

Louis VII the Young
1137–1180

Henry   Robert   Peter   Constance

Mary   Alice   Margaret   Alice   Philip II (Augustus)   Agnes
1180–1223

Louis VIII   Philip   Mary
1223–1226

Louis IX (Saint Louis)   Robert   Alphonse   Charles
1226–1270   King of Sicily

Robert   Blanche
m. Edmund, Earl of Lancaster

Philip III the Bold   John   Peter   Robert   Isabella   Blanche   Margaret   Agnes
1270–1285   m. Beatrice
                                   of Burgundy

Louis I, Duke of
Bourbon, ancestor
of the Bourbon line

Philip IV the Fair   Charles   Louis   Margaret
1285–1314   Count of Valois   m. Edward I
                                             of England

Philip VI, of Valois,
founder of the Valois line
1328

Louis X   Philip V   Charles IV   Isabella
1314–1316 1316–1322   1322–1328   m. Edward II
                                     of England

King Ethelred. The son of this marriage, Edward the Confessor, educated largely at the Norman court, came to the throne of England (1042), and died without heirs (1066). The Witan at once elected Harold, Earl Godwin's son. **William I** of Normandy with a volunteer force (perhaps 5000–6000) collected from Normandy and the Continent, defeated Harold in the **battle of Hastings** (Oct. 14) and was crowned King of England on Christmas Day (p. 168). The *Bayeux Tapestry* forms a unique and probably contemporary record of this expedition.

1060-1108. PHILIP I, enormously fat, but active and vigorous; excommunicated and unpopular with the clergy as the result of an adulterous marriage (1092) and because of his hostility to clerical reform. He defeated (1079) Duke William of Normandy (the *Conqueror*) and steadily supported **Robert Curthose,** William's son, against Anglo-Norman pressure. Systematic expansion of the resources of his house, and regular annexations to its domains in the face of stubborn feudal resistance. The *Chanson de Roland*, the national epic of France, was probably composed during this reign.

The growth of feudalism tended to diminish anarchy and to improve the general security of life, and ultimately led to decisive economic recovery in western Europe, a trend toward urban economy, and the emergence of a bourgeoisie who were beginning to accumulate capital. This development was a determining factor in the economic, social, and monarchical evolution of the 13th century. The **Peace of God** in the 10th century, and the **Truce of God** (first mentioned, 1027), promoted by the Church with Capetian support, were significant rather than effective attempts to reduce warfare.

1108-1328. A period in which the Capetians reduced the great feudatories north of the Loire and began the transformation of the vague ecclesiastical, judicial, and military rights derived from Carolingian tradition into royal powers over the French people as a whole.

1108-1137. LOUIS VI (*the Fat*). A brave soldier, of tremendous physique, intelligent, affable, avaricious, but liked by the peasantry, commercial class and clergy, the first popular Capetian. Consolidation of his Norman frontier (wars with Henry I of England: 1109–1112; 1116–1120), and steady reduction of his lesser vassals as far as the Loire. His charters to colonizers (*hôtes*) of waste lands, and frequent if inconsistent support of the communes, especially on the lands of the Church and the baronage, began the long alliance of the Capetians with

bourgeois interests; Louis' *charter of Lorris*, widely copied in town charters, was a significant sign of the **great urban development** setting in all over Europe in this period. As protector of the Church, Louis gained a foothold in the lands of his vassals. Careers at court were opened to talented clergy and bourgeois: great influence of **Suger** (see below). Louis' compromise with the Church over feudal patronage and investiture initiated the King of France's effective rôle as *eldest son of the Church.* He was the first Capetian to intervene effectively outside his own feudal lands. He defeated the alliance of Henry I of England with the Emperor Henry V, and stopped (1124) a German invasion. The marriage (1137) of his son Louis to Eleanor, heiress of William X of Aquitaine (i.e. Guienne [*Aquitania Secunda*] and Gascony) marked the Capetian effort to balance the Anglo-Norman menace in the north by additions of territory south of the Loire. The Anglo-Norman danger had appeared in aggravated form when in 1129 Geoffrey became Count of Anjou, Maine, and Touraine. He had in 1128 married Matilda (daughter of Henry I of England), and proceeded (1135) to conquer Normandy.

DEVELOPMENT OF ROYAL ADMINISTRATION UNDER THE EARLY CAPETIANS. The court of the king, usually known as the *curia regis*, consisting as it did of magnates, royal vassals, and court officials (mainly chosen from the baronage), was essentially feudal in spirit and tradition. Meeting at royal summons and relatively frequently, its early duties were undifferentiated, its functions judicial, advisory, legislative. The royal administration was in control of the great officers of the crown whose aim was to concentrate power in their own hands, a process which culminated in a virtual monopoly of such power by the **Garlande family** early in the 12th century. Louis VI, after a struggle (1128–1130), terminated their dominance, and thenceforth the Capetians relied increasingly on lesser and more docile nobles, clerics, and bourgeois men of affairs. Such men were career men devoted to the crown rather than to feudal ambitions, and their presence in the *curia regis* began the differentiation of its functions and its subjection to royal rather than feudal influences. Most notable of these careerists was **Suger,** Louis' old tutor, a cleric of humble origin, who became Abbot of St. Denis (1122). An able statesman, his influence was decisive in the reign of Louis and his son Louis VII. Suger began (c. 1136) the new abbey church of St. Denis, the first edifice wholly Gothic in design.

1100-1400. RISE OF TOWNS. The economic revival of western Europe was paralleled by a resumption of town life and development throughout the west, which was most notable in France, where the movement reached its apogee in the 12th century, before the consistent advance of the Capetian monarchy began to retard its progress. Types of town development were by no means uniform, but important general categories can be distinguished: (1) The *commune* proper, a collective person endowed with legal rights and powers (e.g. financial, judicial), able to hold property. As a feudal person the *commune* could have vassals, render and exact homage, establish courts for its tenants, and even declare war and make treaties. Symbols of its independence were the belfry, town hall, and seal. Typical *communes* of northern France and Flanders were the *communes jurées* (e.g. Beauvais, St. Quentin [chartered before 1080], Rouen [chartered 1145], and Amiens [chartered in the 12th century]); in southern France the corresponding *communes* were called *consulates*, which enjoyed even greater rights than in the north, especially in Roussillon, Provence, Languedoc, Gascony, and Guienne. In the south the nobles took an active part in the formation of *consulates* and shared in their government. (2) *Villes de bourgeoisie* (or *communes surveillées*) had elements of communal powers in varying degrees, but lacked full political independence (i.e. they were privileged but unfree). They were found all over France, but especially in the center, and were the prevailing type on the royal domain. Citizens enjoyed specific privileges, but the crown retained judicial and other powers in varying degrees. (3) *Villes neuves* (characteristic of the commercial north) and *bastides* (typical of the south, and usually strongholds) were small rural creations of kings or feudal lords, given a charter from the first, establishing their status. (4) *Peasant associations* and village federations (influential in the north) which sought to define and guarantee the rights of their citizens. Governmentally town development seems to have been hardly the result of conscious effort to introduce a new political dispensation. It was rather an attempt to establish and define the rights of non-feudal groups, and aimed at economic prosperity and personal security. The movement constantly enjoyed royal support, but royal policy toward it was governed by immediate political or financial considerations, and the crown always strove to reduce or control town independence in the interest of its own power. Ultimately monarchy triumphed, but not before the bourgeois groups and the serfs had altered their position to their own advantage.

1137-1180. LOUIS VII (*he Young*), not a strong king, but pious and therefore popular with the clergy. He remained under the influence of Suger until the latter's death in 1151. A papal interdict on the royal lands, resulting from Louis' insistence on his feudal rights, led to intervention by Bernard of Clairvaux.

1147. Louis inspired the **Second Crusade** (p. 260). He induced the Emperor Conrad III and Bernard of Clairvaux to join him and, leaving the kingdom in the hands of Suger, he set out for the east. He returned (1149) beaten, humiliated, and estranged from his wife Eleanor, who had accompanied him. The marriage was annulled (1152), probably due to lack of a male heir. This step cost the Capetians the territories of Poitou, Guienne, and Gascony, for Eleanor at once married Henry, Duke of Normandy, who in 1151 had succeeded his father as Count of Anjou, Maine, and Touraine. The acquisition of Eleanor's domains made Henry master of more than half of France and put him in a position to bring pressure on the holdings of the King of France both from north and the south. When Henry in 1154 became King of England, the so-called Angevin Empire extended roughly from the Tweed to the Pyrenees.

1173. Louis supported **Thomas Becket** (p. 194) against Henry II of England, and was saved from Henry's wrath only through the mediation of the pope, Alexander III, a refugee in France against whom the Emperor Frederick had raised an anti-pope. It was Louis' interest to support the anti-imperial party, because of the pressure of the emperor upon Burgundy.

During the reign of Louis VII the appointment of non-feudal experts to the *curia regis* continued, and their influence on the administration began to be decisive. Grant of town charters also continued. The period was, moreover, one of marked

Cultural progress: The guild of masters (germ of the University of Paris) was recognized (c. 1170) and a number of eminent scholars appeared on the scene: **St. Bernard of Clairvaux** (1090-1153), founder of the Cistercian Order, a great preacher, fervent reformer, and dominant spiritual figure of the west; **Roscellinus** (died c. 1121), champion of nominalism; **Anselm** (d. 1109), Abbot of Bec, later Archbishop of Canterbury, champion of realism; **Peter Abélard** (d. 1142), eminent master at Paris (after about 1115), supporter of conceptualism, a middle ground in the great controversy over universals. Abélard's *sic et non* presented without solution the conflicting theological arguments on 158 important problems.   John of Salisbury (d. 1180), Bishop of Chartres, favored the humanistic rather than the dialectical approach to knowledge.   Peter Lombard, Bishop of Paris (1159), in his *Sententiae* offered a cautious solution of theological and philosophical problems which became a standard text of the Paris schools.   In literature the period produced the *chansons de geste* and the troubadour lyrics.

1180-1223.   PHILIP II (*Augustus*). He began his rule at fifteen and had no time for education (he knew no Latin).   A calculating realist, perhaps the outstanding figure of his time, he was the consolidator of the monarchy and the founder of the organized state. As the "maker of Paris" he paved the streets, walled the city, and began the building of the Louvre.

1180.   A six-year alliance with King Henry II of England enabled Philip to defeat Philip of Artois and the Counts of Champagne, to crush a baronial league against him, and to gain recognition for his title to Artois and Vermandois.   Philip intrigued with the sons of Henry, welcomed the rebellious Richard (1187), and, joining him, defeated Henry (1189), who died the same year.

1191.   Philip, under pressure of public opinion, joined King Richard and Frederick Barbarossa on the **Third Crusade** (p. 260); eclipsed by Richard, he quarreled with him, returned to France, and intrigued against him with John during his (Richard's) captivity (1192–1194).

1194-1199.   Richard, in a pitiless war of vengeance, built Château Gaillard on the Seine and restored the Angevin power in northern France.

1198.   Excommunicated by Pope Innocent III for his divorce of Ingeborg of Denmark, Philip was forced by public opinion to a reconciliation, but sharply refused Innocent's offer of mediation with John, who succeeded Richard (1199).

1202-1204.   The final duel with John for, and conquest of, the Angevin lands north of the Loire.   On King John's refusal to stand trial as Philip's vassal on charges by Philip's vassal, Hugh of Lusignan, Philip declared John's French fiefs forfeited (1203), and supported John's nephew, Arthur of Brittany.   The murder of Arthur (1203) cost John his French support, Château Gaillard was lost (1204), Normandy and Poitou followed, and Philip

emerged master of the Angevin lands north of the Loire.

New royal officials, the *baillis* (*sénéchaux* in the south), paid professionals (often Roman lawyers), superseded the now feudalized *prévôts* as the chief local administrators (financial, judicial, military) on the Capetian lands (c. 1190). In the course of the 13th century *baillis* began to be assigned to regular districts (*baillages*), but they continued responsible to and removable by the king.   As the royal domain expanded, royal administration was extended to it, and the foundation laid for a national, specialized, professional system.

Philip, henceforth master in the north, left the conquest of the south to his successors and devoted himself to statecraft rather than war. He played the barons off against each other, used his position as protector of the Church to weaken them further, and sought the support of the towns and rich bourgeoisie as a balance to the feudality.   Part of this process involved the systematization of the royal finance, the regular exaction of feudal aids and obligations due to the crown as well as the systematic collection of customs, tolls, fines and fees, though as yet there was no such thing as taxation in the modern sense.   The levy of the Saladin tithe (1188) was, however, a forerunner of true taxation.   Philip's reign also saw the formation of a semi-permanent royal army.

1208-1213. The Albigensian-Waldensian Crusade.   The Albigensians (Catharists of Albi) and the Waldensians (followers of Peter Waldo) represented originally a reaction of the lower classes against clerical corruption, but the movement was soon espoused by the nobles, who saw in it a chance to appropriate church lands.   Innocent III, after a vain appeal to Philip, proclaimed a crusade against these heretics.   Philip took no direct part in the action, but allowed his northern vassals to begin the penetration of the south and thus prepare the way for the advance of the Capetian power. Simon de Montfort (the elder), a baron of the Île de France, emerged as the leader of the crusaders.   His **victory at Muret** (1213) sealed the fate of the brilliant Provençal culture, of the leading southern barons, and of the heretics. After a long chapter of horrors the conquest was finally completed in a campaign by Louis VIII (1226).   In the reign of Louis IX the County of Toulouse passed under Capetian administration and the royal domain was extended to the Mediterranean.

1213-1214. The great anti-Capetian Alliance (John of England, Emperor Otto IV the Counts of Boulogne and Flanders, and most of the feudality of Flanders, Belgium and Lorraine).

1214, July 27. BATTLE OF BOUVINES. Philip, in alliance with Emperor Frederick II, defeated the coalition near Tournai and thereby established the French monarchy in the first rank of the European powers, at the same time ruining John of England, assuring Frederick II of the imperial crown, and bringing Flanders under French influence. Militarily speaking the battle was a triumph of Philip's professional cavalry and bourgeois militia over the older infantry.

1223-1226. LOUIS VIII, a pallid reflection of his father. The first Capetian king not crowned in his father's lifetime.

1224. Temporary conquest of the lands between the Loire and the Garonne; the English soon regained all but Poitou, the Limousin and Perigord (1225).

1226. Renewal of the Albigensian Crusade and Louis' **conquest of the south.** Louis began the dangerous practice of bestowing great fiefs as appanages of the princes of the blood, a practice which later had almost fatal consequences to the monarchy (the case of Burgundy).

1226-1270. LOUIS IX (*St. Louis*, canonized 1297). The most chivalrous man of his age and the ideal mediaeval king. Handsome and lofty in character, Louis' careful education prepared him for a unique reign, in which ethics dominated policy. His justice won him national support and made him the arbiter of Europe. His reign was the golden age of mediaeval France.

1226-1234. Minority of Louis IX and regency of his able and devout mother, Blanche of Castile. With the support of the Church, the royal officials and the people, Blanche was able to suppress a number of feudal rebellions (1226–1231). By the **Treaty of Paris** (1129) Raymond of Toulouse surrendered, and his heiress was betrothed to Louis' brother, Alfonso. Louis himself was married to Margaret of Provence and thus began the severance of that province from the empire.

1233. As part of the campaign against heresy, Pope Gregory IX granted independent authority to investigate heresy to the **Dominicans,** requiring the bishops to co-operate with them. Louis later supported the **Inquisition,** despite episcopal objections.

1241. Louis induced the Emperor Frederick II to release the prelates and delegates captured off Genoa while *en route* to a synod at Rome, but, without directly attacking the Church, he associated himself with Frederick's grievances against the pope and refused to intervene against the emperor (1247).

1242. Invasion of France by Henry III of England, in coalition with the rebellious feudal lords of southern France. The whole movement collapsed and was followed by the final submission of Aquitaine and Toulouse (1243).

1244. Louis took the Cross, against his mother's advice, and sailed on his first crusade (1248). His aim was to free Palestine by the capture of Egypt, but the expedition was poorly managed, Louis was captured (1250), and most of his army was put to the sword. Louis himself was ransomed and returned to France.

1258. The Treaty of Corbeil, representing a peaceful adjustment of conflicting claims between France and Aragon, to the advantage of France. Louis' son, Philip, was betrothed to Isabella of Aragon.

1259. Treaty of Paris. Louis, in the interest of amity, yielded Perigord and the Limousin to the King of England, despite protests from both provinces. In return he received the renunciation of English claims to Normandy, Maine, Poitou. Henceforth Guienne became distinct from Aquitaine. This pacific gesture displeased opinion in both countries and weakened the French position in the south as the Hundred Years' War approached.

1265. Louis permitted his brother, Charles of Anjou, to accept the crown of Sicily, a step which later involved France in Italian problems, with decisive consequences.

1270. Louis' second crusade. Probably influenced by Charles of Anjou, who cherished far-reaching Mediterranean ambitions, Louis set out for Tunis. He died of pestilence, without accomplishing anything.

Louis' reign was marked by rigorous insistence on inherent royal rights even at the expense of the Church, and despite episcopal protests. Royal justice was notably efficient and was constantly expanded. The right of appeal from feudal to royal courts was clearly established. The old *curia regis* had already become somewhat differentiated: a *chambre des comptes* and a *parlement* (i.e. high court) were already recognizable. Louis introduced the *enquêteurs,* itinerant investigators, to supervise the *baillis* and *sénéchaux,* but he made few other administrative innovations. Many of his diplomats, *baillis*, and other officials were chosen from the royal household, notably from the so-called *chevaliers du roi*, and from the clergy. Assemblies of royal vassals, irregularly held, gave such "national" sanction as there was to royal policy. Louis was the first king to issue *ordonnances* (i.e. legislation) for the whole realm on his sole authority. By *ordonnance* he outlawed private warfare, the carrying of arms and trial by battle as part of the royal judicial process, and extended the royal coinage to the whole realm. By 1270 the communal movement was already in decline and the crown profited by enforcing a more rigorous control over the towns. Only one new charter (to the port of Aigues Mortes) was granted during the reign. The bourgeois oligarchy of the towns got on increasingly bad terms with the lower orders, often reducing the town finances to chaos. Louis took advantage of this state of affairs to introduce a town audit (1262). The country at large was prosperous in this period, but the financing of the two crusades and of the grandiose schemes of Charles of Anjou led to complaints that royal taxation was leading to bankruptcy and formed a bad precedent for Philip IV.

A brilliant cultural advance accompanied the general material and political progress of the time of Philip II and Louis IX; Perfection of the **French Gothic**: Cathedral of Chartres (c. 1194, Romanesque and Gothic); Amiens (c. 1200); Reims (1210); Louis IX's *Sainte Chapelle*; progress of naturalism in Gothic sculpture. **University of Paris**: Foundation charter (1200); regulations of Innocent III (1215); endowment of Robert de Sorbon (hence Sorbonne) in 1257. Advance of **vernacular literature**: **Villehardouin's** (died c. 1212) *Conquest of Constantinople* (the first vernacular historical writing); **Chrétien de Troyes** and the Arthurian romances; Goliardic verse (with pagan touch); *fabliaux* (risqué, semi-realistic bourgeois tales); *Aucassin and Nicolette* (a *chante fable* marked by irony and realism); **Jean de Meun's** (d. 1305) completion of William of Lorris' *Roman de la Rose* (a satire on the follies of all classes, especially women and clergy); **Jean de Joinville's** *Histoire du roi Saint Louis* (1309), the first vernacular classic of lay biography. **Paris the center of 13th-century philosophy**: harmonization of the Greek philosophy, especially Aristotle (newly recovered during the Renaissance of the 12th century in Latin translations) with Christian orthodoxy: **Vincent of Beauvais'** (d. 1264) *Speculum Maius* (a compendium of contemporary knowledge); **Albertus Magnus** (a German, d. 1280), chief of the great Dominican teachers in Paris; **Thomas Aquinas** (an Italian, d. 1274), the pupil of Albertus Magnus. Thomas Aquinas' *Summa Theologiae* reconciled reason and religion, completed the integration of the classical learning and the Christian theology and remains to this day the basis of all Catholic theological teaching.

1270-1285. PHILIP III (*the Rash*), a hasty, ill-balanced king, victim of his favorites. The death of Philip's uncle, Alfonso of Poitiers, brought Languedoc under royal sway and established the royal power firmly in southern France (1272). The walls of Carcassonne and Aigues Mortes were built, the latter place giving access to the Mediterranean. Unsuccessful candidacy (1273) of Charles of Anjou for the imperial crown. Crusade (1282) against the King of Aragon, Philip acting as papal champion against the successful rival of the House of Anjou in Sicily.

1281-1285. The pontificate of Martin IV brought to an end an anti-French period of papal policy; papal support of Charles of Anjou's ambitious dreams of Byzantine conquest until the **Sicilian Vespers** (p. 294). There followed another period of papal opposition to French ambitions.

1285-1314. PHILIP IV (*the Fair*). His reign had a distinctly modern flavor and was marked by ruthless expansion of the royal power and notable consolidation of the monarchy: royal finance superseded the feudal; Roman lawyers (trained at Bologna and Montpellier) rather than clerics dominated the government; papal pretensions were reduced and the national Church made virtually autonomous under royal domination.

1286. Edward I of England did homage for Guienne.

1293. Philip treacherously confiscated Gascony, which had been temporarily surrendered by Edward as a pledge, after a Gascon-Norman sea-fight.

1294-1298. War with Edward I over Guienne. Philip announced a war levy on the clergy and followed a protest with a violent anti-papal pamphlet campaign. To finance the war Philip debased the coinage. He first made an alliance with the Scots (1295) and excluded English ships from all ports. In 1297, Edward invaded northern France, in alliance with the Count of Flanders, but the war was brought to a close by a truce negotiated by Pope Boniface VIII.

1296-1303. Philip's conflict with **Pope Boniface VIII**, who put forward extreme claims to papal supremacy. The bull *Clericis laicos* (1296) forbade secular rulers to levy taxes on the clergy without papal consent. Philip retorted by forbidding the export of precious metals (a serious threat to the papal finances) and by a vigorous propaganda campaign. Boniface, engaged in a feud with the Colonna in Rome and absorbed in Sicilian affairs, gave way and practically annulled the bull (1297). But the great papal jubilee of 1300 was followed by a resumption of the quarrel, culminating in 1302 in the bull *Unam sanctam*, the most extreme assertion of the doctrine of papal theocracy in the Middle Ages. On the **"Terrible Day"** of **Anagni** (1303, p. 223), Nogaret and Sciarra Colonna attacked the papal palace, demanded the resignation of the pope, and had a violent scene with Boniface. The death of the aged pontiff followed shortly.

1302. The first well-authenticated convocation of the **Estates-General,** including representatives of the towns in their feudal capacity. The meeting was called mainly to insure national support for the king's struggle with the pope.

1302, July 11. Battle of the Spurs (at Courtrai), brought about by the troubles in Flanders. Philip had antagonized the Count of Flanders by his efforts to penetrate his territory, and the count had turned to Edward I of England for support. The Flemish nobility betrayed him (1300) and he lost both his liberty and his county. But French rule soon alienated the independent burghers and led to the massacre of the French (*Matin de Bruges*), followed by the **battle of Courtrai,** in which the burghers defeated the flower of the French chivalry.

1305. Election of Clement V (a Frenchman) as pope. Clement reluctantly accepted French royal domination, lingered in France after his election, and finally took up his residence at Avignon, thus beginning the **Babylonian** or **Avignonese Captivity** of the papacy (p. 223). During the Captivity (1309–1376) the French monarchy exercised an important influence on the papacy. Clement was obliged to quash the bulls of Boniface, to absolve the assailants of Anagni, and to support Philip's suppression of the Knights Templar (see below). Philip may properly be called the founder of **Gallicanism** (i.e. of the autonomy of the French Church).

1306. The Jews were arrested, despoiled, and expelled from France.

1307. The Order of the Knights Templar, a rich, decadent organization which acted as banker to the popes and which was a creditor of Philip, had become almost a state within the state. Philip now launched an attack upon it. He had its lands occupied by royal officers and its property sequestrated. The country was stirred up against the Order by a vigorous propaganda campaign and by an appeal to the States-General (1308). Clement was obliged to co-operate and the Inquisition was made use of in the trial, the entire affair being conducted with unparalleled ruthlessness and horror (torture freely used to extort confessions).

1312. The Order of the Templars was abolished by the **Synod of Vienne.** Its property was transferred to the Hospitalers (except in Spain, and in France where it passed to the crown). Philip made the Temple treasury a section of the royal finance administration.

New economic and social alignments. The rapid expansion of France and especially the wars of Philip III and Philip IV against England and Flanders, raised an acute financial problem. Philip IV tried every device to raise money (feudal *aides*, war levies to replace military service, tallage of towns, special levies on clergy and nobles, "loans" and "gifts," the *maltôte* or sales tax, debasement of the coinage, attacks upon the Jews and Templars), but without finding an adequate solution. It was this situation primarily that explains the emergence of the

Estates-General. Levies on the nobles and clergy had long been arranged in meetings of representatives of these two orders; by negotiations between the towns and the royal agents the burghers had been brought to contribute. Provincial estates had been called frequently during the 13th century. The convocation of the Estates-General simply meant the substitution of national for provincial or local negotiation, and implied no principle of consent or control over royal taxation. The royal revenue was increased perhaps tenfold between the time of Louis IX and the time of Philip IV, but this meant overtaxation of all classes, harmful effects upon economic life, and estrangement of public opinion. Anti-tax leagues were organized and local assemblies drew up lists of grievances. Philip was obliged to call the Estates-General again in 1314, but as the bourgeoisie and the nobility distrusted each other, no effective measures were taken and no permanent constitutional development took place. Characteristic of the period was

Pierre Dubois' *De Recuperatione Sanctae Terrae* (c. 1306), ostensibly an appeal to Philip to undertake a crusade to recover the Holy Land from the Saracens, in reality an extensive program of reform in the interests of stronger national monarchy. Dubois envisaged the formation of a European league to enforce peace through common military action and economic boycott, disputes between parties to be settled by judicial methods. He called also for a system of universal education and for the secularization of church property. (*Cont. p.* 277.)

f. THE IBERIAN PENINSULA, 1037-1284

(1) *Moslem Spain*

1037-1086. THE MULUK AL-TAWA'IF (i.e. *Party Kings*). These were petty dynasties founded on the ruins of the Omayyad Caliphate: the Hammudids of Malaga (from 1016 onward) and of Algeciras (1039–); the Abbadids of Cordova (1031–); the Zayrids of Granada (1012–); the Jahwarids of Cordova (1031–); the Dhul-Nunids of Toledo (1035–); the Amirids of Valencia (1021–); the Tojibids and Hudids of Saragossa (1019– and 1031–). Most of these dynasties were absorbed by the most distinguished of them, the **Abbadids**, who summoned the Almoravids from Africa to aid them against Alfonso VI of Castile.

1056-1147. THE ALMORAVIDS, a Berber dynasty, founded by the Berber prophet **Abdullah ibn Tashfin.** They conquered Morocco and part of Algeria and were called into Spain by the Abbadids to help in the defense against the Christians. They defeated Alfonso of Castile at **Zallaka** (1086) and proceeded to annex Moorish Spain, with the exception of Toledo and Saragossa.

1130-1269. THE ALMOHADES, a dynasty founded by the Berber prophet **Mohammed ibn Tumart.** His successor, Abdul-Mu'min, annihilated the Almoravid army (1114), after which Morocco was conquered (1146).

1145-1150. The Almohades invaded and conquered Moorish Spain, after which they conquered Algeria (1152) and Tunis (1158). They were finally defeated by the Christian kings of Spain in

1212, July 16. The battle of Las Navas de Tolosa, which was followed by their expulsion from Spain. Thereafter only local Moslem dynasties remained, of which the **Nasrids of Granada** (1232–1492) alone offered much resistance to the Christians until union of the Christian states brought about their defeat.

(2) *Castile*

1072-1109. ALFONSO VI, OF CASTILE. He captured Toledo from the Moors (1085) and created his son-in-law, Henry of Burgundy, Count of Portugal (1093).

1086. The Moslems, alarmed by Alfonso's progress, called from Africa the great **Yusuf ibn Tashfin** (d. 1106), leader of the newly dominant sect of Berber fanatics, the Almoravids. Ibn Yusuf landed at Algeciras (1086), and with the support of Seville, began a successful counter-thrust against the Christians (defeat of Alfonso at **Zallaka,** 1086). Yusuf, recalled by the African situation, did not at once exploit his advantage, but on his return to Spain his energetic, puritanic reforms strengthened the Moslems and brought them into an integral relation (c. 1091) with his great African empire which was centered in Morocco. This empire quickly disintegrated on Yusuf's death.

Alfonso resumed the Christian reconquest with the aid of **Rodrigo (Ruy) Diaz** of Bivar, the Cid (*Cid* as applied by the Moslems, means *lord* or *master*). Alfonso's style of "emperor" represented personal prestige and a vague hegemony rather than political reality.

The Cid, a Castilian originally in the service of Sancho II of Castile, later passed to that of Alfonso VI; was exiled (1081); returned to Castilian service (1087–1088); went over to the Moslem king of Saragossa after his second exile. Eventually he became ruler of Valencia. The Cid served both sides, was cruel, selfish, and proud. Despite these characteristics the legendary figure of the man became the great national lay hero of Spain. On his death (1099) Valencia was soon abandoned to the Almoravids.

In the course of the 11th century French influence began to penetrate the peninsula. The Cluniacs, already (1033) strong in Catalonia, Castile, and Aragon, reinforced French influence, and stimulated clerical reform and the reconquest. A literary reflection of this is to be found in the *Cantuar de mio Cid* (c. 1140), which already shows French elements in the cycle of the Cid (a cycle which continued into the 15th century).

1126-1157. ALFONSO VII, crowned "emperor" (1135) on the basis of military ascendancy and an intense feeling of equality with rival monarchs, especially the Holy Roman emperors. The weakening of the Almoravids by luxury, and the rise of rivals (the Almohades)

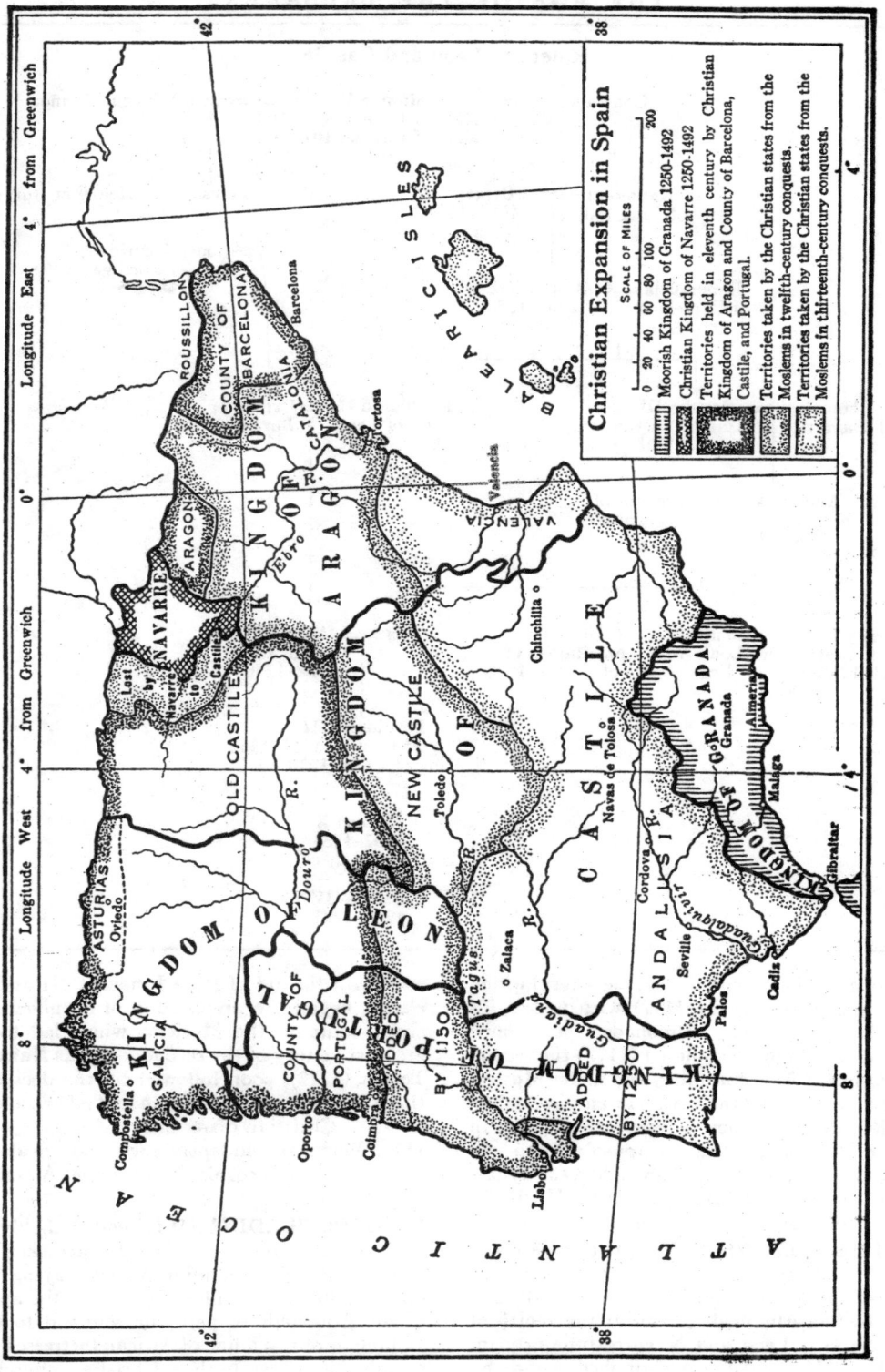

Christian Expansion in Spain

SCALE OF MILES

0 20 40 60 80 100   200

Moorish Kingdom of Granada 1250-1492

Christian Kingdom of Navarre 1250-1492

Territories held in eleventh century by Christian Kingdom of Aragon and County of Barcelona, Castile, and Portugal.

Territories taken by the Christian states from the Moslems in twelfth-century conquests.

Territories taken by the Christian states from the Moslems in thirteenth-century conquests.

Rulers of Leon and Castile

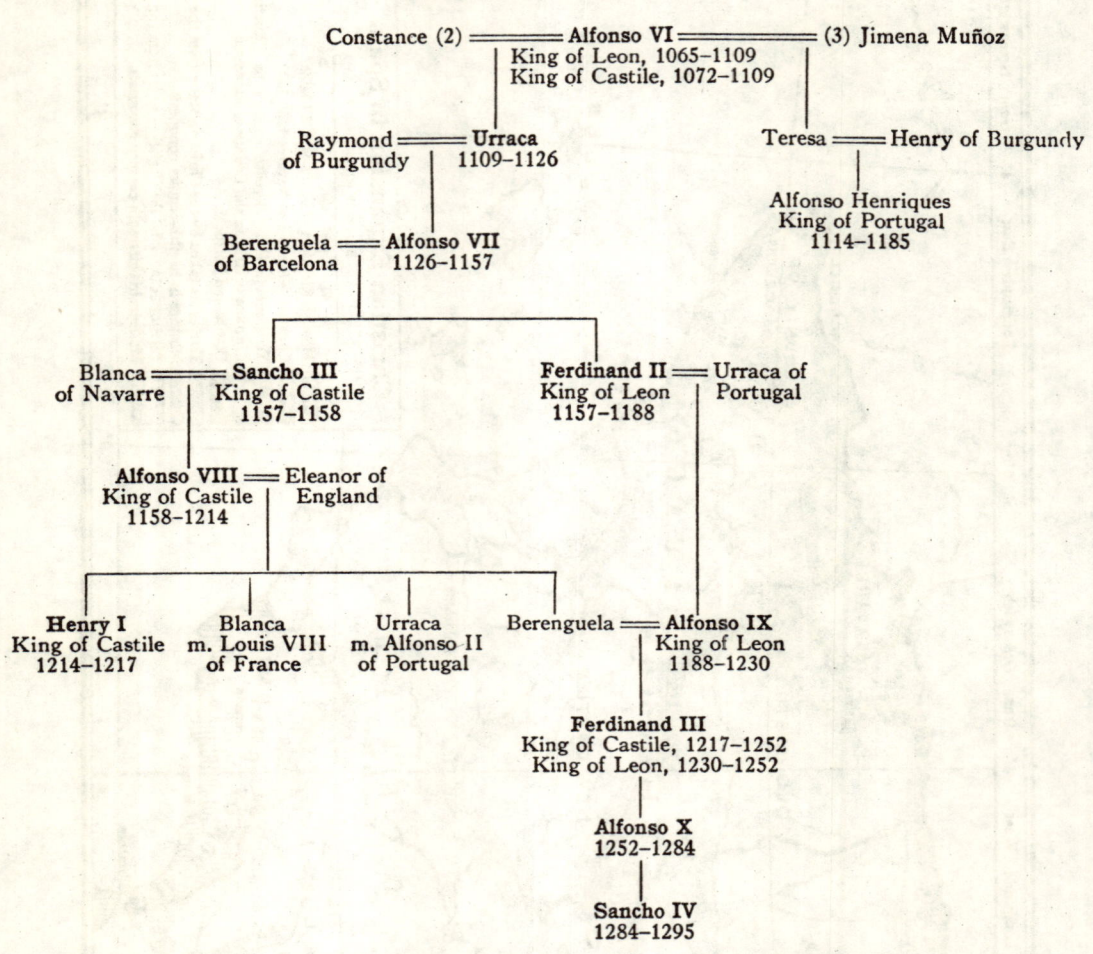

in Africa (c. 1125), made possible a resumption of the reconquest (1144–1147) with wide raids into Andalusia. The Almohades, summoned from Africa (1146), completed (1172) the second restoration of Moslem unity, and made Moslem Spain a province of their African empire, reducing the Arab influence in Spain to nothing in favor of Berber fanatics. Alfonso's death was followed by a minority and an eight-year dynastic crisis from which his son Alfonso VIII finally emerged as master.

1158-1214. ALFONSO VIII. After a series of successful attacks on the Moslems, Alfonso was overwhelmingly defeated (**Alarcos,** 1195) by the Almohades, then at the zenith of their power. Leon and Navarre promptly invaded Castile, but Alfonso triumphed over them,

and, with the aid of Pope Innocent III and the clergy, began the preparation of a unified general assault on the Moslems which led to the greatest victory of the reconquest, **Las Navas de Tolosa** (1212), soon followed by the decline of the Almohade power in Spain and Africa and by Christian dissension.

1179. Portugal's independence and royal title were recognized by Pope Alexander III.

1217-1252. FERDINAND III ended the dynastic war in Castile and attacked the Moors in the Guadalquivir Valley, taking Cordova (1236) and Seville (1248). On the appeal of the Almohade emperor he sent aid to him, gaining in return a line of African fortresses, and permission to establish a Christian church at

Marrakah. His plans for an invasion of Africa were cut short by death. After the capture of Jaen (1246), the emir was allowed to establish himself at Granada, the last Moorish stronghold, as Ferdinand's vassal.

The long history of guerrilla warfare in Castile disorganized tillage, made the people averse to agriculture, led to a concentration of population in the towns, and accounts for the poverty of Castilian agriculture, the tremendous influence of municipalities in mediaeval Castile, the development of a race of soldiers, and the isolation of Spanish thought from general European currents. In general the Moors were not disliked, and intermarriages were not unusual until the 13th century. Then the preaching of crusades as part of the reconquest and papal propaganda prepared the Spanish mind for the burst of intolerance and fanaticism which began in the second half of the 15th century.

The war of Christian reconquest gave birth to three great native military orders, modeled partly on Moorish societies for border defense, partly on the international crusading orders, notably the Templars, already established in the Peninsula. Some members took the regular monkish vows, others did not. Two Cistercian monks assumed (1158) the defense of Calatrava (when the Templars gave it up), and the **Order of Calatrava** which grew up was confirmed by the pope (1164). The **Order of Santiago** (established 1171) was the largest and richest, the **Order of Alcántara** (founded c. 1156) an offshoot of Calatrava, was the most clerical in type. By 1493 these orders had grown to stupendous size (the largest, Santiago, having 700,000 members and vassals, and an annual income of close to a million dollars, present value).

In the period following 1252 fear of the infidel was no longer a dominant force in Iberian politics and the nobles turned from assaults on the Moors to attacks upon the monarchy. The struggle between crown and baronage (which found a parallel all through Europe) was notable in Spain for the depth of governmental degradation which it produced. The new elements in the situation were clearly indicated in the reign of

1252-1284. ALFONSO X (*the Learned*), a versatile savant, distinguished as an astronomer (*Alfonsine Tables*), poet, historian, patron of learning, a pre-eminent lawyer and codifier (*las Siete Partidas*), devoted to the Roman ideal of centralized absolute monarchy, but a futile, vacillating monarch. Lavish concessions to the nobles (1271) to avoid civil war established the aristocracy in a position from

which it was not dislodged until the reign of Ferdinand and Isabella. Debasement of the coinage to relieve poverty produced economic crises; alternate alliance and war with the vassal King of Granada, and hostilities with Aragon, accomplished nothing. The Kingdom of Murcia was regained (1266) with the aid of James I of Aragon, and was then incorporated with Castile.

In foreign affairs Alfonso abandoned the long peninsularity of Spanish sovereigns, made a series of dynastic alliances, and attempted to give Castile an important European position.

1263-1267. Efforts to rectify the Portuguese boundary with advantage to Castile ultimately produced an actual loss of territory (in Algarve); Alfonso began the long effort to regain Portugal, which finally succeeded under Philip II (1580). Claims to (English) Gascony were revived (1253) and abandoned (1254); desultory wars fought with France. A twenty-year effort to win the crown of the Holy Roman Empire (despite papal opposition and public opinion) met with two defeats (1257 and 1273). The death of Alfonso's eldest son Ferdinand (1275) led at once to a bitter struggle over the succession organized by Alfonso's son Sancho.

(3) *Barcelona and Catalonia*

The **Spanish Mark** was established as a result of the conquest of Catalonia by Charlemagne (785-811). The County of Barcelona (erected 817) under the Frankish crown became independent, perhaps as early as the 9th century. By the beginning of the 12th century the Counts of Barcelona had large holdings north of the Pyrenees (notably in Provence), to which they added for a brief period (1114-1115) Majorca and Iviza, and permanently Tarragona.

1137. The union of Catalonia and Aragon, begun by Raymond Berenguer IV of Catalonia, was epochal, for it created a powerful state with access to the sea. Catalonian territories included Cerdagne, a large part of Provence, etc., with the later addition of Roussillon (1172), Montpellier (1204, under French suzerainty), Foix, Nîmes, Béziers (1162-1196).

1213. The battle of Muret (see below) definitely turned Catalonia back into the Spanish orbit.

In the 13th century **Barcelona,** utilizing the skill of her native sailors and the local (mostly Jewish) accumulations of capital, and profiting by Italian commercial pioneering, began an extensive slave trade in Moorish prisoners.

The Houses of Navarre, Aragon, and Barcelona

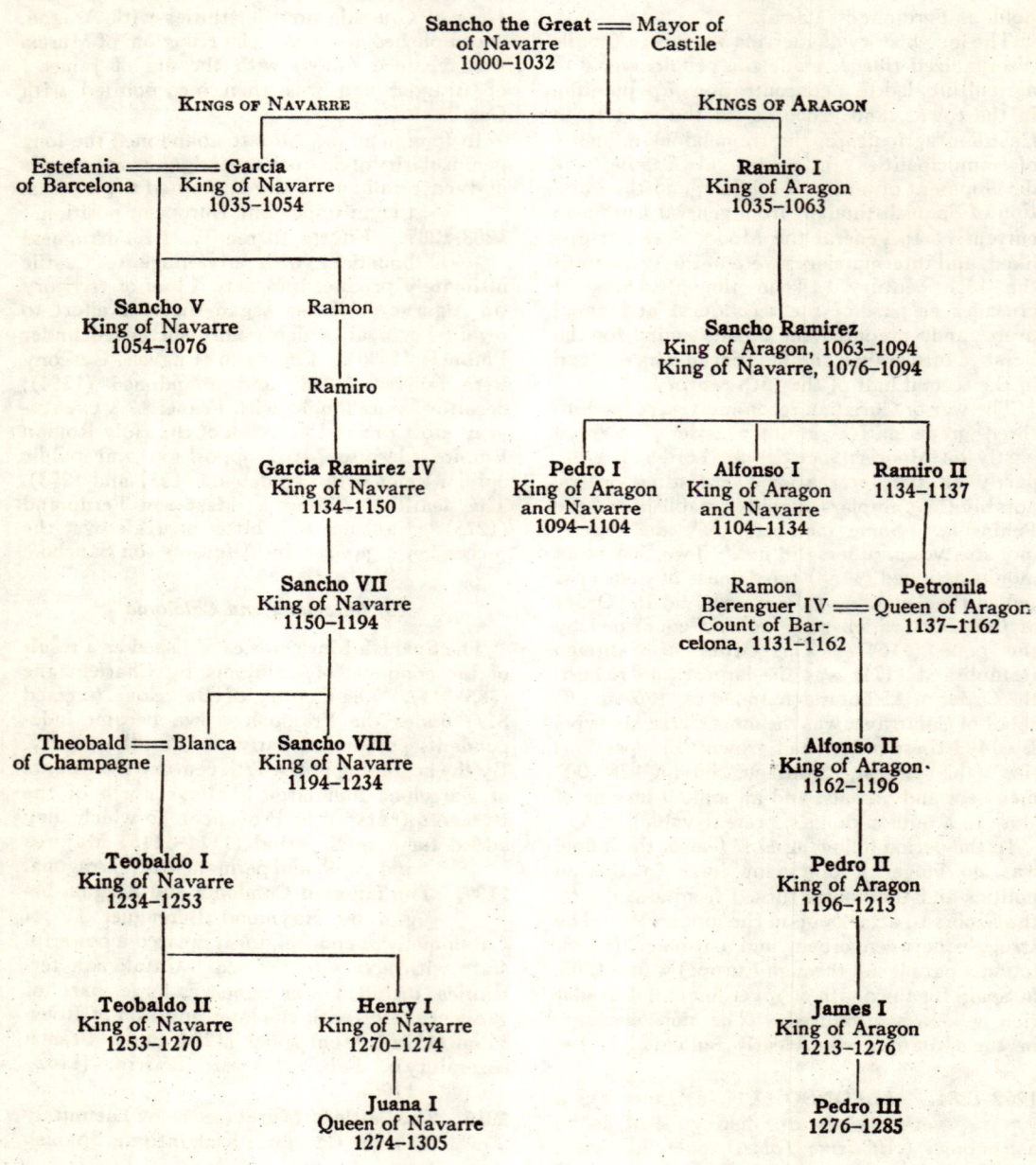

Sancho the Great == Mayor of
of Navarre   Castile
1000–1032

KINGS OF NAVARRE   KINGS OF ARAGON

Estefania ===== Garcia   Ramiro I
of Barcelona   King of Navarre   King of Aragon
                1035–1054   1035–1063

Sancho V   Sancho Ramirez
King of Navarre   Ramon   King of Aragon, 1063–1094
1054–1076   King of Navarre, 1076–1094

                   Ramiro

Garcia Ramirez IV   Pedro I   Alfonso I   Ramiro II
King of Navarre   King of Aragon   King of Aragon   1134–1137
1134–1150   and Navarre   and Navarre
                           1094–1104   1104–1134

Sancho VII   Ramon   Petronila
King of Navarre   Berenguer IV ===== Queen of Aragon
1150–1194   Count of Bar-   1137–1162
                                        celona, 1131–1162

Theobald === Blanca   Sancho VIII   Alfonso II
of Champagne   King of Navarre   King of Aragon
                      1194–1234   1162–1196

Teobaldo I   Pedro II
King of Navarre   King of Aragon
1234–1253   1196–1213

Teobaldo II   Henry I   James I
King of Navarre   King of Navarre   King of Aragon
1253–1270   1270–1274   1213–1276

                       Juana I   Pedro III
                       Queen of Navarre   1276–1285
                       1274–1305

Aragonese imperial expansion in the Mediterranean (Sicily and the Greek Archipelago, pp. 288, 294) gave Barcelona further commercial advantages and made it one of the most active Mediterranean ports.

Ramon Lull (1232–1315) was the greatest Catalonian intellectual figure of the Middle Ages, a vernacular poet, novelist, missionary, mystic, educator, reformer, logician, scientist, and traveler.

(4) *Navarre*

Navarre gained its independence from Carolingian rule in the 9th century and fell heir to the Carolingian rights in Aragon, which was absorbed by Navarre in the 10th century. **Sancho the Great** (970–1035) secured the succession of Castile, conquered most of Leon and temporarily united the Iberian kingdoms. By his will Aragon passed to his son Ramiro (d. 1063) and the union came to an end. On the death of **Alfonso the Warrior** (1104–1134), Navarre returned to its old ruling house until it passed under French control (1234) for two centuries.

(5) *Aragon*

Aragon, beginning as a county on the river Arago under Carolingian control, emerged from Carolingian domination in the middle of the 9th century, passed under the control of Navarre, and then became independent under Ramiro (d. 1063). The period from 1063 to 1134 is marked by confusion, intrigue, some progress against the Moors, and the annexation of Navarre (1076).

1104–1134. ALFONSO I (*the Warrior*) advanced to the Ebro, captured Saragossa (1118), and made raids to the Mediterranean. On Alfonso's death, Aragon chose his brother, **Ramiro,** a monk who emerged from retirement long enough to marry and produce a daughter, Petronilla, whom he married off to Raymond Berenguer IV (1131–1162), Count of Catalonia. He then returned (1137) to his monastery, leaving Petronilla under the guardianship of her husband, and the succession settled. The resulting union of Catalonia and Aragon was a decisive event in Spanish history. After the union the Aragonese kings, preoccupied with Spanish affairs, let Provence drift, and on the death of Alfonso II (1162–1196) it passed to his son Alfonso, nominally under the suzerainty of his brother Peter II (1196–1213), but, in fact, lost for good. Alfonso tried to keep

his Provençal holdings clear of the Albigensian heresy, but Raymond, Count of Toulouse, a supporter of the heresy, sought to win Peter II to his views. Peter went to Rome (1204) for a papal coronation, declared himself a vassal of the Holy See, and bore an honorable part at Las Navas de Tolosa, but was forced by the horrors of the Albigensian Crusade and the legitimate appeals of his vassals to oppose Simon de Montfort at Muret, where he fell.

1213. The battle of Muret marked the real end of Aragonese interests north of the Pyrenees.

1258. By the Treaty of Corbeil the King of France renounced his claims to Barcelona, Urgel (etc.), Cerdagne, Roussillon (etc.). Aragon ceded: Carcassonne, Foix, Béziers, Nîmes, Narbonne, Toulouse (etc.). All rights in Provence passed to Margaret, wife of Louis IX; a marriage was arranged between Louis' son Philip and Isabella, daughter of James I of Aragon.

1213–1276. JAMES I (*the Conqueror*). After the weakness and anarchy of his minority, James, one of the greatest soldiers of the Middle Ages, conquered Valencia in an intermittent campaign (1233–1245), took the Kingdom of Murcia for Castile (1266), and freed the Aragonese frontier of the Moslem menace. James also attempted to establish his overlordship over Tlemcen and Bugia in North Africa, and to secure a hold in Tunis. Against the will of his Aragonese nobles, but with the support of his Catalonian and French vassals, James conquered the Balearic Islands (1229–1235), thus beginning the creation of an Aragonese Mediterranean empire.

SPANISH CULTURE in the middle ages was very largely conditioned by external influences. **Architecture:** (1) **Pre-romanesque** architecture revealed traces of Visigothic, Carolingian, Persian, Byzantine, and Moslem traditions. (2) **Romanesque architecture** showed particularly the influence of Auvergne and Languedoc (e.g. second church of Santiago de Compostella). (3) **The Gothic** was marked by strong elements of the Burgundian style, brought by the Cluniacs. The full tide of the Gothic was probably introduced by the Cistercians (e.g. cathedrals of Toledo, c. 1230; Burgos, 1126; Leon, c. 1230). Catalan Gothic shows German influences (cathedrals of Barcelona, 1298; Gerona, 1312). The later Spanish Gothic revealed French, German, and Flemish currents (e.g. cathedral of Seville, begun 1401; west towers of Burgos cathedral, 1442). (4) **Moorish architecture** had a development of its own: the great mosque of

Cordova (completed 1118), the Alcazar, Seville (c. 1181), and the Alhambra (mostly 14th century).

Foundation of the first universities: Salamanca (1242); Alcala (1293). (*Cont. p. 284.*)

(6) *Portugal to 1279*

1055- Reconquest from the Moors of much of present-day Portugal by **Ferdinand the Great** of Leon and Castile. Ferdinand organized the territory as a county, with Coimbra as the capital.

1093-1112. **Henry of Burgundy,** a descendant of King Robert of France, came to Spain with other knights-adventurers, to fight against the Moors. In return the King of Castile granted him the County of Portugal and gave him the hand of his (illegitimate) daughter, Theresa. Henry himself was a typical crusader, restless and enterprising, whose main hope appears to have been to establish a dynasty in Castile.

1112-1185. **ALFONSO HENRIQUES,** the founder of the Portuguese monarchy and of the Burgundian dynasty. Alfonso was only three years old at the death of his father. His mother Teresa ruled as regent, but soon became involved in a struggle with Galicia and Castile. Being defeated, she agreed to accept Castilian domination, but

1128. Alfonso assumed authority, repudiated the agreement, and, after defeating the Spaniards, drove his mother into exile.

1139. Alfonso, one of the most famous knights of his age, began a long series of struggles against the Moors by defeating them in the **battle of Ourique.**

1143. **Alfonso was proclaimed king** by the Córtes. The pope arranged the **Treaty of Zamorra** between Portugal and Castile, the latter recognizing Portuguese independence, while Portugal accepted the suzerainty of the pope.

1147. The Portuguese took Lisbon and established a frontier on the Tagus.

1169. Further conflicts with Castile led to Alfonso's attack on Badajoz. He was defeated and captured, but soon released.

1185-1211. **SANCHO I,** the son of Alfonso Henriques. His reign was noteworthy for the development of towns and for the establishment of military orders of knighthood. Sancho did much to settle colonists on

Kings of Portugal, Burgundian House

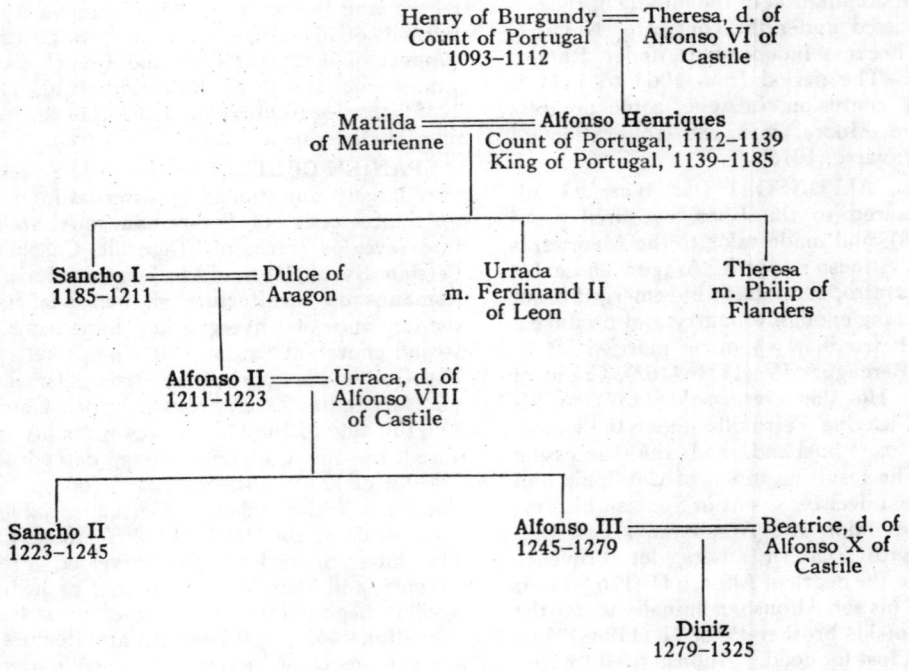

Henry of Burgundy ═══ Theresa, d. of
Count of Portugal │ Alfonso VI of
1093–1112 │ Castile

Matilda ════════ Alfonso Henriques
of Maurienne │ Count of Portugal, 1112–1139
│ King of Portugal, 1139–1185

Sancho I ═══════ Dulce of   Urraca   Theresa
1185–1211 │ Aragon   m. Ferdinand II   m. Philip of
│ of Leon   Flanders

Alfonso II ═══ Urraca, d. of
1211–1223 │ Alfonso VIII
│ of Castile

Sancho II   Alfonso III ═══════ Beatrice, d. of
1223–1245   1245–1279 │ Alfonso X of
│ Castile

Diniz
1279–1325

the lands that were won back in the prolonged wars against the Moors.

1211-1223. ALFONSO II. Beginning of the king's conflict with the clergy, which led to interference by the pope and to restlessness among the nobility.

1223-1245. SANCHO II. His trouble with the clergy and nobility led ultimately to his deposition by the pope, who offered the crown to

1245-1279. ALFONSO III, the brother of Sancho II and Count of Boulogne. His title being weak, Alfonso was much dependent on the Córtes, in which the commons were for the first time represented. **War with Castile** was ended by a peace in 1253. (*Cont. p.* 288.)

2. EASTERN EUROPE

a. THE SLAVS

The **Slavs,** an eastern branch of the Indo-European family, were known to the Roman and Greek writers of the 1st and 2d centuries A.D. under the name of *Venedi* as inhabiting the region beyond the Vistula. The majority of modern scholars agree that the "original home" of the Slavs was the territory to the southeast of the Vistula and to the northeast of the Carpathian Mountains, in the upper basins of the Western Bug, the Pripet, and the Dniester. In the course of the early centuries of our era the Slavs expanded in all directions, and by the 6th century, when they were known to Gothic and Byzantine writers as *Sclaveni*, they were apparently already separated into three main divisions: (1) the western Slavs (the present-day Poles, Czechs, Slovaks, and Moravians); (2) the southern Slavs (the Bulgarians, Serbs, Croats, and Slovenes); (3) the eastern Slavs (the Russians, subsequently subdivided into the Great Russians, the Little Russians or the Ukrainians, and the White Russians).

However, some recent theories insist that the "original" settlements of the Slavs extended much farther south and west than the area indicated above, and thus minimize the importance of the subsequent Slav migrations.

Closely related to the Slavs were the Lithuanians who, together with the Letts and the ancient Prussians, formed the Baltic branch of the Indo-European family. They inhabited the southeastern coast of the Baltic Sea, between the present location of Memel and Estonia.

b. BOHEMIA AND MORAVIA, TO 1306

The earliest recorded attempt at the construction of a Slavic state was that made by

c. 623-658. Samo, who appears to have been a Frankish tradesman traveling in central Europe. Probably taking advantage of the defeat of the Avars by the Greeks in 626, he managed to unite the Czechs and some of the Wends, and succeeded in repulsing not only the Avars, but also the Franks under King Dagobert (631). But on the death of Samo the union of the tribes disintegrated.

870-894. Sviatopluk, a Moravian prince, succeeded in uniting under his authority Moravia, Bohemia, and present-day Slovakia and managed to maintain his position as against the Germans. During his reign the western Slavs were converted to Christianity by the Greek missionaries, **Cyril and Methodius** (d. 885 in Moravia), but in the last years of the century the German clergy redoubled its efforts and won Bohemia and Moravia for the Latin Church, thus establishing the ecclesiastical dependence of the western Slavs on Rome.

906. The Kingdom of Moravia was dissolved as the result of a great defeat by the Hungarians.

929. Death of St. Wenceslas, of the house of Premysl, which had emerged in the late 9th century. Wenceslas was murdered by his younger brother, representing the forces of the heathen reaction, who ascended the throne as

929-967. BOLESLAV I. He seems to have carried on constant warfare against the encroaching Germans, until forced (950) to accept German suzerainty. To the eastward he made many conquests and included Moravia, part of Slovakia, part of Silesia, and even Cracow in his kingdom. Furthermore, he appears to have established a fairly strong royal power over the old tribal chiefs.

967-999. BOLESLAV II, son of the preceding. He apparently continued the policies of his father and saw to the final victory of the Christian faith (foundation of the Bishopric of Prague, 973). Missionaries from Bohemia took an active part in the conversion of Hungary and Poland.

The entire 11th and 12th centuries were filled

with repeated dynastic conflicts between members of the Premysl family and the various claimants appealing to Poland and more particularly to the German emperors for support. The result was an ever-increasing German influence and the gradual integration of Bohemia with the empire.

999–1000. **Boleslav the Brave of Poland** took advantage of the anarchy in Bohemia to conquer Silesia, Moravia, and Cracow. In 1003 he became Duke of Bohemia, but was driven out in the next year by a German army. There followed another period of disorder, marked only by

1031. The reacquisition of Moravia, which thenceforth remained connected with Bohemia.

1034–1055. **BRETISLAV I** (*the Restorer*), who overran Silesia, took Cracow (1039) and for a time ruled Poland, which had now entered upon a period of disruption.

1041. **Emperor Henry III,** alarmed by the expansion of the Bohemian power, invaded the country and advanced to Prague. Bretislav agreed to give up his Polish conquests and pay tribute to the emperor.

1055–1061. **Spytihnev,** son of Bretislav, whose reign was uneventful.

1061–1092. **VRATISLAV II,** who, throughout his reign, loyally supported the German emperor, Henry IV, in his struggle with the papacy and took part in the Italian campaigns. He was rewarded by Henry with a crown (1086), but only for his own person.

1092–1110. **Bretislav II.**

1111–1125. **Vladislav I.**

1125–1140. **Sobeslav I.**

1140–1173. **VLADISLAV II.** Like his predecessors, he supported the German emperors in the main, and was rewarded (1156) by Frederick Barbarossa with an hereditary crown for his aid against the Italian cities.

1173–1197. Another period of dynastic conflict, during which there were no less than ten rulers.

1197–1230. **OTTOKAR I.** He took full advantage of the struggles for the succession which now began to wrack the German Empire. Siding now with one party, now with another, he made the Bohemian king (an imperial elector since the early 12th century) one of the decisive powers in German affairs. On the other hand, a long-drawn conflict with

the clergy (1214–1221) led to the almost complete independence of the Church.

1212. **The Golden Bull of Frederick II** recognized the right of the Bohemian nobility to elect its own ruler.

1230–1253. **WENCESLAS (VACLAV) I.** His reign was marked by large-scale immigration of Germans, encouraged by the ruler, possibly to counteract the growing power of the nobility. Germans had been coming in for a long time (chiefly clergy and nobility), but they now began to open up large forested tracts and to build cities, which were given practical autonomy under German (Magdeburg) law.

1247–1250. Rising of the nobility against the king, possibly in protest against the favor shown the Germans.

1251. The Austrian estates, after the death of the last Babenberg duke, elected Ottokar, son of Wenceslas, as duke.

1253–1278. **OTTOKAR II** (*the Great*), whose reign marked the widest expansion of Bohemian power and was characterized by great prosperity (opening of the famous silver mines, which made Bohemia one of the wealthiest countries in the later Middle Ages).

1255. Ottokar carried on a successful campaign in support of the Teutonic Knights against the heathen Prussians.

1260. After defeating the Hungarians, Ottokar took from them the province of Styria.

1267. A second northern campaign, against the Lithuanians, achieved little.

1269. Ottokar, taking advantage of the interregnum in the German Empire, extended his power over Carinthia, Carniola, and Istria.

1273. Election of **Rudolph of Hapsburg** as emperor. Ottokar refused to recognize him. The Diet of Regensburg (1274) therefore declared all Ottokar's acquisitions void. The emperor, supported by the Hungarians and by some of the Bohemian nobility, attacked Ottokar, who agreed to give up all but Bohemia and Moravia, and to recognize Rudolph's suzerainty even over these.

1278. New war between Rudolph and Ottokar. Ottokar was decisively defeated on the **Marchfeld** (Aug. 26) and killed.

1278–1305. **Wenceslas II,** a boy of seven, for whom Otto of Brandenburg at first acted as regent.

1290. Wenceslas was elected and crowned King of Poland.

1301. His son, Wenceslas, was elected King of Hungary (ruled to 1304).

1305-1306. **Wenceslas III.** He gave up the claim to Hungary and was murdered while en route to Poland to suppress a revolt of the nobles. **End of the Premyslid line.**   (*Cont. p.* 308.)

c. POLAND, TO 1305

The Polish state emerged in the 10th century, the result of the unification of some six tribes under the **Polani,** who were ruled by the members of the semi-mythical **family of Piast.** From the outset the Poles were obliged to fight against the encroachment of the Germans from the west, the Prussians from the north, the Bohemians from the south, and the Hungarians, also in the south.

c. 960-992. **MIESZKO I,** of the house of Piast, the first historical ruler. He conquered the territory between the Oder and the Warthe Rivers, but was defeated by Markgraf Gero and obliged to recognize German suzerainty (973).

966. Mieszko was converted to Christianity by Bohemian missionaries, probably for political reasons, to deprive the Germans of any further excuse for aggression. The acceptance of Latin Christianity meant the connection of Poland, like Bohemia and Hungary, with western European culture.

992-1025. **BOLESLAV I** (*Chrobry = the Brave*). He ascended the throne at 25 and was the real organizer of the Polish state. An energetic, but at times treacherous and cruel ruler, he built up an efficient military machine, laid the basis for an administrative system (*comites = castellani = Burggrafen,* with civil and military powers), organized the Church (establishment of Benedictine monasteries, etc.). Politically his aim appears to have been the union of all western Slavs under his rule. He conquered eastern Pomerania and gained access to the Baltic (992–994), added Silesia, Moravia, and Cracow to his domain (999), and induced Otto III to erect an independent Archbishopric of Gnesen (1000). On the death of Otto he took advantage of the confusion in Germany to occupy Lusatia and Meissen, and in 1003 made himself Duke of Bohemia. The new emperor, Henry II, carried on long wars against Boleslav to break his power (1004-) and ultimately forced the abandonment of Bohemia and Lusatia (1005). But by the **Treaty of Bautzen** (1018) Boleslav was given Lusatia as an imperial fief, and just before his death Boleslav was able to make himself King of Poland (1025).

1025-1034. **MIESZKO II,** a much weaker ruler. The Poles, like the other Slavs, divided the domain among the various sons of a deceased king, thus creating endless dynastic conflict and ample opportunity for intervention by neighboring rulers. During Mieszko's reign most of the territorial gains of Boleslav were lost: St. Stephen of Hungary conquered Slovakia (1027); Bretislav of Bohemia took Moravia (1031); Iaroslav of Russia acquired Ruthenia (1031); Canute of Denmark took Pomerania (1031). In 1032 the Emperor Conrad actually divided Poland between Mieszko and two of his relatives.

1034-1040. A period of violent dynastic struggle and general insurrection, including a heathen reaction (burning of monasteries, massacre of the clergy) and a peasant uprising against the landlords. In the meanwhile Bretislav of Bohemia seized Silesia (1038).

1038-1058. **CASIMIR I** (*the Restorer*), who succeeded, with the aid of the Emperor Henry III, in reconquering his domain, re-establishing Christianity and restoring order. Silesia was recovered (1054). In return Casimir was obliged to give up the royal title (becoming merely a *grand duke*) and to make numerous concessions to the nobility and clergy, thus initiating a baneful practice.

1058-1079. **BOLESLAV II** (*the Bold*), one of the great mediaeval rulers. In the great struggle between the emperor and the pope he consistently supported the latter, as a counterweight to German influence. At the same time he did his utmost to throw off the pressure of the nobility. In his countless campaigns he reconquered upper Slovakia (1061–1063) and marched as far as Kiev, to put his relative upon the Russian throne (1069). In 1076 he reassumed the royal crown, with the pope's approval. But his entire policy estranged the nobility, which ultimately drove him from the throne.

1079-1102. **Vladislav I** (*Ladislas*), **Hermann,** an indolent and unwarlike ruler, brother of Boleslav. He resigned the royal title and attempted to secure peace by supporting the Emperor Henry IV, as well as by courting the nobility and clergy.

1102-1138. **BOLESLAV III** (*Wry-mouth*), who acquired the throne only after a violent struggle with his brother Zbigniew. He was one of the greatest Polish kings, who defeated the Pomeranians (**battle of Naklo,** 1109) and, by the incorporation of Pomerania (1119–1123), re-established the access to the sea. At the same time he defeated the Emperor Henry V (1109, **battle of Hundsfeld,** near Breslau) and checked the German advance. On the other hand, his campaigns in Hungary (1132–1135) had no definite results.

Boleslav completed the organization of the state, in which the great landlords (*nobiles* = magnates), gentry (*milites* = knights = *szlachta*) had become well-defined social classes, the peasantry having steadily lost in the periods of confusion. The Church was reorganized under the Archbishop of Gnesen, by the papal legate Walo. In order to avoid dispute, Boleslav fixed the succession by seniority. Poland was divided into **five principalities** (Silesia, Great Poland, Masovia, Sandomir, Cracow) for his sons; Cracow was established as the capital, and was to go, with the title of *grand duke*, to the eldest member of the house of Piast. In actual fact this arrangement by no means eliminated the dynastic competition, but introduced a long period of disruption, during which the nobility and clergy waxed ever more powerful and the ducal or royal power became insignificant. Only the weakness of the neighboring states saved Poland from destruction.

1138-1146. Vladislav II (Ladislas).
1146-1173. Boleslav IV, an ineffectual ruler, during whose reign the Germans, under Albert the Bear and Henry the Lion, supported by Waldemar of Denmark, drove back the Poles from the entire territory along the Baltic and west of the Vistula (1147). The Emperor Frederick Barbarossa intervened and forced the humble submission of Boleslav (1157).
1173-1177. Mieszko III, a brutal and despotic prince who antagonized the nobility and was soon driven out by them.
1177-1194. CASIMIR II (*the Just*) was practically elected by the magnates, who extorted privileges from him. In the **Assembly of Lenczyca** (1180) the clergy was also given far-reaching concessions. Casimir attempted to preclude further strife by making Cracow and the primacy hereditary in his own line.
1194-1227. Leszek I (*the White*), whose reign was punctuated by constant wars against Mieszko III, who attempted to regain the throne (d. 1202), and against the latter's son Vladislav Laskonogi (1202–1206). The period was one of complete feudal anarchy, with the nobility and clergy controlling the situation.

1227-1279. Boleslav V, an unhappy reign marked by complete disruption and by constant aggression by neighboring states.
1228. Arrival of the **Teutonic Knights,** called to Prussia by Duke Conrad of Masovia (p. 216). Within the next 50 years they conquered Prussia and erected a most formidable barrier to Polish access to the sea.
1241. Beginning of the great **Mongol invasions** (p. 264), of which there were constant renewals throughout the rest of the century. The Poles managed to stave off Mongol domination, but the country was devastated. One result was the calling in of large numbers of German settlers, some of whom cleared forest land and colonized new areas in Silesia and Posen, others of whom settled in the towns. In all cases large concessions in the direction of autonomy were made (*Magdeburg law*). The German influence meant greater and more efficient exploitation of the soil, development of trade, cultural advance.
1279-1288. Leszek II (*the Black*).
1288-1290. Further dynastic and feudal warfare, with the brief reign of Henry Probus.
1290-1296. Przemyslav II. He was crowned king with the consent of the pope (1295), but was murdered soon afterward.
1300-1305. Wenceslas I, son of the King of Bohemia, elected by the nobility but challenged by claimants of the **Piast family.** He soon resigned the position and returned home. (*Cont. p.* 318.)

d. RUSSIA, TO 1263

The **eastern Slavs** settled on the territory of present-day European Russia in the period from the 5th to the 8th century A.D. Little is known of their political history during these centuries, but undoubtedly there were attempts at political organization in the shape of both tribal principalities and city-states formed around important commercial centers. In the 8th century some of the eastern Slavs were under the protectorate of the **Khazars,** a Turkish tribe which established a strong and prosperous state along the lower Volga. After the end of the 8th century the northern part of Russia began to be penetrated by the Scandinavian vikings called in the old Russian chronicles **Varangians** or *Rus* (hence the name of *Russia*). In the course of the 9th century the Varangians

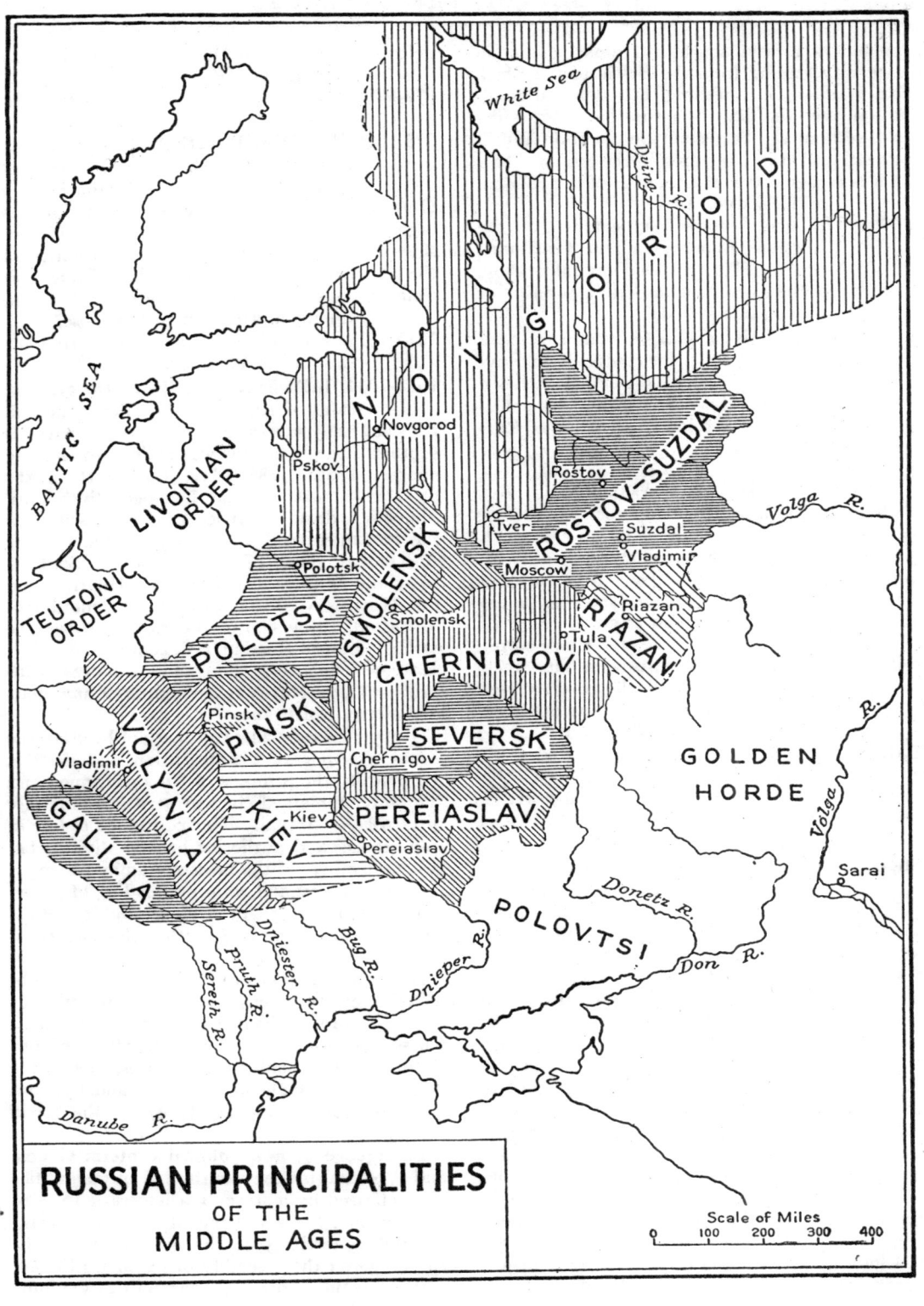

RUSSIAN PRINCIPALITIES
OF THE
MIDDLE AGES

Scale of Miles

0   100   200   300   400

constantly moved southward along the main waterway leading from the Baltic to the Black Sea, gradually establishing their political domination over the Slav communities. According to tradition, the Scandinavian chieftain **Riurik** (Rorik?) ruled in Novgorod in the 860's. Later he was recognized as the founder of the Russian princely dynasty.

860. The first recorded appearance of the Russians (*Varangians*) at Constantinople. This was a raid not unlike those of the Norsemen on Britain and France at the same period.

c. 880-912.   PRINCE OLEG, who succeeded in uniting under his control both Novgorod and Kiev (on the Dnieper River). Kiev subsequently became the political center of a loose federation of Russian states.

911. The Russians again appeared at Constantinople and extracted trade privileges from the Byzantine emperor. Trade became a leading occupation of the Russian princes, who, with their followers (*druzhina*), protected the merchant ships. Russians also began to take service with the Greek emperors in considerable number and came to play an important rôle in the mercenary corps.

945. Further trade agreements with the Greek Empire testify to the ever closer economic connections and no doubt to an increasing cultural contact.

957. The Russian princess, Olga, visited Constantinople and was converted to the Christian faith. This was, however, a purely personal conversion, and may in fact have been Olga's second.

964-972.   SVIATOSLAV, the son of Olga. He was the first of the great conquering princes. In 965 he defeated the Khazars on the lower Volga and proceeded to establish a Russian state in place of the Khazar Empire. Called to the Balkans to aid the Greek emperor against the powerful Bulgars, he carried on a successful campaign (967) and decided to establish himself on the lower Danube. At this time his power extended from Novgorod in the north to the Danube in the southwest and to the lower Volga in the southeast. He was forced to abandon Bulgaria in order to resist the **Patzinaks** (*Pechenegs*), who had entered southern Russia from the east and were threatening Kiev. Having repulsed them (968), Sviatoslav returned to Bulgaria, but he was no more welcome to the Greeks than were the Bulgars. In 971 he was defeated and driven out by the Emperor John Zimisces (p. 180). Sviatoslav was

defeated and killed by the Patzinaks on his way back to Kiev (972).

972-978. A dynastic struggle between the sons of Sviatoslav ended in the victory of

978-1015.   VLADIMIR THE SAINT, in whose reign (c. 990) the Russians were converted in mass to Christianity in the eastern (Byzantine) form. The Russian Church was organized on the Greek pattern and was considered to be under the canonical authority of the Patriarch of Constantinople. From this time on the cultural relation between Constantinople and Kiev was very close.

1015-1019. Further dynastic conflict between the sons of Vladimir.

1019-1054.   IAROSLAV (*the Wise*), the greatest ruler of Russia in the Kievan period. He was finally successful in the struggle with his brother Sviatopolk, but was obliged to leave to another brother, Mstislav, that part of the principality east of the Dnieper River until Mstislav's death in 1036. Iaroslav was then supreme ruler of all Russia. Extensive building activity at Kiev (Cathedral of St. Sophia). Religious activity (metropolitan Hilarion and the Monastery of the Caves). Promotion of education. Revision of the *Russian Law* (the earliest known Russian law code), under Byzantine influence. Dynastic alliances with western states (Iaroslav's daughter, Anna, married Henry I of France).

The period following the death of Iaroslav the Great was one of disintegration and decline. Technically the primacy of Kiev continued and the power remained concentrated in the family of Iaroslav. Actually Kiev continued to lose in importance, and authority became divided between members of the princely family on a system of seniority and rotation, leading of necessity to much dynastic rivalry and countless combinations, sometimes with Poles and Hungarians.

At the same time the Kievan state was subjected to ever greater pressure from the nomads (Patzinaks and Cumans) moving into southern Russia from the east. The period witnessed also a shifting of the older trade routes, due to the decline of the Baghdad Caliphate and the conquest of Constantinople (1204) by the Latin crusaders.

Emergence of new political centers: Galicia and Volynia in the southwest, principalities characterized by a strongly aristocratic form of government; Novgorod the Great, in the north, controlling territory to the east to the Urals. In Novgorod the assembly of freemen (*Vieche*) reached its fullest development; Suzdal-Vladimir in central Russia, the precursor of the Grand Duchy of Moscow. In this region the princely power was dominant.

1113-1125. VLADIMIR MONOMAKH, Prince of Kiev. He carried on numerous campaigns against the Cumans of the steppes and his reign marked the last period of brilliance at Kiev, which soon thereafter became a bone of contention between the Princes of Volynia and Suzdal.

1147. First mention of **Moscow** in one of the chronicles.

1157-1174. ANDREÏ BOGOLIUBSKI, Prince of Suzdal. He repressed the rising power of the nobles (*boyars*), united a large block of territory and established his capital at Vladimir.

1169. Andrei conquered Kiev, which became part of the Vladimir principality. But the new state underwent a marked decline on the death of the ruler.

1199-1205. Zenith of the Galician principality under Prince Roman.

1198. Foundation of **Riga,** which became the center of German missionary enterprise and commercial expansion.

1202. Foundation of the German Order of Swordbearers by Bishop Albert of Livonia (Latvia).

1219. Conquest of Estonia by Waldemar II of Denmark.

1223. BATTLE OF THE KALKA RIVER, near the Sea of Azov. The Mongols (Tatars, see p. 264), under Sabutai, invaded southern Russia from the Transcaucasus region and completely defeated a coalition of Russian princes and Cuman leaders. They retired, however, without pressing their conquests.

1226. The Teutonic Knights (p. 216) were commissioned to conquer and convert Prussia. They united with the Swordbearers in 1237.

1236-1263. ALEXANDER NEVSKI, prince first of Novgorod and after 1252 of Vladimir.

1237-1240. THE MONGOL CONQUEST, under the leadership of Batu. The great armies of the invaders swept over southern and central Russia and into Europe, coming within 60 miles of Novgorod. They took Kiev (1240) and ultimately established themselves (1242) at Sarai on the lower Volga. The **Khanate of the Golden Horde** for two centuries thereafter acted as suzerain of all Russia, levying tribute and taking military contingents, but for the rest leaving the princes in control, respecting the **Russian Church** and interfering little.

1240. Alexander Nevski defeated the Swedes under Birger Jarl on the Neva River and thus broke the force of the Swedish advance.

1242. Alexander defeated the Teutonic Knights in a **battle on Lake Peipus.**

1252. As Prince of Vladimir, Alexander Nevski did his utmost to prevent insurrections against Tatar rule and built up a system of protection based upon submission and conciliation.

1253. Daniel of Volynia attempted to organize a crusade against the Tatars. In order to secure papal aid he accepted the union of the Russian Church with Rome, but his efforts came to nothing.

1263. Death of Alexander Nevski on his way back from the Golden Horde.

RUSSIAN CULTURE in this period was still primarily religious and largely Byzantine in character. Noteworthy churches were built at Kiev, Novgorod, and Cernigov in the 11th and 12th centuries, decorated with fine frescoes. Church literature was active and there appeared further the first chronicles and epics of fights against the nomads. (*Cont. p.* 321.)

e. HUNGARY, TO 1301

896. The Hungarians, organized in a number of tribes, of which the **Magyars** were the leading one, occupied the valley of the middle Danube and Theiss. Under **Arpad** (d. 907) they had come from southern Russia by way of Moldavia, driven on by the Patzinaks (Pechenegs) and other Asiatic peoples. The Hungarians were themselves nomads of the Finno-Ugrian family. For more than half a century after their occupation of Hungary they continued their raids, both toward the east and toward the west.

906. The Hungarians destroyed the rising Slavic kingdom of Moravia.

955. Battle of Augsburg, in which Emperor Otto I decisively defeated the raiding Hungarians. From this time on the Hungarians began to settle down and establish a frontier.

972-997. Geza, Duke of the Magyar tribe, and the organizer of the princely power. He began to reduce the tribal leaders and invited Christian missionaries from Germany (Pilgrin of Passau, 974; **St. Adalbert of Prague,** 993). Christianization had already begun from the east, and was furthered by large numbers of war prisoners.

997-1038. ST. STEPHEN (I), greatest ruler of the Arpad dynasty. He suppressed eastern Christianity by force and crusaded against paganism, which was still favored by the tribal chiefs. Stephen took his stand definitely by the west, married a Bavarian princess, called in Roman churchmen and monks (Benedictines) and endowed them with huge tracts of land. With the help of the clergy he broke the power of the tribal chieftains, took over their land as royal domain, administered through counts (*Ispan*), placed over counties (*Comitat*). The counts and high churchmen formed a royal council. Every encouragement was given to agriculture and trade and a methodical system of frontier defense was built up (large belt of swamps and forests, wholly uninhabited and protected by regular frontier guards; as time went on this frontier was gradually extended).

1001. Stephen was crowned with a crown sent by the pope. He was canonized in 1083.

1002. Stephen defeated an anti-Christian insurrection in Transylvania.

1030. Attacks of the Germans under Conrad II, who tried to enforce German suzerainty over Hungary, were repulsed.

1038-1077. A period of dynastic struggles over the succession, every member of the Arpad family claiming a share of the power, and sometimes calling in the Germans for support.

1038-1046. Peter Urseolo, son of Stephen's sister and the Doge of Venice, succeeded to the throne. He called in German and Italian favorites, aroused the hostility of the Hungarians and was driven out (1041). For a few years Samuel Aba, the brother-in-law of Stephen, occupied the throne, but he in turn was expelled by Peter, who returned with the Emperor Henry III, to whom he swore fealty.

1046. Peter was overthrown in the course of a great **pagan rising** of the tribal chiefs under Vatha, who massacred the Christians and destroyed the churches. This was the last serious revolt of the kind.

1047-1061. Andrew I, who managed to restore the royal power.

1049-1052. The three campaigns of Emperor Henry III against the Hungarians. Andrew managed to hold his own, and in 1058 the emperor recognized Hungary's independence of the empire.

1061-1063. Bela I, brother of Andrew and popular hero of the campaigns against the Germans.

1063-1074. Solomon, the son of Andrew and the candidate of the German party. He was defeated by his cousin

1074-1077. Geza I.

1077-1095. ST. LADISLAS I (canonized 1192), the first great king after St. Stephen. He supported the pope in his conflicts with the emperor, and at home restored order and prosperity.

1091. Ladislas conquered Croatia and Bosnia, but left these regions self-government under a *ban*.

1095-1114. Coloman (*Kalman*) I. Another strong ruler, who, in

1097-1102. Conquered Dalmatia from the Venetian Republic.

1114-1131. Stephen II, in whose reign the dynastic struggles were resumed.

1131-1141. Bela II. He had been blinded by Coloman, and now took a horrible revenge on his opponents.

1141-1162. Geza II. The intestine conflicts were greatly complicated by the efforts of the Greek emperor, Manuel, to extend his sway over Hungary. But a number of campaigns carried out to this end (1097–1102) led to no success, though at one time (1156) the Hungarians recognized Byzantine suzerainty.

1150. Saxon (i.e. Germans from the Moselle region) **settlement** in the Zips and southern Transylvania regions. They were called in to help defend the frontiers against Poland and against the Greeks, and had much to do with developing agriculture, trade, and town-building. In this period many Pechenegs and Szeklers were also established for frontier protection.

1162-1172. Stephen III.

1172-1196. BELA III, who had been educated at Constantinople. He married the sister of Philip Augustus of France and established a close dynastic connection with France. Bela was a strong ruler who successfully defended Dalmatia against Venice.

1196-1204. Emeric I, whose position was challenged by his brother Andrew.

1204-1205. Ladislas III, dethroned by Andrew.

1205-1235. ANDREW II. The most disastrous reign in the Arpad period. Andrew was renowned for his extravagance and for his generosity to his foreign favorites. A crusade to the Holy Land (1217) cost him much money, which he raised by alienating huge tracts of the royal domain, thus paving the way for the emergence of large landed magnates or oligarchs.

1222. THE GOLDEN BULL, forced upon Andrew by the lesser nobility or gentry, led by Andrew's own son, Bela. This document became the charter of feudal privilege. It exempted the gentry and the clergy from taxation, granted them freedom to dispose of their domains as they saw fit, guaranteed them against arbitrary imprisonment and confiscation and assured them an annual assembly to present grievances. No lands or offices were to be given to foreigners or Jews.

1224. The privileges of the Transylvanian Saxons were set down. They were given practical self-government, directly under the king.

1235-1270. BELA IV. A strong ruler who tried desperately to make good the losses of the preceding reign. The magnates, in reply, attempted to set up a rival ruler, and Bela in turn allowed some 40,000 families of the Cumans, who were driven westward by the Mongol invasions, to settle in the Theiss region in the hope of securing support against the magnates.

1241. THE GREAT MONGOL INVASION, which took the country by surprise in the midst of its dissensions. Bela's army was overwhelmingly defeated at Muhi on the Theiss and he was obliged to flee to the Adriatic. The Mongols followed him, but suddenly gave up their conquests when news arrived of the death of the **Great Khan.** But the Mongol invasion left the country devastated. For defense purposes the nobility was allowed to build castles and these soon became bases for feudal warfare and for campaigns against the king himself.

1246. Bela defeated Frederick of Austria, the last of the Babenbergs, who had taken advantage of the Mongol invasion to appropriate some of the western provinces.

1265-1270. Wars of Bela against Ottokar II of Bohemia.

1270-1272. Stephen V, a weak ruler.

1272-1290. Ladislas IV. His efforts to curb the feudal aristocracy were of little avail, but in alliance with Rudolph of Hapsburg he succeeded in breaking the power of Ottokar in the **battle of Dürnkrut** (1278).

1290-1301. Andrew III, last of the native dynasty. He continued the struggle against the domination of the feudal aristocracy, but with little success. *(Cont. p. 322.)*

f. SERBIA, TO 1276

650. Approximate date of the completion of the Slav occupation of the Balkan area. Part of the Slav people extended as far west as Carniola and Carinthia, but these (the Slovenes) were conquered by the Franks in the early 9th century and were thenceforth part of the German Empire.

818. The Croats, who had also been conquered by the Franks, revolted, but were again subdued.

924. Tomislav became King of Croatia, accepting his crown from the pope. He ruled over later-day Croatia and over the territory as far south as Montenegro, though the coastal towns were mostly under Byzantine control.

960. Death of Chaslav, who made the first effort to unite the Serbs. The Serbs, inhabiting a mountainous area, were divided into tribes and clans, under headmen or *zupans*. The grand zupan held an honorary pre-eminence. Technically the territory was under Byzantine suzerainty, which, when the Eastern Empire was strong, was effectively exercised. By the end of the 10th century the inhabitants of present-day Serbia and eastern Bosnia had for the most part accepted eastern Christianity, while western Bosnia and Croatia leaned toward Roman Catholicism. But the conflict of the churches drew the southern Slavs this way and that, becoming frequently an important political as well as religious issue.

1077. Mikhail of Serbia was crowned by a papal legate.

1081-1101. Bodin established a Serbian state in Zeta (i.e. Montenegro).

1102. Croatia was joined with Hungary in a dynastic union, after the defeat of the last ruler, Petar, by King Ladislas. This involved the definitive victory of the western orientation in Croatia and the separation from the other southern Slavs.

1168-1196. STEPHEN NEMANYA, founder of the Nemanyid dynasty in the Raska (i.e. *Rascia* or Serbia proper). Though only grand zupan, Stephen appears to have made considerable progress in uniting the various clans. He definitely adopted the Greek Orthodox faith and persecuted the Bogomils, who were forced across the frontier into Bosnia, which at that time was ruled by a strong prince, Kulin (d. 1204). The death of Manuel I Comnenus (1180) and the subsequent decline of the Eastern Empire gave Stephen an opportunity to establish his independence of Constantinople and to conquer extensive territories to the south. In 1196 he retired to a monastery on Mt. Athos which had been founded by his son, **St. Sava.** Stephen died in 1200.

1196-1223. STEPHEN NEMANYA II, the son of the preceding. The beginning of his reign was marked by a struggle with his elder brother, Vukan, to whom Montenegro had been assigned. The Hungarians, who became an ever greater menace to Serbia, supported Vukan, and Stephen was forced to flee to the Bulgarian court. He returned with an army of Cumans supplied by Kaloyan (see below), who appropriated for himself most of eastern Serbia, including Belgrade and Nish. Stephen's brother, St. Sava, finally mediated between the two contestants and Stephen became ruler of Serbia proper.

1217. Stephen was crowned king by a papal legate (hence *Stephen the First-Crowned*).

1219. St. Sava, fearful of the Roman influence, visited Nicaea and induced the Greek patriarch to recognize him as archbishop of all Serbia and as head of an autocephalous church.

1222. Stephen was recrowned by St. Sava with a crown from Nicaea, thus re-establishing the eastern orientation.

1223-1234. Radoslav, the son of Stephen, a weak ruler, who was deposed by his brother

1234-1242. Vladislav. He married a daughter of Tsar John Asen II of Bulgaria and during this period much of eastern Serbia was under Bulgarian domination.

1242-1276. Urosh I, brother of the preceding two rulers. He married a daughter of the deposed Latin emperor, Baldwin II, and established an alliance with Charles of Anjou, heir of the Latin claims to Constantinople.

1254. The Hungarians, who already held part of northern Serbia, established their suzerainty over Bosnia and Herzegovina. (*Cont. p.* 323.)

g. THE SECOND BULGARIAN EMPIRE

Following the collapse of the First Bulgarian Empire in 1018, Bulgaria was, for 168 years, an integral part of the Byzantine Empire. The more stringent taxation and other grievances led to a serious revolt in 1040, led by **Peter Deljan,** a son of Gabriel Radomir, and confined to the northwest and western parts of the former empire. Delyan had himself proclaimed *tsar*, but the movement suffered from his rivalry with Tikhomir of Durazzo. In 1041 Delyan was defeated and captured by the imperial troops. Another uprising, led by **George Voitech,** in 1072–1073, never assumed the same proportions and was suppressed without much difficulty. During the Byzantine period the country was constantly exposed to marauding raids by the Patzinaks (1048–1054), many of whom settled in northeastern Bulgaria, and by invasions of the Cumans (1064). The **Bogomil heresy** continued to spread, despite persecution by the government (1110 ff.). Under the leadership of the monks it became to a certain extent a reaction to the Greek influence exerted by the higher clergy.

1185. RISING OF JOHN AND PETER ASEN, two Bulgarian lords from the vicinity of Tirnovo. Defeated by the Emperor Isaac Angelus (1186) they fled to the Cumans and returned with an army of the latter. After raiding into Thrace, they accepted a truce which left them in possession of Bulgaria north of the Balkan Mountains.

1189. The Asens attempted to effect an alliance with Frederick Barbarossa and the leaders of the Third Crusade, against the Greeks. This came to nothing, but the Bulgarians resumed their raids into Thrace and Macedonia. An imperial army under Isaac Angelus was completely defeated in **a battle near Berrhoe.**

1196. Peter Asen succeeded to leadership of the movement after the murder of John by boyar (i.e. noble) conspirators.

1197. Peter himself fell a victim to his boyar rivals.

1197-1207. KALOYAN (*Joannitsa*), the younger brother of John and Peter. He made peace with the Greeks (1201) and then engaged (1202) in campaigns against the Serbs (taking of Nish) and the Hungarians, whom he drove back over the Danube.

1204. The collapse of the Eastern Empire (p. 256) gave Kaloyan an excellent opportunity to reaffirm his dominion. By recognizing the primacy of the pope, he succeeded in securing the appointment of a primate for Bulgaria and in getting himself crowned *king* by the papal legate. At the same time he took over the whole of western Macedonia.

1205. Supported by the Cumans and the local Greeks, Kaloyan completely defeated the Frankish crusaders near Adrianople and captured the Emperor Baldwin I.

1206. Kaloyan put down a revolt of the Greeks

and besieged Adrianople and Thessalonica. He was murdered in 1207.

1207-1218. Boril, the nephew of Kaloyan, whose position was not recognized by all other leaders, some of whom attempted to set up independent principalities.

1208. Boril was completely defeated by the Franks under Henry I in the **battle of Philippopolis,** and ultimately (1213) was obliged to make peace.

1217. Ivan (*John*) **Asen,** son of Kaloyan, supported by the Russians, began a revolt in northern Bulgaria. He besieged and took Tirnovo, and captured and blinded Boril (1218).

1218-1241. JOHN ASEN II, whose reign marked the apogee of the Second Bulgarian Empire. John was a mild and generous ruler, much beloved even by the Greek population.

1228-1230. Owing to the youthfulness of the Emperor Baldwin II, a number of Frank nobles at Constantinople projected making John Asen emperor and thereby securing themselves against the aggression of Theodore of Epirus (p. 263). The scheme was opposed by the Latin clergy and ultimately came to nothing.

1230. John Asen defeated Theodore of Epirus at **Klokotnitsa** on the Maritza River and captured him. He then occupied all of western Thrace, Macedonia and even northern Albania, leaving Thessalonica and Epirus to Theodore's brother Manuel, who became his vassal.

1232. John broke with Rome and the Bulgarian Church became independent.

1235. Alliance of John with the Greek emperor of Nicaea against the Franks. The Greeks recognized the patriarch of Tirnovo. Together the allies besieged Constantinople, which was relieved by a fleet and forces from Achaia.

1236. The Hungarians, instigated by the pope, began to threaten the Bulgarians and forced John to withdraw from operations against the Latin Empire.

1241-1246. Kaliman I, the son of John Asen II. His reign was distinguished chiefly by the great incursion of the Mongols, returning from the expedition into central Europe (1241).

1246-1257. Michael Asen, the youngest son of John, and a mere child. The Nicaean emperor, John Vatatzes, took advantage of the situation to conquer all southern Thrace and Macedonia, while Michael of Epirus appropriated western Macedonia.

1254. On the death of John Vatatzes, Michael Asen attempted to recover the lost territories, but was badly defeated by Theodore II Lascaris at **Adrianople** and later (1256) in Macedonia.

1257-1258. Kaliman II, who, with support of the boyars, drove out Michael Asen, only to be deposed and expelled in his turn. He was the last ruler of the Asen dynasty.

(*Cont. p.* 330.)

3. THE NEAR EAST

a. THE EASTERN EMPIRE, 1025-1204

The period of the later Macedonian emperors (to 1050) and the succeeding thirty years was a period of decline, marked by the rule of women, barbarian invasions in the Balkans, the advance of the Normans in Italy and the expansion of the Seljuk Turks (p. 257) in Anatolia. Within the empire there was a steady development of the clerical and bureaucratic nobility in the capital and of the feudal baronage in the provinces, leading ultimately to sharp conflict between the two interests.

1025-1028. CONSTANTINE VIII, the younger brother of Basil II, a man suspicious of the military commanders, who granted many high offices to court favorites.

1027. The Patzinaks, who had invaded the Balkans, were finally driven back over the Danube by the general, Constantine Diogenes.

1028-1050. ZOË, empress. She was the third daughter of Constantine and, though 48 years old at her accession, married three times, associating her husbands in the imperial office.

1028-1034. ROMANUS III (*Argyropolus*), an official 60 years old, first husband of Zoë. He made great efforts to gain popularity by catering to the populace, the nobility, and especially the Church. The patriarchate was permitted to persecute the Monophysites of Syria, thousands of whom fled to Moslem territory. The hatred engendered by this policy helps to explain the Seljuk advance in subsequent years.

1030. Romanus suffered a severe defeat in a campaign against the Moslem emirs who attacked Syria.

1031. The situation was saved by the victories of **Georgios Maniakes,** greatest imperial general of the period.

1032. A combined Byzantine-Ragusan fleet completely defeated the Saracen pirates in the Adriatic.

1034-1041. MICHAEL IV (*the Paphlagonian*), second husband of Zoë. He was a man of lowly origin, who promptly established his brothers (mostly men of energy and ability) in high office.

1034-1035. The Byzantine fleets, manned by the Norseman Harald Hardrada and Scandinavian mercenaries, repeatedly defeated the Saracen pirates off the Anatolian coast and ravaged the coasts of North Africa.

1038. Maniakes and Hadraade, with Scandinavian and Italian mercenaries and with the support of the Byzantine fleets, stormed Messina and defeated the Sicilian Saracens, first at **Rametta** (1038), then at **Dragina** (1040).

1040. Revolt of the Bulgarians under Peter Deljan, a descendant of Tsar Samuel. The revolt was directed against the harsh fiscal policy of the government. The Bulgars attacked Thessalonica, but the city held out. Ultimately the movement collapsed, as the result of dissension among the leaders. Bulgaria was then incorporated in the empire and the autocephalous church of Ochrid became a prey of the patriarchal hierarchy.

1041-1042. MICHAEL V (*Kalaphates*), one of Zoë's favorites. He attempted to secure sole power by shutting the empress in a cloister, but this led to a rising of the Constantinople nobility and to the incarceration of Michael in a monastery.

1042-1054. CONSTANTINE IX (*Monomachus*), the third husband of Zoë, a scholarly person, wholly out of sympathy with the army and with the military aristocracy. He systematically neglected the frontier defenses and the forces.

1042. Maniakes totally defeated the Normans, who had begun the attack on southern Italy, in the **battle of Monopoli** (near Naples).

1043. Revolt of Maniakes, representing the disaffection of the military classes. Maniakes landed at Durazzo and prepared to march on the capital, but he was accidentally shot and killed on the way.

1046. The Byzantine forces occupied Ani and took over the government of Armenia, which became another field for clerical exploitation.

1047. Another military uprising, led by Leo Tornikios, failed.

1048. The imperial generals defeated the advancing Seljuk armies at **Stragna.**

1050. Death of Zoë. Her husband Constantine continued to reign alone.

1051. Expulsion of the Patzinaks from Bulgaria, after years of ravaging and unsuccessful Byzantine campaigns.

1054-1056. THEODORA, empress. She was the elder sister of Zoë, an intelligent, vigorous, and popular ruler, but already advanced in age.

1054. Final schism between Rome and Constantinople. The long-standing friction between the papacy and the eastern patriarch had come to a head with the conquest of parts of southern Italy by the Normans, who were supported by the papacy. The Patriarch Michael Kerularios disputed the claim of Pope Leo IX to jurisdiction in southern Italy. Negotiations were opened, but each side assumed an uncompromising attitude and the rift became unavoidable. The enmity it left behind was of the utmost importance for the development of the next years.

1056-1057. MICHAEL VI (*Stratioticus*), who was overthrown almost at once by a revolt of the Anatolian feudal barons.

1057-1059. ISAAC COMNENUS, proclaimed by the insurgents. He was an able and energetic army man, who promptly abolished a host of sinecures, undertook the reform of the finances, etc. Isaac, already advanced in years, soon found his work too arduous and abdicated in favor of

1059-1067. CONSTANTINE X (*Dukas*), a high official of the finance department. Constantine introduced a period of domination by the civil officials, Church and scholars, during which the army was viewed with suspicion, neglected and driven into hostility.

1060. The Normans took Rheggio, completing the conquest of Calabria.

1064. The Seljuks, under Alp Arslan, took Ani and ravaged Armenia.

1065. The Cumans, having crossed the Danube, flooded the Balkan area as far as Thessalonica. They were finally driven back by local forces.

1067-1071. ROMANUS DIOGENES, who, on Constantine's death, married the widowed empress, Eudoxia. Romanus was an ambitious soldier, who did his best to check the advance of the enemy in the east and the west.

1068. The Normans took Otranto, and then Bari (1071), the last Byzantine outpost. This marked the end of the Byzantine rule in Italy.

1068-1069. Romanus succeeded in repulsing the Seljuks, though they repeatedly raided through the whole of eastern Anatolia.

1071. BATTLE OF MANZIKERT (north of Lake Van). Romanus had concentrated huge forces for a decisive battle, and he rejected all offers of a settlement. In the course of a hard-fought battle he was deserted by Andronicus Dukas and other Byzantine magnates. Romanus was defeated and captured, but then released by the Seljuks. He attempted to regain the Byzantine throne, but was defeated by his opponents and blinded. He died very soon afterward.

1071-1078. MICHAEL VII (*Parapinakes*), a son of Constantine X. His elevation meant another victory for the bureaucratic group. Michael made the great scholar, **Michael Psellus,** his chief adviser and devoted himself to the pursuit of learning. The military system was again allowed to fall into neglect.

1074. The emperor concluded a **treaty with the Seljuks** in order to secure their aid against his uncle, who had set himself up as a pretender. The Seljuks defeated the pretender, but took advantage of the situation to spread themselves over a large part of Anatolia.

1078. Revolt of Nicephorus Briennius in Albania. Another military revolt broke out in Anatolia, led by Nicephorus Botaniates, who was supported by the Seljuks.

1078-1081. NICEPHORUS III (*Botaniates*), emperor after Michael's abdication. His accession was greeted by a number of insurrections in various parts of the army, but these were suppressed by the able general Alexius Comnenus.

1081. Revolt of Alexius Comnenus himself. He seized Constantinople with a force of mercenaries, who thereupon plundered the capital. The victory of Comnenus meant the final success of the military aristocracy and the beginning of a new period of military success.

1081-1118. ALEXIUS COMNENUS, an able general, vigorous administrator, conscientious ruler, and shrewd diplomat. Having to rely upon the great feudal families, he attempted to win their support by lavish grants of honors and ranks. At the same time he tried to use the high clergy to counterbalance the influence of the nobility. He reformed the judicial and financial systems and systematically used his resources in money to buy off the enemies he could not conquer.

1081-1085. The war against the Normans under **Robert Guiscard.** The latter landed in Epirus with a large force and besieged Durazzo (*Dyracchium*). Alexius bought the support of the Venetians with extensive trade privileges (1082), but Guiscard defeated the emperor in the **battle of Pharsalus,** after which he took Durazzo. The war was continued by Robert's son, Bohemund, who again defeated Alexius and in 1083 conquered all Macedonia as far as the Vardar. But the advance was broken by the resistance of Larissa, by the guerrilla tactics of the natives (who hated the heretical Latins), and by the Seljuk cavalry employed by the emperor. In 1085 the combined Byzantine and Venetian fleets defeated the Normans near Corfu. The death of Robert Guiscard at the same time led to dissension among his sons and the abandonment of the Balkan project.

1086-1091. Revolt of the Bogomils in Thrace and Bulgaria. The heretics were supported by the Patzinaks and Cumans and were able to defeat Alexius and a large army (**battle of Drystra** or Dorostolon, 1087). The Cumans then ravaged the entire eastern Balkan region as far as Constantinople until Alexius bought them off, took them into imperial service and used them (1091) to annihilate the Patzinaks (**battle of Leburnion**).

1092. Death of Malik Shah, ruler of the Seljuk empire of Iconium, which controlled almost all of Anatolia. The death of Malik led to disputes as to the succession and paved the way for the partial reconquest of Anatolia.

1094. Constantine Diogenes, a pretender to the throne, crossed the Danube with an army of Cumans and besieged Adrianople, but was then defeated in the battle of **Taurocomon.**

1096-1097. THE FIRST CRUSADE (p. 258). The crusaders, of whom Bohemund was one of the leaders, were looked upon with great suspicion in the east, where there was little interest in a movement organized by the heretical Latin pope. But Alexius was unable to stop the crusaders, and therefore devoted himself to managing the movement. He induced them to promise to do homage to the empire for all territory reconquered from the infidel. The cru-

The Comneni and Angeli

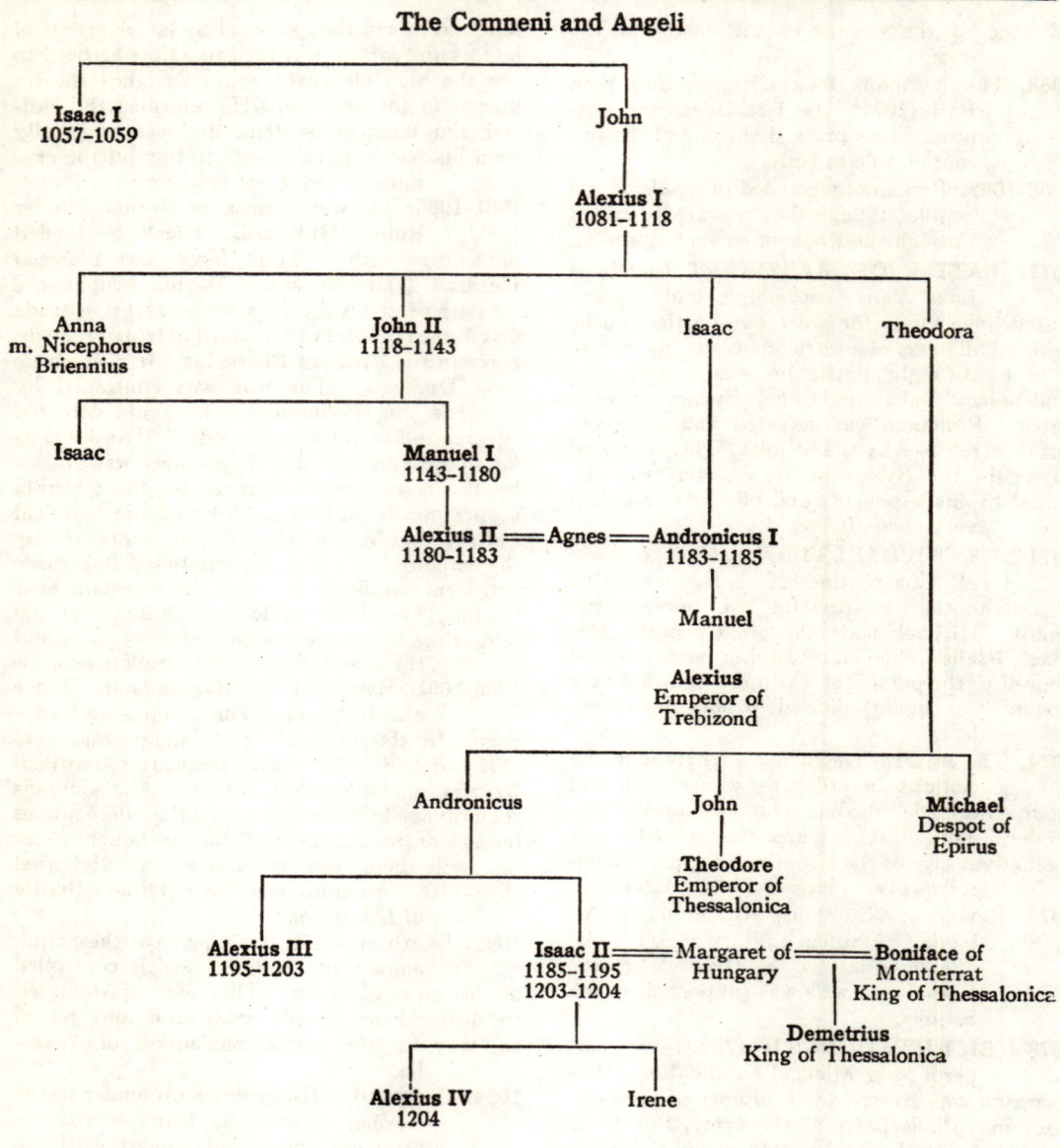

sading **victories at Nicaea** and **Dorylaeum** (1097)
enabled Alexius to recover the entire western
coast of Anatolia.
1098-1108. Second war with the Normans.
The crusaders, having regained An-
tioch (lost to the Turks only in 1085), turned it
over to Bohemund, who refused to recognize
Alexius' suzerainty. War broke out. Bohemund returned to Italy and raised a huge army,
with which he appeared in Epirus (1104). He

failed in his siege of Durazzo, and Alexius wisely
avoided open battle. Ultimately (1108) Bohemund agreed to make peace, recognizing Byzantine suzerainty over Antioch.
1110-1117. War against the Seljuks, who again
advanced to the Bosporus. In 1116
Alexius won a resounding victory at **Philomelion,**
which induced the Turks to make **peace at Akroinon** (1117): they abandoned the entire coastal
area of Anatolia (north, west, and south) and all

of Anatolia west of a line from Sinope through Ancyra (Ankara) and Philomelion.

1111. Trade privileges granted to the Pisans. This was part of the emperor's effort to draw the Pisans away from the Normans and at the same time to counterbalance the extensive trade position of the Venetians in the empire.

1118-1143. JOHN COMNENUS, a ruler of high moral integrity, mild, brave, and sincere. He devoted his attention chiefly to the east, with the object of recovering the old frontier of the Euphrates and of subjecting the Latin states of Syria to the empire.

1120-1121. In a successful campaign against the Seljuks, John recovered southwestern Anatolia. He was diverted from further conquests by continued incursions of the Patzinaks in the Balkans.

1122. The Patzinaks were completely defeated and thenceforth were no longer a threat to the empire.

1122-1126. War with Venice, resulting from John's refusal to renew the extensive trading privileges, which the Venetians had been exploiting to the full. The Venetian fleets ravaged the islands of the Aegean, occupied Corfu and Cephalonia, and ultimately (1126) forced John to renew the privileges.

1124. Intervention of the emperor in behalf of Bela II in Hungary, initiating a policy which continued throughout the century. The objective of the Comneni was to prevent the Hungarians from establishing control over the Slavic regions of Dalmatia, Croatia, and Serbia. By the **Peace of 1126** the emperor secured Branicova, a vital bridgehead on the Danube.

1134-1137. Conquest of Cilician (Little) Armenia, which was allied with the Latin Kingdom of Antioch. John forced Raymond of Antioch to do homage for his domain.

1143. John died from a wound incurred while hunting. He was just about to renew his campaigns in Syria.

1143-1180. MANUEL COMNENUS, the son of John, a noble, intelligent, chivalrous idealist, and yet an adroit statesman and ambitious soldier. He was the greatest of the Comneni and the most splendid. In his reign Constantinople came to be accepted as the capital of the world and the center of culture. Its brilliant art was imitated in the east as in the west. Manuel married a Latin princess (Maria of Antioch) and throughout his career cherished the hope of resurrecting a universal empire. Hence his association with and employment of

Latin nobles, who intermarried with the Greek aristocracy, his constant toying with the idea of reunion with Rome, his designs on Italian territory and his antagonism to the Hohenstaufen emperors. All this tended to arouse much hostility among the Greeks (accentuated by the high-handed activities of the Italian traders), cost the empire inordinate sums of money and involved repeated conflict with the Normans. The emperor's preoccupation in the west at the same time forced him to neglect the east, where the Seljuk Sultanate of Iconium (Rum) was able to effect a marked recovery.

1147-1158. War with Roger of Sicily. The Norman fleets ravaged Euboea and Attica, took and plundered Thebes and Corinth, carried away large numbers of the silk-workers, who were established at Palermo. The emperor, having neglected the Byzantine fleet, was obliged to buy the aid of Venice with extensive trading rights (1148). The Venetians helped to reconquer Corfu (1149) and paved the way for the Byzantine conquest of Ancona (1151). But efforts to extend the Greek power in Italy met with failure (1154) and Manuel in the end had to agree to an inconclusive peace (1158).

1147-1149. THE SECOND CRUSADE (p. 260). The crusaders, having plundered the Balkan region, almost came to blows with the Greeks at Constantinople, but Manuel by diplomacy prevented a clash. The Greeks did nothing to prevent the defeat of the crusaders in Anatolia.

1152-1154. Successful war against the Hungarians, who attempted to make good their claims to Serbia and Bosnia. Peace was made in 1156, the Hungarians recognizing the emperor's suzerainty.

1155. Trade privileges granted to Genoa, the emperor hoping thereby to counteract the domination of the Venetians.

1158-1159. An expedition against Raymond of Antioch forced the latter to renew his homage.

1161. Kilidj Arslan IV, Sultan of Rum, made peace with the empire, recognizing the emperor's primacy.

1165-1168. War with the Hungarians. The imperial forces took Dalmatia and in the final peace (1168) received also part of Croatia. The following years Manuel interfered actively in Hungarian dynastic affairs. Bela III (1173–1196) was practically his vassal.

1170-1177. War with Venice, the natural result of the Byzantine acquisitions in Dalmatia and in Italy. The emperor arrested all Venetian traders in Constantinople and confiscated their goods, but with a neglected fleet he was able to do little. The Venetians conquered Ragusa (1171) and Chios (1171), though they failed in an attack on Ancona (1173). In 1175 the Venetians made an alliance with the Normans against the empire and thereby forced Manuel to yield. By the **Peace of 1176** the trade privileges were renewed and the emperor paid a heavy indemnity.

1176-1177. War against the Seljuks. The Byzantines were defeated at **Myriocephalon** (1176), but in the next year Manuel defeated the enemy in Bithynia, while John Vatatzes drove them out of the Meander Valley.

1180-1183. MANUEL ALEXIUS II, the son of Manuel, who ruled under the regency of his mother, Maria of Antioch. The regent relied almost entirely upon Latins in her service.

1182. Revolt of the populace of Constantinople against the Latins, officials and traders, who were brutally cut down in a great massacre. The mob forced the proclamation of

1182-1185. ANDRONICUS COMNENUS, an uncle of the boy-emperor, who ruled first as co-emperor, but in 1183 had Alexius strangled and became sole ruler. Andronicus had intrigued innumerable times against Manuel and was renowned for his lack of principle. But he was a man of great personal charm, intelligent, vigorous, unscrupulous, and cruel. Through persecution, confiscations, and executions he cleaned the court circle, got rid of the hated Latins, abolished sale of offices, sinecures, etc.; reformed the judiciary, lightened the taxes. All this was a policy directed against the powerful official and landed aristocracy and might, had it been carried through, have led to a thoroughgoing reform of the empire.

1185. The Norman attack. The Normans took Durazzo, sent an army and a navy against Thessalonica, which they stormed, and massacred the Greeks. This attack led to a revolt of the Greek nobility against Andronicus, who was deposed, tortured, and executed.

1185-1195. ISAAC ANGELUS, leader of the insurgents. His accession meant a return to the old negligence and corruption. Within a brief space the entire empire began to go to pieces. In the provinces the powerful feudal families (i.e. Sguros in Greece; Gabras

at Trebizond) began to set up as independent potentates.

1185. Victory of the Byzantine general, Alexius Branas, over the Normans at Demetritsa. By 1191 the Normans were driven out of the Balkans, and even out of Durazzo and Corfu.

1186-1188. The great insurrection in Bulgaria, led by Peter and John Asen. This was due primarily to the extortion of the imperial fiscal agents. The revolt was supported by the Cumans and resulted in the devastation of much of the Balkan region, with the annihilation of much of the Greek population. Though at times successful, the Greek commanders were unable to suppress the movement, which resulted in the formation of a new Bulgarian state north of the Balkan Mountains (1188).

1187. Fall of Jerusalem. Isaac, in fear of another crusade, allied himself with Saladin.

1189. THE THIRD CRUSADE (p. 260). Frederick Barbarossa was welcomed in Bulgaria by John Asen, who offered him an army for use against the empire. But Frederick avoided friction as well as might be, and Isaac did not oppose the crossing of the crusaders into Anatolia. The death of Saladin (1193) relieved the danger from the east.

1190-1194. Continuation of the war in Bulgaria. The Byzantine forces were defeated at Berrhoe (1190) and at Arcadiopolis (1194).

1195-1203. ALEXIUS III, the brother of Isaac, whom he deposed and blinded.

1196. The western emperor, Henry VI, heir to the Norman domains, demanded Durazzo and Thessalonica. Alexius settled for a huge money payment, and Henry's death (1197) removed the immediate threat from that quarter.

1201. Peace with the Bulgars, who were allowed to retain most of the eastern Balkan area, under the younger brother of the Asens, John (*Joannitsa, Kaloyan*, 1197--1207).

1202-1204. THE FOURTH CRUSADE (p. 260). The leaders were the Venetian doge, **Enrico Dandolo,** and **Boniface of Montferrat.** Alexius, the son of Isaac, appealed for aid against his uncle and promised great concessions. Dandolo succeeded in diverting the expedition against Constantinople. The crusaders took Durazzo (1203) and arrived at Constantinople (June, 1203). The emperor thereupon fled to Adrianople (July). His deposed brother, Isaac, was set upon the throne with his son, the accomplice of the crusaders.

1203-1204. ALEXIUS IV. He was wholly under the control of the crusaders and was forced to pay a heavy tribute. Popular discontent led to

1204, Jan. 25. A revolution and the proclamation of

1204. Alexius V (*Dukas*). Alexius IV was killed. The new ruler, refused payments to the crusaders and demanded their withdrawal.

Apr. 12. The crusaders stormed the city, which was given over to a merciless sack. The emperor succeeded in escaping.

(*Cont. p.* 262.)

b. THE SELJUK TURKS

1037. The Seljuks, a sept of the Ghuzz Turks, under the brothers Tughril Beg and Chagar Beg, invaded Khorasan and defeated the Ghaznawid armies. They then conquered Balkh, Jurjan, Tabaristan, and Khwarizm.

1055. Entry of Tughril Beg into Baghdad, where he was proclaimed *sultan*, with the title *King of the East and the West.* Invasion of Byzantine Cappadocia and Phrygia by Tughril Beg.

1063-1073. Alp Arslan, brilliant nephew of Tughril, succeeded the latter. He conquered Georgia and Armenia.

1071. BATTLE OF MANZIKERT (Malaz Kard). Alp Arslan defeated the Byzantine emperor, Diogenes Romanus, and virtually destroyed the Byzantine power in Asia Minor.

1073-1092. Malik Shah, son of Alp Arslan. His vizier, **Nizam al-Mulk,** was one of the ablest administrators ever produced by Asia. At the same time he was a patron of learning, founder of colleges in Baghdad (the Nizamiya) and other principal cities. Under him was undertaken the reform of the calendar by the famous poet, **Omar Khayyam.**

1084. The Seljuks took Antioch.

1090. Rise of the Ismailian fraternity of the Assassins, founded by Hasan Sabbah, a schoolfellow of Nizam al-Mulk, and a Fatimid propagandist. He captured the mountain stronghold of Alamut in the Elburz range in Mazendran. The Assassins later became masters of many mountain fortresses in northern Persia, Iraq, and Syria. The crusaders came into contact with the Syrian branch.

1091. Nizam al-Mulk was murdered by one of Hasan's emissaries, after two expeditions against the Assassins had failed.

1092. Barkyaruk (Rukn al-Din), son of Malik Shah, sultan. Civil war broke out between the new ruler and his brother, Mohammed, over Iran and Khorasan, and separate branches of the Seljuk family attained virtual independence in different parts of the empire, although the main line still preserved the nominal sovereignty down to 1157. The **Seljuk Empire of the East** ultimately fell before the attack of the Kwarizm Shah (1157). The Seljuks of Kirman (1041-1187) were overthrown by the Ghuzz Turcomans; the Seljuks of Syria (1094-1117) by the Burids and Ortuqids; the Seljuks of Iraq and Kurdistan (1117-1194) by the Shahs of Kwarizm. The Seljuks of Rum (Iconium, Koniah), who ruled most of Anatolia, absorbed the Danishmandid princedom in Cappadocia, but were ousted by the Mongols and the Othmanli (Ottoman) Turks (p. 328).

1100-1200. During the 12th century the whole of the Seljuk Empire, excepting Rum, fell into the hands of captains of the Seljuk armies, the so-called *Atabegs* (regents). The **Burid dynasty** of Damascus (1103-1154) was founded by Tughtugin. The **Zangid dynasty** of Mesopotamia and Syria (1127-1250) by Imad al-Din Zangi, whose son, Nur al-Din, was famous as an opponent of the crusaders. The Zangids absorbed the Burids (1154). The **Ortuqid dynasty** of Diyar-Bakr (Diarbekr) was founded by Ortuq ibn Akrab (1101), whose sons, Sukman and Il-Ghazi, both won renown in the wars against the Latin princes of Palestine. The dynasty lasted until 1312. Sukman Qutbi was the first of the Shahs of Armenia (1100-1207). The Atabeg house of Azerbaijan (1136-1225) was founded by Ildigiz, whose son, Mohammed, was the actual ruler of the Seljuk Kingdom of Iraq. The Salgharids held Fars (1148-1287); the Hazaraspids Luristan (1148-1339); and Anushtigin, a Turkish slave of Balkatigin of Ghazna, was the grandfather of the first independent Shah of Kwarizm, Asiz. At one time the rule of the Kwarizm Shah was almost coterminous with the Seljuk Empire.

1095. The crusaders, having invaded the dominions of the Sultan of Rum, took Antioch, with frightful slaughter. They stormed Jerusalem (1099) and founded the Latin Kingdom of Jerusalem. By 1109 Caesarea, Tripoli, Tyre, and Sidon were captured. Constant warfare between the crusaders and the Moslems (Fatimids, Burids, Zangids, Ortuqids, and finally Saladin, the Sultan of Egypt). (*Cont. p.* 328.)

c. THE CRUSADES

PRECURSORS OF THE CRUSADES: (1) **Penitentiary pilgrimages** probably dating from the days of Helena, mother of Constantine; after the Arab conquest of Jerusalem (638) the Holy City was a joint shrine of Christian and Moslem; protectorate of Charlemagne over the Holy Places (recognized by Harun-al-Rashid, 807); abrogated by the mad Caliph Hakim (1010); (2) **Charlemagne's war** of Christian reconquest in Spain; (3) **the Cluniac revival** and its stress on pilgrimages led to a steady increase of pilgrimages (117 known in the 11th century) without serious opposition from the tolerant Moslems until the advent of the Seljuks; (4) **Wars of Christian reconquest** in the west began European reaction to Moslem pressure; Pisan reconquest of Sardinia (c. 1016) with papal support; alliance of Castile and Aragon in the reconquest of Spain (c. 1050); Norman reconquest of Sicily (1060–1090).

1087. **Genoa and Pisa,** by capture of Mahdiyah in Africa, gained command of the western Mediterranean from the Moslems. Appeal of the Greek emperor after Manzikert (1071) to Pope Gregory VII; preparation of an army (alliance with Roger Guiscard) by Gregory (1074) to aid the Greeks.

Transformation by Pope Urban II of military assistance to Constantinople into a new kind of holy war (a sort of ecclesiastical imperialism) under the auspices of the revived and regenerated papacy.

1095. Appeal from the Greek emperor at the **Synod of Piacenza**; Urban's call at the **Synod of Clermont** (1095): Urban, a Cluniac and a Frenchman, speaking to Frenchmen, recited the glorious deeds of the French and tales of Moslem atrocities, made open allusions to the chances of profit and advancement, attacked feudal violence at home, and brought the audience to wild enthusiasms; he himself distributed crosses. Urban's propaganda journeys and the preaching of **Peter the Hermit** and others stirred the west, but had the greatest effect in France and Lorraine, the area most under Cluniac influence. The great rulers were all at odds with the papacy or busy at home; the rest of Europe indifferent, and the Crusades began as they continued, largely under French auspices.

1096-1099. THE FIRST CRUSADE. Five popular, aimless mass migrations (1096), emptying whole villages and often accompanied by pillage and anti-Semitic outbreaks, of which two (perhaps 7000 under Peter the Hermit and perhaps 5000 under Walter the Penniless) reached Asia Minor and were annihilated. The Norman-French baronage flocked to the Cross and converged in three divisions on Constantinople: the Lorrainers under **Godfrey of Bouillon** and his brother Baldwin, via Hungary; the Provençals under Count **Raymond of Toulouse** and the papal legate, Adhemar of Puy, via Illyria; the Normans under **Bohemund of Otranto** (the most effective leader) via Durazzo by sea and land. Perhaps they were 30,000 in all.

The Greek emperor, Alexius Comnenus, expecting mercenaries and unprepared for crusaders, provided food and escort and punished the plunderers. He exacted an oath of fealty from the leaders (Raymond refused) in an effort to insure his title to any recovered "lost provinces" of the Greek Empire.

The Moslem opposition: the Seljuks had merely garrisoned Syria and were not popular with the native population. Moslem unity in Asia Minor ended with the death of Malik Shah (1092), and Syria was divided politically, racially and theologically (Sunnite *vs.* Shiite; the Fatimite capture of Jerusalem (1098) from the Shiites).

1097. **Nicaea,** the Seljuk capital in Asia Minor, taken by the combined Greek and crusading force; defeat of the Moslem field army at Dorylaeum; excursion of Baldwin and Tancred, and rivalry in Cilicia; Bohemund established himself in the Antioch area. Siege and capture (by treachery) of Antioch (1097–1098); counter-siege of the Christians in Antioch by the Emir of Mosul; election of Bohemund as leader. Baldwin's conquest of Edessa (1097); death of Adhemar of Puy (1098); Christian divisions: rivalry of Norman and Provençal (the *Holy Lance*).

1099. **March to Jerusalem** (Genoese convoy and food supply); siege, capture, and horrors of the sack. The death of the papal legate left the organization of the government of Jerusalem to feudal laymen. **Godfrey of Bouillon,** elected king, assumed the title of *Advocate of the Holy Sepulcher* (for pious reasons). The main body of the crusaders soon streamed back home. The Norman effort to dominate the government through their patriarch Dagobert led to his deposition by the anti-Norman party and Jerusalem became a feudal kingdom rather than theocracy under papal domination. The government (as revealed by the *Assizes of Jerusalem*, the most complete feudal code extant) was narrowly feudal, the king a feudal suzerain, not a sovereign, the tenants-in-chief dominant. Besides the feudal organization there were

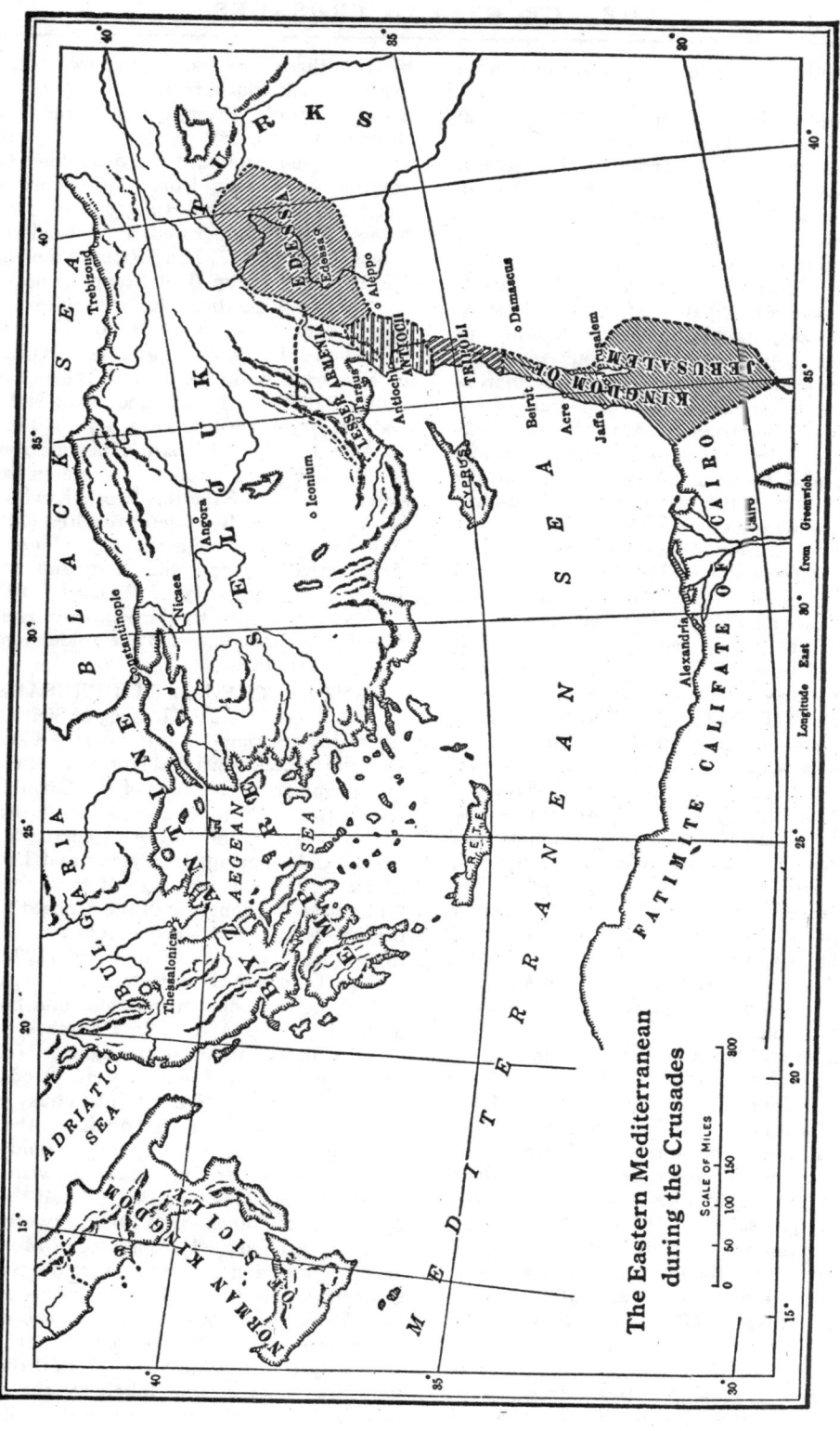

The Eastern Mediterranean
during the Crusades

SCALE OF MILES

0   50   100   150   300

burgher and ecclesiastical organizations, with their own courts.

Continued divisions among the Moslems and the weakness of the Greeks favored the progress of the Latin states: the **Kingdom of Jerusalem,** in close commercial alliance with the Italian towns (Genoa, Pisa, and later Venice), profited by the commerce through its ports and extended south to tap the Red Sea trade. The other states: the **County of Edessa** (established by Baldwin), the **Principality of Antioch** (established by Bohemund), and the **County of Tripoli** (set up by Raymond of Toulouse), were fiefs of Jerusalem (divided into four great baronies and into lesser fiefs). The departure of the main body of the crusaders left the Franks without enough reinforcement to prevent their orientalization and decline. After the capture of Jerusalem (1187) the Kingdom of Jerusalem ceased to be an organized state.

Moslem unification in Syria was completed by the *Atabegs* (regents) of Mosul and signalized by the capture of Edessa (1144). Mosul soon mastered Egypt; Saladin emerged supreme in Egypt (1171), quickly reduced Damascus and Aleppo, and brought Syria and Egypt under a single efficient rule.

1147-1149. THE SECOND CRUSADE. Bernard of Clairvaux, persuaded by Pope Eugenius III, somewhat against his will, preached (1145) the Second Crusade. Emperor Conrad III and King Louis VII of France took the Cross. To avoid conflicts the two monarchs went by separate routes; there never was coherent direction or unity of command. The Norman Roger of Sicily profited by the Second Crusade to seize the Greek islands and to attack Athens, Thebes, and Corinth. Nothing of importance was achieved by the Second Crusade and the movement was discredited throughout Europe.

1184. Saladin's steady advance led to a great appeal to the west; King Philip II of France and Henry II of England declined the crown of Jerusalem, but levied a **Saladin tithe** (1188) to finance a crusade. Christian attack on a caravan (said to be escorting Saladin's sister) provoked Saladin's holy war (1187-1189): **capture of Jerusalem** (1187) without a sack (Saladin's humanitarianism) and reduction of the Latin states to the cities of Antioch, Tyre, Tripoli, and a small area about each.

1189-1192. THE THIRD CRUSADE. Precipitated by the fall of Jerusalem, a completely lay and royal affair despite the efforts of the papacy to regain control. It was supported partly by the Saladin tithe, and was led by the three greatest monarchs of the day: (1) **Frederick Barbarossa** (a veteran of the Second Crusade) as emperor, the traditional and theoretical military leader of Christendom, headed a well-organized and disciplined German contingent starting from Regensburg (1189), which marched via Hungary, entered Asia Minor, and disintegrated after Frederick was drowned (1190); (2) **King Richard I of England** and (3) **King Philip II of France,** who went by sea. Already political rivals, they quarreled in winter quarters in Sicily (1190-1191); Richard turned aside in the spring and took Cyprus which he sold to Guy de Lusignan. The quarrels of Philip and Richard continued in the Holy Land, and Philip returned to France after the capture of Acre (1191). Richard's negotiations with Saladin (Richard proposed a marriage of his sister Joanna to Saladin's brother, who was to be invested with Jerusalem) resulted (1192) in a three-year truce allowing the Christians a coastal strip between Joppa and Acre and access to Jerusalem. Captivity of Richard (1192-1194) and heavy ransom to the Emperor Henry VI. The Third Crusade ended the golden age of the crusades.

1202-1204. THE FOURTH CRUSADE. Emperor Henry VI, King of Sicily (by virtue of his marriage to the Norman Constance) and heir of the traditional Norman plan of creating an empire on the ruins of the Greek Empire, was determined to continue his father Frederick's crusade, and began to encroach on the Greek lands: homage of Cyprus and Lesser Armenia (1195); the marriage of Henry's brother Philip to Irene, daughter of the deposed Emperor Isaac Angelus, established a Hohenstaufen claim to the Greek throne. Henry died 1197.

Pope Innocent III determined to regain control of the crusading movement, and hoping to unite the Greek and Latin Churches, issued a call to the monarchs; it was ignored (Philip II and King John of England were at odds, Germany in chaos, the Spanish rulers busy with the Moors), and the brunt fell again on the French baronage. Egypt, the objective, could only be reached by water; negotiations with Venice (1201): terms, 85,000 marks and half the booty. **Meeting of Hagenau** (1201) between Philip (brother of Henry VI), Boniface of Montferrat, and (?) Alexius; decision to divert the crusade to Constantinople (a return to the plans of Henry VI); Venice may have shared in the decision. As it was impossible to raise 85,000 marks, Venice agreed to fulfill her bargain if the Christian city of Zara were taken by the crusade. Despite Innocent's furious opposition, Zara was taken and sacked (1202); Innocent excommunicated the crusade. Constantinople was entered (1203); Isaac Angelus and his son Alexius IV were restored; Greek opinion was furious at the new exactions to pay the clamorous crusaders, and Alexius V soon succeeded Isaac. The crusaders stormed and took Constantinople (1204), the first **capture of Constantinople** in history, and sacked it with unparalleled horrors. The Latin Empire of the East (*Romania*) replaced the Greek Empire at Constantinople from 1204 to 1261; the first emperor, Baldwin of Flanders; a Latin patriarch, a Venetian (Morosini), replaced the Greek patriarch, and technically the schism was ended; actually the Greeks refused all union. Venice acquired three-eighths of the city, Adrianople, Gallipoli, Naxos, Andros, Euboaea, Crete, and the Ionian islands. Innocent III was horrified and helpless. The government of the Latin Empire was completely feudal under the *Assizes of Romania* (copied from the *Assizes of Jerusalem*). The Greek emperors ruled at Nicaea (1204–1261) until Michael VIII surprised and took Constantinople, 1261. The Fourth Crusade shocked Europe, discredited the papacy and the whole crusading movement, and facilitated the advance of the Turks.

1208. THE ALBIGENSIAN CRUSADE, a European crusade against the Albigensian heretics in southern France, proclaimed by Innocent III (1208) (see p. 230).

1212. The so-called **Children's Crusade,** preached by the lad Stephen of Vendôme and by Nicholas of Cologne in Germany. Stephen's contingent reached Marseilles and was sold into slavery. Nicholas' company was turned back. The whole episode is supposed to have been the origin of the story of the Pied Piper.

1218-1221. THE FIFTH CRUSADE. Innocent III, unwilling to let the crusading idea lapse, preached the Fifth Crusade at the Fourth Lateran Council. Egypt was to be the objective; the date 1217; John of Brienne, King of Jerusalem, was replaced by the papal legate Pelagius as leader (1218). Capture of Damietta (1219); rejection (in the expectation of Frederick II's arrival) of the offers of the sultan (1219) to exchange Jerusalem for Damietta; failure of the march on Cairo; **Treaty of 1221:** eight-year truce, Damietta lost; retreat.

1228-1229. THE SIXTH CRUSADE, of the Emperor Frederick II. Essentially lay, the crusade continued the policy of Frederick's father, Henry VI. Frederick, King of Jerusalem by his marriage (1225) to Yolande

of Brienne, sailed (1227) after careful preparation, returned ill with fever, and was excommunicated. He sailed again (1228); the pope proclaimed a crusade against Frederick's Sicilian lands and renewed the excommunication; Hermann of Salza, Master of the Teutonic Order, remained loyal to Frederick. Frederick, the first crusader to understand the Moslems, negotiated a treaty (1229) with Malik-al-Kamil, nephew of Saladin, Sultan of Egypt; peace for ten years, grant of Nazareth, Bethlehem, Jerusalem, etc., and a corridor from Jerusalem to the coast for the Christians. The Patriarch of Jerusalem opposed Frederick at every turn, and Frederick had to crown himself king (1229) in the Church of the Holy Sepulcher. He returned home at once to repel the papal crusade in his lands. The capture of Jerusalem by a rush of Moslem mercenaries (1244) led to the crusades of King Louis IX of France, but Jerusalem was not again in Christian hands until General Allenby captured it (1917).

The crusades of Theobald of Navarre (1239) and Richard of Cornwall (1240–1241) were forbidden by the pope and were fruitless.

1248-1254. THE SEVENTH CRUSADE, the first of King Louis IX of France. Poorly organized; Damietta taken without a blow; march to Cairo (1249); rout of the army; capture of Louis; massacre of the army; loss of Damietta. Louis, ransomed, spent four years on a pilgrimage to Jerusalem (1251–1254).

1267. Charles of Anjou, aiming at the conquest of Constantinople, became heir (by treaty) to the Latin Empire. He planned to unite Sicily and Jerusalem, but was balked by the Sicilian Vespers (1282).

1269. James the Conqueror, of Aragon, under papal pressure, made a futile crusading expedition to Asia Minor.

1270. THE EIGHTH CRUSADE, the second of King Louis IX and Edward of England (the last of the western crusaders who arrived (1271) and did nothing permanent). Attack on Tunis, possibly at the insistence of Charles of Anjou; death of Louis; the expedition continued by Charles; nothing accomplished.

1274. Preaching of a crusade at Lyons by Pope Gregory X; every ruler took the Cross; Gregory's death ended the project. Acre fell, 1291.

Local and specific crusading expeditions were subsequently undertaken under various circumstances at different times; there was a revival of crusading zeal with the fall of Constantinople

(1453) under papal urging, but the true crusades were over.

The crusades gave rise to great orders of knighthood which combined chivalry and monasticism.

THE KNIGHTS OF ST. JOHN or the *Hospitalers* (black mantle with a white cross), originally a Chilian order founded at Jerusalem by Amalfitan merchants (c. 1070) to care for the Hospital of St. John; militarized (c. 1130) on the model of the Knights Templar; transferred to Cyprus (1291); to Rhodes (1310–1522) (the *Knights of Rhodes*) and then to Malta (*Knights of Malta*). Noble blood was a requisite to knighthood in the order.

THE KNIGHTS OF THE TEMPLE (their house in Jerusalem stood near the Temple) or *Templars* (white mantle with a red cross) founded (c. 1120) by Hugh of Pajens to guide and protect pilgrims; confirmed by the **Synod of Troyes** (1128) and Pope Honorius III. Bernard of Clairvaux drew up their rule, a modification of the Cistercian; they took the threefold monastic vows of poverty, chastity, and obedience, and their rule in general was that of the canons regular. They consisted of knights, men-at-arms, and chaplains. Admission to knighthood in the order was open only to those of noble blood. Organization: by commanderies under a grand master. Transferred to Cyprus (1291), the order was dissolved by the **Synod of Vienne** (1312) (see p. 233).

The other great orders were associated with national or racial influences, and do not represent the older international aspects of knighthood:

The Knights of the Hospital of St. Mary of the Teutons in Jerusalem (*Teutonic Knights*) (white mantle with a black cross) founded (c. 1190); headquarters at Acre. (For their history in Germany, see p. 215.)

The great Spanish orders: **Calatrava** (founded, 1164); **Avis** (Portuguese, founded 1166); **St. James of Compostella** (founded 1175); **Alcantara** (founded, 1183).

Famous orders of chivalry of royal foundation: The **Order of the Garter** (English), founded c. 1344. The **Order of the Star** (French) founded 1351, replaced by the **Order of St. Michael** (1469–1830). The **Order of the Golden Fleece** (Burgundian) founded, 1429, became Hapsburg, 1477.

d. LATIN AND GREEK STATES IN THE NEAR EAST, 1204–1261

Division of the Eastern Empire after the fall of Constantinople: A council, composed equally of crusaders and Venetians, decided to award the imperial crown to **Count Baldwin of Flanders,** while a Venetian (Pier Morosini) was made Patriarch of Constantinople. **Boniface of Montferrat** was made King of Thessalonica and the remaining parts of the empire were assigned to various feudal barons as vassals of the emperor. In Anatolia the crusaders were never able to establish themselves excepting in a part of Bithynia near the Bosporus. In Europe they were constantly exposed to the attacks of the Bulgarians. The Kingdom of Thessalonica at first extended over part of Thrace, Macedonia, and Thessaly, but to the westward the Greek, **Michael Angelus Comnenus,** set himself up as Despot of Epirus and soon began to expand his dominion eastward. Attica and the Peloponnesus were conquered by crusading barons in a short time, and these territories were organized on a feudal basis as the **Lordship of Athens** (Otto de la Roche, 1205–1225; Guy I, 1125–1263; John I, 1263–1280), and the **Principality of Achaïa** (conquered by Guillaume de Champlitte and Geoffroy de Villehardouin in 1205). Achaïa was in turn divided into twelve feudal baronies, a perfect example of the French feudal system. Under the Villehardouin family (Geoffroy I, 1209–1218; Geoffroy II, 1218–1246; Guillaume, 1246–1278) it was well-governed and popular with the Greco-Slavic population, which was considerately treated.

The **Venetians** took as their share of the empire most of the islands and other important strategic or commercial posts. They kept for themselves part of Constantinople, Gallipoli, Euboea, Crete, the southwestern tip of the Peloponnesus (Coron and Modon), Durazzo, and other posts on the Epiran coast, as well as the islands of the Ionian and Aegean Seas. For the most part these possessions were granted as fiefs to the leading Venetian families (Triarchies of Euboea, Duchy of the Archipelago, etc.).

1204–1205. BALDWIN I, Latin emperor.

1204–1214. MICHAEL ANGELUS COMNENUS, Despot of Epirus.

1204. Theodore Lascaris, with most of the Byzantine leaders, established himself in Bithynia; Theodore Mancaphas set himself up at Philadelphia; Leo Gabalas took over Rhodes; Manuel Maurozomes established himself in the Meander Valley; Alexius and David Comnenus organized a state on the north coast of Anatolia, with David at Sinope and Alexius at Trebizond, thus founding the **Empire of Trabizond,** which lasted until the Ottoman conquest of 1461.

**1204. Theodore Lascaris made an alliance with

the Sultan of Rum and with Mancaphas of Philadelphia to resist the advance of the crusaders into Anatolia, but was defeated by the latter under Peter of Bracheuil.

1205. The Bulgars, under Kalojan, defeated Emperor Baldwin and Doge Dandolo **in battle near Adrianople.** Baldwin was captured and died in captivity. The Bulgars then overran much of Thrace and Macedonia, exterminating a large part of the Greek population.

1205-1216. HENRY I, Latin emperor. He was the brother of Baldwin, and the ablest of the Latin emperors.

1206-1222. THEODORE I (*Lascaris*), proclaimed emperor at Nicaea and founder of the Nicaean Empire.

1207. Kalojan and the Bulgarians besieged Thessalonica, but in vain. Kalojan died suddenly, probably murdered.

1207. Theodore Lascaris, allied with the Seljuks of Rum, defeated David Comnenus and drove him back to Sinope. Theodore then concluded a truce with the Emperor Henry, in order to oppose the advance of Alexius of Trebizond, who was now allied with the Seljuks.

1209. Theodore repulsed a second attempt by Peter of Bracheuil and the crusaders to conquer Bithynia.

1210. The Parliament of Ravennika, at which the feudal lords of Greece finally recognized the suzerainty of the emperor at Constantinople. In practice this meant little, and the emperor was left to shift for himself, with such support as the Venetians saw fit to give him.

1211. Theodore Lascaris defeated Alexius of Trebizond and the Sultan of Rum, both of whom were captured. As a result a large part of the Anatolian coast was added to the Empire of Nicaea.

1212. Henry I defeated Theodore at Luparcos and began the invasion of Anatolia. Theodore made peace, abandoning to the Latin Empire part of Mysia and Bithynia.

1214-1230. THEODORE DUKAS ANGELUS, brother of Michael, became Despot of Epirus. He began the work of expansion at the expense of the Latins and Bulgars, taking Durazzo and Corfu from the Venetians (1214).

1216-1217. PETER OF COURTENAY, Latin emperor. He was the brother-in-law of Baldwin and Henry and was in Europe when Henry died. On the way from Durazzo to Thessalonica he was captured by Theodore Dukas of Epirus. He died in 1218.

1217-1219. Regency of Yolanda, the wife of Peter of Courtenay.

1218-1228. ROBERT OF COURTENAY, Latin emperor. His domain was reduced to Constantinople and he spent most of his time soliciting aid in the west.

1222. Theodore Dukas of Epirus captured Thessalonica and extinguished the kingdom. He then had himself proclaimed *Emperor* of the West, and before long had extended his conquests to the vicinity of Philippopolis and Adrianople.

1222-1254. JOHN DUKAS VATATZES, emperor at Nicaea. He proved himself a great ruler as well as an able general. During his reign agriculture was encouraged, trade and industry developed, the finances reformed. The Nicaean Empire enjoyed a period of real prosperity and power.

1224. John Vatatzes defeated the Franks at Poimanenon. In succession he took the islands near the Anatolian coast (Samos, Chios, Lemnos) and subjected Rhodes. An army was even sent across the Straits to capture Adrianople.

1224. Theodore of Epirus defeated an army of the Latin emperor at Serres and then drove the invading Nicaean army away from Adrianople.

1228. On the death of Robert of Courtenay, it was proposed that a regency be established under the Bulgarian ruler, John Asen II (1218–1241) but this suggestion was frustrated by the Latin clergy.

1228-1261. BALDWIN II, Latin emperor. He was the eleven-year-old son of Peter of Courtenay. The reign was a helpless one, during which the emperor was reduced to the point of peddling the Constantinople relics through Europe.

1229-1237. Regency of John of Brienne, former King of Jerusalem, for the boy-emperor. John became co-emperor in 1231.

1230. Theodore of Epirus was defeated and captured by John Asen in the **battle of Klokotnica.** The Bulgarian ruler thereupon appropriated most of the eastern sections of the Empire of the West. Thessalonica and Thessaly passed to

1230-1236. MANUEL, the brother of Theodore.

1235. An expedition sent by John Vatatzes against the Venetians in Crete failed to achieve anything.

1236. An attack of the Nicaean Greeks, allied with John Asen of Bulgaria, on Constantinople. The city was saved by the Venetians and by a force sent by the Duke of Achaia.

1236-1244. **JOHN,** the son of Theodore Dukas of Epirus, became Despot of Thessaly and Emperor of the West.

1236-1271. **MICHAEL II,** Despot of Epirus.

1242. John Vatatzes, in company with Theodore, who had been liberated by the Bulgarians, set out with an army and besieged Thessalonica. He failed to take the city, owing to his lack of sea-power, but John, the Despot of Thessaly, was obliged to give up the title Emperor of the West and to recognize the suzerainty of the Nicaean emperor.

1244. **The Mongol invasion** of Anatolia, after the defeat of the Seljuks in the **battle of Erzingan.** The Mongols reached Ancyra (Ankara). John Vatatzes established friendly relations with them and succeeded to much of the Seljuk territory in central Anatolia.

1246. Second Expedition of John Vatatzes to the Balkans. He conquered northern Macedonia and finally took Thessalonica, deposing Demetrius Angelus, despot since 1244.

1254. Michael II, of Epirus, recognized Nicaean suzerainty. after a defeat by the forces of John Vatatzes.

1254-1258. **THEODORE II** (*Lascaris*), Greek emperor at Nicaea.

1255. Theodore defeated the Bulgarian armies of Michael Asen in northern Macedonia.

1257. Revolt of Michael II of Epirus, who managed to defeat the Nicaean forces sent against him.

1258-1261. **JOHN IV** (*Lascaris*), emperor. He was a mere child and his accession led to a military uprising, led by Michael Paleologus, who became regent.

1259-1282. **MICHAEL VIII** (*Paleologus*), who was first co-emperor with the boy John, whom in 1261 he had imprisoned and blinded. Michael was an able and energetic general, whose great objective was to re-establish the Greek power at Constantinople.

1259. Michael II of Epirus, allied with the King of Sicily and with the Prince of Achaia, attacked Thessalonica, but was defeated and driven back by the Nicaeans (battle of Pelagonia).

1261. **RECONQUEST OF CONSTANTINOPLE.** Michael made an alliance with the Bulgarians and concluded the **Treaty of Nymphaion** with Genoa, promising the Genoese all the privileges hitherto enjoyed by the Venetians. On July 25 a Greek army under **Alexius Strategopulos,** taking advantage of the absence of the Venetian fleet, crossed the Bosporus and retook Constantinople without much difficulty. Baldwin II fled (d. 1273). End of the Latin Empire. (*Cont. p.* 325.)

e. THE MONGOLS

Under the last caliphs, the caliphate had regained its temporal power in Iraq, Mesopotamia, and Fars, and its spiritual authority was greater than at any time since the death of Wathiq (847), but the caliphate was soon threatened by the Mongols, who, in the late 12th century, had advanced from Mongolia.

1206. The Mongol chief, **Temujin** (1162–1227), was proclaimed supreme ruler, *Chinjiz Khan* (Very Mighty King), of all the Mongols. Under his leadership the Mongol armies swept over northern China and over Azerbaijan, Georgia, and northern Persia. Transoxania was invaded and Bokhara taken (1219); Samarcand captured (1220) and Khorasan devastated. Destruction of Merv and Nishapur. Capture of Herat.

1223. **Battle of the Kalka River,** in southern Russia. The Mongols defeated a strong force of Russians and Cumans, but after their victory returned to Asia.

1237-1240. Mongol armies under **Batu** (actually commanded by Sabutai) overran and conquered southern and central Russia and then invaded Poland and Hungary.

1241. The Mongols defeated the Poles and Germans in the **battle of Liegnitz** (Wahlstatt) in Silesia, while another army defeated the Hungarians. But because of political complications arising from the death of the Great Khan, Batu withdrew from western Europe, subjugating, on the way back, Bulgaria, Wallachia, and Moldavia. Subsequently he settled on the lower Volga, where a Mongol (Tatar) state was organized under the name of **Golden Horde,** with Sarai as the capital. The Golden Horde, like other Mongol khanates, recognized the supreme authority of the Great Khan, whose capital was first at Kara-Korum in Mongolia, then at Khanbalyk (present-day Peiping) in China. But after the death of **Kublai Khan** (1294) the unity of the empire was purely nominal.

1245-1253. Continued ravages of the Mongols

The Mongol Empire and Routes to the Far East

SCALE OF MILES
0 100 200 300 400 500   1000

———— Carpini's journey from Cracow to Karakorum

········· Rubruk's journey from the Crimea to
        Karakorum and return to Asia Minor

+++++ Marco Polo's journey from Lesser Armenia
        and return

———— Conquests of Timur (or Tamerlane)

in Mesopotamia, Azerbaijan, Armenia, and Georgia.

1256-1349. THE IL-KHANS OF PERSIA. Hulagu, the grandson of Chinjiz Khan, was sent by his brother, Mangu, to crush the Assassins and extirpate the caliphate.

1256. Suppression and extinction of the Assassins.

1258. CAPTURE AND SACK OF BAGHDAD. Hulagu executed the caliph, Musta 'sim. He then invaded Syria and took Aleppo.

1260. Great victory of the Mamluks of Egypt, under Baybars, at **Ain Jalut.** This victory checked the Mongol advance and saved Egypt, the last refuge of Moslem culture. Baybars revived the caliphate by inviting to Cairo Ahmad Abu-l-Qasim, a scion of the Abbasid house, who was acknowledged as caliph under the title of *Mustansir l' Illah.*

1344-1349. Reign of Nushirwan, last of the Il-Khans of Persia. The dynasty was succeeded by a number of lesser families.

f. MOSLEM EGYPT

868-905. Dynasty of the Tulunids.

935-969. Dynasty of the Ikhshidids. Both these dynasties also ruled Syria.

968-1171. THE FATIMID DYNASTY, under which Egypt became the most brilliant center of Moslem culture. The Fatimids claimed to be descendants of the Caliph Ali, and of Fatima, the daughter of the Prophet. They rose to power as a result of Shi'ite (Ismailian) propaganda among the Berbers, begun about 894 and directed from Yemen. Abu Abdullah, an Ismailian missionary, had won over the powerful Kitama tribe and had overthrown the Aghlabids (909). Obaydullah, son of the Ismailian hidden Imam, then appeared and was proclaimed caliph and mahdi in Qairowan (910). In 922 he reduced the Idrisids, but an attempt to conquer Egypt failed. His son, Al-Qa'im, who succeeded him in 934, was defeated again and again and was besieged in his capital by the Kharijite, Abu Yazid Makhlad. Al-Qa'im's son, Al-Mansur, finally defeated Abu Yazid (947), and brought the whole of North Africa, Sicily, and Calabria under Fatimid rule, though he lost Morocco to the Omayyads of Spain. He was succeeded by his son, Al-Mu'iz, in 952. The latter recovered Morocco and drove the last Byzantine forces out of Sicily (966).

968. Al-Mu'iz took Egypt and transferred the seat of the Fatimid government to Cairo (founded 969).

975-996. Al-Aziz, son of Al-Mu'iz, sultan. He conquered Syria and part of Mesopotamia, and ruled from the Euphrates to the Atlantic.

996-1020. Al-Hakim, son of Al-Aziz, sultan. He was known as the *Mad Caliph,* having affirmed his own divinity. He tried to make Shi'ism the orthodox religion of Egypt. The cult of Hakim as an emanation of deity still survives among the Druses of Syria.

1020-1035. Reign of **Al-Zahir,** marking the beginning of the decline of the Fatimid power. Most of Syria was lost.

1035-1094. Reign of **Al-Mustansir.** The holy cities of Mecca and Medina disclaimed their allegiance (1047) and North Africa threw off the Fatimid yoke. On Al-Mustansir's death civil war broke out among his sons, Nizar and Ahmad. Nizar was defeated and killed, and Ahmad reigned as

1094-1101. Al-Musta'li. He lost Jerusalem to the crusaders (1099). The Fatimid power continued to decline.

1167. Shirkuh, general of the Zangid Nur al-Din of Damascus, entered Egypt to assist the second-last Fatimid, Al-Mustanjid. Shirkuh was appointed vizier, in which office he was succeeded by his nephew, **Salah al-Din** (*Saladin*), who founded the

1169-1250. Ayyubid dynasty. Saladin ruled at first as viceroy of Nur al-Din, but on the latter's death (1173) asserted his independence and consolidated his power over Egypt, part of Nubia, Hijaz, and Yemen.

1172. Saladin drove the Normans out of Tripoli.

1174. Invasion of Syria and conquest of Damascus. Aleppo taken (1183).

1185-1186. Saladin seized Mosul and reduced Mesopotamia.

1187. Battle of Hittin. Saladin destroyed the crusading Kingdom of Jerusalem.

1190-1193. Saladin defended his conquests against the Third Crusade.

g. MOSLEM DYNASTIES OF NORTH AFRICA

788-985. The Alid dynasty of the Idrisids in Morocco, founded by Idris ibn Abdullah, a great-grandson of the Caliph Ali's son Hasan. This dynasty was overthrown by the Miknasa Berbers.

801-909. The Aghlabid dynasty in Tunis, founded by Ibrahim ibn Aghlab, the Abbasid governor of Africa. This dynasty conquered Sicily (827–878), took Malta and Sardinia and invaded southern Italy. The dynasty was ultimately destroyed by the Fatimids.

1056-1147. The Almoravids, a Berber dynasty founded by Abdullah ibn Tashfin, conquered Morocco and part of Algeria and intervened actively in the affairs of Spain.

1130-1269. THE ALMOHADES, another Berber dynasty founded by the prophet, Mohammed ibn Tumart. His successor, Abdul-Mu'min, annihilated the Almoravid armies (1114). Morocco was conquered (1146) and Spain invaded. Algeria was subjugated in 1152, and the Normans driven out of Tunis (1158). Tripoli too was annexed. But in 1235 the Almohades were defeated and gradually ejected from Spain.

1228-1534. The Hafsid dynasty, which succeeded the Almohades in Tunis.

1235-1339. The Ziyanids, successors of the Almohades in Algeria. They were ultimately absorbed by the

1296-1470. Marinids of Morocco, a dynasty founded in 1195 which took the Moroccan capital from the Almohades in 1296.

C. THE LATER MIDDLE AGES

1. WESTERN EUROPE

a. THE BRITISH ISLES

(1) *England*, 1307-1485

1307-1327. EDWARD II. Married to Isabella, daughter of Philip IV of France. Ignorant of his task and bored with the business of kingship, Edward was dominated by his favorite, **Piers Gaveston**, a Gascon. The Scottish war was continued in desultory fashion. The baronage, angered by Gaveston, followed the leadership of Edward's nephew, Thomas, Duke of Lancaster, an ambitious, incompetent person. They forced Edward to accept a committee of reform, the twenty-one **Lords Ordainers** (1310), whose reform ordinances, suggestive of the Provisions of Oxford were confirmed by Parliament (1311). The ordinances required baronial consent to royal appointments, to a declaration of war and to the departure of the king from the realm, this consent to be given through Parliament. Gaveston was captured and slain (1312).

1313-1314. The Scottish War. By 1313 only the castle of Stirling remained in the hands of the English. Edward set out (1314) to relieve the castle; Lancaster and the baronial party refused to support the expedition. At **Bannockburn** (1314) Edward was overwhelmingly defeated, and Scottish independence won.

In Gascony the French kings began a policy of egging Edward's vassals on to resistance, a process which culminated in the French conquest of Gascony and its retention by the French with the consent (1327) of the regents who ruled after Edward's abdication.

1314-1322. Supremacy of Lancaster. Lancaster offered no opposition to Scottish raids; private wars broke out in England; Edward was under a new favorite, Hugh le Despenser. Parliament exiled Despenser (1321). Edward defeated Lancaster at **Boroughbridge** (1322) and beheaded him. The Parliament of York repealed the Ordinances.

1322-1326. Rule of the Despensers, father and son: Scottish truce (1323); decline of the popularity of the Despensers; alienation of Queen Isabella. Isabella went to France (1325).

arranged the marriage of her son, the future Edward III, to Philippa of Hainault, and returned (1326) with Mortimer and foreign troops. Supported by the barons, Isabella gained London, the Despensers were hanged, and the **Parliament of Westminster** (1327), dominated by Isabella and by Edward's enemies, forced an abdication that was tantamount to deposition. Edward was brutally murdered in prison eight months later.

Baronial reform was cynical and selfish in aim, but made no effort to destroy the monarchy. Burgesses and knights sat in the parliaments of 1311, 1322, and 1327, and retained a share in the grant of taxes.

1327-1377. EDWARD III (aged fifteen at his accession). Council of regency and rule (1327–1330) under Mortimer, Isabella's paramour; Bruce's invasion of England forced the acknowledgment of Scottish independence (1328). Edward led the baronial opposition to Mortimer (hanged, 1330) and opened his personal rule (1330).

1337. OUTBREAK OF THE HUNDRED YEARS' WAR. Edward did homage (1329) for his French lands and renewed it (1331). French support of Scottish aggression continued and Edward, profiting by civil war in Scotland, supported Baliol; after a series of expeditions he avenged Bannockburn at **Halidon Hill** (1333). French intrigues to alienate Aquitaine continued; Edward sought allies in the emperor, the German princes, and his wife's relatives in Hainault and Holland, but could not win the Count of Flanders, the vassal of Philip VI. The economic interdependence, due to the wool trade, of England and the Flemish cities, made an English alliance with them inevitable. Philip continued his advance into the English lands south of the Loire (1337) and open hostilities broke out (1338). Edward ravaged northern and eastern France without a decisive battle. Urged on by the Flemings, Edward proclaimed himself King of France (in right of his mother Isabella), and enabled the Flanders towns under James van Arteveldt to support him without violating their oaths.

1340. The naval **victory of Sluys** transferred the mastery of the Channel from France to

England (until 1372). Intermittent truces (1340–1345) were followed by Edward's invasion of France, and

1346, Aug. 26. Great **VICTORY AT CRÉCY** where English longbowmen, supported by dismounted horsemen, routed the undisciplined chivalry and mercenary crossbowmen of France. This tactical innovation, the result of English experiences in Wales and Scotland, began the joint participation of the yeomanry and the aristocracy in war, and gave the English a unique military power and new social orientation. Artillery may have been used at Crécy.

1346. The invasion of Philip's Scottish allies was halted at **Neville's Cross,** and the King of Scotland captured.

1347. **Calais was taken** after a long siege in which artillery was used. (Philippa's intervention in behalf of the burghers of Calais.) Calais remained an English military and commercial outpost in France until 1558.

1347-1355. **A series of truces** with France was ended by the expedition of Edward's son, **Edward, the Black Prince,** to Bordeaux, followed by ruthless plundering raids from there as a base, which enriched the English and alienated the populace.

1356, Sept. 19. **BATTLE OF POITIERS.** The Black Prince, using the tactics of Crécy, defeated King John, capturing him, his son, and the King of Bohemia, as well as the flower of French chivalry.

1359-1360. Edward's last expedition to France penetrated to the walls of Paris; the south had been so devastated that the English could hardly find food.

1360. **PEACE OF BRETIGNY,** ending the first period of the war. (1) France, utterly exhausted and in chaos, surrendered the full sovereignty of Aquitaine, Calais, Ponthieu; and (2) fixed John's ransom; (3) Edward waived his claims to the crown of France.

THE BLACK PRINCE IN THE SOUTH. The Black Prince, ruling as Duke of Aquitaine, supported Pedro the Cruel of Castile against Henry of Trastamara (allied with Charles V and aided by Du Guesclin). Having defeated Du Guesclin and Henry (**Navarrete,** 1367), the Black Prince, disgusted at Pedro's character, his army dissipated by illness, and seriously ill himself, withdrew. Taxation in Aquitaine to pay for the expedition led the southern baronage to appeal to Charles V, who summoned the Black Prince to answer to him as his feudal lord (alleging a

technical defect in the **Peace of Bretigny**). The prince defied Charles, and Parliament advised Edward to resume his claims to the French crown. Du Guesclin avoided open battle, pursuing a warfare of attrition which wore out the Black Prince and alienated the Aquitanians from the English. After the hideous **sack of Limoges** (1370) the Black Prince returned to England (1371) and was replaced (1372–1374) by his brother, **John of Gaunt,** Duke of Lancaster, an incompetent soldier, who lost town after town until only Calais, Cherbourg, Brest, Bayonne, and Bordeaux remained in English hands (1375).

Edward's personal rule and domestic developments in England. Edward, a majestic, affable man, opened his reign with generous concessions to the baronage, and a courteous welcome to the complaints of the middle class. He grew steadily in popularity. He was fond of war and the war was popular; the nation backed him.

Progress of Parliament. The necessities of war finance played into the hands of Parliament, and (after 1325) the knights and burgesses began to establish a privileged position for their common petitions. Without immediate redress when the king broke promises of reform, they were able to apply financial pressure in crises. The king could still legislate outside Parliament by ordinances in council, but Parliament was gaining the initiative: non-feudal levies and changes in levies require parliamentary sanction (1340); a money grant made conditional on redress, and auditors of expenditure appointed (1340–1341); all ministers of the king declared (1341) to be subject to parliamentary approval (soon repealed); demand that a grant be spent as directed (1344); a specific grant voted for defense against the Scots (1348); appointment of parliamentary treasurers and collectors (1377). Parliament continued to sit as a single body, but deliberated in sections: the magnates and prelates sitting in the parliament chamber with the King's Council (thus forming the **Great Council);** the knights and burgesses met separately until 1339–1349, when they began joint sessions (i.e. emergence of **the Commons**) and designated (before 1377) a representative, the speaker, to voice their views in debate. Royal officials ceased to attend the Council-in-Parliament, leaving the council to the prelates and magnates (now sitting virtually by hereditary right). The outline of the **House of Lords** began to appear.

Development of justices of the peace. The conservators of the peace established under Henry III to keep the peace had no judicial powers; the Statute of 1327 allowed them to receive indictments for trial before the itinerant judges. In 1332 their jurisdiction was made to include felonies and trespass. Established as police judges in each county (1360) they were also charged with price and labor regulation. By 1485 they had absorbed most of the functions of the sheriffs. Chosen from the local gentry, under royal commission, they constituted an amateur body of administrators who carried on local government in England until well into the 19th century.

1348-1349. The ravages of the Black Death may have reduced the population one-half; coupled with tremendous war prosperity, this dislocated the wage and price structure, producing a major economic and social crisis. Wages and prices were regulated by a royal ordinance (1349) followed by the **Statute of Laborers** (1351) fixing wages and prices, and attempting to compel able-bodied unemployed to accept work when offered. The labor shortage accelerated the transition (already begun) from servile to free tenures and fluid labor; the statute in practice destroyed English social unity without markedly arresting servile emancipation or diminishing the crisis.

War prosperity affected everybody and led to a general surge of luxury (e.g. the new and generous proportions of contemporary Perpendicular Gothic). Landowners, confronted with a labor shortage, began to enclose for sheep-raising, and the accumulation of capital and landholdings founded great fortunes, which soon altered the political and social position of the baronage. The yeomanry, exhilarated by their joint military achievement with the aristocracy, and their share of war plunder, lost their traditional passivity, and a new ferment began among the lower sections of society.

Growth of national and anti-clerical (anti-papal) **feeling.** Hostility to the Francophil papacy at Avignon: **Statute of Provisors** (1351), an effort to stem the influx of alien clergy under papal provisions (renewed several times); **Statute of Praemunire** (1353), forbidding appeals to courts (i.e. Avignon) outside England (renewed several times); rejection (1366) by Parliament of the papal request that John's tribute (intermitted by Edward, 1333) be renewed, and declaration that no king could make England a papal fief without Parliament's consent; Parliament declared bishops unfit for state offices (1371). **Progress of the vernacular.** English became, by statute (1362), the language of pleading and judgment in the courts (law French retained in documents). English began to be taught in the

schools (1375). Parliament was opened (1399) with a speech in English.

c. 1362. Growth of social tension. Langland's *Piers Plowman*, a vernacular indictment of governmental and ecclesiastical corruption, and an appeal (unique in Europe) in behalf of the poor peasant, appeared. Langland, a poor country parson, typical of the section of the Church directly in contact with public opinion, was the voice of the old-fashioned godly England bewildered and angered by a new epoch. Preaching of scriptural equalitarianism by various itinerant preachers (e.g. John Ball); growing bitterness against landlords and lawyers.

c. 1376. John Wiclif, an Oxford don and chaplain of Edward, already employed (1374) by the government in negotiations with the papacy over provisions, published his *Civil Dominion*, asserting in curious feudal terms that, as Christians hold all things of God under a contract to be virtuous, sin violates this contract and destroys title to goods and offices. Wiclif made it plain that his doctrine was a philosophical and theological theory, not a political concept, but extremists ignored this point. A remarkable precursor of the Reformation, Wiclif advocated a propertyless Church, emphasizing the purely spiritual function, attacked the Caesarian clergy, and insisted on the direct access of the individual to God (e.g. abolition of auricular confession, reduction of the importance of the sacraments, notably penance) and the right of individual judgment. He also was responsible (with Purvey and Nicholas of Hereford) for the first complete, vernacular **English Bible.** He wrote pamphlets, both in Latin and English, and carried on a wide agitation through his poor priests for his doctrines (**Lollardy**) until it was said every fourth man was a Lollard.

1369-1377. Edward, in his dotage, was under the domination of Alice Perrers; the Black Prince (after his return, 1371) was ill and lethargic; government in church and state was sunk in the depths of corruption, society in an orgy of luxury.

1374. John of Gaunt, returning from France, struck a bargain with Alice Perrers, became the leader of the state, set out to use the strong anti-clerical feeling and social unrest for his own ends, and probably aimed at the succession.

1376. The Black Prince, awakened from his lethargy, led the **Good Parliament** in a series of reforms: the Commons refused supply until an audit of accounts; two notorious aristocratic war profiteers (Lyons and Latimer) were impeached before the King's Council (i.e. the future Lords), the first impeachment of officials by Parliament in English history.

1377. After the death of the Black Prince (1376) John of Gaunt's packed Parliament undid the reforms and passed a general poll tax (4d.).

1377. Gaunt, aiming at the confiscation of clerical estates, supported Wiclif, but the bishops, unable to touch Gaunt, had Wiclif called to account. A violent scene between Gaunt and Bishop Courtenay ended with public opinion on the bishop's side and Gaunt in flight. Attempts to discipline Wiclif failed because of public opinion, but his denial of transubstantiation (1380) alienated Gaunt and his aristocratic supporters.

ART AND LITERATURE.

Perpendicular Gothic: Gloucester, transepts and choir (1331–1335); cloisters (1351–1412). Minor arts: *Louterell Psalter* (opening of the 14th century), illuminations. English influence on craftsmen of the Rhineland, Paris, Lorraine.

Popular songs: Anti-French songs in celebration of victories at Halidon Hill, Sluys, the capture of Calais, etc., c. 1377 first mention of Robin Hood.

Historical writing: Higden's *Polychronicon* (before 1363), a brilliant universal history in Latin; Walsingham of St. Albans' (end of the 14th century) *Chronicle*, in Latin, rivaling Froissart in brilliance of description. English translation (1377) of the fictional account of the *Travels of Sir John Mandeville* by Jean de Bourgogne.

The Pearl, a mystical poem of lament for a dead daughter, influenced by the *Roman de la Rose*, and suggestive of Dante's mystical visions.

Geoffrey Chaucer (c. 1340–1400), son of a London burgher, a layman, attached to the circle of John of Gaunt, a diplomat, active at court, later member of Parliament, combined observation with learning. Translator of Boethius' *Consolatio*, etc. Representative of the new cosmopolitanism of English society, he was under Italian and French influences; probably knew Petrarch. Creator of English versification; recaster of the English vocabulary by adding continental grace to the ruder Anglo-Saxon word-treasury. The influence of Wiclif, Oxford, Cambridge, the court, and above all, Chaucer, fixed Midland English as the language of the English people. The *Canterbury Tales* are a witty, sympathetic, sophisticated, realistic picture of contemporary society (omitting the aristocracy). **John Gower** (d. 1408), last of the Anglo-Norman poets, wrote in both Latin and French, and later (perhaps due to Chaucer) in English: *Confessio Amantis*; *Vox Clamantis* (expressing the alarm of a landowner at the Peasants' Revolt).

Foundation of Winchester School (St. Mary's College) by William of Wykeham (1393).

1377-1399. RICHARD II (son of the Black Prince, aged ten at his accession).

1377-1389. Minority. Marriage to Anne of Bohemia (1382); rule by the council under the domination of John of Gaunt; activity of Parliament: insistence by the Commons on the nomination of twelve new councillors. Renewal of war in France (1383): loss of the Flanders trade, complaints at the cost by Parliament. Poll taxes (1370 and 1380); sporadic violence, growing tension in the lower orders of society.

1381. PEASANTS' REVOLT. Efforts by the landlords to revert to the old servile tenures culminated in a peasant rising, the burning of manors, destruction of records of tenures, game parks, etc., assassination of landlords and lawyers, and a march (100,000(?) men) from the south and east of England on London led by **Jack Straw, Wat Tyler,** and others (release of John Ball from prison). London admitted the marchers; lawyers and officials were murdered, their houses sacked, the Savoy (John of Gaunt's palace) burned. Significant **demands:** commutation of servile dues, disendowment of the Church, abolition of game laws. The Tower was seized, Archbishop Sudbury (mover, as chancellor, of the poll taxes) was murdered. Richard met the rebels (Mile End), rapidly issued charters of manumission, and started most of them home. After the murder of Wat Tyler, Richard cleverly took command of the remnant (possibly 30,000), deluded them with false promises, and dispersed them. Cruel reaction ensued: Richard and Parliament annulled the charters; terrible repression followed, and a deliberate effort was made to restore villeinage. This proved impossible and serfdom continued to disappear.

1381. Passage of the **first Navigation Act,** followed by clear signs of growing national monopoly of commerce.

1382. Wiclif, who had alienated his upper-class supporters by a denial of transubstantiation, was discredited by the Peasants' Revolt, and condemned by the Church, and withdrew to Lutterworth (1382–1384), where he continued to foster Lollardy until he died (1384). His body, by order of the Council of Constance, was dug up and burned (1428).

1382. Archbishop Courtenay purged Oxford of

Lollardy, thus separating the movement from the cultured classes and destroying academic freedom, with serious results alike for reform and education in England. Parliament refused to allow persecution of the Lollards. The position of the English Church was not wholly due to its own corruption nor to the paralysis of the Avignonese Captivity, but was partly a result of the fact that secular learning, secular society, and the secular state had overtaken the position of the Church.

1385. Futile expedition of Richard to Scotland; threatened French invasion (1386); general demands for reform in government. Parliament blocked Richard's effort (1385) to set up a personal government, and appointed a commission of reform. The Lords Appellant (led by Richard's uncle, the Duke of Gloucester) secured the impeachment and condemnation (1388) of five of Richard's party (in the *Wonderful*, or *Merciless Parliament*).

1389-1397. Richard's personal and constitutional rule. Truce with France (1389), peace negotiations, marriage to Isabella, infant daughter of Charles VI (1396). Richard was on good terms with Parliament, England prosperous and quiet. Livery and maintenance forbidden by statute (1390); re-enactment of the Statutes of: Provisors (1390); Mortmain (1391); Praemunire (1393).

1397-1399. Richard's attempt at absolutism. Richard, furious at a parliamentary demand for financial accounting, had the mover (Haxey) condemned for treason (not executed). In the next Parliament (Commons, packed for Richard; Lords friendly) three of the Lords Appellant were convicted and executed for treason, Richard was voted an income for life (1398) and the powers of Parliament delegated to a committee friendly to Richard. Heavy taxation, ruthless exactions, and a reign of terror opened the way for the **conspiracy of Henry of Bolingbroke** (exiled son of John of Gaunt).

1399. Bolingbroke landed while Richard was in Ireland, got him into his power on his return, and forced him to abdicate. Richard was thrown into the Tower and later died (murdered?) in prison (1400). Parliament accepted the abdication and, returning to the ancient custom of election, made Henry king. Henry's title by heredity was faulty; his claim was based on usurpation, legalized by Parliament, and backed by public opinion.

1399-1461. THE HOUSE OF LANCASTER.

1399-1413. HENRY IV. The reign, in view of the nature of Henry's title to the throne, was inevitably a parliamentary one.

Henry, an epileptic, was not a great king, but a national monarch was now a necessity to England. To retain the support of the Church, Henry opposed the demand (1404) of the Commons (perhaps a reflection of Lollardy) that church property be confiscated, and applied to poor relief. The request was renewed (1410). The statute, *de Heretico Comburendo* (1401), increased the power of the Church over heresy (primarily, of course, against Lollardy) and was the first law of its kind in England.

1400-1406. Rebellions and invasions: (1) Revolt in behalf of Richard (1400); (2) Scottish invasion (1402) stopped by the Percies, the leading barons of Northumberland, at **Homildon Hill;** (3) Owen Glendower's revolt in Wales (1402-1409) joined by (4) the revolt of the Percies (1403-1404); (5) French landing in Wales (1405); (6) Archbishop (of York) Scrope's rebellion (1405); (7) attack by the Duke of Orléans in Guienne (1406).

1413-1422. HENRY V, a careful king, whose military achievements brought England to the first rank in Europe. Bent on the revival of the Church, he led a strong attack on Lollardy: **Sir John Oldcastle** (Lord Cobham), the leading Lollard, was excommunicated by Archbishop Arundel, but escaped; a Lollard plot against the king's life was discovered; Henry attacked (1414) and captured a Lollard group, most of whom were hanged; anti-Lollard legislation allowing seizure of their books; Oldcastle, the last influential Lollard, executed (1417). Henceforth Lollardy was a lower-class movement driven underground until the Reformation.

1415. Henry, in alliance with Burgundy, reasserted his claims (such as they were) to the throne of France. Relying on the anarchy in France and hoping by military successes to unite the English behind the house of Lancaster, he advanced into France.

1415, Oct. 25. BATTLE OF AGINCOURT. Henry's great victory over vastly superior forces opened the way to

1417-1419. The reconquest of Normandy and an advance to the walls of Paris (1419). The temporary union of the Armagnac and Burgundian factions in France was broken by the assassination (1419) of the Duke of Burgundy, followed by the renewal of Anglo-Burgundian alliance and

1420. The Treaty of Troyes. The dauphin (later Charles VII) was disinherited; Henry V was designated regent of France and successor to the mad Charles VI, was given control of northern France, and was married to

Lancaster and York

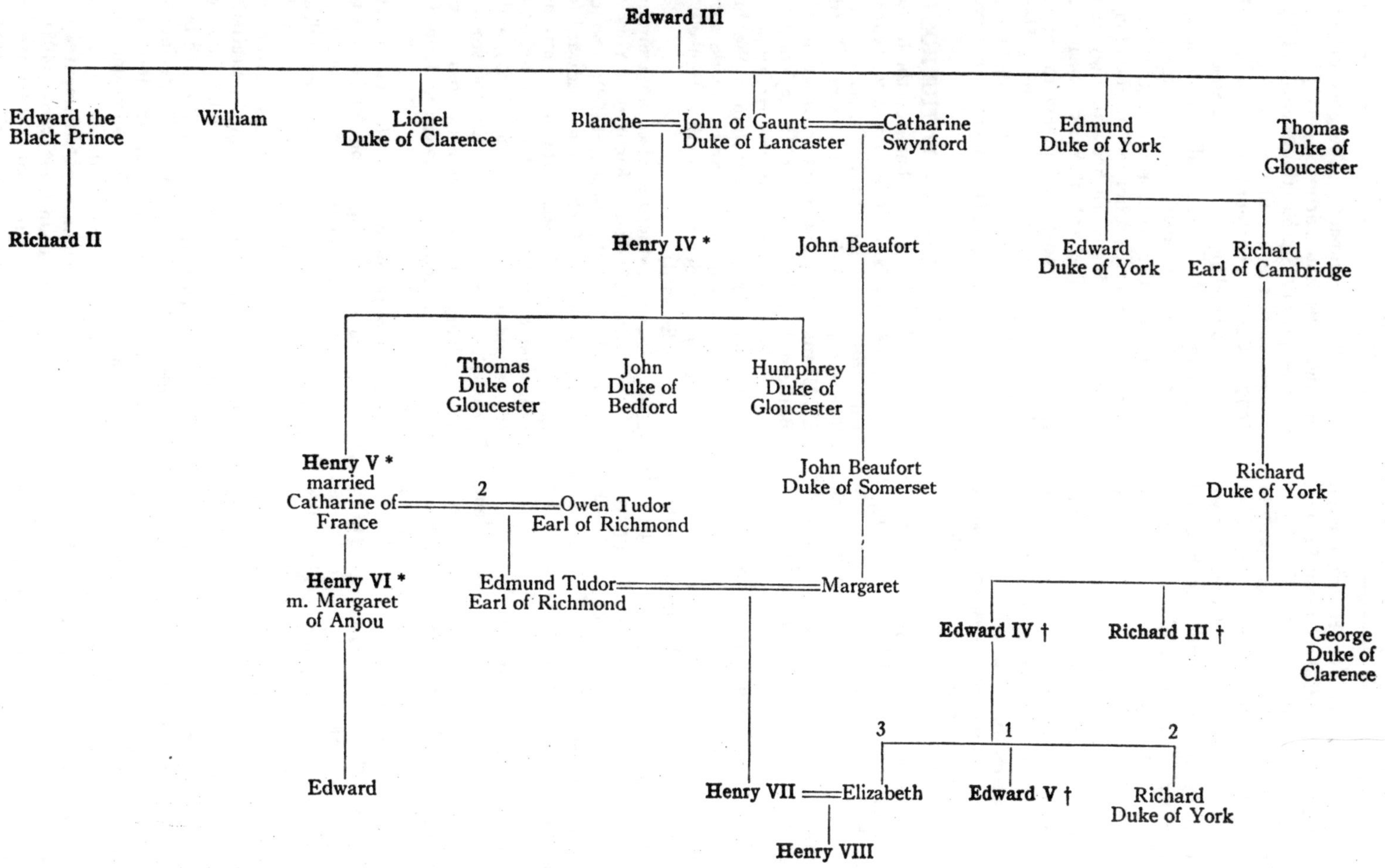

Edward III

Lancaster line (John of Gaunt):

Edward III
- Edward the Black Prince
  - Richard II
- William
- Lionel, Duke of Clarence
- John of Gaunt, Duke of Lancaster = Blanche
  - Henry IV *
    - Henry V * married Catharine of France
      - Henry VI * m. Margaret of Anjou
        - Edward
    - Thomas, Duke of Gloucester
    - John, Duke of Bedford
    - Humphrey, Duke of Gloucester
- John of Gaunt, Duke of Lancaster = Catharine Swynford
  - John Beaufort
    - John Beaufort, Duke of Somerset
      - Margaret
- Edmund, Duke of York
  - Edward, Duke of York
  - Richard, Earl of Cambridge
    - Richard, Duke of York
      - Edward IV †
      - Richard III †
      - George, Duke of Clarence
- Thomas, Duke of Gloucester

Catharine of France (2) = Owen Tudor, Earl of Richmond
- Edmund Tudor, Earl of Richmond = Margaret
  - Henry VII = Elizabeth
    - Henry VIII

Edward IV † (1) = Elizabeth (3); Henry VII (3) = Elizabeth
- (1) Edward V †
- (2) Richard, Duke of York

* Kings of the House of Lancaster.

† Kings of the House of York.

Charles' daughter Catherine. Henry, busy in the reconquest of France, died suddenly, followed shortly by Charles VI (1422).

1422–1461. Henry VI (aged nine months on his accession), acclaimed King of France; his uncle, the Duke of Gloucester, regent (under the council) in England; another uncle, the Duke of Bedford, regent in France.

1424. Bedford defeated the French at **Verneuil**, but his ally the Duke of Burgundy was angered by Gloucester's foolish invasion of Hainault. Bitter feud of Gloucester and Beaufort, Bishop of Winchester and chancellor.

1428–1429. English failure at Orleans (Joan of Arc, p. 282); coronation of Charles VII at Reims (1429).

1431. The English burned Joan of Arc at Rouen and crowned Henry VI King of France in Paris. Steady advance of Charles VII; unpopularity of the war in England; parliamentary resistance to grants; loss of the Burgundian alliance (1435) and of Paris (1436).

1436–1437. Richard, Duke of York (heir to throne), regent in France. He was replaced, after a few successes, by the Earl of Warwick (1437–1439), but later returned to France (1440–1443). Continued rivalry of Beaufort and Gloucester. Beaufort, supported by the king, who liked his peace policy, attended the conference of Calais (1439).

1442. French conquest of Gascony except Bordeaux and Bayonne.

1444. The king's new favorite, the Duke of Suffolk, arranged the marriage of Henry and Margaret of Anjou, concluded a truce of two years, and promised to surrender Maine to Charles VII. Margaret was unpopular in England and Maine was not turned over.

1448. Charles VII, in a vigorous renewal of the war, took Maine, completed the conquest of Normandy (1450), and regained Bordeaux and Bayonne (1451). The English effort to reconquer Gascony failed (1453), leaving only Calais in English hands at the end of the Hundred Years' War.

Domestic disorders. Henry, declared of age (1437), was unfit to rule; the council continued in power, factions and favorites encouraged the rise of disorder. The nobles, enriched by the war and the new sheep farming and progress of enclosures, maintained increasing numbers of private armed retainers (livery and maintenance) with which they fought one another, terrorized their neighbors, paralyzed the courts, and domi-

nated the government. The government lost prestige; Gloucester, arrested (1447) for treason, died in prison, Suffolk (impeached 1450) was killed as he sailed into exile.

1450. Cade's rebellion: a revolt of perhaps 30,000 men of Kent and Sussex, including many respectable small landowners, who marched on London to demand reform in government and the restoration of the Duke of York to power. Admitted to London, the marchers were finally crushed after they resorted to violence. **Richard of York** returned from Ireland and forced his admission to the council (1450). York was regent during Henry's periods of insanity (1453–1454; 1455–1456), but on his recovery (1454) Somerset returned to power.

1455–1485. THE WARS OF THE ROSES: a dreary civil war between the houses of Lancaster and York (the Yorkists wearing a white rose, the Lancastrians (later) a red rose). The nation as such took little part. **Battle of St. Albans** (1455): Somerset defeated and killed. **Battle of Northampton** (1460): the Yorkists defeated the royal army and took Henry prisoner. York asserted his hereditary claim to the throne, and the Lords decided that he should succeed Henry on his death (excluding Henry's son, Edward).

1460. Queen Catherine raised an army in the north, defeated Richard of York, who fell on the field (Wakefield, 1460). Southern England rallied to Richard's son Edward (aged nineteen) who defeated the Lancastrians at **Mortimer's Cross** (1461), but was defeated at the **second battle of St. Albans** (1461), and lost possession of King Henry. London stood firm against Margaret, admitted Edward to the town, and after his victory at Towton acclaimed him king (1461).

Growth of the powers of **Parliament** under the Lancastrians: Profiting by the cloud on the royal title and by the pressing needs for war supply, Parliament reached the zenith of its influence: (1) Grant of supply delayed until the end of the session after redress of grievances; agreement by the king not to alter petitions when drafted into statutes. Petitions began to take the form of bills, which when approved by the king became statutes in the modern sense. (2) Beginnings of the Commons' control over the initiation of financial legislation. (3) Enforcement of reform (1404) in the royal administration; members of the council named in Parliament; appointment of the new council enforced (1405). (4) Parliament forced a reversal of the Haxey judgment (1399), establishing its right to freedom of speech in debate. (5) Opposition to packing began to develop and a statute was padded defining the franchise for elections (1430); this statute was in force until the Great Reform Bill of 1832.

The king could still legislate by ordinances in council. Under Henry VI the autocratic council ruled, and in the end dominated Parliament; finally the chaos of the Wars of the Roses saw the temporary eclipse of Parliament as well as of ordered government.

1461-1485. THE HOUSE OF YORK.

1461-1483. EDWARD IV. Parliament declared the three Lancastrian kings usurpers and Henry VI, his wife, son, and chief adherents, traitors. Edward closed the session with a speech of thanks to the Commons, the first time an English king had addressed that body. The mass of Englishmen now wanted a monarch to keep order in the state, and allow them to attend to trade, industry, and agriculture. Civil war continued intermittently, and Henry VI was finally captured (1465) and put in the Tower. Edward's marriage to the commoner, Elizabeth Woodville, and the beginnings of the creation of a new nobility, angered the older nobles, especially the Earl of Warwick. Edward's sister Margaret was married to Charles the Bold, Duke of Burgundy, and master of the Netherlands (1468). Warwick abandoned the king for his brother, the Duke of Clarence, and began to foment trouble for Edward, now increasingly unpopular (1469-1470). Edward's **victory** (partly due to artillery) at **Stamford** (1470) was followed by the flight of Warwick and Clarence.

1471. Warwick next turned to the Lancastrians (under the astute guidance of King Louis XI of France), returned to England with Lancastrian support. Edward's victory at Barnet (1471), where Warwick was killed. Edward then turned on Queen Margaret at Tewksbury, and defeated her. Henry VI died (in all probability murdered) in the Tower. The only surviving claimant to the crown was Henry, Earl of Richmond, an exile aged 14, descended from John of Gaunt and his mistress, Catherine Swynford.

Edward's vigorous plans for war against Louis XI: Parliamentary grants were too small, so he began a new practice — benevolences (supposedly free, but in fact, forced gifts).

1475. Landing in France, Edward got no support from Charles the Bold, and was bought off by Louis XI. Charles the Bold was killed (1477) and Edward was left without an ally.

1483. EDWARD V, aged twelve. **Richard, Duke of Gloucester,** Edward's uncle, an able man, good soldier, cruel and cynical, skilled at winning popular support, had been appointed guardian by Edward's will. Fearing the Woodvilles (family of Edward's mother), Richard struck at them, taking Earl Rivers and Sir Richard Grey prisoners; the queen mother took sanctuary at Westminster; assassination of Lord Hastings (a supporter of the queen); execution of Grey and Rivers; attacks on the legitimacy of Edward; Parliament declared Gloucester the heir and he was crowned Richard III. Edward was sent to the Tower.

1483-1485. RICHARD III. The Duke of Buckingham, a former supporter of Richard, led (under the skilled direction of Morton, Bishop of Ely) a rebellion in behalf of Henry, Earl of Richmond. The rebellion failed, Buckingham was beheaded, Edward and his brother were murdered in the Tower (1483), and universal indignation was aroused. Richard and the Earl of Richmond were both candidates for the hand of Elizabeth of York, daughter of Edward IV, now heiress to the throne. As she was Richard's niece, even his own followers were shocked.

1485. Henry, Earl of Richmond, landed at Milford Haven, there were open defections from Richard by the nobles, and Henry defeated Richard on **Bosworth Field** (Aug. 22), where Richard fell. The crown of England was found on a bush and passed to the first ruler of the great **house of Tudor,** by virtue of his victory in arms and a later act of Parliament.

Cultural movements. The Italian humanist, Poggio Bracciolini's visit (1418–1423) to England. *The Paston Letters* (1422–1509), a remarkable collection of the correspondence (in the vernacular) of a middle-class English family. *The Libel of English Policie* (c. 1436), a militant nationalistic exposition of the economic value of sea-power. **Eton founded** by Henry VI.

Humphrey, Duke of Gloucester (d. 1447), influential patron of classical learning and Italian humanism, was the donor of 279 classical manuscripts to Oxford, the nucleus of the university library. **Sir John Fortescue** (d. c. 1476), chief justice of the King's Bench, a Lancastrian exile during the anarchy of the Wars of the Roses wrote *On the Governance of the Kingdom of England*, and *De Laudibus Legum Angliae*, contrasting the "political" (i.e. constitutional) spirit of the English Common Law with the absolutism of the Roman Law, and comparing the French monarchy unfavorably with the English. Many of his ideas foreshadowed the policies of Henry VII, in form if not in spirit.

Caxton's printing press set up at Westminster (1476) under the patronage of Edward IV. Malory's *Morte Arthure* printed (1484), the first book in poetic prose in the English language. (*Cont. p.* 375.)

(2) *Scotland*, 1305-1488

1305. The conquest of Scotland by Edward I of England saved the country from civil war. Edward's plan of union seemed possible for a brief period until the emergence of Bruce's grandson, Robert, who turned against the English and maintained himself until the incompetence of Edward II gave him a chance to extend the opposition to the English.

1311-1313. Bruce began a great advance into England and besieged Stirling (1314).

1314, June 24. BATTLE OF BANNOCK-BURN. Bruce completely defeated the English and established himself on the throne, thus postponing for centuries the union with England. Bruce's daughter, Margaret, married Walter "the Steward" and became the founder of the house of Stuart.

1315-1318. Edward Bruce, brother of the king, led an unsuccessful invasion of Ireland.

1323. A truce of five years with England was followed by the **Treaty of Northampton,** which recognized Robert Bruce's title and provided for the marriage of his son David to Joanna, daughter of Edward II.

1329-1371. DAVID II, son of Robert, king. His minority was followed by an incompetent rule.

1332. Edward Baliol, with English support, was crowned, and Bruce fled to France. After Baliol's recall to England, Bruce returned and was defeated and captured at

1346. The battle of Neville's Cross, in an effort to aid France by invading England. He was not ransomed until 1357.

This futile reign gave the Scottish Parliament its chance; the burghs had sent representatives to the Parliament of 1326, but the practice was not a regular one until 1424. On at least two occasions the parliamentary majority went home (1367, 1369), leaving the session to commissions, thus establishing the **Lords of Articles,** who assumed deliberative functions and soon became tools of the crown. Nevertheless, Parliament managed to establish a considerable control over royal acts, and kept its hand on the declaration of war and peace and the coinage. The lower clergy began sending representatives to Parliament (e.g. 1367, 1369, 1370).

1356. Edward Baliol handed over his crown to Edward III.

1363. David Bruce's scheme for a union with England if he died childless was blocked by Parliament's refusal to approve it (1364).

1371. THE STUART LINE was established on the Scottish throne by the accession of

1371-1390. ROBERT II, grandson of Robert Bruce. It maintained itself for three centuries despite a succession of futilities and minorities. The rival **house of Douglas** was finally extinguished (1488).

1390-1424. ROBERT III, king. The arrival of James I (1424) after a long imprisonment (since 1405) in England began a vigorous, if premature reform, reduction of violence, restoration of the judicial process, and new legislation which ended anarchy and disciplined the Church. The country lairds were given representation in Parliament as a support to the crown (1428). James was assassinated, 1437.

1437-1460. JAMES II.

From James I to Charles I (1625) every sovereign was a minor on his accession. The reduction of the Earls of Douglas (1452), followed by confiscation of their lands, enriched the crown. Rosburgh was taken from the English, leaving only Berwick in alien hands.

1460-1488. JAMES III, a feeble figure, was kidnaped (1466) by Lord Boyd, who ruled as governor (by vote of Parliament). The Orkneys and Shetlands were acquired from Norway (1472). France kept Scotland in contact with the Continent. (*Cont. p.* 375.)

(3) *Ireland*, 1315-1485

1315. Edward Bruce, brother of Robert Bruce of Scotland, landed in Ireland and, with the aid of native chieftains, had himself crowned (1316). But he was able to maintain himself only until 1318.

The Anglo-Norman colony began to weaken from internal quarrels while Edward III was preoccupied with the Hundred Years' War. The chieftains thereupon seized their opportunity to encroach still further upon the position of the outsiders. From this period dates the gradual ebb of English influence. The Black Death (1348-1349) made matters even worse.

1366. The Statute of Kilkenny (passed during the viceroyalty of Lionel, Duke of Clarence) had two aims: (1) to maintain the allegiance of the English colony and keep it to the English tradition, and (2) to reduce the grounds of racial conflict. Marriages with the Irish were forbidden, though this was not an entirely new measure. English was enjoined as the speech of the colonists, and English law was insisted on. Nevertheless, the viceroys and governors were unable to maintain order.

1398. Expedition of Richard II to reduce Ireland. This was without permanent results. Under Henry V misery in Ireland reached a new peak and perhaps half of the English colony returned home. The danger in this situation is mentioned in the *Libel of English Policy* (c. 1436). Fear that Ireland might pass into other hands was widespread.

1449. Richard of York arrived as viceroy and ingratiated himself equally with colonists and natives. He departed to England in 1450, but on his return made Ireland virtually independent, with the approval of the Irish Parliament. English rule was repudiated and a separate coinage established. Richard continued this policy until his death, but Edward IV resumed a harsh and anarchic policy. Under Richard III the strongest figure in Ireland was **Kildare,** leader of the Yorkists. (*Cont. p. 375.*)

b. FRANCE, 1314-1483

1314-1316. LOUIS X (*the Quarrelsome*). The real ruler was Louis' uncle, Charles of Valois. A reaction against the monarchy forced concessions from the king. Louis' daughter, Jeanne, was an infant; there was no male heir. A great national council (1316) decreed that there could be no queen regnant in France, and gave the crown to Louis' brother, Philip.

1316-1322. PHILIP V (*the Tall*). There were frequent meetings of assemblies which included burghers. Philip, in an enormous number of royal ordinances, gave definitive form to the Capetian government. He left no male heir.

1322-1328. CHARLES IV (*the Fair*), the last Capetian of the direct line, succeeded his brother Philip, to the exclusion of Edward III of England, grandson of Philip IV. This established the principle, later called the **Salic Law,** that the throne could pass only through males. On Charles' death, an assembly of barons declared that "no woman nor her son could succeed to the monarchy."

1328-1498. In this period the **Capetian house of Valois** freed the soil of France from the alien occupation of the English; completed the creation of French national unity and the establishment of a strong national monarchy; prepared France for its brilliant political and cultural rôle in the Renaissance, and began French expansion south of the Alps.

1328-1350. PHILIP VI (nephew of Philip IV, son of Charles of Valois), the nearest male heir. Jeanne, daughter of Louis X, became Queen of Navarre. Edward III did homage for his French fiefs (1329 and 1331). Brittany, Flanders, Guienne, and Burgundy remained outside the royal sway. The papacy was located in France under powerful French influence; rulers of the Capetian house of Anjou were seated on the thrones of Naples, Provence, and Hungary; French interests were firmly established in the Near East; French culture was dominant in England and northern Spain, and was making headway on the fringes of the empire; Dauphiné, the first important imperial fief added to French territory, was purchased (1336). The king had become less accessible; the kingdom, regarded as a possession rather than an obligation, was left to the administration of the royal bureaucracy.

1338-1453. THE HUNDRED YEARS' WAR. English commercial dominance in Flanders precipitated a political crisis. The communes made the Count of Flanders, Louis of Nevers, prisoner (1325-1326); Philip marched to his relief, massacred the burghers on the field of Cassel (1328), and established French administration in Flanders. Edward III retorted with an embargo on wool export from England (1336); the weavers of Ghent, under the wealthy James van Artevelde, became virtual masters of the country and made a commercial treaty with England (1338). On Van Artevelde's insistence, Edward declared himself King of France; the Flemings recognized him as their sovereign, and made a political alliance with him (1340).

1338. Philip declared Edward's French fiefs forfeited and invested Guienne. Edward was made Vicar of the Empire and his title as King of France was recognized by the emperor. Thus began the **Hundred Years' War,** really a series of wars with continuous common objectives: the retention of their French "empire" by the English, the liberation of their soil by the French.

1340. Philip, by dismissing two squadrons of Levantine mercenary ships, lost his mastery of the Channel until 1372 and was over-

The French Succession, 1328

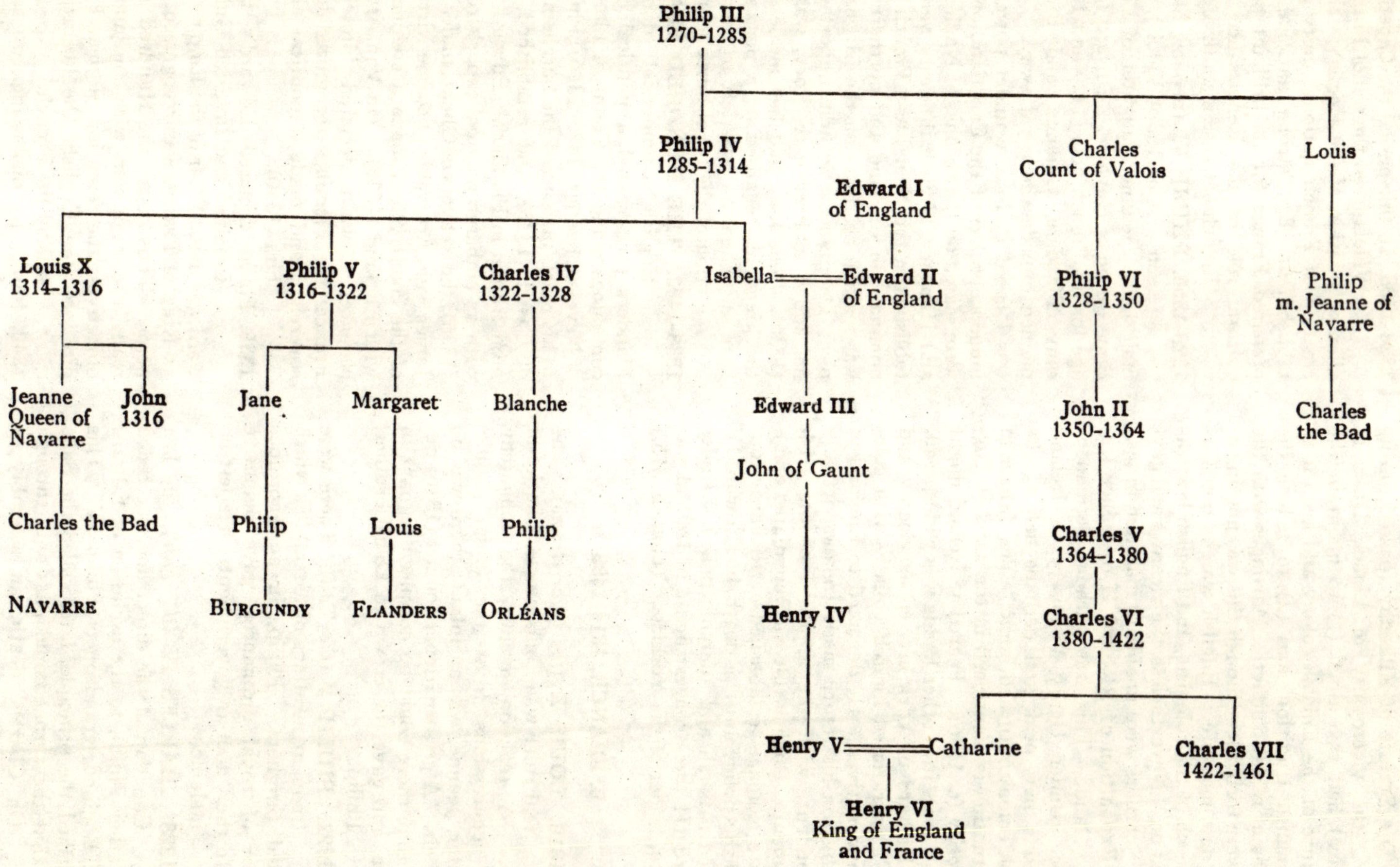

Philip III
1270–1285

Philip IV
1285–1314

Charles
Count of Valois

Louis

Edward I
of England

Philip VI
1328–1350

Philip
m. Jeanne of Navarre

Louis X
1314–1316

Philip V
1316–1322

Charles IV
1322–1328

Isabella

Edward II
of England

John II
1350–1364

Charles
the Bad

John
1316

Jeanne
Queen of
Navarre

Jane

Margaret

Blanche

Edward III

Charles V
1364–1380

Charles the Bad

Philip

Louis

Philip

John of Gaunt

Charles VI
1380–1422

NAVARRE

BURGUNDY

FLANDERS

ORLÉANS

Henry IV

Catharine

Charles VII
1422–1461

Henry V

Henry VI
King of England
and France

The Valois House

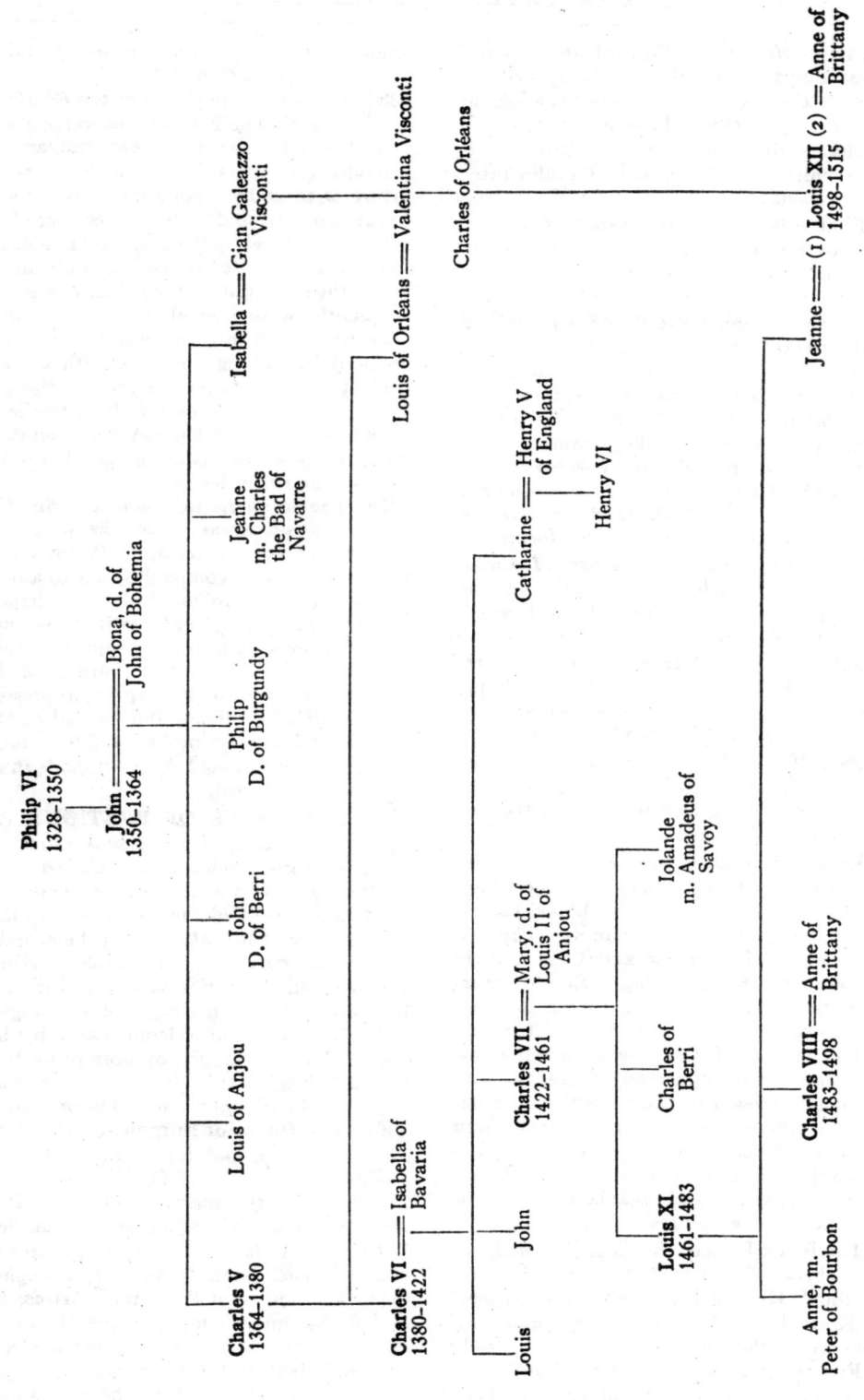

Philip VI
1328–1350

John ══ Bona, d. of
1350–1364   John of Bohemia

Charles V
1364–1380

Louis of Anjou

John
D. of Berri

Philip
D. of Burgundy

Jeanne
m. Charles
the Bad of
Navarre

Isabella ══ Gian Galeazzo
Visconti

Charles VI ══ Isabella of
1380–1422   Bavaria

Louis

John

Louis of Orléans ══ Valentina Visconti

Charles VII ══ Mary, d. of
1422–1461   Louis II of
Anjou

Catharine ══ Henry V
of England

Henry VI

Charles of Orléans

Louis XI
1461–1483

Charles of Berri

Iolande
m. Amadeus of
Savoy

Charles VIII ══ Anne of
1483–1498   Brittany

Anne, m.
Peter of Bourbon

Jeanne ══ (1) Louis XII (2) ══ Anne of
1498–1515   Brittany

whelmingly defeated by Edward at the **naval battle of Sluys** (June 24). This opened the Channel to the English and gave them free access to northern France.

1341-1364. A dynastic contest in Brittany, in which both Edward and Philip intervened.

1341. First collection of the *gabelle* (salt tax) in France; increasing war levies and mounting dissatisfaction.

1346. Edward's invasion of Normandy and overwhelming **VICTORY AT CRÉCY,** Aug. 26 (10,000 English defeated some 20,000 French). The French military system was outmoded, the people unaccustomed to arms, and the chivalry inefficient. Blind King John of Bohemia was slain. · Artillery came into use (1335–1345). Continued war levies led to open refusal (1346) of a grant by the Estates-General of Langue d'Oil, and a demand for reforms. The king attempted some reforms.

1347. Edward's siege and **capture of Calais** gave the English an economic and military base in France which was held until 1558.

1348-1350. **The Black Death** penetrated northern Europe, reducing the. population by about a third, and contributing to the crisis of 1357–1358 in France.

1350-1364. **JOHN II** (*the Good Fellow*), a "good knight and a mediocre king," a spendthrift who repeatedly debased the currency.

1355. English renewal of the war in a triple advance: into Brittany; from the Channel; and from Bordeaux by the Black Prince. Virtual collapse of French finance. The Estates-General of Languedoc and Langue d'Oil (the latter under the leadership of **Etienne Marcel** the richest man in Paris, provost of the merchants), forced the king (ordinance of 1355) to agree to consult the Estates before making new levies of money, a policy already in practice, and to accept supervision of the collection and expenditure of these levies by a commission from the Estates. Charles cleverly induced the Estates to adjourn, debased the coinage in the interest of his treasury, and organized his opposition to the Estates.

1356. **The Black Prince** (the English "model of chivalry") defeated John, the last "chivalrous" King of France **at Poitiers** (Sept. 19). King John, his son Philip, and two brothers were taken prisoner with a multitude of the French aristocracy. The royal authority *in* France was reduced to a shadow; civil chaos

reigned. Charles, the eighteen-year-old son of John, became regent.

1357. Climax of the power of the **Estates-General:** The Estates-General again had to be called and passed the **Great Ordinance** which provided for supervision of the levy and expenditure of taxes by a standing committee of the Estates, regular and frequent meetings of the Estates, poor relief, and many other reforms, but did not attempt to reduce the traditional powers of the monarchy. The Estates had met too frequently, were divided, and had no real coherence or skill in government. They were discredited by Marcel's alliance with Charles the Bad of Navarre (a son of Jeanne, daughter of Louis X) who had a better claim to the throne than Edward III. Charles V fled from Paris and created a powerful coalition against the Estates and Charles the Bad.

1358. The *Jacquerie* (a violent peasant reaction against war taxes, the weight of the ransoms of the captives at Poitiers and the pillage of the free companies) led to a merciless reaction by the nobles. Marcel, already distrusted, was further discredited by intrigues with the revolted peasantry and with the English. Charles, after the murder of Marcel (1358), returned to the capital, repressed disorder with a firm hand, and refused to approve John's preliminary peace (1359), which virtually restored the old Angevin lands in France to Edward.

1360. THE PEACE OF BRETIGNY (Calais) (virtually a truce of mutual exhaustion): Edward practically abandoned his claims to the French crown; Charles yielded southwest·rn France (Guienne), Calais, Ponthieu, and the territory immediately about them, and promised an enormous ransom for John. King John was released on partial payment of the ransom, but returned after the flight of a hostage to die in his luxurious and welcome captivity in England. The southern provinces protested their return to English rule, and there were clear signs of national sentiment born of adversity.

1361. **The Duchy of Burgundy** escheated to the crown, and John handed it to his son Philip as an appanage (1363). Charles negotiated (1369) the marriage of Duke Philip to Margaret, daughter and heiress of Louis de Male, last Count of Flanders, in order to keep Flanders out of English hands. As Mary brought Flanders, the County of Burgundy, Artois, Nevers, and Rethel under control of the Dukes of Burgundy, this marriage added a new danger on the east and north to the Plantagenet threat in the west. Philip further strengthened his house by marriage alliances with the children of the Wittelsbach, Albert of Bavaria, which added holdings in Hainault, Holland, and Zealand.

1364-1380. CHARLES V (*the Wise*), neither strong of body, handsome, nor chivalrous; a pious, refined, realistic statesman of modern cast. He saved France and made it plain to the nation that national well-being depended on the monarchy rather than on the Estates-General.

The reign opened with a bad harvest, plague, and pillage by the free companies (discharged soldiers). The Breton, **Bertrand du Guesclin,** the first great soldier on the French side in the Hundred Years' War, was sent with some 30,000 of these men to support Henry of Trastamara against Pedro the Cruel of Castile, who had become an ally of the Black Prince.

Charles managed to dominate the new financial machinery set up by the Estates-General, continued the war levies (e.g. hearth-tax, *gabelle*, sales taxes) and utilized the peace for general reform and reconstruction: castles were rebuilt, and royal control of them strengthened; permanent companies of professional cavalry and infantry were established; artillery was organized and supported by pioneers and sappers; a military staff and hierarchy of command established in the army (1374); the navy was reorganized, and French sea-power restored. New walls were built around Paris.

The government and finance were reorganized and the general frame of the financial structure fixed until 1789. The grant of the Estates-General of Langue d'Oil (1360) for John's ransom had been for a term of six years; their grant of a hearth-tax (1363) was without a time limit. Following these precedents, Charles was able (1369) to induce the Estates to agree to the general principle that old grants of funds need not be renewed by the Estates unless their terms were to be changed. This freed the king from control by the Estates unless new taxes were needed and meant that the Estates no longer had a vital function. The financial control established by the Estates (1357) was transferred to the royal *chambre des comptes* in Paris.

1369. The appeal of the Count of Armagnac to Charles against the Black Prince and the Black Prince's refusal to appear at Charles' court served as an excuse for the **resumption of the war.** Du Guesclin became (1370) Constable of France (a title usually reserved for great nobles), abandoned chivalrous tactics, and allowed the English to parade through France. Avoiding pitched battle, he harassed the invaders with a picked force. The reconquest of Poitou and Brittany (1370-1372) was followed by the death of the Black Prince (1376); the French fleet, supported by the Castilian, regained control (La Rochelle, 1372) of the Channel, and blocked English transport in the north. By 1380 the English held only Bordeaux, Bayonne, Brest, Calais, Cherbourg, Valais, and their immediately surrounding territory. France was cleared of the enemy, but was in ruins.

1378. With the end of the Avignonese Captivity (1376) the **Great Schism** in the Church began; Charles and his successors supported the French line of popes. On his deathbed Charles forbade the hearth-tax.

1380-1422. CHARLES VI. A minority accompanied by the disruptive rivalry of the king's uncles (the Dukes of Anjou, Berry, and Burgundy, the "Princes of the Lilies"), who exploited France for their own ends. This was followed by the intermittent insanity of the king, and paralysis in the government.

General economic distress, popular unrest, and general revolts, usually against taxes (vigorously repressed): the *Tuchins* (1381) in Languedoc; the *Maillotins* (1382), in Paris, and elsewhere; and the outbreak in Flanders (1382) under Philip (son of James) van Artevelde. The French feudality, under leadership of the Duke of Burgundy, ended this revolt by the victory of **Roosebeke** (1382), following it up with atrocious repression. Flanders on the death of the Count (1384) passed to Burgundy; its pacification was completed in 1385. The hearth-tax was renewed and taxation remained heavy.

1388. The death (1384) of the Duke of Anjou had left the Duke of Burgundy in a position of great power, and Charles, angered at Philip of Burgundy's policies, began his personal rule by replacing the duke by his own brother, Louis, Duke of Orléans, and by restoring (1389) his father's old advisers, men of humble birth (whence their nickname, the *Marmousets*). Louis of Orléans was a refined, talented spendthrift, unpopular in Paris, and Philip of Burgundy (supported by Queen Isabella) was able to pose as a reformer and lead the opposition, bringing the rivalry of Burgundy and Orléans into the open.

1392. Charles' first (brief) **attack of insanity** was soon followed by longer seizures; Philip of Burgundy (as regent) replaced Louis of Orléans in power and the situation returned to what it was before 1389.

1396. Twenty-year truce with England; annihilation of the French knights on a crusade to free Hungary from the Turk (Nicopolis, p. 330).

1404. John (*the Fearless*) an able, ambitious man, became **Duke of Burgundy.** After the sudden transfer of Isabella's support to Louis of Orléans, John's orders led to the assassination of Louis, Duke of Orléans (1407). John became the hero of Paris, but caused the emergence of two great factions in France and began the civil war of the **Armagnacs** against the Burgundians. The Armagnacs, named for their head, the Count of Armagnac (father-in-law of Charles, the new Duke of Orléans), were strong among the great nobles, drew their strength from the south and southeast, were a reactionary, anti-English, war party. The Burgundians, supported by the people, the University of Paris, and the Wittelsbachs, were strong in the north and northeast, favored peace, were pro-English, and supported Pope Clement VII and his papal successors.

1413. The Cabochian revolt (named for the skinner, Simon Caboche) in Paris forced attention to reform, and led to the **Cabochian Ordinance** (1413), inspired by the University of Paris and aimed at efficiency in government rather than democracy. It provided for three councils to conduct public business, and a general detailed program of reform. The Armagnacs returned to control in Paris and led a feudal reaction, which destroyed all hope of reform and opened the way for the English. The Duke of Armagnac (Constable, 1415) repeated the traditional military errors of the feudal class, which understood tournaments but not war.

1415, Oct. 25. THE BATTLE OF AGINCOURT: Henry V, with 10,000 men, defeated three times that number of French; the Duke of Orléans was taken prisoner; **Normandy was reconquered** (1415–1417) by the English, undoing for the time the work of Philip Augustus; the dauphin (later Charles VII) fled to the south of France (1418); the Burgundians returned to power and there was a massacre of Armagnacs in Paris (1418).

1419. Rouen fell; the Burgundians, alarmed at the English advance, began negotiating with the Armagnacs; John of Burgundy was assassinated at a conference with the dauphin at the Bridge of Montereau, and the Burgundians returned to the English alliance.

1420. Charles, under Burgundian influence, and supported by his wife Isabella, accepted the **Treaty of Troyes** (which repudiated the dauphin as illegitimate), adopted Henry V of England as his heir and immediate regent (with the approval of the University of Paris and the Estates-General, 1421). Charles' daughter, Catharine, was married to the future Henry V and, also under the treaty, the English were allowed to retain all their conquests as far as the Loire. King Henry V drove the forces of the dauphin across the Loire and began the steady conquest of France which continued uninterrupted until his death (1422). The dauphin remained at Bourges (whence his nickname, *the Roi de Bourges*).

1422-1461. CHARLES VII (*the Roi de Bourges*, not crowned until 1429). Physically weak, bowed and lethargic from misfortune, the puppet of unscrupulous advisers until the advent of a better group (including Dunois, Richemont, brother-in-law of the Duke of Burgundy, La Hire, *et al*), after 1433, when he became known as "Charles the Well-Served." **Regency of the Duke of Bedford** (1422–1428) for the infant Henry VI of England, who was recognized as King of France in the north, supported by the Burgundians, and crowned in Paris (1436).

1424. Bedford's decisive victory at Cravant was followed by the defeat of the Armagnacs and the Scots at Verneuil.

1428. The English began the siege of Orléans. **Jeanne Darc** (later D'Arc in Charles' patent of nobility) born in 1412 at Domrémy, was of comfortable village family, illiterate, but a good seamstress. A devout mystic, she began to have visions at the age of thirteen.

1429. Jeanne presented herself to the king at Chinon, and was allowed to lead an army (with the empty title of *Chef de Guerre*) to the relief of Orléans. The relief of the city, followed by **Charles' coronation** (1429) at Reims, was the turning point of the war and marked a decisive change in the spirit of the king and the nation. Jealous ministers (e.g. *La Trémoille*) of Charles soon undermined Jeanne's position, despite the progress of the royal cause.

1430. Jeanne was captured at Compiègne by the Burgundians, ransomed by the English. Without intervention by Charles on her behalf, she was tried for witchcraft. The process was probably a typical ecclesiastical trial. After her confession and its repudiation she was burned (1431) by the English at Rouen ("We have burned a saint"), and Charles returned to his old ways.

1432. Charles favored the **Council of Basel,** which was pro-French and anti-papal.

1435. Separate Peace of Arras, reconciliation with Burgundy: Charles agreed to punish the murderers of Duke John of Burgundy and recognized Philip as a sovereign prince for life.   Burgundy was to recognize Charles' title; the Somme towns were to pass to Burgundy (subject to redemption).   The English refused to make peace on acceptable terms.   **Charles recovered Paris** (1436).

1436-1449. Period of military inaction, utilized by Charles for reforms of the army paid for from the *taille*.   The Estates-General agreed to permanent taxation for support of the army. Charles entered Paris and was welcomed (1437).

1437-1439. Famine, pestilence, the anarchy of the *écorcheurs*, but steady progress against the English.

1438.   THE PRAGMATIC SANCTION OF BOURGES: assertion that a church council is superior to a pope; suppression of the annates; provision for decennial councils; maintenance of the autonomy of the French national Church (*Gallicanism*) and its isolation from Rome.

1440.   The Praguerie, part of a series of coalitions of great nobles against the king, with support from the dauphin (later Louis XI), was put down; the dauphin was ordered to the Dauphiné, where he continued his intrigues.

1445-1446.   Army reforms: establishment of the first permanent royal army by the creation of 20 companies of élite cavalry (200 *lances* to a company, 6 men to a *lance*) under captains chosen by the king; a paid force, the backbone of the army, assigned to garrison towns; regularization of the auxiliary free archers (*francs-archers*), a spontaneous body dating from the reign of Charles V (opposed by the nobles), under royal inspection (1448) and under territorial captains (1451).   Establishment of artillery (the Bureau brothers).

1444. Charles the dauphin made a **treaty of alliance with the Swiss cantons.**   The alliance was strengthened (1452) and an alliance made with the towns of Trier, Cologne, *et al.* (1452), and with Saxony, as part of a developing anti-Burgundian policy.   Intermittent support for the house of Anjou in Naples and the house of Orléans in Milan.   Under **Jacques Coeur,** the merchant prince of Montpellier, royal finances were reformed, control of the public revenue by the king established, and French commercial penetration of the Near East furthered (c. 1447).

1449-1461.   Expulsion of the English: Normandy and Guienne regained; Talbot slain (1453).

1456. Retrial and **rehabilitation of Jeanne Darc,** to clear Charles' royal title.

1461-1483.   LOUIS XI (*the Spider*), of simple, bourgeois habits, superficial piety, and feeble, ungainly body, the architect of French reconstruction and royal absolutism.   He was well-educated, a brilliant diplomat, a relentless statesman, an endless traveler throughout his kingdom.   He perfected the governmental system begun under Charles V (revived by Charles VII), and established the frame of the constitution until 1789.   The recognized right of the king to the *taille*, the *aides*, and the *gabelle* made a good revenue available for defense and diplomacy.   Louis improved and perfected the standing army with added emphasis on the artillery, but seldom waged war.   Feudal anarchy and brigandage were stopped; a wise economic policy restored national prosperity despite grinding taxes.

1461. Louis' first step in the reconstruction of the kingdom was a *rapprochement* with the papacy by the formal **revocation of the Pragmatic Sanction of Bourges.**   Little of the royal power was sacrificed, and the national Church remained under the firm control of the crown.   Louis steadily reduced urban liberties and began the extinction of local and provincial administrative independence in the interests of royal centralization.

1462.   Acquisition of Cerdagne and Roussillon; redemption of the Somme towns (1463) revealing the resumption of national expansion.

1465.   League of the Public Weal, a conspiracy against Louis by the Dukes of Alençon, Burgundy, Berry, Bourbon, Lorraine.

1465. Louis' defeat by the league at Montl'héry.   The **Treaty of Conflans** restored the Somme towns to Burgundy, and Normandy to the Duke of Berry.   Louis began to evade the treaty at once, and split the league by diplomacy.

Louis' greatest rival was **Duke Philip the Good** of Burgundy.   Philip was head of the first union of the Low Countries since the days of Charlemagne, a curious approximation of the ancient Lotharingia, which included: the Duchy and County of Burgundy, Flanders, Artois, Brabant, Luxemburg, Holland, Zealand, Friesland, Hainault.   The dukes lacked only Alsace and Lorraine and the royal title.

1467. The accession of **Charles the Bold** as Duke of Burgundy opened the final duel with Burgundy.

1468. Anglo-Burgundian alliance; marriage of Charles the Bold to Margaret of York.

1468. The affair at Péronne: Charles, assuming Louis' treachery in the revolt of Ghent, arrested him at a conference at Péronne.

1469. The Emperor Sigismund ceded Charles' rights in Alsace; Charles occupied Alsace and Lorraine (1473). Louis formed an alliance with the Swiss(1470) and seized the Somme towns (1471).

1474. Louis formed the **Union of Constance** (a coalition of the foes of Burgundy, under French subsidies) which opened the war on Charles.

1475. **Edward IV,** an ally of Charles, invaded France; Louis met him at Piquigny and bought him off.

1476. Charles' conquest of Lorraine and war on the Swiss cantons: defeat of Charles at Granson and Morat.

1477, Jan. 5. DEFEAT AND DEATH OF CHARLES AT NANCY (triumph of the Swiss pikeman over cavalry); end of the Burgundian menace. Louis united the Duchy of Burgundy to the crown and occupied the County of Burgundy (Franche Comté). Flanders stood by the daughter of Charles, Mary of Burgundy, and was lost to France forever. Mary hurriedly married the Hapsburg Prince Maximilian, the "heir" to the empire.

1480. On the **extinction of the house of Anjou,** Anjou, Bar, Maine, and Provence fell to the French crown. Bar completed Louis' mastery on the eastern frontier.

The most significant internal fact of the reign is the development of a clear basis for royal absolutism. Only one meeting of the Estates-General was held (1469), and on that occasion the Estates asked the king to rule without them in future. Legislation was henceforth by royal decree, a situation which facilitated Louis' thoroughgoing reform of the government and administration.

Philippe de Commines, a Fleming who left the service of Charles the Bold for that of Louis, produced in his *Memoirs* the finest piece of critical history since the days of the great historians of antiquity, and was a precursor of Machiavelli.

François Villon (b. 1431), a lyric poet of the first rank.

Jan (d. 1440) **and Hubert van Eyck,** Flemish painters in the service of the court of Burgundy, perfected oil technique; religious painting; portraiture, raising the painter's art to the highest stage of proficiency and perfection.

(*Cont. p.* 387.)

c. THE IBERIAN PENINSULA

(1) *Castile*, 1312-1492

The successors of Alfonso X were not conspicuous for capacity. Frequent minorities and constant dynastic contests still further weakened the authority of the crown. Most outstanding of the Castilian rulers in this period was

1312-1350. ALFONSO XI, who decisively defeated the joint attack of the Spanish and Moroccan Moslems. His **victory at Rio Salado** (Oct. 30, 1340) ended the African menace forever and was the chief battle in the whole history of the reconquest.

Throughout the **Hundred Years' War** (p. 277) Castile supported France, but attempted to avoid hostility with England as much as possible.

1350-1369. PETER (*Pedro, the Cruel*). His reign was in fact little more than a nineteen-year dynastic conflict with his half-brother, the bastard **Henry of Trastamara.** The French, alienated by Peter's outrageous treatment of his wife, Blanche of Bourbon, supported Henry and sent Du Guesclin to Spain. The English (the Black Prince) supported Peter. Henry was defeated at **Navarrete** (1367), but the English were soon estranged by Peter's vicious character. Ultimately Henry defeated and killed Peter (1369).

1369-1379. HENRY II (Trastamara), who renewed the alliance with France. The Castilian fleet, by its victory over the English in the **battle of La Rochelle** (1372), restored command of the Channel to the French. Peace between Castile on the one side and Portugal and Aragon on the other concluded at **Almazan** (1374).

1375. **Rapprochment of Castile and Aragon,** through the marriage of Henry's son, John, to Eleanor, daughter of Peter the Cruel.

Castilian leadership in the reconquest of Moslem Spain led to a maximum of local and municipal self-government between the middle of the 12th and the middle of the 14th century. The Córtes apparently originated from councils of nobles dating from Visigothic days. The Castilian rulers freely granted *fueros* (charters of self-government) to towns in the early stages of the reconquest, and definite elements of democracy appeared in municipal government in this period. By calling the burghers to the Córtes, the kings found allies against the baronage, and this process began in Castile and Leon

The House of Castile

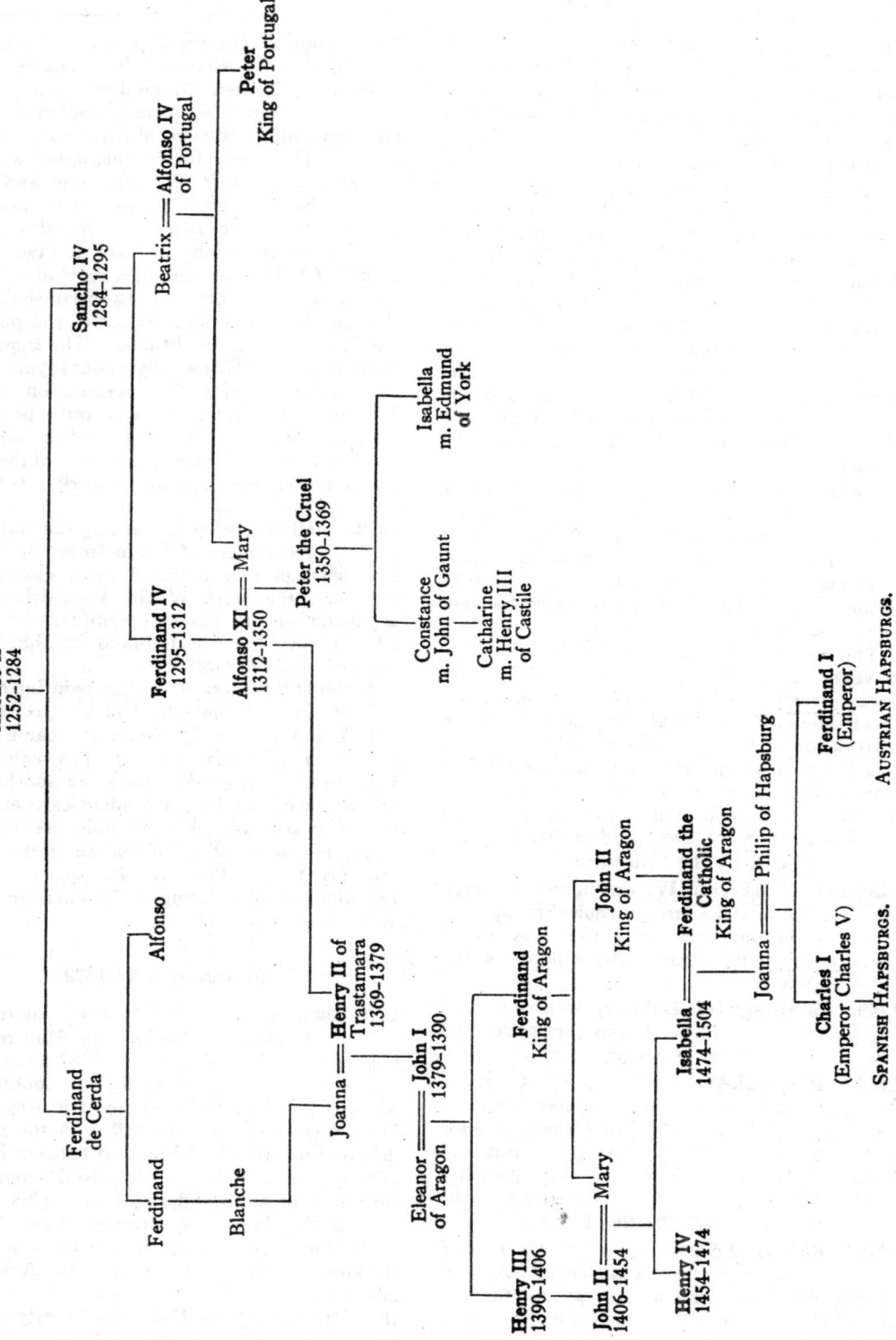

Alfonso X
1252-1284

Ferdinand
de Cerda

Sancho IV
1284-1295

Alfonso

Ferdinand

Blanche

Beatrix ═ Alfonso IV
of Portugal

Ferdinand IV
1295-1312

Peter
King of Portugal

Alfonso XI ═ Mary
1312-1350

Peter the Cruel
1350-1369

Joanna ═ Henry II of
Trastamara
1369-1379

Constance
m. John of Gaunt

Isabella
m. Edmund
of York

Catharine
m. Henry III
of Castile

Eleanor ═ John I
of Aragon   1379-1390

Ferdinand
King of Aragon

Henry III
1390-1406

John II ═ Mary
1406-1454

John II
King of Aragon

Henry IV
1454-1474

Isabella ═══ Ferdinand the
1474-1504   Catholic
               King of Aragon

Joanna ═ Philip of Hapsburg

Charles I
(Emperor Charles V)

SPANISH HAPSBURGS.

Ferdinand I
(Emperor)

AUSTRIAN HAPSBURGS.

at least as early as 1188 (in Aragon probably not before 1250). The Córtes reached its zenith in the 14th and 15th centuries, but petitions to the crown were received and embodied in legislation as early as the 13th century.

Urban groups, the *hermandades* (brotherhoods), sworn to defend the laws of the realm and the lives and property of their members, were clearly developed in the 13th century (e.g. Sancho's, 1282, directed against his father, Alfonso X) and usually supported the kings in periods of crisis (minorities, succession struggles, baronial assaults). The decline of the *hermandades* is associated with the municipal decline and the appearance of the royal *corregidores* in the towns (14th century), but it is not clear whether the crown hastened the decay of the towns and the brotherhoods or sought to stave it off.

Despite all this support, the battle of the kings with the aristocracy, firmly entrenched during the early stages of the reconquest, was a losing one. The nobles were exempt from taxes and from many laws; in general the same was true of the clergy, and some of the great bishops were virtual sovereigns.

The status of the lower classes of Castile was, however, far from desperate: Jew and Moslem were protected for their economic value, though the tendency toward jealousy and toward the segregation of the Jews was already appearing and the Jewish population was declining. The status of rural workers and serfs tended to improve by the definition and limitation of the landlord's rights. Slavery had probably disappeared by the 15th century.

1454-1474. HENRY IV, during whose reign the feudal anarchy reached its apogee. The monarchical power was saved primarily through the support of the towns.

1469. Marriage of Isabella, stepsister and heiress of Henry IV, to **Ferdinand,** heir of the King of Aragon.

1474. ISABELLA succeeded to the Castilian throne. Isabella's succession was challenged by the daughter of Henry IV, supported by Alfonso V of Portugal. But the Córtes of Segovia (1475) recognized Isabella and Ferdinand and the latter defeated the Portuguese in 1476 (**battle of Toro**).

1479. FERDINAND succeeded to the rule of Aragon, Catalonia, Valencia. A form of dyarchical government was set up for the united Castilian and Aragonese crowns. Rule of the Catholic kings (Ferdinand and Isabella).

Restoration of the royal power in Castile: by revising the town charters, the towns were made centers of resistance to feudal aggression; formation of the *Santa Hermandad,* a union of Castilian towns in the interest of royal authority and order. The great feudal magnates were deprived of many of their possessions and rights and a royal administration was gradually established. The *Libro de Montalvo* (1485), the first codification of Spanish law. **Concordat of 1482** with the pope, carefully restricting the power of Rome over the Spanish Church: the king became grand master of the powerful religious orders of knighthood. **The Inquisition** (established in 1478) wholly under royal control, used primarily for the persecution of the Marranos (converted Jews secretly practicing their old faith). Confiscations of property did much to increase the financial power of the rulers and to strengthen them in the work of subduing the feudal opposition.

1492. Fall of Granada, marking the end of the reconquest of Spain from the Moors. This was speedily followed by a spiritual reconquest, the work of the Inquisition. The **expulsion of the Jews** (possibly as many as 200,000) in 1492 was followed by that of the Moors in Castile (1502).

Art and literature. Castilian painting showed the influence of the school of Giotto (after c. 1380), and in the 15th century came under Flemish inspiration (visit of Jan van Eyck, 1428–1429). In general literature and learning followed the same foreign tendencies as architecture and painting: French influence came in early, followed later by Italian and English (notably Dante, Petrarch, Boccaccio, Gower). Introduction of printing at Valencia (c. 1474) and in Castile (c. 1475).

(2) *Aragon,* 1276-1479

1276-1285. PETER III, who was married to Constance, daughter of Manfred and heir of the Hohenstaufen. In 1282 he sailed on a long-planned expedition for the **conquest of Sicily** (which he disguised as an African crusade). He landed at Collo, was called to the throne, defeated Charles at Anjou and became Peter I of Sicily (1282–1285), refusing to do homage to the pope for his island kingdom. This expansion of the Aragonese Kingdom gave Aragon for a time predominance in the western Mediterranean. But it estranged the Aragonese aristocracy, as well as the towns. The nobility therefore formed the **Union for Liberty** and, in the Córtes of 1283, extorted from Peter a

The House of Aragon

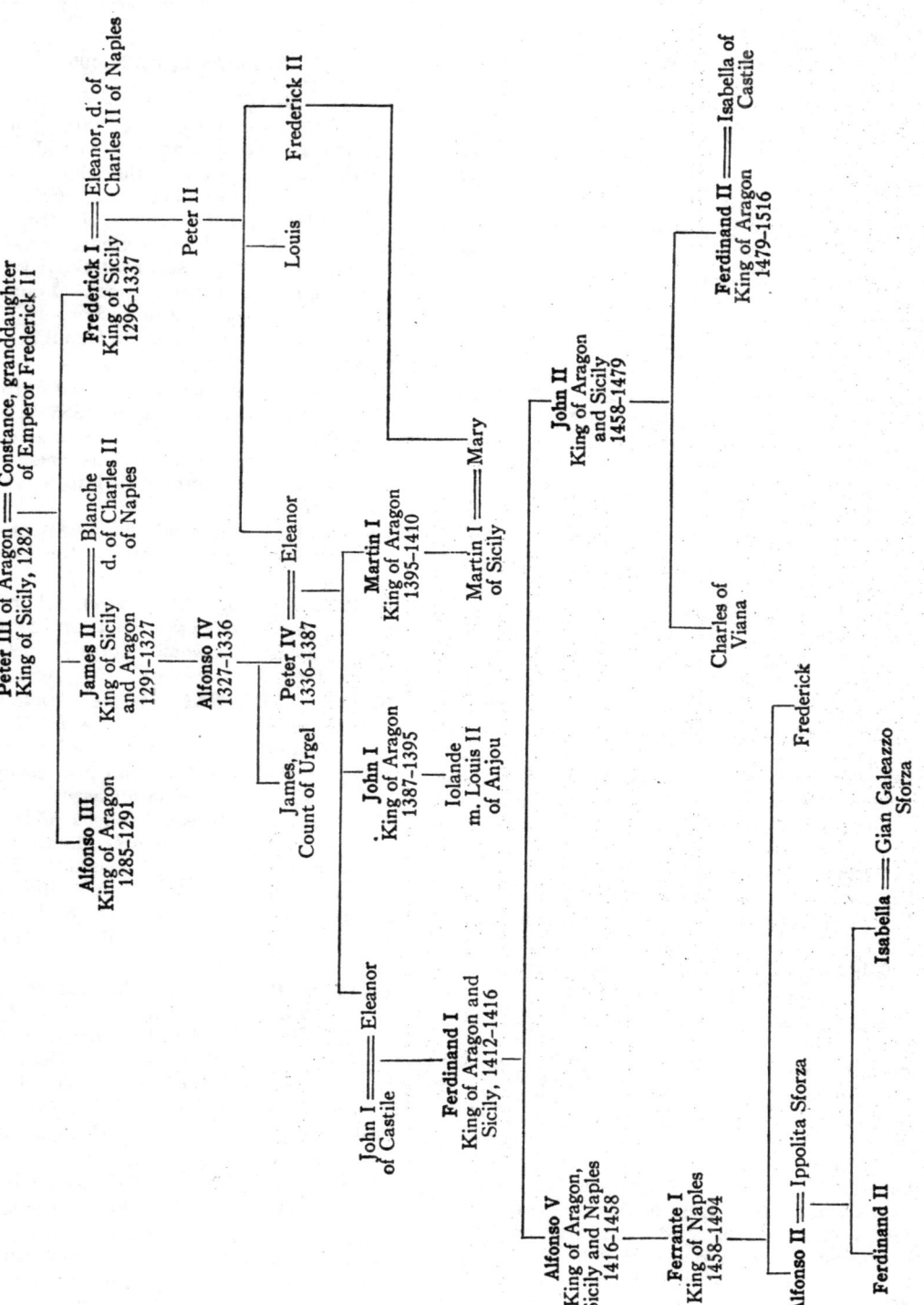

General Privilege which defined the rights and duties of the nobles, affirmed the principle of due process of law, and provided for annual meetings of the Córtes.

1285-1291. ALFONSO III was obliged to make a sweeping regrant of the Privileges of Union (1287), the so-called *Magna Carta of Aragon.*

1291-1327. JAMES II (King of Sicily, 1285-1295). He exchanged the investiture of Sardinia and Corsica for that of Sicily (1295), which thereupon passed to his brother Frederick, who established the separate Sicilian dynasty. James began the expulsion of the Genoese and Pisans from Sardinia (1323-1324), a process not finally completed until 1421. For a period Aragon held the Duchy of Athens (first indirectly through Sicily, 1311-1377, then directly, to 1388), thanks to the activity of the **Grand Catalan Company** (p. 327).

1327-1336. ALFONSO IV.

1336-1387. PETER IV. He was virtually a prisoner of the revived union of the nobility and had to confirm their privileges. But, after a victory over the union (at **Epila,** 1348), he broke up the coalition and gradually restricted the power of the aristocracy in Aragon and Valencia. The clergy and the towns had far less power than in Castile, while the rural workers and serfs suffered a much harder lot.

1377. On the death of Frederick III of Sicily, Peter IV, as the husband of Frederick's sister, sent his son Martin as viceroy to Sicily.

1387-1395. John, king.

1395-1410. Martin, king. He reunited Aragon and Sicily (1409). On his death the native dynasty came to an end.

1410-1416. Ferdinand I, of Castile, a grandson of Peter IV, succeeded to the throne.

1416-1458. ALFONSO V (*the Magnanimous*). His attention was engrossed by the desire to conquer Naples. After long diplomatic intrigues and occasional combats, he succeeded (1435), being recognized as king by the pope in 1442. Alfonso, a lover of Italy and passionate *dévoté* of the Renaissance, shifted the center of gravity of the Aragonese Empire and subordinated the interest of Aragon to that of Naples. Aragon was ruled by his brother John, as viceroy. On the death of Alfonso, Naples passed to his son Ferrante (1458-1494).

1458-1479. John II, king.

1479-1516. FERDINAND II, king. **Union of Aragon with Castile.** (*Cont. p.* 393.)

(3) *Portugal, 1279-1495*

1279-1325. DINIZ (*the Worker*), the best-known and best-loved king of mediaeval Portugal. An ardent poet, he did much to raise the cultural level of the court. His interest in agriculture and constant effort toward economic development (commercial treaty with England, 1294) resulted in greater prosperity. Beginning of **Portuguese naval activity** (under Venetian and Genoese guidance). Foundation (1290) of the University of Lisbon, which was soon (1308) moved to Coimbra.

1325-1357. ALFONSO IV (*the Brave*), whose reign was scarred by dynastic troubles. The **murder of Inez de Castro** (1355), the mistress and later the wife of Alfonso's son Peter, at the behest of Alfonso. This episode, the subject of much literature, led to a revolt of Peter.

1340. The Portuguese, in alliance with Castile, defeated the Moors in the **battle of Salado.**

1357-1367. PETER I (*the Severe*), a harsh and hasty, though just ruler, who continued his predecessors' efforts in behalf of the general welfare.

1367-1383. FERDINAND I (*the Handsome*), a weak ruler whose love for Leonora Telles led him to repudiate his betrothal to a Castilian princess and so bring on a war with Castile.

1383. Regency of Queen Leonora in behalf of Ferdinand's daughter, Beatrice, who was married to John I of Castile. This arrangement led to strong opposition among the Portuguese, who detested both the regent and her lover and resented all control from outside.

1385-1433. JOHN I, an illegitimate son of Peter I, established the **Avis dynasty** after leading a successful revolt and driving the regent out of the country. He was proclaimed king by the Córtes of Coimbra, but his position was at once challenged by the Castilians, who twice invaded Portugal and besieged Lisbon.

1385, Aug. 14. THE BATTLE OF ALJUBAR-ROTA, in which the Portuguese defeated the Castilians. A decisive date in the history of the country, this battle established the independence of Portugal beyond all possibility of challenge. With the Avis dynasty Portugal entered upon the greatest period of her history. The king himself was an able and enlightened ruler, who enjoyed the aid of five outstanding sons, of whom **Henry the Navigator** (1394–1460) became the greatest figure in the history of the epoch-making discoveries of the 15th century (p. 369).

1386, May 9. **The Treaty of Windsor,** by which England and Portugal became permanently allied. King John married Philippa, the daughter of John of Gaunt. The dynasty thereby became part English.

1411. **Peace was finally concluded with Castile.**

1415, Aug. 24. The Portuguese took **Ceuta** from the Moors, thus initiating a policy of expansion on the African mainland.

1433-1438. **Edward** (Duarte) **I,** a learned and intelligent prince, eldest son of John. His short reign was marked by a terrific epidemic of the plague and by

1437. **The disaster at Tangier,** where the Portuguese were overwhelmingly defeated. They were obliged to promise to return Ceuta, and to leave in Moorish hands the youngest brother of the king, **Ferdinand** (*the Constant*

Kings of Portugal

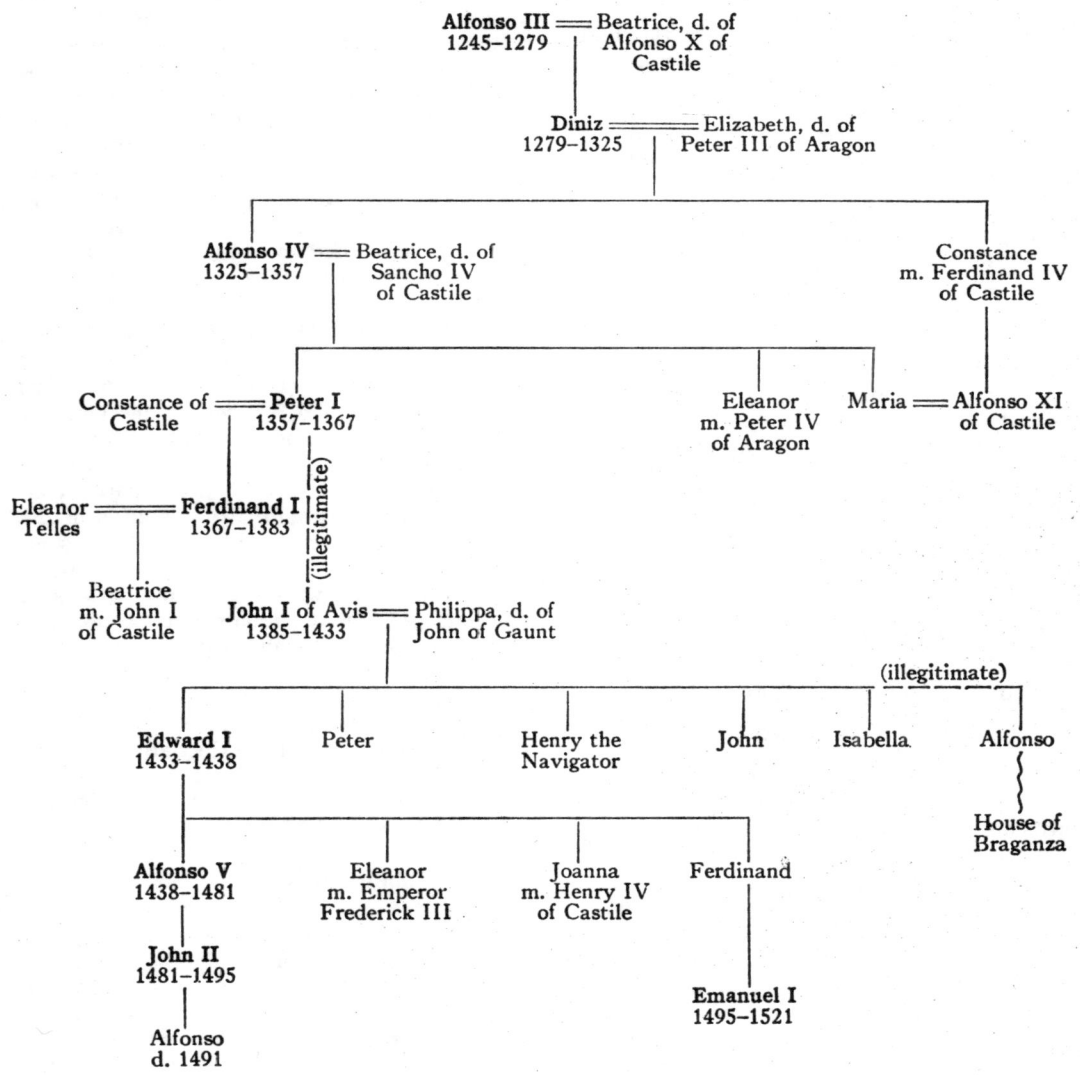

Prince), who died in captivity after five years of suffering. Ceuta was not returned.

1437-1481. ALFONSO V (*the African*), an attractive and chivalrous ruler, but lacking the hard-headed realism of his predecessors. The reign began with the regency of the king's mother, Eleonora, a Spanish princess, who again was confronted with Portuguese opposition to a Spanish connection. The nobility revolted, the regent fled, and the king's uncle, Peter, was made regent. His able and enlightened rule came to an end when the king, having reached his majority, allowed himself to be persuaded by favorites to make war on Peter. The latter and his son were defeated and killed in the **battle of Alfarrobeira** (1449).

1446. The Ordenaçoes Affonsinas, the first great law code of the Portuguese, representing an amalgam of Roman, Visigothic, and customary law.

1463. Campaigns against the Kingdom of Fez. The Portuguese captured Casablanca and

1471. Tangiers.

1476. Battle of Toro. Defeat of the Portuguese by the Castilians, after Alfonso, who had married a sister of Isabella, attempted to dispute the latter's succession to the throne.

1481-1495. JOHN II, an energetic prince who at once undertook to restrict the property and power of the nobility, which had become very great during the preceding reign. This led to a revolt of the nobles, led by **Ferdinand of Braganza** and supported by the Catholic Kings of Castile and Aragon. The revolt was suppressed in 1483; Braganza and many of his followers were executed. The royal power thenceforth was more firmly established than ever before. (*Cont. p.* 396.)

d. ITALY AND THE PAPACY

(1) *The Papacy*, 1305-1492

1305-1378. THE AVIGNONESE PAPACY (*Babylonian Captivity*): during seven pontificates the popes, exiled from the spiritual capital of the west, preferred to contend against the pressure of the French crown rather than face the disorder of Rome and Italy.

1310-1313. Expedition of the Emperor Henry VII to Italy (p. 305). Henry asserted his independence of the spiritual power and claimed control of Italy. Clement V and Philip IV (opposed to him as a rival of the Angevins) combined against him.

1316-1334. JOHN XXII, who supported the Angevins in Naples. His attempt to decide the validity of Emperor Louis IV's title led to a long struggle (1323-1347). Louis was supported by the German people, who resented the Avignonese papacy, and by the Franciscans. John was unable to return to Italy because of the continued anarchy.

1334-1342. Benedict XII, and

1342-1352. CLEMENT VI, whose pontificate was marked by the

1347. REVOLUTION OF COLA DI RIENZI at Rome. With the support of the populace, Cola overthrew the rule of the patricians, set himself up as tribune of the people and summoned an Italian national parliament. Expelled by his opponents (1348), he returned in 1352 and was appointed senator by the pope (1354), but was in the same year slain by his baronial opponents. The lords of the Papal States resumed control and were, to all intents and purposes, independent of papal authority.

1352-1362. INNOCENT VI. He sent the Spanish cardinal, Albornoz, to Italy and the latter succeeded in reducing the powerful barons to obedience, thus making possible an eventual return of the pope.

REFORM OF THE CURIA during the Avignon period. General work of centralization and departmentalization: (1) the *camera apostolica*; (2) the chancery; (3) justice; (4) the penitentiary (punishments and dispensations). Centralization put important clerical appointments throughout Europe under direct papal control through an extraordinary extension of the papal rights of reservation and provision; made a virtual end of local elections, filled ecclesiastical offices with aliens and strangers, and outraged public opinion everywhere. A parallel reorganization and departmentalization of the papal financial administration led to a new efficiency in the levy and collection of papal taxes, fees, etc., which bore hard on the clergy, and drained large sums from the national states, stirring public opinion still further, especially in England. Significant items of the budget of John XXII: war, 63.7%; upkeep and entertainment, 12.7%; alms, 7.16%; 0.4% stables; 0.33% art; library, 0.17%.

Vying with the growing magnificence of the monarchies of Europe, the Avignonese popes and cardinals became proverbial for their pomp and luxury, and these tendencies spread to the episcopate despite the thunders of the Franciscans and the decrees of local synods. The insubordination of outraged reformers like the

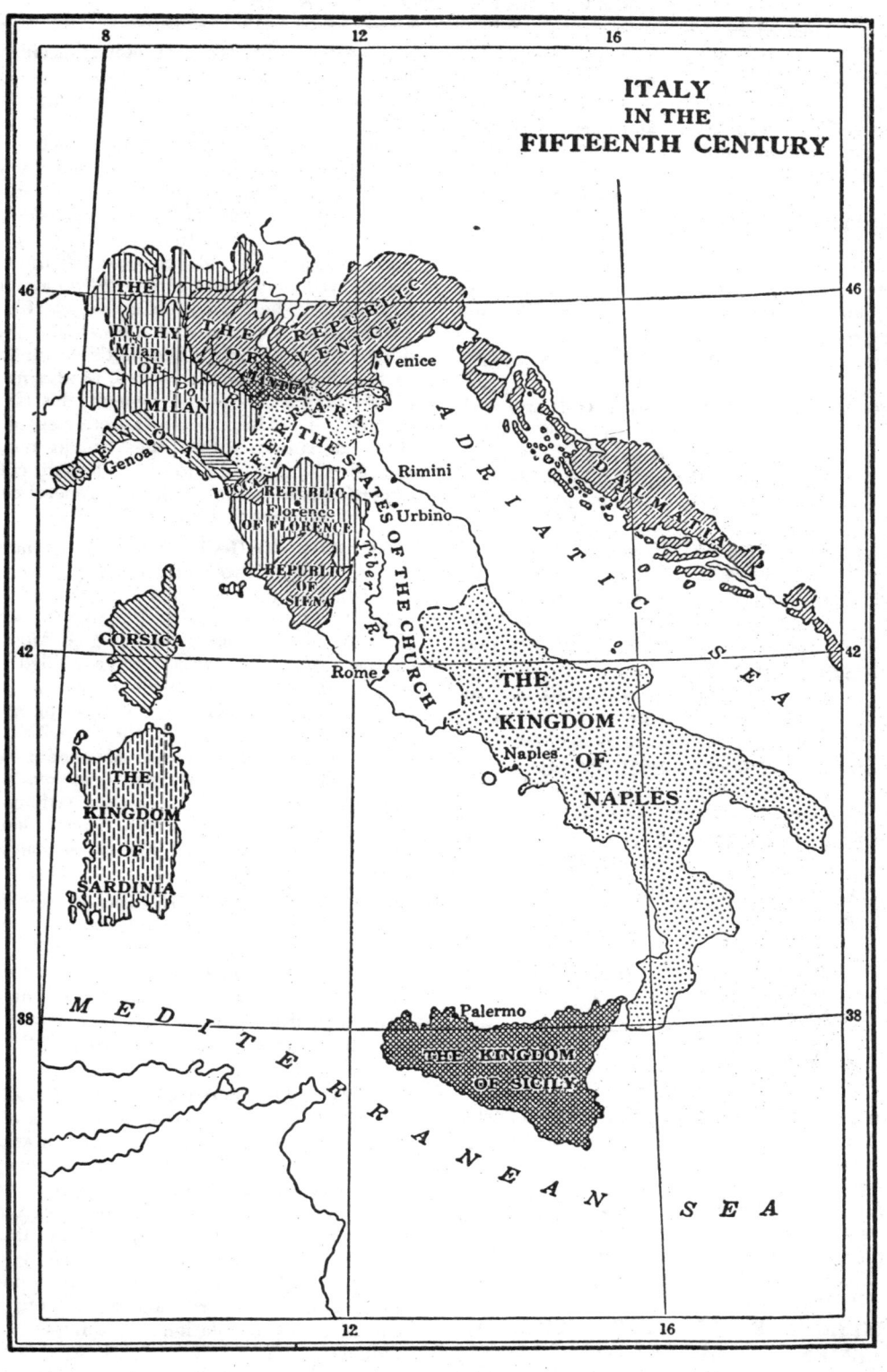

ITALY
IN THE
FIFTEENTH CENTURY

THE
DUCHY
OF
Milan •
MILAN

Genoa

LUC

REPUBLIC
Florence •
OF FLORENCE

REPUBLIC
OF
SIENA

CORSICA

THE
KINGDOM
OF
SARDINIA

THE REPUBLIC OF VENICE

Venice

FERRARA

THE STATES OF THE CHURCH

Rimini •

• Urbino

Tiber R.

Rome •

DALMATIA

ADRIATIC SEA

THE
KINGDOM
OF
NAPLES

Naples

MEDITERRANEAN SEA

Palermo
THE KINGDOM OF SICILY

8   12   16

46   46

42   42

38   38

12   16

Fraticelli, the Bohemian preachers, and **Wiclif** soon penetrated to the masses.

Virtually every pope (notably Clement V and John XXII) made serious and honest efforts to combat these alarming developments, but the general anarchy in Europe made success impossible. There was a notable **expansion of missions to the Far East:** China (an archbishop and ten suffragans, 1312; fifty Franciscan houses, 1314; missions to Persia). Rome, the ancient spiritual center of the west, was reduced to an anarchic, poverty-stricken, provincial city, and clamored for the return of the popes. Petrarch's extreme denunciations of the Avignonese popes had little justification.

1362-1370. URBAN V. Return to Rome with the co-operation of Emperor Charles IV; the city a dismal ruin; return to Avignon on the entreaties of the cardinals (a majority of whom were French).

1370-1378. GREGORY XI visited Rome and died before he could leave. The conclave, under threat of personal violence from the Roman mob, yielded to demands for an Italian pope, electing

1378-1389. URBAN VI, a blunt, avaricious man, who alienated the cardinals by announcing that his reform of the Church would begin with the Sacred College.

1378-1417. THE GREAT SCHISM: the papacy divided and dishonored. Thirteen cardinals, meeting at Anagni, elected

1378-1394. CLEMENT VII, thus dividing western Christendom into obediences:

The Roman Line	The Avignonese Line
Urban VI	Clement VII
(1378–1389)	(1378–1394)
Boniface IX	Benedict XIII
(1389–1404)	(1394–1423)
Innocent VII	
(1404–1406)	
Gregory XII	
(1406–1415)	

Allegiance to the rivals was determined partly by practical considerations, but often was settled after careful study of the claims of each and consultation with the clergy (e.g. King Charles V of France, John of Castile); England's decision was based largely on hostility to France; Scotland's on its hostility to England; in Naples and Sicily the rulers and their subjects took opposite positions.

EMERGENCE OF THE CONCILIAR MOVEMENT: The basic ideas were inherent in such writers as **Marsiglio of Padua;** specific arguments that a general council is superior to a pope, can be called by a king, and is competent to judge a pope or call a new conclave, were advanced in 1379 (**Henry of Langenstein**) and from then on grew in importance. King Charles VI of France (influenced by the University of Paris) called a **national synod** (1395), which voted overwhelmingly to urge the resignation of both popes. The Avignonese cardinals approved with only one negative; the popes refused to resign. The French clergy voted (1398) to withhold papal taxes and dues, and were endorsed by the king. Benedict's cardinals deserted him in panic and he fled, producing a reaction of public opinion against the King of France. Two Roman popes were elected with the understanding that they would resign if Benedict XIII would do so. The two colleges of cardinals joined in a call for a general council to meet at Pisa, 1409.

1409. THE COUNCIL OF PISA: attended by 500 prelates and delegates from the states of Europe. Two parties: (1) a moderate majority with the sole aim of ending the schism; (2) radical reformers (including d'Ailly and Gerson from Paris), who were compelled to accept postponement of reform to a council supposed to meet in 1412. After hearing specific charges against both popes, the council deposed both. The conclave chose **Alexander V** (d. 1410) and then the ecclesiastical *condottiere*, Cardinal Baldassare Cossa, a man without spiritual qualities. Neither the Roman nor the Avignonese pope resigned, and the schism was a triple one.

1410-1415. JOHN XXIII, expelled from Rome by Ladislas of Naples, was forced by the Emperor Sigismund to issue a call for the **Council of Constance** (1414) in return for protection. This marked the passing of the initiative in reform from the King of France to the Roman Emperor, a return in theory to the days of the Ottos.

1414-1417. THE COUNCIL OF CONSTANCE: one of the greatest assemblies of mediaeval history; three aims: (1) **restoration of unity to the Church;** (2) **reform in head and members;** (3) **extirpation of heresy,** particularly the Hussite heresy (p. 309). Following university practice, voting was by nations and the numbers of the Italian prelates did no good to Pope John. John, seeing a chance to divide the council and the emperor, allowed the imprisonment of Hus (in violation of the imperial safe-conduct).

Hus, heard three times by the whole council (and cleverly induced to expand his doctrine that sin vitiates a clerical office to include civil office as well), lost Sigismund's support, was condemned and executed (1415) as was his companion, Jerome of Prague (1416).

John XXII, having agreed to resign if his rivals did so, fled the council, was brought back, tried, and deposed (1415); **Gregory XII** resigned (1415); Sigismund, unable to induce Benedict XIII to resign, won away his supporters, and isolated him. Reform was again postponed, but two decrees are significant: *Sacrosancta* (1415), asserting that a council is superior to a pope; and *Frequens* (1417) providing for stated meetings of general councils.

The conclave elected Cardinal Colonna as Martin V. Christendom ignored the obstinate Benedict, and the schism was over.

1417-1431. MARTIN V (Colonna), a Roman of Romans, declared it impious to appeal to a general council against a pope and dissolved the **Council of Constance.** Evasion of general reform and the threat of general councils supported by powerful monarchs, through the negotiation of concordats with the heads of states (i.e. by dealing with the bishops through lay rulers, a complete negation of the theory of a universal papal absolutism, and a virtual recognition of national churches). **Recovery of the Papal States:** most of the cities were under their own lords who bore *pro forma* titles as papal vicars but were in fact independent. Concentration on Italian political problems at the expense of the universal spiritual interests of Christendom.

1431-1447. EUGENIUS IV, an obstinate Venetian who favored summoning the **Council of Basel.**

1431-1449. THE COUNCIL OF BASEL, dominated by strong anti-papal feeling. Dissolved by Eugenius because of negotiations with the Hussites, the council ignored the order and decreed (with the support of the princes) that no general council can be dissolved without its consent, continued in session, and summoned Eugenius and the cardinals to attend. Eugenius ignored the summons, but was forced (1433) to accept the council. Temporary compromise with the Hussites registered in the *Compactata.* **Reforms voted:** abolition of commendations, reservations, appeals to Rome, annates, etc.; provision for regular provincial and diocesan synods; confirmation of the right of chapter elections; appeal from a general council to a pope pronounced heresy. Already divided over these re-

forms, the council split over reunion with the Greek Church. Eugenius and his cardinals ignored a second summons, were pronounced contumacious; Eugenius dissolved the council and called another to meet at Ferrara; the papalists left Basel. The rump council continued to meet, deposed Eugenius (1439), elected Amadeus of Savoy,

1440-1449. FELIX V, because he could pay his own way. Moved to Lausanne, the council continued with dwindling numbers and prestige.

1438-1445. THE COUNCIL OF FERRARA-FLORENCE (under the presidency of Eugenius). After months of futile discussion (over the *filioque* question, unleavened bread at the sacrament, purgatory, and papal supremacy), the Greeks were forced to accept the Roman formula for union (1439) and the schism between east and west, dating from 1054, was technically healed. As the Greeks at home repudiated the union, it was of no effect. Isidore of Kiev and Bessarion remained as cardinals of the Roman Church.

1438. A French national synod and King Charles VII accepted the *Pragmatic Sanction of Bourges* embodying most of the anti-papal decrees of the Council of Basel (basis for the Gallican Liberties). The *Pragmatic* checked the drain of money from France to the papacy.

1439. The Diet of Mainz accepted the *Pragmatic Sanction of Mainz,* abolishing annates, papal reservations, provisions, and providing for diocesan and provincial synods.

Aeneas Sylvius Piccolomini, sent to win Germany back for the papacy, came to an agreement with Emperor Frederick III on such cynical terms that the German princes flocked to Felix V, but a provisional concordat, embodying the *Pragmatic of* 1439 enabled Aeneas Sylvius to detach the princes one by one.

1448. Concordat of Vienna, Eugenius' greatest triumph, accepted the supremacy of a general council, but restored the annates and abandoned most of the restrictions on papal patronage.

1449. Dissolution of the Council of Basel: abdication of Felix V (who became a cardinal). Papal celebration of the triumph over the conciliar movement in the **Jubilee of 1450.** Postponement of moderate reform made the radical Reformation of the 16th century inevitable.

1447-1455. NICHOLAS V, former librarian of Cosimo de' Medici, scholar, humanist, collector of manuscripts, founder of the **Vatican**

Library. Rome temporarily a center of humanism: Nicholas' circle included: **Poggio Bracciolini, Alberti,** and **Lorenzo Valla** (a scientific humanist and critic who had just demolished the *Donation of Constantine* as a forgery). Plans for a new St. Peter's.

1453. The Turkish capture of Constantinople (p. 331) ended the Greek Empire of the East and removed all serious rivalry by the patriarch to the position of the Roman pope.

1455-1468. CALIXTUS III (an Aragonese), an aged invalid, anti-humanist, energetic supporter of war against the Turk, an ardent nepotist (three Borgia nephews, one of them later Pope Alexander VI).

1458-1464. PIUS II (Aeneas Sylvius Piccolomini). In his youth a gay dog; in later life austere; most brilliant and versatile of the literary popes, a humanist, lover of nature, eloquent essayist, orator, and Latin stylist. A short, bent man with smiling eyes, a fringe of white hair, seldom free of pain, a tireless worker, always accessible. Advocate of papal supremacy, obstinate foe of conciliar reform. His appeals for a crusade ignored by a preoccupied Europe, he gallantly took the Cross himself to shame the princes of Christendom, and died at Ancona. His family was large and poor and he was a nepotist.

1467-1471. PAUL II, a Venetian, rich, kindly, handsome, a collector of jewels and carvings, founder of the Corso horse-races. A strong centralizer, supporter of the Hungarian crusade. The Turkish victory at **Negroponte** (1470) gave the Turks mastery of Levantine waters.

1471-1484. SIXTUS IV (della Rovere) aimed to consolidate the Papal States and reduce the power of the cardinals; methodical nepotist (three nephews, the Riarios, one of them later Pope Julius II).

1475. Rapprochement with Ferrante of Naples; alienation of the Medici who were replaced as papal bankers by the Pazzi. The Riarios organized with Sixtus' knowledge, if not approval, the **Pazzi Conspiracy** (assassination of Giuliano de' Medici, 1478). This destroyed the alliance of Florence, Naples, Milan, to maintain the Italian balance of power and led to a war involving most of Italy; the war was terminated by the capture of Otranto (1480) and by the diplomacy of Lorenzo de' Medici. Sixtus' coalition with Venice led to the Ferrarese War (1482–1484). Sixtus and Julius II were the great beautifiers of Rome: **Sistine Chapel** (c. 1473), paving

and widening of streets and squares; patronage of **Ghirlandaio, Botticelli, Perugino, Pinturicchio,** *et al.*

1484-1492. INNOCENT VIII, a kindly, handsome Genoese, a compromise cipher, the first pope to recognize his children and to dine publicly with ladies. A baronial revolt (1485–1487) in Naples (supported by Innocent and, *secretly*, by Venice) led to a revival of the Angevin claims to Naples. Florence and Milan, fearing French intervention in Italy, opposed the war, and peace and amnesty were arranged. Ferrante's cynical violation of the amnesty led the exiles (on Ludovico Sforza's advice) to call in King Charles VIII of France. Sforza struck an alliance with Charles to protect Milan and opened the road into Italy to this alien invader (1494). Italy was not again to know full independence from foreign domination until the end of the 19th century.

Girolamo Savonarola (1452–1498), a Dominican, Prior of San Marco in Florence (1491), eloquent reforming preacher and precursor of the Reformation, was already denouncing the new paganism of the Renaissance, the corruption of the state and the papacy, and foretelling the ruin of Italy. *(Cont. p. 401.)*

(2) *Sicily and Naples,* 1268-1494

1268-1285. CHARLES I (Angevin), King of Naples and of Sicily (1268–1282). His grandiose scheme for the creation of a Mediterranean empire in succession to the Byzantine (a revival of the Latin Empire under French auspices) was frustrated by the **Sicilian Vespers** (1282) and the war in Sicily which continued until 1302. Sicily maintained its independence and offered the crown to **Peter III of Aragon** (husband of Constance, heiress of the Hohenstaufen), an ally of Constantinople against Charles. Peter accepted the offer (1282), ejected the Angevins and established the house of Aragon on the throne.

1282- SICILY UNDER ARAGONESE RULE: Peter (1282–1285); **James** (1285–1295). James exchanged the investiture of Sardinia and Corsica for that of Sicily, and Sicily passed to his brother, **Frederick** (1295–1337). Frederick brought to a close the war with Naples (**Peace of Caltabelotta,** 1302), marrying the daughter of Charles I and accepting the stipulation that the Sicilian crown should pass to the Angevins on his death. This agreement was not fulfilled, with the result that the struggle continued until, in 1373, Joanna of Naples abandoned Sicily to the Aragonese in return for tribute. Sicily was

The House of Anjou

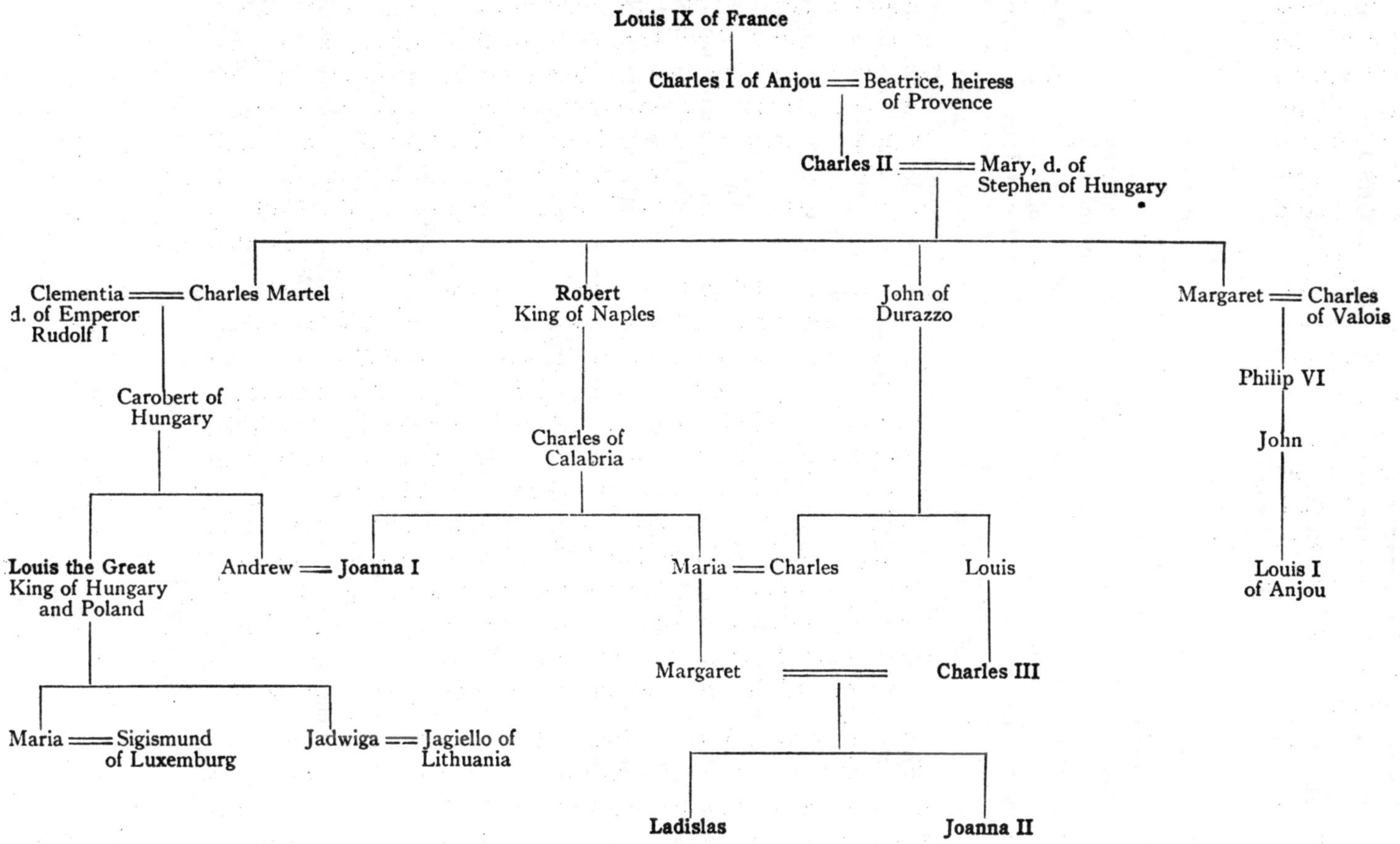

Louis IX of France

Charles I of Anjou == Beatrice, heiress of Provence

Charles II === Mary, d. of Stephen of Hungary

Clementia === **Charles Martel**
d. of Emperor Rudolf I

Robert King of Naples

John of Durazzo

Margaret == Charles of Valois

Carobert of Hungary

Charles of Calabria

Philip VI

John

Andrew == **Joanna I**

Maria == Charles

Louis

Louis I of Anjou

Louis the Great King of Hungary and Poland

Margaret ==

Charles III

Maria == Sigismund of Luxemburg

Jadwiga == Jagiello of Lithuania

Ladislas

Joanna II

ruled as a viceroyalty until the reunion with Aragon in 1409.

1285-1309.   Charles II (Angevin) of Naples.

1309-1343.   Robert (Angevin) of Naples. He was the leader of the Italian Guelfs and, having been appointed imperial vicar on the death of Emperor Henry VII, planned to create an Italian kingdom.

1343-1382.   Joanna I, Queen of Naples.

1382-1386.   Charles III, a grandnephew of Robert.

1386-1414.   Ladislas, son of Charles III, finally succeeded in establishing some measure of order in the kingdom and began a vigorous campaign of expansion in central Italy. In 1409 he bought the States of the Church from Pope Gregory XII, but his designs were blocked by Florence and Siena.

1414-1435.   JOANNA II, sister of Ladislas. The amazing intrigues of this amorous widow with her favorites, successors designate, and rival claimants to the throne kept Italian diplomacy in a turmoil, and culminated in a struggle between **René,** the Angevin claimant (supported by the pope), and **Alfonso V of Aragon** (supported by Filippo Maria Visconti). This conflict ended in the triumph of Alfonso, who secured Naples in 1435 and was recognized as king by the pope in 1442.

1435-1458.   ALFONSO (*the Magnanimous*) reunited the crowns of Naples and Sicily and made Naples the center of his Aragonese Mediterranean empire (p. 288). He supported Filippo Maria Visconti of Milan, who apparently willed his duchy to him on his death. Alfonso avoided arousing Italy by claiming the duchy, but Ferdinand of Aragon later revived the claim. Alfonso's pressure drove Genoa into the arms of France. Loyal to the pope, Alfonso supported Eugenius IV against Francesco Sforza. He centralized the administration, reformed taxation, and arranged a series of dynastic marriages in Italy. But he failed to subdue his barons entirely. He preferred Italy to Aragon, was a passionate *dévoté* of Italian culture and acted as a Renaissance Maecenas, the patron of Lorenzo Valla. The **Academy of Naples** was composed mostly of poets. Alfonso divided his domain, Aragon and Sicily passing to his brother, John, and Naples (correctly called the Kingdom of Sicily) going to his illegitimate son

1458-1494.   FERRANTE (Ferdinand I), one of the most notoriously unscrupulous Renaissance princes. He triumphed in his struggle for the succession with the aid of Francesco Sforza and Cosimo de' Medici (who was alarmed at the presence of the French in Genoa). Ferrante generally supported the triple Italian alliance (p. 299) except for the period 1478–1480.

The Neapolitan Anjous

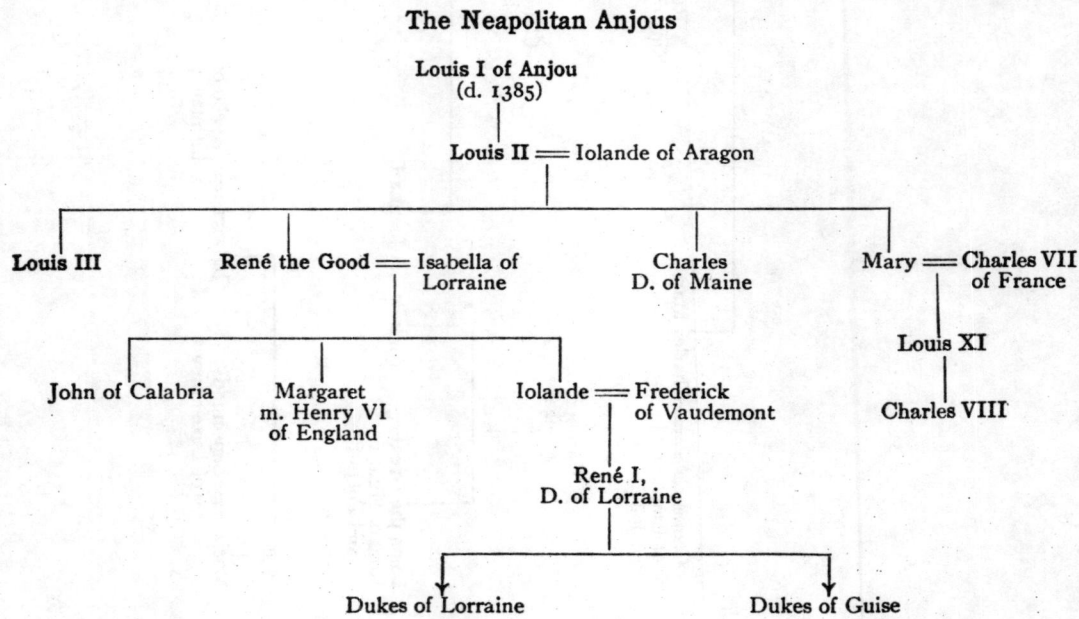

Pope Innocent V, angered at Ferrante's suspension of tribute, supported the Angevin pretender, and Ferrante made a hollow peace until he could crush a baronial revolt. Then, supported by the Colonna and Orsini in Rome, he turned on Innocent, who was saved only by Lorenzo de' Medici. Innocent (1492) guaranteed the succession in Naples. Alexander VI stood by the bargain, and opposed Charles VIII's demand for investiture.

THE CLAIMS OF THE VALOIS KINGS TO NAPLES. Based on (1) the marriage of Margaret (daughter of Charles II of Naples) and Charles of Valois, the parents of King Philip VI; and on (2) the claims of the so-called "second" house of Anjou founded by Duke Louis I (d. 1385) of Anjou, Count of Provence. Louis was grandson of Philip VI, and grandfather of (1) Mary, wife of Charles VII of France, mother of Louis XI; and of (2) Duke Louis III (d. 1434) and his brother René of Lorraine (d. 1486).   (*Cont. p.* 404.)

(3) *Florence, to 1492*

EARLY HISTORY. The **Margraviate of Tuscany,** set up by the Carolingians, extended from the Po to the Roman state under the Margrave Boniface (d. 1052) whose daughter, the great **Countess Matilda** (1052–1115), was probably the strongest papal supporter in Italy. Associated with her in the government was a council of *boni homines*, whose administration during her frequent absences, and after her death, laid the foundation for the emergence of the commune. Florence, already a great commercial center, opposed the Ghibelline hill barons, who preyed on her commerce. The burghers continued Guelf in sympathy; trade and financial connections with France made them Francophil and friendly to Charles of Anjou. Under Matilda the **guild organization** emerged, which came to form the basis of the city government. Control of the government was concentrated in the hands of the great guilds (one of which included the bankers). Consuls appeared after 1138. The populace was divided into two great groups, the *grandi* (nobles) and the *arti* (guilds). Consuls were chosen by the *grandi*.

On the breakup of the margraviate following Matilda's death, Florence began her advance, and by 1176 was master of the dioceses of Florence and Fiesole. The institution of the *podestate* after 1202 was favored by the feudal elements and the lesser guilds. Intermittent rivalry of the noble houses continued. Wars were fought with Pisa, Lucca, Pistoia, Siena. Under the *podestà* the commune developed a strong organization paralleled by the growth of the *popolo* under its *capitano*.

The great struggle of **Guelf and Ghibelline** was reflected in Florentine civil strife. After a Guelf régime, Frederick of Antioch (son of Frederick II) as imperial vicar instituted the first mass expulsion in Florentine history by driving out the Guelfs (1249).

1252. **The first gold florin** was coined, and soon became the standard gold coin of Europe.

1260. **Siena,** with the aid of Manfred and the Florentine Ghibellines, inflicted a great defeat on the Florentine Guelfs (**Montaperti**), beginning a Ghibelline dominance which lasted until Manfred's death (1266). This was followed by a reaction, and the expulsion of the Ghibellines. Under the Ghibelline régime the *popolo* lost all share in the government.

In the reaction following the Ghibelline régime, Ghibelline property was confiscated to support persecution of the Ghibellines. Under Charles of Anjou the formulae of the old constitution were restored; the party struggle continued. The Sicilian Vespers (1282) weakened Charles, strengthened the commune, and the Florentine "republic" became in effect a commercial oligarchy in the hands of the greater guilds.

1282. By the **Law of 1282** nobles could participate in the government only by joining a guild. The last traces of serfdom were abolished (1289) and the number of guilds increased to 21 (7 greater, 14 lesser).

1293. **The Ordinance of 1293** excluded from the guilds anyone not actively practicing his profession, and thus in effect removed the nobles from all share in the government.

Two factions arose: the Blacks (*Neri*), extreme Guelfs led by Corso Donati; **the Whites** (*Bianchi*), moderate Guelfs (and later Ghibellines) under Vieri Cerchi. The Neri favored repeal of the Ordinance of 1293.

Emperor Henry VII was unable to capture Florence, but

1320-1323. **Castruccio Castracani,** Lord of Lucca, humiliated the city in the field. Growing financial troubles, partly the result of Edward III's repudiation of his debts to the Florentine bankers, culminated in the failures of the Peruzzi (1343) and Bardi (1344), and damaged Florentine banking prestige. The government was discredited and civil war ensued. **Walter of Brienne** (Duke of Athens) was called in, reformed the government, began a usurpation, and was expelled (1343). The restored commune was under the domination of the business men who had three objectives: access to the sea (hence hostility to Pisa), expansion in Tuscany (to dominate the trade roads), and support of the popes (to retain papal banking business). Social conflict continued and grew as the oligarchy gained power and the Guelfs opposed the increasing industrial proletariat. The lesser guilds were pushed into the background, the unguilded were worse off. The first social revolt came in 1345.

1347-1348. Famine followed by the **Black Death** reduced the population seriously, but recovery was rapid.

1351. The commutation of military service for cash marked the decline of citizen militia and the golden age of the *condottieri*. War with Milan resulted (1351) from Giovanni Visconti's attempt to reduce Florence and master Tuscany.

1375-1378. Papal efforts to annex Tuscany led Florence into a temporary alliance with Milan.

1378. Continued pressure by Guelf extremists to exclude the lesser guilds, led to a series of violent explosions. **Salvestro de' Medici,** Gonfalonier, ended the *admonitions* which were the basis of the Guelf terrorism, and a violent **revolt of the** *ciompi* (the poorest workmen) broke out. The *ciompi* made temporary gains, but Salvestro was exiled, and by 1382 the oligarchy was back in the saddle and even *admonitions* were revived.

FLORENTINE CULTURE: Precursors of the Renaissance. (1) **Dante** (1265-1321): *Vita Nuova,* in the Tuscan vernacular; the *Divine Comedy,* a brilliant poetic synthesis of mediaeval ideas and culture which established Tuscan as the literary vernacular of Italy; *De Vulgare Eloquentia,* a defense of the vernacular, written in Latin. **Petrarch** (1304-1374), of Florentine origin, greatest of Italian lyrists, brilliant Latinist, the first great humanist; he never mastered Greek. Interested in every aspect of humanity, a lover of nature, a universal mind. **Boccaccio** (1313-1375), friend of Petrarch, knew both Greek and Latin, the first modern student of Tacitus, collector of classical manuscripts, first lecturer on Dante (1373). His *Decameron,* an epitome of bourgeois sophistication. Founder of Italian prose. **Giotto** (1276-1337), architect (employed on the cathedral), sculptor, painter, revealing Renaissance tendencies. **Villani** (d. 1348), *Chronicle* with clear bourgeois elements. **Chrysoloras** (called from Constantinople) the first public lecturer on Greek in the west (1396-1400); he had many famous humanists as pupils.

1382-1432. A half-century of oligarchic domination in Florentine politics, in many ways the zenith of Florentine power. Constitutional reform (1382) broadened popular participation in government, but nothing much was done for the *ciompi,* and sporadic revolts continued as the Guelfs slowly regained power.

1393. **Maso degli Albizzi's** long control of the government began with the exile or disenfranchisement of the Alberti and their supporters. Capitalism had destroyed the guild organization as a vital political force, and Albizzi ruled for the advantage of his own house and the *Arte della Lana* (wool) with which he was associated. Democratic elements in the state had vanished.

1397-1398. Florence resisted the Visconti advance into Tuscany.

1405. **Pisa was bought** and reduced to obedience (1406), giving Florence direct access to the sea. Leghorn was purchased (1421) and the *Consuls of the Sea* established. Filippo Maria Visconti's drive into Tuscany led Florence to declare war. The peace party was led by **Giovanni de' Medici,** a wool dealer and international banker, probably Italy's richest man. Several defeats of Florence were accompanied by a decline of Florentine credit and a number of serious bankruptcies. Alliance with Venice and defeat of the Visconti, who accepted peace on onerous terms (1429); Venice monopolized the gains of the war.

1427. **Taxation reform,** the *catasto,* an income tax intended to be of general and democratic incidence, supported (?) by the Medici.

1433. The fiasco of the war on Lucca (1429-1433) led to Cosimo (son of Giovanni) de' Medici's imprisonment as a scapegoat, and his sentence to ten-year exile. The next election to the Signory favored the Medici, and Cosimo was recalled (1434). Rinaldo degli Albizzi, Rodolfo Peruzzi, *et al.,* were in turn exiled, and the Medici dominance in Florence began, opening three centuries of close identity between the fortunes of the family and those of Florence. Cosimo, without holding office, dominated the government, determining who should hold office.

1434-1494. DOMINATION OF THE MEDICI.

1434-1464. COSIMO (*Pater Patriae*).

1440. Florence and Venice in alliance defeated Filippo Maria Visconti at **Anghiari.** The *castato* was replaced by a progressive income

The Medici Family

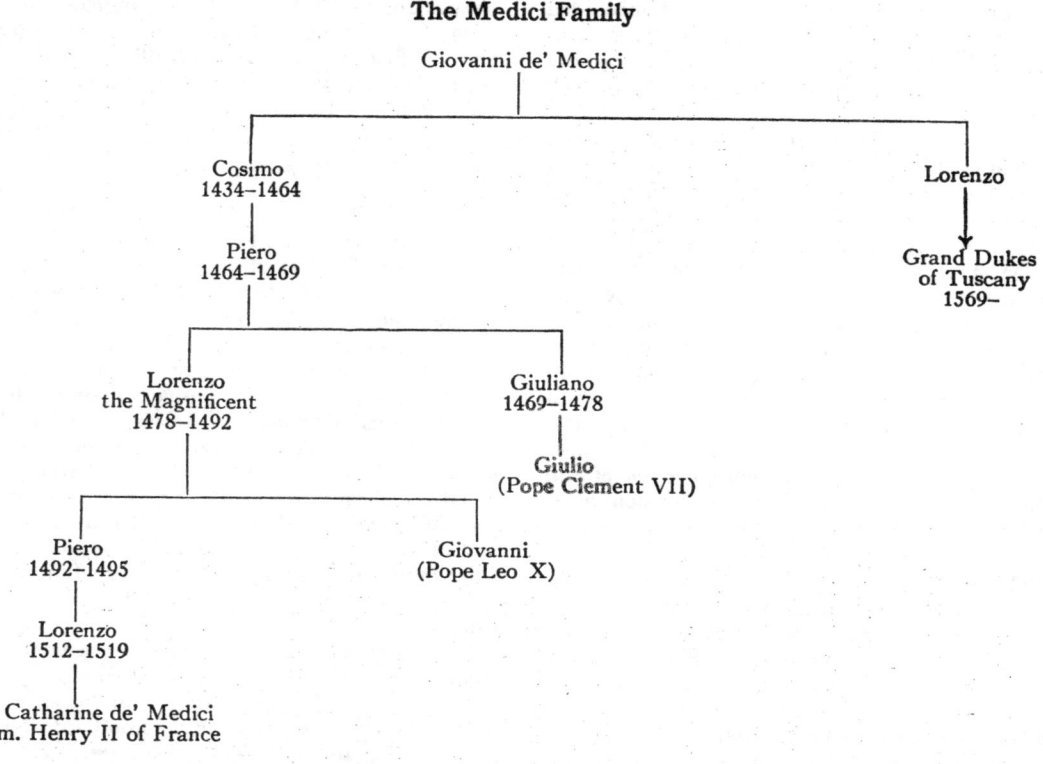

Giovanni de' Medici

Cosimo
1434–1464

Lorenzo

Piero
1464–1469

Grand Dukes
of Tuscany
1569–

Lorenzo
the Magnificent
1478–1492

Giuliano
1469–1478

Giulio
(Pope Clement VII)

Piero
1492–1495

Giovanni
(Pope Leo X)

Lorenzo
1512–1519

Catharine de' Medici
m. Henry II of France

tax designed to lighten the burdens of the poor (i.e. the Medici adherents). Cosimo supported Francesco Sforza's contest for the Duchy of Milan and aided him in his war with Venice. For commercial reasons he favored France, but backed Ferrante of Naples against the Angevin claims. He was thus the real creator of the **triple alliance** of Florence, Milan, and Naples in the interest of the Italian equilibrium and security.

1464-1469. Piero the Gouty, son of Cosimo, a semi-invalid who was opposed by Luca Pitti.

1469-1478. Lorenzo and Giuliano de' Medici, and

1478-1492. LORENZO DE' MEDICI (*the Magnificent*) alone. Lorenzo continued the general policy of Cosimo. He enjoyed the power and prestige of a prince, though he had neither the title nor the office. His marriage to Clarice Orsini was the first princely marriage of the Medici.

1471. Lorenzo's effort to conciliate Pope Sixtus IV netted him a confirmation of the Medici banking privileges and the appointment as receiver of the papal revenues.

1474. Pope Sixtus and Ferrante of Naples were asked to join the alliance of Florence, Venice, and Milan (concluded in 1474), but Ferrante, feeling isolated, and Sixtus, angered at Lorenzo's opposition to his nephews, the Riarios, drew together. Italy became divided into two camps. The Pazzi family, rivals of the Medici, were given the lucrative position as receivers of the papal revenues.

1478. The Pazzi Plot. The Riarios (apparently not without Sixtus' knowledge), plotted to have Lorenzo and Giuliano assassinated in the cathedral at Easter mass. Giuliano was killed, Lorenzo wounded. The Medici almost exterminated the Pazzi and hounded the fugitives all over Italy. Sixtus laid an interdict on Florence, excommunicated Lorenzo; Alfonso of Calabria invaded Tuscany. Venice and Milan stood by Florence, Louis XI sent Commines as his representative. Ferrante engineered a Milanese revolt, the Turks diverted Venice at Scutari, plague broke out. Desperate, Lorenzo visited Ferrante (the cruelest and most cynical despot in Italy), and by his charm and the threat of a revival of Angevin claims, arranged (1480) a peace. Florence suffered considerable losses, but Lorenzo was a popular hero and succeeded in establishing the *Council of Seventy*, a completely Medici organ, the instrument of *de facto* despotism, but a source of real stability in government.

Lorenzo's brilliant foreign policy was costly; he had neglected the family business, and apparently used some of the state money for Medici purposes; he also debased the coinage. Florentine prosperity, under the pressure of rivals, heavy taxation, and business depression, was declining. Nonetheless, Lorenzo, the leading statesman of his day, brought a twelve-year calm before the storm to Italy, resuming the Medici alliance with Naples and Milan to balance the papacy and Venice, and to keep a united front against alien invasion. Florence, on good terms with Charles VIII, regained most of her Tuscan losses. **Savonarola,** Prior of San Marco (1491), had already begun his denunciations of Florentine corruption and his attacks on Lorenzo (p. 294).

1492. PIERO succeeded Lorenzo on his death. Son of an Orsini mother, married to an Orsini, he supported Naples, angered Florence, and threw Ludovico Sforza into alliance with the Neapolitan exiles who summoned Charles VIII.

1494. Charles' invasion began the age-long subjugation of Italy to alien invaders who dominated the national evolution until 1870. Piero, alarmed at public opinion, fled the city.

Florence, center of the Italian Renaissance. For over a century the Medici were the greatest patrons of the Renaissance, and led the rich bourgeoisie of Florence in fostering the most brilliant development of culture since the days of Pericles. **Cosimo** was an enthusiastic patron of manuscript collectors, copyists, and humanists, established the **library of San Marco** and the **Medici library.** The Council of Ferrara-Florence sat in Florence (1439) and brought a number of learned Greeks who stimulated Platonic studies in Florence. Under Cosimo's auspices **Ficino** was trained to make his great translation of Plato (still ranked high) and the **Platonic Academy** was founded. **Lorenzo,** a graceful poet (carnival songs, etc.), ardent champion of the vernacular, and lover of the countryside, a generous patron, drew about him a brilliant circle. He continued the support of Ficino. Florentine leadership in Renaissance: (1) **painting: Massaccio** (1401–1429?), **Botticelli** (1444–1510), **Leonardo da Vinci** (1452–1519) (sculptor and polymath); (2) **architecture: Brunelleschi** (1377–1446); **Alberti** (1405–1471); (3) **sculpture: Donatello** (c. 1378–1455), **Ghiberti** (1386–1466)

Verocchio (1435–1488); **Michelangelo** (1475–1564) (also painter, poet, architect); (4) **history and political theory: Machiavelli** (1469–1527); **Guicciardini** (1485–1540); (5) **romantic poetry: Pulci** (1432–c. 1487). *(Cont. p. 404.)*

(4) *Milan, to 1500*

EARLY HISTORY. Milan, ancient center of the agriculture of the Lombard Plain, self-sufficient in food, master of important passes (Brenner, Splügen, St. Gothard) of the Alps, was for a long time surpassed in wealth only by Venice.

Establishment of Pavia as the Lombard capital (569). Emergence of Milan as the center of Italian opposition in the Lombard Plain to alien and heretical domination. Rise of the archbishop as defender of native liberty and orthodoxy laid the basis for the evolution of archepiscopal temporal power (military, administrative, judicial) exercised through his viscounts. The end of Lombard domination (774), followed by Carolingian destruction of the great Lombard fiefs, strengthened the episcopal power still further.

The spirit of municipal independence emerged from intense rivalries for the archepiscopal see and the necessities of defense; Milan became an island of safety and justice in the Lombard Plain, a populous, self-sufficient, city-state. Under **Archbishop Heribert** (1018–1045) the *carroccio* (arc of municipal patriotism) was set up; expansion in the Lombard Plain began (reduction of Lodi, Como, Pavia). The moat was dug after Emperor Frederick I's destruction (1162); the city was rebuilt by its allies Bergamo, Brescia, Mantua, and Verona. (For the Lombard League and the wars with Frederick, see p. 221.) Rapid growth, extension of the walls (after 1183). Chief industry armor manufacturing and the wool trade, later silk manufacture; irrigation made the plain productive.

Government: (1) *Parlamento* (*consiglio grande*) (membership successively reduced to 2000, 1500, 800). (2) *Credenza,* a committee of twelve for urgent and secret business. (3) *Consuls* (the executive) elected for a year, responsible to the assembly.

Rise of the Della Torre and the Visconti. Bitter warfare between populace and nobles led to the rise of two great families, the Della Torre (lords of the tower, i.e. castle) and the Visconti (i.e. the viscounts).

1237–1277. Rule of the (Guelf) **DELLA TORRE.** Martino established the *catasta,* a tax of democratic and uniform incidence. The title *signore,* i.e. Lord of Milan, established

Rulers of Milan

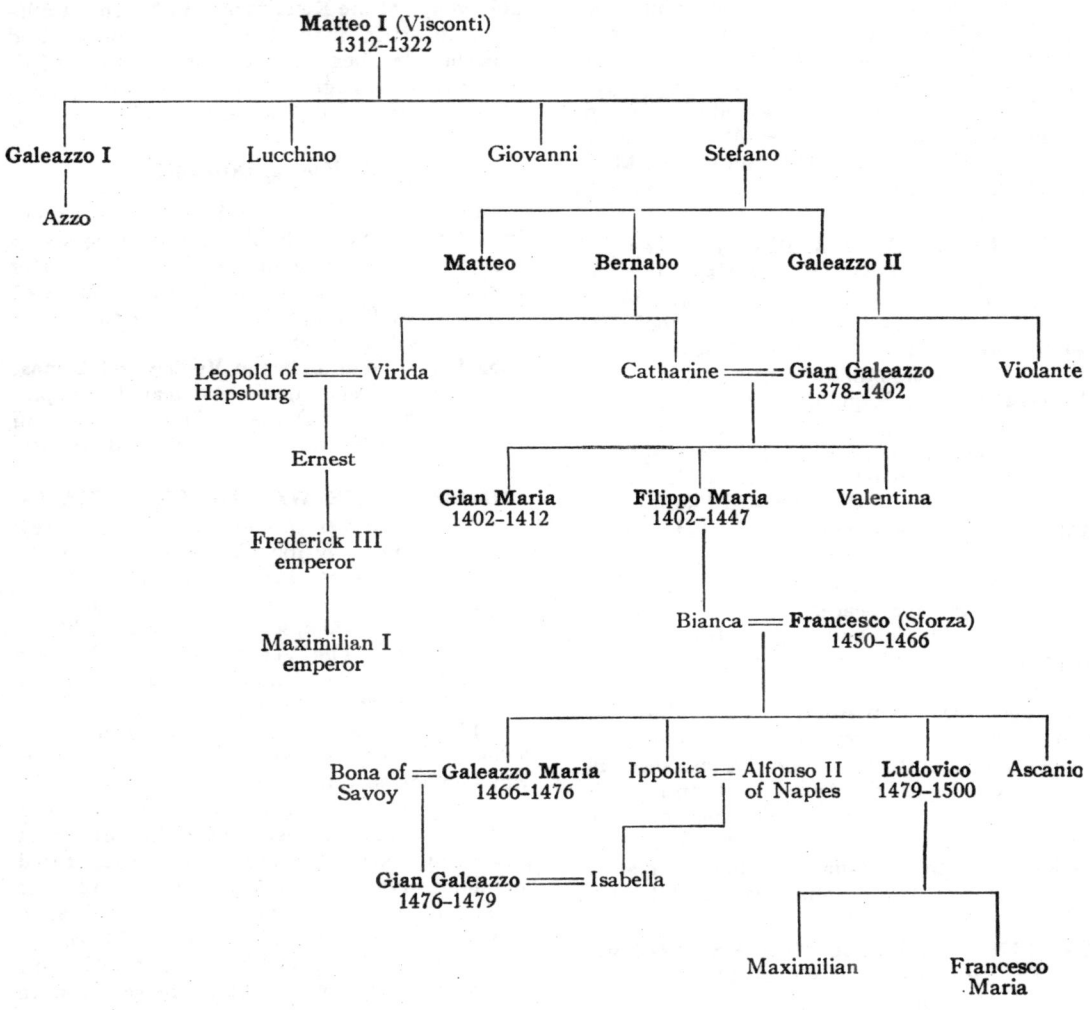

(1259): defeat and capture of the (Ghibelline) Visconti and their adherents. Milan established her power over Bergamo, Lodi, Como, and Vercelli.

1277-1447. Rule of the **VISCONTI.** Established by Archbishop Otto Visconti. Brief restoration of the Della Torre (1302) in a Guelf reaction with outside support. Establishment (1312) of the Visconti supremacy (Matteo designated *imperial vicar*). Ruthless Visconti rule and expansion over northern Italy (including Genoa). Stefano's sons, Bernabo, Galeazzo, Matteo, divided the domains but ruled jointly until Matteo was assassinated (1354) by his brothers. Intolerably harsh joint rule of

Bernabo (1354–1385) at Milan and Galeazzo (1354–1378) at Pavia; ostentatious patronage of learning and art.

1378-1402. **GIAN GALEAZZO** succeeded his father Galeazzo and did away with Bernabo (1385), thereafter ruling alone (1385–1402). Gian Galeazzo married Isabella, daughter of King John of France; one of his daughters married Lionel, son of Edward III of England; another, Valentina, married Louis of Orléans (the source of Louis XII's claims to Milan). Gian Galeazzo began the creation of a northern Italian kingdom: mastery of Verona, Vicenza, Padua (1386–1388); Tuscan advance blocked by Florence (1390–1392) and by the rebellion of

Padua. Created hereditary duke (1395) by Emperor Wenceslaus, he added Pisa and Siena (1399), Assisi and Perugia (1400) to his domains, and routed (1401) Elector Rupert III (in Florentine pay). The *Certosa* and *Duomo* were begun. Gian Galeazzo's death (1402) saved Florence and opened a period of anarchy in Milan under his sons Gian Maria (1402–1412) and Filippo Maria (1402–1447), which undid much of their father's work.

1402–1447. FILIPPO MARIA, after the assassination (1412) of Gian Maria, regained Gian Galeazzo's lands (even Genoa). Venice joined Florence against Filippo and took Bergamo, Brescia (1425). Filippo, last of the Visconti, was followed by

1447–1450. The Republic and the supremacy of Francesco Sforza, the condottiere, son-in-law of Filippo, who fought his way to mastery, defeating Venice and conquering the Lombard Plain.

1450. Francesco Sforza was invested with the ducal title by popular acclaim.

1450–1500. Rule of the SFORZA. Francesco, eager for peace, came to terms with Cosimo de' Medici and Naples (the so-called triple alliance for the Italian balance of power). Louis XI was on intimate terms with Francesco and made him his political model. Francesco completed the Certosa and the Duomo with Florentine architects under Renaissance influence and began the *Castello*. Patron of the humanist Filelfo, Francesco gave his son Galeazzo and his daughter Ippolita a humanist education; Ippolita was famous for her Latin style. His court was full of humanists and learned Greeks.

1466–1476. GALEAZZO MARIA SFORZA was assassinated after a cruel but able rule. His son

1476–1479. GIAN GALEAZZO, husband of Isabella of Naples, under the regency of his mother, supported Florence against Naples after the Pazzi conspiracy (1478). Gian Galeazzo's uncle Ludovico usurped the duchy (1479).

1479–1500. LUDOVICO (*il Moro*), alarmed at his isolation after the death (1492) of Lorenzo de' Medici, supported the appeals of Neapolitan refugees to Charles VIII of France, whose expedition (1494) began the destruction of Italian independence. In Charles' train came Louis of Orléans, who, as Louis XII (1498–1515), added claims to Milan to his other Italian claims, took Milan (1499) and captured Ludovico (1500), who ended his days (1508) as prisoner of Louis.

Ludovico's generous patronage marked the **golden age of the Renaissance in Milan.** Ludovico, an artist, man of letters, economist, and experimenter, beautified the city, improved irrigation, bettered agriculture. He was the patron of Bramante and Leonardo. (*Cont. p. 403.*)

(5) *Venice,* 1310–1489

In the early 14th century Venice already dominated the trade of the Adriatic and possessed many colonies throughout the Near East. Her position in the eastern trade was challenged primarily by Genoa, at that time at the height of her power.

1353–1355. War between Venice and Genoa. The Venetians were defeated at **Sapieanza** (1354) and suffered the loss of their fleet. Peace was mediated by Milan.

1378–1381. THE WAR OF CHIOGGIA between Venice and Genoa. This grew out of the grant, by John V Palaeologos, of the island of Tenedos, key to the Dardanelles. Luciano Doria, the Genoese admiral, defeated the Venetians at **Pola,** seized Chioggia and blockaded Venice. The Venetians, under **Vittorio Pisano,** blocked the channel and starved out the fleet of Pietro Doria, forcing its surrender. From this blow Genoa never recovered. Henceforth Venice was mistress of the Levantine trade, which made an outlet for her goods over the Alpine passes more urgent than ever. The war with Genoa had demonstrated the importance of a mainland food supply and thereby inaugurated an inland advance which had a decisive influence on Italian politics. Venice had already taken Padua from the Scaligers of Verona (1339), but by agreement had turned it over to the Carrara family. Treviso and Belluna, however, were retained.

1388. Treaty of the Venetians with the Ottoman Turks, the first effort to assure trade privileges despite the rise of the Turkish power.

1405. Venice seized Padua, Bassano, Vicenza, and Verona after the breakup of the Visconti domains (1402) and the defeat of the Carrara family.

1416. First war of Venice against the Ottoman Turks, the result of Turkish activity in the Aegean. The **Doge Loredano** won a resounding victory at the Dardanelles and forced the sultan to conclude peace.

1423. The Venetians took over Saloniki as part of a plan of co-operation with the Greek emperor against the Turks.

1425-1430. Second war against the Turks. The Turkish fleets ravaged the Aegean stations of the Venetians and took Saloniki (1430). The Venetians were obliged to make peace in view of

1426-1429. The war with Filippo Maria of Milan, by which the Venetians established a permanent hold over Verona and Vicenza, and gained in addition Brescia (1426), Bergamo (1428), and Crema (1429).

1453. Participation of the Venetians in the **defense of Constantinople** against Mohammed II (p. 331). After the capture of Constantinople, Mohammed proceeded to the conquest of Greece and Albania, thus isolating and endangering the Venetian stations.

1463-1479. THE GREAT WAR AGAINST THE TURKS. Negroponte was lost (1470). The Turks throughout maintained the upper hand and at times raided to the very outskirts of Venice. By the **Treaty of Constantinople** (1479) the Venetians gave up Scutari and other Albanian stations, as well as Negroponte and Lemnos. Thenceforth the Venetians paid an annual tribute for permission to trade in the Black Sea.

1482-1484. War with Ferrara, as a result of which Venice acquired Rovigo. This marked the limit of Venetian expansion on the mainland. The frontiers remained substantially unaltered until the days of Napoleon.

1489. Acquisition of Cyprus (partly by gift, partly by extortion), from Catharine Cornaro, widow of James of Lusignan.

Venetian culture in the Renaissance. Preoccupied with her commercial empire, her expansion on the mainland, and the advance of the Turk, Venice, despite her wealth, unique domestic security, and the sophistication of wide travel, *long* stood aside from the main currents of the early Renaissance. Her architecture remained under Gothic and Byzantine influences until the end of the 15th century, and the Palazzo Vendramini (1481) is perhaps the first important example of the new style. **The Bellinis** (Jacopo, 1395–1470, and his two sons) were the most notable early Venetian painters, and there was little promise of the brilliant if late achievement of the 16th century. The printing press apparently appealed to the practical Venetian nature and the Senate decreed (1469) that the art should be fostered. Much of the finest early printing issued from the Venetian presses of the 15th and 16th centuries.   *(Cont. p. 403.)*

e. THE HOLY ROMAN EMPIRE

1273. The election fell to **Rudolf of Hapsburg** (b. 1218), who ranked as a prince, wished to restore and retain in his family the Duchy of Swabia, and had three daughters to marry off. The Hapsburgs (from *Habichts-Burg*, Hawk-Castle) originally (10th century) of the district of Brugg (junction of the Aar and Reuss) had steadily expanded their lands in the Breisgau, Alsace, and Switzerland, emerging as one of the leading families of Swabia.

1273-1291. RUDOLF I. Indifferent to the Roman tradition, he concentrated on the advancement of his own dynasty, and founded the greatness of the Hapsburgs on territorial expansion of the family holdings and dynastic marriages. Edicts for the abolition of private war and support of local peace compacts (*Landfrieden*).

1276-1278. Struggle with Ottokar, King of Bohemia, over the usurped imperial fiefs of Austria, Styria, Carinthia, Carniola (p. 242). Rudolf expelled Ottokar from Austria by force (1276), but allowed him to retain Bohemia and Moravia (after homage) as a buffer against Slavdom; dynastic alliance with the Hapsburgs. Ottokar was ultimately defeated and killed (1278, Aug. 26, **battle of the Marchfeld**); investiture of Rudolf's sons with the imperial fiefs of Austria, Styria, Carniola (1282) established the Hapsburgs on the Danube until 1918.

Rudolf threw away the last remnants of Frederick II's great imperial fabric: confirmation of papal rights in Italy and Angevin rights in southern Italy (1275); renunciation of all imperial claims to the Papal States and Sicily (1279).

1291. Alarmed at the rapid rise of the Hapsburgs to first rank, the electors passed over Rudolf's son, choosing instead **Adolf of Nassau** in return for substantial considerations.

1291. Revolt of the three Forest Cantons, Uri, Schwyz, and Unterwalden, and formation of a (Swiss) confederacy (p. 311).

1292-1298. ADOLF, a strong imperialist, and able. He supported the towns and lesser nobles and entered into alliance with Edward I of England against Philip IV of France to protect the imperial fiefs of Franche Comté, Savoy, Dauphiné, Lyonnais, and Provence, long under French pressure; the alliance came to nothing, as the German princes were indifferent. The

The House of Hapsburg

Rudolf I
Emperor, 1273–1291

Albert I ═══ Elizabeth
Emperor of Tyrol
1298–1308

Matilda
m. Louis II
of Bavaria

Catharine
m. Otto III
of Bavaria

Hedwig
m. Otto
of Brandenburg

Clementia
m. Charles
Martel of
Hungary

Judith
m. Wenceslas
of Bohemia

Agnes
m. Albert II
of Saxony

Rudolf
m. Agnes
d. of Ottokar
of Bohemia

Rudolf
King of Bohemia
1306–1307

Agnes
m. Andrew III
of Hungary

Frederick

Elizabeth
m. Frederick IV
of Lorraine

Leopold

Albert II

Henry

Anna

Otto

Frederick

Margaret
m. Meinhard
of Tyrol

Frederick

Albert III ═══ Beatrice of
Brandenburg

Leopold ═══ Virida, d. of
Bernabo Visconti

Rudolf

Albert IV

William
m. Joanna II
of Naples

Leopold

Ernest

Frederick

Albert

Elizabeth ═══ Albert V
d. of Emperor   King of Hungary
Sigismund   1437
King of Bohemia
1438
Emperor, as
Albert II
1438–1439

Frederick III ═══ Eleanor of
Emperor 1440–1493   Portugal

Anne
m. William III
of Saxony

Elizabeth
m. Casimir IV
of Poland

Magdalen ═══ Ladislas Posthumus
d. of Charles   King of Hungary, 1450
VII of France   King of Bohemia, 1454

Maximilian ═══ Mary of
Emperor 1493–   Burgundy
1519

Cunigunde
m. Albert II
of Bavaria

princes, alarmed at Adolf's advance in Meissen and Thuringia, deposed him (1298), electing Rudolf's rejected son Albert.

1298-1308. ALBERT I (Albrecht). Firm reduction of the ecclesiastical electoral princes (aid of the French and the towns); double dynastic marriage with the Capetians; acquisition of the crown of Bohemia (on the extinction of the Premyslids, 1306); Albert supported the Angevin Carobert's acquisition of Hungary; the Rhineland was filled with Francophil clerical appointees of the pope, and the election of 1308 was dominated by French influence. Charles of Valois procured the election of Henry of Luxemburg, brother of the Archbishop of Trier.

1308-1313. HENRY VII (*Luxemburg*), Francophil, devoted to Italian culture, and bent on restoring the empire. The marriage of his son John to the sister of King Wenceslas of Bohemia brought the throne of Bohemia to the house of Luxemburg (1310–1489).

1310-1313. Expedition to Italy at the urging of Pope Clement V and the Ghibellines; order restored, Milan, Cremona, Rome reduced; imperial coronation (1312); alliance of the pope and King Philip IV of France to save Naples from Henry.

1314-1347. LOUIS IV (*Wittelsbach*). A Hapsburg anti-king, **Frederick the Hand-**some, and civil war (until 1322). Bitter papal opposition (1323–1347, refusal of confirmation of Louis' title to the empire); Louis, backed by the German people, against the Avignonese pope. Violent war of propaganda: **Marsiglio of Padua** (*Defensor Pacis*, 1324) and **William of Occam,** defending the imperial position, gave wide currency to pre-Reformation ideas; **Dante's** *De Monarchia*; papal supporters, **Augustino Trionfans** and **Pelagius.**

1327-1330. Louis' futile expedition to Italy and "lay" coronation (1328); his demand for a general council welcomed by the Italian Ghibellines.

Effort to give the German monarchy a formal constitution.

1338. The Day at Rense: formation of a strong electoral union (*Kurverein*); declaration by the electors that election by a majority of the electors without papal confirmation is valid. The **Diet of Frankfurt:** declaration (the *Licet juris*) that the electors are competent to choose an emperor (i.e. papal intervention is not necessary); in effect the Holy Roman Empire was divorced entirely from the papacy.

1346. Louis was deposed, but fought against his successor, Charles (son of King John of Bohemia, who had been elected after an open alliance with the pope).

1347-1378. CHARLES IV (*Luxemburg*). Con-

The House of Luxemburg

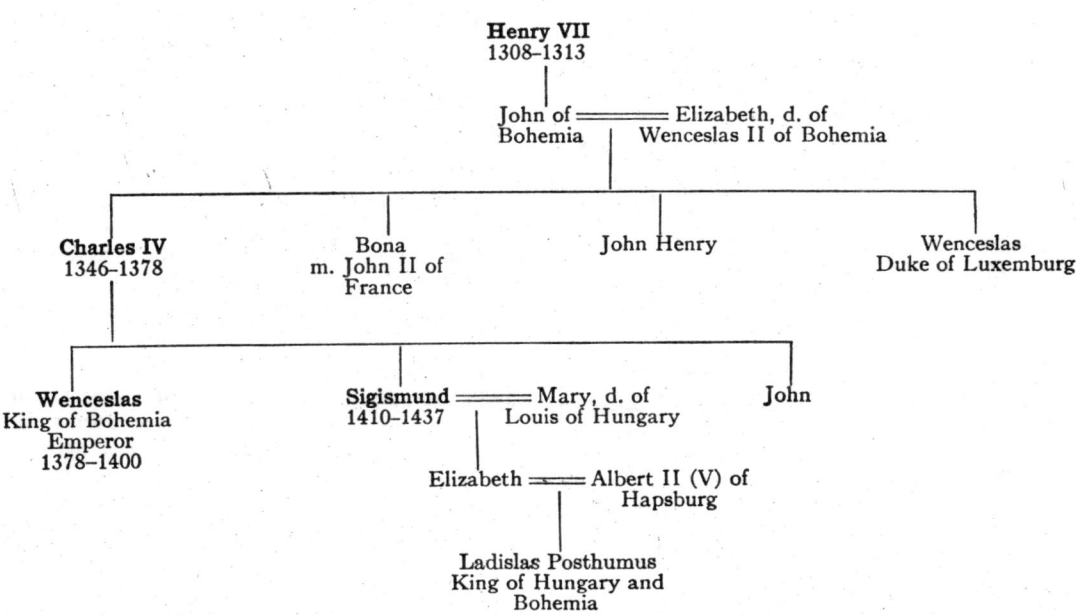

centration on the advancement of his dynasty (in Silesia, the Palatinate, Lusatia, Brandenburg) and on the progress of Bohemia. Prague became one of the chief cities of the empire (the University founded, 1348). The **Black Death** (1348–1349); the Flagellants; anti-Semitic massacres. Promulgation of the Swabian League and numerous *Landfrieden* reduced private warfare. Dauphiné and Arles continued to drift into the French orbit.

Further elaboration of a formal constitution of the empire.

1356. THE GOLDEN BULL (in force until 1806) transformed the empire from a monarchy into an aristocratic federation, to avoid the evils of disputed elections. Seven **electors**, each a virtual sovereign: the Archbishops of Mainz, Trier, and Cologne, the Count Palatine of the Rhine, the Duke of Saxony, the Margrave of Brandenburg, the King of Bohemia. Secular electorates to be indivisible and pass by primogeniture. Elections to be by majority vote and without delays; urban leagues forbidden without specific license; other restrictions on the towns. No mention of papal rights or claims. The electors to exercise supervision over the empire, a new function. The crown to remain in the house of Luxemburg.

Charles openly regarded the empire as an anachronism, but valued the emperor's right to nominate to vacant fiefs.

1364. Treaty of Brünn with the Hapsburgs, whereby either house (Luxemburg or Hapsburg) was to succeed to the lands of the other upon its extinction.

Little improvement in internal anarchy; climax of localism and the *Faustrecht*; the only islands of order and prosperity were the walled towns; the only basis of order were the town leagues (e.g. revival of the **Rhine League** (1354); the **Swabian League**); bitter warfare of classes, and princely opposition to the towns. Charles' vain appeal to the princes of Europe to resist France and end the Avignonese Captivity. Apogee of the **Hanseatic League** (p. 312).

1378–1400. WENCESLAS (Wenzel, son of Charles IV, King of Bohemia, 1378–1419). Formation of the **Knights' League** (*League of the Lion*) followed by a series of political quarrels between the knights and lords on one side and the towns on the other, ending in the town war (1387–1389) and the defeat of the towns, but not their ruin. Rising Bohemian nationalism: revolts, 1387–1396.

1400. Deposition of Wenceslas for drunkenness and incompetence. He refused to accept the decision, and the result was that at the end of the confused period (1400–1410) there were **three rival emperors** (Sigismund, Jobst, and Wenceslas) to correspond to the three rival popes.

1410–1437. SIGISMUND (*Luxemburg*; King of Bohemia, 1419–1437; King of Hungary by marriage). His main concern was to end the Great Schism, and he succeeded the King of France as protagonist of conciliar reform by forcing Pope John XXIII to call the **Council of Constance** (p. 292). Establishment of the **House of Wettin** in Saxony (1422); the **Hohenzollerns (Frederick)** in Brandenburg (1415). Sigismund's failure at Constance not merely alienated Bohemia, but also ended any hope of German unification.

1410. Utter defeat of the Teutonic Knights by the Polish-Lithuanian army at **Tannenberg;** beginning of the decline of the Teutonic Knights.

1411. Peace of Thorn, halting of the Slavic advance.

1420–1431. Emergence of **BOHEMIAN NATIONALISM** and the **HUSSITE WARS** (p. 309).

1433. Called to the **Council of Basel** (p. 293), the Hussites finally accepted the *Compactata* (which embodied the *Four Articles*), but the Church by its devious dealings alienated them, and they began a final break from the Roman Church. Bohemian nationality asserted itself increasingly in the 15th century, and Bohemia never returned to the German orbit.

Sigismund struggled against the Turkish advance (1426–1427) and was crowned at Rome (1432). In the election of 1438, Frederick of Brandenburg (candidate of the political reformers in Germany) withdrew, making the choice of Albert of Hapsburg (Sigismund's son-in-law) unanimous. Albert also succeeded Sigismund on the thrones of Hungary and Bohemia. Henceforth the imperial crown in practice became hereditary in

1438–(1740) 1806. THE HOUSE OF HAPSBURG.

1438–1439. ALBERT II.

1439. The Pragmatic Sanction of Mainz (abolition of annates, papal reservations, and provisions), a preliminary agreement between the papacy and the emperor, left the German Church under imperial and princely control and postponed reform till the days of Martin Luther.

1440–1493. FREDERICK III. The last emperor crowned (1452) at Rome by the

The House of Wittelsbach

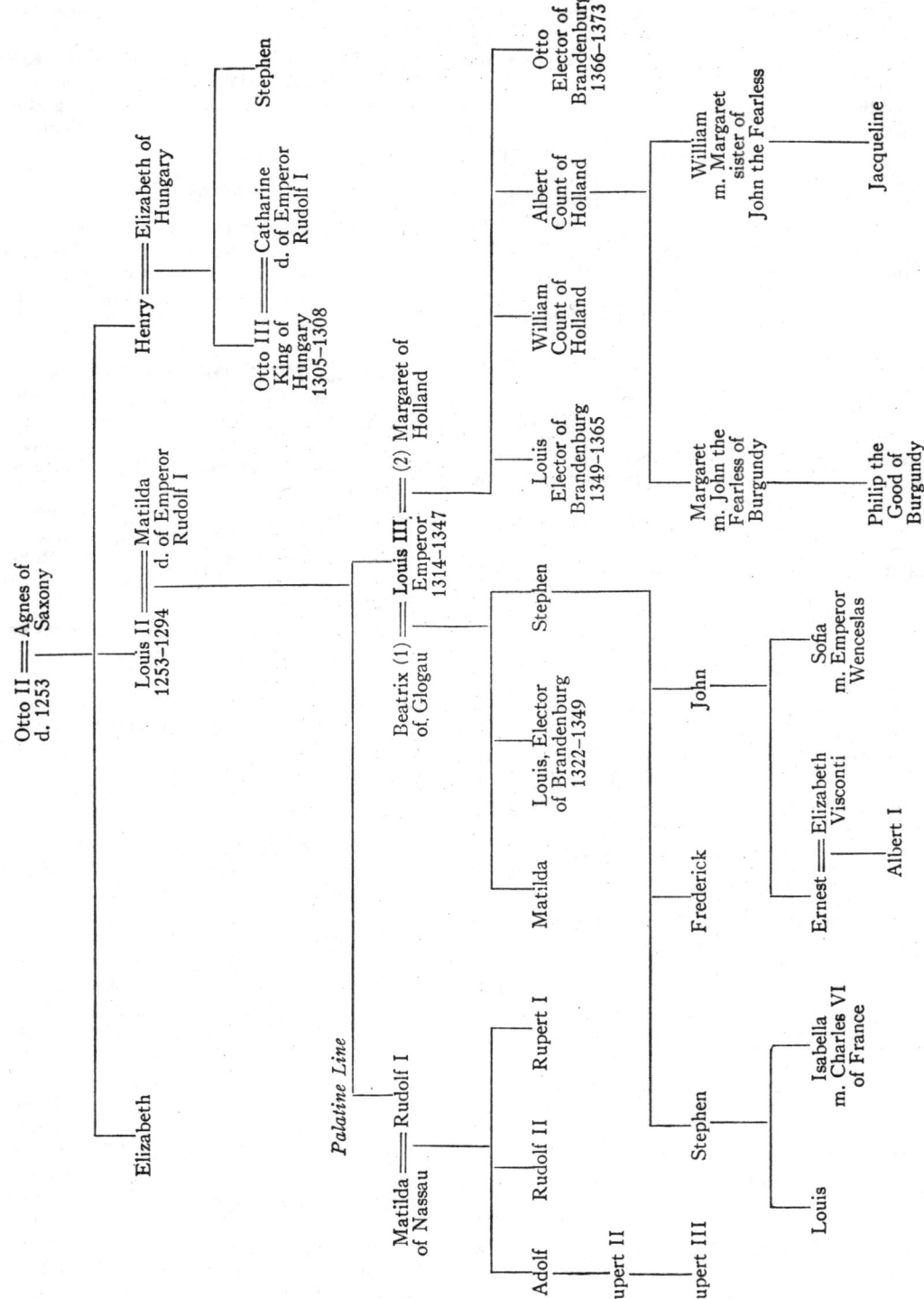

pope; a handsome, placid *fainéant,* amateur astrologer, botanist, mineralogist, he ignored the existence of diets, debates, and appeals for crusades.

Ladislas Posthumus (d. 1457), nephew and ward of Frederick, became Duke of Austria (1440), was acknowledged King of Hungary (1445) and elected King of Bohemia (1440) with a council of regency. **George Podiebrad** (champion of the *Compactata*) emerged (1452) from the Bohemian civil war (Catholics vs. Utraquists) as regent of Bohemia, and later king (1458–1471) (p. 309).

1448. The Concordat of Vienna: a compromise on cynical terms between the pope and the emperor on the reform issue: The papacy triumphed over the conciliar movement for reform, by dividing profits with the princes and emperor; external episcopal jurisdiction was excluded, the princes retained rights of presentation, obtained a share in episcopal taxation, and established an authority over the German Church which survived even the Reformation.

1453. The capture of Constantinople (p. 331) and end of the Eastern Empire left the Roman Empire without a rival and brought the Turkish menace to the frontier of Germany.

c. 1455. The Mazarin **Bible** printed at Mainz, the first book printed from movable type in Europe.

1456. Hunyadi (without imperial support) repulsed the Turk from Belgrade.

1458. Election of Hunyadi's son **Mathias Corvinus,** King of Hungary (to 1490) and **George Podiebrad,** King of Bohemia (to 1471), the climax of national spirit in Bohemia and Hungary.

1462. Pius II's annulment of the Compactata and the excommunication and deposition (1466) of Podiebrad reopened the Bohemian religious wars. **Ladislas** (elected 1468) succeeded on Podiebrad's death, as King of Bohemia (1471–1516), becoming King of Hungary in 1490 (see below).

1473. Frederick, faced with the threat of (French) Burgundian expansion in the empire, avoided giving Charles the Bold, Duke of Burgundy, the royal title (p. 284), and married his son Maximilian to Charles' daughter Mary (1477), bringing the Hapsburg fortunes to their zenith, and giving reality to his own monogram: **A.E.I.O.U.** (*Austriae est imperare orbi universo,* or, *Alles Erdreich ist Oesterreich unterthan.*)

1485. Expelled from Vienna by Mathias Cor-

vinus, Frederick became a cheery imperial mendicant.

1486. Maximilian, elected King of the Romans, became the real ruler of Germany and began the creation of the Hapsburg dynastic empire.   (*Cont. p.* 404.)

(1) *Bohemia,* 1306–1471

1306. The Premyslid dynasty came to an end with the death of Wenceslas (Vaclav) III. There followed an interregnum, during which the Bohemians were driven out of Poland. The interregnum ended with the election of

1310–1346. JOHN OF LUXEMBURG, son of the Emperor Henry VII. The circumstances of his accession forced John to issue a charter guaranteeing the rights and privileges of the nobility and clergy. Thus limitations of the royal power were fixed by written law. At the same time the national diet, theretofore called only on special occasions, became a regular institution. During this reign Bohemian overlordship over Upper Lusatia and Silesia was established.

John supported the Teutonic Knights against the Lithuanians and participated in three campaigns (1328, 1337, 1346). For a time (1331–1333) he ruled western Lombardy, as well as the Tyrol (1336–1341). John found his death in the battle of Crécy, where he fought on the side of the French. While he had shown little concern for Bohemian domestic affairs, he had made Bohemia a power in international politics.

1347–1378. CHARLES I (Charles IV as German Emperor), the son of John of Luxemburg. His reign is regarded as the "golden age" of Bohemian history. A series of charters issued in 1348 established an order of dynastic succession and determined Bohemia's place in the Holy Roman Empire. Moravia, Silesia, and Upper Lusatia were to be indissolubly connected with the Bohemian crown. By the **Golden Bull** (1356, see p. 306) the King of Bohemia was given first place among the empire's secular electors. At the same time Bohemia's internal independence was guaranteed. Acquisition of Lower Lusatia (1370) and Brandenburg (1373). Charles ruled as a constitutional king and spared no effort to promote material well-being and cultural progress. A new code of laws, the *Maiestas Carolina,* was published. Prague was rebuilt and beautified. The **University of Prague** founded (1348), the first university in central Europe.

1378-1419. WENCESLAS (Vaclav) IV, son of Charles. Gradual weakening of the connection with the German Empire. Loss of Brandenburg (1411). Continued conflicts with the barons. This was hastened by the development (since the end of the 14th century) of a national-religious movement which culminated in **Hussitism. John Hus** (1369-1415), a professor at the University of Prague and a popular preacher in the vernacular, was deeply influenced by the teaching of Wiclif and the Lollards in England. He attacked sale of indulgences, demanded reforms in the Church, challenged the primacy of the pope, and emphasized the supreme authority of the Scriptures. He also supported the native element in the university in the struggle which ended in the exodus of the alien Germans (1409), becoming rector of the university. Excommunicated by the pope and eager for vindication, he went to the **Council of Constance** (1415) under a safe-conduct from the emperor. His arrest in violation of this guaranty, his trial and burning (July 6), identified religious reform with Bohemian nationalism and split the empire in the

1420-1433. HUSSITE WARS. Refusal to recognize Sigismund as king. The reformers divided into two groups: (1) The moderate **Calixtines,** with the university as a center, favored separation of religious and political reform and formulated their program in the **Four Articles of Prague** (1420): full liberty of preaching, the cup to the laity (*Utraquism*), exclusion of the clergy from temporal activity and their subjection to civil penalties for crime. (2) The radical **Taborites,** under extreme Waldensian, Catharist, and Wiclifite influences, with a program of democracy and apostolic communism. The papal proclamation of a **Bohemian Crusade** (not opposed by the Emperor Sigismund) united the nation behind **John Ziska,** a brilliant soldier, who led the Hussites in a series of victories (1420-1422). Ziska's "modernization" of tactics: improved, mobile artillery, use of baggage wagons for mobile cover. Ziska's death (1424) did not affect the movement. Under a priest, **Procop the Great,** the Hussites defeated one crusade after another (1426, 1427, 1431) and carried the war into neighboring regions of Germany, on one occasion (1432) advancing as far as the Baltic. Then civil war broke out between the Calixtines and the Taborites (led by Procop the Great), the latter suffering defeat (1434).

1431-1436. The Council of Basel. The Hussites finally accepted a compromise, the *Compactata* (1436), recognizing them as true sons of the Church and conceding them the cup in the communion.

1436. Sigismund was finally accepted as king by all parties. He attempted a Catholic reaction, which was cut short by his death in the following year. Disputes continued between the Catholics and the Hussites, complicated by factional struggles between Hussite moderates and radicals and by social tension between nobility, townsmen and peasantry.

1437-1439. ALBERT OF AUSTRIA (son-in-law of Sigismund), elected king. An opposition group chose Ladislas, King of Poland. Albert died in the course of a civil war.

1439-1457. LADISLAS POSTHUMUS, the son of Albert. The Emperor Frederick III acted as his guardian, and for many years kept him from Bohemia. In the midst of continued factional conflict, a young nobleman, **George of Podiebrad,** rose to power.

1448. George seized Prague and became head of the Hussites. He was recognized as administrator of the kingdom (1452) and devoted himself to the task of reconciling Catholics and Hussites. The radical wing of the latter was completely suppressed by the **capture of Tabor** (1452). George ultimately succeeded in bringing the young king to Prague, but Ladislas died before he could accomplish much in behalf of the Catholics.

1459-1471. GEORGE PODIEBRAD elected king. Policy of conciliation: vigorous persecution of the Bohemian Brotherhood, a puritanical sect with outspokenly democratic leanings, dating from the teaching of **Peter of Chelchich** (d. 1460), and, like the Taborites, rejecting all subordination to Rome. George, an avowed Hussite of the moderate school, was technically a heretic and soon found himself in conflict with the pope.

1462. The pope denounced the agreements of Basel, and deposed George (1465). Thereupon the Catholic nobility of Bohemia elected **Mathias of Hungary** as king. George defeated him in a series of engagements, but the issue was undecided when George died.

(*Cont. p.* 424.)

(2) *The Swiss Confederation, to* 1499

Lake Lucerne and the original **Forest Cantons** belonged to the Duchy of Swabia, and the expansion of powerful Swabian families during the

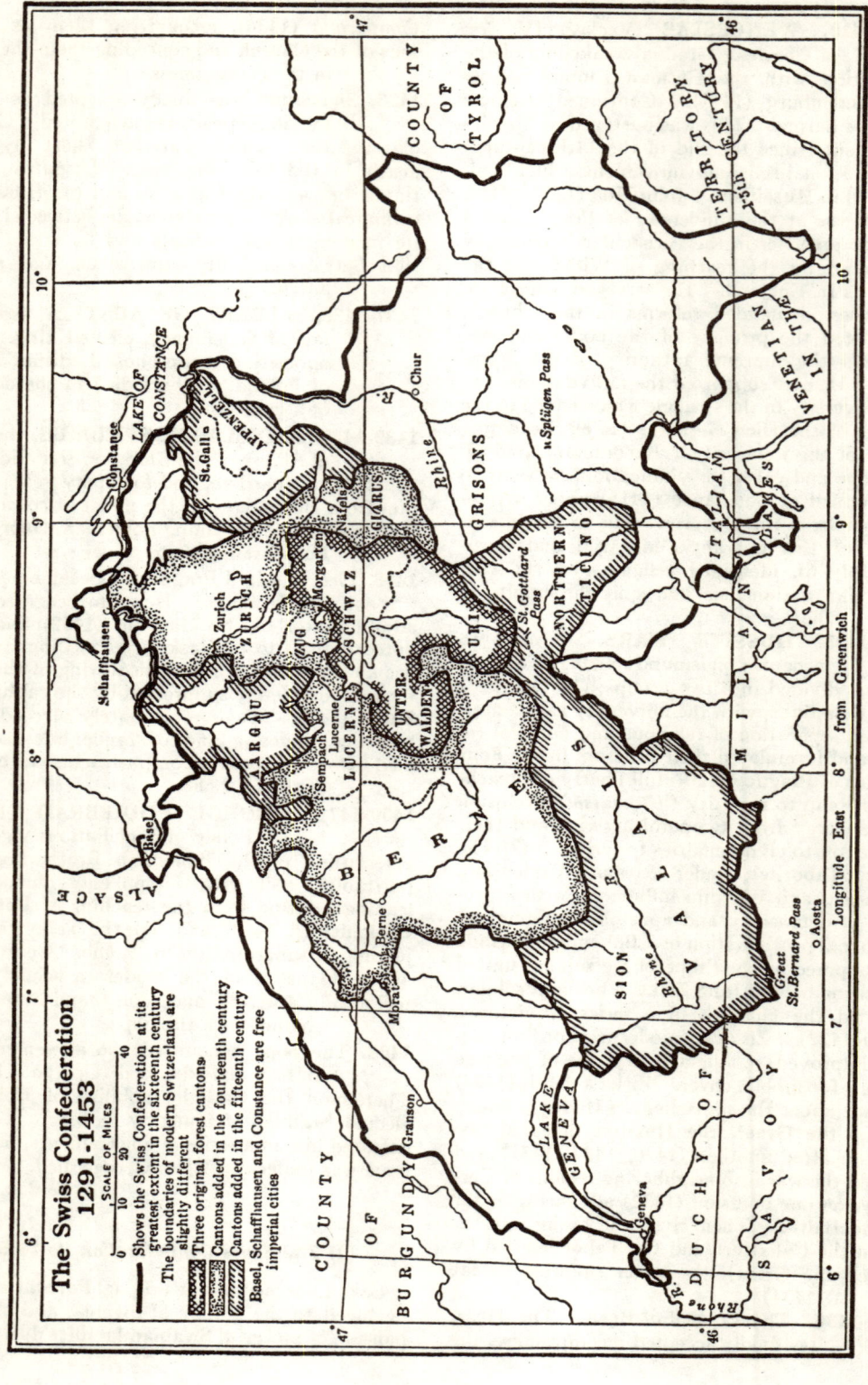

**The Swiss Confederation
1291-1453**

SCALE OF MILES
0   10   20   40

—— Shows the Swiss Confederation at its
greatest extent in the sixteenth century
The boundaries of modern Switzerland are
slightly different
Three original forest cantons
Cantons added in the fourteenth century
Cantons added in the fifteenth century
Basel, Schaffhausen and Constance are free
imperial cities

Great Interregnum led the Forest Cantons to a determined effort to replace feudal allegiances to various nobles with a single direct allegiance to the emperor. Most powerful of the Swabian families was the rising **house of Hapsburg** (whose original lands expanded in the 13th century into the Aargau, Breisgau, and Alsace). **Rudolf III** (b. 1218) of Hapsburg sought to restore the Duchy of Swabia under his house.

The Forest Cantons of Uri (already acknowledged independent of any but a loose imperial allegiance in 1231), **Schwyz,** and **Unterwalden,** emerged as champions of local independence and masters of the St. Gotthard Pass into Italy. Rudolf during the Interregnum expanded his suzerainty, but as emperor was too busy to assert it.

1291. First (known) **League of the Three Forest Cantons,** an undertaking for mutual defense, a kind of constitution, but not an independent federal league, as the cantons did not claim independence. Emperor Adolf confirmed the status of Uri and Schwyz, Henry VII that of Unterwalden, and henceforth the three Forest Cantons were thought of as a unit. The Swiss sent Henry VII three hundred soldiers for his Italian expedition, the first recorded use of Swiss troops outside their own borders.

1315, Nov. 15. Battle of Morgarten. Leopold of Austria, in an effort to crush the Swiss and punish them for support of Louis IV against the Hapsburg Frederick the Handsome, was thoroughly beaten at Morgarten, a battle which began the brilliant career of the Swiss infantry in Europe. Renewal and strengthening of the league and its confirmation by Louis IV.

1332-1353. Additions to the three Forest Cantons: Canton of Lucerne (1332); Canton of Zürich (1351); Canton of Glarus (1352); Canton of Bern (1353), bringing the number to seven, half of which were peasant cantons, the other half urban.

1386, July 9. BATTLE OF SEMPACH. The confederation, supported by the Swabian League, defeated the Hapsburg Leopold II of Swabia. In 1388 another victory was won at **Näfels.**

1394. Twenty-year truce between the confederation and the Duke of Austria. Austria abandoned claims on Zug and Glarus. The confederation became solely dependent on the empire, which amounted to practical independence.

The confederation was controlled by a **federal diet** (1393), but the cantons retained the widest possible autonomy. Throughout the succeeding period there was but little evidence of union.

The various cantons followed their own interests (Lucerne and Schwyz looked to the north; Bern to the west; Uri to the south) and wrangled among themselves. Only the threat from Austria invariably united them against the common enemy. In the meanwhile the 15th century was marked by continual struggles and conflicts with neighbors, as a result of which further territories were brought into the confederation and some approach was made to natural frontiers.

1403. The Canton of Uri began expansion southward, to get control of the passes to the Milanese. In 1410 the whole Val Antigorio was conquered, with Domodossola. The Swiss were driven out by the Duke of Savoy in 1413, but in 1416 regained mastery of the country.

1415. Conquest in the north of the Aargau, from Frederick of Austria, at the behest of his rival, the Emperor Sigismund.

1419. Purchase of Bellinzona, which, however, was seized by the Visconti of Milan (1422).

1436-1450. Civil war between Zürich and some of the neighboring cantons over the succession to the domains of the Count of Toggenburg. Zürich allied itself with Emperor Frederick IV (1442), but was defeated by Schwyz (1443); Zürich besieged (1444). Frederick called in the French, but after a defeat near Basel, the French withdrew. The emperor made **peace at Constance** (June 12, 1446) and in 1450 peace was made within the confederation. The general effect of the war was to strengthen the confederacy.

1460. Conquest of the Thurgau from Austria gave the confederation a frontier on Lake Constance.

1474-1477. The great war against **Charles the Bold of Burgundy,** whose designs on Alsace were regarded as a menace to the confederation. The Swiss allied themselves with the South German cities. This combination was joined by the emperor (perpetual peace, Mar. 30, 1474: Austria again renounced claims to Swiss territory). Louis XI of France also joined, but in 1475 both the emperor and the king withdrew again. Great victories of the Swiss at **Grandson** (Mar. 2, 1476), **Morat** or Murten (June 22, 1476), and at **Nancy** (Jan. 5, 1477) sealed the fate of Charles' plans and established the great military reputation of the Swiss, who were thenceforth sought far and wide as mercenaries.

1478. War with Milan. Victory of the Swiss at Giornico (Dec. 28). Alliance with the pope, who was allowed to engage Swiss forces.

1481. Solothurn and Fribourg were admitted to the Confederation after a long dispute among the members. The **Diet of Stans** drew up a covenant by which federal relations were regulated until 1798. Henceforth the urban cantons were in a majority.

1499. War with the emperor over disputed territories in the east. The emperor was supported by the South German cities, while the Swiss enjoyed the support, especially financial, of the French. The Swiss won a series of victories (especially **Dornach,** July 22) and forced the emperor to conclude the **Treaty of Basel** (Sept. 22) which granted the confederation independence of the empire in fact, if not formally (this came only in 1648). By the inclusion of **Basel and Schaffhausen** (1501) and later **Appenzell** (1513), the confederation rounded out its northern frontier.

The Swiss at the end of the 15th century enjoyed immense military prestige, but within the confederation there was much social unrest, especially among the peasants, and a good deal of demoralization in the towns. **Hans Waldmann,** bürgermeister of Zürich (1483–1489), was only the most outstanding of the typical ruthless, mercenary, cynical figures which dominated the scene and which remind one of the contemporaneous Italian despots. (*Cont. p. 414.*)

(3) *The Hanseatic League*

Hansa (Old French *Hanse*; Med. Latin *Hansa*), meaning a group, company, or association.

Associations (*Hansas*) and partial unions of North German towns date from the 13th century and were an important aspect of the great town development of Germany in that period.

c. 1000. German traders were established on the island of Gothland and in London.

c. 1150–c. 1250. Revival of the German river trade, notably along the Rhine, centering in the towns of Cologne, Dortmund, Soest, and Münster. At the same time the German expansion toward the Slavic east extended the sphere of German trade along the Baltic coasts. In the later 12th century the German settlement on Gothland (**Wisby**) became autonomous and established an offshoot at **Novgorod** (*St. Peter's Yard*) which became the focus of the important Russian trade.

1226. Lübeck (founded 1143) secured an imperial charter from Frederick II. Hamburg followed in 1266–1267.

1237. Wisby secured trading rights in England, and soon afterward in Flanders.

1241. Lübeck and Hamburg formed an alliance to protect the Baltic trade routes.

1256. The Wendish towns (Lübeck, Stralsund, Wismar, Rostock, Greifswald, and later Lüneburg) held their first recorded meeting. Lübeck began to emerge as the dominant North German town, a position which it retained throughout the history of the Hanseatic League. Most of the commercial towns followed the *Code of Lübeck*, which was an early source of unity between them. By the end of the century the Wendish towns had taken the leadership from the Gothland merchants.

1282. The **Germans in London** formed a corporation and established their own guildhall and steelyard. Other German yards were opened at York, Bristol, Yarmouth, Lynn, and Boston. The London trade was dominated by Cologne, but the yards at Lynn and Boston were under the control of Lübeck and Hamburg.

THE HANSEATIC LEAGUE. No date can be fixed for its organization, which was evidently the result of the lack of a powerful German national government able to guarantee security for trade. Its formation was no doubt facilitated by the mediaeval affinity for co-operative action and for monopoly. The term *Hanseatic League* was first used in a document in 1344. The exclusion of Germans abroad (1366) from the privileges of the Hansa indicates a growing sense of unity, but league members spoke of the association merely as a *firma confederatio* for trade, and throughout its history it remained a loose aggregation. This looseness of organization allowed a maximum of independence to its members and was not modified until the league was put on the defensive in the 15th century. The league never had a true treasury or officials in a strict sense; its only common seal was that of Lübeck; it had no common flag. Assemblies of the members (*Hansetage*) were summoned by Lübeck at irregular intervals and were sparsely attended, except in times of crisis. The objectives of the league were mutual security, extortion of trading privileges, and maintenance of trade monopoly wherever possible. The chief weapon against foreigners or recalcitrant members was the economic boycott and (rarely) war. Primarily concerned with the North European trade, the Hansa towns dealt chiefly in raw materials (timber, pitch, tar, turpentine, iron, copper), livestock (horses, hawks, etc.), salt, fish (cod and especially herring), leather, hides, wool,

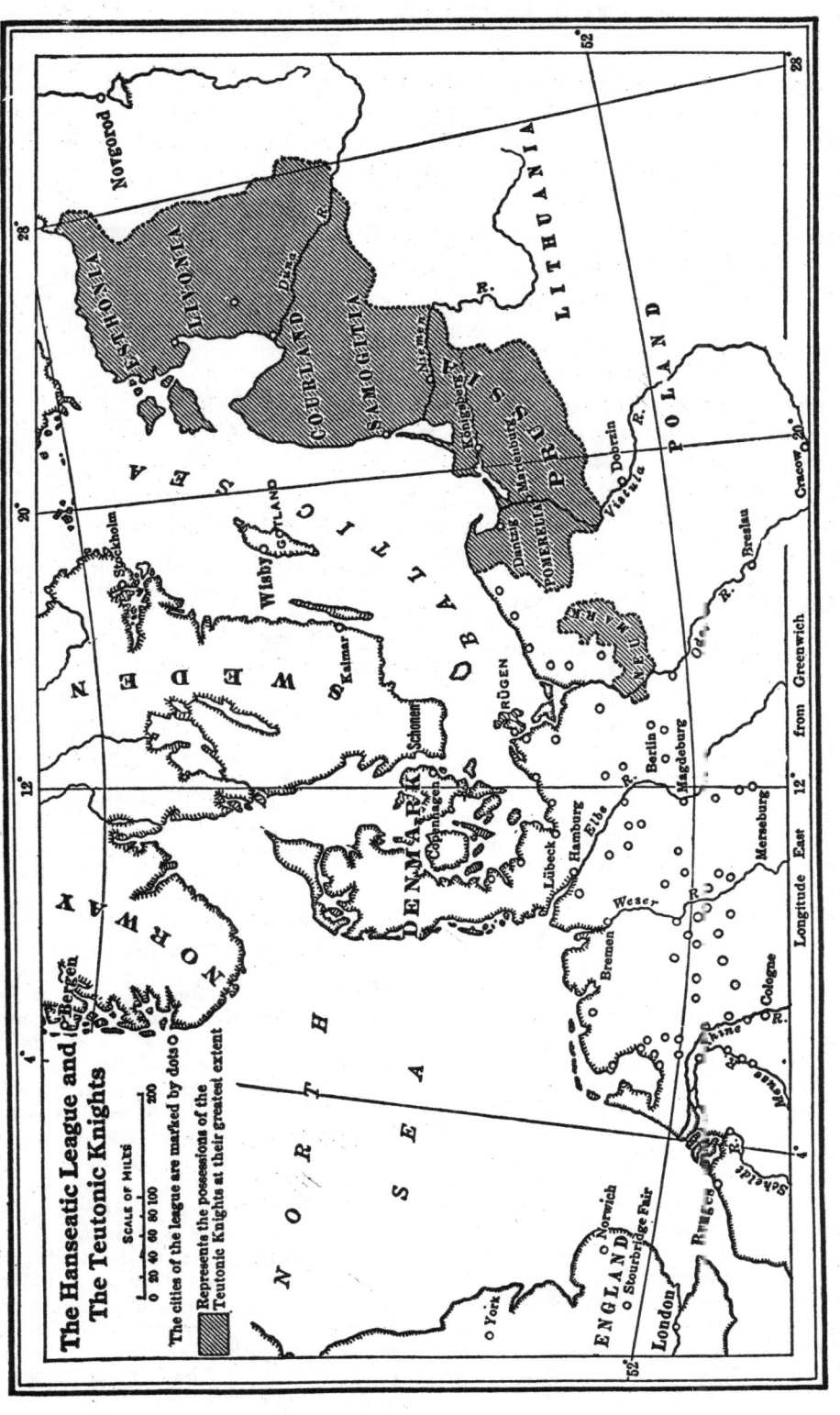

The Hanseatic League and
The Teutonic Knights

SCALE OF MILES
0 20 40 60 80 100   200

The cities of the league are marked by dots ○

Represents the possessions of the
Teutonic Knights at their greatest extent

grain, beer, amber, drugs, and some textiles. The four chief *kontors* were Wisby, Bergen, London, and Bruges.

1340-1375. WALDEMAR IV of Denmark, who freed his country of the German domination and took up the struggle against the powerful Hansa towns. He threatened the Hanseatic monopoly of the herring trade by his seizure of Scania, and in 1361 cut the Russian-Baltic trade route by his capture of Wisby. In 1362 he defeated the German fleets at **Helsingborg.** By the **Peace of Wordingborg** (1365) the Hansa was deprived of many of its privileges in Denmark.

1367. THE CONFEDERATION OF CO-LOGNE, effected by a meeting of representatives of 77 towns, organized common finance and naval preparations for the struggle. Reconstruction of Scandinavian alliances to meet the threat from Waldemar. After a series of victories, the German towns extorted from the Danish *Reichsrat*

1370. THE PEACE OF STRALSUND, which gave the league four castles in Scania (dominating the Sound), control of two-thirds of the Scanian revenues for 15 years, and the right to veto the succession to the Danish throne unless their monopoly was renewed by the candidate. The treaty marked the apogee of Hanseatic power and virtually established control over the Baltic trade and over Scandinavian politics. The Baltic monopoly was not finally broken until 1441, after a war with the Dutch. Wisby itself never recovered from Waldemar's sack, and was long a nest of pirates (e.g. the famous **Victual Brothers**).

FLANDERS. The Germans in Bruges received a special grant of privileges in 1252, which allowed them their own ordinances and officials. They later (1309) established exemption from the usual brokerage charges levied on foreigners and eventually won an influential voice in the affairs of the city, notably in foreign policy. The revised statutes of the Bruges Kontor (1347) recognized the division of the Hanseatic League into thirds: The Wendish-Saxon; the Prusso-Westphalian; and the Gothland-Livland thirds. Bruges was the most ardent champion of Hanseatic unity, and, with Lübeck, was the chief source of such cohesion as the League attained. A boycott in 1360 brought the town into complete submission to the League.

ENGLAND. The Hansa towns, by maintaining friendly relations to the crown, were able to ignore the growing national hostility to alien traders (directed at first mainly against the Italians) and to avoid granting reciprocal privileges to the English in return for their own exclusive rights (notably those claimed under Edward I's *Carta Mercatoria* of 1303). One source of Hanseatic influence derived from loans to the crown, especially during the Hundred Years' War. The English themselves began to penetrate into the Baltic (c. 1360) and growing public resentment against the league led to increased customs dues, but Richard II in 1377 renewed the privileges of the league, thus firmly establishing the Hanseatic power in England. The Sound was opened to the English in 1451, and the league, profiting by the Wars of the Roses, secured full title to the steelyard in London (1474) and the renewal of rights in Boston and Lynn. Not until the days of Elizabeth were the Hanseatic privileges finally reduced.

DECLINE OF THE LEAGUE. Externally the league was weakened by the disorders of the Hundred Years' War; by the rise of Burgundy and the new orientation thereby given to Dutch trade (e.g. Brill wrested the monopoly of the herring trade from the league); and by the great discoveries and the opening of new trade routes. But above all, the monopolistic policies of the league aroused ever sharper opposition in the countries where the league operated (notably in England, Holland, Scandinavia, and Russia; Ivan III destroyed the Novgorod Kontor in 1494). **Internally** the league continued to suffer from lack of organization. The inland towns held aloof from the Baltic policy and Cologne sent no representatives to the assembly until 1383. The assembly itself was summoned only at irregular intervals. The delegates were strictly bound by their mandates and their votes were subject to review by their home towns. Decisions were not binding on all members until 1418. In the 15th century the league was further weakened by the struggle within the member towns between the democratic guildsmen and the patrician oligarchy. The league threatened the expulsion of "democratic" towns. The German princes (notably the Hohenzollerns of Brandenburg) gradually reduced the freedom of various powerful members of the league and rivalries broke out within the league itself (Cologne and the Westphalian towns stood together, as did Danzig and the Prussian towns, especially after 1467). The South German towns opened direct trade relations of their own with Flanders, Breslau, Prague, and other centers, and began to establish their own fairs. Leipzig, for example, replaced Lübeck as the center of the fur trade.

1629. The Assembly entrusted the guardianship of the common welfare to Lübeck, Hamburg, and Bremen.

1669. The last assembly (attended by five towns) was held. The league by this time was the merest shadow of its former self, but its Kontors survived in Bergen until 1775, in London until 1852, and in Augsburg until 1863.

(4) *The Teutonic Knights*

The 14th century marked the apogee of the power of the **Teutonic Order** in eastern Europe. The Knights began the penetration of Poland, where Germans settled some 650 districts and where the middle class of the towns became German in speech and law, much to the alarm of the rulers and nobles. At the same period the Knights advanced into Lithuania, a huge region extending from the Baltic to the Black Sea, the last heathen area in Europe. German colonization and town-building first opened and civilized this region.

1326–1333. THE FIRST POLISH WAR, marking a sharp reaction to German penetration and putting the order for the first time on the defensive. With the aid of John of Bohemia, Louis of Hungary, Albert of Austria, Louis of Brandenburg, and others, the order emerged triumphant and the Poles were obliged to conclude a truce.

1343. PEACE OF KALISCH. The Poles, despite papal support of their claims to Pomerelia, were obliged to recognize the Order's possession of the territory, in return for a promise of aid against the Lithuanians. Poland was thus cut off from the Baltic.

1343–1345. The Estonian Revolt, one of the worst *jacqueries* of the Middle Ages. Estonia was taken by the Order from the Danes in 1346.

1385. Union of Poland and Lithuania under Jagiello and Jadwiga, thus creating a strong barrier to the further advance of the Germans and indeed, sealing the ultimate fate of the Order.

1410, July 15. Defeat of the Knights in the **battle of Tannenberg** by a huge army of Poles and Lithuanians. Poland, unable to exploit the victory, concluded

1411. THE FIRST PEACE OF THORN, which cost the Knights only Samogitia and an indemnity.

1454. The Prussian Revolt, a great uprising against the oppressive rule of the Order

in which the Prussian nobility and towns took part. The movement was supported by the Poles, and Casimir of Poland declared war on the Order.

1466. SECOND PEACE OF THORN. Prussia was divided: (1) **West Prussia** (including Danzig, Kulm, Marienwerder, Thorn, and Ermeland) went to Poland, thus cutting East Prussia off from the rest of Germany and securing for Poland access to the sea. (2) **East Prussia** was retained by the Order, with Königsberg as capital. East Prussia, Brandenburg, and Memel were all to be held as Polish fiefs. The Order was opened to Polish members. This peace marked the definitive end of the German advance until the partitions of Poland.

The decline of the Order continued (growing commercialization, exclusiveness, lack of new blood, loss of discipline, Slavic pressure) despite efforts at reform by various grand masters.

1525. East Prussia was finally secularized by the grand master, Albert (Hohenzollern) of Brandenburg, and became a fief of the Hohenzollerns under the Polish crown.

1561. The **Livonian holdings** were similarly transformed and became the Duchy of Courland.

The Order itself survived in Germany until 1809 and was later revived in 1840 under Hapsburg auspices with its original functions (e.g. ambulance service in war).

f. SCANDINAVIA

(1) *Denmark*, 1320–1387

The active and on the whole successful reign of **Eric Menved** (1286–1320) was followed in Denmark by a period of weakness and decline, marked by the ascendancy of the nobility and the constant advance of German influence.

1320–1332. CHRISTOPHER II, elected king after a capitulation, the first in Danish history, limiting the royal power in the interest of the nobility and clergy. The Hansa towns, having acquired a monopoly of trade in Denmark, soon became dominant in Danish politics.

1332–1340. A period of complete anarchy. Christopher was driven from the throne by Gerhard, Count of Holstein, who parceled out the territories of the crown, established German nobles in all the important fortresses, and gave the German traders full rein. Gerhard was murdered in 1340.

1340-1375. WALDEMAR IV, the youngest son of Christopher and one of the greatest Danish kings. At home he did his utmost to break the German influence and to restrict the power of the nobility and the clergy. The Church was subordinated to the royal power and the nobles and towns obliged to perform their military obligations. Abroad Waldemar devoted himself to the reconquest of the territories lost by his father. In wars with Sweden, Holstein, and Schleswig he regained Zeeland (1346), most of Fünen and Jutland (1348), and Scania (1360). His seizure of Gothland (1361) brought him into direct conflict with the powerful Hansa towns, which were supported by Sweden.

1361-1363. First War against the Hansa. Copenhagen was sacked, but Waldemar defeated the Hansa fleets at **Helsingborg** (1362) and forced the Hansa to accept peace (1363) which greatly curtailed their privileges.

1368. A revolt against heavy taxation led to Waldemar's flight. His return (1370) was purchased by tremendous concessions. Meanwhile

1368-1370. THE SECOND WAR WITH THE HANSA had broken out. The German towns were supported by Sweden, Norway, Holstein, Mecklenburg, and even by some of the Danish nobles. Waldemar, badly defeated, was obliged to accept

1370. THE PEACE OF STRALSUND, renewing the privileges of the German Hansa, turning over the larger part of the revenues of four places, and accepting interference in the royal succession. This treaty marked the ascendancy of the Hansa in the Baltic.

1376-1387. Olaf, grandson of Waldemar, who, until his death, ruled with his mother Margaret as regent.

1387-1412. Margaret, mother of Olaf, was queen, ruling at the same time Norway and Sweden and thus uniting Scandinavia.

(2) *Sweden,* 1319-1387

1319-1365. MAGNUS VII (*Smek*), aged three at his accession and, until 1333, ruler under the regency of his mother. He was a weak and ineffectual ruler, but through his mother succeeded (1319) to the Norwegian crown and, during the troubled period in Denmark, managed to acquire, temporarily, Scania, Halland,

and Bleking (given up again in 1360, to Waldemar IV). His long minority and his reliance on unworthy favorites led to a striking weakening of the royal power and an equally striking rise of the aristocratic party (first *Riksdag*, including burghers, 1359). Magnus was ultimately deposed and was succeeded by

1365-1388. Albert of Mecklenburg, who from the outset was merely a tool of the nobility. The magnates eventually deposed him and defeated him, calling to the throne

1388-1412. MARGARET, the regent of Denmark.

(3) *Norway,* 1320-1387

1320-1343. Magnus VII, who was also King of Sweden. In 1343 he turned over Norway to his son

1343-1380. Haakon VI, who was married (1363) to Margaret of Denmark.

1380-1387. Olaf, the son of Haakon and Margaret, already King of Denmark, succeeded to the throne. His death ended the Norwegian line.

1387-1412. MARGARET, mother of Olaf, was elected to the throne, thus introducing into Norway the system of election already in practice in Denmark and Sweden.

(4) *The Union of Kalmar to* 1483

1387-1412. MARGARET OF DENMARK, ruler of all three Scandinavian kingdoms. She had her grand-nephew, Eric of Pomerania, elected king of all three countries in 1389, but retained effective power herself.

1397. Coronation of Eric. Margaret presented a draft for the union of the three kingdoms. Vague and incomplete, the plan provided for a single king, established rules of succession, and set up a system of common defense. It was never ratified by the councils of the three kingdoms, but as long as Margaret lived, it worked relatively well. The union left the internal government of each kingdom much as it was. Margaret, an able despot (the Lübeck delegates called her "the lady king"), repressed the nobles, maintained order, and began the recovery of the Danish royal domain. In general the Danes profited by the union, and Danes and Germans were gradually insinuated into power in Sweden and Norway. Effective government of Scandinavia was centered in Denmark.

Rulers of Denmark, Norway, and Sweden (1263–1533)

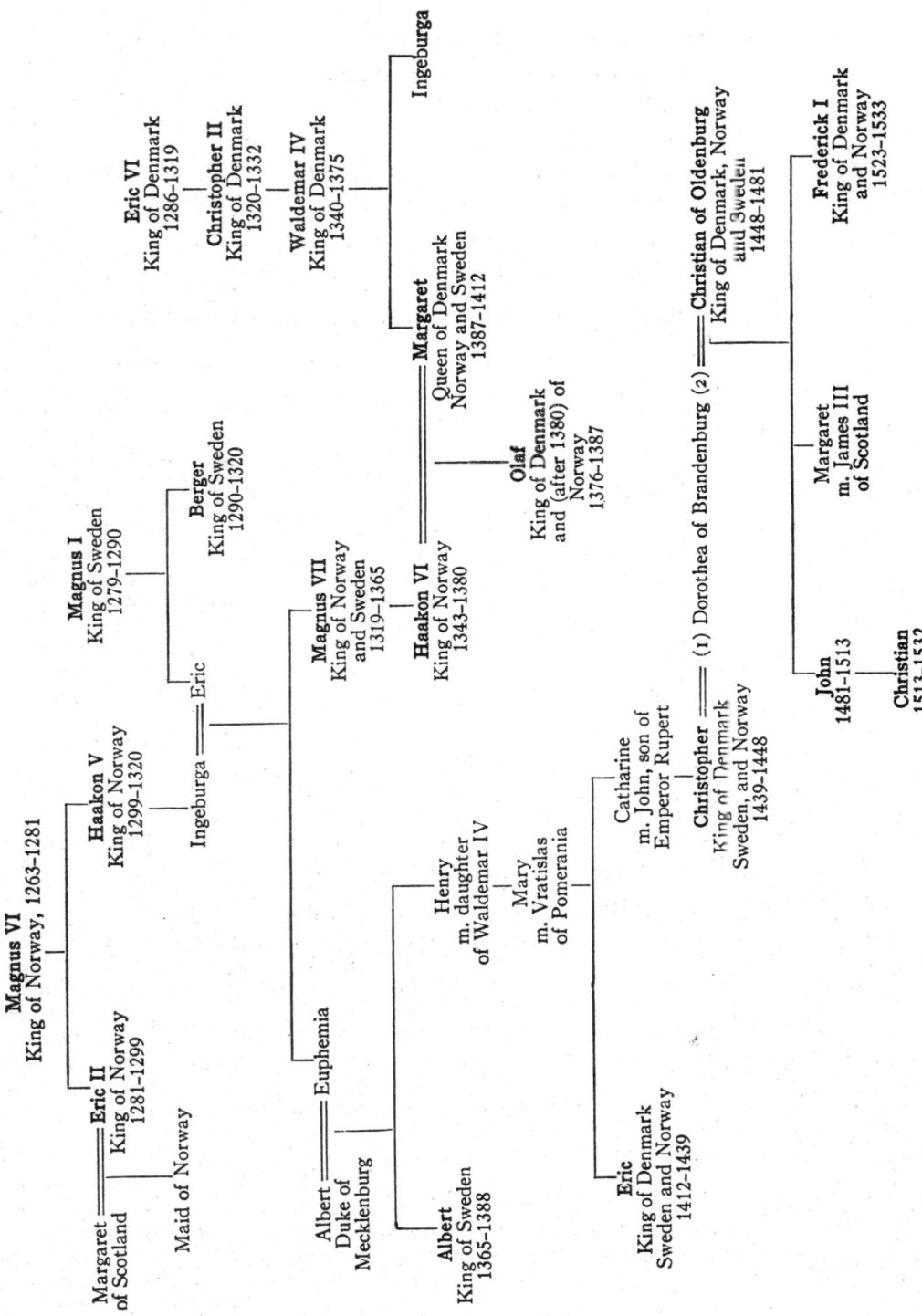

1412-1439. **ERIC**, Margaret's successor, proved himself less able. His efforts to regain control in Schleswig led to a long contest with the Dukes of Holstein, who, in alliance with the Hansa towns, finally conquered Schleswig completely (1432). At the same time much unrest developed among the peasantry (especially in Sweden, where **Engelbrecht Engelbrechtson** emerged as a leader of the lower classes).

1434. Engelbrecht marched through eastern and southern Sweden, seizing castles and driving out bailiffs, until the **Diet of 1435** recognized his demands, electing him regent. This diet included representatives of all four orders and for four hundred years continued to be an important institution. The movement of revolt spread to Norway, where it was taken up and controlled by the nobles. Eric finally took flight and the Danish council called in

1439-1448. **CHRISTOPHER of Bavaria,** cousin of Eric, who again ruled all three countries (elected in Sweden, 1440; in Norway, 1442). His reign marked the nadir of the monarchy, for Christopher was entirely dependent on the Hansa towns and was obliged to renew all their privileges, despite protests from the Danish burghers.

1448-1481. **CHRISTIAN I** (of Oldenburg) was elected by the Danish council under a capitulation which left all real power in the hands of that body. He had to accept a similar engagement on assuming the crown of Norway. The Swedish nobility, on the other hand, elected **Knut Knutsson** as king with the title of **Charles VIII** (1449–1457). Charles tried to secure the throne of Norway, but was ousted by Christian.

1457. Charles VIII was driven out of Sweden by a revolt inspired by the Church. Christian I was then crowned, but the real power was in the hands of the Stures (Sten, Svanee, and Sten the Younger). Christian kept a great state, but his court, like that of Christopher and Eric, was filled with Germans, and he was financially dependent on the Hansa cities. The **union of Schleswig and Holstein,** each autonomous under the crown of Denmark, was arranged in 1460. Christian founded the **University of Copenhagen** (1479).

Sweden in the later 15th century: The crown was a plaything of the nobles, while the clergy supported the King of Denmark. A rising commerce and industry was, however, creating a burgher class which was soon to assert itself. Sten Sture the Younger, who came into power with the death of Charles VIII, repulsed Christian of Denmark (1471) with the aid of the towns (especially Stockholm) and returned to the reforms of Engelbrecht. The **University of Uppsala** was founded (1477) and **printing** was introduced soon afterward. (*Cont. p.* 416.)

2. EASTERN EUROPE

a. POLAND, 1305-1492

The history of Poland in this period was concerned chiefly with the efforts of the kings to reunite the various duchies and to establish the royal power. This policy was opposed, with success, by the nobility, which, as elsewhere in Europe, managed to extract countless privileges and to erect a type of oligarchical government. Externally the Poles were involved in a long struggle with the Teutonic Knights, designed to secure an outlet to the Baltic. This conflict alternated with a policy of expansion to the southeast, toward the Black Sea.

1305-1333. **VLADISLAV IV** (*Lokietek*), under whom Poland regained its independence after a brief period of Bohemian domination. Vladislav was obliged to continue the struggle against Bohemia, and was not crowned until 1320. For protection he concluded dynastic alliances with Hungary (his daughter married Charles Robert of Anjou) and Lithuania (his son Casimir married the daughter of Gedymin). He did much to reunite the various duchies and established a new capital at Cracow. But he failed to secure Pomerania, which in 1309 passed from Brandenburg to the Teutonic Order. A papal decision in 1321 awarded the region to Poland, but the Knights ignored the order to turn it over, and continued their raids into Polish territory (1326–1333).

1333-1370. **CASIMIR III** (*the Great*), an astute and cautious statesman. He introduced an improved administration, reduced the influence of the German town law (a new law code published), developed national defense and promoted trade and industry (extensive privileges to the Jews, 1334). In 1364 he founded a school at Cracow, which became a university in 1400 and the chief intellectual center of eastern Europe.

POLAND, LITHUANIA
AND RUSSIA
IN THE 15TH CENTURY

Scales of Miles
0   200   400   600

In **foreign affairs** Casimir abandoned claims to Silesia and Pomerania, turning his attention toward the southeast, where dynastic problems in the Ukraine called forth dangerous rivalry between Poles, Lithuanians, and Hungarians. By an agreement with Hungary (1339), Casimir, who had no direct heir, promised that on his death the Polish crown should pass to Louis, the son of Charles Robert of Hungary. Louis was to reconquer the lost territories and to respect the privileges of the Polish nobility. This marks the beginning of the disastrous elective system, which gave the magnates an unequaled opportunity for extracting further rights (first real diet — *colloquia* — in 1367). In 1340 Casimir seized Halicz, Lemberg, and Volhynia. War ensued with Lithuania over Volhynia, and ultimately the Poles retained only the western part (1366).

1370-1382. LOUIS (of Anjou). He paid but little attention to Poland, which he governed through regents. To secure the succession to his daughter Maria (married to Sigismund, son of Emperor Charles IV) he granted to the nobility the *Charter of Koszyce* (Kaschau), the basis of far-reaching privileges.

1382-1384. Opposition to Sigismund led to the formation of the **Confederation of Radom** and civil war between the factions of the nobility.

1384-1399. JADWIGA (Hedwig), a daughter of Louis, was elected queen.

1386. Marriage of Jadwiga to Jagiello, Grand Duke of Lithuania, who promised to become a Christian and to unite his duchy (three times the size of Poland) with the Polish crown. As a matter of fact, though the marriage prepared the way for union, Jagiello was obliged to recognize his cousin, **Witold,** as Grand Duke of Lithuania, and the connection continued to be tenuous.

1386-1434. JAGIELLO (title **Vladislav V**). He had great difficulty in keeping his fractious nobility in order and in 1433 was obliged to grant the *Charter of Cracow*, reaffirming and extending their privileges.

1410, July 15. BATTLE OF TANNENBERG (Grünwald), a great victory of the Poles, using Bohemian mercenaries under John Ziska and supported by the Russians and even the Tatars, against the Teutonic Knights. The Poles thereupon devastated Prussia, but Jagiello, unable to keep his vassals in order, concluded the

1411, Feb. 1. FIRST PEACE OF THORN,

which left matters much as they were and failed to secure for the Poles an access to the Baltic.

1434-1444. VLADISLAV VI, son of Jagiello, succeeded to the throne. Since he was only ten years old, the country was ruled by a regency. Vladislav's brother, Casimir, was offered the Bohemian throne by the Hussites (1438), and Vladislav himself became **King of Hungary** (1440). Thenceforth he devoted himself to Hungarian affairs, leaving Poland in the hands of the magnates. Vladislav lost his life in 1444 at the **battle of Varna** (p. 331) against the Turks.

1444-1447. An interregnum, followed by the reign of

1447-1492. CASIMIR IV, brother of Vladislav. He was able to make use of a rift between the great nobles (magnates) and the gentry (*szlachta*). The *Statute of Nieszawa* greatly limited the power of the former and granted substantial rights to the latter (no laws to be passed, no war to be declared without their consent). At the same time the independence of the church was curtailed (bishops to be appointed by the king).

1454-1466. War against the Teutonic Order. The Poles took advantage of the Prussian Union (Prussian nobles and towns in opposition to the Order). The war was carried on in desultory fashion, marked by constant shifting of the feudal forces and of the mercenaries from side to side, but the Poles ultimately gained the upper hand and secured

1466, Oct. 19. THE SECOND PEACE OF THORN, by which Poland finally secured an outlet to the Baltic. Poland acquired Kulm, Michelau, Pomerania, Marienburg, Elbing, and Christburg. The Order became a vassal of the Polish crown, and half its membership became Polish.

1471-1516. Vladislav, the son of Casimir, became King of Bohemia, which involved a long and indecisive war with Hungary (1471–1478). Eventually Vladislav became King of Hungary also (1490). (*Cont. p. 419.*)

b. LITHUANIA

Of the early history of Lithuania little is known. The numerous heathen tribes were first brought to some degree of unity by the threat of the German Knights (after 1230).

c. 1240-1263. Mindovg, one of the Lithuanian chieftains, in order to deprive the

Knights of their crusading purpose, accepted Christianity and was given a crown by Pope Innocent IV. He later broke with the Teutonic Order (1260) and relapsed into paganism. He was killed by one of his competitors. Of the following period almost nothing is known.

1293-1316. Viten re-established a Lithuanian state.

1316-1341. GEDYMIN, the real founder of Lithuania. Blocked by the Germans on the Baltic, he took advantage of the weakness of the Russian principalities to extend his control to the east and south (acquisition of Polotsk, Minsk, and the middle-Dnieper region). **Vilno** became the capital of the new state.

1341-1377. OLGERD, the son of Gedymin, was the ablest of the dynasty. Defeated by the Knights (1360) he too turned eastward. Siding with Tver in the dynastic conflicts of Russia, he advanced several times to the very outskirts of Moscow. During his reign the domain of Lithuania was extended as far as the Black Sea, where Olgerd defeated the Tatars (1368).

1377-1434. JAGIELLO, the son of Olgerd, married Jadwiga of Poland (1386) and established the **personal union with Poland.** Through him Lithuania became converted to Roman Catholicism and the Polish and Lithuanian nobility gradually became assimilated. In 1387 and 1389 Moldavia and Wallachia, and in 1396 Bessarabia accepted Lithuanian suzerainty.

1398. Jagiello was obliged to recognize his cousin, **Vitovt** (Witold) as Grand Duke of Lithuania. Vitovt hoped to re-establish the independence of the country from Poland, but his failure in a crusade against the Tatars greatly weakened him.

1447. Casimir IV of Poland, having been Grand Duke of Lithuania before his accession, once again united the grand duchy and the Polish kingdom. (*Cont. p.* 419.)

c. RUSSIA, 1263-1505

The period following the death of **Alexander Nevski** (1263) was marked by the continued and repeated disruption of the Russian lands, due to the complicated and unfortunate system of succession in the princely family. Russia was under the **suzerainty of the Tatars,** who played off one candidate against another, thus increasing the confusion and perpetuating the weakness of the country. The **rise of Moscow** (first

mentioned 1147) to prominence among the Russian principalities was perhaps the most important development looking toward the future. Centrally located, Moscow was in the most favorable position to serve as nucleus for a revived Russian state.

1325-1341. IVAN I KALITA (*Moneybag*), Grand Prince of Moscow. His was the first of a series of noteworthy reigns. Extremely cautious and parsimonious, Ivan bought immunity from Tatar interference and was ultimately entrusted by the Tatars with the collection of tribute from the other princes.

1341-1353. Simeon I continued the policy of his predecessor and was placed, by the Tatar overlord, above all the other princes.

1353-1359. Ivan II Krasnyi (*the Red*).

1359-1389. DMITRI DONSKOI (of the Don), who ascended the princely throne at the age of nine. His reign was filled with a struggle against **Michael of Tver,** his chief rival, who was supported by Olgerd of Lithuania. At the same time he began the conflict with the Tatars, whose power was fading, but who also enjoyed the support of Lithuania.

1380, Sept. 8. THE BATTLE OF KULIKOVO. Dmitri completely defeated the Tatar armies before the Lithuanians arrived. The victory was in no sense decisive, for the Tatars on several occasions thereafter advanced to the very gates of Moscow. But Kulikovo broke the prestige of the Tatar arms and marked the turning point.

1389-1425. Basil I. He annexed Nishni-Novgorod and continued the struggle with the Tatars and the Lithuanians, without forcing a decision.

1425-1462. Basil II, whose reign was distinguished by a relapse into anarchy. A long civil war with his rivals, Yuri and Shemyaka, was followed by Tatar invasion (1451, the Tatars beaten back from Moscow). Nevertheless the Moscow principality managed to maintain itself. In 1439 Basil refused to accept the union of the Eastern and Western Churches, arranged for at the Council of Florence. Thenceforth the Russian metropolitan, who had moved to Moscow in the time of Ivan Kalita, became more and more the head of an independent Russian Church.

1462-1505. IVAN III (*the Great*), who may be regarded as the first national sovereign of Russia. By a cautious but persistent policy he annexed most of the rival principalities and, after a series of wars, subjected Novgorod, where the patrician elements tended to side with Lithuania. In 1471 Novgorod was obliged to renounce the alliance of Lithuania and to pay tribute. After a second war, in 1478, Novgorod's independence was ended and the troublesome upper classes were deported to central Russia. In 1494 Ivan drove out the German merchants and closed the Hanseatic Kontor. Thus he acquired the huge territory of Novgorod, extending eastward to the Urals. Indirectly he greatly reduced the danger of Lithuanian interference. The annexation of Tver (1485) put an end to the most formidable rival of Moscow.

1472. Marriage of Ivan with Zoë (Sophia), niece of the last Greek emperor of Constantinople. This was arranged by the pope in the hope of bringing the Russians into the Roman Church, but all efforts in that direction failed. The marriage was of importance in establishing the claim of Russian rulers to be the successors of the Greek emperors and the protectors of Orthodox Christianity (theory of the Three Romes, of which Moscow was to be the third and last). It also served to introduce into Moscow the Byzantine conception of the autocrat (Ivan took the title of *Tsar*, i.e. Caesar) and the practice of court ceremonial. Rebuilding of the grand ducal palace (Kremlin) with the assistance of Italian architects brought in by Zoë. The court hierarchy (precedence in rank of princes and nobles, etc.).

1480. Ivan threw off the Tatar yoke after a last Tatar advance on Moscow. Ivan avoided open warfare, but took advantage of the disunion among the Tatars. The Khan of the Crimea (Mengli Girai) became his ally against the Lithuanians.

1492. Invasion of Lithuania, made possible by dynastic troubles in Lithuania and Poland. A **second invasion** (1501) led to the conclusion of peace in 1503, which brought Russia many of the border territories of White Russia and Little Russia. Moscow had by this time become an important factor in European affairs and enjoyed a considerable prestige. Resumption of active diplomatic relations with western countries. (*Cont. p. 421.*)

d. HUNGARY, 1301-1490

At the beginning of the 14th century Hungary was already an essentially feudal country, in which the great magnates and the bishops, richly endowed with land, ruled as virtually independent potentates ("little kings"), while the lower nobility, organized in the *Comitats* (provincial governments), had, to a large degree, control of the administration. The nobility, freed of taxation, was responsible for defense, but acted only as it saw fit.

1301-1308. The **extinction of the Arpad dynasty** led to a period of conflict, during which Czech, German, and Italian parties each attempted to put their candidates on the throne. **Wenceslas,** son of the King of Bohemia, only thirteen years old, was first elevated, but could not maintain himself. The same fate befell **Otto of Bavaria.**

1308-1342. CHARLES I (Charles Robert of Ánjou), a grandson of Mary, the daughter of Stephen V, was elected and founded the brilliant and successful Anjou line. Charles established his capital at Visegrad and introduced Italian chivalry and western influences. After 15 years of effort he succeeded in subduing the "little kings" of whom **Mathias of Csak** and **Ladislas of Transylvania** were the most powerful. Recognizing the hopelessness of suppressing the nobility entirely, he regulated its position and obliged it to furnish specified contingents to the army. Regulation of taxation (first direct tax); encouragement of towns and trade. Charles left the royal power well entrenched, but only as part of an avowedly feudal order.

1342-1382. LOUIS (*the Great*), the son of Charles, a patron of learning who established a brilliant court at Buda. He attempted to solidify the position of his house in Naples and embarked on a successful expedition to Italy to avenge the murder of his brother Andrew (1347). In conjunction with Genoa he carried on a long struggle with Venice, which ended in the **Peace of 1381:** Venice ceded Dalmatia and paid tribute. In the east the Hungarian power made itself felt throughout the Balkans: Serbia, Wallachia, and Moldavia recognized the suzerainty of Louis; foundation of the border districts (*banats*) south of the Danube and the Save, as protection against the Turkish advance. **War against the Turks:** Hungarian victory in northern Bulgaria (1366).

1370. Louis became King of Poland but paid little attention to his new obligations. In Hungary he continued the work of his father: the *jus aviticum* (1351) restricted the freedom of the great magnates to dispose of their property.

1382-1385. Mary of Anjou, queen. She was married to Sigismund of Luxemburg, who became guardian of the kingdom. His position was challenged by Charles of Durazzo and

Naples, who had many adherents, especially in southern Hungary and Croatia.

1385-1386. Charles II (of Naples). He was assassinated after a very brief reign, which led to a new revolt in Croatia.

1387-1437. SIGISMUND (of Luxemburg), who became German Emperor in 1410 and King of Bohemia in 1436. His reign marked a great decline in the royal power, due in large measure to Sigismund's constant absence from the country and his practice of selling royal domains in order to get money for his far-reaching schemes elsewhere. In general Sigismund relied on the towns and lesser nobility against the great magnates (who imprisoned him for four months in 1401). Hence the grant of ever greater rights to the Comitats.

1396. The diastrous **crusade of Nicopolis** against the Turks (p. 330). Loss of Dalmatia to the Venetians. Hussite invasions of Hungary, resulting from Sigismund's attempts to gain the Bohemian throne.

1437-1439. Albert of Hapsburg, the son of Sigismund, also German Emperor and King of Bohemia. He was obliged to sign far-reaching capitulations (nobles not obliged to fight beyond the frontiers).

1437. First victory of John Hunyadi over the Turks. Hunyadi was a powerful frontier lord of uncertain origin.

1440-1444. Vladislav I (Vladislav VI of Poland), a weak ruler, whose reign was distinguished chiefly by the continued victories of Hunyadi (1443). Crusade against the Turks.

1444, Nov. 10. Disaster at Varna and death of Vladislav.

1444-1457. Ladislas V, the son of Albert of Hapsburg, also King of Bohemia. He was only four years old at his accession and Hunyadi was therefore appointed governor of the kingdom until 1452.

1456. Crusade against the Turks, preached by John of Capistrano and led by Hunyadi. The Turks were turned back from the siege of Belgrade, but Hunyadi died in the same year.

1458-1490. MATHIAS CORVINUS (*the Just*), the son of John Hunyadi and one of the greatest of the Hungarian kings. He was fifteen at his election, but soon distinguished himself as a soldier, statesman and patron of art and learning. Intelligent, firm, crafty, yet just and noble, he re-established the power of the crown and made Hungary the dominant power in central Europe, if only of the brief space of his reign. He once again broke the power of the oligarchs and drew on the support of the lesser nobility. Development of a central administration; regulation and increase of the taxes. Great wealth and luxury of the court. The *Bibliotheca Corvina*, consisting of more than 10,000 manuscripts and books, many beautifully illuminated by Italian artists. Mathias the patron of Renaissance learning. Famous law code (1486). Creation of a standing army (*Black Troop*), composed first of Bohemian, Moravian, and Silesian mercenaries. This gave Mathias one of the most effective fighting forces in the Europe of his day. **Mathias' aims:** to secure the Bohemian throne and ultimately the empire and then to direct a united central Europe against the Turks. Long struggles against **George Podiebrad** of Bohemia ended with George's death in 1471, after Mathias had been proclaimed King of Bohemia (1470). Equally prolonged struggle against Emperor Frederick III, who had been elected King of Hungary by a faction of nobles in 1439. Frederick was finally bought off (1462), but trouble continued. Mathias, disposing of much greater funds and forces than Frederick, conquered not only Silesia and Moravia, but also lower Austria. His capital established at Vienna (1485). Mathias died at 47, leaving Hungary the dominant state in central Europe and a decisive factor in European diplomacy.

(*Cont. p. 425.*)

e. THE SERBIAN STATES, 1276-1499

By the end of the 13th century the Serbian states, like others of eastern Europe, had evolved a strong secular and clerical aristocracy which, to a large extent, controlled even the more outstanding rulers. In view of the general unsettlement of the law regarding succession and inheritance, the tendency toward dynastic conflict and territorial disruption was very pronounced. In the western Balkans the situation was further complicated by the rivalry of the western and eastern forms of Christianity, to say nothing of the persistence of the heretical Bogomil teaching, especially in Bosnia.

1276-1281. Dragutin, with the aid of the Hungarians, seized the Serbian throne from his father, **Urosh I.** Having been defeated in battle by the Greeks, he abdicated after a short rule.

1281-1321. Milyutin (*Stephen Urosh II*), the brother of Dragutin. He was a pious and yet dissolute ruler, but above all a political and religious opportunist. Taking full advantage of the growing weakness of the Byzantine Empire, he gradually extended his possessions in Macedonia, along the Adriatic, and, in the north, toward the Danube and the Save.

1321-1331. Stephen Dechanski (*Stephen Urosh III*), the illegitimate son of the preceding. His reign was marked chiefly by the great victory of the Serbs over the Greeks and Bulgarians near **Küstendil** (Velbuzhde) in 1330. The Serbs now held most of the Vardar Valley.

1331-1355. STEPHEN DUSHAN (*Stephen Urosh IV*), the greatest of the Serbian rulers in the Middle Ages. Dushan began his career by deposing his father, who was strangled soon afterward. For most of his reign he attempted to maintain friendly relations with Hungary and Ragusa, in order to have a free hand to exploit the dynastic war in the Byzantine Empire between the Palaeologi and John Cantacuzene. By 1344 he had subjected all of Macedonia, Albania, Thessaly, and Epirus. His daughter was married to the Bulgarian tsar and Bulgaria was under Serbian supremacy.

1346. Dushan set up his capital at Skoplye (Usküb) and proclaimed himself *Emperor of the Serbs, Greeks, Bulgars, and Albanians*. At the same time he set up a Serbian patriarchate at Peč (İpek), for which he was anathematized by the Greek patriarch. Dushan established a court wholly Byzantine in character, with elaborate titles and ceremonial. In the years 1349–1354 he drew up his famous law code (*Zakonnik*), which gives an invaluable picture of Serbian conditions and culture at the time.

1349. Attack upon Dushan by the ruler of Bosnia. This led to the invasion of Bosnia by the Serbs, who found much support among the Bogomils, resentful of the Catholic proclivities of their rulers. The conquest of Bosnia was not completed because of Dushan's diversion elsewhere.

1353. Dushan defeated Louis of Hungary, who had been instigated by the pope to lead a Catholic crusade. The Serbs now acquired Belgrade.

1355. Dushan died at the age of 46 as he was en route to Constantinople. Thus perished his hope of succeeding to the imperial throne and consolidating the Balkans in the face of the growing power of the Ottoman Turks (p. 330).

1355-1371. Stephen Urosh V, a weak ruler who was faced, from the outset, by the disruptive ambitions of his uncle Simeon and other powerful magnates. He was the last of the Nemanyid house.

1358. Hungary obtained most of Dalmatia, after defeating Venice. Ragusa became a Hungarian protectorate.

1371. Battle of the Maritza River, in which the Turks, having settled in Thrace, defeated a combination of Serbian lords.

1371. Zeta (Montenegro) became a separate principality under the Balsha family (until 1421).

1371-1389. Lazar I, of the Hrebelyanovich family, became *Prince* of Serbia.

1375. The Greek patriarch finally recognized the Patriarchate of Peč.

1376. TVRTKO I, Lord of Bosnia from 1353–1391, proclaimed himself *King of Serbia and Bosnia*, taking over parts of western Serbia and controlling most of the Adriatic coast, excepting Zara and Ragusa. Tvrtko was the greatest of the Bosnian rulers and made his state for a time the strongest Slavic state in the Balkans.

1389, June 20 (traditional June 15). **BATTLE OF KOSSOVO,** a decisive date in all Balkan history. Prince Lazar, at the head of a coalition of Serbs, Bosnians, Albanians, and Wallachians, attempted to stop the advance of the Turks under Murad I. Murad was killed by a Serb who posed as a traitor, but his son Bayazid won a victory. Lazar was captured and killed, due to the reputed desertion of Vuk Brankovich. Henceforth Serbia was a vassal state of the Turks.

1389-1427. STEPHEN LAZAREVICH, the son of Lazar I. He was a literary person, but withal an able statesman. During the early years of his reign he loyally supported the Turks, being present with his forces at the **battles of Nicopolis** (1396) and **Angora** (1402). In return the Turks recognized him as *Despot of Serbia*, and supported him against Hungary and other enemies.

1391. Death of Tvrtko I of Bosnia; gradual disintegration of the Bosnian Kingdom.

1392. Venice acquired Durazzo, beginning the process of establishment on the Dalmatian and Albanian coasts. Scutari was acquired in 1396, and when, in 1420, Venice secured **Cattaro,** she possessed practically all the fortified coast towns.

1393. Hungary recovered Croatia and Dalmatia from the Bosnian Kingdom. Hungarian campaigns against Bosnia itself continued for years, until the native elements in 1416 called in the Turks.

1427-1456. GEORGE BRANKOVICH, the nephew of Stephen Lazarevich, Despot of Serbia. He built himself a new capital at Semendria (Smederovo) on the Danube and attempted, with Hungarian support, to hold his own against the Turks. This policy led to a Turk invasion (1439) and conquest of the country, the Hungarians, however, saving Belgrade. But in 1444 Brankovich, with the aid of **John Hunyadi** (p. 323), recovered his possessions and the Serbian state was recognized in the **Treaty of Szegedin.** Thereafter Brankovich deserted Hunyadi and tried to maintain himself through close relations with the Turks.

1456-1458. Lazar III, the son of George Brankovich. On his death he left his kingdom to

1458-1459. Stephen Tomashevich, the heir to the Bosnian throne. Stephen, as a Roman Catholic, was much disliked by the Serbs, who consequently offered less resistance to the Turks.

1459. The Turks definitively conquered and incorporated Serbia with the empire.

1463. The Turks overran and conquered Bosnia.

1483. Turkish conquest of Herzegovina (Hun).

1499. Conquest of Zeta (Montenegro) by the Turks.

f. THE EASTERN EMPIRE, 1261-1453

After the recapture of Constantinople by the Greeks in 1261, the **Empire of the Palaeologi** was still a relatively small domain, consisting of the former Nicaean Empire, the city of Constantinople and its immediate surroundings, the coastal part of Thrace, southern Macedonia with Thessalonica, the islands of Imbros, Samothrace, Lesbos, and Rhodes. In Anatolia the northeastern part was still held by the Greek Empire of Trebizond, which in the course of the 13th century had managed to hold a balance between the Seljuk Turks and the Mongols and had become the great entrepôt of the eastern trade coming to the Black Sea by way of Persia and Armenia. The city and the court reached its highest prosperity and brilliance under the Emperor **Alexius II** (1297-1330), whose reign was followed by a period of dynastic and factional struggle, marked by unbelievable degeneracy and cruelty. The reign of **John Alexius III** (1350-1390) marked a second period of splendor,

but the 15th century was one of decline. The empire came to an end with the Ottoman conquest in 1461 (last ruler, **David,** 1458-1461).

The European territories of the earlier empire were divided between the Greek Despotate of Epirus and the Greek Duchy of Neopatras (Thessaly, Locris), the Latin Duchy of Athens, the Latin Principality of Achaia, and the Venetian Duchy of the Archipelago.

1261-1282. MICHAEL VIII (*Palaeologus*). He was the ablest of the Paleologi, a man who devoted himself to the restoration of Byzantine authority throughout the Balkan area, persisting despite many setbacks.

1261. Michael established a foothold in the southeastern part of the Peloponnese (Morea), which was widely expanded in the ensuing period. **Mistra** (Misithra) became the capital of a flourishing principality and one of the great centers of late-Byzantine culture.

1262. Michael II of Epirus was forced to recognize the suzerainty of the Constantinople emperor. In a series of campaigns much of the despotate was regained for the empire (Janina taken, 1265).

1264-1265. Constant raids of the Bulgars into Thrace led to a formidable campaign against them and the reconquest of part of Macedonia.

1266. Charles of Anjou became King of Sicily. He made an alliance with Baldwin II, the last Latin emperor, and, through the marriage of his son with the heiress of the Villehardouins, extended his authority over Achaia. He soon became the most formidable opponent of the Greeks, for by the **Treaty of Viterbo** (1267) he took over the claims of Baldwin II.

1267. Michael permitted the Genoese to establish themselves at Galata, across from Constantinople. This was part of his policy of encouraging the Genoese at the expense of the Venetians, to whom, however, he had to grant privileges also (1268).

1271. Death of Michael II of Epirus. Charles of Anjou had already taken Corfu (1267) and now undertook the conquest of the Epiran coast, the essential base for any advance on Thessalonica and Constantinople. Durazzo was taken in 1272. **John Angelus,** driven out of Epirus, set up as Lord of Neopatras (to 1295). **Nicephorus I** was the titular ruler of a much-reduced Epiran state (to 1296). Charles of Anjou proclaimed himself *King of Albania* and entered into alliance with the Serbs, who had begun the construction of a large state by advancing down the Vardar Valley.

1274. THE COUNCIL OF LYON. Michael, in order to escape from the Angevin danger, accepted the Roman creed and the primacy of the pope, thus effecting the reunion with Rome. This move, purely political in intent, met with vigorous resistance on the part of the Orthodox Greek clergy and in the long run only served to accentuate the antagonism of Greek and Latin.

1274. Campaigns of Michael against the Angevins in Epirus. These campaigns were carried on year after year, with varying success.

1278. The death of William of Villehardouin, Prince of Achaia, gave the Greeks an opportunity to expand their holding in the southeastern part.

1281. Michael VIII won a great victory over the Angevins at Berat. Thereupon Charles made an alliance with the papacy and with Venice, with which the Serbs and Bulgars were associated. Michael in reply effected a rapprochement with Peter of Aragon.

1282. The Sicilian Vespers (p. 294). This blow at the Angevin power in Sicily served to relieve the pressure on the Greek Empire.

1282–1328. ANDRONICUS II, the son of Michael, a learned, pious, but weak ruler, whose first move was to give up the hated union with Rome and conciliate the Orthodox clergy.

1285. Venice deserted the Angevin alliance and made a ten-year peace with the Greeks.

1295–1320. MICHAEL IX, son of Andronicus, co-emperor with his father.

1296. The Serbs, continuing their advance, conquered western Macedonia and northern Albania. Andronicus was obliged to recognize these losses (1298).

1302. Peace between the Angevins and the Aragonese. Andronicus, once again exposed to Angevin ambition, engaged **Roger de**

The Palaeologi

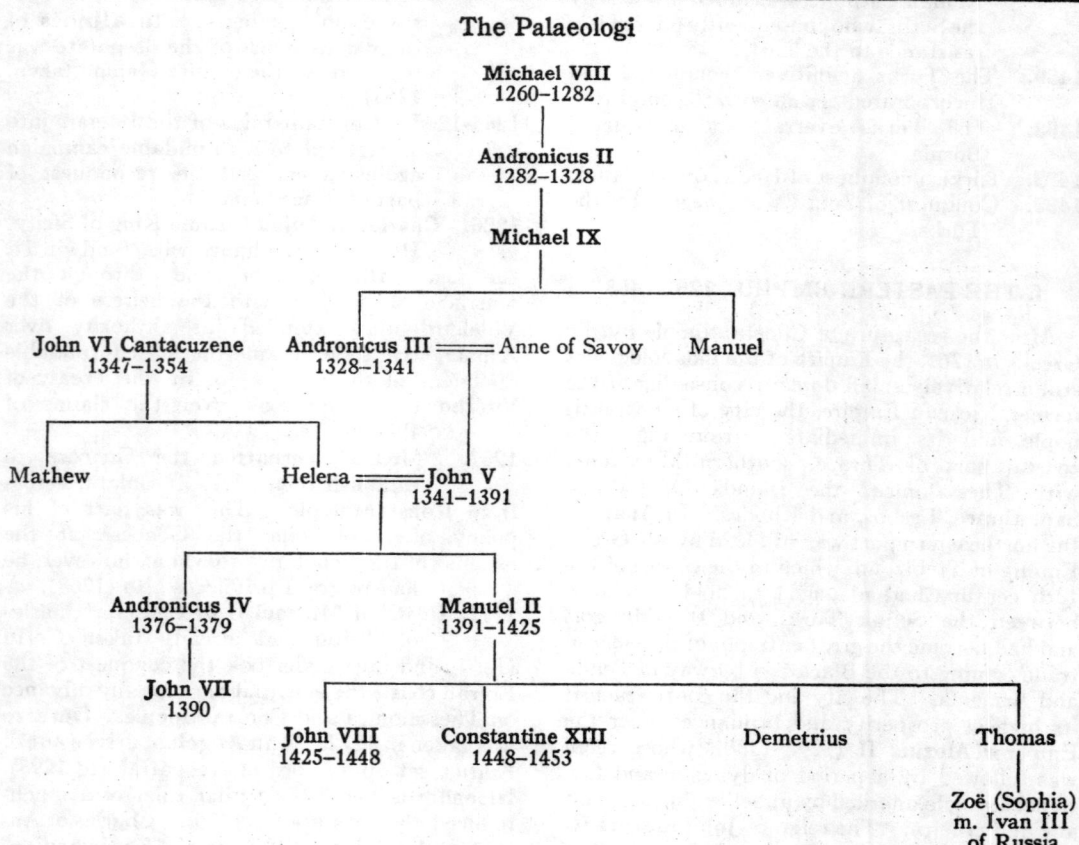

Michael VIII
1260–1282

Andronicus II
1282–1328

Michael IX

John VI Cantacuzene   Andronicus III ══ Anne of Savoy   Manuel
1347–1354   1328–1341

Mathew   Helena ══ John V
                          1341–1391

Andronicus IV   Manuel II
1376–1379   1391–1425

John VII
1390

John VIII   Constantine XIII   Demetrius   Thomas
1425–1448   1448–1453

Zoë (Sophia)
m. Ivan III
of Russia

Flor and 6000 Catalan mercenaries (the *Catalan Company*) to fight against the Italians. They raised havoc at Constantinople, where 3000 Italians are said to have been killed in the disorders.

1304. The Catalans repulsed an attack of the Turks on Philadelphia, but they then turned and attacked Constantinople (1305–1307), without being able to take it.

1305. Murder of Roger de Flor. The Catalan Company became a veritable scourge, roaming through Thrace and Macedonia and laying the country waste.

1311. The Catalans, having advanced into Greece, took the Duchy of Athens, where they set up a dynasty of their own.

1321–1328. Civil war between the emperor and his grandson Andronicus. In the course of the struggle much of the empire was devastated.

1325. Andronicus was obliged to accept his grandson as co-emperor.

1326. RISE OF THE OTTOMAN TURKS in northwestern Anatolia. In 1326 they took Brusa from the Greeks, and in 1328 Nicomedia (p. 330).

1328–1341. ANDRONICUS III, the grandson of Andronicus II, who finally forced the emperor's abdication (d. 1332). Andronicus III was a frivolous and irresponsible ruler, wholly unequal to the great problems presented by the rise of the Turkish and Serb powers (Sultan Orkhan, 1326–1359; Tsar Stephen Dushan, 1331–1355).

1329. The Greeks managed to take the important island of Chios from the Genoese.

1330. The Serbs defeated the Bulgars in a decisive battle and put an end to the Bulgar power.

1334–1335. Andronicus conquered Thessaly and part of Epirus from the despot, John II Orsini.

1336. The Greeks reconquered Lesbos.

1340. Stephen Dushan, having conquered the Albanian coastal territory (as far as Valona) from the Angevins, drove the Greeks out of the interior and took Janina.

1341–1376. JOHN V, the son of Andronicus III, ascended the throne as a child, under the regency of his mother, Anna of Savoy.

1341–1347. CIVIL WAR IN THE EMPIRE. John Cantacuzene, supported by the aristocratic elements, set himself up as a rival emperor. John V was supported by the popular elements. In the ensuing war much of Thrace and Macedonia was ravaged. The war proved to be the undoing of the empire, since both sides freely called in Serbs or Turks to support them.

1341–1351. THE HESYCHAST CONTROVERSY in the Greek Church, which added to the confusion. The controversy was really a conflict between the mystic teachings emanating from the monasteries of Mt. Athos (founded 962 ff.) and the rationalism of the clergy. The Hesychasts (*Zealots*) supported Cantacuzene and were victorious with him. In the interval the dispute led to a great popular, almost socialistic rising in Thessalonica, where the extremists set up an almost independent state (1342–1347).

1343. The Venetians, taking advantage of the civil war, seized Smyrna.

1346. Stephen Dushan was crowned Emperor of the Serbs and the Greeks and made preparations to seize Constantinople and replace the Greek dynasty.

1347. Cantacuzene managed to take Constantinople, through treachery.

1347–1354. JOHN VI (*Cantacuzene*), sole emperor. He made his son Manuel despot of the Morea (1348). The Serbs held all of Macedonia.

1351. Stephen Dushan besieged Thessalonica.

1353. The **Ottoman Turks,** called in by Cantacuzene, defeated the Serbs.

1354. The Turks established themselves in Europe, at Gallipoli, thus beginning their phenomenal career of expansion (p. 330).

1355. John V took Constantinople and forced the abdication of Cantacuzene (d. 1383). At the same time Dushan, having taken Adrianople, was advancing on the capital. His sudden death (1355) led to the disintegration of the Serb Empire and to the removal of a great threat to the Greeks. On the other hand, it left the Christians an easier prey to the advancing Turks.

1365. The Turks, having overrun Thrace, took Adrianople, which became their capital.

1366. John V, who had been captured by Tsar Shishman of Bulgaria, was liberated by his cousin, Amadeo of Savoy.

1369. John V appeared before the pope at Avignon and agreed to union of the churches, in order to secure aid of the west against the Turks.

1376-1379. ANDRONICUS IV, the son of John V, who dethroned his father with the aid of the Genoese.

1379-1391. John V, supported by the Turks, managed to recover his throne.

1386. The Venetians recovered Corfu, which they held until 1797.

1388. The Venetians purchased Argos and Nauplia.

1389. Battle of **Kossovo** (p. 324). End of the great Serb Empire.

1390. John VII, a grandson of John V, deposed the latter, but after a few months the old emperor was restored by his second son, Manuel.

1391-1425. MANUEL II, an able ruler in a hopeless position. By this time the empire had been reduced to the city of Constantinople, the city of Thessalonica, and the province of Morea. The Turks held Thrace and Macedonia.

1391-1395. The Turks, under Bayazid I, blockaded Constantinople, and only the Christian crusade that ended in the disastrous **battle of Nicopolis** (1396) gave the Greeks some respite.

1397. Bayazid attacked Constantinople, which was valiantly defended by Marshal Boucicault. This time the advance of the Tatars under Timur distracted the Turks. The defeat and capture of Bayazid in the **battle of Angora** (1402), led to a period of confusion and dynastic war among the Turks.

1422. The Turks again attacked Constantinople, because of Manuel's support of the Turkish pretender Mustapha, against Murad II.

1423. The Venetians bought the city of Thessalonica.

1425-1448. JOHN VIII, the son of Manuel, whose position was, from the outset, desperate.

1428. Constantine and Thomas Palaeologus, brothers of the emperor, conquered Frankish Morea, with the exception of the Venetian ports. In these last years the Morea was the most extensive and valuable part of the empire.

1430. The Turks took Thessalonica from the Venetians.

1439. THE COUNCIL OF FLORENCE. John VIII, having traveled to Italy, once again accepted the union with Rome and the papal primacy. As on earlier occasions this step raised a storm of opposition among the Greeks and to some extent facilitated the Turk conquests.

1444. A second crusade from the west ended in disaster when the Turks won a decisive victory at **Varna.**

1446. The Turks frustrated an attempt of the Greeks to expand from the Morea into central Greece. Corinth fell into Turkish hands.

1448-1453. CONSTANTINE XIII, the last Byzantine emperor.

1453. The siege and capture of **Constantinople** by **Mohammed the Conqueror** (p. 331). End of the **Eastern Empire** after a thousand years of existence.

1460. Conquest of the Morea by the Turks. End of the rule of the Palaeologi in Greece.

1461. Conquest of the Empire of Trebizond, the last Greek state, by the Turks.

BYZANTINE CULTURE in the time of the Palaeologi. The territorial and political decline of the empire was accompanied by an extraordinary cultural revival, analogous to the Renaissance in Italy. The schools of Constantinople flourished and produced a group of outstanding scholars (philosophy: **Planudes, Plethon, Bessarion**). In theology the dominant current was one of mysticism (**Gregory Palamas** and the *Hesychasts*; **George Scholarius**). Historical writing reached a high plane in the work of **John Cantacuzene, Nicephorus Gregoras,** and, in the last years of the empire, of **Phrantzes, Ducas, and Chalcocondylas.** Art, especially painting, was distinctly humanized and three different schools (Constantinople, Macedonia, and Crete) cast a flood of splendor over the closing years of the empire. **Mistra,** the capital of the Morean province, became in the early 15th century the center of a revived Greek national feeling and a home of scholars and artists.

g. THE OTTOMAN EMPIRE, 1300-1481

The presence of the Turks in central Asia can be traced back to at least the 6th century A.D. (**Orchon inscriptions,** dealing with the period 630–680). These Turks, of the Oghuz family, were conquered by the Uighurs in 745 and continued under their rule until 840, when they in turn were conquered by the Kirghiz, coming from the west. In the 9th and 10th centuries the Turks were converted to Islam, and in the 11th century, having pushed their advance into southeastern Russia and Iran, began to attack the Byzantine Empire. The **Seljuks,** a branch of the Turks, took Baghdad in 1055, and in the following two centuries built up an imposing empire in Anatolia and the Middle East (p. 257).

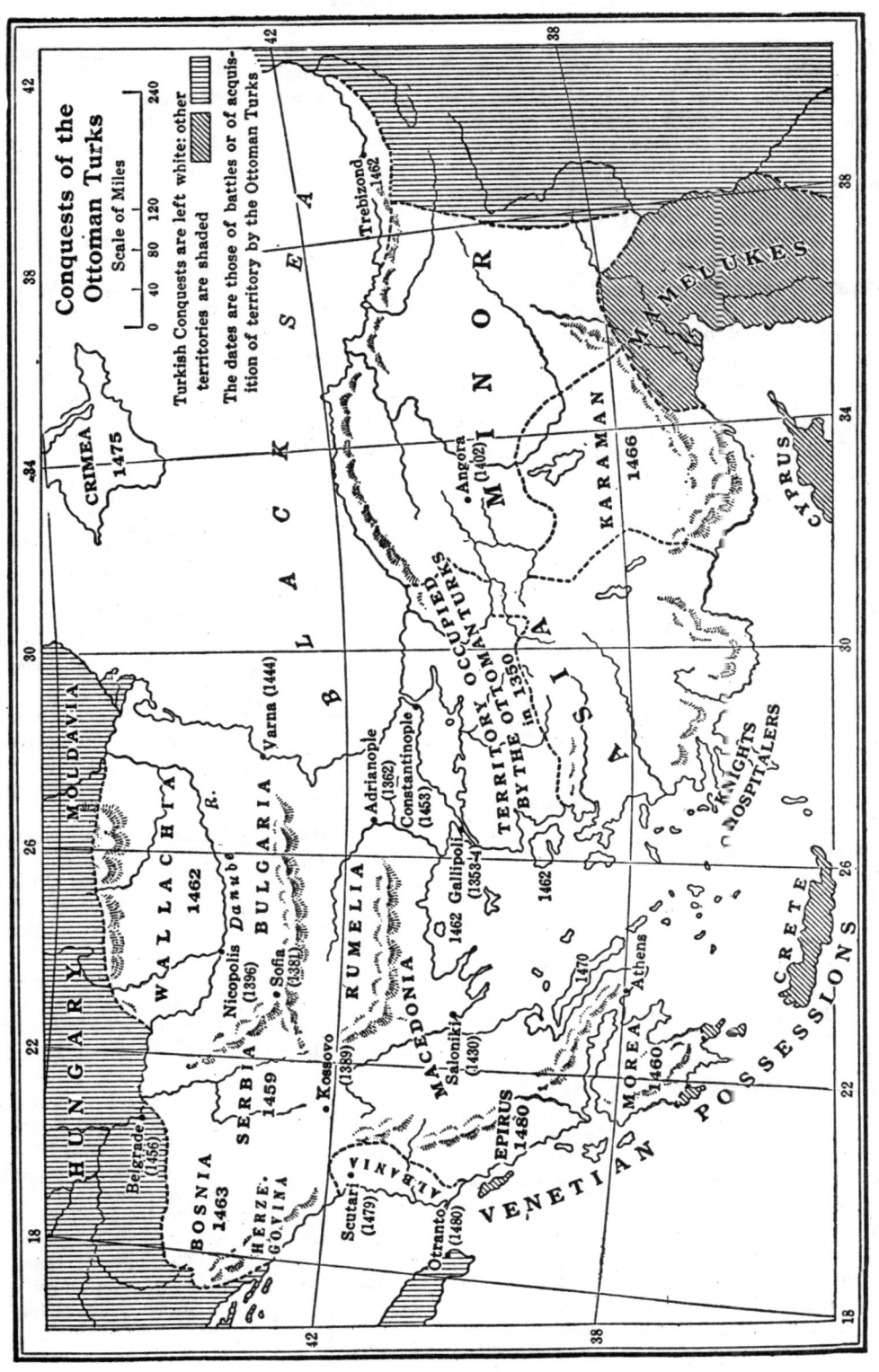

**Conquests of the
Ottoman Turks**

Scale of Miles

0   40   80   120   240

Turkish Conquests are left white; other
territories are shaded

The dates are those of battles or of acquisition of territory by the Ottoman Turks

CRIMEA
1475

B L A C K   S E A

Trebizond
1462

MAMELUKES

CYPRUS

M   I   N   O   R

KARAMAN
1466

•Angora
(1402)

A   S   I   A

KNIGHTS
HOSPITALERS

TERRITORY OCCUPIED
BY THE OTTOMAN TURKS
IN 1350

MOLDAVIA

HUNGARY

WALLACHIA
1462

Danube R.

Nicopolis
(1396)

BULGARIA

Varna (1444)

•Sofia.
(1381)

•Adrianople
(1362)

Constantinople
(1453)

Belgrade
(1456)

BOSNIA
1463

SERBIA
1459

•Kossovo
(1389)

RUMELIA

1462

Gallipoli
(1353-4)

1462

HERZE-
GOVINA

ALBANIA

Scutari
(1479)

Otranto
(1480)

MACEDONIA

Saloniki
(1430)

EPIRUS
1480

1470

MOREA
1460

Athens

V E N E T I A N   P O S S E S S I O N S

CRETE

1243.   The Mongols, under Chinjiz (Jenghis) Khan, defeated the Seljuks at Kösedagh. Anatolia under Mongol suzerainty; disintegration of the Seljuk Empire in Anatolia; appearance of local dynasties in many places, especially along the Aegean coast.

1289. Traditional date of the **death of Ertogrul,** half-legendary leader of a Turkish tribe serving as frontier guards on the border of the Byzantine Empire.

1290-1326.   OSMAN (Othman) I, traditional founder of the Ottoman dynasty. He continued the work of his father, but gradually extended his territory at the expense of the Byzantine Empire, which was weakened by the transfer of many of its frontier guards to the Balkans. The Turks were almost certainly more civilized and less nomadic than has generally been supposed. There is evidence to show that Osman had at his command well-organized forces (*Akhi,* a type of semi-religious and possibly mercantile as well as military society). But the Turkish advance seems to have taken the form of gradual infiltration more than outright conquest.

1317-1326. Siege of Brusa by the Ottoman Turks. The town was finally starved into submission.

1326-1359.   ORKHAN I, the first well-authenticated ruler and obviously the organizer of the empire.

1329. The Turks defeated a Byzantine force under Andronicus III at **Maltepe.**

1331. Nicaea taken by the Turks.

1337 or 1338. Nicomedia (Ismid) taken by the Turks.

1345. The Ottomans first crossed into Europe, called in by the Emperor John Cantacuzene, to support his claims against the Empress Anna. Orkhan married Theodora, daughter of Cantacuzene.

1349. The Turks again called in by Cantacuzene, to aid him against the Serbian conqueror, Stephen Dushan.

1354. First settlement of the Turks in Europe (Tzympe, on Gallipoli), as a result of a third appeal by Cantacuzene for aid. They spread rapidly through Thrace. On Orkhan's death the state was already well-organized (first Ottoman coins) and the Turkish ruler was able to dictate to the Byzantine emperors.

1359-1389.   MURAD I.

1365. Adrianople taken by the Turks, who soon made it their capital (1366), replacing Brusa. Organization of the **Janissary corps** (date uncertain) composed of captives taken in war, and later of levies of Christian children.

1365. Ragusa made a commercial treaty with the Turks, paying tribute.

1366. Crusade of Amadeus of Savoy. He took Gallipoli, but was soon obliged to abandon it. Victory of Louis of Hungary near Vidin.

1369-1372. Conquest of Bulgaria to the Balkan Mountains. Shishman, ruler of Bulgaria, became a vassal of the Turks.

1371. Defeat of the Serbs by the Turks at **Cernomen** on the Maritza River; conquest of Macedonia by the Turks. Raids into Albania and Greece. Continued interference of the Turks in Byzantine affairs.

1385. Capture of Sofia by the Turks.

1386. Capture of Nish. Lazar of Serbia became a Turkish vassal.

1387. Genoa made a treaty with Murad.

1388. Venice made a treaty with the Turks.

1389, June 20 (June 15 traditional). **BATTLE OF KOSSOVO.** Murad defeated a coalition of Serbs, Bulgars, Bosnians, Wallachians, and Albanians. Lazar was killed in battle, Murad assassinated just after it, by a Serb.

1389-1402.   BAYAZID I. He began his career by having his brother Yakub strangled. The Serbs were treated leniently and Bayazid turned his attention to Anatolia.

1391. Invasion of Karamania (the leading Anatolian emirate) by Bayazid, who conquered part of it. Several of the other emirates peacefully absorbed. By 1395 the Ottoman Empire extended east to Sivas.

1391-1398. First siege of Constantinople by the Turks. Bayazid made and unmade emperors and extracted a heavy tribute.

1396.   CRUSADE OF NICOPOLIS, led by Sigismund of Hungary, supported by Balkan rulers and by French, German, and English knights, as well as by the Roman and Avignon popes. Venice and Genoa negotiated with both sides. The knights assembled with great pomp at Buda and proceeded along the Danube to Nicopolis, pillaging and slaying. On Sept. 25 they met the Turks about four miles south of Nicopolis. The knights ignored all advice and pressed forward; after an initial success they were completely overwhelmed and many captured. Forces were about 20,000 on each side.

1397. Invasion of Greece by the Turks, who advanced as far as Corinth, though they did not take Athens.

1400. Invasion of Anatolia by the Mongols under **Timur** (p. 335). They took Sivas. Provocative attitude of Bayazid.

1402, July 20. **BATTLE OF ANGORA** (Ankara). Bayazid, deserted by most of his Turkish vassals, was completely defeated and captured. Timur restored many of the Turkish emirs and advanced to Nicaea and Brusa. The Ottoman Empire on the verge of dissolution. Dispute of Bayazid's sons for the succession.

1403. **Mohammed** defeated his brother **Musa** and became sultan of the remaining Asiatic possessions (retirement of Timur from Anatolia, 1403). **Suleiman** became sultan of the European territory.

1405. Suleiman crossed to Anatolia and drove Mohammed into the mountains. Most of the emirs reinstituted by Timur were reduced to obedience.

1406. On Suleiman's return to Europe, Mohammed regained control in Anatolia. He sent his brother Musa to Wallachia to attack Suleiman from the north.

1410. Musa took Adrianople, but was defeated by Suleiman.

1411. Suleiman, having returned to Anatolia, was captured and strangled. His place in Europe was taken by Musa.

1413. Mohammed crossed to Europe, defeated and killed Musa, and re-established his power over the whole empire.

1413-1421. **MOHAMMED I** (*the Restorer*). He devoted most of his energy to consolidating his authority.

1416. **First war with Venice,** due chiefly to Turkish activity in the Aegean. The Doge Loredano destroyed a Turkish fleet off Gallipoli, whereupon Mohammed wisely made peace.

1421-1451. **MURAD II.**

1422. **Mustafa,** a supposed son of Bayazid, supported by the Greek emperor, John VIII, defeated Murad's troops near Adrianople, but failed to get any support from Anatolia. He was ultimately captured and executed. Murad, in revenge, began to besiege Constantinople, but soon gave up the attempt.

1423. The Venetians took over Saloniki from the Greeks, as part of a plan of co-operation against the Turks.

1425-1430. **War between Venice and the Turks.** A Turkish fleet ravaged the Aegean stations of Venice, and in 1430 the Turks took Saloniki. They then conquered most of Albania and Epirus. The Venetians, having become involved in war with Milan, were forced to make peace.

1442. The Turks, having invaded Hungary, were defeated by **John Hunyadi,** a frontier lord of uncertain origin, most famous of the fighters against the Turks.

1443. **Crusade against the Turks,** instigated by the pope and composed of Hungary, Poland, Bosnia, Wallachia, and Serbia. The crusaders, led by Hunyadi, took Nish and advanced to Sofia. Murad thereupon made the ten-year **Truce of Szegedin,** with **Vladislav** of Hungary; by it Serbia was freed and Wallachia abandoned to Hungary.

1444. Murad voluntarily abdicated in favor of his fourteen-year-old son, Mohammed. The Hungarians, encouraged by the pope, thereupon broke the truce and renewed the crusade (Sept.). They advanced through Bulgaria to Varna, where they were to meet the ships of Venice that were to carry them to Constantinople. But the Venetians stayed at Gallipoli and did not even prevent Murad from crossing from Anatolia. Murad resumed the throne and on Nov. 10 completely defeated the crusaders at **Varna** (Vladislav killed).

1448, Oct. 17. **Second battle of Kossovo.** Murad defeated Hunyadi, who had again invaded Serbia.

1451-1481. **MOHAMMED II** (*the Conqueror*). He was only 21 when he succeeded his father, but seems to have been unusually well-educated and, like others of the early sultans, a man of pronounced intellectual tastes. From the very outset he devoted his attention to the capture of Constantinople, the center of intrigue against Turkish rule.

1452. Mohammed completed the **Castle of Europe** (*Rumili Hissar*) at the narrowest point of the Bosporus, opposite the older **Castle of Asia** (*Anadoli Hissar*). This assured freedom of passage between Anatolia and Europe and at the same time controlled the supplies of Constantinople. Its erection led to war with the Byzantine emperor, Constantine.

1453, Feb.-May. **SIEGE OF CONSTANTINOPLE,** at that time largely depopulated and very poor. Constantine had only some 10,000 men at his command and was unpopular because of his efforts to reunite the eastern and western churches. He received some aid from the Venetians and Genoese, but his chief asset was the tremendous wall-system of the city. The Turks concentrated between 100,000 and 150,000 men outside the city. They had a substantial fleet, but this was shut out from the Golden Horn by an iron chain. Most important was the heavy artillery, built by a Hungarian renegade, Urban, for Mohammed. The walls were continually bombarded, but the defenders managed to close the breaches. Finally Mohammed had some 70 light ships dragged overland from the Bosporus to the Golden Horn. These forced the defenders to divide their attention. On May 29 the Turks delivered a great attack on the Romanos Gate and forced an entry. Constantine was killed in the mêlée and many of the defenders escaped on Venetian and Genoese ships. The city was given up to pillage for three days. Mohammed tried at first to populate it with Turks, but had indifferent success. He then repopulated it with Greeks and other Christians, chiefly artisans, and gave the Greek patriarch, **Gennadios,** considerable civil as well as religious authority over the Orthodox inhabitants throughout the empire. Somewhat later similar authority over the Armenian community was given to the Armenian patriarch (millet system). Constantinople (Istambul) soon became the Turkish capital. Churches were transformed into mosques (notably **Santa Sophia)** and palaces built (**Old Serai,** completed 1458; **New Serai,** completed 1467). The seat of government became more firmly fixed and Mohammed evolved a complete administrative system, with an elaborate system of training (palace school; slave household). Much of the court ceremonial was borrowed from the Greeks, though the institutions were fundamentally Turk.

1456. Mohammed besieged Belgrade, after repeated raids by Hunyadi, who relieved the city, but died soon afterward (Aug.). Thereupon Mohammed subdued Serbia (1456–1458) and Bosnia and Herzegovina (1458–1461), where many of the upper classes accepted Islam. In the same years the Turkish fleet took most of the Genoese stations in the Aegean and an army overran the Morea, deposing the last Palaeologi.

1456–1463. The Albanian campaign, against **Scanderbeg** (George Castriota), a *condottiere* educated at the Turkish court, who had escaped in 1443. Scanderbeg was in the pay of Alphonse of Aragon-Naples until 1458 and thereafter in the pay of Venice. He was repeatedly driven back by the Turks, but from his stronghold at Kroia he maintained a vigorous resistance. When he died (1467), Albania was quickly conquered and incorporated in the empire.

1463–1479. FIRST GREAT WAR BETWEEN THE TURKS AND VENICE, resulting from interference with trade and from the Turkish threat to the Venetian stations on the Greek and Albanian coasts. The humanist pope, Aeneas Silvius (Pius II), attempted to organize a crusade and Hungary joined Venice. But only a small and miscellaneous force was collected at Ancona.

1468. The Turks raided Dalmatia and invaded Croatia.

1470, July. The Turks, with a huge fleet and landing force, conquered Negroponte (Euboea) from the Venetians.

1473. The Venetians induced the Persians to attack the Turks, while they raided the Anatolian coasts. The Persians were defeated at Erzingan.

1477–1478. The Turks took Kroia, Alessio, and Drivasto in Albania. Scutari was twice besieged and Turkish raiders reached the very outskirts of Venice.

1479. Peace between Venice and the Turks. The Venetians gave up Scutari and their Albanian stations, but they kept Dulcigno, Antivari, and Durazzo; they gave up Negroponte and Lemnos and paid an annual tribute of 10,000 ducats for permission to trade in the Black Sea.

1480. A Turkish force occupied Otranto in southern Italy.

1480–1481. Siege of Rhodes, held by the Knights of St. John, last Christian outpost in the eastern Mediterranean. Mohammed died before the siege could be successfully completed. (*Cont. p.* 426.)

D. AFRICA DURING THE MIDDLE AGES

AFRICA

(For the history of Mediterranean Africa see pp. 266–267)

The earliest history of Africa is shrouded in obscurity. In the north the original inhabitants appear to have been of some white stock (the ancestors of the Berbers), while south of the Sahara the country was populated by Negrillos, a small race of Negroes of whom the Pygmies, Bushmen, and Hottentots are probably the descendants. The Negrillos were evidently pushed to the northwest and south by a great invasion (possibly c. 30,000 B.C.) of a larger Negro race arriving from the other side of the Indian Ocean and landing on the central part of the eastern coast. From the newcomers the Bantu derive. A second great invasion from overseas followed and pushed the Negrillos even farther to the west, though there seems to have been much intermixture in the region north of the equator, forming the various Sudanese tribes. In all likelihood there was also a good deal of infiltration of Semitic stocks into the northern part of the continent, both west (Carthage) and east (Syria). The earlier inhabitants were chiefly hunters, but the Negro invaders brought pastoral and agricultural pursuits and introduced polished stone and iron. Very few monuments of the earlier ages have survived. The great stone ruins (**Zimbabwe**) of Rhodesia have been variously dated from the 10th century B.C. to the 15th century A.D. They may have been built by the Bantu, though the weight of expert opinion seems to favor the Sabeans from the Yemen (10th century A.D.) or Dravidians from India.

c. 1st to 6th century A.D. The **Kingdom of Axum** in northern Ethiopia and in southwestern Arabia (obelisks of Axum); direct contact with the Greek world; conversion of the country to Christianity by **Frumentius** (early 4th century). The connection with the Christian east was broken by the Arab conquests (640–).

640-710. CONQUEST OF NORTH AFRICA BY THE ARABS, beginning with Egypt and spreading westward (p. 184 et seq.).

c. 980. Settlement of Arabs from Muscat and Persians from Shiraz and Bushire along the eastern coast, south as far as Cape Corri-

entes. They founded the towns of Mogdishu, Melinde, Mombasa, Kilwa (Quiloa), and Sofala and traded with the natives of the interior in slaves, ivory, and gold that was shipped to India and Arabia.

10th century. Apogee of the Kingdom of Ghana (capital Kumbi), which had been founded in the 4th century, supposedly by people of Semitic extraction. It extended from near the Atlantic coast almost to Timbuktu and was an essentially Negro state consisting of a group of federated tribes with a surprisingly developed culture (visits of the Arabs Ibn Haukal and Masudi in the late 10th century). There appears to have been an active trade with Morocco by way of the Sahara.

1054. Beginning of the **Islamic conquest** of West Africa by the Almoravids under Abdallah ben Yassin. Several of the native dynasties were converted, though the masses appear to have retained their original beliefs.

1076. The Almoravids pillaged Kumbi, the capital of Ghana, which never entirely recovered. Its decline was evidently hastened by the growing barrenness of the region. The **breakup of the Ghana Empire** led to the formation (11th century) of succession states (Diara, which existed till 1754), Soso, the two Mossi states south of the bend of the Niger, and Manding. The ruler of Manding was converted to Islam, as was also the ruler of Songhoy, a great empire which sprang up (c. 690) on the middle Niger and came to divide West Africa with Manding.

1203. **Sumanguru,** greatest of the rulers of Soso, plundered Kumbi.

1224. Sumanguru conquered and annexed Manding.

1235. **Sun Diata,** powerful king of the Mandingos, defeated the ruler of Soso and re-established his independence. In 1240 he destroyed Kumbi.

1307-1332. Apogee of the Mandingo Empire under **Gongo Musa,** who extended his dominions until they covered most of West Africa, after defeating and subjecting the Songhoy Empire (1325). Brilliant culture of Timbuktu (founded 12th cent.).

1352-1353. The great Arab traveler, **Ibn Batuta,** having crossed the Sahara, visited the Mandingo Empire, of which he wrote a description.

1433. The Tuaregs from the Sahara took and sacked Timbuktu.

1433. **The Portuguese explorers** first rounded Cape Bojador, beginning a long series of expeditions along the coast (p. 369).

1468. The Songhoy ruler recaptured Timbuktu from the Tuaregs.

1471. The Portuguese founded the post of San Jorge d'el Mina on the Guinea coast.

1487. The Portuguese reached Timbuktu overland from the coast.

1490. The Portuguese ascended the Congo for about 200 miles and converted the King of the Congo Empire (14th cent.–). They established a post at **São Salvador** and exercised a wide influence in the region until the end of the 16th century.

1493-1529. **Greatness of the Songhoy Empire** under **Askia Mohammed,** who conquered the larger part of the Mandingo Empire and pushed his conquests to the east beyond the Niger. Visit of Leo Africanus (1507).

1505-1507. The Portuguese took Sofala and Kilwa from the Arabs and founded Mozambique. In 1513 they ascended the Zambezi, establishing posts at Sena and Tete. Missionaries probably penetrated much of the hinterland, but details are not known.

(*Cont. p.* 369.)

E. ASIA DURING THE MIDDLE AGES

1. PERSIA

1349. The end of the troubled reign of **Nushirwan** was also the end of the dynasty of the Il-Khans of Persia. They were succeeded by

1336-1411. The Jalayrs, in Iraq and Azerbaijan;

1313-1393. The Muzaffarids in Fars, Kirman and Kurdistan;

1337-1381. The Sarbadarids in Khorasan.

The Muzaffarids and Sarbadarids were overthrown by Timur, and the Jalayrs by

1378-1469. The **Turkomans of the Black Sheep,** who ruled Azerbaijan and Armenia until they were succeeded by

1387-1502. The **Turkomans of the White Sheep.**

1369-1405. **TIMUR** (*Tamerlane*), the vizier of the Mongol Chagatay Khan Suyurghatmish, usurped the power of his master. Between the years 1380 and 1387 he overran Khorasan, Jurjan, Mazandaran, Sijistan, Afghanistan, Fars, Azerbaijan, and Kurdistan. In 1391 he completely defeated Toqtamish, the Khan of the Golden Horde.

1393. Timur took Baghdad and reduced Mesopotamia. After an invasion of India (1397) he marched against Anatolia and routed the Ottoman Turks at **Angora** (p. 331). The empire of the Timurids (until 1500) was soon restricted to Transoxania and eastern Persia.

1404-1447. **SHAH RUKH,** fourth son of Timur, whose reign was noted for its splendor. He carried on successful campaigns against Kara Yusuf, head of the Turkoman dynasty of the Black Sheep (1390-1420), who ruled Azerbaijan, Shirvan, and other regions of the northwest. Kara Yusuf was obliged to recognize the suzerainty of the Timurids, though Kara Yusuf and his successor, Kara Iskender (1420-1438), and

Jehan Shah (1435-1467) were effective rulers of all northwestern Persia. Jehan Shah for a brief period (1458) held even Herat.

1452-1469. **Abu Said,** last of the Timurid dynasty. This period was marked by the great expansion of the Turkoman power under

1453-1478. **UZUN HASAN,** of the dynasty of the White Sheep. This dynasty had established itself under Hasan's grandfather, Osman Beg Kara Iluk (d. 1435) and ruled the territory about Diabekr. Hasan rapidly extended his authority over Armenia and Kurdistan. His defeat by the Ottoman Turks (1461) turned his attention eastward, and led to five large-scale raids into Georgia.

1467. Uzun Hasan defeated and killed Jehan Shah of the Black Sheep and took over his territories.

1469. Uzun defeated, captured and killed Abu Said, the Timurid sultan, who had marched against him. Thereupon Hasan became effective ruler of Armenia, Kurdistan, Azerbaijan, and Iran. He entered with Venice into a treaty directed against the Ottoman Turks, but the artillery that was sent him never reached him, and he was defeated by Mohammed II in

1473. The battle of Terchan. On his death he was succeeded by his son

1478-1490. **JAQUB,** who continued his father's policies and gave the country firm and enlightened rule.

1492-1497. **ROSTAM SHAH,** who succeeded to the throne after a severe dynastic conflict. His death was followed by confusion and by the emergence of the new Safavid dynasty, under Shah Ismail. (*Cont. p.* 531.)

2. INDIA

a. NORTHERN INDIA

The **White Huns** or Hephthalites, a branch of the Mongol Juan-juan who dominated Central

Asia (407-553), had occupied Bactria (425) and, after defeat by Sassanid Bahram Gor (428), Gandhara. Victory over Sassanid Peroz (484) freed them for raids from the Punjab into Hindustan.

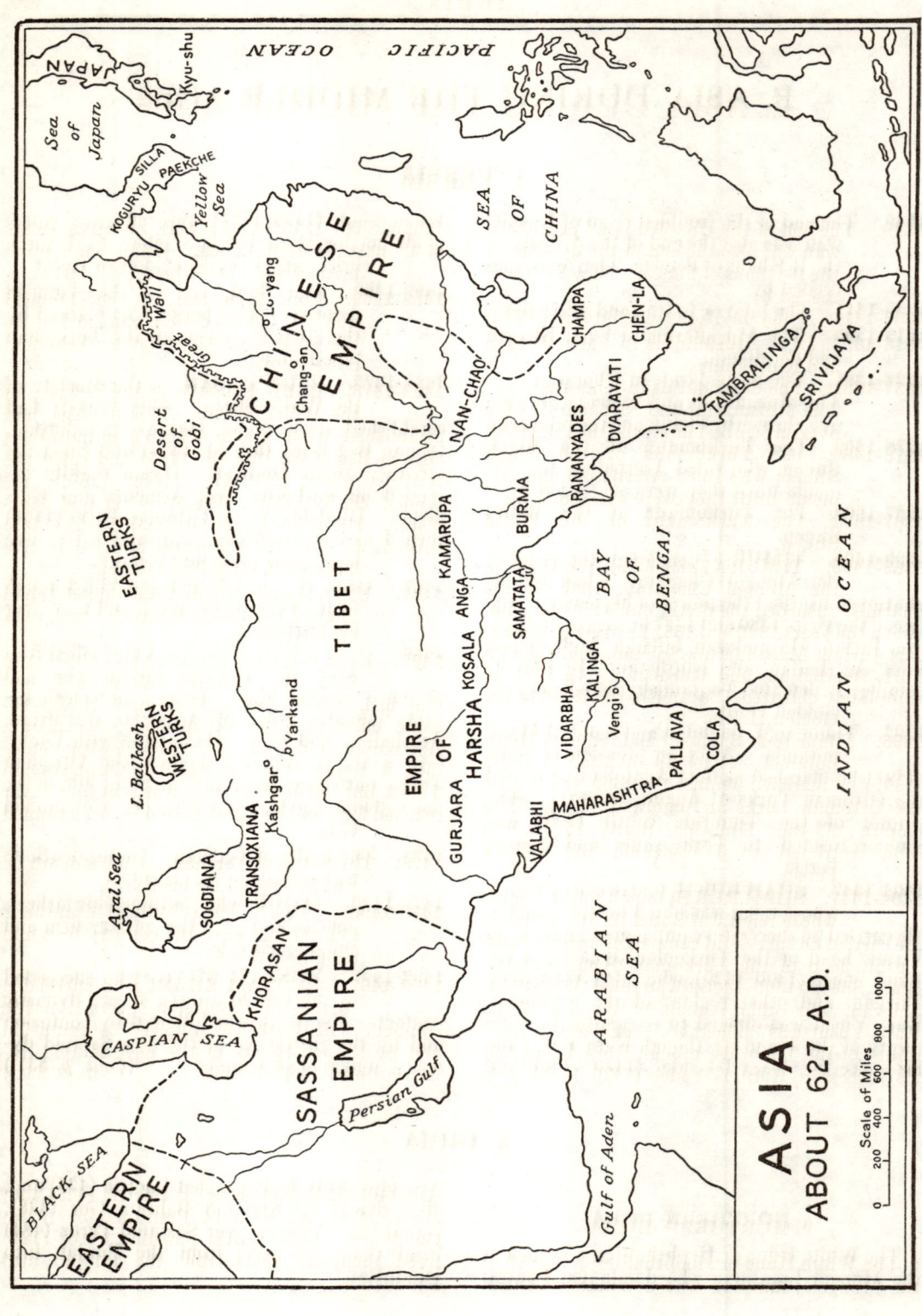

ASIA
ABOUT 627 A.D.

PACIFIC OCEAN

JAPAN

Kyu-shu

Sea of Japan

KOGURYU SILLA
PAEKCHE

Yellow Sea

Great Wall

Lo-yang
Chang-an

CHINESE EMPIRE

SEA OF CHINA

CHAMPA
CHEN-LA

Desert of Gobi

NAN-CHAO

TAMBRALINGA

SRIVIJAYA

EASTERN TURKS

TIBET

KAMARUPA

DVARAVATI

RANANYADES

BURMA

ANGA

KOSALA

SAMATATA

BAY OF BENGAL

INDIAN OCEAN

WESTERN TURKS

L. Balkash

Yarkand

Kashgar

EMPIRE OF HARSHA

VIDARBHA

KALINGA

Vengi

PALLAVA

COLA

Aral Sea

TRANSOXIANA

SOGDIANA

GURJARA

MAHARASHTRA

VALABHI

ARABIAN SEA

KHORASAN

CASPIAN SEA

SASSANIAN EMPIRE

Persian Gulf

Gulf of Aden

BLACK SEA

EASTERN EMPIRE

Scale of Miles

0   200   400   600   800   1000

c. 500–502. Toramana ruled as far as Eran (E. Malwa, inscrip. of his 1st year).

502–c. 528. Mihirakula from Sialkot controlled Gwalior (inscrip. of 15th year) and Kashmir. Bhanugupta probably expelled him from Eran (510). Yasodharman of Mandasor (?) boasts (533) of victory over him. Although the Huns in Central Asia were crushed by Turks and Sassanians (553–567), their chiefs kept rank in the Punjab and Rajputana till the 11th century.

606–647. HARSHA, fourth King of Thaneswar north of Delhi (new era Oct. 606), succeeded his brother-in-law as King of Kanauj (royal title 612), and quickly conquered an empire across northern India, to which he left no heir. He received an embassy (643) from the Emperor T'ang T'ai-tsung. A poet and dramatist, he patronized men of letters. He is well known through **Bana's** poetic romance *Harshacharita*, which is fashionably studded with recondite vocabulary drawn from lexicons of rare words; and by the *Hsi yü chi* (*Record of Western Lands*) of his guest, the pilgrim **Hsüan-tsang,** whose exact observations in India (630–643) have given priceless guidance to modern archaeology. Hsüan-tsang too, after long study at Nalanda, brought together in his *Vijnaptimatratasiddhi*, the classic anthology of texts and comment of the Yogachara or Dharmalakshana school.

Tantrism meanwhile sought to secure for its adepts in magic arts, through esoteric texts (*tantra*) and charms, rapid attainment of Buddhahood or at least supernatural powers. Partial syncretism with Sivaism led to a cult of Vairochana and various new divinities, largely terrible or erotic. Spells (*dharanis*) appear early (Ch. trans. 4th cent.), but the *Panchakrama* is in part the work of Sakyamitra (c. 850). Tantrism seems to have flourished chiefly along the northern borderland. Buddhism, however, progressively disappeared from India from the 9th century, lingering in Bengal and Bihar until the Moslem conquest (1202). It was largely absorbed by Hinduism or united with it.

647. A second Chinese embassy, under Wang Hsüan-ts'e, having been attacked by a usurper on a local throne (Tirhut, north of Patna ?), secured 7000 troops from Amsuvarman, King of Nepal, and 1200 from his son-in-law, Srong-tsan-sgampo, King of Tibet; captured the malefactor, and haled him to Ch'ang-an (648).

c. 730–c. 740. YASOVARMAN, King of Kanauj, an author, patronized the Prakrit poet **Vakpatiraja** and **Bhavabhuti,** a Sanskrit dramatist ranked by Indian criticism next to **Kalidasa.**

c. 725–1197. The Pala Buddhist kings ruled Bengal (till c. 1125) and Magadha. Leading rulers: Dharmapala (c. 770–c. 833), and Devapala (c. 833–c. 881), who endowed a monastery founded at Nalanda by Balaputradeva, King of Sumatra.

c. 1125–c. 1225? Senas from the Carnatic gradually advanced from North Orissa into Bengal.

c. 1169–c. 1199. Lakshmanasena patronized Jayadeva, whose *Gitagovinda*, mystic call to love of Krishna, is hailed by Keith as a world masterpiece in union of sound with sense. Tightening of caste restrictions was accompanied by origin of **kulinism:** prohibition of marriage of any girl below her own caste, which led to infanticide; and rise in caste by marriage to man of higher caste, which led to polygamy of high-caste husbands to collect dowries.

b. WESTERN INDIA

Western India, thanks to many impregnable fortresses in Rajputana, was usually divided among local dynasties from the time of the Gupta power to the advent of the Mohammedans.

c. 490–766. A dynasty of Maitrakas, foreigners of the Rajput type, usually independent at Valabhi in Surashtra, created a Buddhist scholastic center which rivaled Nalanda. Their gifts reveal that Buddhist images were honored with *puja* of the kind devoted to Hindu gods.

c. 550–861. THE GURJARA horde of central Asiatic nomads established a dynasty of twelve kings at Mandor in central Rajputana. Two retired to Jain contemplation, and a third to self-starvation.

712– Arab raids from Sind devastated Gujerat and Broach (724–743) and finally shattered the Maitraka dynasty (766).

c. 740–1036. THE GURJARA-PRATHIHARA DYNASTY, by uniting much of northern India, excluded the Moslems till the end of the 10th century. Prominent early rulers were Nagabhata I (c. 740–c. 760), who defeated the Arabs; Vatsaraja (c. 775–c. 800); and Nagabhata II (c. 800–836), conqueror of Kanauj.

746–c. 974. The Chapas (or Chapotkatas), a Gurjara clan, founded Anahilapura (or Anandapura, 746), the principal city of western India until the 15th century.

831–1310. A Dravidian dynasty of Chandellas

(in present Bundelkhand) built numerous Vaishnava temples, notably at Khajuraho, under Yasovarman (c. 930–954) and Dhanga (954–1002).

c. 840–c. 890.   Mihira, or Bhoja, devoted to Vishnu and the Sun, ruled from the Sutlej to the Narmada, but failed to subdue Kashmir.

c. 950–c. 1200.   The Paramaras of Dhara, near Indore, were known for two rulers: Munja (974–c. 994) who invaded the Deccan, and Bhoja (c. 1018–1060), author of books on astronomy, poetics, and architecture, and founder of a Sanskrit college.

c. 974–c. 1240.   The Chalukya or Solanki Rajput clan, led by Mularaja (known dates 974–995) ruled from Anahillapura over Surashtra and Mt. Abu.

977–1186.   The Ghaznavid (Yamini) **dynasty** ruled at Ghazni and Lahore. It was founded by **Sabuktagin** (977–997), a Turkish slave converted to Islam, who extended his rule from the Oxus to the Indus and broke the power of a Hindu confederacy which included King Jaipal of Bhatinda, the Gurjara-Prathihara King of Kanauj, and the Chandella King Dhanga.

998–1030.   MAHMUD OF GHAZNI made 17 plundering raids into the Punjab (defeat of Jaipal, 1001) to Kangra (1009), Mathura and Kanauj (1018–19), Gwalior (1022), and Somnath (1024–26). Vast destruction, pillage of immensely rich Hindu temples, and wholesale massacre resulted only in enrichment of Ghazni and annexation of the Punjab. Ghazni, heir to the rich artistic heritage of the Samanids of northeastern Persia, was now one of the most brilliant capitals of the Islamic world. **Alberuni** (973–1048) of Khiva, the leading scientist of his time, followed Mahmud to the Punjab, learned Sanskrit, and wrote the invaluable *Tahkik-i Hind* (*Inquiry into India*).

1093–1143.   The Chalukya ruler, Jayasimha Siddharaja, a patron of letters, although himself a Saiva, organized disputations on philosophy and religion, and favored a Jain monk, **Hemachandra,** who converted and dominated **Kumarapala.**

1143–1172.   Kumarapala. As a good Jain, he decreed respect for life (*ahimsa*), prohibited alcohol, dice, and animal fights, and rescinded a law for confiscation of property of widows without sons. He also built (c. 1169) a new edifice about the Saiva temple of Somanatha, which had been reconstructed by **Bhimadeva I** (1022–1062) after destruction by the Moslems.

1151–1206. The Shansabani Persian Princes of Ghur (Ghor) having burned Ghazni (1151), drove the Yamini to the Punjab and deposed them there (1186).

1172–1176.   Ajayapala, a Saiva reactionary, ordered the massacre of Jains and sack of their temples until he was assassinated, when Jain rule was restored under a mayor of the palace whose descendants displaced the dynasty (c. 1240).

Two Jain temples at Mt. Abu are the work of a governor, **Vimala Saha** (1031), and a minister **Tejpala** (1230). Built of white marble with a profusion of ornamented colonnades, brackets, and elaborately carved ceilings, they are the most elegant version of the northern or Indo-Aryan architectural style.

Kashmir, already (c. 100 A.D.) an important home of the Sarvastivadin Buddhist sect, remained a center for Buddhist studies (till the 10th cent.; degenerate before the Moslem conquest, 1340) and of Sanskrit literature (until today). Its history from c. 700 is rather fully known through the *Rajatarangini* of **Kalhana** (c. 1100), the sole early Indian historian who consulted literary sources and inscriptions but accepted even absurd tradition without criticism.

1175–1206.   Mohammed of Ghur, Mu'izz-ud-Din, undertook conquest of Hindustan by capture of Multan and Uch. He ruled from Ghazni as governor for his elder brother, **Ghiyas-ud-Din Mohammed,** whom he succeeded as ruler of Ghur (1203).

1192.   A battle at Taraori (14 m. from Thaneswar) decisively crushed a new Hindu confederacy led by the Chauhan King of Ajmer and Delhi. Cumbersome traditional tactics, disunited command, and caste restrictions handicapped the Hindu armies in conflict with the mounted archers from the northwest. Victory led to occupation of Delhi (1193), to conquest of Bihar where the organized Buddhist community was extinguished (c. 1197), Bengal (c. 1199), and the Chandella state in Bundelkhand. Mohammed appointed **Kutb-ud-din Aibak,** a slave from Turkestan, viceroy of his Indian conquests and left him full discretion (1192, confirmed 1195).

1206–1266.   A dynasty of slave kings, the first of six to rule at Delhi (until 1526), was founded by Aibak (killed playing polo, 1210).

The numerically weak early Moslem rulers in India were forced to employ Hindu troops and civilian agents, welcome allegiance of Hindu landholders, and afford their native subjects much the same limited protection (including tacit religious toleration) and justice to which they were accustomed. Rebels, both Hindu and Moslem, were slaughtered with ruthless barbarity.

1211-1236. Shams-ud-din Iltutmish, ablest slave and son-in-law of Aibak, succeeded to his lands in the Ganges Valley only, but recovered the upper Punjab (1217), Bengal (1225), the lower Punjab with Sind (1228), and Gwalior after a long siege (Feb.–Dec. 1232). He advanced to sack Ujjain (1234).

1229. He was invested as Sultan of India by the Abbasid Caliph of Baghdad.

Islamic architects brought to India a developed tradition of a spacious, light and airy prayer chamber covered by arch, vault, and dome, erected with aid of concrete and mortar, and ornamented solely with color and flat linear, usually conventional, decoration. This formula was applied with recognition of local structural styles and of the excellence of Hindu ornamental design. Aibak built at Delhi (1193–96) with the spoils of 27 temples a mosque of Hindu appearance to which he added (1198) an Islamic screen of arches framed with Indian carving. He began (before 1206) a tower for call to prayer, which was finished (1231–32) and named *Kutb Minar* to honor a Moslem saint (d. 1235) by Iltutmish, who also enlarged the mosque in strictly Islamic style.

Upon the death of Iltutmish actual power passed to a group of 40 Turks who divided all offices save that of sultan, and controlled the succession.

1266-1290. A new dynasty at Delhi was founded by **Balban** (d. 1287), a slave purchased by Iltutmish (1233); made chamberlain (1242), father-in-law and lieutenant (1249–52 and 1255–66) of King Mahmud (1246–1266). Balban as king, aided by an effective army and corps of royal news-writers, repressed the 40 nobles, ended highway robbery in south and east, and rebellion in Bengal. His son repelled the Mongols established in Ghazni (since 1221), but was killed by them (1285).

The **tomb of Balban** is the first structure in India built with true arches instead of Hindu corbelling.

1290-1320. The Khalji dynasty of Delhi was founded by **Firuz** of the Khalji tribe of Turks, long resident among the Afghans. Senile mildness led him to release in Bengal 1000 Thugs (murderers in honor of Siva's consort Kali) captured in Delhi.

1296-1316. Ala-ud-din, his nephew and murderer, bought allegiance with booty secured by surprise attack upon Devagiri in

Maharashtra (1294–95). He consolidated the empire.

1297. He conquered and despoiled Gujarat with its rich port Cambay. Frequent revolts prompted a program of repression which included espionage; confiscation of wealth (esp. of Hindus), endowments and tax-exempt lands; prohibition of liquor and all social gatherings.

Mongol invasions (1299 and 1303) led to

1303. Decrees which by fixing low prices for all products permitted reduction of army pay and increase of strength to nearly 500,000 cavalry. Mongol armies were destroyed (1304 and 1306) and expeditions, usually led by a eunuch, Kafur, entitled Malik Naib, effected

1305-1313. Conquest of Malwa (1305) and the Deccan: Devagiri (1306–1307, annexed 1313), Warangal (1308), the Hoysala capital at Dvarasamudra and that of the Pandyas at Madura (1310–11), and the central Deccan (1313), with enormous treasure.

The *Alai Darwaza* (1311), southern gateway of a proposed vast enlargement of Aibak's mosque, represents the finest ornamental architecture of the early Delhi sultanate, fortunately continued in Gujarat. **Amir Khusrav** (1253–1325), greatest Indian poet to write in Persian, was son of a Turk who had fled before Jenghiz Khan to Patiala. He was prolific as court poet to Ala-ud-din and later in religious retirement. Another excellent Persian poet of Delhi was **Hasan-i-Dihlavi,** who died at Daulatabad (1338).

1320-1413. The Tughluk dynasty was founded by the old but vigorous **Ghiyas-ud-din Tughluk** (d. 1325), a pure Turk who boasted 29 victories over the Mongols. He reduced to provincial status Warangal (1323) and eastern Bengal (1324). He encouraged agriculture, corrected abuses in tax collection, and perfected a postal system by which runners covered 200 miles a day. At Multan he erected a splendid octagonal tomb of Persian character for the saint, Rukn-i-Alam. Increasing austerity marked the architecture of his house.

1325-1351. Mohammed Tughluk hastened to the throne by deliberate parricide. A half-mad military genius, his administrative measures were warped and defeated by his own unwisdom, inordinate pride, inflexibility, and ferocious indiscriminate cruelty. Revolt of a cousin in the Deccan (1326) led to

1327. Transfer of the capital to Devagiri, renamed *Daulatabad,* handsomely rebuilt with European feudal fortifications about an impregnable rock citadel. As a punitive measure

1329. All remaining citizens of Delhi were forced to move thither. He raised taxes so high in the Doab as to force rebellion and then destroyed both fields and cultivators.

1330. Emission of copper fiat money equivalent to the silver *tanga* of 140 grains failed because of easy counterfeiting.

1334. **Ibn Batuta,** a Moorish traveler, was welcomed with fantastic gifts like other foreigners who might help in world conquest. He left on a mission to China (1342).

1334-1378. Madura revolted under a Moslem dynasty, ended by Vijayanagar.

1337-38. An army of 100,000 horse, sent through Kangra into the Himalaya to conquer Tibet and China, was destroyed by rains, disease, and hill-men; and with it resources needed to avert

1338. **Loss of Bengal** to the house of Balban, independent until 1539. Moslem architects used at Gaur, its capital, local brick and terra cotta to build, e.g., the bold Dakhil Gateway (1459–74?).

1340. Mohammed sought recognition (received 1344) from the caliph in Egypt. He vainly tried to restore prosperity by redistricting, and appointing undertakers to supervise fixed (unscientific) crop rotation, and to maintain a mounted militia. Increased penal severity culminated when he began

1344-45. Wholesale extermination of his centurions, revenue collectors who usually failed to meet his quotas. Rebellion begun by them in Gujarat led to permanent loss of the whole South.

1346-1589. Shah Mirza (1346–1349) founded a Moslem dynasty in Kashmir. He substituted the usual land tax of one-sixth for the extortionate rates of the Hindu kings.

1347-1527. **The Bahmani dynasty,** founded by rebels against Mohammed Tughluk, who elected **Bahman Shah** (1347–1348), at first ruled four provinces: Gulbarga, Daulatabad, Berar, and Bidar. The capital at Gulbarga and many other fortresses were built or strengthened with European science to serve against Gujerat, Malwa, and Khandesh in the northwest, the Gonds, Orissa, and Telingana in the northeast, and Vijayanagar in the south.

1351-1388. **Firuz Tughluk** (b. 1305) restored rational administration. He exacted tribute from Orissa (1360), Kangra (1361), and Sind (1363). He refused to disturb the Bahmani Kingdom of the Deccan, its tributary Warangal,

or the rebels from it, the Khans of Khandesh between the Tapti and Narbada (independent 1382). He built several towns, notably Jaunpur north of Benares (1359), many mosques, palaces, hospitals, baths, tanks, canals, and bridges; but with cheap materials and little artistic quality. His successors were too weak to prevent further dissolution of the empire.

1358-1375. The Bahmani **Mohammed I** gave lasting organization to the government of the new dynasty.

1363-1364. Warangal was forced to cede Golconda, with much treasure.

1367. Victory of the Bahmani over immense but ineffectual armies of Vijayanagar. It was the first of several successes and was won with artillery served by Europeans and Ottoman Turks. The subsequent massacre of 400,000 Hindus led to agreement to spare non-combatants. The **Great Mosque at Gulbarga** was completely roofed with domes.

1392-1531. Malwa (formally independent in 1401) was ruled by the Ghuris and the Khaljis (1436). **Hushang Shah** (1405–1435) fortified the capital at Mandu above the Narbada, and erected there the durbar hall *Hindola Mahall*, together with a great mosque. These buildings are impressive through structural design rather than surface ornament.

1394-1479. Jaunpur, with Oudh, became independent under the Sharki (eastern) dynasty, founded by the eunuch, Malik Sarvar, and his adopted sons, probably of African Negroid descent. The second ruler, **Ibrahim Shah** (1402–1436), was a cultured and liberal patron of learning.

1396-1572. Gujerat prospered under a Moslem Rajput dynasty.

1398-1399. **INVASION OF TIMUR** (*Tamerlane*) of Samarkand, who had already conquered Persia, Mesopotamia, and Afghanistan (p. 335). He desolated the whole Kingdom of Delhi. Crossing the Indus (Sept. 24), he marched 80 miles in a day and night (Nov. 6–7) to overtake fugitives at Bhatnair, massacred 100,000 Hindu prisoners before Delhi (Dec. 12), sacked the city (Dec. 17), stormed Meerut (Jan. 9), and fought his way back along the Himalaya to the Indus (Mar. 19).

1411-1442. **Ahmad Shah** of Gujerat built Ahmadabad as a capital and beautified it with the *Tin Darwaza* (Triple Gateway) and *Great Mosque*, one of the most imposing structures in the world.

1414-1526. **THE KINGDOM OF DELHI,** reduced to the Jumna Valley, with tenuous control over the Punjab, was ruled by the Sayyids, who laid nebulous claim to Arab descent from the Prophet, but could collect their revenues only by force. Later the Afghan **Buhlul Lodi** (1451-1489) founded the Lodi dynasty.

1420-1470. Zain-ul-Abidin, learned and tolerant, permitted Brahman rites in Kashmir, employed convicts on public works, and exacted communal responsibility for order.

1422-1436. Ahmad Shah Bahmani enrolled 3000 foreign mounted archers, who, like the Turks, Arabs, Mongols, and Persians, when employed as ministers, earned by superior qualities and disdain the hostility (massacre 1446) of the native-born Deccanis, Africans, and Muwallads, half-breed offspring of the latter.

1429. Bidar, rebuilt under Persian decorative influence, became capital.

1458-1511. Mahmud I of Ahmadabad, called *Begarha* (*Two Forts*) because of his conquest of Girnar (with Kathiawar, 1469-1470) and Champanir (near Baroda, 1483-1484), when 700 Hindu Rajputs preferred ritual death (*jauhar*) to Islam. He built magnificently and in exquisite taste: the Great Mosque at Champanir; the palace at Sarkhej; the step-well at Adalaj; and the pierced stone window-screens of Sidi Sayyid's mosque. The tiny Rani Sipari mosque at Ahmadabad (1514) displays harmonious perfection of the ornamental style.

1463-1482. Mohammed III Bahmani conquered the Konkan and Telingana to both coasts. He died at 28 of drink, the curse of nearly all his house, and of remorse at having slain (while drunk) his best minister, Mahmud Gavan, the builder of the large quadrangular college at Bidar.

1490. Ahmadnagar (1490-1633), Bijapur (1490-1686), and Berar (1490-1574) became in fact independent of Mahmud (1482-1518), the incompetent prisoner of his minister, Kasim Barid, whose dynasty mounted the throne of Bidar in 1527 (till 1619).

c. SOUTHERN INDIA

100-200. King Karikalan of early Tamil poems is credited with construction of a great irrigation dam on the Kaveri River, east of Trichinopoly.

c. 300-888. The Pallava warrior dynasty of foreign (Pahlava?) origin, using Prakrit and later Sanskrit, held from Kañchi (near Madras) hegemony of the Deccan, which it disputed with the Chalukyas of Vatapi (550-753),

the Rashtrakutas of Malkhed (753-973) and the Chalukyas of Vengi (611-1078).

c. 500-753. The first Chalukya dynasty in Maharashtra advanced from Aihole on the upper Kistna to near-by Vatapi (or Badami, c. 550) and to Banavasi (566-597) at the expense of the Kadambas. Construction of the earliest temples at Aihole was followed by that of Mahakutesvara (c. 525) and completion of the cave-temple to Vishnu at Vatapi (578).

c. 575. The Pallava **Simhavishnu** seized the Chola basin of the Kaveri, which his family held until after 812.

c. 600-625. The Pallava **Mahendravarman I,** converted from Jainism to Sivaism, destroyed a Jain temple, but dug the first (Saiva) cave-temples in the south (at Trichinopoly, Chingleput, etc.). From his reign date **Buddhist monasteries** (in part excavated) and *stupas* on the Samkaram Hills (near Vizagapatam).

609-642. The Chalukya **Pulakesin II** placed his brother on the throne of Vengi, where he ruled as viceroy (611-632), repulsed an attack by Harsha of Kanauj (c. 620), sent an embassy to Khosroes II of Persia (625), and enthroned a son, who headed a branch dynasty in Gujerat and Surat (c. 640-740). Hsüan-tsang (641) describes the prosperity of the country just before the Pallavas pillaged the capital (642), a disaster which was avenged by pillage of the Pallava capital, Kañchi, by Vikramaditya (c. 674).

611-c. 1078. The Eastern Chalukyas of Vengi (independent after 629-632), were continually at war with Kalinga on the north, the Rashtrakutas on the west, and the Pandyas on the south.

c. 625-c. 645. The Pallava **Narasimhavarman** defeated Chalukya Pulakesin II (c. 642) and took Vatapi. He defeated also his southern neighbors and enthroned Manavalla in Ceylon (?). He improved the port of Mamallapuram, near Kañchi, and cut there the first of five *raths,* monolithic sanctuaries in the form of cars, the earliest monuments of the Dravidian style; also the cliff-relief depicting the descent of the **River Ganges** from Heaven.

c. 675-c. 705. The Pallava **Narasimhavarman II** built in stone and brick the Shore temple at Mamalla, and the central shrine of the Kailasa temple at Kañchi, completed by his son.

c. 700. Conversion of the Pandya Srimaravarman to Sivaism by Tirujnana Sambandhar, the first of 63 *nayanmars* or Tamil saints, led the king to impale 8000 Jains at Madura in a single day, since celebrated by the Saivas. Another saint, Manikka Vasagar (9th cent.) wrote poems of his own religious experience which correspond to our *Psalms*. The Tamil Vaishnavas, too, had their saints, twelve *alvars*, who also expressed emotional religion and whose works were collected c. 1000–1050.

733–746. The Chalukya **Vikramaditya II** thrice took Kañchi, and distributed presents to the temples. He imported Tamil artists and his queen commissioned Gunda, "the best southern architect," to build the temple of Virupaksha. The frescoes of Ajanta caves 1 and 2 are believed to date from this period. So too the Saiva and Vaishnava sculptures of the Das Avatara cave-temple at Ellora.

c. 735–c. 800. Nandivarman II, a collateral kinsman twelve years of age, accepted the Pallava throne offered him by the ministers and elders, who defended him against rival claimants.

753–973. The **Rashtrakuta dynasty** of Canarese kings, already enthroned in North Berar (631) and in Gujerat (c. 700) was elevated to empire by Dantidurga, who soon overthrew the Chalukyas.

758–772. Rashtrakuta **Krishnaraja I** cut from the cliff and decorated with Saiva sculpture the Kailasa(natha) temple at Ellora to rival that of Kañchi. To the same Canarese dynasty if not to the same reign belong the equally classic Saiva sculptures of the cave-temples at Elephanta (an island in Bombay harbor). The successors of Krishnaraja were Govinda II (779) and Dhruva (783), who defeated the Pallava Nandivarman II and the Gurjara Vatsaraja.

774–13th cent. The **Eastern Gangas** ruled Kalinga, waging constant war with the Chalukyas of Vengi and the Princes of Orissa.

c. 788–c. 850. Samkara of Malabar revitalized the Vedanta, creating an unobtrusively new but consistent synthesis of tradition, which he speciously traced to the *Upanishads* and to Badarayana, author of the *Brahma sutra*. His doctrine became accepted as orthodox Brahmanism. He taught a rigorous monism (*advaita*) which admits release for the soul only in union with *brahman* through the higher knowledge that the phenomenal world (and individual personality) do not exist save for those who think objectively. For these latter, however, engrossed in worldly phenomena (*maya*), he recognized that a simpler kind of knowledge was necessary; and for them he was a practical apostle of Sivaism. Although he denounced Buddhism he imitated its moral teaching by opposition to sectarian extravagance, its ecclesiastical strength by organization of an ascetic order for zealous youth (hitherto debarred till later life from religious activity). He founded four scholastic monasteries (*maths*) which still survive at Sringeri (Mysore), Puri (Orissa), Badrinath (the Himalaya), and Dwaraka (western Kathiawar). Ramanuja (c. 1055–1137) of Kañchi also interpreted the Vedanta. For him souls are distinct from *brahman*, whose representatives they are, and from the material world with which they are entangled. It is through piety toward Vishnu and his saving grace that they may recover their divine nature.

c. 790. The Chalukya **Vikramaditya II** was defeated by the Rashtrakuta Dhruva (779–794).

794–813. Rashtrakuta **Govinda III** seized Malwa with Chitor from the Gurjaras, and enthroned his brother as head of a second Rashtrakuta dynasty in Gujerat (till c. 900). He took from the Pallava (c. 800) tribute and territory as far as the Tungabhadra.

c. 812–844. Pallava **Nandivarman III** helped Govinda III to crown Sivamara II as Ganga King of Mysore. At the same time

c. 812– Pandya **Varaguna I** imposed suzerainty on the Pallavas.

817–877. Rashtrakuta **Amoghavarsha I** moved the capital from Nasik to Malkhed, the better to carry on war against the Chalukya of Vengi. He abdicated and died in saintly Jain fashion. The last of his line found death in Jain starvation (982).

c. 825–1312. The **Yadavas,** early suzerains of a score of petty vassal kings, occupied in turn three capitals: (modern) Chandor and Sinnar (1069), both near Nasik, and the fortress of Devagiri (c. 1111) renamed Daulatabad (1327). They fell heir to the northern possessions of the Chalukyas of Kalyani.

843–1249. The **Silaharas,** another petty dynasty, under Chalukya or Rashtrakuta suzerainty, provided forty-five kings in three different areas along the west coast north of Goa. The Parsis (Parsees), refugees in Kathiawar, had probably already reached Thana near Bombay during the 8th century.

844–888. Gunaga **Vijayaditya III** of Vengi fought successfully against western and northern enemies and by the defeat of the Pallava Aparajita and the Pandya Varaguna II helped the rising Chola to supersede both. His association of two brothers as kings-consort led ultimately to succession struggles which placed eight kings on the throne in ten years (918–927).

c. 844-870. Pallava **Nripatungavarman** recovered Tanjore and obtained the submission of Varaguna II (862-) and of Ganga Prithivipati I.

c. 870-888. Pallava **Aparajitavarman,** with Ganga Prithivipati, crushed Varaguna II, but was himself defeated and killed by the Chola Aditya I. Numerous Pallava chiefs continued to rule locally. Perunjinga, in the Tamil South, claimed imperial titles for at least 31 years.

888-1267. **The Chola dynasty of Tamil kings** from Tanjore, under **Aditya I** (870-c. 906), with the aid of the Chalukyas of Vengi, replaced the Pallavas at Kañchi. The Chola territory extended along the east coast from Telugu to the Pandya lands.

927-934. A royal inscription is the earliest extant specimen of Telugu literature. It records the erection of a Saiva temple and sectarian hostel.

973-c. 1190. The Chalukyas of Kalyani (near Bombay) were restored to power by Taila II (or Tailapa), who spent his reign fighting the Cholas and Paramaras.

985-1014. Chola **Rajaraja I** acquired hegemony over the Deccan.

994. Conquest of the Cheras and Pandyas justified the title *Thrice-crowned Chola,* marking the first historical union of the southern peninsula.

999. The conquest of Vengi drove a usurper from the East Chalukyan throne and was extended (1000) to Kalinga.

1001-1004. A successful **invasion of Ceylon** permitted assignment of Singhalese revenues to the Saiva Great Pagoda of Rajarajesvara, which Rajaraja I built at Tanjore, the masterpiece of baroque Dravidian architecture. He also endowed a Buddhist monastery built at Negapatam by a king of Srivijaya (Sumatra).

1014-1042. Rajendra Choladeva, who had helped his father since 1002.

1014-1017. A second invasion of Ceylon secured the regalia and treasure of the Pandya kings, so that a son of the Chola could be consecrated king of Pandya.

1024. An **invasion of Bengal** enabled the Chola to assume a new title and establish a new capital near Trichinopoly.

c. 1030. By use of sea-power, the Chola exacted tribute from Pegu, Malaiyur (Malay Peninsula), and the empire of Srivijaya.

1040-1068. Rashtrakuta **Somesvara I** founded Kalyani, the capital until c. 1156. He drowned himself with Jain rites in the Tungabhadra, the sacred river of the South.

1042-1052. Chola **Rajadhiraja I,** who had aided his father since 1018. He was killed in battle at Koppam against Somesvara I of Kalyani.

1062-1070. Chola **Virarajendra** defeated the Chalukyas and gave his daughter to Vikramaditya VI. He founded a vedic college and a hospital. His two sons fell into conflict and extinguished their line by assassination (1074).

1073-1327. **The Hoysalas,** at first a petty dynasty, ruled at Dvarasamudra (Halebid) in Mysore.

1074-1267. **The Chalukya-Chola dynasty,** founded by Rajendra, son and grandson of Chola princesses, King of Vengi (1070-), who took the vacant throne of Kañchi (1074) and thenceforth ruled Vengi through a viceroy. His authority was recognized by the Ganga King of Kalinga.

1075-1125. **Vikramaditya VI** of Kalyani began a new era in place of the Saka era, but with small success. One of his many inscriptions is at Nagpur in the northern Deccan, while in the south one of his generals repelled the Hoysalas. His people enjoyed unwonted security. He built temples to Vishnu, but made gifts also to two Buddhist monasteries which must have been among the last in the south to withstand Hindu reaction and absorption. **Bilhana of Kashmir,** in return for hospitality, a blue parasol, and an elephant, wrote the *Vikramankacharita* in praise of his host.

1076-1147. **Anantavarman Codaganga** extended his authority from the Ganges to the Godavari, and built at Puri (south of Cuttack) the temple of Jagannath (Vishnu) which, at first open to all Hindu castes, is now barred to fifteen. The great Sun temple, in form of a solar car, known as the *Black Pagoda,* at Konarak, may be earlier than its attribution to Ganga Narasimha (1238-1264).

1111-1141. **Bittideva,** independent, fought successfully against Chola, Pandya, and Chera. As viceroy before accession he was converted from Jainism to Vishnu by Ramanuja, at that time a refugee from Saiva persecution by the Cholas. He began construction at Belur and Halebid of temples in a distinctively ornate Hoysala style, featured especially by a high, richly carved plinth of stellate plan.

c. 1150-1323. **The Kakatiyas** reigned in the east at Kakati or Warangal between the Godavari and the Kistna. They held an important kingdom under **Ganapati** (1197-1259) and his daughter (1259-1288), whom Marco Polo knew.

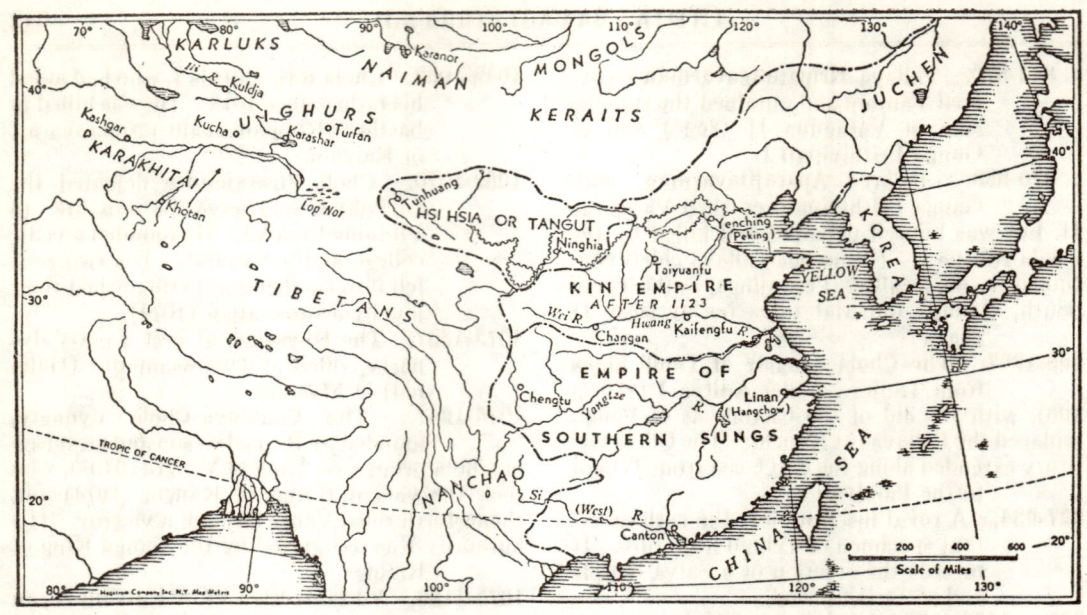

CHINA

IN THE LAST HALF OF THE
TWELFTH CENTURY

INDIA

TO THE MOHAMMEDAN
CONQUEST

MAPS FROM STEIGER'S *A HISTORY OF THE FAR EAST*. USED BY PERMISSION OF THE PUBLISHERS, GINN AND COMPANY.

c. 1156-1183. A revolt against the Rashtrakuta ruler **Taila III** (known dates 1150-1155) led to usurpation by a general who was soon assassinated by Basava, who was in turn compelled to commit suicide. Basava created and organized the Lingayat sect of fanatic, anti-Brahman worshipers of Siva under a phallic emblem. The movement at the outset appeared in the form of a religious and social (equalitarian) war.

1183. Taila's son **Somesvara IV** regained Kalyani, but was unable to resist the Hoysalas (last date 1189).

1292-1342. The Hoysala ruler **Viraballala III** inherited an empire comprising most of southern India.

1327. After sack of Halebid by **Mohammed Tughluk**, Viraballala moved his capital to Tiruvannamalai (South Arcot).

c. 1335-1565. **Vijayanagar** (present Hampi), founded by two brothers from the region of Warangal, fought steadily against the Moslem sultans north of Kistna and Tungabhadra. It became an important center for Brahman studies and for Dravidian nationalism and art. **Madhava** wrote at Sringeri (c. 1380) the *Sarva darsana samgraha*, which remains the classic summary of the various Brahman philosophical points of view.

1520. Division of the Moslems into five rival sultanates (late 15th cent.) gave Krishnadeva (c. 1509-1529) a chance to win a victory over the Sultan of Bijapur.

1542-1565. Ramaraja sought to profit by further division of the Moslems but provoked a coalition which crushed him and razed Vijayanagar

d. CEYLON

846. The capital was moved south to Polonnaruva to escape Tamil invasions, which later culminated in

1001-1017. **The two great invasions** (1001-1004 and 1014-1017) by Chola Rajaraja and his son Rajendra.

1065-1120. **Vijayabahu** ruled prosperously despite further incursions (1046, 1055).

1164-1197. **Parakramabahu I** repelled the Tamils (1168), invaded Madura and united the two rival monasteries.

1225-1260. **Parakramabahu II** repelled two attacks (c. 1236 and c. 1256) by a King of Tambralinga (Ligor on the Straits of Malacca), with Pandya help.

1284. The king sent a relic of the Buddha to Kublai Khan. (*Cont. p.* 535.)

3. CHINA, 618-1471

618-907. **THE T'ANG DYNASTY,** founded by
618-626. **LI YÜAN** (T'ai Tsu) and his son Li Shih-min. The T'ang used Loyang and Ch'ang-an as eastern and western capitals. Sui institutions were in general retained. The central administrative organization remained essentially unchanged from this time until 1912. The emperor ruled through daily audience with a grand council composed of (1) heads of a secretariat and chancery, which for safety divided transaction of business (a feature later discarded); (2) representatives of the six ministries of civil office, finance, ceremonial, war, justice, and public works; and (3) specially appointed dignitaries. The censorate and nine independent offices, notably a clan court and a criminal high court, together with three technical services including the national college and flood-prevention bureau, reported to him directly. Although the empire was divided into ten (627), later fifteen (733) districts for supervisory purposes, the prefectures (*chou*) depended directly from the central administration, the prefect being responsible for duties corresponding

to those of the six ministries. Each prefecture sent an annual quota of candidates to join graduates of two state universities in civil-service examinations. These led to the eighth or ninth (bottom) ranks in the official hierarchy. Appointment to a corresponding office depended on a further searching examination before each term until the sixth rank was reached. Promotion was based on performance.

627-649. **The reign of T'AI TSUNG** (Li Shih-min) is illustrious not alone because of the military conquests which established stimulating contacts with Iranian and Indian civilizations, but still more for the liberal, tolerant spirit of the emperor and his patronage of art and letters.

630. The Eastern Turks, who had attacked Ch'ang-an in 624 and 626, were crushed.

631-648. Chinese suzerainty was acknowledged by the petty states of western and eastern Turkestan. The Western Turks were divided and defeated (641).

635. A Nestorian missionary, A-lo-pen, was officially welcomed to Ch'ang-an; and

given (638) both freedom of the empire and an imperial church at the capital.

641. A Chinese princess was married to the first King of Tibet, Srong-tsan-sgam-po, and helped convert Tibet to Buddhism, later (after 749) modified by Padmasambhava towards Tantrism.

645. Hsüan-tsang, returned from a pilgrimage to India, recorded his precise observations, and headed a commission which translated 75 books in 1335 volumes, creating for the purpose a consistent system for transcription of Sanskrit. He introduced the scholastic doctrine of **Vasubandhu** (which still survives), that the visual universe is only a mental image. The **Pure Land** or **Lotus School** of Buddhism for the next seventy years enjoyed far more popular favor. Based on texts translated in the 2d and 5th centuries, it is called the *Short-Cut School* because it teaches direct salvation by faith in Amitabha and invocation of his name. Religious **Taoism,** fully organized on the Buddhist model, now also received imperial patronage on the ground that Lao-tzu, whose surname legend gives as Li, was the ancestor of the ruling house. A 4th century apocryphal text, *Hua Hu Ching,* which claims Lao-tzu to be a prior avatar of Buddha, was actively debated. It was proscribed (668) but again tolerated (696). Imperial commissions completed or newly compiled eight standard histories to bring the series down to date from the Three Kingdoms and prepared the first literary encyclopedia, *I Wen Lei Chü.*

653. A dynastic legal code with commentary was revised (737) and carried abroad.

657-659. Dispersal of the **Western Turks** (T'u-chüeh), some of whom eventually migrated across southern Russia to Hungary while others followed Mahmud of Ghazni to India.

671-695. I-ching made the pilgrimage to India by sea, stopping to learn Sanskrit in Srivijaya (southeastern Sumatra), a state which became tributary (670-73), and remained powerful until the close of the 14th century.

684-704. Empress **Wu** temporarily altered the dynastic title to *Chou* (690-704), and decreed use of deformed written characters.

712-756. HSÜAN TSUNG, popularly known as Ming Huang, ruled over a court of brilliant High Renaissance literary and artistic attainment. He founded the **Academy of Letters** (725) and established schools in every prefecture and district in the empire (738). **Li Po** (705-762) and **Tu Fu** (712-770) created and excelled in lyric verse. In painting, continuous

composition was substituted for episodic treatment. **Wu Tao-hsüan** (c. 700-760) ranks foremost among figure-painters. **Li Ssu-hsün** (651-c. 720) and **Wang Wei** (698-759) created two of the first and most influential landscape styles. Slackening of genuine religious enthusiasm is conspicuous alike in the tone of Buddhist votive inscriptions and in the monumental realism of the sculpture which becomes increasingly secular, then perfunctory. T'ang potters freely borrowed forms of Iranian flask and ewer, Indian ritual drinking vessel, and Greek amphora. They made these resplendent with new colors in soft lead glaze applied over slip with new technical versatility. From about this time dates probably also the first true porcelain with high-fired felspathic glaze. The Buddhists, too, now enlarged the seal and produced wood blocks for printing on paper (earliest extant printed book dated 868).

732. Manichaeism was condemned as perverse doctrine, but was permitted to Persians and Tokharians who had introduced it (694 and 719) and who were favored for their competence in astronomy and astrology.

738. The title *King* was conferred on a T'ai ruler who (730) united six principalities as **Nan Chao** with capital at Ta-li (741). After two disastrous efforts at conquest (751 and 754), the T'ang made peace (789-794), leaving the kings of Nan Chao full autonomy. They still had to be repelled, twice from Ch'eng-tu (829 and 874), once from Hanoi (863).

745. Uighur Turks overthrew the Eastern Turks and set up their own empire on the Orkhon, ruling from Ili to Tibet and the Yellow River. Their *kaghan* was given a title and a Chinese princess (758).

747. Kao Hsien-chih led an army across the Pamirs and Hindukush, but

751. Defeat by the Arabs at Talas lost Turkestan to China.

751-790. Wu-k'ung made the pilgrimage to India through Central Asia on the eve of displacement of Buddhism by Islam.

755. Revolt of An Lu-shan, a foreign adventurer from Manchuria who had been adopted by the emperor's favorite concubine, Yang Kuei-fei, and had united three military commands, plunged the empire into particularly sanguinary and destructive civil war.

756-757. The emperor fled to I-chou (renamed Ch'eng-tu) which now developed rapidly as a cultural center. He there abdicated in favor of his son. Despite gradual suppression of the rebellion by Kuo Tzu-i and Li Kuang-pi, power remained in hands of territorial military leaders.

762-763. The Uighur kaghan sacked the eastern capital at Loyang, then in rebel hands, but was himself there converted to Manichaeism, which became the Uighur state religion.

763. The Tibetans, by a surprise attack, sacked Ch'ang-an. Through fear of the Uighur, who tried to convert the T'ang, Manichaeans were allowed to build temples in the capitals (768) and seven other cities (771 and 807). The kaghans were given rich gifts of silk, and a princess (821).

840-841. **Overthrow of the Uighur Empire** by the Turkish Kirghiz and Karluk led to migration of many tribes from the Orkhon to the Tarim basin, where they carved out a second Uighur empire in which the Turkish language extinguished the Indo-European dialects.

841-846. **The reign of Wu Tsung,** under Taoist influence, was filled with persecution of Manichaeans (843), Buddhists, Nestorians, and Mazdeans (845). Buddhism alone was now naturalized and able to survive. The most prominent place in an epoch of increasing anarchy was taken by the **Ch'an** (Skt. *Dhyana,* Jap. *Zen*) **sect** which offered refuge in introspective contemplation. **Bodhidharma,** an aged Persian who had come to Loyang from India prior to 534, was now hailed as fabulous founder of the school, although in fact he was still obscure as late as 728.

CULTURAL PROGRESS continued despite military alarms. **Wei Pao** was commanded (744) to prepare an authentic version of the *Canon of History* by collation of variant manuscripts. It was included, together with all three competing rituals and all three commentaries on the *Annals,* among twelve classics which were cut in stone at Ch'ang-an (836-841). **Po Chü-i** (772-846) wrote excellent poetry, while **Han Yü** created and set the classic model for the essay style. The first historical encyclopedia, the *T'ung Tien,* was compiled (766-801) by **Tu Yu;** and the practice of writing monographs on individual prefectures and districts was begun.

907-959. **Five dynasties** of short duration asserted imperial authority but seldom exercised it outside the Yellow River Basin: Later Liang (907-923), Later T'ang (923-936), Later Tsin (Chin) (936-947), Later Han (947-950), and Later Chou (951-960). Among ten competing secession states the most considerable were southern Han at Canton (904-971), and

southern T'ang which from Nanking ruled much of the east and south (937-975).

932-953. **Nine classics were first printed** from wood blocks, as cheap substitute for stone engraving, at the Later T'ang capital at Loyang by **Feng Tao,** who had seen the process in Shu (Szechuan). The text was that of the stone inscriptions of 836-841.

907-1123. **KHITAN MONGOLS** under their dynastic founder Ye-lü A-pao-chi (907-926) conquered all Inner Mongolia, the Kingdom of Po Hai in the Liao Valley, and 16 northern districts of China. His suzerainty was recognized even by the Uighurs. His son Ye-lü Te-kuang (927-947) both helped set up the Later Tsin dynasty at Ta-liang (modern K'ai-feng) and destroyed it. He took Yen-chou (Peking) as his own southern capital (938), and adopted the Chinese dynastic name *Liao* with periodic reign-titles (947-1125).

960-1279. **THE SUNG DYNASTY** marks the advent of modernity, not only in governmental and social organization, but in thought, belief, literature, and art; not least in the diffusion of learning through print. It was an age of humanism, of scholar statesmen who were at once poets, artists, and philosophers. The first half of the dynasty is often distinguished as the Northern Sung (960-1127) when the capital was at K'ai-feng, then variously called Ta Liang, more properly Pien-liang, or Pien-ching.

960-976. **Chao K'uang-yin** or (Sung) T'ai Tsu gradually restored unity and order under accustomed forms with the help of a paid army.

965. The Annamese secured independence before South China could be subdued and shortly (c. 982) sacked the Cham capital Indrapura before Chinese pressure forced them to peace. Although the Chams (c. 1000) moved their capital south to Vijaya (Cha-ban, near Binh-dinh), the Annamese resumed the war (1043) and sacked it also.

967. The emperor deliberately refused to invade the territory of the native kings of Nan Chao in Yünnan, a policy observed by his successors. He permitted temporary autonomy to the King of Wu Yüeh (modern Chekiang) who had retained his throne (897-978) by pledging loyalty to each Chinese dynasty.

972 ff. **The Buddhist canon** was printed in Szechuan by imperial order from 130,000 blocks. It was reprinted with additions in Fukien (1080-1104), and elsewhere thereafter.

976-997. **T'ai Tsung** completed reunion of the

empire (979), but was twice repulsed from Peking by the Liao (979 and 986).

997. Division of the empire into 15 provinces (*lu*) later extended to 18 (1023–31) and 23 (1078–85).

990-1227. The Western Hsia (Hsi Hsia) Kingdom of Tangut on the northwest frontier with capital at Ning-hsia appealed often to arms (996–1042) despite grant of the imperial surname *Chao* and office (991, 997, 1006), tribute (1043) and royal investiture (1044).

1004. An invasion by the Liao reached the Yellow River near Pien-Liang. They were granted annual tribute. These payments, increased in 1042, and the hire of a large standing army bade fair to bankrupt the treasury.

1006. Granaries for emergency relief were established in every prefecture. In 1069 grain so stored was valued at 15 million strings of cash.

1069-1074. WANG AN-SHIH (1021–1086) carried out a program of radical reform with the full confidence of Shen Tsung (1068–85), and in face of bitter opposition of conservative statesmen.

Through a new **financial bureau** (1069) he cut the budget 40% and raised salaries to make honesty possible for ordinary officials. To avoid excessive transport costs and to control prices he empowered the chief transport officer to accept taxes in cash or kind, to sell from the granaries, and to buy in the cheapest market, using capital of 5 million strings of cash. Further to protect poor farmers against usurers and monopolists, loans of cash or grain were offered in spring against crop estimates to be repaid in autumn with interest of 2% a month (moderate in China). Ambitious officials forced these loans upon merchants and others who did not want them. Objection to both principle and administration of these measures, which were accompanied by alarming centralization of power and disregard for precedent, led to wholesale resignations and transfers of the best officials whose help alone might have made them successful. **Conscript militia** were organized (1070) and trained for police purposes and national defense. The standing army of over a million inefficient men was gradually cut in half. By 1076 the militia, volunteer guards, and border bowmen numbered over 7 million men. **Cash assessments** graded in proportion to property were substituted (1071) for compulsory public services which had borne too heavily upon thrifty rural families. The exemption of officials, clergy, and small families was reduced by half. Necessary local services were now per-

formed by paid volunteer agents. **State banking and barter offices** were opened (1072) first at the capital and later in every prefecture, with the object of controlling prices for the popular benefit.

1074-1085. The reform program was continued, despite complaints of excessive cash levies and other malpractices, until the emperor's death, for a time (1075–1076) by Wang himself.

1085-1093. Regency of the hostile grand dowager empress (under the reign title Yüan Yu) and recall of Ssu-ma Kuang, Su Shih, and the conservative faction to rescind the whole of the reform scheme (1085–1086). Extreme reaction in turn provoked reaction. On the death of his grandmother,

1093-1100. Che Tsung again favored reform, as did his younger brother

1101-1125. Hui Tsung who permitted Ts'ai Ching to proscribe (1102) 98 of the Yüan-Yu partisans, finally (1104) 309 conservatives, living and dead, headed by Ssu-ma Kuang. Eventually much that was good in the measures of 1070 and 1071 was retained. Hui Tsung, himself an able painter, was an active patron of the arts and letters. He founded the imperial academy of painting, and sponsored catalogues of his collections of painting and of archaic bronzes, some of which were obtained by excavation.

The Northern Sung is the golden age of **landscape painting,** when compositions of majestic breadth and exquisite detail were rendered in monochrome and color on long rolls or broad panels of silk. **Tung Yüan** (late 10th cent.) and **Kuo Hsi** (c. 1020–90) combined mastery of continuous composition and linear technique with that of suggestion of atmosphere through gradations of ink-tone. **Li Kung-lin** (c. 1040–1106) excelled in vigorous contrasts of light and shade, of broad and delicate line, and in airy architectural renderings in ruled and measured style. **Mi Fei** (1051–1107) used hardly any lines, building mo ntains and forests from graded accumulations of blobs of ink.

Scholarship flourished no less. Two great encyclopedias were compiled by imperial order, the *T'ai P'ing Yü Lan* (977–983) and the *Ts'e Fu Yüan Kuei* (1005–1013). **Ou-yang Hsiu** (1007–1072), a prominent statesman, helped edit the New History of the T'ang, compiled the first repertory of early inscriptions, and wrote a new type of poetic criticism as also a monograph on the peony. **Ssu-ma Kuang's** cardinal work, the *Tzu Chih T'ung Chien,* is an integrated history of China, 403 B.C.–A.D. 959, compiled 1066–1084. **Su Shih** (1036–1101), better known as **Su Tung-p'o,** was distinguished as an independent statesman, and one of China's greatest essayists, poets, and calligraphers. **Wang An-shih** held his own with these as a brilliant writer of state papers and classical expositor.

Use of tea, first mentioned as substitute for wine under the Wu dynasty (222–280), spread through North China.

It is not known when or by whom the **principle of magnetic polarity,** known to the Chinese at least since the 1st cent. A.D., was applied in the mariner's compass with floating needle. The Malays in the 16th century employed, like the Chinese, a compass rose with 24 points, in contrast to the Arab rose of 32 points; which suggests, but does not prove, that the Malays received both compass and rose from the north. The compass is plainly mentioned by Chinese writers of the early 12th century. The volume of maritime commerce swelled greatly as Arabs in the 9th and 10th centuries entered into competition with Persians at Canton and Ch'üanchou (Zayton), later at Lin-an. It was trade in cotton goods which brought 17 (70?) families of Jews from Persia and India to settle at the capital Pien-liang, where they built a synagogue (1163) and remained unmolested until gradually absorbed.

1114-1234. Jurchen Tungus tribes overthrew their Khitan rulers in Manchuria (1114–16) and, with short-sighted Chinese aid, seized all the Liao lands in China (1122–23). Ye-lü Ta-shih of the Khitan led the remnant of his people to found a new state, Kara-Khitai, in eastern Turkestan (1130) and Turkestan proper (1141–1211). Meantime

1122. The Jurchen prince declared himself emperor of the **Chin (or Kin) dynasty.** He attacked the Sung so vigorously that although

1125. Hui Tsung abdicated in favor of his son,

1126. Ch'in Tsung and his father were both captured with the entire court in the capital. Hui Tsung died in captivity (1135).

1127-1279. THE SOUTHERN SUNG. A junior prince fled southeastward across the Long River from city to city, even by sea to Wen-chou; but, when the Chin retired north of the Long River (1130) and set up the puppet buffer state of Ch'i (1130–37), the capital was established (1135) at Lin-an (modern Hang-chou). The gallant general Yüeh Fei won several successes until put to death by Ch'in Kuei who made

1141. A peace dictated by economic exhaustion, accepting as frontier the line of the Huai and upper Han rivers.

1161. **Explosives** were used by Yü Yün-wen in defeating the Chin at Ts'ai-shih (in Anhuei near Nanking). The Chin, like the Liao before them, avidly absorbed and adopted Chinese culture.

Early Chinese philosophers devoted nearly all their effort to the practical study of ethics. Buddhism, however, insistently raised the problems of ontology and epistemology. It is the merit of the Sung philosophers to have achieved a synthesis of ancient ethics with a new rationalized metaphysics. **Chou Tun-i** (1017–1073) revived a diagram of the ancient diviners to illustrate his conception of causation: emergence of paired forces from primal unity, and differentiation of natural phenomena by their interaction. **Ch'eng Hao** (1032–1085), the leading member of a commission which initiated the valuable Public Services Act of 1071, was in philosophy a mystic synthesist who found benevolence in all things. His brother **Ch'eng I** (1033–1107) was an analyst who discovered in the *Li Chi* the *Ta Hsüeh* or "Great Learning," a short work on method which stresses knowledge as essential to self-improvement on which all human welfare depends. Ideas of the school were systematized and crystallized by **Chu Hsi** (1130–1200), who equated as universals Primary Unity, an impersonal but just and benevolent Heaven, and Righteousness, which correspond to the physical, metaphysical, and ethical spheres. From these proceed as coordinates the dual modes of production, the decrees of Heaven, and the processes of self-improvement. The final products are, respectively, the diversity of natural phenomena, conscience, and character. All these activities of parallel evolution are expressions of a universal divine law. Acceptance of knowledge as an element in self-improvement, and consequent emphasis on objective study, pointed the way towards scientific research; but this tendency was promptly combated by **Lu Chiu-yüan** (1139–1192), who stressed the teaching of Mencius that goodness springs from within.

Painters under the Southern Sung reproduced most often the mild misty landscapes of the Hang-chou region rather than the beetling crags found south of Ch'ang-an which had often inspired northern artists. **Ma Yüan** (1190–1224), **Hsia Kuei** (c. 1180–1230), and their school placed special emphasis on economy of line and representation of mists and clouds. Secular painters came increasingly under domination of conventions which grew up in the academy founded by Hui Tsung, and elegance, charm, and impeccable taste tended to replace more virile virtues; but religious painters, both Buddhist and Taoist, continued to produce vigorous work until the close of the dynasty. **Ch'en Jung** (c. 1235–1255) ranks as China's greatest painter of dragons.

Sung ceramists applied to pottery and porcelain in forms of subtle and sophisticated elegance both incised and molded decoration, together with a wide variety of high-fired glazes, some of which have never since been equaled. Although most wares were ostensibly monochrome, the potters learned to control color-transmutation of their pigments. The potters of Tz'u-chou for the first time employed penciled decoration both under and over glaze.

c. 1190-1294. THE MONGOLS. In central Asia Temujin (c. 1155–1227) created a new Mongol empire which was rapidly expanded by strategy and a military machine employing discipline, extreme mobility, espionage, terrorism, and superior siege equipment.

1194. **The Yellow River,** after repeated alterations of its bed, flowed south of the Shantung massif until 1853.

1206. **Temujin was proclaimed** *Chingiz Khan* ("Emperor within the Seas") at Karakorum. He employed as chancellor a Uighur scholar Tatatonga, who applied to Mongol the Uighur script which was derived from Phoenician through Aramaic, Old and New Sogdian. Enforcement of peace and order within the empire promoted both commerce and cultural exchanges.

1211-1222. The Chin were driven south to the Yellow River (from Yen-ching, 1215).

1227. After several campaigns (1205, 1207, 1209) the Hsi Hsia Kingdom was destroyed, with massacre at Ning-hsia. Temujin bequeathed the empire to a grandson and three sons: to **Batu,** son of his eldest Juchi, Kipchak in Russia; to **Chagatai,** the former Kara-khitai empire; to **Ogedei,** Outer Mongolia; and to Tului (regent 1227–1229), eastern Mongolia and North China.

1229-1241. **Ogedei** was elected khan by plenary kuriltai on the Kerulen.

1231. **Ye-lü Ch'u-ts'ai** (1190–1244), a sinicized scion of the Khitan royal house and adviser to Temujin since 1215, proved his ability to collect taxes in China by traditional methods, and was appointed chancellor. Korye (Korea) was conquered and placed under 72 Mongol residents.

1233. Pien-liang fell after a flanking campaign by Tului through Han-chung and Szechuan (1231–1232), and a long siege by

Sabotai in which the Chin defenders used explosive bombs.

1234. The Chin Empire was annexed. Belated Chinese attack provoked Mongol seizure of Szechuan (1236–1238).

1237. **Ye-lü Ch'u-ts'ai** secured 4030 scholars, one quarter of whom were freed from slavery, through civil service literary examinations; and restored full civilian administration.

1237-1241. Sabotai subjugated Russia and led an invasion through Hungary to Cattaro which was recalled only by death of Ogedei (p. 247).

1246-1248 or 1249. **Guyuk,** son of Ogedei and his widow Turakina (regent 1242–1246), was elected khan in presence of Plano Carpini, envoy of Innocent IV.

1251-1259. **Mongka,** son of Tului, was elected over the son of Guyuk's widow (regent 1249–1251).

1252-1253. Mongka's brother Kublai crushed Nan Chao. The king was named *maharaja* and hereditary administrator under the eyes of a Mongol garrison commander and Chinese resident. More autonomy and an imperial princess were conferred in 1284.

1254. Mongka, the son of a Nestorian woman and employer of a Nestorian chancellor, told William of Rubruck, envoy of Louis IX of France, that religions are like the fingers of one hand. He yet favored Buddhism, and after public disputation (1255) proscribed Taoist books for forgery. Kublai shortly followed this example (1258).

1257. The capital was transferred to Shang-tu, north of present Peking.

1258. The Mongols pillaged Hanoi, while, at the other end of the empire, Hulagu with a Nestorian wife and general destroyed the Abbasid Caliphate of Baghdad.

1260-1368. **THE YÜAN DYNASTY** (as distinguished from the Mongol Empire) was effectively founded when **Kublai** (1214–1294) had himself elected khan by his own army at Shang-tu (1260), although he adopted the dynastic title only in 1271. He ruled in China according to Chinese precedents. His dynastic name is Shih tsu.

1264. **The Mongol Empire** was reunited by capture of Kublai's brother Arikboga, who had been proclaimed khan at Karakorum (1260). Twice (1277 and 1287–1288) its unity was defended against Khaidu, head of the house of Ogedei. Kublai's authority was respected by his brother Hulagu and the succeeding Ilkhans of Persia, and in theory by the Golden Horde on the Volga. He transferred (1264) the winter capital to Yen-ching where he constructed Khanbalig, modern Peking (1267). He erected an astronomical observatory on the city wall, wherein were installed bronze instruments cast by Kuo Shou-ching (1279).

1268-1273. A siege of Hsiang-yang and Fan-ch'eng on the Han was ended after 4 years 5 months only by engineers and machines from Mesopotamia. There-after the Mongols were free to descend towards the sea.

1276. Capitulation of the empress-regent and boy-emperor at Lin-an (Hang-chou) was followed by capture of Canton (twice, 1277) and destruction of a fleet carrying the last youthful Sung pre-tender (1279).

1281. Disastrous attack upon Japan. An as-sault in 1274 having failed, a Mongol army of 45,000 from Korea joined (June) a tardy armada with 120,000 men from the southern Chinese coast in landing at Hakozaki Bay. The invaders were repulsed by the well-prepared Jap-anese until (Aug. 15) a typhoon destroyed their fleets, leaving them to death or slavery.

1282-1283. An army sent by sea from Canton to subdue Champa took the capital Vijaya, but was forced by epidemics to withdraw.

1285 and 1287-1288. Abortive expeditions against Annam and Champa by land and sea were massacred and repulsed, but secured admission of vassalage.

1287. The Mongols pillaged Pagan, capital of Burma, received homage (1297), and returned (1300) to pacify competing Shan chiefs.

1289-1323. The Siamese kingdoms of Sukhotai and Lopburi presented tribute.

1292-1293. A naval **expedition to Java,** after temporary success, was forced to re-embark.

1295-1307. Temur Oljaitu, grandson of Ku-blai, was the second and last effective ruler of the Yüan dynasty.

1296. A Mongol embassy accompanied by Chou Ta-kuan found Chen-la (Cam-bodia) much weakened by the attacks of Suk-hotai, which had now become a powerful state under its second ruler Rama Kamheng.

ECONOMIC DEVELOPMENTS. Kublai devoted special attention to economic matters: The Grand Canal was restored (1289-1292) from the former Sung capital, Lin-an at Hang-chou

(the Kinsay of Marco Polo), now a great and rich city, to the Huai River, and carried north to the outskirts of Peking. Imperial roads were improved, and postal relays of 200,000 horses established. Charitable relief was organized (1260) for aged scholars, orphans, and the sick, for whom hospitals were provided (1271). Im-perial inspectors every year examined crops and the food supply with a view to purchase when stocks were ample for storage against famine.

The T'ang first employed paper money orders, to which the Sung and Chin added various bills of exchange. When issue of paper currency was suggested to Ogedei (1236), Ye-lü Ch'ü-ts'ai se-cured limitation to value of 100,000 oz. of silver. Under Kublai, a Mohammedan financier, Saiyid-i Edjill Chams al-Din Omar (1210-1279), kept annual issues at an average of 511,400 oz. (1260-1269). His successor Ahmed Fenaketi increased emissions (1276-1282) to 10,000,000 oz. annually. After Ahmed's murder, inflation increased until a Uighur, Sanga, reduced the rate of printing to 5,000,000 oz. (1290-1291). Circuit stabilization treasuries (1264 and 1287) were given reserves inadequate to redeem the flood of bills at $2\frac{1}{2}\%$ discount, the official rate of 1287. The issue of 1260 depreciated until replaced 1 for 5 by that of 1287, which again was replaced 1 for 5 in 1309. All printing was discontinued in 1311; but the credit, financial and moral, of the dynasty was already on the wane. The southern provinces of the empire rapidly fell from its control.

Marco Polo, in the service of the khan (1275-1292), traveled widely in Cathay (from Khitai, hence North China), and Manzi (South China), and to Burma (p. 368). Through his "Division of the World" he first brought detailed and accurate knowledge of eastern Asia to Europe. In his time, and even in that of the Arab, Ibn Battuta (c. 1345), Zayton (Ch'üan-chou) was the busiest deep-sea port in the world, leading Kinsay (Lin-an), Foochow (Fu-chou), and Can-ton in shipping silks and porcelains to Java, Malaya, Ceylon, India, and Persia in exchange for spices, gems and pearls. The itineraries given by Chao Ju-kua (1225) imply in the pre-cision of their bearings the use of a compass needle mounted on a dry pivot.

THE MOSLEM COMMUNITIES of Persian and Arab traders at these ports were small com-pared to those which now grew up in North China and in Yünnan. Saiyid-i Edjill as gov-ernor of Yünnan (1274-1279) built the first two mosques in what became a stronghold of Islam. Most popular religion with all the Mongols was Buddhism. Kublai welcomed a gift of relics of the Buddha from the raja of Ceylon. He conferred the title *Teacher of the State* upon a Tibetan lama Phags-pa, whom he employed to convert the Mongols and to whom he entrusted government of the three provinces of Tibet.

NESTORIAN CHRISTIANS enjoyed full protection. The Patriarch of Baghdad created an archbishopric at Peking (1275); churches were built in Chen-kiang (1281), Yang-chou, and Hang-chou; and a special bureau was created (1289) to care for Christianity. **Mar Yabalaha**, pilgrim from Peking to Jerusalem, was elected patriarch (1281), and his companion Rabban Sauma was sent by him and Argun, Ilkhan of Persia, to Rome and France. He negotiated with Pope Nicholas IV an entente between the Nestorian and Roman churches. **John of Montecorvino** was the first of several Roman missionaries to China (1294–1328). He baptized 5000 converts and was named by the pope (1307) Archbishop of Peking. He received a three-year visit from **Oderic of Pordenone** who reported to Europe the custom of foot-binding, which had spread through South China under the Southern Sung, but which was unknown to the Chin and early Yüan.

LITERATURE: the Mongol period introduced the novel and the drama, the latter accompanied by raucous percussion music. Although neither was at once admitted as a form of polite letters, both are now recognized to possess artistic merit.

PAINTING: one group of artists continued traditions of the Southern Sung while another boldly swept away the mists which had shrouded landscape. **Ch'ien Hsüan** (1235–c. 1290) is perhaps the greatest painter of flowers and insects. **Chao Meng-fu** (1254–1322) was particularly adept at depicting the horses and other live-stock which were prominent in Mongol economy. Yüan porcelain reveals in arabesques no less than in the technique of penciling in cobalt blue directly on clear white paste the debt of Chinese potters to Persian models. From these also is derived the Byzantine form of cloisonné enamel.

1368–1644. THE MING DYNASTY was founded by **Chu Yüan-chang** (Ming T'ai Tsu, 1328–1398), a monk turned insurgent amidst anarchy, who seized Chiang-ning (Nanking) in 1356, set up there an orderly government, and proceeded to annex the holdings of surrounding southern war-lords until in 1368 he was strong enough to drive the Mongols from Peking with Shensi, Kansu (1369) and Szechuan (1371). Like all the emperors of this and the following dynasty he ruled under a single reign-

title, **Hung-wu** (1368–1398), which is accordingly often used instead of his personal name.

1382. Yünnan was completely conquered, and its prince executed at Nanking. The whole territory of China was now under direct government.

1388. The Mongols were driven from Karakorum and defeated on the Kerulen.

1392–1910. The Li dynasty was founded in Korea upon the ruins of that of Wang, which had reigned since 918 (p. 354).

1403–1424. THE YUNG LO REIGN of Ch'eng Tsu was established by violence against his nephew, who disappeared in a palace fire (1402).

1403–1433. A series of naval expeditions through the southern seas was motivated by desire for commerce and military prestige, but also by uneasiness lest the deposed nephew emerge thence to claim his throne. Secret inquiry by Hu Jung within the empire also was protracted (1407–1416, 1419–1423). A claimant actually appeared in Honan in 1440.

1405–1407. Cheng Ho, the chief eunuch (a Mohammedan whose real surname was Ma), brought back in chains the Prince of Palembang (Sumatra), who had been defeated in battle, as he did

1408–1411. The King of Ceylon and his family, who had attacked the mission. As a result of

1412–1415. A third cruise as far as Hormuz, sixteen southern states sent tribute. Cheng Ho was appointed to lead two more embassies during this reign: 1416–1419 (as far as Aden), and 1421–1422. Other eunuchs led additional missions.

1410, 1414, 1422–1424. Campaigns into Outer Mongolia were directed at destruction of whatever chieftain or group momentarily possessed sufficient prestige to threaten re-creation of the Mongol power.

1421. Transfer of the capital to Peking was mooted in 1409, decreed in 1420. Wisdom of the move is reflected by the fact that the northern frontier was never successfully violated during the five centuries Peking remained capital, save when the Manchus were invited in.

1428–1788. The later Le dynasty in Annam, after a quarter century of fighting, secured recognition of independence (1431) from Hsüan Tsung in the Hsüan Te reign (1426–1435). The royal title was conferred in 1436.

1431-1433. Cheng Ho led a seventh and final embassy to twenty states. As result tribute was sent by Mecca and ten others.

1449. Emperor Ying Tsung (1436-1449 and 1457-1464) was captured in battle by the chief of a new Mongol confederation (Oirat) of four tribes. Although released next year, he recovered his throne from his brother Ching Ti only in 1457.

c. 1470-1543. Dayan, a descendant of Chinghiz, restored unity to Mongolia, but divided it among his own descendants.

1471. Annam finally annexed its southern neighbor, Champa.   (*Cont. p.* 541.)

a. BURMA

From early times Burma was under Indian influence. By the 3d century A.D. expanding Hindu peoples had established commercial settlements on the Tenasserim coast and at the principal river mouths which developed into small kingdoms in contact with the Tibeto-Burman tribes of the Irrawaddy Valley. Commercial relations with China were less influential, although an embassy from a Burmese state reached Ch'ang An in 802.

1044. Anawrata seized royal power at Pagan and by his patronage of Hinayana Buddhism and conquests, both north and south, made it the political, religious, and cultural center of Burma; the Burmese written language was developed and Buddhist scriptures translated; architectural monuments followed the inspiration of Ceylon and southern India; able rulers succeeded Anawrata.

1106. A Burmese embassy at the Sung capital in China was received as from a fully sovereign state.

1287. Following the rejection of Mongol demands for tribute (1271 and later), Burmese raids into Yünnan, and the death of Narathihapate (who ruled 1254-1287), Mongol forces looted Pagan and destroyed its power. The invasion of Shan tribes, forced southward by the Mongols, led to the division of Burma into a number of petty states, chief among them being Toungoo (estab. 1280), Pegu in southern Burma, and Ava in the middle and lower Irrawaddy Valley (estab. as capital 1365).
          (*Cont. p.* 547.)

b. SIAM

During the early centuries of the Christian Era, the Khmer peoples of the Menam Valley came under the influence of Hindu civilization, and about the 6th century there was organized, in the region of Lopburi, the **Kingdom of Dvaravati,** which was Buddhist rather than Brahman in religion, and from which during the 8th century migrants to the upper Menam Valley established the independent and predominantly Buddhist Kingdom of Haripunjaya, with its capital near the present Chiengmai. Early in the 11th century Dvaravati was annexed to Cambodia; but Haripunjaya retained its independence until the 13th century, when it was overrun by a migration of Tai, or Shan, peoples from the north. This migration, accelerated by the Mongol conquest of the Tai state of Nanchao in 1253, led to foundation at Sukhothai (1256) of Sien or Syām (Siam) which attained wide hegemony under Rāma Kamheng, inventor of Siamese script (1283) and victor over the Khmers. Another Thai, Rāmādhipati, seized the smaller southern state of Lopburī, annexed Sukhothai to it, and built a new capital at Ayuthia (1351-1767). The Siamese from the first were under the influence of Hīnayāna Buddhism, derived from Burma, and of Chinese political institutions. Toward the end of the 13th century a form of writing had been invented for the Siamese language.

1357-1460. Siamese **invasions of Cambodia** finally led to the abandonment of Angkor and collapse of the Khmer Empire.

1371. A Siamese embassy at Nanking inaugurated tributary relations with the newly founded Ming dynasty.

1376-1557. Intermittent friction between Siam and the Thai state of Chiengmai in the northern Menam Valley ended only with the destruction of Chiengmai by the Burmese.

During the 14th and 15th centuries strong Siamese influence was exerted over the disunited states of Burma and the northern part of the Malay Peninsula.   (*Cont. p.* 547.)

c. MALAYSIA

Early Indian commercial settlements in Sumatra and Java, at first Brahman in religion and later influenced by Buddhism, became the centers of organized states. Toward the end of the 7th century A.D., **Srivijaya** became the dominant state of Sumatra and built up a commercial empire which at its height (c. 1180) controlled the Straits of Malacca and of Sunda, all of Sumatra and the Malay Peninsula, and the western half of Java; its authority was recognized as far away as Ceylon and Formosa, and in many colonies throughout the East Indies. The **Sailendra dynasty,** whose capital was at Palembang, were ardent patrons of Buddhism, as is shown in the great Borobudur stupa in central Java (c. 775–825). The consolidation of petty Javanese states, begun after the middle of the 9th century, led to the rise of **Singhasari** in eastern Java, which under Kartanagara (who ruled 1268–1292) challenged and finally destroyed the power of Srivijaya.

1293. A Mongol expedition, sent to avenge insult offered by Kartanagara, was forced out of Java by a new kingdom, **Madjapahit**, which during the 14th century built up a commercial empire with authority extending over Borneo, Sumatra, and parts of the Philippines and of the Malay peninsula, and profited by an extensive trade with China, Indo-China, and India. After the

1389. Death of Hayam Wuruk, the power of Madjapahit disintegrated.

1405-1407. The first Chinese expedition under Cheng Ho established tributary relations between many Malay states and the Ming Empire; and the authority of Madjapahit rapidly gave way to that of the Mohammedan Arabs. During the 15th century Mohammedan commercial operations, based chiefly on Malacca, were extended to the whole archipelago, and some 20 states accepted Islam as the state religion. *Cont. p. 547.*)

4. KOREA

612. Emperor Yang-ti of the Sui dynasty of China invaded Koguryŏ, but was repulsed.

645-647. Two T'ang expeditions against Koguryŏ failed.

663. The T'ang destroyed Paekche.

668. The T'ang and Silla together destroyed Koguryŏ.

670. Silla robbed the T'ang of Paekche and southern Koguryŏ, but did not break its allegiance to China.

670-935. SILLA PERIOD.

670-780. Height of Silla power and culture, when Buddhism and art flourished, particularly at the capital near the modern Kyŏngju (J. Keishū).

780-935. Period of political decline, but of closer relations with and increasing imitation of China.

c. 880. Serious rebellions broke out.

918. The state of **Koryŏ** was founded in west central Korea.

935. Silla peacefully submitted to Koryŏ.

935-1392. KORYŎ PERIOD.

935-1170. Height of Koryŏ power and culture centering around the capital, Kaesong (modern Sŏngdo, J. Kaijō) in west central Korea and P'yŏngyang, the secondary capital.

936. Koryŏ destroyed Later Paekche, thus uniting Korea once more.

996. **The Khitan** (Liao dynasty) forced Koryŏ to recognize them, and not the Sung dynasty of China, as overlords of Korea.

1044. A great wall was completed across northern Korea as a defense against the Manchurian peoples.

1123. **The Juchên** (Chin dynasty) forced Koryŏ to recognize their suzerainty.

1170. Military officers seized the government and proscribed Buddhism.

1196. **The Ch'oe family** established its control over the government with the title of *Kongnyŏng*.

1223. Beginning of over 200 years of attacks on coastal regions by Japanese pirates.

1231. **The Mongols** invaded Korea, and the Ch'oe removed the government to the island of Kanghwa off the west coast.

1258. The Im (Lim, J. Rin) family supplanted the Ch'oe as *Kongnyŏng*.

1259. Koryŏ submitted to the Mongols, and the Koryŏ kings through intermarriage became merely a branch of the Mongol imperial family and their representatives in Korea. This situation and the rise of Confucianism at this time led gradually to the unquestioning acceptance of Chinese suzerainty and leadership in political and cultural matters.

1356. Koryŏ revolted successfully against the Mongols.

1356-1392. Period of great disorder. The Koryŏ kings, who had depended on Mongol prestige for their authority, were unable to suppress their unruly vassals, and the Japanese pirates were at their worst.

1369. Koryŏ submitted to the Ming dynasty of China.

1392. I (Li, J. Ri) **Sŏnggye** declared himself king after a series of *coups d'état* and assassinations, thus founding the

1392-1910. I (Li, J. Ri) **DYNASTY** with its capital at Kyŏngsŏng (modern Sŏul [Seoul], J. Keijō). This new dynasty based its claims to legitimacy on its championing of the Ming cause as opposed to the Mongols, considered by them not to be the legitimate rulers of China. Like their predecessors they remained unswervingly loyal and subservient to China.

1392–1494. Period of greatest prosperity and cultural development.

1419–1451. King Sejong was a patron of learning, and in his time the native phonetic script called *ŏnmun* was introduced. During this reign the Japanese pirates ceased to ravage the Korean coast, and the northeastern corner of present-day Korea was brought under Korean rule. (*Cont. p.* 548.)

5. JAPAN, 645–1543

645–784. PERIOD OF THE IMITATION OF CHINA. An edict outlining the general principles of national reorganization was promulgated as early as 646 (the *Taika Reform*), but it was only in the course of several decades that the principles were put into practice and even then the reforms often remained on paper. The major features of the new system were: (1) the nationalization of the land, in theory; (2) the adoption of the T'ang system of land distribution and taxation; (3) the reorganization of local government and other measures intended to increase the authority of the central government in the provinces and its income from them, and (4) the reorganization of the central government. The principles and many of the details of the reforms were borrowed directly from China, but in Japan, dominated as it was by an hereditary aristocracy, it was well-nigh impossible to carry them out in full, and from the start they were basically modified in practice. (1) Although the land was nationalized in theory, in actuality the large hereditary estates of the clan chiefs were returned to them as lands held as salary for their official positions and ranks. (2) The land was to be periodically divided among the agriculturalists in accordance with the membership of each family as determined by census, and uniform taxes were to be levied on all alike. These were (a) the land tax (*so*), paid in rice; (b) the corvée (*yōeki*), often commuted at a fixed rate into a textile tax; and (c) the excise (*chō*) levied on produce other than rice. The system was too closely patterned after the Chinese and functioned badly in Japan from the beginning. Powerful families and institutions, hungry for land, were always ready to deprive the public domain of taxpaying lands, and the peasants, impoverished by taxes, were often anxious to transfer themselves and their lands from the taxpaying public domain to the care of privately owned manors (*shōen*). As a result the history of economic development during the next several centuries is primarily the story of the return of the land into private hands and the emergence of large tax-free estates owned by the court nobility and great religious institutions. (3) The improvement of means of communication helped in the centralization of government and in the collection of taxes, but, although the officials of the provincial governments were to have been appointees of the central government, in practice local leaders retained their supremacy by occupying the lower posts, and it soon became the accepted custom for the high provincial officials to remain at the capital and to delegate their powers to underlings in the provinces. (4) An essential and permanent feature of the reforms was the complete reorganization and great elaboration of the central government. A department of religion (*jingikan*) and a great council of state (*dajōkan*) were established as two parallel organs controlling the spiritual and political aspects of the state. Below the great council were eight ministries, and below them in turn many smaller bureaus. The organization was too ponderous for the Japan of that day. Moreover, with the collapse of the economic supports of the central government through the growth of tax-free estates, this elaborate organism was literally starved to death. Although in theory it continued little changed until the 19th century, actually during most of that period it was merely a skeleton devoid of most of its former powers. In adopting the Chinese form of government the Japanese made one significant change. The official hierarchy of Japan remained a hereditary aristocracy, and with rare exceptions there was little opportunity for the able or learned of low rank to rise far in this hierarchy.

This period was the **classic era of Japanese culture.** Poetry and prose in pure Chinese were composed, and native Japanese poetry reached an early flowering. Japan in the preceding century had already been imitating continental artistic styles, and now the art of T'ang China found fertile soil in Japan and produced there many of the greatest extant examples of Far Eastern art of that day in the fields of architecture, sculpture, painting and the applied arts.

663. The Japanese withdrew from Korea, after the defeat of a Japanese army and fleet, sent to the aid of Paekche, by a combined force from China and Silla (662). Thus ended the first period of Japanese continental expansion. The fall of Paekche in 663 and of Koguryŏ (a North Korean kingdom) in 668 left Silla supreme in the peninsula and resulted in a great immigration of Korean refugees into Japan.

697. The Empress Jitō (686–697) abdicated in favor of her grandson, **Mommu** (697–707). This was the first case of the accession of a minor and the second of the abdication of a ruler, but both were soon to become the rule.

702. New civil and penal codes known as the *Taihō Laws* were promulgated. This may have been the first complete codification of the laws embodied in the reforms commenced in 646, although there is mention of an earlier code. These laws, together with a revision of 718 (*Yōrō Laws*, not enforced until 757), have come down to us only through later commentaries, the *Ryō no Gige* of 833 and the *Ryō no Shūge* of 920. A supplementary code, the *Engishiki*, was completed in 928.

710. Heijō (or Nara) was laid out on the model of Ch'ang-an, the T'ang capital, as the first permanent capital of Japan. The period during which it was the capital is known as

710–784. THE NARA PERIOD.

712. The *Kojiki*, which records the history of the imperial line since its mythical origins, was written in Chinese characters (used to a large extent phonetically) to represent Japanese words. This is Japan's oldest extant book.

720. The *Nihonshoki* (or *Nihongi*), a more detailed history of Japan written in Chinese, was compiled. It was continued to 887 by five other official histories written in Chinese, which together with it constitute the **Six National Histories** (*Rikkokushi*).

724–749. Shōmu's reign, which included the brilliant Tempyō year period (729–748). This and the period during which Shōmu dominated the court as the retired emperor (749–756) marked the apogee of the Nara Period and its classic semi-Chinese culture.

737. The death of the four grandsons of Kamatari delayed for several decades the complete domination of the imperial court by the Fujiwara clan.

741. Government monasteries and convents (*Kokubunji*) were ordered erected in each province.

752. The dedication of the **Great Buddha** (*Daibutsu*) at Nara marked the completion of the devout Shōmu's most cherished project.

The 53-foot bronze figure of the Buddha Rushana (Skt. *Vairocana*) and the huge hall built over it was a tremendous undertaking for the Japanese court and gave witness to the great Buddhist fervor of the time. Many of the objects used in the dedication service together with the personal belongings of Shōmu form the basis of the unique collection of 8th century furniture and art preserved at the imperial treasury in Nara (the *Shōsōin*, commenced in 756).

Shortly before the erection of the Great Buddha the famous monk, **Gyōgi** (670–749), is said to have propagated the concept that Buddhism and Shintō were two aspects of the same faith. Such beliefs served as a justification for the growing amalgamation of the two religions, which was to lead by the 12th century to the development of **Dual Shintō** (*Ryōbu Shintō*), in which Shintō gods were considered to be manifestations of Buddhist deities. Faced with a highly developed foreign religion backed by all the prestige of the more advanced Chinese civilization, the simple native cult became for a period of almost 1000 years the handmaiden of Buddhism in an unequal union.

754. The Chinese monk **Ganjin** (also pronounced Kanshin, etc.; Ch., *Chienchên*, d. 763), after five unsuccessful attempts to reach Japan, finally arrived at Nara, where he set up the first ordination platform (*kaidan*) and firmly established the **Ritsu** (Skt. *Vinaya*) **Sect,** which stressed discipline rather than doctrine. The Ritsu Sect together with five other sects formed the so-called **Nara Sects,** the oldest sectarian divisions of Japanese Buddhism. These others were the **Sanron** (Skt. *Madhyamika*) **Sect,** said to have been introduced in 625; the **Hossō** (Skt. *Dharmalaksana*) **Sect,** brought from China by Dōshō (d. 700), who had gone there to study in 653; the **Kegon** (Skt. *Avatamsaka*) **Sect,** which was largely responsible for the cult of Rushana, the universal and omnipresent Buddha; the **Kusha** (Skt. *Abhidharmakosa*) **Sect;** and the **Jōjitsu** (Skt. *Satyasiddhi*) **Sect,** which last two may never have existed as independent religious bodies in Japan.

759. The *Man'yōshū*, a collection of over 4000 poems in pure Japanese, composed largely by the court nobility between 687 and 759, was compiled shortly after the latter date. It was followed in later centuries by similar anthologies. In 751 the *Kaifusō*, a small collection of poems in Chinese had been compiled; it likewise was continued by similar works.

764. A clash for power between **Fujiwara Nakamaro** (also known as Emi Oshikatsu), the leading statesman during Junnin's reign

(758–764), and Dōkyō, the monk favorite of the retired nun empress, Kōken (749–758), led to the death of Nakamaro, the exile of Junnin, his subsequent assassination, and the reascension to the throne of Kōken as the Empress Shōtoku.

764–770. Dōkyō was all-powerful during Shōtoku's reign and may even have aspired to the throne. Strong opposition and Shōtoku's death led to his ultimate downfall. Perhaps because of the memory of Dōkyō's influence over Shōtoku, for almost nine centuries thereafter no woman occupied the throne.

781–806. The reign of the energetic **Kammu** witnessed the conquest of much of northern Hondō in a prolonged but successful border struggle with the Ainu. After several initial failures the natives of this region, both Ainu and intractable Japanese frontiersmen, were definitely brought under the imperial sway by **Sakanoue Tamuramaro** (d. 811). His campaigns concluded centuries of slow advance into Ainu territory. After a final outbreak in 812 the Ainu menace in the north never again assumed major proportions.

794. Kammu moved the capital from Nagaoka, where it had been since 784, to Heian, the modern Kyōto, where it remained until 1868. The reasons for his abandoning of Nara are not definitely known but were probably: (1) a desire to make a new departure politically and economically; (2) a desire to escape the oppressive influence of the powerful Nara monasteries; (3) the superior location of Nagaoka and Kyōto, which had better water communications with the sea; and (4) the influence of the Hata family (?), which had lands in that region. The reasons for the sudden removal of the capital from Nagaoka to Kyōto, a few miles farther inland, are still more obscure, but may have been connected with Kammu's fear that the first site had incurred the curse of certain spirits. The establishing of the capital at Kyōto marked the beginning of

794–1185. THE HEIAN PERIOD, a long era marked by few violent upheavals but one in which the transition from the period of the imitation of China to the feudal and more strictly Japanese Kamakura period was slowly made. These centuries were characterized by a somewhat effete dilettantist court society, becoming increasingly divorced from political and economic realities; the gradual decline and collapse of the economic and political system borrowed from China; the growth of tax-free manors; the slow emergence of a new military

class in the provinces; the full glory and subsequent decline of the Fujiwara family; the appearance and development of the Buddhist sects and cults which dominated much of Japan's religious history; a sounder understanding of the borrowed Chinese civilization and a greater ability to synthesize it with what was natively Japanese, or to modify it to fit the peculiar needs of Japan; a resultant growing cultural independence of China, and the reappearance of more purely Japanese art and literature.

800–816. New offices in the central government, which were to affect profoundly the whole administration, appeared at this time. These were: (1) the *kageushi* (audit office) (c. 800), which in time usurped the prerogatives of the original audit and revenue offices; (2) the *kurōdo-dokoro* (bureau of archivists) (810), which gradually attained control of palace affairs and became the organ for issuing imperial decrees; (3) the *kebiishichō* (police commission) (c. 816), which in time became the primary law enforcement organ of the state and eventually created outside of the official codes its own code of customary law.

804. Tendai and **Shingon,** the two leading sects of the Heian period, were founded by **Saichō** (Dengyō Daishi 767–822) and **Kūkai** (Kōbō Daishi 774–835) respectively. Both monks accompanied the eleventh embassy to the T'ang in 804. Saichō returned to Japan the next year to found the Tendai Sect, named after Mt. T'ien-t'ai in China. The syncretistic inclusive nature of the philosophy of the sect appealed to the Japanese, and its central monastery, the Enryakuji, which Saichō founded on Mt. Hiei overlooking Kyōto (788), became the center from which sprang most of the later significant movements in Japanese Buddhism. Kūkai returned from China in 806 bringing with him the Shingon or Tantric Sect, a late esoteric and mystic form of Indian Buddhism. Because of his tremendous personality and the natural appeal of Shingon to the superstitious propensities of the people, the new sect won considerable popular support, and the Kongōbuji monastery on Mt. Kōya, which Kūkai founded (816), became one of the great centers of Buddhism. Tendai and Shingon were more genuinely Japanese in spirit than were the Nara sects, and the Shingon Sect in particular furthered the union of Shintō and Buddhism.

838. The twelfth and last embassy to the T'ang was dispatched. When in 894 Sugawara Michizane (845–903) was appointed to be the next envoy, he persuaded the court to discontinue the practice on the grounds that China was disturbed and no longer able to teach Japan. Although some unofficial intercourse continued between the two countries, this brought to an end the three centuries of the greatest cultural borrowing from China and marked the beginning of a period in which peculiarly Japanese traits asserted themselves increasingly in all phases of Japanese life.

858. The complete **domination of the Fujiwara clan** over the imperial family was achieved by Yoshifusa (804–872) when he became the *de facto* regent of the child-emperor, Seiwa (858–876). In 866, after Seiwa had attained his majority, Yoshifusa assumed the title of regent (*sesshō*), becoming the first non-imperial regent. Seiwa was the first male adult emperor to have a regent. The typical inner family control which the Fujiwara exercised over the emperors can be seen in the relationship that existed between Seiwa and Yoshifusa, for the latter was both the grandfather and the father-in-law of the young ruler. It was the definite policy of the Fujiwara to have a young imperial grandson of the head of the clan occupy the throne and to have him abdicate early in favor of another child. The period of the domination of the Fujiwara family is often called

866–1160.   THE FUJIWARA PERIOD.

880. **Fujiwara Mototsune** (836–891) became the first civil dictator (*kampaku*), a post thereafter customarily held by the head of the clan when an adult emperor was on the throne, while the post of regent came to be reserved for the clan head in the time of a minor emperor.

889. The branch of the warrior **Taira clan** which was to rule Japan for part of the 12th century was founded when a great-grandson of Kammu was given this surname. The clan was established in 825 by another imperial prince. In 814 the rival military **clan of Minamoto** was founded by other members of the imperial clan, and in 961 the princely progenitor of the later Minamoto rulers received this surname. The descendants of such imperial princes, reduced to the rank of commoners, often went to the provinces to seek their fortunes, and there some of them merged with the rising class of warriors, who were soon to dominate the land.

891. The **Emperor Uda** (887–897), who was not the son of a Fujiwara mother, made a determined effort to rule independently without Fujiwara influence and refused to appoint a new civil dictator after Mototsune's death. To further this end he used the brilliant scholar, **Sugawara Michizane** (845–903), as his confidential minister, but after Uda's abdication (d. 931),

Fujiwara Tokihira (871–909) managed to obtain the removal of Michizane to a provincial post, where he soon died. He was posthumously loaded with honors and deified because it was believed that his vengeful spirit had caused certain calamities. Tokihira throughout his official career strove valiantly but in vain to stem the tide of governmental corruption and disintegration.

905. The *Kokinshū*, an anthology of over 1000 poems in Japanese, was compiled by Imperial order in a revival of interest in Japanese poetry. For over a century almost all literary effort and scholarship had been devoted to prose and poetry in the Chinese language, but **Ki Tsurayuki** (d. 946) wrote the preface to the *Kokinshū* in Japanese and followed it in 935 by a travel diary (*Tosa Nikki*) also in Japanese. Within the short compass of a century Japanese prose was to rise to great heights of literary achievement. An important contributing factor to the revival of Japanese literature at this time was the fact that in the preceding century a simple syllabary for writing Japanese phonetically had been evolved from the complicated Chinese characters.

930. The offices of regent and civil dictator were revived after a lapse of four decades when **Fujiwara Tadahira** (880–949) became regent in 930 and civil dictator in 941.

935–941. Civil strife in the provinces broke out on an unprecedented scale, giving witness to the rise of the provincial military class. From 936 until his death in 941 Sumitomo, a member of the Fujiwara clan and a former provincial official, controlled the Inland Sea as a pirate captain, while in eastern Japan an imperial scion, Taira Masakado, after waging war on his relatives and neighbors, declared himself emperor (940), but was presently killed.

949. The **Emperor Murakami** (947–967) did not appoint a successor to Tadahira, but after the former's demise

967–1068. The successive heads of the Fujiwara clan occupied the posts of **regent** and civil dictator almost uninterruptedly for a full century. This was the heyday of the Fujiwara clan and the core of the so-called Fujiwara period. Court life was ostentatious and extravagant and was characterized by amatorial dilettantism and moral laxity. At the same time petty jealousies and intrigues disrupted the Fujiwara clan, members of the provincial warrior class began to appear on the capital stage as petty military officers and came to be used by the court nobles in their disputes, manors continued to grow apace, further limiting government resources and the general collapse of the central government continued unabated.

985. The *Ōjōyōshū* by the monk **Genshin** (942–1017) gave literate expression to new religious currents which were stirring the nation. A belief had sprung up that the age of *mappō* ("the latter end of the law"), a period of degeneracy to come 2000 years after the Buddha's death, had already commenced. There was a growing belief in the **Pure Land** (*Jōdo*), Paradise of Amida (Skt. *Amitabha*) and salvation through his benign intervention in favor of the believer and not only through one's own efforts, as earlier Buddhism had taught. Emphasis was increasingly placed on *nembutsu*, the repetition of Amida's name or a simple Amidist formula. **Kūya** (903–972), an itinerant preaching monk, was the first articulate voice to express this new religious movement, and Genshin gave it sound literary formulation. It continued to develop, and in the 12th and 13th centuries produced important new Buddhist sects.

995-1028. **FUJIWARA MICHINAGA'S** (966–1028) rule over clan and state saw the zenith of clan power and some of the most brilliant decades of artistic and literary achievement of the epoch. Although he was never officially civil dictator and was regent for only a short period prior to his official retirement in 1017, he was perhaps the most powerful leader the Fujiwara produced. At this time the classic prose literature of Japan reached its height in the *Genji Monogatari* (c. 1008–1020), a long novel by **Murasaki Shikibu,** a court lady, and in the *Makura no Sōshi* (Pillow Book) (c. 1002) a shorter miscellany by another court lady, **Sei Shōnagon.** The refined and somewhat feminine art of the epoch also was at its height. **Jōchō** (d. 1057), a famous Buddhist sculptor, was already active, and Michinaga's successor, **Yorimichi** (992–1074, regent 1017–1020; civil dictator 1020–1068), built the *Byōdōin*, the outstanding architectural work remaining from the age.

1039. Armed Enryakuji monks invaded Kyōto to force their will upon the government, but were driven off by Taira troops at Yorimichi's command. Such descents upon the capital, known as "forceful appeals" (*gōso*), were common during the 11th and later centuries and sometimes led to actual fighting. The turbulence of the monks, who fought fiercely among themselves as well as with the court, made it necessary for the court to appeal to the Taira and Minamoto for military aid, and the warrior clans consequently became more influential at court.

1051-1062. In the **Earlier Nine Years' War** Minamoto Yoriyoshi, on imperial command, destroyed the **Abe,** a powerful military clan of northern Japan. Thereby he firmly established the prestige of his branch of the Minamoto clan in eastern and northern Japan. Yoriyoshi's ancestors had already started the military renown of the house, and its status at court as "the claws and teeth of the Fujiwara" greatly increased its power.

1068-1073. The **Emperor Sanjō II,** who was not the son of a Fujiwara mother, ruled directly without the interference of the Fujiwara. Although the latter continued to occupy the posts of regent and civil dictator, they never again gained full control of the government. Sanjō II established a records office (*kirokujo*) to examine title deeds of manors in an effort to check their growth, but in this attempt he was blocked by the opposition of the Fujiwara.

1083-1087. In the **Latter Three Years' War** Minamoto Yoshiie (1041–1108) destroyed the Kiyowara family of northern Japan, thereby increasing Minamoto prestige in that region.

1086-1129. The **Emperor Shirakawa** (1073–1086) continued to rule after his abdication as a retired emperor (*jōkō*) and after 1096 as a priestly retired emperor (*hōō*). He built up a complete governmental organization of his own (*insei*, camera government) which was continued during much of the next two and a half centuries by other retired emperors and priestly retired emperors, but after 1156 they lost control of the government to the warrior clans.

1129-1156. The **Emperor Toba** (1107–1123) ruled after Shirakawa's death as a priestly retired emperor.

1156. Civil war (the *Hōgen no Ran*) broke out between the reigning emperor, **Shirakawa II** (1155–1158), and the retired emperor, Sutoku (1123–1142). Both were supported by prominent members of the Fujiwara, Minamoto, and Taira clans. Shirakawa II's partisans, among whom were numbered Minamoto Yoshitomo (1123–1160) and Taira Kiyomori (1118–1181), were victorious. Sutoku was exiled, and many of his supporters were executed. This war brought no lasting peace and was soon followed by

1160. A second civil war (*Heiji no Ran*), in which Minamoto Yoshitomo and an adventurous young Fujiwara noble, Nobuyori (1133–1160), gained temporary control of the capital by a successful *coup d'état*, but were soon crushed by the Taira. This war left

1160-1181. **Taira Kiyomori** in control of the

nation. The two wars of 1156 and 1160 had not been a struggle for power between the court and the military clans, but the result had been to make a single victorious warrior, backed by personal troops, the dominating figure in Japanese politics. Shirakawa II as retired emperor (1158–1192) had some influence in the government, but in 1167 Kiyomori had himself appointed prime minister (*dajōdaijin*), and gave important posts in the central and provincial governments to his clansmen. Kiyomori married his daughters into both the imperial and the Fujiwara families. In 1180 his infant grandson, Antoku, was placed on the throne. Thus he attained the same hold over the imperial family that the Fujiwara had once had.

1175. The Pure Land (*Jōdo*) **Sect** was founded by Genkū (Hōnen Shōnin) (1133–1212). It was the first of the Amidist Sects, and this event marked the beginning of a great new sectarian movement.

1179. The death of Shigemori (1138–1179), Kiyomori's eldest son and perhaps the wisest of the Taira, removed a stabilizing check on Kiyomori, whose desire for more power was leading him to excesses which were alienating the sympathies of the imperial family, the court nobility and the Buddhist monasteries. The rapid adoption on the part of Kiyomori and his family of the customs and mentality of the court nobles also estranged many of the provincial supporters of the clan.

1180. An abortive uprising against the Taira led by an imperial prince and by Minamoto Yorimasa (1106–1180), together with certain monasteries, started a general uprising of the remnants of the Minamoto clan under the leadership of Yoshitomo's son, Yoritomo (1147–1199), backed by Taira and other clansmen of eastern Japan.

1183. The Taira were driven out of Kyōto by Yoshinaka (1154–1184), a cousin of Yoritomo. A long campaign in the Inland Sea region followed and culminated in

1185. The battle of Dan no Ura, at the western outlet of the Inland Sea, where Yoritomo's younger brother, Yoshitsune (1159–1189), annihilated the Taira. The child-emperor, Antoku, whom the fleeing Taira had taken with them, died in the battle. The elimination of the Taira left Yoritomo, as head of the Minamoto clan, the virtual ruler of the nation and marked the beginning of the first period of feudal rule in Japan known as

1185–1333. THE KAMAKURA PERIOD. The outstanding feature of the era was the clear division between the now powerless civil and religious government of the imperial court at Kyōto and the military government (*Bakufu*) of the Minamoto established at Kamakura, near the clan estates in eastern Japan and away from the enervating influence of the court nobility. The transition from civil to feudal military rule had begun with the Taira and was not completed until centuries later, but it was in the Kamakura Period that the most drastic changes occurred and the political and economic institutions of the next several centuries began to take shape.

Feudalism. The usurpation of the powers of the imperial court was largely unconscious and developed naturally out of the economic and political conditions of the late Heian period. Primary factors in this evolution were: (1) The wars of the 11th century had hastened the transfer of the prerogatives of ownership of the great manors of the nobles to the military men who resided on these manors as bailiffs or wardens and who often had feudal ties with the warrior clans. The actual ownership of the estates usually remained unchanged, but ownership was robbed of most of its meaning by a complicated series of feudal rights (*shiki*) which ranged from rights to cultivate the land up through an ascending scale of rights to the income from it. (2) Because of the breakdown of the old centralized government and the need for self-defense feudal military groups had grown up in the provinces with their own "house laws," governing the conduct and the relations of the members of a single group. Moreover, a feudal code of ethics had been developed which emphasized personal loyalty to a feudal chief rather than to a political ideal. (3) Minamoto prestige had for long induced landed warriors to commend themselves and their lands to the Minamoto for the sake of protection. The victory over the Taira greatly increased Minamoto feudal authority both through new additions of this sort and through the confiscation of vast Taira lands. The single Minamoto feudal union consequently had grown so large that it now controlled the nation, and its military government, and not the impotent Kyōto administration, was the real government of the land.

Foreign Relations. For four and a half centuries only a few Japanese monks had gone abroad, and foreign trade had been in the hands of the Koreans and Chinese, but in the Kamakura period the Japanese once more began to take part in foreign commerce. At the same time they began to raid and plunder the coasts of both Korea and China, and in time they became a serious nuisance and occasionally even a national menace to both countries.

Art. Kyōto, though remaining the scene of a colorful court life, was forced to share honors with Kamakura as a center of art and culture. Many Kyōto scholars moved to Kamakura to aid in the civil administration of the military government, and the warrior class brought a new creative energy to art and literature, which were approaching sterility in the late Heian period. Significant artistic trends were: (1) a final great flowering of sculpture before its gradual extinction in following centuries; (2) the introduction from China of two new architectural styles known as the Chinese (*Karayō*) and the Indian (*Tenjukuyō*) styles, which came to blend with the traditional style (*Wayō*); and, (3) the perfection of the narrative picture scroll (*emakimono*). Significant literary trends were: (1) the increasing use of Japanese in preference to Chinese; (2) the revival of native poetry in the *Shin-kokinshū*, an imperial anthology of 1205; and, (3) the popularity of historical military tales written in rhythmical prose.

Religion. The Kamakura period was one of great religious and intellectual ferment. It witnessed the birth and development of new sects growing out of the popular movements of the late Heian period. It saw the introduction of the **Zen Sect** from China and the growth of a military cult glorifying the sword, Spartan endurance and loyalty. From these two elements was born the combination of the aesthetic and mystical penchants of the Zen monk with the qualities of the Kamakura warrior — a combination which remains one of the chief characteristics of the Japanese people.

1185-1199. Yoritomo, as the feudal military dictator, organized the new military government with the aid of Kyōto scholars like Ōe Hiromoto (1148-1225). Already in 1180 he had created a *Saburai-dokoro* to perform police duties and to control affairs of the warrior class. In 1184 he had established an administrative board, renamed the *Mandokoro* in 1191. In 1184 the *Monchūjo* had also been established as a final court of appeal. Impartial administration of justice characterized the rule of the Kamakura military government and was one of the chief reasons for its long duration.

In 1185 Yoritomo appointed constables (*shugo*) in some of the provinces and placed stewards (*jitō*) in many of the large manors. A few such appointments had been made in preceding years, but now this system was expanded in order to strengthen his influence in regions over which he had hitherto had no direct control. The constables were special military governors in charge of the direct vassals of the Minamoto. The stewards, who represented Yoritomo on estates not otherwise under his control, levied taxes on the estates for military purposes. Thus the fiscal immunity of the manors was violated, and Kamakura retainers were scattered in key positions all over the country. The constables and stewards gradually grew in importance in the economic and political life of the provinces and in time developed into the feudal lords of later centuries.

1189. Yoshitsune was killed at the orders of Yoritomo, who apparently was jealous of the fame the latter had won as the brilliant general responsible for the greatest victories over the Taira. Yoritomo similarly disposed of other prominent members of the family, including his cousin Yoshinaka (1184), who as a warrior ranked next only to Yoshitsune, his uncle Yukiie (1186), who was one of the prime movers in the Minamoto uprising, and his brother Noriyori (1193), who also was one of the clan's great generals. His cruel treatment of his own relatives contributed to the early extinction of the family.

1189. Yoritomo crushed the powerful Fujiwara family of northern Japan on the grounds that they had killed Yoshitsune, albeit at his own command. The northern Fujiwara in the course of the previous century had become a great military power and had made their capital, Hiraizumi, a brilliant center of culture. Their elimination removed a serious menace to Minamoto supremacy.

1191. Eisai (1141-1215) propagated the Rinzai branch of the Zen (Skt. *Dhyana*) Sect after his return from a second study trip to China. The Zen Sect enjoyed the official patronage of Kamakura and the special favor of the warrior class in general.

1192. Yoritomo was appointed *Seiidaishōgun* ("barbarian-subduing great general"), or *shōgun* for short. He was not the first to bear this title, but he was the first of the long line of military dictators called *shōgun*.

1199-1219. Transition period from Minamoto to Hōjō rule. Yoritomo was succeeded as head of the Minamoto by his eldest son, Yoriie (1182-1204), who was not appointed *shōgun* until 1202, but his mother, Masako (1157-1225), actually ruled with the aid of a council headed by her father, **Hōjō Tokimasa** (1138-1215). The latter, though a member of the Taira clan, from the start had cast his lot with Yoritomo and had exercised great influence in the Kamakura councils before Yoritomo's death. The Hōjō, though loyal to the military government, unscrupulously did away with Yoritomo's descendants and crushed their rivals among the other Minamoto vassals.

1203. Yoriie was exiled and his younger brother, Sanetomo (1192–1219) was made *shōgun* by Tokimasa. The following year Yoriie was murdered.

1205. Tokimasa was eliminated from the government by Masako and his son, Yoshitoki (1163–1224), who then became regent (*shikken*) of the *shōgun*, a post held by successive Hōjō leaders, who were the real rulers.

1219. The Minamoto line came to an end when Sanetomo was assassinated, probably with Hōjō connivance, by his nephew, who in turn was executed.

1219-1333. THE PERIOD OF HŌJŌ RULE as regents for weakling *shōgun* of Fujiwara and imperial stock was characterized by administrative efficiency and by justice.

1221. An uprising under the leadership of the retired emperor, **Toba II** (1183–1198), was the gravest menace the Hōjō had to face, but was quickly crushed. Two prominent Hōjō leaders were left in Kyōto as joint civil and military governors of the capital region (*Rokuhara Tandai*). The estates confiscated from the defeated partisans of Toba II gave Kamakura much needed land with which to reward its followers, and the abortive uprising gave the Hōjō a chance to extend the system of constables, stewards and military taxes to regions hitherto unaffected by it.

1224. **Shinran Shōnin** (1173–1262), a disciple of Genkū, founded the **True Pure Land** (*Jōdo Shin*) **Sect** as an offshoot from the Pure Land Sect of his master. The True Pure Land Sect introduced innovations such as marriage for the clergy. It was destined to become the most popular of all Japanese Buddhist sects with Zen its only close rival.

1226-1252. Fujiwara nobles as figurehead *shōgun*.

1229. **Dōgen** (1200–1253) introduced the Sōtō branch of the Zen Sect after his return from study in China.

1232. The *Jōei-shikimoku*, a law code based primarily on custom rather than on earlier sinicized law codes, was adopted for all those directly under the feudal rule of Kamakura. It remained the basis of law codes until modern times.

1252-1333. Imperial princes as figurehead *shōgun*.

1253. Nichiren (1222–1282) **founded the Lotus** (*Hokke*) **Sect,** popularly known as the *Nichiren Sect*. In it the Lotus Sutra was venerated much as the Amidist Sects venerated Amida. A fiery religious and political reformer, Nichiren was an ardent nationalist, and his writings illustrate the gradual emergence of a definite national consciousness at this time. Imbued with the turbulent nature of its founder, the sect had a stormy career.

1274. FIRST MONGOL INVASION. The Mongols, already masters of Korea and most of China, repeatedly sent embassies (1268–1273), enjoining the Japanese to submit, but the Kamakura government under the bold leadership of the regent, Hōjō Tokimune (1251–1284), refused. Finally in 1274 the Mongols dispatched an expedition aboard a Korean fleet. The islands of Tsushima and Iki were reduced, a landing was made in Hakata (Hakozaki) Bay in northern Kyūshū, and an inconclusive encounter, in which superior weapons and military organization gave the Mongols the advantage, was fought with the local warriors. But the same night, because of their insecure position and the threat of a storm, the invaders set sail for Korea.

1281. SECOND MONGOL INVASION. Mongol envoys sent to Japan in 1275 and again in 1280 were summarily executed, and the military government hastily prepared defense works in western Japan. In 1281 the Mongols embarked a huge force on two large fleets, one Korean and one Chinese, and again, after capturing Tsushima and Iki, landed in northern Kyūshū. Although the invaders numbered some 150,000, the Japanese checked their advance on land with walls they had prepared for this emergency and worsted them on the sea because of the greater mobility of their smaller craft in close quarters. After almost two months of fighting a terrific storm destroyed a large portion of the invading armada, and the remainder departed with serious losses. The Mongols continued plans for another invasion of Japan until the death of their emperor, Kublai (1294), and the Japanese continued their defense preparations still longer.

The Mongol invasions no doubt spurred on Japan's nascent national consciousness, but it also contributed greatly to the final collapse of the Kamakura government. Military preparations against the Mongols had seriously taxed the nation's resources, and at the end of the two invasions the military government, lacking land confiscated from the enemy, was without the usual means of rewarding its vassals for their valiant efforts. This state of affairs helped undermine the loyalty of the warrior retainers of Kamakura. At the same time the monasteries were becoming increasingly unruly, the court nobility was beginning again to intrigue with disaffected warriors against the Hōjō, and the latter themselves had lost the virtues of frugality and justice which had once characterized the family.

The Hōjō during the final decades of their rule began to resort to **Acts of Grace** (*Tokusei*) cancelling certain indebtedness in an effort to save the lands of their vassals from mortgages, but such obviously unfair measures antagonized certain powerful interests and failed adequately to protect the Kamakura vassals.

1331-1333. THE IMPERIAL RESTORA-TION of **Daigo II** and the fall of the Hōjō. The energetic and able emperor, Daigo II (1318–1339), after bringing to an end in 1322 the domination of the court by retired emperors, organized an abortive plot to overthrow the Hōjō as early as 1324. In 1331 open warfare broke out between Daigo II, supported by his able sons, some of the large monasteries in the capital region, and various local nobles and warriors like **Kitabatake Chikafusa** (1292–1354) and **Kusunoki Masashige** (1294–1336), the two outstanding patriot heroes of mediaeval Japan. The following year the emperor was captured and exiled to Oki, but in 1333 he escaped. Most of western Japan declared for the imperial cause. Ashikaga Takauji (1305–1358), one of the two chief generals dispatched by the Hōjō from eastern Japan, deserted to Daigo II's standards, and the sudden capture of Kamakura by another prominent Hōjō vassal, Nitta Yoshisada (1301–1338), brought the military government of Kamakura to an end.

1333-1336. Daigo II in a short period of personal rule, failing to face economic and political realities, attempted to revive the civil imperial rule of the 8th century. However, he did make his able son, Morinaga (1308–1335), *shōgun* and appointed his leading generals military governors of large sections of the land. Because of his dissatisfaction with his share of the spoils in northeastern Japan,

1335. Takauji revolted against the throne. Defeating the Nitta, Kitabatake, and other loyal families,

**1336. **Takauji drove Daigo II out of Kyōto and set up a new emperor from a branch of the imperial family which had been jealously contending the throne with Daigo II's branch for several decades. He thereby became the virtual dictator of the central government, and,

although he was not appointed *shōgun* until 1338, with his capture of Kyōto commenced

1336-1568. THE ASHIKAGA (or Muromachi) **PERIOD.** The Ashikaga *shōgun* continued the outward forms of the military rule of the Minamoto and Hōjō, but during most of the first and last centuries of the period open warfare disrupted the nation, and at best the Ashikaga exercised only a shadowy control over the great feudatories who made their appearance at this time. The age was characterized by quickly shifting allegiances and by political instability, which at times amounted to anarchy. There was a general redistribution of feudal and economic rights, and the Kyōto nobility, which now lost most of its few remaining lands and provincial sources of income, was reduced to penury. The complicated feudal relations of the Kamakura period broke down into simpler, more compact divisions with practically independent lords, often the former provincial constables, ruling large territories, which were in turn subdivided into smaller units administered by their direct vassals. The collapse of clan unity and an organized feudal system necessitated stronger solidarity within the smaller family and feudal units. The division of patrimonies among heirs was abandoned, and women were reduced to the subordinate status they are still allotted. Lords exercised a closer paternalistic supervision over their vassals, and the latter in turn served their lords with greater personal loyalty.

The **overseas trade** and pirate enterprises of the Japanese increased in the Ashikaga Period; the central government once more established official relations with China; and another important period of borrowing from abroad commenced. Foreign trade stimulated the growth of towns and provincial ports, such as Sakai (part of the modern Ōsaka), Hyōgo (the modern Kōbe), and Hakata (part of the modern Fukuoka). Despite political disruption and incessant warfare, a phenomenal economic development took place. Nascent industries grew and expanded, and trade guilds (*za*), usually operating under the patronage of some religious institution, appeared and flourished. However, the unrestricted multiplication of various levies and of customs barriers proved a serious curb to the development of trade.

Kyōto was once more the undisputed political and cultural capital, and there the warrior class and the court nobility tended to fuse. Constant warfare made the period in some respects the intellectual dark ages of Japan, but political disunity helped to diffuse learning throughout the land. Zen monks dominated the intellectual and artistic life of the nation and through their intimate contacts with China, where many had lived and studied, expanded Japan's intellectual and artistic horizons. Although this was a great age of Zen, the other sects, particularly the Amidist sects, flourished and sometimes developed powerful military organizations. It was still a thoroughly Buddhist age, but intellectual life began to free itself from the bonds of Buddhism, Sung Confucian philosophy was introduced from China, and stirrings of new life appeared in Shintō, where for the first time systematic syncretic philosophies were developed.

Despite the violent internecine strife of the early and late Ashikaga period, in the middle decades literature and art, ruled by Zen standards of restraint and refinement, flourished. The *Literature of the Five Monasteries*, as the Zen school at Kyōto was called, revived poetic composition in Chinese, and a great lyric drama called *Nō* appeared. The Sung style of painting, often in monochrome and usually of landscapes, reached its height in Japan with such great masters as **Shūbun** (c. 1415) and **Sesshū** (1420–1506), and the two greatest Japanese schools of painting, the **Tosa** and **Kano**, flourished. The independent architectural styles of the Kamakura period were blended to form a composite style. Minor arts like landscape gardening and flower arrangement grew up, and the tea ceremony was popular among the upper classes. Under Zen tutelage there developed a refined simplicity of taste and a harmony with nature which has had a lasting influence on Japanese art and psychology.

1336–1392. CIVIL WARS OF THE YOSHINO PERIOD. When Takauji drove Daigo II out of Kyōto and set up a rival emperor, Daigo II and his partisans, the Kitabatake, Kusunoki and others, withdrew to the mountainous Yoshino region south of Nara, where Daigo II and three imperial successors maintained for almost six decades a rival court, called the *Southern Court* because of its location. During this period, known as the *Yoshino period* or the *Period of the Northern and Southern Dynasties*, civil war convulsed Japan. In support of the legitimacy of the southern court

1339. **Kitabatake Chikafusa** wrote the *Jinnō-shōtōki*, a history of Japan imbued with extreme nationalistic and patriotic sentiments. It is an important landmark in the growth of a national consciousness and the imperial cult.

1392. **The reunion of the two courts.** Although at times the Yoshino warriors even captured Kyōto, the hopes of the southern court

gradually waned. Eventually in 1392 peace was made, and Kameyama II (1383–1392) of the southern line abdicated in favor of **Komatsu II** (1382–1412) of the northern line, with the understanding that the throne should henceforth alternate between members of the two branches of the imperial family, as it had done for several reigns preceding that of Daigo II. However, the northern line never yielded the throne to its rivals despite futile uprisings in their behalf. Official history regards the southern line as the legitimate rulers during the Yoshino period.

1395–1408. **Rule of Yoshimitsu** as retired *shōgun*. Yoshimitsu, the third Ashikaga *shōgun* (1369–1395), after crushing his principal opponents, uniting the two imperial courts and bringing the Ashikaga power to its apogee, passed on the title of *shōgun* to his son and retired as a monk to his Kitayama estate on the outskirts of Kyōto. The **Golden Pavilion** (*Kinkaku*) he erected there is the outstanding remaining architectural work of the day, and his coterie of artists was the center of the artistic movements of the most creative epoch of the Ashikaga Period. There **Kan-ami** (1333–1384) and his son **Se-ami** (1363–1444) perfected the highly refined *Nō* drama from earlier dramatic and Terpsichorean performances. The luxurious but artistically creative life of the Kitayama estate was continued for several decades after Yoshimitsu's death by his successors.

1449–1490. **Rule of Yoshimasa** as *shōgun* (1449–1474) and retired *shōgun*. This was the second great creative period of Ashikaga art. In his Higashiyama estate on the edge of Kyōto, Yoshimasa built the **Silver Pavilion** (*Ginkaku*), which as an architectural work ranks second only to the Golden Pavilion of Yoshimitsu, and here he and a brilliant group of artists and aesthetes, presided over by Nō-ami (1397–1476), enjoyed a life of luxury and artistic elegance.

At the same time the complete collapse of what little authority the Ashikaga exercised over the nation became apparent, and there was great social unrest, resulting in numerous popular uprisings. Under the pressure of popular demands, Yoshimasa, like other Ashikaga *shōgun*, repeatedly issued Acts of Grace (*Tokusei*), which, unlike those of the Kamakura period, were sweeping debt cancellations for the benefit of the whole debtor class.

1465. The monks of the Enryakuji destroyed the Honganji, the central monastery of the True Pure Land Sect in Kyōto. Such affrays between the great monasteries were common at this time. Rennyō (1415–1499), the eighth hereditary head of the sect, fled to the region north of Kyōto, where his teachings met with great success and his numerous followers built up a military organization to defend their interests.

1467-1477. The Ōnin War, ostensibly a contest over the succession in the Ashikaga and other great military families, was actually a reshuffling of domains and power among the feudal lords, who divided into two camps under the leadership of two great war lords of western Japan, **Yamana Mochitoyo** (Sōzen) (1404–1473) and his son-in-law, **Hosokawa Katsumoto** (1430 [1425?]–1473), long the chief minister (*kanryō*) of the military government (1453–1464, 1468–1473). Kyōto was soon laid waste, but both leaders died in 1473, and exhaustion eventually brought peace in 1477. However, local struggles went on unabated. In fact, the Ōnin War was merely the prelude to over a century of almost uninterrupted warfare. This period, which is aptly called the *Epoch of a Warring Country,* witnessed a continual shifting of fiefs and power, the elimination of many of the old feudal families, and the emergence of a new group of territorial lords, now known as *daimyō.*

1488. The True Pure Land Sect believers north of Kyōto defeated and killed a local lord. This is considered the first of the *Ikkō-ikki,* or Uprisings of the Ikkō Sect, another name for the True Pure Land Sect. Such uprisings became increasingly common and acted as a medium for popular manifestations of discontent.

1493. Hosokawa Masamoto (1466–1507) drove the *shōgun,* Yoshitane (1490–1494, 1508–1521) out of Kyōto and set up a puppet *shōgun* (1494), acts which were repeated by his adopted son, Takakuni (1484–1531), in 1521. Yoshitane's successors suffered similar indignities as the prestige of the Ashikaga dwindled further. (*Cont. p.* 548.)

F. PRE-COLUMBIAN AMERICA

The aborigines of America, varying among themselves in certain racial characteristics, migrated from Asia to North America in successive waves by way of the Bering Strait. These migrations began at a very early date, and apparently continued until relatively recent times. The migrants, when they arrived, were in a very primitive state. Becoming isolated from other peoples they slowly expanded throughout both continents, and developed autochthonous cultures which ranged from savagery to a relatively high degree of civilization. Many groups at a comparatively early date attained the agricultural stage, and the Inca of Peru achieved the use of bronze. The use of iron and the principle of the wheel were unknown. The dog universally, the turkey, the duck, and, in the Peruvian highlands, the llama, alpaca, and guanaco were the only existing domestic animals, the llama being the sole beast of burden.

At the time of the discovery the peoples of highest culture, most complex society, and greatest political importance were the Aztec, with their center in the Valley of Anáhuac; the Maya of Yucatan and portions of Mexico and Central America; the Chibcha of the Colombian plateau; and the Inca, whose empire centered in the highlands of Peru. Between the higher civilizations of Mexico, Yucatan, and Central America and between those of the Andean region there was extensive interchange of culture over a lengthy period, and it is possible that there was cultural interchange between the peoples of Central America and those of the Andean region. The civilizations of the Aztec and the Inca were built upon preceding cultures of a high order.

THE AZTECS were originally a minor tribe of the great Nahua group. This group evolved the high Toltec civilization which, receiving through cultural transmission mathematical and astronomical knowledge and a calendar from a lowland people, possibly the Maya, reached its height in the 13th century and declined thereafter, being followed by the transitional Chichimec culture. Reaching the shores of Lake Tezcuco in 1325, the Aztecs erected an impregnable capital, **Tenochtitlán,** in the marshes of the lake and, through superior political and military capacity and alliance, extended their control over central and southern Mexico from the Gulf to the Pacific and established colonies in Central America. In 1519 Tenochtitlán was a city of some 60,000 householders and the Aztec Empire included perhaps 5,000,000 inhabitants. The government was relatively centralized, with an elective monarch, provincial governors appointed by the central authority, a well organized judicial system, and a large and efficient army. The Aztecs attained a high degree of development in engineering, architecture, art, mathematics, and astronomy. Principal buildings were of mortar and rubble faced with stucco. There existed a body of tradition, history, philosophy, and poetry which was orally transmitted. Picture writing which was rapidly approaching phonetic was evolved. Music was rudimentarily developed. Agriculture was far advanced and commerce and simple industry flourished. The working of gold and silver and the production of pottery and textiles were highly developed. The religion of the Aztecs was polytheistic, and although it included many lofty concepts the deity of war, Huitzilopochtli, was the principal god and his worship led to the development of one of the most extensive systems of human sacrifice which has ever existed. The priesthood constituted a powerful group, political as well as religious. Certain of the peoples subjected by the Aztecs were restive under their domination and were prepared to rebel at the first opportunity. In the mountains to the east of Lake Tezcuco there existed the powerful republic of Tlaxcala, which, maintaining its independence, regarded the Aztec as hereditary enemies. These conditions created a situation favorable to the Spaniards during the conquest.

THE MAYA before the Christian Era established themselves in the peninsula of Yucatan, Tabasco, Chiapas, northern, central, and eastern Guatemala, and western Honduras. They developed a civilization which, reaching its apogee well before 1000 A.D., was in certain cultural aspects the highest in the New World. The Maya culture in the earlier period extended with considerable uniformity throughout the greater part of their general area, but after about 1000 A.D., tended to center in the northern part of the peninsula of Yucatan. During the period of highest development the Maya did not evolve a unified empire, the area being divided into city states governed by politico-religious rulers or ruling groups. Art, architecture, mathematics, engineering, and astronomy were far advanced, and the Maya had evolved the conception of zero, a vigesimal numerical system, and a calendar more accurate than the Julian. Temples and other major buildings were constructed of stone and mortar and were faced with carved stone. A system of causeways existed. Codices were formed for religious and astronomical purposes, but writing did not exist. A body of traditions, history, and religious prophecies were orally preserved. Religion was polytheistic and relatively humane, and the priestly class, exercising political authority as well as religious, possessed, with the ruling groups, a monopoly of learning. Widespread commerce existed, and weaving and pottery making were well developed. Agriculture was on an exceedingly high level. Civil war occurred during the 13th century and certain Mexican groups conquered the Maya of northern Yucatan. Mexican cultural influences were consequently introduced, especially in art, and religion. In the same century a greater degree of political cohesion appears to have been established in the northern part of the peninsula, and this resulted in a period of peace which endured until the 15th century, when internecine strife led to the destruction of Mayapan in 1451 and the abandonment of the great cities Chichen Itzá and Uxmal. The Maya civilization was decadent culturally and politically when the Spaniards arrived, although certain of the independent provinces were relatively powerful militarily. The Maya of Yucatan numbered perhaps 400,000 to 500,000 on the eve of the Spanish conquest.

THE CHIBCHA. The political organization of the Chibcha, who numbered some 1,000,000, was comparatively cohesive. The Zipa at Bacatá and the Zaque at Tunja were the political rulers, and supreme religious authority was held by the high-priest known as the *Iraca*. The Chibcha possessed a well-developed calendar and numerical system and employed pictographs. Extensive commerce and simple industry existed, ceramics and textiles being highly developed. In gold working the Chibcha were in certain respects unequaled. The Chibcha employed wood and thatch in the construction of buildings.

THE INCA, with their capital at Cuzco, successors to the high coastal and upland cultures of Chimú, Nasca, Pachacamac, and Tiahuanaco, which flourished during the early centuries of the Christian Era, extended their control over the area from Ecuador to central Chile along the coast and inland to the eastern slopes of the Andes including the Bolivian plateau. Expansion was particularly rapid from the 14th century onward and one of the greatest of the conquerors, **Huayna Capac,** lived until the eve of the Spanish conquest. The empire, with a population of perhaps 6,000,000 to 8,000,000, was a thoroughly organized absolute, paternal, socialistic, and theocratic despotism. All power emanated from the Inca as the ruler and representative of the Sun Deity, whose worship constituted the religion of the Inca. There existed a close-knit and graduated system of provincial and local administration. Each individual had a fixed place in society, and the state benignly provided for the welfare of all. The army was large and well organized, and a system of post and military roads extended to all portions of the empire. In mathematics and astronomy the Inca were not as accomplished as the Maya and Aztec, but in engineering, architecture, and the production of textiles and ceramics they were far advanced. The Inca did not evolve writing, but possessed a device to aid memory in the form of the *quipu*, through which governmental records were kept, tradition was preserved, and messages were sent. In gold working a high degree of skill was attained. Commerce, entailing extensive navigation along the coast, was well developed. A great body of oral tradition and poetry existed, and music was comparatively well developed. Principal buildings were of stone. Politically the Inca were the most advanced of the peoples of the New World. At his death Huayna Capac, contrary to practice, divided the empire between Huáscar, his son by a lawful wife, and Atahualpa, his son by a concubine. A civil war followed, in which Atahualpa, shortly before the arrival of the Spaniards, triumphed and imprisoned his half-brother.

G. THE GREAT DISCOVERIES

1. ASIA

The Crusades left Europe with a greatly expanded horizon, with much more extensive trade interests and connections, and with an accentuated hostility toward Islam. The great conquests of the Mongols in the 13th century (**Jenghiz Khan**, 1206–1227; period of greatness under **Kublai Khan**, 1259–1294), in uniting most of Asia, the Near East, and eastern Europe under one sway opened direct communication between Europe and the Orient and raised the prospect of an alliance against the Moslems.

1160–1173. Rabbi **Benjamin of Tudela** (in Navarre) traveled through Persia, central Asia, and to the very confines of China, but for religious reasons his records had little influence on Christian Europe. The same was true of the researches of the great Arab geographer **Yaqut**, who lived in the late 12th and early 13th centuries and wrote a great geographical dictionary.

1245–1247. Travels of **John of Pian de Carpine**, an Umbrian sent to the court of the Great Khan to propose an alliance against Islam and if possible to convert the Mongols. Traveling by way of southern Russia and the Volga, Carpine crossed central Asia and reached the Mongol court at Karakorum. Though well received his mission proved abortive.

1253–1255. Mission of **William of Rubruck**, a Fleming sent by St. Louis of France to the court of the Great Khan. Rubruck followed much the same route as Carpine and left one of the finest travel accounts of the Middle Ages.

1255–1266. First journey of the **Polo brothers**, Nicolo and Maffeo, Venetian traders in the Black Sea, who traveled to central Asia, spent three years in Bokhara and proceeded thence to China. They returned to Acre in 1269, bearing letters to the pope from the Mongol ruler.

1271–1295. Second journey of the Polos, accompanied this time by Nicolo's seventeen-year-old son, **Marco**, greatest of all mediaeval travelers. They took the route Mosul–Baghdad–Ormuz–Kerman–Khorasan–Pamir–Kashgar and thence across the Gobi Desert to the court of the Great Khan. The Mongol ruler was so favorably impressed that he took them into his service. During the next fifteen years Marco became acquainted with much of China, Cochin-China, Burma, and India. The Polos returned by sea by way of Sumatra, India, and Persia. Marco's famous *Book of Various Experiences* was dictated, probably in 1297, while he was a prisoner in Genoa. It was almost immediately popular and colored the whole geographic outlook of the succeeding period. Marco died in 1324.

1290–1340. During this period lively trade relations sprang up between Europe and Asia. Specific records are few, but such as they are they indicate the existence of commercial colonies and missionary groups in Persia (Tabriz), in India (Gujerat and Malabar coast), and in China (Peking and other cities). The great trade routes from Central Asia through southeastern Russia and the Black Sea, and from Trebizond through Persia were wide open. Embassies were constantly passing between western rulers and the Ilkhans of Persia, whose emissaries on various occasions came as far as England (1287, 1289, 1290, 1307).

1289. The pope sent out Friar **John of Monte Corvino** to take charge of the newly established Archbishopric of Peking. John remained at his post until his death in 1328 and seems to have built a flourishing Christian community.

1324–1328. Friar **Oderic of Pordenone** traveled to China, leaving one of the best accounts of the country.

1328. The pope established a Bishopric of Quilon and sent out **Jordanus of Severac** to take charge.

1338–1346. **John Marignolli** was sent out to Peking as legate of the pope.

1340. **Francesco Pegolotti**, a Florentine trader at the Genoese station at Kaffa (Black Sea, founded 1266), wrote his *Merchants' Handbook* (*Della Pratica della Mercatura*), most valuable business manual of the time, which gives an unrivaled account of the commercial communications with Asia.

1368. Overthrow of the Mongol domination in China. Under the succeeding Ming dynasty foreigners were again excluded. The conquests of Timur the Great, shortly after, served to block the Near-Eastern trade channels once more.

2. AFRICA

During the Middle Ages much of Africa was familiar to the Arabs. **Ibn Batuta,** greatest of Arab travelers, between the years 1325 and 1349 journeyed from his home in Morocco across northern Africa, through Egypt, the Near East, Arabia, eastern Africa, and thence to India. Later he traveled northward to the Crimea and thence through central Asia to India. After spending eight years at Delhi, he went on to Ceylon and China. On his return to Morocco in 1349, he set out across the Sahara and visited Timbuktu and the Niger region. His remarkable journeys serve to record not only the Arab trade from Egypt down the east coast to Africa and to India and beyond, but also the regular caravan trade from southern Morocco across the desert to the **Kingdom of Ghana** (i.e. Guinea) in Nigeria.

1225. Under the tolerant rule of the Almohades and Marinides in Morocco, the Franciscans and Dominicans were allowed to establish their missionary centers in the country. By the end of the 13th century Christian and more particularly Jewish European merchants were engaged in the trans-Saharan trade, dealing chiefly in gold and ivory. In 1447 the Genoese Antonio Malfante penetrated far to the south.

1316. Having heard of a Christian king in East Africa (legend of **Prester John,** widespread in Europe after the spurious letter of 1165), the pope sent eight Dominicans to Ethiopia. Others seem to have been sent in the course of the century.

1402. **An Ethiopian embassy** reached Venice. There were others in 1408 and 1427. In 1452 Ethiopian emissaries arrived at Lisbon and in 1481 at Rome. The object of these embassies, and of those sent in return (especially by the pope in 1453) was to establish a Christian alliance against the Moslem Mamelukes in Egypt and later against the Ottoman Turks. Nothing came of this project, but the exchange of missions served to acquaint Europe with that part of Africa.

1270. Beginning of **Portuguese exploration** of the west coast of Africa. The Portuguese Malocello visited the Canary Islands (1340–1341). These were assigned by the pope to the crown of Castile (1344).

1291. The two Genoese, Doria and Vivaldo, set out to find a route to India by sea; they never returned and nothing is known of their explorations.

1394-1460. PRINCE HENRY THE NAVIGATOR, the greatest patron of cosmography and discovery. Through his mother a grandson of John of Gaunt. Prince Henry, as general of the *Order of Christ*, was able to turn the crusading enthusiasm as well as the funds of the order into the fields of science and discovery. From 1418 onward the prince sent out, almost annually, expeditions carefully prepared and ably conducted. There can be little doubt that the religious factor dominated the work of the prince, though the scientific and commercial factors were hardly less important. That Prince Henry hoped to open up direct communications with Guinea by sea is clear. That he hoped ultimately to find a sea-route to Ethiopia and thence to India has been questioned by some, but is reasonably certain.

1418-1419. Exploration of the **Madeira Islands,** some of which had been known before. The **Azores,** some of which appear on the *Medicean Portolano* of 1351, but probably as imaginary islands, were discovered between the years 1431 and 1437.

1425. Expedition sent by Prince Henry to conquer the Canaries from Castile. Thereafter the prince tried hard to secure the islands by negotiation and so exclude Castile from any share in the West African trade. Further attacks were made upon them in 1450–1453, but by the **Treaty of Alcaçovas** (1480, Mar. 6) they were definitely assigned to Castile, while West Africa, Guinea, and the islands of the ocean were assigned to Portugal.

1433. After more than ten years of repeated efforts, the Portuguese (under Gil Eannes) succeeded in doubling **Cape Bojador.** The advance then became rapid. Gold and natives were brought back and slave-raiding (later forbidden by Prince Henry) began.

1444. Nuño Tristam reached the Senegal River.

1445. Dinis Dias rounded Cape Verde. By this time the most barren part of the coast was passed and a lively trade with West Africa (c. 25 caravels a year) developed.

1455-1457. Alvise da Cadamosto (Cà da Mosto), a Venetian in the service of Prince Henry, explored the Senegal and Gambia Rivers and discovered the Cape Verde Islands.

1469. After the death of Prince Henry there was a slackening of activity and the King, Alfonso V, for financial reasons leased the Guinea trade for five years to **Fernão Gomes,** with the stipulation that exploration be carried forward at least 100 leagues annually.

1470-1471. Under Gomes' auspices, **João da Santarem** and Pedro de Escolar reached Mina on the Gold Coast, where the Portuguese established a factory (fort, 1482) and did a rich trade in gold.

1472. Fernando Po discovered the island which bears his name. Lopo Gonçalves crossed the equator and Ruy de Sequeira reached latitude 2° south.

1481. With the accession of **John II** (1481-1495) the crown once more took in hand the work of exploration, and with greater energy than ever.

1482-1484. Diogo Cão reached the mouth of the Congo River and Cape St. Augustine. In 1485-1486 he advanced to Cape Cross and Cape Negro.

1487. King John organized expeditions by land and by sea in the hope of reaching Ethiopia and India. **Pedro de Covilhã** and Alfonso de Paiva were sent out by way of Cairo and Aden. Covilhã reached India and on his return followed the east coast of Africa as far south as the mouth of the Zambesi.

1487, Aug.—1488, Dec. VOYAGE OF BARTOLOMEU DIAS. Having followed the African coast, Dias was driven by a great storm (Dec.–Feb.) south of the tip of Africa. He turned east and soon discovered hills running to the northeast, showing him that he had rounded the **Cape of Good Hope.** He followed the east coast of Africa as far as Mossel Bay and the Great Fish River and then was obliged by his crew to return.

1497, July 8—1499, Aug. 29 or Sept. 9. VOYAGE OF VASCO DA GAMA. This would have been undertaken sooner, excepting for internal troubles in Portugal and disputes with Castile arising from the discoveries of Columbus. Da Gama left with four ships to find the way to India, the feasibility of the route being perfectly clear after the discoveries of Covilhã and Dias. He rounded the Cape in Nov. 1497, reached Quilimane (Jan. 1498),

Mozambique (Mar.), and then Mombasa. Despite trouble with the jealous Arab traders, he was finally able to get a pilot from Melindi. He reached Calicut on the Malabar coast (May 22). He started for home in Aug. 1498, touched Melindi (Jan. 1499) and rounded the Cape (Mar.). The exact date of his arrival at Lisbon is disputed.

1500, Mar. 9.—1501, June 23. VOYAGE OF CABRAL, who set out with 13 ships to establish Portuguese trade in the east. After touching Brazil (p. 374) he went on to India, which he reached in Sept. The fleet loaded pepper and other spices and arrived safely in Lisbon. From this time on Portuguese trading fleets went regularly to India, and Lisbon soon became the chief entrepôt in Europe for oriental products.

1501. Vasco da Gama was sent out with 20 ships to punish the Arabs and to close the Red Sea, in order to cut the trade route through Egypt to Alexandria.

1505. Francisco de Almeida sent out as first governor of India. He took Quiloa and Mombasa on the African coast and established forts at Calicut, Cananor and Cochin on the Malabar coast.

1509, Feb. 2. Almeida destroyed the fleet of the Moslems in the **battle of Diu,** thus definitely establishing Portuguese control in Indian waters.

1509-1515. Governorship of **Alfonso de Albuquerque,** who in 1507 had conquered Ormuz on the Persian Gulf. Albuquerque made Goa the capital of the Portuguese possessions (1510), and in 1511 took Malacca. He opened communication with Siam, the Moluccas and China.

1513. Jorge Alvarez first landed near Canton.

1517. Fernão Peres de Andrade appeared with a squadron at Canton.

1542. Antonio da Mota and two companions, driven by a storm, first reached Japan.

1557. The Portuguese established themselves at Macão (near Canton) and initiated regular trade with China.

The opening of the direct route to India at once began the revolution in the conditions of trade between Europe and Asia. The Mamelukes in Egypt had controlled the main routes, from the Persian Gulf to Syrian ports and from the Red Sea to Alexandria, and from these ports the Venetians shipped to western Europe. The Egyptian sultan kept the consignments small (210 tons of pepper per year) and the prices were therefore high. By 1503 the price of pepper in Lisbon was only one-fifth what it was in Venice. When the Portuguese succeeded in blocking the Red Sea route, the Egyptian-Venetian trade was more or less ruined. The conquest of Syria and Egypt by the Turks (1516–1517), though frequently described as a stimulus to the discovery of new routes, had almost nothing to do with the situation. On the contrary the Turkish sultans (notably Suleiman, 1520–1566) did what they could to reopen the Near-Eastern routes.

3. AMERICA

a. PRE-COLUMBIAN DISCOVERIES

790. **Irish Monks,** searching for religious retreats and for new fields of missionary enterprise, reached Iceland, after discovering the Faroe Islands in the 7th century.

874. **The Norsemen** (Normans, Vikings) arrived in Iceland and settled.

981. The Norsemen, under **Erik the Red,** discovered Greenland and settled on the southwest coast (985–986).

1000. **LEIF ERICSSON,** returning from Norway to Greenland, was driven onto the American coast, which he called *Wineland* (Vinland), from the grapes he found there. Wineland was probably Nova Scotia.

1003-1006. THORFINN KARLSEFNI set out from Greenland with three ships to settle Wineland. He and his party spent three winters on the American continent. There is no general agreement regarding the localities visited by him, which have been placed by different authorities as far apart as Labrador and Florida. One recent writer puts the *Helluland* (Flat-stone Land) of the Greenlandic-Icelandic sagas in northeastern Labrador; *Markland* (Wood Land) in southern Labrador; *Furdustrand* (Wonder Strand) on the north side of the Gulf of St. Lawrence; *Straumfjord* (Stream Fjord), where the first and third winters were spent, on Chaleur Bay (New Brunswick); and *Hop* (Lagoon) on the New England coast, either north or south of Cape Cod. Another recent writer is convinced that Karlsefni visited only the Labrador coast and both sides of the northern peninsula of Newfoundland, Straumfjord being, perhaps, in the vicinity of Hare Bay. Wineland was first mentioned in the *Hamburg Church History* of **Adam of Bremen** (1074 ff.), but most of our knowledge derives from the Norse sagas written down in the 14th century. Supposed Norse remains on the American continent (*Dighton Rock, Old Stone Mill* at Newport) have all been rejected by scholars as spurious, with the exception of the Kensington Stone, found near Kensington, Minnesota, in 1898, under the roots of a tree 70 years old. The stone contains a long runic inscription recording the presence there of a group of Norsemen in 1362. The stone and the inscription are clearly not forgeries, and a majority of geographers as well as many historians are disposed to accept the authenticity of the record. The philologists are less favorable, because of irregularities in the language that are hard to explain. Within recent years a Norse grave, with sword, shield, and two axes, is reported to have been found in Ontario.

How long the Norsemen continued to visit America is obviously an open question. The last definite mention, apart from the Kensington Stone evidence, is for 1189 A.D., but there is some reason to believe that they came at least as far as southern Labrador for ship's timber as late as 1347. After that date the Greenland colonies declined, though the West Colony (in southeast Greenland) continued to exist until at least 1400 and ships appear to have gone there periodically, probably trading in walrus hides and tusks.

1470-1474. Between these years two Germans in the Danish service, **Didrick Pining** and **Hans Pothorst,** undertook a voyage to Iceland and the west. Pining was a great seaman and the terror of the English; from 1478 to 1490 he was governor of Iceland, but the evidence does not show that he and Pothorst went beyond Greenland. On a globe of 1537 (the *Gemma Frisius* at Zerbst) it is stated that a famous pilot, **Johannes Scolvus** (claimed by some to have been a Pole — Jan Szkolny), reached the Arctic regions at this time. It has been held by some scholars that he must have accompanied Pining and Pothorst, but, since Labrador (mentioned in the sources) was a name generally used for Greenland, it seems unlikely that Scolvus went beyond the old Norse settlements. In any event there is no proof of realization of any pre-Columbian discovery, or of any influence on later attempts.

A great many theories have been advanced in recent years, notably by the Portuguese, but also by others, to show that the Portuguese knew of the existence of America before Columbus sailed. Most of the theories rest upon conjecture and clever deductions. All we can say is that, after the translation of Ptolemy's *Geography* into Latin (1410), the idea of the sphericity of the earth (never entirely lost during the Middle Ages, cf. Roger Bacon's *Opus Majus* of the late 13th century) spread rapidly in scientific circles and revived the idea of reaching Asia by sailing westward. Prince Henry the Navigator, for all his interest in the African route, sent expeditions to the west. Between 1431 and 1437 the Portuguese discovered seven of the Azores. Flores and Colvo were discovered in 1451–1452. It is clear that after 1450 many Portuguese expeditions set out in search of legendary islands (St. Brandan's, Brazil, Antillia or Island of the Seven Cities, etc.) and, according to some scholars, the Lisbon government enforced a policy of rigorous secrecy with regard to new findings. Nevertheless, no present evidence of Portuguese knowledge of America before 1492 can be regarded as probable.

b. THE VOYAGES OF COLUMBUS

1451, bet. Aug. 26 and Oct. 31. CRISTOFORO COLOMBO (Span. Cristóbal Colón) born near Genoa, the son of Domenico Colombo, a weaver. Almost nothing definite is known of his youth (unreliability of the biography by his son Fernando). He was probably himself a weaver and probably went to sea only in 1472, when he made a trip to Chios. He seems to have come to Portugal in 1476 and to have made a voyage to England in 1477 (the story of his visit to Iceland is rejected by almost all authorities). In 1478 he appears to have made a voyage to the Madeiras and in 1482 possibly to the Guinea coast. In 1480 he married the daughter of Bartholomew Perestrello, hereditary captain of Porto Santo, near Madeira. By this time Columbus must have learned much about Portuguese discoveries and certainly about the ideas current in Lisbon. His appeal to the great Florentine geographer, **Paolo Toscanelli**, and the latter's reply (?1482) urging a voyage to the west, have been called in question by some writers and may be spurious. In any event the idea of seeking India or China in the west was not novel.

1483 or 1484. Columbus appealed to King John II of Portugal to finance a voyage to the west, but whether to seek new islands or a route to Asia is not clear. At this very time the king was authorizing self-financed expeditions to the west of the Azores (1486, Ferman Dulmo) and he might have licensed Columbus had the latter been willing to finance himself. Others maintain that the Portuguese already knew that Asia could not be reached in this way. Apparently Columbus, whose geographical knowledge appears to have been very incomplete, was regarded as a vain boaster. His project was rejected.

1486. Columbus, through the mediation of some Franciscan monks, was able to submit his project to **Ferdinand and Isabella** of Spain. His religious fervor and personal magnetism impressed the queen, but the project was again rejected by experts.

1492. After being recalled to court, Columbus finally induced the queen to finance his expedition. It is not yet clear whether he set out to discover new islands and territories, or whether his object was to find a route to the Indies. He was made admiral and governor of the territories to be discovered, but also carried letters to the Great Khan (Emperor of China), which makes it probable that his purpose was twofold.

1492, Aug. 3—1493, Mar. 15. The First Voyage. Columbus left Palos in command of three ships (*Santa Maria*, Juan de la Cosa, *Pinta*, Martin Alonso Pinzón, *Niña*, Vicente Yáñes Pinzón), with about 90 men. Taking a fresh departure from Gomera (Canary Islands), on Sept. 6, he made the island of **San Salvador** (Oct. 12), sailed through the Bahamas to Cuba (Oct. 28), which he thought to be a province of China, and to Hispaniola (Dec. 5), which he thought to be Japan. Near Cape Haitien the *Santa Maria* was wrecked (Dec. 25), after which Columbus established 39 men ashore in a fort named **Navidad.** He sailed in *Niña* from Samaná Bay (Jan. 16, 1493), called at Santa Maria (Azores) on Feb. 17–24, was blown into Lisbon (Mar. 4), and reached Palos (Mar. 15), the same day as the *Pinta*. He announced that he had discovered the Indies, which many doubted, but the Spanish sovereigns believed (hence *West Indies* and *Indians*).

1493, May 4. The Line of Demarcation. At the instance of the Spanish rulers, who feared counterclaims by Portugal, Pope Alexander VI granted to the Catholic kings exclusive right to and possession of all lands to the south and west toward India, not held by a Christian prince on Christmas Day, 1492, beyond a line drawn one hundred leagues west of the Azores and Cape Verde Islands.

1493, Sept. 25–1496, June 11. SECOND VOYAGE OF COLUMBUS. He left with 17 ships and 1200–1500 men to establish Spanish power. On this voyage he discovered most of the Lesser Antilles, Puerto Rico and Jamaica, explored the southern coast of Cuba and circumnavigated Hispaniola, where he founded the town of Isabella. He left his brother Bartholomew in charge, who in 1496 transferred the settlement to the southern coast (Santo Domingo).

1494, June 7. TREATY OF TORDESILLAS, between Portugal and Spain. The line of demarcation was moved to 370 leagues west of the Cape Verde Islands, Portugal to have exclusive rights to all lands to the east of it, and Spain of all lands to the west.

1498, May 30–1500, Nov. 25. THIRD VOYAGE OF COLUMBUS. Discovery of Trinidad Island (1498, July 31) and South America (Aug. 1) on the Orinoco delta. He explored the Gulf of Paria and the coast westward to Margarita Island, then sailed to Hispaniola, where a revolt of Spanish colonists had taken place. He requested the crown to send out a judge. The government sent out to the Indies **Francisco de Bobadilla** (1499), who sent Columbus and his brother to Spain as prisoners. Columbus was released and treated with distinction, but, despite the earlier rights granted him, was never restored to his former authority or monopolistic grants. With Bobadilla direct royal control was established.

1502, May 11–1504, Nov. 7. FOURTH VOYAGE OF COLUMBUS. He sailed along the coast of Central America from Trujillo (Honduras) to the Gulf of Darien (Rep. of Panama) in search of a strait, attempted a settlement in Veragua, which the Indians broke up, spent a year shipwrecked at Jamaica, was rescued and returned to Spain.

1506, May 21. Columbus died in relative obscurity at Valladolid. It is reasonably clear that he believed to the end of his days that he had discovered outlying parts of Asia, despite the fact that ever since 1493 the conviction had spread among experts (e.g. **Peter Martyr**) that a New World had been discovered.

c. POST-COLUMBIAN DISCOVERIES

1497, May 2–Aug. 6. VOYAGE OF JOHN CABOT. Cabot was an Italian merchant (born in Genoa, naturalized in Venice) who had traveled in the Near East and settled in Bristol, England, whence expeditions had been fitted out to seek the mythical island of Brazil. His object was to find a short route in high latitudes to the source of the spices. With one ship (*Mathew*) and 18 men, under a patent from Henry VII, he reached land (June 24), probably Cape Breton Island, and was back at Bristol Aug. 6. Cabot saw no natives but was convinced that he had discovered the country of the Great Khan and intended to return, seeking the passage to India.

1498, May–? SECOND CABOT VOYAGE. John Cabot, possibly accompanied by his son Sebastian, sailed from Bristol with four English ships, but nothing certain is known of this voyage, not even that Cabot returned, although his pension was paid to someone until September, 1499. Line of English flags along coast of North America on map of Juan de la Cosa (c. 1500–08).

1498. John II of Portugal sent **Duarte Pacheco Pereira** to discover lands on his side of the Line of Demarcation, but there is no certain knowledge that he found anything.

1499, May–1500, June. Voyage of Alonso de Ojeda in the service of Spain. He discovered the mouth of the Amazon, sailed along the northern Brazilian and Guiana coasts, and westward to the Magdalena R.; a native settlement on piles in the Gulf of Maracaibo was called *Venezuela* (Little Venice). **Amerigo Vespucci** (1495–1512), a Florentine resident in Seville, was on this voyage, and wrote an account antedating it by 2 years and not mentioning Ojeda.

1500, Apr. 22. The Portuguese **Pedro Álvares Cabral**, having sailed from Lisbon (March 9) with a fleet of 13 vessels, sighted Mt. Pascal, Brazil (17° S.L.), explored the coast for 40 miles, and continued his voyage to India. He named it *Terra de Vera Cruz*, which Manuel II changed to *Santa Cruz*. On this discovery, as well as the Line of Demarcation, Portugal based her title to Brazil.

1500. João Fernandes, *lavrador* (landowner) of Terceira, Azores, with Pedro de Barcelos, rediscovered Greenland, which the English of Bristol (in a voyage of 1501 in which Fernandes was a partner) named "Land of the Labrador"; a name later transferred through misunderstanding of maps to the present Labrador.

1500. Gaspar Corte-Real of Terceira discovered Newfoundland (unless previously discovered by Cabot) which he called *Terra Verde*.

In 1501 he explored Labrador, Newfoundland and Nova Scotia with three ships; two returned but his was lost. His brother Miguel was lost on a voyage to Newfoundland in 1502, but that island, called *Terra de Corte-Real* or *Terra de Bacalhau* (codfish) was largely explored by the Portuguese and the principal bays and capes were named by them.

1501, May—1502, Sept. SECOND VOYAGE OF AMERIGO VESPUCCI, this time in the service of Portugal. The voyage took him south along the Brazilian coast to about 32° S.L. if not farther. It was from the published account of this voyage and from Vespucci's conviction that what had been found was a *New World* that the geographer **Martin Waldseemüller** was led to propose that this New World be called *America* (1507). The name was at first applied only to South America and the use of it spread slowly until its general adoption toward the end of the 16th century.

Further explorations need not be listed in detail. **De Bastidas** traced the coast from Panama to Port Manzanilla (1500–1502); **Vicente Pinzón** followed the mainland from the Bay of Honduras to beyond the easternmost point of Brazil (1508); **Ocampo** circumnavigated Cuba (1508), which was conquered by **Diego Velázquez** (1511); **Juan Ponce de Leon,** the governor of Puerto Rico, discovered Florida (1512).

1513, Sept. 25. Vasco Nuñez de Balboa crossed the Isthmus of Panama and discovered the Pacific Ocean.

1515-1516. Juan Diaz de Solis, chief pilot of Spain, searching for a strait to the Pacific, explored the coast of South America from near Rio de Janeiro to the Rio de la Plata, where he was slain.

1517. Francisco Hernández de Córdoba discovered Yucatan, finding traces of large cities and great wealth.

1518. Juan de Grijalva followed the coast north from Yucatan to the Panuco River.

1519. Alvárez Pineda completed exploration of the Gulf of Mexico by coasting from Florida to Vera Cruz and back. **Francisco de Gordillo** advanced up the Atlantic coast to South Carolina (1521), and **Pedro de Quexos** as far as 40° N.L. (1525). At the same time (1524–1525) **Esteban Gómez,** sailing from Spain, followed the coast from Nova Scotia in the north to Florida in the south.

1519-1522. CIRCUMNAVIGATION OF THE GLOBE BY FERDINAND MAGELLAN (Fernão de Magalhães, 1480–1521). Magellan was sent out by the Spanish crown to find a strait to the Moluccas. He reached the Brazilian coast near Pernambuco, explored the estuary of the Rio de la Plata and, after wintering at Port St. Julian, passed through the strait which bears his name and entered the South Sea, to which the name *Mare Pacificum* was given. After following the coast to about 50° S.L. he turned northwest and after months of sailing reached the Ladrones and Philippines. In the latter place he was killed in a skirmish with the natives. One of his vessels, under **Sebastian del Cano,** continued westward and reached Spain, thus completing the circumnavigation of the globe.